D1273179

CONSTITUTIONAL GOVERNMENT AND POLITICS

CONSTITUTIONAL GOVERNMENT
AND POLITICS

Printed in the United States of America

I-M

CONSTITUTIONAL GOVERNMENT AND POLITICS

NATURE AND DEVELOPMENT

BY

CARL JOACHIM FRIEDRICH

Associate Professor of Government
Harvard University

HARPER & BROTHERS PUBLISHERS

NEW YORK AND LONDON

1937

A. Pisano — *Alinari*

THE SCIENCE OF GOVERNMENT
A Figure on the Cathedral Campanile at Florence

To Len

for Liesel

CONTENTS

PREFACE

I have enjoyed so much help and stimulation from the discussion with friends throughout the years during which this book has reached its present scope that I am utterly incapable of setting a suitable memorial for each of them individually. Wherever I could, I have tried to emphasize in the bibliography such special debts. But some of the greatest benefits I have derived from men and women who have not written anything, and their share in shaping my thoughts must remain obscure.

It may be permissible to mention, however, those who have taken part in the arduous and trying task of reading the manuscript and the proof, mending and polishing my knotty Teutonic diction. Jane Barbour, William Yandell Elliott, Rupert Emerson, H. Schuyler Foster, William P. Maddox, George Pettee, David Reisman, Jr., Frederick M. Watkins, Harold Winkler, and the whimsical person to whom this volume is dedicated, have all lent a helping hand. But I have refused many of their suggestions even though they were supported by weighty authority. In order to forestall unnecessary misunderstanding, it may be said outright that a good many American folk phrases are consciously used.[1] I love the living language, and as long as Fowler will let me do it, I'll enjoy some of its vagaries. You cannot live among farmers without calling a chore a chore.[2]

Well, the chore of this book has been the bibliography. It is mainly put in so as not to disappoint those who venerate sound (German?) scholarship. As far as I am concerned, it might all be washed out. When I look at it all, I can not help thinking of Rabelais' rollicking mockery at the citations from the Bible and the Digest with which sixteenth-century books used to be studded. I mourn the amount of time wasted in checking the dates and exact titles of volumes and page references, and I shudder at the number of mistakes which are left. May the reviewers have mercy with—my assistants. I shall be forever grateful to these faithful souls.

This book is written for those who are puzzled about the future of constitutional government and democracy. It tries to show the present

[1] Some American pedants have found fault with this "slangy" style before, though no English reviewer has objected to it.

[2] The English spelling is "chare."

disturbances in proper perspective by setting them off against the ground swell of long-range secular trends. Some time ago, just about when Hitler came into power, I concluded an article with the following sentence: "In any case, Germany will remain a constitutional, democratic state, with strong socializing tendencies whose backbone will continue to be its professional civil service."

The doings of the Nazis make me look like a fool. But I would rather misjudge man by expecting him to do better than he will. I am quite frank to own that I never expected such a violent attack upon the fundamentals of our culture. But what is more, in the long run I hold firm to the sentence as written. Within the lifetime of this generation, the present barbarities will be abandoned, and finer, more noble conceptions of life will reassert themselves. There are great latent reservoirs of faith in a higher morality which were overgrown with the slime of nineteenth-century decadence. I do not propose to know how the creative sensibilities will manifest themselves. I will confess to a faith in their potential strength. This book wants to be a wheelbarrow of stuff toward the new structure which is going to be reared in the not too distant future.

Carl Joachim Friedrich

Part I

MODERN GOVERNMENT IN THE MAKING

CHAPTER I

THE FORMS OF GOVERNMENT AND THE INSTRUMENTS OF POLITICAL ACTION: FROM ARISTOTLE TO MODERN POLITICAL SCIENCE

1. *Introductory: the essence of science.*—2. *Social sciences cannot benefit from applying methods of natural sciences to them.*—3. *John Stuart Mill's historical method.*—4. *The value of common human experience.*—5. *Human nature as a datum minus psychological explanation.*—6. *Basic hypotheses derived from common sense notions are critically examined by political science when applied to more complex institutional and procedural phenomena.*—7. *Uncertainty of the materials and subjective bias of the student.*—8. *Political science and history.*—9. *Law.*—10. *Economics.*—11. *Power presupposes common objectives.*—12. *Power a human relationship; its nature controversial.*—13. *Consent and constraint both real forces, generating power.*—14. *Both consent and constraint together determine the intensity of a political situation (first hypothesis).*—15. *Concentration of power and disunity (second hypothesis).*—16. *The rule of anticipated reactions (third hypothesis).* 17. *Aristotelian and modern views contrasted as static and dynamic.*—18. *Conclusion.*

Introductory: the essence of science.—Ever since the days of Aristotle, the study of politics has oscillated between the extremes of pure description and political ethics, between a panorama of the Constitution of Athens, and a discussion of justice and the good life. Since both these topics are of perennial interest to expert and general public alike, they have flourished and contributed their share to the betterment of human understanding of the nature and conditions of our living together—as well as our inability to live together. Friendship and enmity, peace and war, these are microcosm and macrocosm of political interest, and reasonably accurate description as well as searching metaphysical contemplation are essential parts of our comprehending the human experiences involved. But the peculiar province of science in the modern sense is neither the description nor the metaphysical delimitation of the vista to be inspected. To be sure, modern science presupposes both. It is not possible to be a physicist without having some general notion as to what constitutes the field of physics. It is no accident that the great founders of modern physics, like Isaac Newton, considered themselves natural philosophers. Nor is it feasible to be a physicist without the power of observing and accurately describing the specific phenomena thus included in the field of physics. But the peculiar essence of modern physics lies in something transcending these specific phenomena, in the discovery of "laws" governing recurrent phenomena; in short it lies in establishing descriptive formulæ of a more comprehensive kind, covering a whole series of individual events. We say deliberately: descriptive formulæ; for nothing would be more misleading than to construct an antithesis between description in general and the formulation of such "laws" or "rules." Every such "law," "rule," or, to use the most modern expression, every such "hypothesis," is a description of what are believed to be observed phenomena. It is an hypothetical generalization covering a considerable number of phenomena having certain qualities or properties in common. When we say generalization, we do not, however, necessarily imply a prejudice in favor of induction as the logical method of science; for the process through which the more general descriptive formulæ, or hypotheses, are reached, is a philosophical, and perhaps a psychological, problem of great complexity, still highly controversial. All we do say is that such general descriptive formulæ must correspond to the observed phenomena covered by them, and if any observation is made and verified which contradicts the formulæ, the formulæ must be so altered as to make allowance for the "stubborn facts," as William James once so aptly called such a deviating observation.

Social sciences cannot benefit from applying methods of natural sciences to them.—Even those who agree with the preceding remarks may be apprehensive, lest the author propose to advance the claim that political science be ranked with physics as a mode of scientific endeavour. For where are the exact methods of observation? Where the carefully controlled experiments in a laboratory constructed with all the refinements of modern engineering science? Looked at from this angle, political science appears to be precisely where it was in the days of Aristotle. Much of this the author is ready to grant. And yet, he makes bold to claim as much genuine science for politics as for physics, if not more. The nineteenth century notion that the social sciences are backward, and that this backward state can only be remedied by applying to them the methods of the physical sciences is no longer tenable. To be sure, as illustrious a student of the social world as John Stuart Mill subscribed to these propositions in his justly celebrated *System of Logic*. But as we shall presently see, he re-interpreted such an important part of these tenets as in fact to abandon them. At any rate, these generalizations about the relative scientific "value" of the different fields of human knowledge are subject to two fatal objections. In the first place, they contain a simple *petitio principii*; for in order to prove the alleged backward state, the methods of the social sciences are being compared with those of the natural sciences. Thus the social sciences are said to lack the "exactness" of experiment, or of quantitative measurement, and so forth. But the application of the methods of the natural sciences to the social sciences could only be justified if the objects of the social sciences were the same as those of the natural sciences. No effort, of course, is made to prove this evidently untenable position. Yet, only if this could be maintained, would the application of the methods of natural science be justified. In spite of his willingness to render lip-service to these generalizations, John Stuart Mill proceeded to destroy the foundations upon which they rested. In three brilliant chapters he showed why neither the geometrical, i.e., abstract deductive method, nor the chemical, i.e., experimental method, nor yet the physical, i.e., concrete deductive method is applicable to the study of society. We will not follow him into these negative arguments, but turn toward his positive suggestion that the sciences of society must employ a method adapted to their peculiar needs, the historical or inverse deductive method.

John Stuart Mill's historical method.—In spite of the fact that Mill was misled into the bypaths of sociological metaphysics by the speculations of Comte, which so deeply impressed him, his exposition of this inverse deductive method contains the germ of the most fruitful methodological thought in the field of the generalizing social sciences. It is true that Mill was still beset with the belief in universal laws which haunted the scientists of his age; but it is not very difficult to adapt his ideas to the conceptions of a more critical age. The decisive point is that he rightly perceives that verification in all fields concerned with man and society means linking an empirical generalization or hypothesis with the simple facts of human nature as they are known to us through common human sympathy. Many generalizations in the special social sciences, such as economics and politics, do not, to be sure, refer to the total human personality. Being dedicated to the study of certain phases of human nature which manifest themselves in the effort to secure power or wealth, their generalizations cannot be referred to or linked with other problems. Any concrete social situation built of actual human beings will contain all the elements of human nature, and will therefore require consideration from the viewpoint of the several social sciences. It is difficult for a person accustomed to the thought processes of the natural sciences to appreciate how essential this verification by reference to human nature is to the social sciences. Yet, as Mill said, such inverse deduction is as real a process of verification as, and no less indispensable than, verification by specific experience where the hypothesis is originally obtained by the direct way of deduction. This, then, is the crucial point: How do we come by our hypotheses? But before we venture an answer, we must dispose of two preliminary problems.

The value of common human experience.—Let me be challenging. The much flaunted exactitude of methods in the natural sciences, —is it not perhaps simply a substitute for the peculiar insight which the student of human affairs can count upon? Is not the social scientist lucky in that he is himself one of the atoms, so that the ways of atoms are familiar to him? Is it not maintainable that the first "law" of thermodynamics is not nearly so certainly true as that "men lie"? Ah, your proud scientist retorts, will you, old cynic, deny that there are men who never lie? Not at all, the answer should be, but if they do not, it is probably due to a peculiar and relatively infrequent motivation such as that which would spring from their not only having, but actually practising the faith in an ethic which prohibits that comfortable practice. In other words, your student of human affairs can not only give a general descriptive formula, but he can also *understand* the aberrations from such recurrent phenomena quite readily. The physicist can merely note that every so often an atom deviates from the norm, but he is at present completely at a loss when it comes to accounting for it. Far be it from me, however, to belittle the achievements of modern natural science; they are the more imposing precisely because the naturalist has to work without the guide of common human sympathy. However, it is thoughtless, indeed, to deprive ourselves in the social sciences of the invaluable aid which mutual human understanding can give us, merely because the natural sciences have had to evolve techniques for getting along without it.

Human nature as a datum minus psychological explanation.—It may here be objected that such reference to human nature casts the social sciences out upon the high seas of psychological controversy. Must we admit that economics and politics change with the changing fashions in the most controversial of all sciences? Is there a pragmatic, a Freudian, a behavioristic, and finally a *Gestalt* variety of politics? If this were so, it would indeed be fatal. How is it, then, that the significant generalizations, the primary hypotheses of political science and economics, seem to be quite independent of psychological controversy? Largely because they are concerned with a very simple order of data which every one of these psychologies accepts. Their differences arise over the question of how to account for such data and it is a matter of relatively minor importance to the political scientist how the aspect of human nature which is known to all of us as the desire for power is to be accounted for. To put it in another and more radical way, the social sciences are concerned with what Santayana has so aptly called "literary psychology," not the specific and subtle phases of it in which Santayana is so much interested, but rather the general and obvious base lines of common human conduct, prevailing notions of the most evident sort. How does such mutual human understanding operate within the particular field of political science?

Basic hypotheses derived from common sense notions are critically examined by political science when applied to more complex institutional and procedural phenomena.—All the more important base-line "hypotheses," the general descriptive formulæ from which political studies must start, are offered to it in the form of so-called common-sense notions. For many of them proverbs can be given as equivalents. That is one of the reasons why efforts to set forth these hypotheses in any labored form invariably produce an impression of platitudinous pedantry. The very general propositions regarding human conduct in politics are too well known to all. It is certainly not very interesting to learn that men desire justice, but do not practice it, or that men are guided by emotions in making decisions. That those possessing power tend to abuse it is another "hypothesis" not worth proving, although all the natural sciences cannot boast of a single "hypothesis" of equal importance to mankind. But there is another level of generalizations, perhaps more transitory, certainly more complex, where the "common understanding" is either silent or given to over-simplification as well as to outright error.

This is the field of institutional and procedural phenomena. The proposition that democracy is in all places a workable form of government was often assumed during the past generation, but careful observation would prove the "hypothesis" to be wrong. That the American president's duty to see to the execution of the laws cannot be discharged without his possessing the power to hire and to fire all the ranking officials without consulting anyone is an "hypothesis" underlying the famous decision of the United States Supreme Court in the *Myers Case*, and is there asserted as an axiomatic truth; yet to "prove" this proposition is probably impossible, since well-recorded experience points in the opposite direction. Here you have occasions of great, widely recognized significance, affecting the lives of millions of people. It is the task of the political scientist to examine these and other hypotheses in the light of all available experience, and to criticize the current assumptions as to the workings of institutional and procedural devices. Since the constant forward march of events generates ever-new assumptions of this type, the scientific effort of students of politics is directed toward these assumptions rather than in search of "hypotheses" of their own creation, though these do repeatedly offer themselves as alternatives to false popular notions.

Uncertainty of the materials and subjective bias of the student.—But is not political science fatally hampered in this effort by the inevitable uncertainty of the materials it works with, and the equally certain subjective bias of the student himself? The answer is: No. Hampered it is, but not fatally so. For it is by no means the pretension of political scientists, any more than of other scientists (we hope) to produce infallible knowledge. All they wish to supply is a more comprehensive knowledge, *a better* understanding of matters politic, than is available to the chance observer or the mere practitioner. It would be most unscientific, to be sure, for the student of politics to deceive himself about his personal bias, as unscientific as it would be for the naturalist to neglect the chances of error resulting from the interference of uncontrollable factors such as gravitation and weather, as well as from the psychological inaccuracies of observation. Again we have the antithesis between exactitude and understanding, or, to put it negatively, between the naturalist's groping in the dark as to what factors he is confronted with and the sociologist's vagueness as to the extent of the interference created. But these limitations upon effectiveness in coping with such sources of error do not alter the fact that scientific effort presupposes their admission as deplorable, yet unavoidable, conditions of scientific work. The farther removed from present-day controversy the facts to be considered are found, the less serious is the danger resulting from such personal bias, until we reach the phenomena which are so remote that their interpretation is no longer affected by the frequency of their occurrence. Now, as far as these data in between the remote past and the immediate present are concerned, modern critical (scientific) history has brought to light an enormous amount of factual data of great relevance. It is this storehouse of relevant facts which made the author unwilling to grant the whole truth of the claim that political science is today where it was in the days of Aristotle, when it comes to exact methods of observation. Many people who fail to appreciate the considerable difference this historical research makes to modern political science are simply unaware of it. Also, they are unaware of the refinements in historical criticism paralleling the refinements of modern laboratory technique. It has with justice been said that history is the laboratory of mankind. The fairly accurately recorded experiences of human beings can thus be made available for the testing of commonly accepted general descriptive formulæ or hypotheses. To do this as well as possible is the task of political science.

Political science and history.—It would, of course, be blasphemous to describe history as a mere fact-gathering subsidiary to political science (and sociology). History has its own peculiar province in seeking to understand historical individuality, whether of a person, a movement, or a nation. This is why a good many studies are admittedly historical as well as political in scope. Bryce's *American Commonwealth* is essentially an historical monograph, but of great value to the political scientist. How could this be otherwise, when one of the most nourishing roots of modern political science is institutional history? From this standpoint it must be admitted that a great deal of the best work done in Departments of Government in the universities is fundamentally historical in nature. The main feature distinguishing a good book on American or English government is usually the author's familiarity with the general problems of politics. Much of the value of Bryce's achievement lay in that direction, and so did that of Lowell, Merriam, or Beard, to mention only three of the more distinguished names. All these men had, or have, a vivid personal sense of historical individuality, coupled with a genuine insight into the more generally accepted "hypotheses" regarding politics. As a result, these writers succeed in giving at once a sense of a reliable factual foundation and a stimulus to reflection about general ideas. Somehow, you not only learn a great deal about America and American government through reading Bryce, but you also commence to understand politics. This results, of course, to some extent from all good history, but there is naturally a great deal more to history than just politics. This is not the place for considering the relative educational value of history and political science. What we are concerned with is to bring out the difference in focus of the two. To clinch the argument by a specific example: If an historian considers the materials of early English party history, he is likely to do it for the purpose of better understanding England in the seventeenth century, or English government at that time, or even the personality of Shaftesbury. If a political scientist uses the same materials, he is probably testing some general hypothesis about the origin of parties. Both these inquiries are vital, and they can greatly benefit each other. The tendency to deprecate each other's work is deplorable, and unworthy of the fellowship of scholars.

Law.—If the relations between students of history and politics are sometimes strained by lack of genuine appreciation of each other's ends, this is even more frequently the case between students of law and those of government, at least in the United States. For in Europe, a great deal of important work in political science has been done by jurists concerned with public law. From Bodin down to Jellinek the annals of political science cannot be written without taking constant account of the legalist. To be sure, most of these legal studies of politics plainly show their juristic mode of thought. What is the distinguishing feature of this legal approach? It is a particular vocabulary taught by the particular legal system. In modern times, this is usually a national legal system. Thus all the work of German political scientists during the nineteenth century bears the earmarks of the leading concepts of German public law. There are many ways of interpreting law, its nature and its functions; they all imply that the student of legal problems is essentially concerned with the interpretation of authoritative words and phrases. Professor Powell's sarcastic gibe: "Due process is what the Supreme Court says it is," undeniably is correct. The "state" is, for the American lawyer, what the courts say the Constitution means by that word. If someone speaks of the American state, meaning thereby the federal union rather than Massachusetts, Vermont, and the rest, he has transcended the law. If he has taught students to talk that way, he may some day to his distress find them pleading in court that the state can do things which according to the Constitution (and the Supreme Court) only the federal government can do. Now the political scientist not only cannot accept these national legal vocabularies, but he must transcend them. Being by definition interested in the things which happen in the most diverse places and at the most diverse times, no verbal pattern with very distinctive and limited meanings can suit him. At the same time, his interest in the work of the student of legal phenomena must be of the very keenest, since so much political activity becomes manifest in matters legal. Thus Bryce had to be a lawyer as well as an historian to write his *American Commonwealth*. Particularly in modern times, so much political activity is focused upon, and revolves around, the making of law that political science without law is a phantom. Many students of law are unwilling to admit the reverse. Why? Because common ideas about politics are afloat all about us, and can be picked up by any intelligent person, while their critical evaluation and testing by political science has not progressed far enough, in most cases, to impress the layman.

Economics.—If political science is thus differentiated by method from law and history, though sharing a great part of their materials, the opposite may be said and has been said of it in relation to economics. Here you have a generalizing social science which tries by a variety of scientific methods to verify distinct hypotheses regarding recurrent social events. These economic hypotheses (or laws, as they used to be called) are primarily concerned with the acquisition and distribution of wealth, i.e., scarce consumable goods and their equivalent, money. If the method of political science is similar, what is its distinguishing content? The answer at present most readily offered is that political science is concerned with the acquisition and distribution of power. But what is power? Is not wealth itself a form of power? To this latter question we must simply reply: No. Wealth may be converted into power, but it is not in itself power. Similarly power can, of course, often be converted into wealth, and for both processes there are large masses of supporting historical evidence. A study of the conditions under which wealth is converted into power, and vice versa, is a borderline field of very significant inquiry which the economist approaches through a heading such as monopoly, whereas the political scientist approaches it through corruption, plutocracy, and the like. But what is power? Hobbes, in a famous definition, described it as the present means to secure some future apparent good. That such a definition is much too broad must be apparent when we consider power as contrasted with wealth, since so much wealth is precisely what Hobbes claims power to be: present means to secure future apparent goods. This would not be a fatal objection to Hobbes' definition; for it may well be that some types of power and wealth are identical, that the two groups of phenomena overlap. But a dime, though certainly present means to secure future apparent goods, is not "power" in any but a rather strained sense. This criticism of Hobbes' definition is not being advanced, however, as a preface to a better definition, but rather as a stepping stone to a more radical assertion. For we maintain that no adequate scientific answer can be given to the question: "What is power?" All we can state are some of the properties of power which are relevant to political inquiry. For the rest, we must depend upon common sense agreement which would concede that neither a house, nor a love affair, nor yet an idea is power when taken by itself. They can all become instruments in the hands of one seeking power. But in order to convert them into power, this power-seeker must find human beings who value one of these things sufficiently to obey his orders in return.

Power presupposes common objectives.—This, then, is the first axiom concerning power: that it presupposes two or more human beings, and ordinarily it presupposes a group of such beings, pursuing common objectives, interests, or values. It is, therefore, impossible to study politics as the process of acquiring, distributing, and losing power without taking into consideration the major objectives of the human beings involved in the situations studied. This does not, however, cast us out upon the uncharted seas of teleological metaphysics. For common sense observation shows us that certain objectives are constantly recurring among human groups,—why, we do not know. Such are order and security on the one hand, happiness and prosperity on the other. Such "objectives" may seem vague; they certainly are comprehensive. Just the same, the Declaration of Independence uttered not merely aspirations, but unalterable facts when it claimed life, liberty, and the pursuit of happiness as the goals of politics. A moment's thought will show further that order and security and all that goes with these objectives are neutral, the area within which they are sought is capable of indefinite expansion, and there is no logical reason why ultimately all mankind should not be united in securing them. Happiness and prosperity, on the other hand, are distinctive and exclusive. They divide human beings from each other. As the proverb has it: "One man's owl is another's nightingale." Germans like to do one thing, Americans another. If the Russians have all the manganese, the French cannot have it, and so forth. From the efforts to secure the latter objectives conjointly with the former result all the political situations which we know.

Power a human relationship; its nature controversial.—The fact that power presupposes several human beings implies the further fact that power is a certain kind of human relationship. (Second axiom.) While this has always been accepted as axiomatic by political thinkers, the nature of this type of human relationship has been described by some as if it were a quality or substance found in some human beings and from them radiating as it were to others. The definition of power by Hobbes which was cited in an earlier paragraph puts Hobbes into the group of thinkers expounding such a "substantive" concept of power. A diagram might indicate more clearly the way in which this substantive view of power appears:

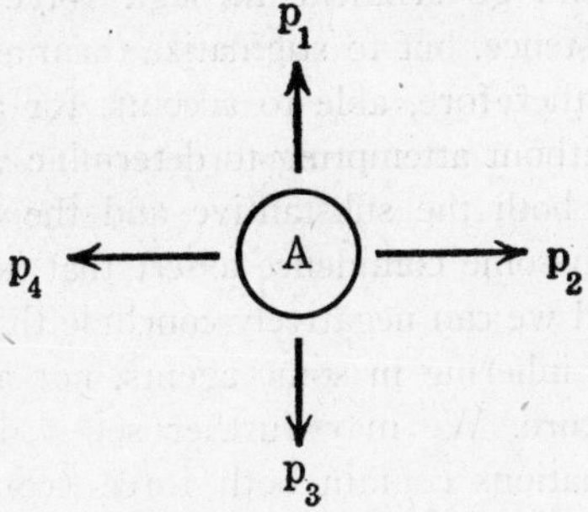

A=agent possessing power
p_1, p_2, p_3, p_4 = powers possessed by agents

Other thinkers have been led to stress the mutual nature of the power situation,—in other words the fact that in order to have power one has to find people over whom to have power. Power, in this case, is not inherent in some of the individuals composing the group, but in the relationship itself. Such a "relational" concept of power is found in Locke's philosophical writings, though his political tracts are contradictory in this respect. It, too, might for a better understanding of the matter be represented by a simple diagram:

$$A_1 \bullet \xleftrightarrow{\quad p \quad} \bullet A_2$$

A_1, A_2 = agents involved in power relationship
p = relationship containing power

Neither of these diagrams should be taken too seriously, of course; they merely aid in grasping the contrast between the "substantive" and the "relational" concept of power.

Consent and constraint both real forces, generating power.—What is the importance of attributing to power the quality either of a substance or of a relationship? Where the substantive concept of power prevails, the thinker has been inclined to neglect the phenomena of genuine consent, interpreting them as propaganda, symbols, myths, and so forth. As was the case with Hobbes in the seventeenth century, so it is with many modern writers, particularly of the psychological school today. Where the relational concept has been emphasized, as in Locke, the monarchomachs, or contemporary socialist utopians, there has been a tendency to neglect the phenomena of conquest and government through force or constraint, to recognize their existence, but to stigmatize them as tyranny. Neither of these views is, therefore, able to account for all of the facts as we know them. Without attempting to determine whether we should therefore abandon both the substantive and the relational view of power, we can with some confidence assert that neither view can be really adequate, and we can negatively conclude that power is neither simply a substance inhering in some agents, nor a relationship of a strictly mutual nature. We may further set it down as axiomatic that all power situations contain both force (constraint) and consent, but in greatly varying ratios, with power based on either force (constraint) or consent alone constituting an unreal extreme or limit. (Third axiom.) In graphic representation the foregoing statements could be put down thus:

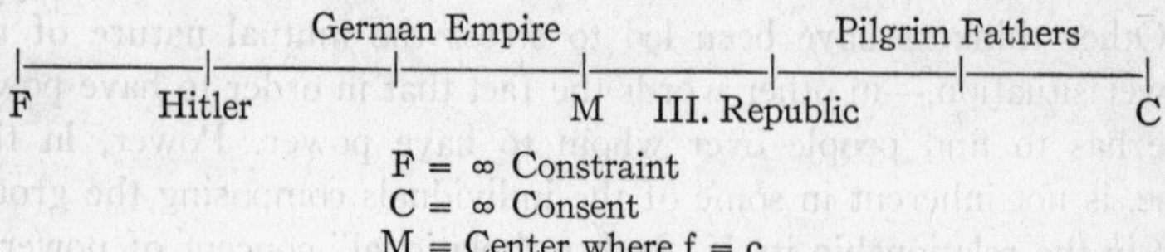

This cursory analysis of force (constraint) and consent would not be complete without emphasizing the implication that constraint and consent are not logical opposites. In other words, both constraint and consent are something real, they *do* something, they do not merely denote the absence of something else. It is wrong, therefore, to look upon consent as non-constraint, or upon constraint as non-consent. Each of them is more than the negation of its opposite; each is a living force generating power.

Both consent and constraint together determine the intensity of a political situation (first hypothesis).—Another consideration of great significance is closely bound up with this axiom regarding the constant presence of constraint and consent in power situations. The Hitlers, Mussolinis, and Stalins claim, of course, that their governments rest upon the consent of the governed. So may a hold-up occur with the "consent" of the victim. Yet few people would confound rape with a love affair. To clarify this aspect, it has been said that consent must be voluntary; but all consent is voluntary in the sense that it is being willed. The only adequate method of dealing with this problem is to seek to discover observable indices for the relative amount of consent and constraint (force) present in a variety of power situations. As both are positive, real forces, their presence must be positively ascertained. We may say tentatively, for example, that a high degree of constraint on the part of a given government is indicated by frequent killings, many suicides, large-scale confiscations, numerous types of corporal punishment, and so forth. Consent in large measure would, on the other hand, be indicated by voluntary donations, relative infrequency and lightness of punishments, public manifestations of great enthusiasm such as parades, and finally willing sacrifice of life by the governed. But what shall we say when both these indicators are present in large measure? Power situations are evidently not only differentiated according to the ratio of consent and constraint, but also according to the absolute amount of both. This absolute amount of both consent and constraint determines what we may call the intensity of a political situation. This is our first hypothesis, derived from the axioms, and quite important. There unquestionably is a very real difference between a political situation in which both consent and constraint are rather low, as in the United States today, and one in which both consent and constraint are rather high as is supposedly the case in contemporary Italy. Since this intensity is determined by the absolute amount of either consent or constraint or both, it is perhaps most readily represented by the diagonal of the parallelogram of these two forces: consent and constraint. In that case its numerical value would equal the square root of the sum of squares of the numerical values of consent and constraint. But since we are not at the present time in a position to state numerical values for either consent or constraint, case analysis will be offered in Chapters II, III, XIV and XXV.

Concentration of power and disunity (second hypothesis).—From the preceding hypothesis and its corollaries it may be deduced that neither military conquest, nor economic purchase, nor religious persuasion can be interpreted as synonymous with either constraint or consent, though this has often been done in politics. To be sure, there is a greater probability of constraint in military conquest, and a greater probability of consent in religious persuasion; but the calling in of the Norsemen by the nobles of Kiev, or the calling in of the French by the Separatists in the Rhineland (to mention a more recent, though less important example) show elements of consent in situations involving military conquest. Likewise the Inquisition and the Elizabethan and Fascist oaths of allegiance show elements of constraint in situations presumably based upon religious persuasion. This whole set of facts—and they are recurrent in human affairs—is traceable to the fact that communities are divided, rather than united; at least they contain elements of division. While certain objectives are common to members of a given group, others are not at all. If the objectives in a community were ever completely alike, all the fundamental decisions would be made by the community as a whole without any friction. But if the objectives in the community are divided, there are apt to be authoritative decisions. If the division becomes so profound as to forestall even vital decisions, rulership will be assumed by a minority which succeeds in detaching itself from the divisions in the community. In the hands of this minority power will be concentrated. In other words, a tendency toward the concentration of power is the concomitant of a rather divided community, while a united community can function with rather dispersed powers. The full implications of the second hypothesis will become clear only in the course of the second part.

The rule of anticipated reactions (third hypothesis).—The interaction of constraint and consent not only shows how vitally the distribution of power is connected with the structure of the community in terms of its objectives; it also gives us a decisive clue as to the nature of influence. Apart from power, influence is probably the most important basic concept of political science. In popular parlance, influence is recognized to be a form of power. But it is very evasive, because most influence operates by changing the conduct of people without any outward appearance of change. Though the element of constraint may be of great weight, it almost always appears to be entirely obscured by manifest consent. The influence of public opinion, or of parliament upon the conduct of governmental affairs is as devoid of ascertainable manifestations as the influence of a courtesan upon her royal master. Why should this be so? Because the person or group which is being influenced *anticipates the reactions* of him or those who exercise the influence. Once, when being asked (in private) how much English public opinion influenced the conduct of English foreign affairs, Sir Eyre Crowe, a keen permanent official of the Foreign Office, replied that there was only one instance, the Venezuela imbroglio, when the Foreign Office had been obliged to change its policy in response to public opinion. The implication of this statement was that the influence of public opinion is very small. Sir Eyre Crowe forgot that almost daily the policy-making officials deliberated upon what would be the reaction of the public to this, what the reaction of Parliament to that move. By correctly anticipating these reactions, the Foreign Office avoided getting embroiled and having to reverse its course; but was it therefore free from being influenced by Parliament and the public? The fatal hesitancy of the Foreign Office in clarifying its position with regard to a war in Europe—a hesitancy which Poincaré and others claimed to have been a major "cause" of the outbreak of the World War—was entailed by Lord Grey's fear of the reaction of the British (Liberal) public. He believed that the cabinet would have to resign if it announced that it was prepared to enter the war against Germany on the side of France and Russia. Sir Eyre Crowe himself was bitterly opposed to this policy, believing it to be an error of the first magnitude. Considered opinion agrees with him today, and yet it also agrees with Grey that the Cabinet would have had to resign. Was that not influence of Parliament and public opinion, influence of the most fatal sort? In the light of these considerations, we can formulate a third rule regarding the primary qualities of power, or rather the particular form of power known as influence, the rule of anticipated reactions: Any political context in which we observe one or more instances in which a previous decision or action is reversed is likely to be permeated by the *influence* of the individual or the group to whom the reversal can be traced in the specific case. The decisive importance of this third hypothesis will appear in the course of the third part when we consider parliamentary government.

Aristotelian and modern views contrasted as static and dynamic.—This brief survey of power as the focal point of modern political science brings to light the deep abyss which separates our approach from that of Aristotle. Aristotle as well as Plato was concerned with static problems of classification in terms of (a) the number of rulers, and (b) a general moral judgment as to the objectives pursued by the government. It is consequently not without some truth that a student of imagination and ability when sent to consider contemporary European politics in terms of Aristotelian political theory reported that the place of greatest interest to a true Aristotelian would be the Republic of Andorra. This static, numerical, and moral approach had another implication. It looked upon all change as intrinsically bad, except in terms of the fixed moral judgments regarding objectives. Such a view forms the most complete contrast imaginable to our modern viewpoint. For our whole approach is dynamic in its interests. Monarchy, the very word which for Aristotle essentially meant rule by one man when directed to good purposes, has for the modern mind become a term denoting rather certain selective and functional ideas. Broadly speaking it designates a peculiar type of constitutional legitimacy founded upon the pure blood of the monarch, who, no matter how limited may be the extent of his governing functions, is thereby enabled to represent the organic unity of the people. The monarch is the symbol of the living growth of a unified culture pattern of which the constitutional order is but an aspect. What made France a monarchy in the time of Richelieu was not the rule of one man—Richelieu—but the fact that there existed an hereditary king from whom he derived his authority and legitimate powers. Beyond these considerations, the modern scientific approach is interested in questions of historical fitness, i.e., in relative value judgments which take account of the "character" of a particular group or nation. This interest is akin to modern painting's love of portraiture, contrasted with which we may liken the Aristotelian analysis to the abstract beauty of the human body in Greek sculpture. From such historical considerations there results a very different attitude toward change. Change is looked upon as intrinsically necessary. The question is therefore how to turn such change to good account, how to adapt political life to the changing social context in order to secure the most advantageous conditions, and as a minimum the continued survival of the group in question.

Conclusion.—We conclude that modern political science is largely a critical examination of common sense notions concerning the working of political institutions and procedures. Three axiomatic truths regarding the nature of power lie at its foundation, namely that power ordinarily presupposes a group of human beings with some common objectives, that it manifests a relationship between them, and that it is generated as the joint effect of consent and constraint. Most of the materials of political science are taken from history and law, and the common-sense notions are examined in the light of this historical experience, as if they were scientific hypotheses formulated for the purpose of discovering general rules or "laws" of politics. Since most of the common-sense notions regarding the working of political institutions and procedures are at least partially inaccurate, different and strictly scientific hypotheses may also be developed by the political scientist, and of these we have offered three leading examples. The whole tenor of this discussion has shown that modern political science is not concerned with the forms of government, nor is it concerned with *the* ideal form of government. It is concerned with the instruments or techniques of political action in terms of the objectives they are supposed to serve. We shall therefore focus the discussion of the first part by considering the major objectives of modern government and the techniques for their achievement. Such a discussion will, it is hoped, show that a consideration of these objectives is compatible with an empirical scientific approach to the whole gamut of political phenomena.

CHAPTER II

THE CORE OF MODERN GOVERNMENT: BUREAUCRACY

A. Its Background

1. Introductory.—2. The progress of unitary government gradual and intermittent.—3. Determinants of this progress.—4. The economic factor.—5. The military factor.—6. The geographical factor.—7. The religious factor.—8. Nationalism as a factor.—9. Possibility of other determinants.—10. The Roman law as a formative force.—11. Sovereignty and the power to make laws.

Introductory.—The cradle of modern government has been variously recognized in the kingdoms of France and England, in the Italian city state, in the Roman Catholic Church, and even in the Sicilian realm of the brilliant Emperor Frederick II. All these claims are based upon one aspect common to these several political bodies: the possession of a bureaucracy, a body of servants devoted to prince, *civiltà,* or church. Deprived of the halo cast about them by the success of their endeavors, these people appear to have been a gang of henchmen united in the determination to strengthen their lord against various rivals. What caused historians later to acclaim some of these gangs as public servants is the fact that a certain number of lords succeeded in identifying their own with the public interest. This is particularly true of the princes claiming a wide territorial realm, for the very creation of those larger communities whose interest they ultimately claimed to represent was due in large measure to their own successful efforts to compete with political authorities of a more narrowly local sort.

The progress of unitary government gradual and intermittent.—This struggle between more or less local holders of power raged for many centuries, and it is quite arbitrary to single out a particular ruler, such as Henry VIII of England, or Louis XI of France as the "founder." The fact of the matter is that this long-drawn-out conflict had many ups and downs. Its course is marked by decided up-swings of royal power and of the services which they controlled, only to be followed by retrogressions accompanied by the inevitable dispersion of power. Nor was this process by any means a uniform one in the several countries—a word one hesitates to use when speaking of periods in which boundaries were as fluctuating as they were then. Under the Norman and early Plantagenet kings, England made remarkable strides toward centralization, but the period of *Magna Charta* is marked by the ascendancy of the local powers. The consolidation which followed was almost entirely lost during the Wars of the Roses, which in turn paved the way for Tudor absolutism. In France the development was no less turbulent, and subject to the "law of the pendulum," so generally characteristic of political processes, yet it resembled the English case in that it steadily progressed toward greater consolidation of the nation. In Germany and Italy, on the other hand, the forces of disintegration gained the ascendancy, when we consider the nation as a whole; but within the more limited areas of city states and principalities, centralizing forces were also victorious. The histories of Florence and Venice, no less than those of Bavaria and Brandenburg-Prussia bear witness to this trend.

Determinants of this progress.—Various causes, military, economic, geographic, religious, and nationalist, have been offered to explain this progress of territorial expansion. We are not going to take a stand regarding these rival doctrines, but shall limit ourselves to describing these several factors, treating them as so many conditions the confluence of which seems to have attended the development of modern governmental activities. For as scientists we are not concerned with final causes, but with intermediary conditions which are found to accompany certain observed results. It is the old story of the camel which collapses under a single blade of straw, having previously been loaded to the very limit of its capacity. This is a concrete illustration of the general logical principle that if several causes are necessary for producing a given result, then there is no good reason for considering one more important than another. With this general principle firmly in mind, we can explore the several "causes" or determinants for centralization and bureaucratization.

The economic factor.—The primary economic determinant is to be found in the expansion of trade, which created a need for better police protection and security in transportation and communication. The story of these activities is a long and complicated one, but there is little disagreement concerning the fundamental facts as revealed in the mounting trade figures in Venice, Florence, Antwerp, London, Frankfort, and many other centers of urban progress. The citizenry of London and Paris, as well as the imperial cities of Germany, were on the whole willing supporters of the princely overlord against local feudal barons, regarding him as the likeliest guarantor of the public peace. But in Italy where the development of trade was perhaps most marked, the cities did not support such a central head, in fact offered the most violent opposition to imperial as well as papal pretensions. Here traders preferred to rely upon the growing power of their own city, a tendency which culminated in the brilliant ascendancy of the Medici in Florence to the very headship of the state. By increasing the security of commercial intercourse, these political developments provided a fertile field for the expansion of trade activities. During the later phase of the evolution of modern government when differentiated bureaucracies were being established all over Europe, the industrial revolution with its growing number of manufacturing establishments is said to have "caused" the expansion of governmental services. But while there can be no doubt that the growth of these industries provided an important concomitant condition of governmental expansion, evidence is plentiful which would point toward the governments' growing the industries. In fact, the term mercantilism, generally used for characterizing this age, suggests just that type of governmental participation and stimulation in the economic realm.

The military factor.—The military cause or determinant is most clearly seen when we consider the development of various weapons and techniques of warfare during these centuries. If we compare the military establishments of early modern times with those prevalent in the Middle Ages, we discover three important technical differences: (1) they are very much larger, (2) their main force consists of infantry, (3) they are equipped with fire arms and guns. Besides these three technical differences, there are three important administrative contrasts: (1) the military establishments are permanent (standing armies), (2) they are mercenary, or at least regularly paid, (3) they possess a central command, entrusted to a professional officer corps. The story of how all these changes came about is an intricate one, and differs considerably for the various countries. To mention just one important example, in England the military establishment was predominantly naval, while on the Continent the army occupied the center of attention, for obvious reasons. But army and navy exercised a similar effect upon the growth of modern government. In the first place, as irregular forces become standing mercenary armies, expensively equipped, they require ever increasing sums for their sustenance and thereby oblige the prince to perfect his tax-gathering machinery. Officials must be hired and organized, not only to collect the taxes, but to break down local resistance, and to give assistance to those groups in the community which promise larger tax returns through the development of industry and manufacture. Again, the large size of the armies presupposes the organization of offices for collecting the food for men and horse as well as for distributing it. Finally the development of a professional officer corps suggests a similar hierarchy for the administrative services. Obviously, if one starts from this military development as a fact, he could undertake to explain the entire evolution of modern government from that angle. Actually this military development itself is as much caused by the evolution and growth of modern government; for in the struggle with local lords, as well as in the conflicts which arose between the several kingdoms, we recognize the most powerful stimulants to this military progress. For modern infantry first appeared in Switzerland, where peasants on foot defeated the Austrian duke's baronial cavalry, and it appeared again in the Hundred Years' War when the newly organized archers gave the victory to England, until Charles VII of France succeeded in establishing his regular infantry. Again we find that military and governmental development stimulate each other as concomitant aspects of the same process.

The geographical factor.—Attempts to explain the evolution entirely in terms of geography are likewise foredoomed to failure. For while the insular situation of England obviously at once invited her subordination to one government, and facilitated such centralization by making foreign assistance to the weaker party relatively difficult, if not impossible, it does not suffice to explain its actual consummation. England has always been an island. In other words, the difficulty under which any geographic explanation labors is the static character of all geographic conditions. Growth is change, and cannot be explained by what has always been. Consequently we find that those who would make us believe that geography was the final cause, always slip in an unexplained, but firmly asserted "natural" tendency of the state to grow. This natural tendency toward growth once accepted, it is shown how the governments of England, France, Switzerland, and so forth grew the way they did, because mountains, rivers, plains, and other such "facts" conditioned the particular form of their growth. There is little in the geography of Burgundy, to pick an example at random, which would lead us to conclude affirmatively that it was to become part of France rather than Germany. Nor can the general assertions about the relation of climate to national character, first expounded by Aristotle, be considered adequately tested scientific hypotheses. Of the three causes or conditions which we have considered so far, the geographic would appear to be the least conclusive as the specific element, though from the point of view of the natural scientist the most "natural."

The religious factor.—The determinants or conditions which we have so far discussed have been of the material sort, and their efficacy has been expounded by people of a material bent of mind. We must now look for a moment at determinants of an idealist type which condition men's behavior through their minds without reference to a material force. The broadest and most inclusive interpretation of this type is that which sees modern governments essentially as attempts at a realization of the social teachings of the Christian churches. While medieval political life was devoid of moral and legal restraints, except in so far as the Church was able to bring pressure to bear upon individual rulers, the Reformation carried this into the daily life of the individual citizen. The concepts of duty and discipline are cited as essential constituent elements of modern governmental behavior patterns, and these are said to have been spread by the Reformation and then to have been instilled into Catholic rulers by the Counter-Reformation. Again, as in our previous cases, it is possible to offer abundant proof for these contentions. The life-stories of individual leaders, such as Cromwell and Coke, the Great Elector and Henry IV, Gustavus-Adolphus, and the princes of Orange, reveal the force of these ideas in shaping their own conduct as well as the standards which they set for their officials. But there is nothing in the evidence which would not allow a person determined to "prove" the economic or any other material interpretation to turn the argument right around and insist that religion would not have possessed this formative power, if the conditions for the growth of such large-scale governmental administrative machinery had not been favorable to or even determinative of such a development. Thus the unbiased observer is once more forced to the conclusion that these religious ideas were a concomitant condition of the evolution of modern government, no more, no less. The same can be said of the secular form Hegel gave to these notions when he ventured to explain the growth of governments in terms of the eternal spirit which presumably manifested itself in history through certain ideas to be realized by certain governments.

Nationalism as a factor.—Another important explanatory "cause" of modern governments is the nation, or the national spirit. In some ways this explanation is closely linked to the preceding one, in that it is fundamentally religious in the sense in which nationalism has been described as the modern religion. Both in England and France this nationalist explanation has flourished, on account of the strength of the national tradition in these countries. Fundamentally, it is proposed under this theory that modern constitutional government (England) or modern centralized governmental machinery (France) is the work of a "national genius," a collective group spirit as it were, which created the government as we know it. As in our previous explanations, considerable amount of proof can be offered in support of this contention. Letters and statements of politicians and officials abound with more or less unctuous references to their devotion to the national cause, and there can be no question that the development of a public, as compared to a royal, service was greatly aided by the emergence of national consciousness. The nation as the sum total of the cultural environment offered a welcome substitute for the person of the king. Cromwell and Richelieu are alike in their allegiance to their country, their nation. The French revolution immensely intensified these sentiments, and carried them into lands, like Germany, where they had previously not taken root. The answer to these arguments, once they are made out to prove that the nation caused the modern state, springs from this very fact that modern states arose where there was no nation, nor any national spirit, countries like Prussia and the Hapsburg domains which rivaled France in the perfection of a modern governmental machinery.

Possibility of other determinants.—After this survey of major causes, determinants, or conditions, whichever we prefer to call them, it remains to suggest that the selection of these conditions is in a scientific sense quite arbitrary. Political psychologists of the Freudian bent of mind will rebuke us for not mentioning the changing sex behavior as the ultimate cause. Perhaps this factor is as important a concomitant condition as any of the ones we have discussed; but nobody has as yet undertaken to unearth the material which would establish the link between sex repression and the building of modern governments, though a casual inspection of a long line of such builders suggests the fruitfulness of such an investigation: Elizabeth, Cromwell, Richelieu, Wallenstein, Gustavus-Adolphus, the Great Elector, Frederick the Great, Napoleon, and so forth. Nor can the concomitant deterioration of sex repression (morals) and governmental efficacy be entirely accidental. Willy-nilly, we must lay these conditions aside as being too remote and obscure for adequate observation and analysis, just as the student of plant life is limited by the capacity of his microscope, the student of the heavens by that of the telescope. The example of the sexual factor is useful primarily in serving as a warning against any rash conclusions and final closing of the books. Though we mark down five causes or conditions as primarily relevant for an understanding of the growth and development of modern government, its centralization and bureaucratization, we should forever be ready to examine new evidence which might enrich our comprehension and test the adequacy of our hypotheses.

The Roman law as a formative force.—Having sketched the background of conditions of our modern governmental bureaucracy, it remains for us to say a few words about its legal background, in other words the forms in which it emerged. For law is essentially the embodiment of the established forms of recurrent social behavior patterns. This is the reason why all political, economic, and sociological studies are impossible without an adequate analysis of the legal forms within which a particular activity or process has been clothed. But this analysis must not be a legal analysis, in the sense in which the legal scholar must carry it on. The legal scholar is interested in specific rules and concepts of law and in the relation of the various concepts to each other. The political scientist is interested in the system of law as a whole, the political function it serves, because of the formal elements it happens to contain. Concretely speaking with reference to our subject of centralization and bureaucratization, we find that royal judges everywhere (imitating the papal legates) tended to employ the Roman law during the later Middle Ages and early modern times. It was long believed that this was not so in England, but more recent investigations have shown this to be largely untrue; the impact of the Roman law is merely more obscure, because it lay farther back in time in England. Until the idea of man-made law, of legislation, was definitely established, the greatest obstacle in the king's or prince's efforts toward centralization and expansion of the royal jurisdiction was the multitude of local laws, embodied in eternal custom. As against this obstacle, there offered itself one ideal weapon, a system of law, more ancient and therefore almost divine, the law of the Roman Empire as embodied in the Institutes, the Digests, and the Code of Justinian. Emperor and Pope alike sought weapons in its provisions against traditional local customs, only to be followed by the several national kings. This is the importance of the famous doctrine of French lawyers, that the French king is *imperator* (emperor) in his own kingdom. He can, therefore, draw upon the Roman law. In it were presumably embodied the principles of a common law of the whole kingdom. Through it, the jurists, called *Legistes*, slowly succeeded in breaking down the feudal organization. It is perfectly obvious that in this process of interpretation and application the Roman law was twisted and arbitrary selections from its tenets gave it a wholly different flavor from the one it had possessed when it regulated the social life of the Eastern Roman Empire. Yet, it so happened that the Roman law, being the law of a highly developed commercial community, contained many principles which were better adapted to the needs of the emerging commercial classes than the local customs of a cruder agricultural society. Its urbanity, you might say, strengthened its position rather considerably, and insured it the support of the rising townsfolk everywhere. The essential political significance of the impact of Roman law has at times been overlooked, because it came much earlier in England and France than in Germany. The imperial aspirations of the German kings had prevented its "nationalization," and therefore the true "reception" as the process was baptized by German scholars, came only when ultimate political authority passed to the several territorial princes in the sixteenth and seventeenth centuries. Then suddenly these princes commenced to put the Roman law to the same use to which it had earlier been put by the kings of France, England, and Spain; for they no longer needed the local law for combating imperial pretensions. But here as there it served the purpose of consolidating and centralizing scattered feudal realms, facilitating commerce, and last, but not least, rendering abstract and impersonal the relation of official and prince, as well as that of prince and people, by the Roman doctrine of magistracy. In Frederick the Great's celebrated phrase: "I am the first servant of my state," there appears an echo of the Roman *magister* (servant), though no Roman magistrate could ever have ventured to claim the state as his own, as Frederick did.

Sovereignty and the power to make laws.—This is the politically relevant element in the concept of sovereignty, that it rendered impersonal the relation of the king to his subjects. Under feudalism, the principle of the relation between the lord (*princeps*) and the vassal was personal "mutuality." Such personal relationship must needs be limited in extent, and was therefore ill-adapted to wide territorial realms. The hierarchy of the mutual relationships which feudal society had tried to evolve in the effort to bridge the gap had shown a dismal tendency toward distintegration and anarchy. This tendency had resulted from the growth of complex intermediary authorities which opposed the prince's rule. To escape from this confusion it was then asserted that no true government existed unless there was somewhere an authority for making laws binding upon all the inhabitants of a given territory. The true achievement which lay in this process has been obscured by the struggle over the control of such a government. It was forgotten that it was necessary first to create a government, before the question of its control could even arise. And it was furthermore forgotten that this question of control could arise earlier in England than in France, because Tudor absolutism had consolidated previous efforts to establish an effectively centralized bureaucracy, at a time when France was in the grip of an extended civil war. From this civil war the crown emerged with a considerable army at its command which made it possible to crush the *Fronde,* while Cromwell's Model Army triumphed over the weak royal forces in England. This military ascendancy of the French crown, stimulated as it was by the possibilities of foreign invasion, delayed the outbreak of the struggle over the control of the government for one hundred and forty years. There is no reason to question these conclusions of de Lolme, set forth long ago in his *Government of England.* The needs of potential military conflict formed a chain of interacting causes which delayed the advent of popular control. It was the recognition of this fatal effect of international anarchy which led Immanuel Kant to point out the vital connection between peace and popular control of government. If only a family of democratic republics could keep the peace, it was true also that only a world government uniting the several national governments could assure the continued maintenance of popular control. Nor should it be forgotten that England was an aristocracy, or even an oligarchy, rather than a democracy, until 1832. The people at large seem to be better at controlling a government once it is set up than at creating one. It was in the pre-democratic period, therefore, that the concept of sovereignty was destined to play its most significant role in modern government.

CHAPTER III

THE CORE OF MODERN GOVERNMENT: BUREAUCRACY

B. Its Nature

1. *Introductory.*—2. *The example of Brandenburg's Council as revealing the four elementary constituents of a bureaucracy.*—3. *The Great Elector's Council as showing two more constituents.*—4. *These six elements distinguished as functional and behavior aspects.*—5. *The differentiation of functions.*—6. *Centralization and integration.*—7. *The hierarchy.*—8. *Unitary central direction more easy in monarchies.*—9. *More of hierarchy.*—10. *Discipline.*—11. *Qualification for office.*—12. *Relation to educational system.*—13. *Publicity.*—14. *Objectivity.*—15. *Precision and continuity.*—16. *Discretion versus secretiveness.*—17. *Conclusion.*

Introductory.—At the beginning of the previous chapter we called the body of servants devoted to the prince a bureaucracy. We might have called it officialdom, magistracy, government service or what not, as long as it is clearly understood (1) that we are talking of a group of human beings, not some mysterious super-entity as is suggested by the word "state," and (2) that these human beings perform definite functions which the community at large considers worth while. In primitive agricultural communities, these functions are directly attached to the possession of the land, usually becoming hereditary. Such was the foundation of the feudal system. Hereditary offices attached to the land offered the most promising means of securing a certain amount of law and order over widespread areas under primitive conditions of communication. It was a very inefficient system, allowing wide latitude for personal abuse, and great variations from one locality to the next. One way of coping with the attendant evils was for the royal overlords to extend their personal estate, through marriage, escheat, and so forth. As the royal domain grew, it became of vital importance that a central body of direction be created to prevent new disintegration at the center. This process we find took place in England, France, Spain, Prussia, Austria, and other realms.

The example of Brandenburg's Council as revealing the four elementary constituents of a bureaucracy.—These central bodies of royal servants are the beginnings of our modern administrative systems. In Brandenburg-Prussia where the process came fairly late, we are particularly well supplied with documentary evidence. In 1598, when Joachim Friedrich became Elector of Brandenburg, absolutism was unknown in his lands. Under his predecessor, Brandenburg was ruled by the Estates (Parliament). But Joachim Friedrich wanted to create a rule by officials (*Beamtenregiment*), a bureaucracy. Most educated people siding with the Estates, he resolved to draw upon foreigners, men brought to Brandenburg from other territories (they were, of course, Germans) and made into a Council by the order of 1604. This document together with one amending it in 1651 shows, in embryo, the vital constituent elements of a government service, or bureaucracy. Admitting openly that he was motivated to take his step by the example of other states (presumably France), this prince wished to bring about centralized control, where a great confusion of councils had prevailed before. The councillors should be allowed to speak and vote freely, and for the sake of order, the votes should be counted. That the transactions might be remembered, the prince's private secretary should keep records, and bring them forth again, when needed. This practice of keeping records, characteristic of an effective government service, does not prevail in the English cabinet even today, though all the lower offices keep careful records of all transactions in Britain as elsewhere. The confusion resulting from the failure to keep records disrupts the continuity of the service. All these records should, however, be kept strictly secret. In keeping with this secrecy was the further provision regarding the mails. The prince's chamber secretary was to bring all the letters unopened to the prince, who would read them and decide upon the answer either with or without consulting the councillors. The provision that every councillor who was given a letter for answering should make out a receipt for it points to the fact that many letters were lost by being taken away from the office. The elementary constituents of a bureaucracy as revealed by this document are thus four: (1) centralization of control and supervision, (2) safeguards for the independence of judgment of each member of the organization, (3) keeping of records and files, (4) secrecy.

The Great Elector's Council as showing two more constituents.—In the succeeding decades, certain difficulties appeared which had to be dealt with if the bureaucracy was to triumph over the Estates (Parliament). These arose partly from the acquisition of additional territories, and partly from the attendant multiplication of functions. The unification of a number of territories and provinces under one princely house was for Prussia, as it was for Austria, the most important impulse toward the development of an efficient bureaucracy, as it had been in France and England before. The aim was to make Brandenburg-Prussia strong, to win respect for her outside, and to make her prosperous and progressive. By the ordinance of 1651, the authority of the privy council is extended to all the different parts of the realm. Moreover, each councillor is assigned certain definite and specific functions which he must perform in the name of the prince. In accordance with this differentiation of functions, each councillor is to receive the mail which refers to his functions, read it, make comments, and then submit it to the prince and the other councillors. When the business at hand is familiar to all, council is to be held. In this procedure we recognize the beginnings of the discretionary power of the inferior regarding what shall come to the attention of his superior. In the council, the councillor specially in charge shall have the first vote, the votes shall be registered; but the ultimate decision is reserved for the prince. When we inspect the list of duties or functions, we also find a beginning made in the direction of distributing functions according to the qualification of the several councillors; court work is assigned to lawyers, diplomatic work to high nobles having experience therein, and so forth. The further elementary constituents of a bureaucracy as revealed by this document are therefore two: (1) the differentiation of functions, and (2) qualification for office. All the later documents merely re-affirm and expand upon these six elementary aspects, and therefore have no special interest for us here. Nor would it be impossible to show the same elements operative in England or France; merely because the development was much more gradual and goes back much further, it would be a much longer tale.

These six elements distinguished as functional and behavior aspects.—The six elements of a bureaucracy discovered in this analysis fall naturally into two groups. Three of them order the relations of the members of the organization to each other, namely, centralization of control and supervision, differentiation of functions, and qualification for office (entry and career aspects), while three embody rules defining desirable habit patterns of all the members of such an organization, namely, objectivity, precision and consistency, and discretion. Since the relations of the members of the organization are elaborated and defined with reference to the functions to be performed, we may call the first group of elementary criteria functional aspects, while the second group of criteria may be designated as behavior aspects of bureaucracy. Let us now turn to a more detailed analysis of the functional aspects. The first two functional aspects, namely centralization of control and supervision and differentiation of functions, are in a sense related; for the centralization of control and supervision is itself a kind of differentiation of a particular function, viz., the function of control and coördination. Central supervision is necessary only when a differentiation has previously existed. This is why centralization stands in close relation to integration. They both coördinate diffuse functions. But while centralization coördinates spatially diffused functions, such as the feudal age bestowed upon early modern times, integration coördinates technically differentiated functions, such as arose from the early differentiation of functions at the center. We may therefore speak first of the differentiation of functions.

The differentiation of functions.—The differentiation of functions means that offices or functions are distributed carefully and rationally among the members of a given organization, like a government service, and are then arranged into a whole, thus producing a more or less elaborate system of competencies or jurisdictions. This differentiation seems such an obvious prerequisite of an administrative task of any magnitude that it is frequently given only the most cursory attention. And yet, literally hundreds of years of the history of modern government were consumed in evolving even the most elementary distinctions, and in discovering by trial and error that, all things considered, functional differentiation is superior to regional differentiation, though a certain amount of both are always necessary. Nor is the process of differentiation yet by any means complete. To be sure, every modern government today has a separate ministry (department) of foreign affairs, of finance, of commerce, of labor, and so forth, and what cannot be readily classified is thrown into the ministry of the interior. But here the simplicity ends. There are the greatest variations between the several governments when we go into further detail. Students of administration are wont to consider the problems which arise under this heading as those of departmentalization, but in reality the problem is intimately related to the broader questions of constitutional framework. In the United States, for example, tariff problems do not only occupy the Department of Commerce, and the State Department handling foreign affairs, but also a special Tariff Commission which owes its existence to the separation of powers. In European countries where that constitutional device has not developed along the same lines, we do not find such a body. Brief reflection upon this and many other similar items will show that a rule embodying the principle of differentiated functions is more frequently pronounced in general terms than put into practical effect. Constant experimentation and work are necessary in order to keep the differentiation of functions of a government service abreast of developing communal needs.

Centralization and integration.—The afore-described technical differentiation of functions may, as we have pointed out, be complicated by a regional differentiation. Under such regional differentiation, also often referred to as decentralization, a whole series of governmental functions is assigned to an individual or a body having jurisdiction over a territorial subdivision, such as a province, a department, a county, a town, and so forth. The functions of such local authorities will invariably overlap to some extent the functions of technically differentiated central authorities. For this reason, a certain measure of supervision and control is invariably found necessary, and is usually vested in ministries of the interior (France, Prussia, and so forth), but may be lodged elsewhere for historical reasons (England: Board of Health). This central authority then acts as an intermediary and integrator between technically and regionally differentiated functions. This often causes a great deal of red tape, when the central authorities have themselves widely scattered local representatives. It might be very much easier for the local assessors to deal with the fiscal agents of the ministry of finance, but apart from personal contacts they are dependent upon the ministry of the interior for effective coördination. This set of situations shows vividly the close relationship between functional differentiation and central supervision and control. For when we pass from the top level of offices in a large organization, say the treasury, to the next lower one, the differentiation must be carried forward into the regulation of activities of individual officials on that level. Each official's sphere of competency is smaller, and comprised within a higher official's competency along with several other officials. There is, then, a double differentiation, namely (1) a technical differentiation on each level, and (2) a differentiation between more routine and more discretionary activities, as we go up and down the line in each organization. But because of its peculiar significance for the development and rationalization of a government service, we must isolate this type of differentiation as a distinct process. Historically speaking, functional differentiation commences at the top, and gradually is extended downward, limiting in its course the sphere of regional differentiation, or, as it is usually called, local self-government (home rule). But as it proceeds downward, it constantly raises problems of integration with regard to differentiated functions, and problems of centralization with regard to functions not yet technically differentiated, but regionally dispersed. These problems of integration and of centralization, of supervision and control, may be lumped together under the heading hierarchy.

The hierarchy.—The hierarchy, then, is a concomitant of the rational distribution of functions. As soon as an organization grows to any size the large number of officials who exercise partly conflicting functions stand in constant need of integrating and coördinating leadership. This seems obvious enough, and yet the implications of administrative leadership have received rather inadequate attention, except in connection with private business management. The urgency of such administrative leadership springs from two related and recurrent problems. On the one hand, the detailed and specific functions of the lower-downs need constant re-interpretation in terms of the larger objectives which they presumably serve. On the other hand, the obstacles and difficulties encountered in the exercise of these detailed and specific functions require consideration with a view to the possible improvement or alteration of these larger objectives or purposes. Even so general a statement shows that the semi-military, authoritarian nature of a government service is by no means a gratuitous addition of petty autocrats, but inherent in the very nature of the processes which form the essence of all administrative services. It is curious that this point requires emphasizing in an age which exhibits examples of this same authoritarian, hierarchical control on all sides, since large scale business corporations are conducted on precisely this pattern.

Unitary central direction easier in monarchies.—The need for administrative leadership explains to some extent why monarchies have been so peculiarly well-adapted to developing a high-class government service. If the powers of control and coercion connected with the various offices and functions are arranged in more or less concentric circles which become smaller as we ascend to the higher regions, a single individual (or bureau acting as a unit) would presumably have ultimate control and power. Moreover, such an individual or group must be himself a part of the hierarchy, though not necessarily chosen from among it. This unitary central control characteristic of a fully developed hierarchy may, of course, be quite effectively exercised by elective officials, provided there is a sufficient amount of continuity and agreement between successive office holders as to the fundamentals of governmental activities. The English cabinet in the latter half of the nineteenth century succeeded in building up a remarkable public service corps; it may be well, however, to keep in mind that the English Prime Minister has often been called a practical dictator, once he has entered No. 10 Downing Street with a safe majority in the House of Commons. Lord Balfour well expressed the unity in fundamentals which alone will make this system work: "It is evident that our whole political machinery presupposes a people so fundamentally at one that they can safely afford to bicker." But when the realm is scattered, and the constituent elements are fundamentally at odds, as was true of the continental kingdoms and is still true of the German Reich or the British Empire, then one-man executive leadership (monocracy) can be secured most effectively through hereditary monarchy.

More of hierarchy.—Even though a trend toward unitary leadership be inherent in the hierarchical aspect of bureaucracy, or effective government service, it seems undesirable to overemphasize this point. Hierarchy in our opinion should describe more generally any determinate system of distributing the powers of control and coercion by subordinating officials performing very specific and tangible functions to other officials, who supervise and direct a determinate number of these officials, who in turn may be supervised and directed by a still more limited number of "higher-ups." Nor need this scale of subordination and control be restricted to individual officials. A hierarchy may subordinate one group of officials to another group of officials acting together as a unit. Or individual officials lower down may be subordinated to a group higher up. The Prussian Cabinet, the Swiss (Executive) Council, American executive commissions, and practically all judicial systems are of this structure. In

Anglo-Saxon countries, although the power of specific coercion of the higher courts to determine the decisions of lower ones is limited, the power of reversing decisions produces a similar effect crystallized in the rule of *stare decisis*. This rule limits narrowly the discretion of lower courts. However, an element of discretion remains, and this fact has led some writers to overemphasize the difference between courts and administrative bodies. In terms of actual conduct, the difference is quite small; for although the hierarchical principle seems to imply flawless subordination, the extent to which any given hierarchy conforms to that standard is limited by other competing principles which are essential for its life, such as the principle of differentiating and distributing functions. A higher official will hesitate to reverse the decision of a lower official, when he feels, as is often the case, that the lower official has a better knowledge of the facts in detail. This tendency in turn is also made a point of attack by those enamoured of the judicial form of governmental action; such writers forget that a certain discretion exercised by the lower officials contradicts their first allegation of strict centralization; they also forget that such discretion is found in the judicial realm too. The question of whether judicial or administrative action should be provided for is only to be answered in respect of the purposes or objectives to be achieved. There is nothing inherently beautiful in either. Both are techniques for accomplishing certain purposes, as we shall show further on. And both are comprehended within the governmental services or the bureaucracy, as that term is here understood.

Discipline.—Almost all administrative hierarchies have well-defined rules of discipline, according to which acts of alleged insubordination are judged. Some rudimentary discipline is inherent in any hierarchy. The rigor of the discipline should be studied by the political scientist in relation to the purpose for which the administrative set-up has come into existence. Moralizing should at all costs be avoided, though it is one of the most common inclinations of popularized thought on politics. Often, the word bureaucracy appears for propaganda purposes in this connection. But if the purpose of the particular hierarchy is kept in mind, a better understanding will result. A purpose which is likely to be defeated by delay in execution will produce a more rigorous discipline than one which is not imperiled by being postponed. An army at war and business enterprises in highly competitive fields offer good examples of rigorous discipline, while ordinary government service, in peace time, and business enterprises in distinctly monopolistic fields offer examples of rather lax discipline, unless their execution is intrinsically fraught with danger, like the railroad business, which shows high disciplinary standards. The comparatively static condition of most governmental activities during peace time has made it possible to subject all disciplinary action to fairly elaborate judicial procedure; its main purpose is to protect the official against arbitrary exercise of the disciplinary power. His punishment and removal cannot take place until he has been accused, indicted, examined, and pronounced guilty, either by a regular court, or by a court composed of his peers.

Qualification for office.—Our third functional criterion, the qualification for office, has received so much of the attention of students of public administration in the United States, that the problem of government personnel is treated by many people as identical with that of qualification for office. In view of this preoccupation with the problem of qualification, it is curious that the cognate problem of training for the service has received only cursory examination until now. Yet the system of public schools and universities as we find it in Europe originated to a considerable extent in the requirements of the government for well-trained officials. Speaking broadly, such a system of public schools and universities fulfills the function of coördinating educational facilities with the differentiated hierarchy of official functions through an elaborate system of standardized examinations. If such coördination is effective it becomes possible to consider the degrees from the several educational institutions as constituting at least in part satisfactory evidence that the person passing such examinations and holding the corresponding degree is qualified for a certain function in the hierarchy. Civil Service Commissions, as we find them in the United States, may turn out to be an effective substitute for such a system of coördinated schooling, for they tend gradually to bring about a mutual adaptation of the required qualifications for service and of the training which is given to acquire them. But the European governments in days gone by could not rely upon such a coördinator, because there were few schools to coördinate, and so they undertook to organize schools and universities themselves. Nor is it inconceivable that state schools and universities in this country will become subject to a certain amount of guidance from their governments, if the requirements of the governments for well-trained officials go on increasing as they have of late.

Relation to educational system.—To illustrate the foregoing general statement by a concrete example, let us take the German Post and Telegraph Office. Its service is divided roughly into three broad categories, the lower, the middle, and the higher service, the positions corresponding to the private, the non-commissioned officer, and the officer in the army. Similarly, the schooling is divided into three layers, normal schools, middle (American high) schools, and universities. The normal schools carry children to the age of fourteen, and graduation from them is required for entry into the lower service of the Post Office. The middle schools carry young men and women up to about eighteen (but usually taking them at ten), and the graduation from them (sometimes without the last two years) is required for entry into most of the positions in the middle service, as well as for admission to the university. A degree in law, or engineering, based upon academic training, is required for the higher service. Very similar arrangements prevail throughout continental Europe. In the United States there is a marked contrast in the upper range of the service. In this field, where the requirements for qualification are in Europe most rigorous, the spoils system continues to hold sway, while in the subordinate positions an approximation to the standards of a developed bureaucracy is found to prevail.

Publicity.—The foregoing analysis of the functional aspects of a developed bureaucracy would be incomplete, if we did not discuss briefly a feature which these several aspects gradually acquire to an ever increasing extent. This is the feature of determinateness and publicity. It will be recalled that we found all the elementary aspects present in the embryonic bureaucracy of the Brandenburg councils of the seventeenth century. What they then lacked was determinateness and publicity. In a sense, it is possible to assess the stage of development of a given bureaucracy by examining the extent to which its functional aspects are determinate and publicly known. We must link determinateness with publicity, because it is never insured unless full publicity enables any reasonably intelligent and interested person to judge for himself whether equality of treatment is safeguarded, favoritism, nepotism, arbitrariness, and so on, excluded. Only if that confidence exists, will the governmental services attract that high calibre of personnel which is an essential prerequisite for its ultimate success.

Objectivity.—Having examined the functional aspects of bureaucracy, we may now cast a passing glance at the three behavior aspects of bureaucracy. It is not necessary to examine them in detail, because their meaning is rather apparent. There has, however, been an inclination in English-speaking countries to belittle the first criterion. Yet objectivity, the unswerving loyalty to objective considerations of the needs of the service, has been an outstanding characteristic of the British, no less than of other successful bureaucracies. It is quite erroneous to attribute this devotion to "duty" to the fact that the cabinet is responsible to Parliament; more often than not this objectivity has to assert itself against, rather than on behalf of cabinet policy. It is dictated by a certain craftsman-like pride in achievement which derives its satisfaction from the respect and admiration it arouses in fellow craftsmen rather than in the public at large. It is never to be had without long training for a craft, for only such apprenticeship instills certain standards of perfection. The danger of such an attitude is a certain narrowness of outlook, and a failure to see the particular action in relation to its wider implications. Prussian bureaucracy suffered grievously from this over-perfection. Bismarck once exclaimed indignantly that the efficiency of her department heads would ruin Prussia. Herbert Hoover's administration of the United States Department of Commerce is another case in point.

Precision and continuity.—That precision and continuity are essential to effective administration is so evident that it has given rise to the rather extreme notion that any policy is better than a vacillating policy. The resulting rigid adherence to precedent usually is at the bottom of the public indignation about red tape. An intimate knowledge of the requirements of a certain field of governmental activity is necessary before it is really possible to distinguish between superfluous red tape and inherently desirable routine work. In the same way, imprecision, which is often so helpful a quality in human relations and in politics, is absolutely fatal to administrative work, as it throws the complex machinery into confusion. It is the same difference as between driving an ox-cart and an express train. The first may be esthetically much more charming.

Discretion versus secretiveness.—Discretion also has its shadowy side, when it develops into secretiveness. Disgusted at the secrecy which shrouded governmental transactions, reformers in the past have tended to assume that anything which is secret is *ipso facto* bad. Yet they have usually given the lie to this view when it came to their own affairs. The truth of the matter is that in the age when liberal leaders fought for subjecting governmental activities to popular control, it was often a matter of eliminating a certain policy which in itself was considered undesirable. This was particularly true in the field of foreign affairs where courts were suspected of plotting wars. Similar objections arose in various realms of domestic policy as well, for example, regarding favors to landed nobility. In other words, the real target of criticism was the policy or objective; but the methods or techniques were equally condemned. In opposing this popular fallacy, we might formulate the following rule, which is rather the reverse of the infamous notion that the end justifies the means: Means are not necessarily bad, because the end is bad; in other words, an end does not disqualify the means, though it often discredits them. Discretion well expresses the desirable mean between loquacity and secretiveness. It suggests that a vivid sense of relative importance is as essential to good administration as to the good life. If a governmental activity is very important, touches the life of many people, and is generally agreed upon, it should be given corresponding publicity. If it is of a special nature, or still in an uncertain state, it should be kept away from general discussion. No government service, no bureaucracy can develop, unless it discovers and trains a sufficient number of persons who are capable of the good judgment which such decisions require.

Conclusion.—We have now sketched the nature of a government service or bureaucracy in broad outline. Six fundamental criteria of such a bureaucracy have stood out—three functional and three behavior aspects. They are found in a small administrative body such as the Brandenburg council in the seventeenth century, and they pervade a vast administrative machine such as that of the British Empire encircling half the globe. Their forward march is accompanied by ever-increasing determinateness and publicity, and that is the reason we can evaluate a bureaucracy's development by this criterion. It is a process of great portent for the future of mankind, and the very core of all government. We must now turn to a consideration of the main objectives which this growing force sought to realize.

CHAPTER IV

THE OBJECTIVES OF MODERN GOVERNMENT AND ITS TECHNIQUES FOR THEIR ACHIEVEMENT

A. Territorial Expansion, Security, and the Military Establishment

---

1. *Introductory.*—2. *The connection between territorial expansion and security.*—3. *Insecurity.*—4. *Outside attacks.*—5. *British navy and continental armies akin.*—6. *Size of armies.*—7. *The development of arms.*—8. *The bearing of the relative strength of aggressive and defensive weapons upon government.*—9. *The evolution of arms and science.*—10. *Government control of universities.*—11. *A reference.*—12. *The provisioning of armies.*—13. *The problem of revenue.*—14. *The situation of estates on the continent.*—15. *Commissioners and the emergency power.*—16. *Civil and foreign war.*—17. *Disarmament and supernational government.*—18. *Who is the enemy?*—19. *The importance of the military establishment for maintaining any government: conclusion.*

Introductory.—Certain of the conditions which we found to form the background of modern bureaucratized government constitute at the same time central objectives. In fact, if they did not constitute objectives, they could not form conditions for the development of these governments. For such is the nature of human and social, as compared to subhuman and anorganic life, that many of its most essential conditioning factors must and do pass through the forge of human consciousness where they are wrought into swords of wilful purpose. Thus the geographic factor exerts its most powerful influence where a determinate will for territorial expansion exists. This desire for territorial expansion is deeply rooted in the human breast; anyone who has possessed land or lived with farmers knows the urge toward acquiring the adjoining plot. The great kings of Europe who built our modern governments were fundamentally such land-hungry farmers.

The connection between territorial expansion and security.—When several such farmers live in close proximity, the question of security at once arises. Everyone has heard the ancient tales about the peasant who in the depth of night went out to his field to shift the stone which divided his field from that of his neighbor. Where there are no courts to decide the ensuing quarrel, armed conflict will be the only method of settling the dispute, unless one of the parties gives in. Thus the idea of security arises as a corollary to the will for territorial expansion, for the dread of foreign invasion haunts those who dream of territorial acquisitions.

Insecurity.—Rare are the occasions when a government has admitted blatantly its intentions for territorial conquest, except in the colonial sphere, even in the stark days of the seventeenth century. Louis XIV, Frederick the Great, and Napoleon are among the few who have dared to speak out frankly and admit the brutal facts. And even they sought support for their aggressive schemes in the records of the past, Louis XIV citing Cæsar and Charlemagne. Usually, each government insisted upon its own pacific intentions, and its need for security, as they do to this day. But when the scientific observer places the various declarations side by side and compares them with the actual behavior of their authors, he clearly perceives that insecurity results from a will for territorial expansion. These objectives in turn generate armed conflicts. Therefore each of the contestants must seek to increase its armed strength. Thus an expansion of the military establishment became the obvious corollary objective of those who sought territorial expansion and talked of security.

Outside attacks.—It would, however, be unjust and incorrect to attribute the entire dynamic evolution toward vast military establishments to the ugly passion for territorial conquest, innate in these peasant-kings. The tendency toward ever-increasing armaments also received a tremendous impetus from the onslaught of the conquering Turk. After the Reformation had swept away the halo of a united religion which had sanctioned the medieval empire, the Hapsburgs found a new justification for asking the united support of the German princes in their struggle against the huge armies of the Moslem. Nor can we deny that military and administrative methods were deeply affected by them. The extraordinary military successes of the Ottoman Turks hastened the abandonment of feudal, and the adoption of modern, bureaucratic methods; the standing armies of the Sultans made the organization of similar troops in the Hapsburg realms almost inevitable. We have here a particularly striking instance of the diffusion of political techniques strengthening the emerging traits created by independent invention. Once these traits had fully established themselves, and a central bureaucracy had consolidated the scattered Hapsburg dominions and organized them for the support of a large standing army, it did not take long to destroy the Turkish power, at the beginning of the eighteenth century. These techniques must now be considered.

British navy and continental armies akin.—But first a warning should be inserted regarding Great Britain. There has been a tendency to sentimentalize the English development as essentially different from that on the Continent. This is only true in a strictly technical sense, but not with reference to the general observations bearing upon the evolution of modern governmental methods. England was at least as aggressively expansionist as other European governments. Finding her road to European conquest blocked by the consolidation of the French kingdom, she limited herself on the Continent to balance of power diplomacy (see next chapter), and turned her dominant attention to conquest overseas. For this reason her military development is predominantly naval. But the needs of this royal navy engendered, as was remarked before, the same administrative problems as did those of the army in other European countries. The decisive turn comes, as might be expected, during the reign of Henry VIII, as a natural concomitant of his policy of expansion and rivalry with the Hapsburg and Bourbon princes. In 1546 he established the Navy Board as a central administrative body. Naval development continued unchecked through the reign of Elizabeth, but under the Stuarts the increasing hostility of Parliament made it impossible for the kings to get the necessary funds. The striking contrast of the Commonwealth period illumines in an exceptionally distinct manner the dependence of modern military development upon unimpeded executive leadership, such as the dictatorship of Cromwell afforded. It is well known that the decisive defeat of the Dutch in 1653-1654 was of crucial importance to nascent British imperial aspirations. The victory would have been impossible without the rapid expansion of the naval forces under the administrative leadership of the Cromwellian Navy Commissioners. The English crown's natural preoccupation with the navy, notably in the case of Charles I, weakened the government in its struggle with the squirearchy and the great property owners. The eventual ascendancy of the latter classes made the English government oligarchic; it did not alter the already accomplished centralization upon which the naval power of England depended.

Size of armies.—Nothing shows more vividly the trend of the development than the bare figures of the size of the several armies. In medieval days armies were small—people were astounded at the French army of 32,000 men at Crécy in 1346. Four hundred years later, in 1750, Austria, France, and Prussia had armies of 297,000, 182,000, and 190,000 men respectively. Nor were these armies collected temporarily and for a specific purpose as was the French army at Crécy; they were permanent, standing armies who had to be fed, clothed, and sheltered all the year round. Soon this matter of provisions became the touchstone of victory. To revert once more to the Hapsburg victory over the Turks, it is interesting to find that Prince Eugene of Savoy has been described as "a provider and husbander of resources, as well as a leader of armies," and that "he set to work with a firm hand to organize the finances which he found in the worst possible condition with debts of enormous proportions . . ." (Henderson.) Similarly, the attention of the Great Elector and his Prussian successors was to a considerable extent concentrated on building up an effective administrative machine to safeguard once and for all the financial and provisional rear of their big armies. Toward this aim, the French and later the English Treasury contributed on a large scale; indeed it would have been utterly impossible for Brandenburg-Prussia to maintain such a large army on its own resources. But we shall postpone a further consideration of these fiscal and economic aspects, and now turn to another aspect of a strictly military kind, namely the development of arms.

The development of arms.—Along with the constant growth of the size of the armies, there took place a constant improvement in the effectiveness of the arms which these armies employed. If the Middle Ages were on the whole an epoch in which defensive weapons were stronger than aggressive ones, that relative superiority was now reversed. To be sure, fortresses continued to play a decisive role in the East, where the Turkish onslaught broke under the walls of Vienna, though even here only after outside reinforcements under a Polish king made a successful counter-attack against the beleaguering forces. But usually, the force of attack was strengthened more by the new weapons of firearms, guns and machine guns, than the force of defense. The trench warfare of the World War seemed momentarily to give supremacy to defensive techniques—Verdun!—only to be broken once more by the advent of the tank and poison gas.

The bearing of the relative strength of aggressive and defensive weapons upon government.—The relative strength of defensive and aggressive weapons is of fundamental importance to government and politics, as long as armed conflict takes place, for the superiority of defensive weapons strengthens the chances of local resistance, and therefore entails a dispersion of political authority. Aggressive weapons, conversely, strengthen the chances of successful attack by growing units, and therefore help the concentration and centralization of political authority. This has been true since the dawn of civilization, when tribes of horsemen, equipped for successful attack by their greater swiftness, first succeeded in building large territorial dominions. But while these horsemen, and later similar conquerors down to the bombarding battleships of modern imperialism, fell upon alien civilizations, the curious and striking aspect of modern army development in Europe was a constant parallel forward march of a group of competing units, each at once ready to adopt a new device introduced by one of its opponents, and by its civilization fully equipped to do so. This is as true of the spread of Swiss compact infantry technique in the fifteenth century as it is of the firearm and the gun in the sixteenth, of rapid troop movements in the seventeenth, of the goose-step and sudden cavalry attacks in the eighteenth, of the loose infantry technique evolved by the *levée en masse* of the French Revolution and its attendant compulsory military service—the nation in arms—of the ironclad, the machine gun, the aeroplane, poison gas, and so on in more recent years. Here is a long list of some of the most remarkable achievements in the development of modern weapons and military techniques, each of them signifying a new impetus to potential aggression.

The evolution of arms and science.—If we consider this evolution in retrospect, we see at once that it is intimately linked to modern science, and thereby to the whole context of modern industrial civilization. Every great discovery, we find, has its counterpart and concomitant effect in new engines of destruction. So intimately are the two related to each other that if governments and peoples should resolve tomorrow to abandon armaments, they would face a major economic crisis. If they wished to avoid it, they would have to nationalize the armament industry or place orders on a large scale for peace time products to be made by the same factories. This close link between bathtubs and trench mortars, between the progress of civilization and science and the intensification of warfare is often forgotten. Professor Haber's invention of synthetic nitrogen during the World War repaid the German government for the millions it had spent on research. This and many similar "achievements" illustrate the close connection between man's struggle with nature and the struggle with our fellow men. These bonds will have to be severed if war is to stop, and what the effects of such a step upon the progress of science will be, no one can foretell. Perhaps it will go on, now that our industrial society has reached maturity and may carry science forward on its own momentum. At any rate, science appears to be a technique closely associated with the military techniques evolved by governments seeking expansion and security.

Government control of universities.—As long as this connection exists between science and the engines of war, governments are bound to take a decisive interest not only in science but in the institutions where it is developed and taught. That is one of the reasons why war-minded European governments have always controlled universities and other institutions of higher learning. Harold Nicolson, in a recent novel, undertook to picture the intense excitement which surrounds any new invention affecting the course of a future war; cabinets fall, and the whole politics of a large country like England are shown to revolve around questions raised by the discovery of a new metal-alloy with the help of which more formidable aeroplanes can be built. Naturally, the greatest importance must be attached by the government concerned to insuring the loyalty of the inventor. This is, of course, much easier when the inventor is an official of the government, as all state university professors are. The chances of winning a war are of such decisive importance to expansionist governments that large amounts of purely "academic" work might well be supported with a view to the gambling prospect of a major discovery of that kind. For this reason, academic work is another technique closely associated with the military techniques evolved by governments seeking expansion and security.

A reference.—Other associated techniques, such as tax gathering and the stimulation of trade and industry, should now be discussed, were it not preferable to treat them in a separate chapter (see Chap. VI). Their development also serves modern government's second major objective, namely, the fostering of prosperity, and their importance and ramifications are so considerable that the thread of our argument would be lost in any attempt to consider them at this point. We will thus lay them aside for the moment, even though the whole subject of provisioning the armies is intimately bound up with it. To this technique of provisioning itself we must, however, devote a brief sketch.

The provisioning of armies.—Arming, feeding, and clothing soldiers arose very gradually into the prominence which it occupies within the scheme of modern governments. In medieval days every soldier, knight as well as hired mercenary, had to bring his own arms and clothes, had to buy his own food. Heavy guns made a first dent in this system; cities and princes commenced to set up armories from which to supply their troops. Soon it was discovered that other arms, too, might be secured on advantageous terms and rented out to the mercenaries, deducting fees from their pay. Similarly, the purchase of clothes wholesale made possible considerable savings; standardization of these clothes into *uni-forms* readily suggested itself as the next step. Regarding food, a mixed system prevailed for a long time. But as armies grew, troop commanders found themselves shouldered with the task of providing canteens where the soldiery might secure food at reasonable prices. Graft and corruption were difficult to avoid. Therefore it seemed imperative, particularly to princes with a sense for economy, to take over entirely the feeding of troops, particularly after the general draft got under way. Perhaps the early beginnings of this system of governmental provisioning must be sought in countries with a considerable navy. It was palpably impossible to let marines do their own buying of food. Therefore in maritime nations like the English, governments entered at a very early date into the "retail business" of feeding their navies.

The problem of revenue.—Now it is perfectly apparent that for all these activities of organizing and keeping intact arsenals and armories, of collecting, storing, and distributing food stuffs and drinks, and of purchasing, storing, and handling uniforms, considerable administrative organizations had to be set up, once armies grew into large standing bodies. For a time, attempts were made to handle these problems within the context of the medieval constitutional order by multiplying councils and boards, partly under royal, partly under parliamentary direction. Incredible confusion resulted. Where a strong and capable administrator-king attempted to cut the Gordian knot by independent measures, his activities encountered very serious difficulties from a constitutional viewpoint. Since the levying of additional taxes was in varying degrees subject to the consent of the Estates (Parliament), the princes had great difficulty in securing the necessary revenue. Debasing the currency was a temporary expedient often resorted to. The chartering of colonial trading companies helped some governments, but the returns were much less considerable than was commonly hoped for. The seizure of church lands helped the Protestant princes. Both transactions were obviously of a predatory nature. It has never been determined how much the government of Holland or the king of England gained from these enterprises, because they were not regular stockholders. Whatever they were able to extract from organizations like the East India Company they received in the form of charter fees, loans, and so forth. What benefit kings derived from the confiscation of church lands, and the like, is almost as difficult to determine. But a very rough estimate, based on extant sources, and probably representing a minimum, suggests that these confiscations yielded Henry VIII £1,890,500 between 1524 and 1547. The military significance of such loot can roughly be gauged by comparing it with the cost of a medium-sized man-of-war, such as the *Ark Royal,* the flagship for which Queen Elizabeth paid £5000. Had these sums been used by the English kings to organize and equip a sizable army, as Charles V and his Hapsburg successors in Spain and Austria did with their American gold, they might well have triumphed over the parliamentary forces. But since the road to territorial expansion lay overseas, they were obliged to concentrate on the navy, and as colonial revenue was slow in coming into the royal treasury, they had to wrangle with a Parliament which was quite aware of the dangers of allowing the king to build up military support.

The situation of Estates on the Continent.—Estates' assemblies on the Continent were, of course, no less alive to the threat which any rapid expansion in royal military forces contained for their own position. But the immediacy of dangers from abroad made it difficult, if not impossible, for them to refuse to grant the revenues which the prince demanded, and, what was worse, proceeded to collect anyway, if the Estates were slow in making the grant. In other words, the continual imminence of foreign invasion gave to continental monarchs the entering wedge for expanding their revenues. They could appeal to the "emergency power," a power always recognized even in England as part of the royal prerogative. This power was, of course, also often invoked for the purpose of quelling civil disturbances; in both forms it can be traced to the constitutional law of the Roman Republic, and we shall return to it when we come to consider dictatorship. There is perhaps no other intrinsic reason than this royal prerogative for explaining why Continental Estates did not proceed to develop their parliamentary armies along the lines of Cromwell's Model Army. It was quite common in the sixteenth and the first half of the seventeenth century for representative assemblies to maintain their own military establishments, a situation which is so contrary to our unitary conception of modern government. But they were seldom as ably led as the Model Army, and if they attempted to swing into action, as happened in Bohemia after 1618, the civil war at once embroiled them in foreign complications and actual invasion, in the course of which the monarchical cause could more surely count upon support from foreign princes than the Estates. Thus the battle on the White Hill (near Prague, 1620) was lost, because the Bohemian Estates and their elected king could not secure adequate foreign support. Would the Parliaments of Cromwell and William III have fared better, if they had needed such aid?

Commissioners and the emergency power.—Estates and princes alike were dependent upon a host of intermediary officials, commissioners or commissaries, as they were called, but the princes could much more effectively employ such agents on account of their claim to "emergency power" under the prerogative. Such commissaries often appeared with the armies in the field and just collected money, grain, horses, and what not, claiming simply that it was needed. Thus constant deprivations of the civilian population, particularly of the peasantry, but also of the cities, took place because of an alleged impending threat to peace and security. Such commissions varied greatly in scope; some, as in the cases just cited, were merely sent to do one particular errand, others had more or less plenary powers to accomplish a certain result, such as quelling disturbances and reëstablishing the authority of the prince. But in all these cases, the decisive point is a specific need requiring immediate or, as it is nowadays often called, "direct" action. It is an interesting and striking fact, and one well illustrating the persistence of political techniques within a given culture pattern, that with the advent of the dictatorship of the proletariat in Russia and the innumerable occasions for direct action (the legal order having practically vanished), the commissary instantaneously appeared on the scene as the People's Commissar,—an agent of the revolutionary leaders and the mass behind them. The same thing had happened during the French Revolution, and there can be little doubt that the word came from there into Russia, though the technique itself is inherent in the very situation requiring direct action. Thus we may say in conclusion that direct or emergency action and its executors, the commissaries, are an important concomitant technique of modern military evolution. In so far as military operations are involved in civil war, this technique is necessarily characteristic also of revolutionary periods.

Civil and foreign war.—This close proximity of political techniques suggests a kinship between civil and foreign warfare, between internal and external armed conflict, which is of broad significance. It is a curious commentary upon the unrealistic quality of much nineteenth century political thought that it failed completely to perceive the close relationship which exists between civil and foreign war. In fact, the only group which is characterized by a distinct propensity toward foreign as against civil war is the modern nation and the princes under whose leadership it arose. Equally powerful group cohesion is, however, generated by religious and class interests, and both these groupings tend to lead toward civil war. Thus the "pacifism" of revolutionary socialists preaching the doctrine of class warfare turns out to be little more pacific than the pacifism of a government which keeps its peace with one adversary to concentrate all its force upon crushing the other.

This bellicose spirit of militant socialism should make us sceptical regarding the prospects of eternal peace in a fully socialized world. To be sure, self-contained empires such as Russia may be more pacific since they possess all they need. This attitude has been maintained by both Lenin and Stalin. But the very exclusiveness of socialist governments with their trade and production monopolies augures ill for international coöperation. Therefore new causes for war seem to be lurking in the struggle for raw materials and markets; the attitude of British labor, or at least sections of it, toward Egypt and India are rather significant in this connection: beneath altered phrases the will for empire remains unshaken. There is, then, no inherent reason why a family of socialist nations, embittered by the whole-hearted participation of the masses, might not be engaged in armed conflicts at least as fierce as those fought between expansionist monarchies. The preceding digression may help in avoiding any undue optimism concerning the future. The mere adoption of socialism will not abolish nor even minimize the danger of war. No matter how considerable might be the solidarity of the labor class when confronting their employers, this solidarity weakens when the labor classes of various countries confront each other.

Disarmament and supernational government.—If socialism is rather uncertain, disarmament must likewise be doubted as an effective means for maintaining peace. Armaments do not, as the foregoing shows, "cause" wars; military establishments are the governmental techniques for realizing the territorial objectives, expansion, security, defense. As long as these objectives remain, the close connection between the progress of civilization, science, culture, and military undertakings will make it inevitable that disarmament turn into a change of armaments. For in an industrial society such as ours the abolition or limitation of certain types of weapon at present in use cannot ban the spectre of the enemy's inventing a wholly new weapon with correspondingly devastating effect. It is, in other words, not the possession of arms, but the disposition to use them, which must be uprooted. (In practice, the advocacy of disarmament may, to be sure, afford a rather valuable propaganda technique for such uprooting.) Such a change in outlook and purpose can only be brought about by rendering territorial questions relatively unimportant. In 1866 the several German states, such as Prussia and Bavaria, were fighting each other, and the victorious Prussians appropriated large amounts of territory, such as the entire kingdom of Hanover. Today such a proceeding seems to most Germans hard to imagine. The problem of territorial division has largely become a question of administrative expediency. If a civil war situation flared up between Bavaria and the Reich in 1923, it was not over territorial questions, but concerned the political organization of the whole country, the problems of monarchy, socialism, and so forth. The territorial objectives have been minimized, if not eliminated, by creating a government comprising the several German states. Thus we can see that modern military techniques with their predominantly aggressive potentialities afford the most persuasive argument for supernational government as the only effective guaranty for lasting peace between nations, because only such government will lessen the urge of the territorial objectives. Even the chances of civil war would be somewhat decreased in such a larger context. For many facts point toward the conclusion that size mitigates the possibility of friction developing into fighting; the whole is so much larger than any of its parts. These considerations apply to supernational government, even if such a government does not comprise the entire globe. That was the strength of the Pan-European idea, and the League of Nations was probably ill-advised to throw so many obstacles into the path of those who undertook to propagandize it.

Who is the enemy?—In fact, being opposed to an effective power outside helps greatly to maintain supernational government. After all, the German states were unified against external interference. The same thing is true of the United States of America. A federal union seems invariably to form in response to outside pressure (see below, Chap. XIII). But maybe the pressure could be of a different sort. André Maurois has imaginatively depicted mankind united against the people of the moon. Another poetical soul has seen the world brought together in the effort to build a building as high as Mont Blanc, presumably engaging their attention for more than a hundred years. Still others have urged the war against microbes as a sufficiently powerful unifying objective—the health work of the League representing a first vanguard engagement. Economic crisis may also call forth supernational organization of a governmental type. It too has its beginnings in the League as at present constituted. But all things considered, these promising seedlings are apt to be crushed, if the existing territorial rivalries continue to engender a feeling of violent insecurity and a consequent determination to remain armed. Unfortunately, even the unification of Europe would not eliminate these rivalries; for neither the inclusion nor the exclusion of Soviet Russia would give her a natural boundary. If, therefore, territorial exigencies in conjunction with the inventive genius of modern science are resolvable only by creating a world super-government, the question of the conditions under which such world super-government is possible becomes an urgent one indeed. Whether or not the League of Nations fulfills these conditions, we are not yet able to say. Not until we have analyzed a considerable number of other factors, can we hope to approach that question.

The importance of the military establishment for maintaining any government: conclusion.—Before we conclude this more limited consideration of the territorial objectives and the military establishment, we must call attention to one other aspect, well illustrated by rather recent developments. We have seen how the exigencies of external pressure facilitated the monarchs' military ascendancy. We have seen how in times of release from external pressure, the prince could broaden his military ascendancy into a general political ascendancy. He became a monocrat, almost a despot. When, in the course of events after the French Revolution, this central control was wrested from the princes and appropriated by the "people" through its representatives, the control of the military establishment passed into their hands. Maintenance of this control has always seemed of vital importance to those who reflected upon the conditions of successful constitutional government, from Cromwell to Gambetta. It is a striking confirmation of their views that the collapse of constitutional orders in post-war Europe has occurred, where that monopoly of control over military techniques (violence) was not or could not be maintained. Germany, Austria, Russia, and Italy all suggest the trend of development in countries where the government surrenders this monopoly of military power which the autocratic governments of seventeenth and eighteenth century Europe labored so persistently to establish. In Russia, the Kerenski government allowed itself to be so misled by the wiles of Entente diplomacy and the liberal doctrinaire's indifference to the vital condition of effective control over the military forces that it continued an increasingly unpopular war, and thus hastened the disintegration of the regular army. Trotzki has expressed it well when he says, "The mass of the soldiers shaken by the revolution was looked upon by Kerenski as clay with which he could do as he pleased. . . . He ordered a new offensive (in June). . . . It soon was clear that no 'democratic army' stood behind Kerenski; . . ." Lenin and Trotzki knew that they must strike while the army was defunct. Foreign observers have agreed with reactionary generals in making the same point. In Germany, the Communists were unable to employ similar tactics, because the moderate Socialists were making peace. A sufficient body of the army and police remained loyal to cope with the situation. But due to these services in a transition period, the army was able to entrench itself sufficiently to escape from all serious efforts at effective democratization. In this endeavour they were greatly helped by the provisions of the Treaty of Versailles which forced Germany to reduce her army to a small professional force; a liberalist indifference toward military problems of government common amongst the new leaders of the democracy did the rest. As a result, the democratic leaders later were placed at the mercy of generals who were admittedly quite indifferent to the fate of the new regime. "Private" armies, both Communist and National Socialist, scheming for the overthrow of the "system," were allowed to grow up alongside a rather puny "private" army of defenders of the new constitution. For a time, each of these "armies" numbered about 100,000 men, Red Fighters, Brownshirts, Steel Helmets, and National Banner Men; they balanced each other, with the official army and the police endeavouring to keep the "peace." But when the Steel Helmets made common cause with the Brownshirts, and the official army was won over, too, the democratic and constitutional forces found themselves cornered and utterly without that "monopoly of armed force" which the maintenance of government requires. The course in Austria has been very similar. In Italy, where the situation is somewhat obscured by the gradual emergence of Mussolini's power, the "humiliations" of the peace treaty had undermined the position of the parliamentary leaders in the popular mind. The army was profoundly affected. It is significant that the proclamation of the Fascists after their March on Rome stated, first of all, that the march was not made against the army. What is more, the government's intention to declare a state of siege was thwarted by the king's refusal to sign, and this refusal was motivated by urgent advice given the king that "the army would not fight." These situations suggest that a government's loss of its monopoly of military force is a concomitant of its imminent collapse. Lenin in Russia, Hitler in Germany, Mussolini in Italy have all shown by their later actions that they were most anxious to remove the weakness which had given them success. They may not be successful, but their military policies show a clear realization of the dangers to which a government is exposed which does not rest upon a firm basis of military support. The political scientist must likewise conclude that the military establishment is a necessary concomitant of all government, that it transcends territorial objectives and ultimately is rooted in the general objective of security. Group dissensions within are as threatening as external conflicts. The people of the United States, whose most dangerous war has undoubtedly been the Civil War, should be the last to overlook the lessons which this political rule can teach. Disarmament can not be considered without reference to the potential revolution.

CHAPTER V

OBJECTIVES AND TECHNIQUES

B. The Reduction of External Friction through Diplomacy

1. *Introductory.*—2. *Diplomacy and war.*—3. *The art of negotiating.* —4. *Foreign and domestic affairs.*—5. *The language of diplomacy.*—6. *The system of ambassadors.*—7. *The Foreign Service as an organized administrative service.*—8. *The balance of power.*—9. *The "social" function of the professional diplomatist.*—10. *The post-war international bureaucracy.*—11. *Technical experts abroad.*—12. *The new diplomatist: a conclusion.*

Introductory.—The contents of the previous chapter seem to suggest that the living-together of modern nations constitutes one continuous warfare, interrupted by brief periods of relaxation caused by utter exhaustion. Contemplating the history of Europe during the last four hundred years a gloomy philosopher would certainly be tempted to reiterate Heraclitus' sinister phrase that war is the father of all things. It is, however, equally justifiable to take the diametrically opposed view that an intrinsically peace-loving family of nations has occasionally seen its underlying harmony disturbed by wars which were essentially breakdowns of an unstable equilibrium. Still, most of the time the inevitable friction resulting from territorial and other maladjustments has been successfully reduced by a technique wholly different from warfare, namely, diplomacy. Diplomacy, the textbooks tell one, is (or at least was) "the application of intelligence and tact to the conduct of official relations between the governments of independent states" (Satow). Napoleon's mocking sally to Talleyrand that "treaties might be signed by diplomats, but they are made by soldiers" notwithstanding, war would thus appear as the breakdown of diplomacy, since it is the artless application of brute force. Conversely, diplomacy is not merely the application of tact and intelligence to foreign affairs, but it strives to avoid war, and yet to realize a maximum of potential objectives of a government, whenever those objectives reach beyond the boundaries of the country concerned. These latter have loomed ever larger with the expanding industrialism of the modern age.

Diplomacy and war.—The proposition that diplomacy strives to avoid war is often questioned on the supposedly realistic ground that the diplomacy of a Louis XIV, a Napoleon, or a Bismarck was more concerned with preparing war than with avoiding it. This is undoubtedly true, and if it had been asserted that it was the objective of diplomacy to avoid *all* war, the objection would be well taken. But when the diplomacy of certain aggressive statesmen was employed to isolate a particular enemy so as to facilitate his defeat, the diplomat's task in effecting such isolation consisted in an effort to maintain peace with the enemy's potential allies. The failure of Louis XIV's diplomacy is generally admitted in his inability to prevent the great alliance which was formed by England, the Netherlands, and the House of Hapsburg, and which resulted in his being checked by the series of wars which ended in the peace of Utrecht (1713-1714). Likewise Frederick the Great was almost crushed beneath the combination of Russia, France, and Austria, which Maria Theresa succeeded in bringing together against him; a brilliant strategist and army leader, this extraordinary Prussian king was handicapped by his ineffective diplomacy. Napoleon Bonaparte, another remarkable soldier, also affords a striking illustration of how superior military strength will suffer defeat, if not aided by skillful diplomacy; the alliance of Russia, England, Austria, and Prussia, as well as many minor countries, could not be combated in the field, and statecraft would have anticipated its emergence and tried to prevent it. The marvel of Bismarck's diplomacy, on the other hand, lay precisely in his careful elimination of potential allies of whoever happened to be his particular opponent. In Prussia's war with Austria he succeeded in keeping out France, England, and Russia (1866), while in Germany's war with France he similarly kept peace with Austria, Russia, and England. It is small wonder that after the brilliant victories which his diplomacy had prepared, he spent the rest of his days haunted by the spectre of coalitions which might be brought together against Germany. It was in an effort to prevent such coalitions that Bismarck became so interested in maintaining peace throughout Europe; the catastrophic consequences of the failure of later German governments to follow his lead are too well known to require more than mention. Throughout all these great cycles of recent history a tendency can be observed: the dominant objective of successful diplomacy is the maintenance of peace. Toward this dominant objective point the many minor efforts at eliminating friction necessarily engendered by the conflicting interests of the various countries. Ideally, diplomacy would be perfect if through mere art in negotiation it could realize the maintenance of peace, while at the same time securing such advantages as are demanded by the people, a prince, big business, or whoever happens to determine the policy of the government in the final analysis.

The art of negotiating.—Unfortunately, the so-called "sovereigns," whether princes, peoples, or interest groups, are and have been in the habit of demanding things which no diplomat, no matter how skillful, could secure without envisaging the ultimate use of armed force against someone. We have here confronting us a paradox which has puzzled the students of diplomacy, both of democratic and of autocratic governments. There is the desire for peace, and the concurrent insistence upon things which cannot be had without recourse to war, because someone else's vital interests are involved. This suggests the need for differentiating between ultimate goals of foreign policy and the negotiations involved in realizing them. Apparently, when talking of diplomacy as a governmental technique, one considers it mainly in terms of the art of negotiation. The two, however, are often fused in reality. The ultimate goal of Bismarckian diplomacy, German unification under Prussian leadership, was supported, perhaps even demanded, by a considerable body of the German people; in fact it was a popular, rather than a monarchical objective. To be sure, Bismarck shared it whole-heartedly and his efforts were devoted to its realization. Bismarck the diplomat was, however, concerned with how to bring about this end with the least sacrifice. He was convinced that it could not be done without resort to war; but only Austria and France were unalterably opposed to German unification under Prussian leadership: the Austrians to Prussian leadership, the French to unification. So he prepared a single-handed encounter with each of these implacable enemies, keeping his peace with the rest of Europe. This case (and many others) shows that the distinction between ultimate goals of policy and the negotiations required to realize them is a rather difficult one, except superficially. A closer analysis of reality reveals that the actual negotiation generates a policy, and a given policy imposes certain and peculiar methods of negotiation. To say, therefore, that we wish to consider diplomacy largely as the art of negotiation means really defining our standpoint and method of approach; actual foreign affairs consist of an undifferentiated complex context which is compounded of policies and negotiations.

Foreign and domestic affairs.—To define the term foreign affairs is not as easy as the constant use of the phrase would lead one to believe. The various human activities involved in carrying on the relations between nations are fairly clearly discernible by examples: Poincaré making a speech on the war debts, the German Parliament ratifying the Locarno Treaty, Sir Esme Howard, the British ambassador, calling upon President Coolidge, the disarmament conference being held at Geneva, a clerk in the Foreign Office deciphering a message from one of the embassies; these and many similar floating pictures suggest themselves in varied succession. Perhaps the phrase foreign relations would be more indicative of their true nature; for these activities together constitute the relationship through which nations and their governments are bound together. Nations at any rate are not truly independent in any factual sense, even though governments may be. But legally their relations are treated *as if* they were independent of each other. This leads to many difficulties, both in learned analysis and in popular views. The United States are a particularly happy hunting ground for those who have been and are inclined to treat foreign relations as if nations were in fact independent of each other, thus making the fatal mistake of treating as a fact what is a legal fiction. What is more, even to treat foreign relations as a separate thing amounts to committing a similar mistake; for the distinction between foreign and domestic affairs is a fiction also. Particularly under modern industrial conditions, is there when speaking of major policies any such thing as a purely domestic concern? Law may treat the tariff, the restriction of immigration, the regulation of various fields of production, governmental subsidies, and all such measures of governmental policy as strictly domestic, but are they in fact? Matters of governmental organization likewise are anything but domestic, unless they concern minor details. Were the coming of the Nazis, of the Fascists, of the Communists purely domestic matters? How could Wilson have insisted upon the disappearance of monarchy in Germany, if governmental organization had no bearing upon foreign relations? Similarly did not the question of maintaining monarchy inject itself into the League of the Three Emperors and the Holy Alliance? Searching students of foreign relations and diplomacy have always known that foreign and domestic affairs constitute a whole which one is bound to discover, if he digs deep enough. One of the great turning points of pre-war European diplomacy was the conclusion of the Franco-Russian alliance (1894); historians have shown how powerful a role Russia's need of large loans played in her shifting from Germany to France. Another great turning point was Germany's refusal to enter into negotiations for an alliance with Great Britain (1900); the latest evidence seems to point toward the fear bourgeois Germany had of rising German socialism as the real foundation for the big fleet program which stood in the way of such an alliance (see below, Chap. XIX). From this vantage point one perceives the difficulty of maintaining the time-honored principle of the "primacy (priority) of foreign over domestic policy"; the two are so much part of one pattern or web that the meaning of the principle is obscure.

The language of diplomacy.—The supposed failure of diplomacy to eliminate war has made people forget what a great advance over earlier conditions its carefully worked-out and subtle technique represents. The oft-quoted wisecrack that ambassadors are honest men sent abroad to lie for the good of their country is less than a half-truth. Many statements which to the average lay reader of diplomatic documents would seem to be "lies" or pretenses are in fact conventional phrases which carry to the informed recipient precisely the meaning they possess in the mind of the person who uttered them. When the President of the United States, in his letter of credence for the American ambassador to Mexico speaks of "the desire to cultivate to the fullest extent the friendship which has so long subsisted between the two governments," he obviously is not "lying," and when the ambassador on suitable occasions repeats such phrases, his candor cannot on that account be questioned. Formally amicable relations between two governments constitute a "friendship" in the soothing language of diplomacy. It was, therefore, an extraordinary breach of diplomatic tradition when the government of the Soviet Union announced that it would teach unfriendly powers "to keep their swinish snouts out of our potato patch." Such language is very dangerous in the intercourse between powerful nations. It has been the purpose of diplomatic etiquette to avoid these dangers by carefully prescribed traditional restraints in conduct and language. The British Foreign Office "was aghast," we are told, at the breach of diplomatic etiquette which Lord Curzon committed, when, in 1923, he "proceeded to quote the text of messages and instructions exchanged between the Soviet government and their representatives in Persia and India which had been intercepted" by the British Intelligence Service. The Foreign Office was aghast not because the statements were untrue, but because "never, even in the most embittered diplomatic controversy, had information thus obtained been cited as evidence." In other words, governments maintain a secret service to spy upon their "friends," but they will never, never admit it. Yet, labelling this failure to admit such a generally recognized practice as deceit would be little short of absurd.

The system of ambassadors.—The elaborate system of ambassadors and other plenipotentiaries which one is inclined to take for granted today is another major achievement of the evolution of modern diplomacy. The practice of sending such representatives was commenced by the medieval church and from it spread first to the city states of Renaissance Italy. From there it was taken over and developed, as so many other practices, by the monarchical governments north of the Alps. Yet, regularized practices developed very slowly. Ambassadors were often given a discourteous reception, if they were not actually maltreated. Many protracted struggles arose over questions of etiquette, and the prestige connected with them. How imperfect the arrangements still were at the end of the Thirty Years' War, toward the middle of the seventeenth century, can be gleaned from the fact that almost four years were consumed in clearing up innumerable questions of etiquette, before the peace conference could commence to sit at Muenster and Osnabrück in 1645. Nor were the succeeding negotiations easy: they lasted for fully three years. The slow development of tradition in the subsequent hundred and fifty years brought into existence a whole code of diplomatic conduct which was codified by the Congress of Vienna in 1815. This was some twenty-five years after the professional diplomat had almost accidentally made his debut. It happened in France where, after the Revolution had swept away the titled ambassadors of the old regime, the conduct of affairs had been left in the hands of their secretaries. The latter were mostly commoners who had acquired a semi-permanent professional status by the force of custom and circumstance. To be sure, seasoned and quasi-professional diplomats had existed in the monarchical service wherever a man held his post for a considerable length of time, but the service as a whole was amateurish, except perhaps that of the Catholic Church and the Republic of Venice. Even a casual reading of the instructions handed to French ambassadors of the period will reveal that fact. These instructions often read like an elementary introduction into the nature of the relations of the two governments concerned. Only during the nineteenth century did a professional bureaucracy take hold of the field of foreign affairs. It is worth passing notice perhaps that with the exception of the French service under the Third Republic and of course that of the United States, these services were dominated by titled noblemen; they were considered the exclusive province of the upper crust of society, like the corps of cavalry officers. Just the same, or perhaps as a result of this circumstance, the diplomatic corps developed certain characteristics which bear scrutiny beyond that given the official when we considered modern bureaucracy.

The Foreign Service as an organized administrative service. —It is obvious that our three functional criteria, namely, differentiation of functions, integration, and hierarchical organization, as well as professionalization are likely to prevail. The differentiation is partly along geographical and partly along functional lines. It varies from government to government, as one country or another looms large in importance. Thus Germany appears of greater significance to France than to the United States, South American countries more important to the United States than to the Soviet Union. Sometimes policy trends are discernible in these arrangements, as when the German Foreign Office handles the League of Nations as part of Western Europe (France). Functional differentiation appears in such sections as the legal, the commercial, and the cultural. As far as the commercial work is concerned, foreign services have for a long time recognized a distinction between the consular and the "diplomatic" service, though the tendency to separate these two services as careers is now generally criticized as unsound. Both these services are, as field services, in turn clearly distinguished from the work in the central foreign office (Department of State in the United States), but again without differentiating the career. Even in the arrangements for these field services' policies trends can be shown. After the Franco-Prussian War, the French abandoned a number of consulates in Germany. After the World War, Great Britain, France, and Germany changed their missions in the ABC states to embassies, thus recognizing the enhanced power of the new world. As far as integration and hierarchical organization is concerned, the foreign services present distinct problems. The great distance between the central directing office and the field offices necessitates a large measure of autonomy, even under modern communication conditions. Not only ambassadors, but consuls as well, are very much their own masters in all matters not specifically directed from the central office. While the embassy in a large country, like the United States, may have general direction of affairs, it is not definitely the hierarchical superior of the various consulates in its territory; they may and often do communicate directly with the home office. Within the last fifty years, clearly defined professional requirements have become established in all the major countries, with the United States following suit by the Rogers Act (1924). Each country in its own way, and in keeping with its peculiar traditions of preparing and testing for the administrative services of the government, has set up its own system. It would be far-fetched and tedious to describe the detailed provisions here. Suffice it to say that the higher ranks of the service (except for political appointments in the top rank of the United States service) are, in all the leading countries, manned by men and women possessing some type of academic university training. Besides these three functional criteria, certain behavior patterns have been held essential to effective administrative services. These—that is, objectivity, continuity, and precision, as well as discretion—are essential aspects of a good diplomatic service. Therefore, a good diplomatist is, in the words of one of them, "indifferent to public applause, has devoted some thirty years to the study of foreign pyschology, is unaffected by vanity, dislikes controversy, eschews all forms of publicity, and is not subject to acute time pressure or overwork. In addition, as a trained expert in a common science working with other experts, he is intent upon producing a piece of work which will satisfy his own professional standards." (See below, Chap. XV, for a discussion of this type of standard and its effect upon maintaining responsible conduct.) According to the same author, "a man who has spent some thirty years in the diplomatic service acquires, inevitably, an international frame of mind." He comes to have a kind of masonic feeling for other diplomatists and to feel that parliamentary and public opinion is foolish and ill-informed. While the latter attitude is often found among professional administrative officials in national services as well, it seldom is held with as much show of good ground. There are always citizens who know as much as any government official about most governmental tasks (though most citizens do not), but there are rarely, if ever, citizens who have a full grasp of all the implications of a given decision in the field of foreign affairs. (See below, Chap. XXII, for a further discussion of parliamentary control.) This "international frame of mind," is subtly adjusted to a rapid, though careful, calculation of the effects which a given move will have throughout the network of international relationships. This chess-player's attitude may and often does result in a neglect of underlying trends of long-range significance, particularly of social and economic forces. But the diplomatist is, on the other hand, acutely aware of the balance of power at any particular moment, and highly sensitized to the prestige connected with certain developments or the damage to prestige of certain others.

The balance of power.—Having mentioned the balance of power, it seems desirable to comment upon it at somewhat more length. The phrase balance of power has, since the sixteenth century, when it was first used by Guiccardini and other Florentine historians, been a euphemistic description of any particular distribution of the power amongst nations which happened to be acceptable to the person using the phrase. The French, after 1871, said they wished to *restore* the balance of power in Europe which the unification of Germany had disturbed. The Germans held that they must *maintain* the balance of power which the French desire for revenge threatened. These observations have been reversed since the World War. Thus it can be seen that the balance of power does not necessarily refer to the maintenance of the *status quo*; it may also be the basis for arguing that this status be changed. Since the phrase describes any kind of distribution of power, the history of the balance of power is obviously identical with the history of foreign relations. In his well-known sketch *The Great Powers*, Ranke has given a brilliant essay showing what can be done in that way; there is no need for duplicating this effort here, though the new knowledge we possess would make this undertaking quite worth while. Whatever the actual balance, that is, distribution of power, may happen to be, the idea affords a ready argument in international negotiation, and presumably even a foundation for international law. As such, it has always had its greatest vogue when it was a question of checking the tendency toward concentration of power in the hands of a single government. The desirability of "redressing the balance of power" was thus invoked against the Hapsburg world empire by Francis I during the first half of the sixteenth century. It was, in turn, brought forth against Louis XIV by William III. Maria Theresa used it against Frederick the Great, the tottering French monarchy against the British Empire under George III and Pitt, everybody against Napoleon I. In the course of the nineteenth century, the scope of its application was widened. The United States, by the Monroe Doctrine, forbade the extension of balance of power politics to the American continents, and thereby maintained its own supremacy with considerable success. But we begin to hear of a balance of power in the Balkans, in the Near East and in the Far East. More recently, the most decisive balance of power is said to be grouped around the Pacific. All this is heresy in terms of the true Wilsonian. The Fourteen Points undertook to banish the balance of power from the world. No longer were people to be bartered about from sovereignty to sovereignty, as the balance of power diplomats had done; instead all nations were to determine their own status under an all-embracing League of Nations. But even had the League become truly all-embracing, and even had the treaties terminating the World War been negotiated on the basis of the Fourteen Points, it is doubtful whether the balance of power argument would have disappeared. The problem of the distribution of power is almost as pressing in a federation as it is in a family of nations. How could Wilson, an American native of the South, have failed to perceive this? Had he forgotten the lesson of the Civil War? Was not the whole story of the genesis of that baneful conflict a tale of balancing power of state against state, till the final rupture occurred? Has not the same happened under the Swiss Confederation (see Chap. XIII), and under the German Union almost at the same time? If one cannot share Wilson's unrealistic inclination to contrast the League and the balance of power, he need not be as despondent concerning the future of the League either. Both are mechanisms for conducting international negotiations, and who would question that the League or some similar organization offered the superior technique, if for no other reason than that it contains whatever is useful of the balance of power within itself. For it became apparent soon after the war, that there was much need for considering the balance of power within the League, and successive international crises brought out the importance of careful attention to that problem (an effort hateful to many League enthusiasts). Whatever the future of the League and other international organizations, the problem of the distribution (balance) of power will, therefore, remain a matter of prime concern to all professional diplomats, and we will very probably continue to use the concept as a convenient standard or idea in terms of which to discuss the shifting scene of international power relationships. It is an outstanding behavior aspect of the professional diplomat to be "power-conscious."

The "social" function of the professional diplomatist.—We have already dwelt upon the great importance attached to social etiquette in the conduct of international negotiations. It has been shown how deeply this regard for etiquette and procedure is embedded in the intensity of the power struggle, its sensitizing effect and its heightening of the feeling for all questions of prestige. In private life, people are apt to smile about someone who makes a great fuss over who should go first to the dinner table. But where each person is a public person, representing a nation jealous of its prestige, this is no small matter, and the salutary effects of etiquette are seen in the rule of seniority, which ranks each representative according to the length of time he has been accredited to the particular government (with the papal *nuncio*, however, ranking ahead of all others). This custom attests to the fiction of equality between all the states, great and small: no balance of power intrudes itself into the dinner parties. This is more important than may be thought at first glance. Countless memoirs, written by distinguished diplomats, such as Sir Cecil Spring-Rice and Walter Hines Page, attest to the fact that much of their most important information is gathered at social functions of one sort or another. Since the seventeenth century the houses of distinguished diplomats have been the center of a brilliant social life. It is the glamour of this past which often draws young men into the foreign service. They forget that it, too, has been sullied by the smoke of the machine age. Most members of the foreign service spend a large proportion of their lives in relatively small and remote cities, often not even capitals of unimportant countries. But even in the great metropolitan centers of London, Paris, and Berlin, it is not today a matter of court intrigues and cabals of the high aristocracy, but rather dull dinner parties for press magnates and industrial tycoons with an occasional journalist or parliamentarian to brighten up the atmosphere. But of course it is social life just the same. Consequently, no person can make a success in the foreign service unless he is able to handle social relations effectively. This fact, too, differentiates the professional diplomat from other officials; a fifth behavior aspect is social presence. Since social grace is acquired more easily by those who grow up with a silver spoon in their mouth, the monopoly of the nobility, later shared with the wealthy upper middle class, is quite understandable, though not necessarily beneficial for the service.

The post-war international bureaucracy.—What has so far been said concerning qualifications remained very largely true until the World War. But since that time, considerable changes have come about. The creation of the League of Nations and constant international conferences widely participated in by governmental officials outside the foreign service proper have set the stage for intergovernmental relationships of a technical sort in the many fields which require international action, such as communications, transportation, and health. In these realms, diplomacy is not the acknowledged technique for handling business. Rather do we find the administrative technique of state bureaucracies within federal systems, whenever coöperation between several component states is required. This technique is fundamentally characterized by a solicitude for the opinion of every constituent member. Since it is impracticable to coerce a recalcitrant member of the coöperating group, every effort has to be made to avert any member from becoming recalcitrant. Naturally, such coöperative efforts are rendered considerably more difficult when the constituent members belong to different nations and even different cultures. Yet the fact that such coöperative undertakings were commenced long before the World War in specific fields, such as that of the Universal Postal Union, shows conclusively that their rapid development after the war and under the ægis of the League is by no means gratuitous; the League merely affords a convenient administrative device for holding the various activities together, since they are of course interrelated.

Technical experts abroad.—In view of the central importance which the bureaucracy has had for the growth and development of the modern state and modern government, this expansion of administrative services into the international field is decisive. As these international activities grow, ambassadors and other diplomats in the foreign field find themselves surrounded by commercial, agricultural, and labor experts who are in direct communication with their corresponding ministries at home. The presence of such experts is usually the cause of considerable friction in the foreign legations. Independent and often conflicting points of view are at times held and expressed by these experts on issues of international significance, particularly within their own bailiwick. Thus a commercial attaché may favor the lowering of tariff rates at a time when the representative of the foreign office considers such a plea very inopportune. From the point of view of integration, the complaints of the professional diplomat are undeniably justified. But from the point of view of governmental growth the lack of integration and centralization may open up new avenues of international progress, just as in centuries past expanding technical services served (as we have seen in Chap. II) as the vanguards of national unification.

The new diplomatist: a conclusion.—In the long run, external friction is unquestionably reduced by administrative internationalism; for each participant becomes in time a bit more internationally minded. He perceives that the most diverse cultural backgrounds and personal habit patterns may be combined with high achievement in a given specialty. This is true to such an extent that the resulting situation has given rise to the query whether the regular, old-fashioned diplomatic service is needed any longer at all. The answer is that the regular old-fashioned diplomatic service is not at all old-fashioned, if it is good. The modern diplomat will look upon himself as a liaison officer who will promote coöperation and understanding on all sides. He will induct experts into the general set-up of a foreign country, will furnish them introductions as well as an adequate meeting ground, will smooth out difficulties wherever he can; in short, he will act according to the first paragraph of the general instructions of the American Department of State to foreign service officers: "He creates good will and common understanding, and, with restrained and critical leadership born of mature experience and profound knowledge of men and affairs, he uses these as instruments for enhancing international confidence and coöperation among governments and people." A man of this type is a far cry from the honest fellow sent abroad to lie for the good of his country.

CHAPTER VI

OBJECTIVES AND TECHNIQUES

C. Prosperity, the Police, and Legislation

Prosperity and expansion, a dual objective.—When discussing the governmental business carried on in support of the military establishment, we passed lightly over some of the most important activities, such as tax gathering and the stimulation of trade and industry (see Chap. IV, ¶11). We did so because these activities were not only vital to the objective of territorial expansion, but perhaps even more bound up with general prosperity. It is, of course, possible to merge these two objectives into one, by claiming that prosperity was wanted and needed because it facilitated the maintenance of armies and navies, and therefore territorial expansion. Or it may reversely be claimed that territorial expansion was sought because of the added opportunities for insuring prosperity, particularly in the case of colonies. While the close relationship and interaction of these two major objectives cannot be denied, it seems on the whole more adequate to admit a twofold objective, rather than force the interpretation of relevant facts by merging them into one. By keeping the two objectives apart, we also escape the acrimonious controversy as to which of the two is really the dominant purpose.

The common factor of growth.—If a unified focus is wanted, and admittedly there is a great appeal in unity to our logical faculty, growth of the community would seem to be the drive behind territorial expansion and prosperity. At certain times, communities undeniably tend to grow. The whys and wherefores of such growth are as mysterious and inexplicable as all growth. All we know is the fact: communities grow. If governments are to remain the central organization of such growing communities, it stands to reason that they should grow, too. This undeniable situation curiously enough has given rise to controversies no less furious than futile. To a detached reader it would seem that the violence of this conflict over the "organic" nature of governments, states, and communities is due to the nineteenth century error of considering anything justified, once it had been shown to be natural. Therefore, to show that communities "naturally" grow was taken as proof that statesmen were "justified" in whatever measures they adopted to insure such growth. Seeley in England and Treitschke in Germany are leading examples of European thought on this subject, while the manifest destiny school of historians provided America with similar notions. In order to buttress their view that governments do tend to grow they have gone further and asserted that governments, or rather states, are organisms. From John of Salisbury in the twelfth century down, writers have revelled in relating various parts of the government to various parts of the human body. The prince was said to be the head, his councillors the nerves, the army the hands and feet, and so forth. Even to this day, these analogies survive in speaking of the president of a country as its head. It is easy to ridicule this "organic" concept, particularly in its more extravagant forms, and to point out that governments are composed of human beings, each with his own will and consciousness. Since nobody has ever seen the entity apart from these separate human beings, it is indeed doubtful whether it exists in the same way as the body of an animal exists apart from the cells composing it. Yet, on the other hand, these human beings composing the government are living human beings, and there is no very tangible reason why we should not assume that the government and the nation live too. If they do, they will tend to grow, for a certain length of time, as all living things do. But it is better to consider the foregoing remarks as an aside, useful, perhaps, in showing how difficult it is to work out a unified objective for all governments, and then to return to the more apparent duality of territorial expansion and prosperity. For it is high time that we return to the techniques employed in realizing the second objective, prosperity.

Prosperity and government expenditure.—Prosperity appeared to be an intrinsically desirable state of affairs to all those princes who looked upon their countries in the same way in which a proprietor looks upon his estate. This desire for good husbandry may be motivated by a love of lavish expenditure, as we find it in France, in Austria, or during the Restoration in England, as well as in many of the minor courts of Europe. Nor ought we merely to scoff at these extravagant masters; for much of the enjoyment of later generations is derived from the masterpieces of art, architecture, and music which the prodigal expenditures of these courts called forth. As the cathedrals of the medieval church were lifted skyward upon the backs of serfs, so the castles and picture galleries of Europe were born of the extortions of vainglorious princes. Mozart and Beethoven were made possible by the autocratic Austrian government, no less than Raphael and Leonardo by the tyrants of renaissance Italy. Nor were all the governments ruthlessly extortionate in design. Many a good prince loved prosperity for its own sake, as the poet tells us of Count Eberhard of Württemberg, who could without misgivings rest in any farmer's hut of the Black Forest, so much was he beloved by his people. In fact, the princes often leaned in the direction of protecting the common people against the nobles, and in England, where the nobility and squirearchy together with a small group of rich commercial families had superseded the prince and become the mainstay of the government, the lot of the poorer classes was, if anything, worse than on the Continent. Farmers were pitilessly driven from their homes to make way for the vast landed estates which in time transformed England into a country of parks. The justice of peace made war upon the peasantry within the framework of a law bearing all the earmarks of class legislation. Thus a vast overseas emigration set in which followed the path of colonial expansion and empire. It is obviously improper to talk of England as a democracy in those days when modern government was in the making.

Police or administrative action.—A whole welter of different policies was initiated by these incipient modern governments for the purpose of fostering prosperity at home. The establishing and the nurturing of manufactures may for the moment serve as an example. Here was something that seemed to benefit the community and therefore recommended itself as a policy. Now it is no accident that the word policy is so intimately related to that of police. Both derive from the old French *policie*. The Oxford Dictionary tells us that the general connotation of police is "civil administration," which is charged, of course, with the several courses of action adopted by the government (policies). The second connotation of police is "public order" and that of course is to be maintained by these several policies. It is, therefore, hardly surprising to find early modern governments preoccupied with the problem of police. After our modern industrial society had gotten well under way, and we had begun to reap the profits of the manufactures and the commerce which these governments had initiated, it became the fashion to decry their attitudes and techniques as paternalistic. The vast capacity of human beings to forget made them assume more and more that this industrial society had been produced by "nature," and that any organized effort of the community or its government to take a hand in it would be an "interference." But if we use a homely analogy, the interference appears to be no greater than that of a gardener who, having sown vegetables, proceeds to pull up those which he finds too thickly grown. It is by no means an accident, but a revival of ancient precedents, if today in the United States the "police power" is so often called upon to interfere in the industrial sphere.

Early legislation.—Administrative action was, however, not enough. A great many ancient customs stood in the way of the desired development of manufacturing industries. Under time-honored charters given to cities in a period when urban handicraft was predominant, craft-guilds had entrenched themselves as exclusive and monopolistic associations. To break their resistance, new rules had to be worked out and established. Both general and special legislation, in other words, were needed to clear the way for infant industries. It was this need which, more than anything else perhaps, contributed to the appeal of Bodin's famous doctrine of sovereignty. For this sovereignty consisted of all but constitutionally unlimited legislative power; in other words, the power to make laws without regard to any previous laws already existing. Without such a power, Bodin and his contemporaries argued, there was no real government at all. In medieval times, by and large, the oldest law was considered the best law, and when popes, emperors, and kings sought to overcome the confusion of local customs, they had recourse to the Roman law, as we have seen before (see Chap. II, ¶10). Certainly in so far as the government was there to work out and apply *policies* which would enhance the *general* welfare, the power to make general rules was essential. We are thus compelled to recognize legislation, or the purposeful making of new rules, as a second technique of modern government in its pursuit of prosperity. This association of the legislative with the police power seems startling nowadays, for we have come to look upon the police as a particularly virulent form of administrative action, and under the separation of powers doctrine it is customary to differentiate sharply between administrative and legislative activities. It will be seen later that this differentiation could not take place until power had been concentrated for once in the hands of progressive yet autocratic princes, under the Tudors in England, under Henry IV and Louis XIV in France, under Fredrick William I and Frederick the Great in Prussia. Each time, when their successors slipped into "unprogressiveness," they were overthrown, either through revolution, or war, or both.

The ordinance.—This general discussion of formal techniques of police action and legislative reform would not be complete without calling attention to the fact that their legal instruments were often the same, at least on the Continent of Europe. The ordinance was not only employed for specific action, but for broad legislation as well. In fact, much of the most important early legislation of France is found in the *Ordonnances de Roi,* and the same is true in other countries. Even in England, under the Tudors and Stuarts, much actual legislation of paramount significance is embodied in royal ordinances and decrees, though the subservience of Parliaments under Henry VIII and Elizabeth often made it easy and advisable for the prince to "pass the buck" to the representatives of the "people," as the limited group of nobles and wealthy burghers represented in the commons were naïvely called. It is from this past record that we can understand the recent emergence of rule-making activities on the part of executive or administrative authorities, for this again usually takes the form of making ordinances. In continental countries, where monarchical government is less remote, such law-making ordinances have continued to be recognized as part of the executive's work. We shall go further into this question when we consider the separation of powers (see Chap. XI). Now we must return to ask just what things these governments did in order to bring about what they conceived to be prosperity. If administrative police action was the general technique for furthering the general welfare, what particular activities were developed to deal with the several objectives or purposes derived from the general purpose of prosperity? And what were those purposes?

Accumulation of gold and silver the central goal.—Just as a simple farmer measures his wealth by the number of coins he has stowed away in his chest, so the princes of those days and the governments over which they presided looked upon the actual gold and silver in their treasuries as the only reliable measure of prosperity. Their entire policy was directed toward increasing these treasures, or at least preventing their decrease. In the course of this period various devices were worked out to satisfy this craving for money in the most primitive sense of the term. Apart from simply prohibiting the export of precious metals, a device which goes back to the Middle Ages, we find essentially the following techniques of fostering prosperity. First, there are the policies aiding manufacture and commerce. This was done by granting certain enterprisers privileges and monopolies, such as were granted the East India Company or the Hudson Bay Company. These two happened to be trading companies, but the same device was readily available for industrial enterprises. At the same time, the government assumed the right to supervise and even direct these enterprises. Likewise the government undertook to hinder or prohibit certain exports and imports. Secondly, governments groped their way towards a well-defined monetary policy calculated to assist their struggle to attract as much precious metal into their coffers as possible. Lastly, governments undertook to colonize on a large scale, thus insuring their industrial community raw material supplies as well as markets. If one wishes to glean from one document the policy in its several ramifications, the English Navigation Act of 1651 is as good an illustration as any. We must now turn to a brief consideration of each of these policies.

The trade balance and tariffs.—The governmental activities directed towards aiding industry and commerce could be divided, as we said, into the granting of privileges and monopolies and the attendant regulation on the one hand, and into measures affecting the trade balance on the other. It is from this preoccupation with the trade balance that the whole system derived its name: mercantilism. The fact that England first abandoned mercantilism has led to our forgetting that she also probably first consciously embraced it. At any rate, England practiced mercantilism together with all other European governments. For mercantilism was not merely an economic theory (and a wrong one at that), it was a very powerful formative force in the growth of modern government. In fact there are those who would claim it as the cradle of modern government (Sombart).

Now, the effort to interfere directly with the flow of trade took, as we said, the form of impeding or prohibiting certain imports and exports. This policy was carried out by means of general legislation, as in the Navigation Act, and tariffs were employed on a very considerable scale. It is impossible to say at what point commercial tariffs commenced to develop out of the older fiscal tariffs. It seems that they emerged more or less gradually as people found that the manufacture of goods subject to a fiscal tariff, that is, a tariff for revenue purposes only, offered a margin of protection against foreign competition. Certain it is that at the time of Colbert these ideas were fully worked out and that the greatness of this remarkable minister of Louis XIV lay rather in the zest with which he pursued the policy than in his discovery of it. The French tariff of 1581 was certainly a protective tariff. Protective tariffs dominated throughout the seventeenth and eighteenth centuries, and the commercial treaty negotiated in 1786 between France and England made the first real breach in the system. This tariff policy consisted in placing high duties upon the export of raw materials and unfinished products, and high duties upon the import of finished products, while at the same time facilitating the export of finished products, and the import of raw materials. It is easy to see why the contemporary trend of economic nationalism is sometimes called neo-mercantilism.

The stimulation of trade and industry through monopolies.—This direct method of affecting the balance of trade favorably was complemented by the policy of stimulating industry and commerce through the granting of more or less extensive monopolies. Such grants were usually in the form of specific action, rather than of general legislation. Every American knows that the Massachusetts Bay Company received a charter from the king of England. Few have stopped to consider what this meant with regard to the growth of modern government. The granting of charters was a device carried over from medieval days, when it was the legal technique for bringing municipal corporations within the context of a feudal order. In the period when modern governments emerged from the medieval context, such charters were turned to the rather different use of licensing corporations for diverse commercial purposes. These were the regulated companies of the England of the eighteenth century. The device of creating such corporations and granting such privileges was employed on so vast a scale as to revolutionize the whole economic life of the several peoples. Naturally, administrative authorities had to be developed to supervise and regulate these undertakings, at home and abroad. The multiplication of central authorities in England, France, Austria, and other states is directly related to the rapid expansion of trade and manufacture under governmental guidance and supervision. Ministries of commerce and boards of trade developed everywhere, and local commissioners were sent out to break down the resistance of old-fashioned craft-guilds. The development of such industries would keep the money at home. The arts and manufactures must be promoted, according to the preamble of the Edict of Henry IV of 1603, "for they are . . . the only means of preventing the taking of gold and silver out of the kingdom and thus enriching our neighbors." Therefore he sends out his intendants to discover what industries might be started and where, and to find persons interested and able to undertake such efforts.

Enforcement.—It is obvious that this policy of stimulating trade and commerce entailed regulation and supervision of industrial and business life on a large scale. There was no point in decreeing tariffs, unless the border control was made effective for dealing with smugglers. Nor was it worth while to grant a manufacturing monopoly to a particular enterpriser, unless an effort was made at the same time to set up authorities to enforce that privilege. The English government, which granted many trading monopolies to colonizing companies, solved the problems of enforcement by delegating governmental authority to the commercial corporations themselves. By this policy they really allowed the establishment of a separate government which in course of time might elect to declare itself independent, as the American colonies did. After this experience, the British changed their policy, and commenced to reabsorb the great commercial corporations within the government. There is a grain of truth, therefore, in Lloyd George's remark that George Washington founded the British Empire by teaching the British how to govern an empire. At home, governmental authority was more readily retained and central administrative bodies continued to regulate and supervise until the full-grown industrial society swept away most of these restrictions. The process on the Continent was quite similar, except that it lagged behind England by several decades. In fact, in the countries east of the Rhine the governments never quite released their grip on industry and commerce, or, to put it another way, industry and commerce could never quite get along without the support of the government (English competition being too powerful). Consequently, all these countries look with a greater equanimity upon governmental restrictions, and even collectivism on a comprehensive scale, now that the breakdowns of industrial society have made men eager for remedial action.

Stable money.—The amassing of gold and silver being, as we saw, the central goal of mercantilist governments, it was only natural that they should also attempt to affect the flow of precious metals by a suitable monetary policy. Perhaps it is a travesty to call the activities in which early modern governments engaged a monetary policy. Certainly they had little in common with the subtle and complicated operations which are today comprehended under that term. Nor can they be said to have been very successful at the outset. During the entire Middle Ages, the purchasing power of the monetary units created by Charlemagne (pound, shilling, penny) had declined along with a constant decrease in their metallic weight. For example, in England, a silver-penny's weight in troy grains fell from 22 to 12 between 1300 and 1464. This fall continued during the sixteenth and seventeenth centuries. The utter confusion into which such handling of the monetary units plunged trade and commerce caused the city of Florence, the forerunner of so much that is significant in the modern government, to establish as early as 1252 a stable monetary unit, the florin, later adopted by Edward III for England, but not maintained stable by his successors. Not until the eighteenth century did England get a monetary unit with a fairly stable metallic content. This followed upon the rapid deterioration of silver coins during the "clipper period" at the end of the previous century (from 1672 to 1696, when all silver was re-coined). In other European countries, the decline continued all during the eighteenth century. Yet there can be little question that an ordered fiscal economy was impossible as long as such uncertainty as to the monetary units prevailed. With rising prices, tax returns were bound to fall below the requirements, even though the salaries of the officials were not adjusted to the rising price level. This consideration alone would show that a modern government with its extensive purchasing of materials and supplies must seek to maintain a stable monetary system. Yet for the longest time the temptation of getting something for nothing by making the coins smaller was irresistible. It was fundamentally inflation, of course. It must, therefore, have aided the debtor class, that is, industry. But whatever effects it had in this direction were certainly quite unintentional. Nor was all of the weight decrease intentional, as a matter of fact. Certain scholars, at least, have argued that technical inefficiency in the coining of money had a good deal to do with it.

Its obstacles.—Minting coins was a very complicated process which made certain variations in weight difficult to avoid. This fact was seized upon by shrewd men who discerned a chance of making money by sorting the coins. In the language of an Englishman of the late seventeenth century: "But tho' all the pieces together might come near the pound weight or be within remedy; yet diverse of 'em compared one with the other were very disproportionable; as was too well known to many persons who pick'd out the heavy pieces and threw 'em into the Melting pott, to fitt 'em for exportation or to supply the Silver Smiths. And 'twas a thing at last so notorious, that it 'scap'd the observation of very few." Once all the heavier pieces had been withdrawn from circulation, the inducement to coin at the lower level was obviously great. Since, according to Gresham's Law this poorer coin forthwith commenced to invade adjoining countries and to drive the better coin off the market (by making the latter desirable for hoarding), the governments of those countries would willy-nilly be driven to debase their coins also. This was particularly true as long as money consisted of metallic coins, and the governments looked upon wealth in terms of the amassing of precious metals. They were not in the happy position of the American government after the war, which could cheerfully let Europeans hoard American dollar bills, since they were nothing but paper representing the credit of the government. On the other hand, the peculiar dangers of that situation in case the government's credit collapsed were much less pronounced under the earlier conditions.

Paper money.—On the whole, governments were pretty helpless in dealing with monetary conditions. The more extravagant courts, like those of the Hapsburgs and the Bourbons, were almost always heavily in debt, and they often had recourse to quite dubious practices in order to escape the burden. The most notorious of these was the huge stock swindle into which the French government allowed itself to be persuaded around 1720 by the Scotch adventurer John Law. This man had the notion that the government's debt might be taken care of by forming a colonial corporation and selling its stock to the public. When the ensuing speculative boom collapsed, the idea of paper money, implicit in it, was utterly discredited, though with sound handling it might have made history. About the same time, the English government made the first very tentative steps in that direction through the organization of the Bank of England, which issued notes to the amount of its capital (£2,000,000). These notes were at first issued in very large denominations (£20), and constituted hardly more than two per cent of the total currency. Even in 1796-1797 there were only approximately £10,000,000 available, or about ten per cent. Yet a significant beginning had been made here, soon to be followed by other governments. The Bank of France was established by Napoleon in 1800 and followed the English example. In the meantime, methods of coining had been steadily improving, and by the beginning of the nineteenth century governments were already on the road toward effective management and control of this difficult technique, so vitally important for real prosperity.

Colonial policy.—Finally, a word must be said regarding the colonial policy of early modern governments. Though colonial policy is usually treated as a part of foreign policy, it exerted the profoundest influence upon the growth of modern government, and formed an absolutely essential part of its mercantilist scheme. As we have said before, colonies made it possible to safeguard markets for a country's industrial products and, what was even more important at first, to control sources of raw material supply. Gold, around which mercantilist policy has been found to revolve, was brought back from America in large quantities by the Spanish *Conquistadores*, and its impact upon government was so decisive that one writer has gone so far as to say that "modern government emerged from the silver mines of Mexico and Peru and from the gold mines of Brazil" (Sombart). This is of course meant only as a necessary, not as a sufficient condition: without such an abundant production of precious metals modern government could not have blossomed forth as it did. For one thing, the arms of Hapsburg would not have been nearly as potent against the popular forces in Germany without American gold. Likewise, it is quite imaginable that the Stuarts might have triumphed in England, if the North American trading companies which they had chartered had discovered gold, instead of land for colonists. England, by this natural circumstance, was forced to travel the slower road of converting agricultural produce into wealth. This gave superior strength to the great commercial families (Whigs), and strengthened the aristocratic rather than monarchical forces. But as American gold was claimed by the *Conquistadores* for the royal chest of Spain, so the agricultural produce of the colonies was restricted to London merchants. The Navigation Act of 1660 (1.

Charles II, c. 18) well expresses in its Article XIII the prevailing temper of the time: "No sugar, tobacco, cotton-wool, indigo, ginger, fustic, and other dying woods, of the growth or manufacture of our Asian, African, or American colonies shall be shipped from the said colonies to any place but to England, Ireland, or to some other of His Majestys said plantations, there to be landed."

Continuation and conclusion.—Much of this tale is very familiar to Americans, since these policies stand at the threshold of their national history. Yet it seems desirable to recall the facts here, in order to show how profound a relation they bore to the early growth of modern government. Besides the policies already mentioned, colonial mercantilism prohibited colonies from manufacturing those products which the mother country produced, the mother country claimed a monopoly of transportation to and from the colonies, and imposed duties between the several colonies and between the colonies and the mother country. This entailed a vast amount of additional governmental activity, and ministries for the colonies became a settled part of the great colonizing nations. And since these colonies consisted almost invariably of conquests beyond the seas, and were hotly contested, they required very considerable military forces, both land and naval, but particularly the latter. Here, then, is another vital point of contact between the mercantilist policy of furthering prosperity by governmental action, and the absolutist policy of territorial expansion, the one involving administrative and the other military efforts on an unprecedented scale.

CHAPTER VII

OBJECTIVES AND TECHNIQUES

D. The Reduction of Internal Friction through Judicial Methods

1. *Introductory: the antiquity of judicial techniques.—2. The differentiation of* jus dicere *and* leges dare *in seventeenth century England.—3. The two rival conceptions of a higher law.—4. "Artificial reason."—5. The rule of precedent and the judicial process.—6. Judicial organization in continental Europe.—7. The lawyers' guild.—8. The background of the Act of Settlement.—9. Frederick the Great and the miller.—10. Cocceji's reforms.—11. Judicial restraint as the beginning of constitutional government.—12. Administrative law.—13. The* Conseil d'Etat.—14. *French administrative justice and American problems.—15. Conclusion.*

Introductory: the antiquity of judicial techniques.—One of the most ancient governmental techniques is unquestionably the judicial method of settling disputes between members of the group. Far back in prehistoric times, verdicts were pronounced and punishment meted out to the evil-doer in accordance with traditional customs. The legendary Germanic chieftain, with long beard, sitting under an oak tree and performing this crucial function is not peculiar to our own racial group, as the Romantics once imagined; he could be duplicated from practically every other land. This tribal chieftain, if successful, eventually emerged as a king surrounded by a group of elder statesmen, a council of wise men, the Witenagemot of Anglo-Saxon times. Its members were counselors of the king, the bishops, the ealdormen, and the thegns. Besides exercising many other functions of government, this great council sat as a high court of justice over all persons and causes. The function of a high court was later inherited by Parliament, or rather the king in Parliament, as the ancient phrase goes. This judicial work, indeed, was perhaps the central function of Parliament. It is one of the most significant developments under modern government that this function was ultimately differentiated from the law-making, the legislative function, and attributed in large part to separate organs and officials. Indeed, from the legal point of view, the most significant feature of modern government is precisely this differentiation of the judicial process. This was clearly perceived by Montesquieu who considered an independent judiciary the core of constitutional government. In the *Spirit of the Laws* he observes: "There is no liberty yet, if the power to judge is not separated from the legislative and executive power. . . . In the majority of the kingdoms of Europe, the government is moderated, because the prince leaves the exercise of the judicial power to his subjects." Montesquieu's idea of a moderated government corresponds, in general, to our notion of a constitutional government. (See below, Part II.)

The differentiation of *jus dicere* and *leges dare* in seventeenth century England.—Differentiation of the judicial process could, of course, not commence, until the idea of "making" laws had become distinct. In the Middle Ages there existed, broadly speaking, no such idea. Law was assumed to be something already in existence, fixed and immutable. All that was necessary was to find out what this law was, to interpret and determine it. Custom was supposed to be the fountain of this law. But custom is local, and the inconveniences which resulted from the great variety of rules seriously troubled medieval rulers. As we have already pointed out (see above, Chap. II, ¶ 10), one ideal weapon, the Roman law, was available against this multiplicity of local laws. It fitted in with the prevailing notion that law is something immutable, but had the advantage of stemming from a single source. What was more, the Roman law was patterned on the needs of a highly civilized society, built on commerce and industry. It was, to that extent, a welcome instrument to the commercial and industrial, as against the feudal landowning classes. Emperor, pope, and king alike sought refuge and relief in its provisions. However, the struggle between royal and papal authority, which was so significant an aspect of the later Middle Ages, made national kings turn away from the Roman law. More particularly in England, a common law, expounded by the king's judges, rapidly amalgamated the more useful ideas of the Roman law with the broader principles of Germanic customs. This development is most strikingly illustrated by the work of Bracton (1216-1272). When the great rupture of the Reformation eventually enabled national judicial systems to consolidate themselves by eliminating most of the ecclesiastical jurisdiction altogether, England was thus already possessed of a body of consolidated national law. On this law judges could base their decisions in opposing the royal claims to supremacy in the field of law-making which Bodin's sovereignty had so ingeniously vindicated for the royal authority. Coke's famous claim that the king is under the law assumed a significance under such conditions which it could not have had when no national law was extant. Whether this meant a denial or an assertion of parliamentary supremacy, we shall see below (Chap. XVI), but just now we must examine somewhat further the question of whether there was supposed to be a higher law than the law made by whoever had the authority to make laws.

The two rival conceptions of a higher law.—In Dr. Bonham's case, Sir Edward Coke, then Chief Justice of the Court of Common Pleas, claimed "that in many cases the common law will controll acts of Parliament and sometimes adjudge them to be utterly void." The difficulty in extracting the true meaning of this statement lies in the fact that "acts" of Parliament could, in that period, refer to judicial decisions as well as to legislative enactments. While the process of legislation had definitely commenced, it was not clearly recognized as such by most people. To be sure, Sir Thomas Smith in his *English Commonwealth*[1] distinctly speaks of a legislative function apart from the judicial function of Parliament. Francis Bacon's entire work on the common law is also permeated by this distinction, which is implied in his celebrated dictum that the common law is more worthy than the statute law. Yet it is not easy to fix with any exactness the beginnings of the legislative activity which has become one of the main characteristics of modern Parliaments, nor to assign the causes of its growth (McIlwain). Probably the many statutes consequent upon the Reformation and involved in the separation of the Church of England from the Catholic Church represent a first genuine outburst of legislation in the modern sense. Here was a genuine rupture in the community, and whatever was done in the form of parliamentary enactment could not but appear in the light of man-made law to those opposed to it. Sir Thomas More was executed because he would not subscribe to "legislation" making the king's marriage legal. And when, under Mary, the opposing faction gained the upper hand, and repealed a good many statutes, only a blind man could have failed to perceive that laws were made and unmade by human beings. Yet the older idea constantly recurs. "King Henry VIII,"

[1] II, ii, and II, v-vii.

Bacon recalls, in suggesting the making of a Digest of English Law to James I, "was authorized by Parliament to nominate thirty-two commissioners to purge the canon law, and to make it agreeable to the law of God, and the law of the land." This idea that all laws should be related to the "fundamental law" of the land gained ground constantly, until, at the trial of the Earl of Stafford, in 1641, a member of Parliament declared that if any question arises concerning either a custom or an act of Parliament, "the Common Law of England, the First, the Primitive and the General Law, that's the Rule and Expositor of them, and of their several extents," must be decisive. In other words, the common law was supposed to contain within itself broad basic principles regarding the procedure and limitation of governmental organs which no one of them could undertake to change. The attempt to eliminate this idea of a fundamental law by resuscitating the Roman doctrine of a law of nature as the rule of right reason, a doctrine which was so eminently successful on the Continent as the path-maker of monarchical absolutism, failed utterly. Bacon, after first putting the common law above the statute law in worth, wanted to place the law of nature above them both. But since he meant by that the rule of right natural reason, he encountered the fierce opposition of Sir Edward Coke, who in answer evolved the doctrine of the "artificial reason of the law." This peculiar notion has been of such decisive significance in the development of the judicial process that we must stop to examine it for a moment.

"Artificial reason."—The doctrine grew out of an argument as to whether the king was or was not above the law. Sir Edward Coke, as Chief Justice of the Court of Common Pleas, had been restricting the jurisdiction of the ecclesiastical Court of High Commission. He was asked to discuss the matter with the clergy in the presence of King James, November 13, 1608, and roundly asserted that he would not be able to accept the Romanist interpretation of the clergy. James, taking exception to this dogmatic view, declared that he was the supreme judge, and under him were all the courts. To this Coke replied: "The common law protecteth the King." "That is a traitorous speech," King James shouted back at him in great anger; "the King protecteth the law, and not the law the King. The King maketh judges and bishops." He then proceeded to denounce Coke so vehemently, shaking his fists at him, that Coke "fell flat on all fower" before the King, and humbly begged his pardon. But the matter did not long rest there. In 1616, a similar quarrel ensued over whether the king could stay a court proceeding which he considered contrary to his prerogative. Under the leadership of Coke, then Lord Chief Justice of King's Bench, the judges had claimed such a proceeding to be contrary to law. To this claim, James answered that although he never studied the common law of England, yet he was not ignorant of any points which belong to a king to know.[1] Thereupon his idea that "natural reason" unrelated to a knowledge of the law of the land could be employed in interpreting statutes was rejected by Coke in the most explicit form. "Reason is the life of the law, nay the common law itself is nothing else but reason; which is to be understood as an artificial perfection of reason, gotten by long study, observation and experience, and not as every man's natural reason . . . by many successions of ages [the law of England] has been fined and refined by an infinite number of grave and learned men, and by long experience grown to such a perfection, for the government of this realm, as the old rule may be justly verified of it, that no man out of his private reason ought to be wiser than the law, which is the perfection of reason." Thus reason is clearly not a standard, philosophical or otherwise, brought to the law from outside, but the essence of the law itself, acquired in the process of learning the law. This notion is not only historically significant, but has a certain general validity. For it is only when general rules, embodied in legislative enactments, are transformed into detailed statements applicable to everyday life, that they become part of the living law. We can appreciate the significance and value of this process, even though we are no longer able to consider the tentative "hypotheses" of legal judgments as eternal truths. If the whole community is more sceptical, such hypotheses may be as important and influential as absolute and immutable laws once were. And even though we appreciate the irrational forces which affect judicial conduct, "the traditional beliefs, acquired convictions, and the deep-rooted prejudices" which mold the judge's interpretations of the law, we continue to realize the essential service which is rendered by the man or woman who struggled to find the just decision in the light of all the available facts and rules. For even if the fabric of the law be considered a huge web of effective make-believe, the life of the community and the maintenance of government are dependent upon it.

The rule of precedent and the judicial process.—The rule of artificial reason which permeates the judicial process is in turn so

[1] Bacon, *Works,* II, 493.

firmly grounded in the tradition of *stare decisis*, that is, the idea that the courts must abide by rules set up in previous decisions, that some consideration must now be given to this important technique of the judicial process. Rules set up by previous decisions are called *precedents*. That judges are guided by such precedents is hardly surprising. "It takes effort and time to solve problems. Once you have solved one it seems foolish to reopen it. . . . Both inertia and convenience speak for building further on what you have already built; for incorporating the decision once made, the solution once worked out, into your operating technique without reëxamination of what earlier went into your reaching your solution" (Llewellyn). In other words, the following of precedent is firmly rooted in human nature, and characteristic of all human activity. It is the governmental equivalent of what, in the community at large, we know as folkways, and of what, in the individual, we know as habit. Is it surprising that it should share with habit and folkways the tendency to be considered desirable in itself? And even if the judges were willing to discard their previous decisions, the lawyers at the bar pleading their cases are constantly reminding the judges of these former decisions, and thus keep the courts conscious of such precedents. What is more, the precedents not only stabilize and unify governmental practices, but they make available to the inexperienced newcomer the accumulated experience of the past. Perhaps they also heighten the sense of responsibility of the judge who confronts an unprecedented situation, since he knows that the precedent which he sets may become the guiding star of many judges following him. It would, however, be foolish to assume—and the last sentence already suggests it—that all cases can be decided by precedent. As a matter of fact, precedent makes for change as well as stability. How? Essentially through the use of two rather contradictory views of precedent which one might call the strict and the loose view (Llewellyn). According to the strict view, the judge must make certain just what it was that the precedent decided, he must confine the case to its particular facts. This view is applied to unwelcome precedents. It is the technique for freeing the lawyer and the judge of precedents. The loose view, on the other hand, maintains that the court has decided any or all points on which it chose to rest a case, no matter how broad the statement. This loose view accordingly provides lawyer and judge alike with a technique for capitalizing welcome precedents. The doctrine of precedent is therefore two-faced, and if applied to the same precedent at the same time, it yields contradictory results. It is apparent now how this equivocal "rule" provides for both stability and change, by offering a technique for getting rid of previous rules, as well as for bringing in previous rules. Broadly considered, it is a most extraordinary make-believe calculated to maintain the unity of the legal system (relatively speaking, of course!) and to bind the new judge to the experience of the past. But since this ingenious make-believe does not prevail on the European Continent, we may well ask the supplementary question of how the objectives it serves are being realized there.

Judicial organization in continental Europe.—Do continental judges fail to follow precedent? Of course not. As we observed in the previous paragraph, precedent is so much a reflection of general human and therefore official traits that we find it wherever human beings pursue the same tasks for any length of time. But their following of precedent is clothed in a different garb, namely what is known as the custom of judicial action (*usus fori*). Continental practice focuses attention on the corporate activity of the courts, rather than individual pronouncements. This is in keeping with the fact that in these countries we find a definite profession whose members form an hierarchically organized bureaucracy of judicial officials (including prosecutors). Into this bureaucracy men enter after appropriate training and remain for the rest of their lives. At the top of the system is a ministry of justice which supervises the system, attends to promotions and in general acts as a directing force in making judicial experience available to the legislature. As a consequence, ministries of justice have been the spearhead in promoting the recurrent great codifications of continental law, of which Cocceji's judicial reforms under Frederick the Great in Prussia marked the beginning, while the *Code Napoleon* is perhaps the most striking single achievement along these lines. Thus we find that the two most important practical objectives of the doctrine of precedent, (1) to bridge the gap between experience and inexperience, (2) to maintain relative unity of the legal system, are here achieved through administrative devices, to wit, an adequate apprentice training and a judicial career leading to the higher judicial positions of grave responsibility. Reliance upon authoritarian, administrative devices, as compared to believed-in traditional group-ways resting upon common consent, is in keeping with the general lines of differentiation between the political traditions of England and America as compared with those of France and Germany. In order to appreciate fully the significant cleavage which underlies this differentiation in the judicial process, it will be helpful to describe a little more fully the particular group with whose ways we are here concerned, that is, the lawyers' guild in the broadest sense. Obviously the decisive point is that in England and America judges usually are appointed from among the practising lawyers, so that there does not exist any distinct judicial profession. Instead, judges are included in the lawyers' guild.

The lawyers' guild.—The lawyers' guild in English-speaking lands is one of the most ancient and honorable professions. It goes back to the thirteenth century. At that time, England had acquired centralized institutions and was in the process of acquiring a national common law as well. This common law was being developed by royal judges, as we have seen, and drew extensively on national sources. Since the universities (under ecclesiastical guidance) taught Roman and Canon law, the practice grew up of teaching the common law in fraternal organizations of which the four so-called Inns of Court were the most important. The education given at these Inns was primarily of a practical nature; it was an education which trained students for their work both at the bar and on the bench. In connection with this development, the custom grew up that the judges must be taken from among the practising lawyers, rather than from the universities where the Roman and Canon law was taught. Eventually these Inns of Court acquired the exclusive right to call men to the bar, through calling them to the so-called bar of the Inn. Thus legal education became a monopoly of the professional class itself, uniting as it did in one body both judges and advocates. This development of an all-inclusive professional guild was of the greatest political consequence. For while at first and well into the sixteenth century the common lawyers constituted a force strengthening the monarchical position in its struggle with the Catholic Church and the local feudal lords, their allegiance shifted gradually as the royal prerogative commenced to absorb the Romanist pretensions of the church, after having largely destroyed the feudal residues of local power. Thus the position taken by Sir Edward Coke that the king is under the law is a consistent expression of the traditional group-ways which the legal guild had developed in the preceding age.

The background of the Act of Settlement.—It is only upon this background of a solidified legal profession priding itself upon its mastery of the "artificial reason" of the law, that the emergence of judicial "independence" can be evaluated. Truly communal control effected through the lawyers' guild had become so well established that "independence" from authoritarian governmental control left the interests of the community unimpaired, or at least seemed to do so. Without adequate consideration of this collegiate control, judicial independence would indeed spell that judicial "tyranny," the danger of which continental observers have constantly been inclined to emphasize. But the irresponsibility of such a tyranny is avoided by just this fraternal community of bench and bar. It made and continues to make the English and the American judge highly sensitive to the criticism of his brethren off the bench. (For a more elaborate discussion of the problems of responsibility see below, Chap. XV.) As long as judges held office during royal pleasure, they were in some difficulty, whenever "the royal pleasure" ran contrary to predominant legal sentiment. This was often the case during the better part of the seventeenth century. Coke made the common law, as we have seen, the basis of his attacks upon James' conception of the prerogative as of divine right. Is it surprising that James' instinctive feeling toward lawyers should have been hostile? Bacon tells us that the king realized that "ever since his coming to the crown, the popular sort of lawyers have been the men, that most affrontedly in all Parliaments have trodden upon his prerogative." On the other hand it was rather natural that the legal brotherhood should have felt that the royal displeasure should not be exhibited, unless it amounted to displeasure with the conduct of judicial business, according to the established law of the land. But since governments during the seventeenth century seemed much inclined to interpret the royal pleasure in quite an arbitrary fashion, the demand arose that judges should hold office during good behavior, or as the ancient phrase goes *quamdiu se bene gesserint*. This aspiration was realized in the Act of Settlement, which thereby supplemented the Bill of Rights in a very important regard. But what good behavior meant cannot be fully appreciated in its political implications, unless it be realized that the standard of conduct here implied is set by the collegial and fraternal organization, the compelling force of whose professional ethics was thus given governmental recognition.

Frederick the Great and the miller.—The utterly different situation on the Continent is perhaps most strikingly illustrated by the famous case of the miller Arnold which occurred under Frederick the Great in Prussia, in 1779/80. Here a technically correct, but substantially unjust decision led to the summary dismissal and imprisonment of six judges. They had incurred the royal displeasure, because they did *not* employ the rule of right reason, artificial or otherwise, and rendered a judgment which favored the wealthy landowners to the detriment of a simple peasant-miller. Frederick's despotic, yet popular, action was widely acclaimed throughout Europe; yet in Prussia it had the unhappy consequence that the officials were besieged on all sides with direct complaints to the king. The king himself was profoundly worried, lest he had punished an innocent man. It was so affirmed after his death. Perhaps the most striking result of this case was, however, the king's resolution to have a general code prepared. This code was to be based upon reason and the Prussian common law. It was, in other words, conceived in the same terms as Francis Bacon's celebrated proposal for the codification of the laws of England. But where Bacon's plan foundered upon the solid rock of opposition of the lawyers' guild, the Prussian code was completed in 1794, and thus became the first of a long series of codifications which characterize the law of European constitutional governments in the nineteenth century. These codes mark, broadly speaking, the passing from the arbitrary government of absolutist monarchy to the legalized government which followed it. But they are, at the same time, striking expressions of the authoritarian conception of government, which subjects the judicial process to general rules, rules which are no less arbitrary from the viewpoint of a judicial tradition, when they are supposed to be the commands of a popular assembly.

Cocceji's reforms.—In disposing of the case of the miller as he did, Frederick the Great lapsed back into a way of thought and action which had been very common under his father, Frederick William I. This great administrator and builder of the absolutist government of Prussia was filled with a deep distrust of the judicial courts. He looked upon them as the last refuge of feudal privilege and patrician intrigue. The upper classes, represented in the Estates' Diets (parliaments) as in England, were so strongly entrenched in these local courts that Frederick William saw no other escape than to develop separate jurisdictions where judicial functions would be exercised by his own administrative officials, like those of the General Directory. His endeavors in this direction stand in close parallel to the development of the Court of Star Chamber and the Court of High Commission under the Tudors in England. But whereas the jurisdiction of these bodies was bound to remain limited by the fact that England was already a united realm with a strongly developed judicial system expounding a national common law, the kingdom of Prussia consisted of scattered fragments in each of which the established courts attempted to maintain a local law. They consequently lost ground constantly in their effort to maintain their jurisdiction intact against the inroads of administrative justice. However, the arbitrary decisions handed down by agencies which tended to decide according to a standard of expediency or utility rather than according to the law, produced in time a marked reaction which led to the demand for a common law. This common law and the consequent return to a system of strictly judicial procedure of regular courts were also the guiding ideals of Frederick's great chancellor and judicial reformer, Samuel von Cocceji. Under his influence the king decided to submit himself and all his administrative officials to the law. Thus in 1748 he decreed that "neither the General Directory nor the Chambers of War and of the Public Domain shall mix in cases all of which shall be brought before the regular courts and judicial boards and decided therein," and furthermore that "the judicial boards should decide the case according to the written law." And even though later certain cases had to be excepted from this general instruction, and were declared suable before administrative tribunals, it was provided that in all these cases the same procedure should be used as that employed in the ordinary courts,—in other words, due process of law was guaranteed. We have here, together with the recognition of the rule of law, the emergence of the idea of administrative law. A perusal of the several exceptions shows that the idea of administrative law is rooted in the continental notion of a royal or public domain (the Roman *fiscus*), of the public needs in military, tax, and police matters, and in the maintenance of a disciplinary code in the official hierarchy itself. These exceptions are, obviously, closely related to those fields of governmental activity in the United States where administrative rules and regulations, as well as administrative adjudication, are growing by leaps and bounds. A treatment of judicial process cannot be considered complete without some attempt at analyzing this administrative law, so-called.

Judicial restraint as the beginning of constitutional government.—A generation ago, this subject was the occasion of a heated controversy in which Dicey maintained that administrative law (*droit administratif*) was utterly alien to English and American legal traditions, and that any growth of it must be viewed with profound alarm. In his statement of the problem he harked back to the time-honored argument that law when administered by administrative agencies becomes arbitrary and bureaucratic. We are facing here the fundamental problem of how to enforce responsibility, a topic of great complexity which will be fully considered elsewhere (see below, Chap. XV). It is unquestionably desirable to have a king cherish the noble sentiment that he is the first servant of his state, but it is not enough, if he is left to himself when it comes to determining whether he has lived up to this standard. Now the least objectionable technique, from the point of view of monarchy, is, or at least appears historically to have been, the proposition that the king is bound by the law. We have seen how this rule was insisted upon by Sir Edward Coke in his struggle with James I, and how it underlay the judicial reforms of Cocceji. But here again, the question immediately arises as to who is to say what the law is. In other words, the problem of who controls the courts is politically the decisive question. Just as the control of many courts by the Catholic Church had seemed an unbearable situation from the point of view of national monarchies in the late Middle Ages, so the control of the courts by the patrician classes represented in Parliaments and Diets had carried with it implications for the proposition that the king is under the law, which aroused bitter struggles. And since the patrician classes were quite prepared to interpret the law in their own favor whenever controversy arose, their control of the courts was resented not only by the king, but by the common people as well. Looked at from the angle of a detached power analysis, this issue is related, therefore, to the conflict of various groups in the community, each attempting to secure supremacy, and the common man who supposedly controls this latter-day democracy cannot be said to have been on the side of judicial supremacy at a time when courts were closely linked to the patrician class. And yet, it cannot be doubted that the era of modern constitutional government commences with the establishment of judicial restraints upon the executive branch of the government. This is due to the fact that such judicial restraints mark the beginning of a division of power in the community which the advocates and builders of absolute monarchy had denied. They, like their modern brethren advocating dictatorial forms of government, were persuaded that nothing but a complete concentration of power could hope to overcome the grave disorders which religious disunity had produced, and which are akin to the social disorders of our time. For, as we pointed out in the beginning and shall show more fully in the next chapter, only divided power makes for constitutional, legalized government.

Administrative law.—From this point of view, administrative law, that is, the administration of certain bodies of law by administrative agencies, is undoubtedly a step in the direction of the concentration of powers. It is, therefore, bound to be welcomed by all those who have a leaning in the direction of dictatorial techniques, provided they are employed in support of objectives which they approve. Since, broadly speaking, the expansion of governmental activities is the goal of reformers or "progressives" of various descriptions, we find these groups actively supporting the expansion of administrative jurisdiction. This was natural as long as no Fascist rival had arisen to seek the use of governmental authority for the bolstering up of rapidly declining profits in either business or agriculture or both. But it should, of course, be apparent that efficiency, expediency, and utility are formulas which can be diverted to various ends, as nothing is inherently and ultimately efficient, expedient, or useful. It all depends finally upon what you want to do or have. On the other hand, it cannot with any show of factual evidence be claimed that the existence of administrative law, that is, the exercise of judicial functions by administrative agencies in limited fields, heralds the disappearance of the "supremacy of law" or of constitutional government (*Rechtsstaat*). On the contrary, the development of administrative law in France and elsewhere is the crowning achievement of the constitutional era. For it does not signify the supremacy of administrative officials over the law, but its exact opposite, namely the standardization of all administrative conduct in terms of legal rules. This is immediately apparent when we discover that the central concern of administrative law has been the legal limitation of administrative "discretion." Thus the first principle of administrative law is that no administrative measure which imposes a burden upon anyone can be taken without legal authorization. Through this principle "discretion" is enclosed within the narrowest possible limits. It may, in fact, be claimed that the exercise of judicial functions by administrative officials, which so thoroughly frightened Dicey, is, when seen in historical perspective, an indication of the fact that large areas of formally administrative activity are actually judicial in nature, or are in the process of being judicialized. In view of this fact, Professor Frankfurter cannot be blamed for describing Lord Hewart's strictures on the new "tyranny" as a piece of lurid journalism, though to the writer Lord Hewart's essay seems rather a bit of "learned" tilting at windmills. But just as Don Quixote's indignation over royal oppression was a laudable and intrinsically sound, though misdirected, motive for his spirited attack upon the windmills, so the Lord Chief Justice's concern over the extension of administrative jurisdictions contains an element of truth. This aspect of the matter is well-expressed by Harold Laski when he writes: "If administrative tribunals are to command public confidence it may be suggested that their membership must satisfy certain historic canons on which public confidence appears to depend. Their composition must be stable in character. The minister or department head must not be able to change their membership at his discretion or to overrule their findings on issues of fact. . . . The men appointed to such tribunals must be known and chosen for their competence in the theme of their particular jurisdiction. Such tribunals should moreover always contain a legal element. These canons are in fact satisfied by the French and German systems; it cannot be said that they have yet been satisfied in the tribunals which the necessities of the modern state have led Great Britain and the United States to erect."

The *Conseil d'Etat.*—It may be well to examine a bit more closely the apex of the French system, the *Conseil d'Etat.* It is a common mistake to describe the French council of state as primarily, if not exclusively, a judicial body. In fact, this council combines its judicial activities with very important administrative functions, particularly in the field of ordinance-making (*réglements* and *décrets*). The judicial functions constitute the work of merely one section of the council. It is, however, significant that the regular members of the council, the thirty-five regular councillors, the thirty-seven masters of petitions, and the eighteen auditors, are the only ones to participate in the work of this judicial branch of the council. Moreover, the majority of these members are career men who have entered the council as assistant auditors (*auditeurs de seconde classe*) on the basis of a competitive examination, and have been promoted on merit. Still one-third of the councillors and one-fourth of the masters of petitions may be taken from outside the council. It would, however, be very far from the mark to suppose that these members are spoilsmen without any preparation; usually they are career men from the active administration and university professors who, the French believe, add a valuable element of flexibility to the council's work. In terms of what we have seen regarding the nature of judicial work, it is more objectionable that even the regular members of the council hold office at the pleasure of the government. Remembering the rule of anticipated reactions, we cannot accept the argument of Professor Garner that this is in fact not serious, since there have been no cases of arbitrary dismissal since 1879, or even of the exercise of official pressure. At the same time, the fact that the council is engaged in administrative as well as judicial work makes tenure during good behavior rather impracticable. It is here, as in the case of administrative commissions in the United States, a question of the right balance of advantages and disadvantages; for the loss of administrative experience may not be sufficiently balanced by the gain of complete judicial independence. Certainly thorough familiarity with many branches of administration (the regular members are rotated from section to section at from one to three year intervals) is no mean gain to men who are called upon to settle judicially contentions or disputes (*contentieux*) which arise over administrative activity. To be sure, many such disputes are raised and settled in ordinary courts, even in France, though the bulk is brought before the council of state. Administrative law may not, therefore, be defined in terms of the jurisdiction of the council of state—a tendency which is ever-present in common law countries. It is much more comprehensive, and includes, in the language of Professor Hauriou, that branch of public law which regulates (1) the organization of public administration and of the several administrative officers; (2) the powers and privileges which these administrative officers possess in order that they may operate the public services; (3) the exercise of these powers and privileges through the prerogative, specially through the procedure of official action (*action d'office*), and the disputes which result therefrom. If, therefore, we now turn to a consideration of these questions of administrative adjudication under the council of state, we must never forget the much broader sphere of the administrative law, nor the wide administrative competencies of the council itself.

French administrative justice and American problems.—Perhaps the most important question which arises in connection with a separate set of administrative courts is that of a conflict of jurisdiction between such courts and the ordinary judicial courts. In France that problem is settled by the organization of a separate court of conflicts (*Cour de Conflits*) which, as M. Hauriou has rightly pointed out, is essentially a court interpreting the constitution, since the whole separation of administrative from other adjudication rests upon the French doctrine of the separation of powers (see below, Chap. XII). There is no reason why in the United States this sort of problem could not be settled by the Supreme Court, which is the interpreter of the Constitution, anyway. It is, in this connection, worthy of note that a suit regarding an alleged conflict of jurisdiction can only be brought by an administrative court, because according to the French conception it is a matter of protecting matters involving the government against interference by the ordinary courts. In the United States, it would undoubtedly be more in keeping with constitutional traditions if that question could be raised by ordinary courts as well. But there is another side to the development of truly judicial bodies in the administrative field, which is equally fundamental, and which seems to stand in the way of building up a high administrative court on the French model, as has been suggested. The French administrative courts have grown out of what is known in France as consultative, as contrasted with active, bodies of administration. This idea of consultative, advisory bodies goes back to the *Ancien Régime*, was retained during and after the revolution, and remains a significant feature of French, as of other European, administrative systems. In the personnel of these consultative bodies there was a sort of passive administrator. In the United States, consultative bodies are of very minor significance, though the Governor's Council in Massachusetts shows the persistence of these older (monarchical) forms. In the federal government they are not entirely lacking. What is more, these consultative bodies have not been active in usurping the growing amount of judicial work which modern administration entails. In keeping with the tendencies of the federal government, administrative boards and commissions with quasi-judicial as well as quasi-legislative functions have been created everywhere. Their work is quite uncoördinated. In France, where such a consultative body existed at the center of the government, it offered a personnel which was at once conversant with administration and yet not actively involved in the administrative decisions. It could, therefore, lay claim to a position of neutrality and impartiality such as a judicial body must possess if its decisions are to be accepted as final. French writers are correct in emphasizing the fact that the council of state and the lower administrative courts are *public* bodies, and thus clearly distinguished from the secret working of any kind of appeal to active administrators. Even though the latter device has through long periods of history proved a satisfactory instrument for the maintenance of political order (Catholic Church), there can be no question of comparing such an appeal with any sort of appeal to an independent administrative judiciary. It remains to remark that the procedure before the council of state is essentially an inquisitorial procedure, that is, the case is conducted by the judges themselves. This is the final point of real difficulty in applying the remarkable experience of the French council of state to American problems; for this kind of procedure does not satisfy the American constitutional standard of due process of law. Even though it be admitted by most students of these problems that "due process of law" means a relatively slow and expensive procedure, nothing but a constitutional amendment could probably overcome this obstacle.

Conclusion.—In conclusion, it may be pointed out that judicial activities, which from time immemorial down to the present day have constituted the core of governmental work, began, in the course of the nineteenth century, to be applied to the government itself. This process can theoretically be understood only in terms of a self-limitation of the government, if the government is thought to be the one and only source of power, as political theorists in the seventeenth, eighteenth, and nineteenth centuries were inclined to maintain when expounding the doctrine of the "state." But once the people through a constitution divide the powers of government between several different bodies, and thereby create an independent judiciary, it is no longer necessary, for the sake of logic, to think of judicial checks upon the executive and administrative establishment in such artificial terms (and that is the reason why we are omitting a summary of the whole mass of legalistic theorizing which fills continental literature on this subject). Casting aside the outworn legal rule that "the king can do no wrong" which still clogs the minds of American jurists, we can see and describe the growth of administrative law as an extension of the judicial branch of the government to keep abreast of the ever-widening sphere of administrative activities entailed by the expansion of our industrial civilization. In the eloquent phrases of William A. Robson, the ablest expositor of administrative law in England, we may conclude: "The judicial power which has been given to administrative bodies will be exercised wisely, and the results are likely to be good. . . . I am convinced that Administrative Tribunals have accomplished, and are accomplishing, ends which are beyond the competence of our courts of law as at present constituted. Furthermore, those ends seem to me socially desirable ones which compare favorably with the selfish individual claims based on absolute legal rights to which the formal courts are so often compelled to lend ear. I believe that administrative law as it has developed in modern England is filling an urgent social need which is not met by any other branch of the law; and that there is no inherent reason, if due care and foresight are exercised, why it should be unfitted to take its place side by side with the common law and equity and statute law in the constitutional firmament of the English governmental system." Since the division of judicial from executive power rests, however, upon the development of modern constitutional government, we have been anticipating in these last few paragraphs the constitution as a political process and a political institution. Historically considered, it took many generations of bitter struggle, before the constitution triumphed over the bureaucracy. To be sure, modern bureaucracy was itself organized by the great national monarchies in their fight against the medieval constitutional state, with its division of power between church and state. But once that battle was won, the tyrannical implications of such concentration of power became too manifest not to call forth new movements for a secular constitutional order. In the course of these endeavors, the medieval ideas of popular rights and governmental limitations emerged in new and startling garbs. The thought of men like Locke and Bentham is deeply embedded in the institutional transformations of their times. We must now turn to a consideration of these problems.

constitution. [illegible], those who spoke in the [illegible] of [illegible] who [illegible] with the [illegible] on [illegible] [illegible] or [illegible] [illegible] [illegible] of the law [illegible] the [illegible] [illegible] [illegible] [illegible] [illegible] the common law and [illegible] law in the constitutional [illegible] of the English [illegible] [illegible] [illegible] [illegible] [illegible] [illegible] [illegible], however, [illegible] [illegible] we have been [illegible] in [illegible] that [illegible] constitution as a [illegible] process and a [illegible] [illegible] [illegible] [illegible] [illegible] [illegible] [illegible] [illegible] [illegible] [illegible] over the [illegible] [illegible] [illegible] [illegible] [illegible] [illegible] [illegible] by the [illegible] [illegible] [illegible] their fight [illegible] [illegible] [illegible] [illegible] of [illegible] [illegible] and state [illegible] [illegible] [illegible] [illegible] [illegible] [illegible] [illegible] [illegible] [illegible] [illegible] [illegible] [illegible] [illegible] [illegible] [illegible] [illegible] [illegible] [illegible] of popular rights and governmental [illegible] [illegible] [illegible] [illegible] [illegible]. The [illegible] of men like Locke and [illegible] [illegible] [illegible] in the [illegible] [illegible] of [illegible]. We must now [illegible] to a consideration of these problems.

Part II

CONSTITUTIONALIZING MODERN GOVERNMENT

CHAPTER VIII

THE MAKING OF A CONSTITUTION AS A POLITICAL PROCESS

Introductory.—A certain Senator from the South, whom out of kindness we shall leave unnamed, when told that a measure he defended was unconstitutional expostulated in reply: "When the Constitution comes between me and the virtue of the white women of South Carolina, I say: To hell with the Constitution." Autocrats and revolutionaries of all ages have always spoken in a like vein. By doing so they have revealed their common opposition to restraints placed upon political and governmental action, regardless of its content. As a political process, the constitution can be described as analogous to the rules of the game insuring fair play. This is the meaning of the word constitution in its political sense, as distinguished from its meaning in law, in history, and in medicine. The political scientist inquiring into the political process of constitutionalizing a government must study the technique of establishing and maintaining effective restraints on political and governmental action. He must not allow himself to be sidetracked by other concepts.

Confusion of meanings.—We may recognize as outstanding *three* non-political concepts of a "constitution," the philosophical, the legal, and the historical. The first of these is a generic concept, the other two specific. What I mean by specific is that the historian may speak of the Constitution of Athens, the Constitution of Medieval England,

and the Constitution of the United States, and by each mean something particular or specific, found only at the time and place with which he is concerned. Similarly, the constitutional lawyer of America, England, or France is talking about *the* constitution when he discusses the particular constitution with the legal connotation with which he is familiar in terms of a whole "system of law." Philosophical concepts of the constitution, finally, are usually generalizations from several such historical or legal particulars with which the author happened to be acquainted, or thought he was. In the case of European philosophers their concepts of a constitution are usually derived by contrasting the meaning commonly attached to the word constitution (*constitution, Verfassung*) in their own country at the time of their writing with what the Roman law and Aristotle presumably suggested as being the meaning of constitution in classical antiquity.

Three general descriptive concepts defined.—Long lists of such "meanings," historical, legal, and philosophical, can easily be compiled for the amusement of those who possess a botanical turn of mind. It seems more profitable and less time-consuming to summarize such an inventory in terms of a few dominant concepts. Aristotle's concept of a constitution—or rather his concept of *politeia* which is commonly translated as constitution—refers to the whole order of things in a city. Hegel, who owes a great deal to Greek philosophers in his political philosophy, entertains a very similar idea. Akin to this conception is the notion that the constitution designates the actual organization of the government in broad outline, so that we can speak of a monarchical constitution, a democratic constitution, and so forth. Finally there is found the idea, current among lawyers with a philosophical bent of mind, like Coke, that the constitution embodies the basic legal conceptions of the community, their outlook on life or *Weltanschauung*, in so far as it can be embodied in general legal rules. It is obvious that these three descriptive, general concepts of what a constitution is apply to all political communities, to a Fascist and Communist dictatorship just as much as to the United States or England. However, a normative turn may be given, and often has been given to the last of the three. One merely has to emphasize the difference between the legal conceptions of the community and the actions of the government when the latter are challenged in court. We shall presently return to this aspect of the question.

Two specific procedural concepts.—Besides these general descriptive concepts we find two concepts which are based upon specific procedural aspects. Those who expound the first would maintain that a constitution must be *written,* in order to be a constitution, that it must be embodied in a document. Superficial though this view may seem to us today, it was widely held during the age of constitution-makers in the past century and a half. It was bound to be challenged by students of the English political system like Lord Bryce; for English law makes considerable use of the concept of constitution without having a written document to argue from. The other concept of a constitution in terms of a formal aspect is characterized by insistence upon a democratic mode of amendment. Such a concept is elusive because of the uncertainties surrounding the word democratic. Is not a popular plebiscite like that held under the Empire of the Third Napoleon or under Hitler more democratic than the need of sanction by the House of Lords, required in England until 1911? If so, it obliges us to use the concept of a constitution when speaking of the arbitrary rule of a dictator, merely because he happened to be popularly approved (see below, Chap. IX).

The constitution a technique of effective regularized restraint.—The five basic concepts which we have so far enumerated may for convenience's sake be labelled as philosophical (totalitarian), governmental, legalistic, documentarian, and procedural. As has been stated before, this quintet could without difficulty be multiplied, more or less at pleasure, but five concepts seem sufficiently bewildering, when it is merely a matter of discarding them to return to the political inquiry in a sixth concept. The question may well be asked why we should have bothered to speak of them at all. It seemed necessary because the philosophical and legal connotations have wide currency, while the political connotation in which it is here used is rather less common. Now to recall the definition given at the outset of this chapter: it was said that to render a government constitutional required establishing and maintaining effective restraints upon political and more especially upon governmental action. This definition, while adequate for the purpose of distinguishing the political from the philosophical, legal, and other concepts of the constitution, must now be elaborated by another important qualification: the restraints must be regularized. At the same time, a few comments upon the required standard of effectiveness will be in order. It should be evident that the existence of merely legal restraints is in no wise an indication of the existence of a constitutional order in the political sense. All the cumbersome formalism of the Roman republican constitution cannot alter the fact that Rome in the first century before Christ had become an aristocratic absolutism, with power concentrated in the hands of the senate. Similarly, the legal separation of powers under the British constitution as expounded by Blackstone during the second half of the eighteenth century cannot blind us to the fact that power in England was largely concentrated in the hands of the aristocracy whose political will found expression in Parliament. On the other hand, a restraint might be very effective and thoroughly regularized, without being necessarily legal unless law is very broadly defined as including all custom. Thus many of the most important restraints of the English constitution, such as the alternation of government between two or three parties, are very effective. But unless such restraints are regularized, they cannot be said to have value as constitutionalizing factors. Madame Pompadour scolding the king at her bedside, or a Brownshirt rebellion against Hitler, while possibly very effective checks upon the arbitrary whims of an unconstitutional ruler, cannot be classed as even rudimentary constitutional devices. The restraint which they produce is wholly irregular and hence unpredictable. Obviously, the lines determining what is a regularized procedure are blurred. Since time enters into this question, a practice which at one time is wholly irregular, and at another fully regularized must, for a certain period, have been hard to classify. Yet the end points are relatively easy to determine; in a political system such as that of the United States, a decision of the Supreme Court will often (but by no means always) mark the point of ultimate regularization, as happened not long ago with the presidential pocket veto.

The English and American development not uniformly constitutional.—To this broad political concept of a constitution it may be objected that it is a generalization derived from English and American political development. But while it is true that English and American constitutional development afford us some admirable illustrations for the abstract concept, actual developments, at least in England, have at times veered far toward a scheme of powers concentrated in the hands of a landed aristocracy, aided by other big property owners. When Sir Edward Coke waged his historic battle with James I, he did it, to be sure, in the name of the constitution. Taking the constitution to mean the basic legal conceptions of the community, he welded this alleged "rule of law" into a powerful weapon for restraining royal action. The king's claim that the royal prerogative was beyond the law was flatly denied. Coke would, however, allow Parliament to exercise the concentrated power which he withheld from the king in the name of the law. Thus the particular importance of his struggle lay, admittedly, in his insistence "upon the exclusive right of Parliament to change the laws of England, his vigorous opposition to the claim of any right, even by the king himself, to change the law of the land." But while Coke still meant by "Parliament" the "king in Parliament," or "the ancient body politic composed of kings, Lords and Commons," a decade or two later that medieval aspect of Coke's thought was forgotten. Parliament emerged as the unrestrained power. Once parliamentary supremacy was established, it was not long before a new opposition developed to restrain parliamentary absolutism, ending in the dictatorship of Cromwell. The eventual settlement after the Glorious Revolution was more permanent, but in the end the concentration of power in Parliament entailed the American Revolution and the Reform Bill (1832). From this sketch it can be seen that what appears to the legalist or the historian as an unbroken period of constitutionalism (simply because men in authority called it so), must from the standpoint of political science and its peculiar concept of a constitution as a process of effective and regularized restraints appear in a varying light, oscillating between constitutional and unconstitutional periods. In other words, our more specifically political concept of a constitution is thus freed from the admixture of individualistic and democratic ideology. According to the former, a constitutional government would be one in which so-called personal liberties would be recognized. But an analysis of the personal rights recognized in eighteenth century England will show them to be the rights which mattered to the ruling oligarchy of the landed gentry. Later on, in the United States, constitutional government was being confused with democracy. But radical democracy may and often does mean majority tyranny, and therefore does not satisfy our requirements for a constitutional process.

Restraint as a question of degree.—Upon further reflection, it will be apparent that no government can, in the light of the preceding discussion, be described as strictly constitutional. Nor will a completely unconstitutional order be discoverable amongst the governments known to us. Like all true political concepts, the notion of constitutional government is essentially descriptive of two poles: very strong restraint and very weak restraint. Between these two poles, all actual governments can be ranged. The unreal limits are "complete restraint" and "no restraint," thus:

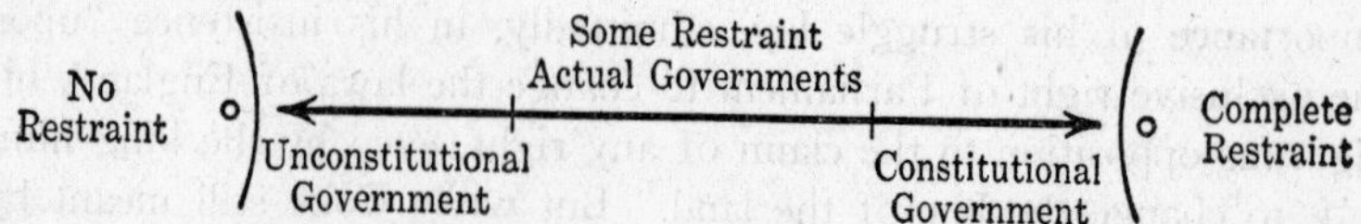

For rough descriptive purposes, governments near the no-restraint pole could be classed as unconstitutional, governments near the complete-restraint pole as constitutional; in the middle there would remain an area of uncertainty. Thus Germany today would be in the first class, the United States in the second; Prussia in 1860 (before Bismarck's usurpations) might be put into the third along with England before 1832 or present-day Austria. There is, however, no way of pushing this analysis much further at present, since adequate means for measuring restraint are not yet available.

A general comparison.—Besides the quantitative analysis which must be postponed until quantitative measuring rods are worked out, there is, however, the functional and qualitative analysis of the constitution as the process by which governmental action is effectively restrained. This analysis has by no means been completed. It can be pushed much further. In the first place it is possible to describe the several restraints which have actually proved effective in the historical experience of mankind. This task will be undertaken with some care in three later chapters (XI, XII, XIII). Then there is the problem of who decides what restraints shall be employed and under what conditions; finally, there is the question how such a system of restraints is generally related to various forms of government. Each particular form of government has its particular tendency toward concentration of power, and the so-called "pure" forms of Aristotle are all characterized by such a concentration of power in the hands of one, a few, or the many, as the ancient formula goes. No actual government ever conformed to these pure types, though a good many of the Greek city states seem to have come perilously near to the no-restraint pole of our figure.

The medieval constitutionalism.—The governments of western civilization with which we are here primarily concerned have rarely come anywhere near to the extremes of purity achieved by Greek city states, for reasons which are extremely controversial. Whatever they may be, the fact remains that restraints have been relatively strong, except in the Italian city states of the Renaissance, and possibly the recent dictatorships (see below, Chap. XIV). The restraints were as often external as internal. To overlook this is a grave error, rather frequently committed by those who allow their political thinking to be fettered by legal and historical particularities. The medieval church and the Holy Roman Empire rendered constitutional the government of many communities which might otherwise have fallen prey to the merciless ascendancy of tyrants. Unquestionably, the eclipse of the ecclesiastical power during the later Middle Ages and upon the advent of the Reformation paved the way for absolutism, first in England, later in France and other continental countries. The remarkable services which such absolute rulers rendered in the course of their bloody reigns have been indicated in the previous discussion of bureaucracy. We must now consider the efforts made and the techniques employed in restraining them, efforts which were often clouded by the thunderstorms of revolutionary upheavals.

The dilemma of Cromwell.—Though it is unquestionable that the city states of Italy, the Low Countries, and Germany anticipated the constitutional evolution of modern government, we shall not here undertake to discuss or even outline that development. Nor shall we enter into an examination of the nature of medieval constitutionalism. We proceed at once to England where the problem of a constitution was first encountered squarely in the age of Cromwell. It is well-known that the *Instrument of Government* which the more radical followers of Cromwell in his Model Army submitted to him in 1649 was not accepted. But even though this prophetic document with its strongly democratic bias failed to become the first English "constitution," Cromwell was haunted by a sense that his arbitrary exercise of power needed a sanction. This sanction he sought to obtain from Parliaments which were elected in rapid succession. Yet since they endeavored to restrain him as well as to sanction his rule, they were dissolved one after the other. The long-drawn-out story of Cromwell's conflicts with his several Parliaments serves, therefore, as an admirable illustration of the fact that once the *de facto* government controlling power by force of arms seeks to secure the approval of the community, it will find itself confronted by demands for effective restraint. This statement is subject to one exception. If a purely formal plebiscite, that is, a vote of the single subject or citizen either accepting or rejecting the government as a whole, is employed for the purpose, "the ayes will have it." There is a simple psychological reason for that: the majority of human beings dislike the futile gesture of pure negation.

The constitution as the decision regarding the organization of the government.—It is for this reason that we have put forward the proposition that the constitution as a political process is invariably concerned with the technique of establishing effective restraints. The seemingly broader definition of a constitution as the fundamental decision about the form of government is misleading. This is so because there often is no conscious decision—as in the case of Cromwell, who simply drifted along—and furthermore because the resolution of an all-powerful tyrant to maintain his tyranny cannot be called a constitution without rendering the meaning of the term absurd. However, the establishing of such restraints does invariably involve a fundamental decision about the organization of government. We may therefore say that every constitution implies at the same time a fundamental decision, but that not every such decision necessarily implies a constitution. Thus if it be clearly understood that unconstitutional government is never meant, we can accept the definition of the constitution as the fundamental decision about the organization of the government. We shall see presently why this definition is important.

By whom this decision is made.—Who, it may now be asked, must make such a decision in order to render it fundamental? All that we can truthfully say in answer to this question is: not too few. It used to be customary to answer: the people. Yet, did the electorate which stood back of the Commons in England during the seventeenth century represent more than a fraction of the people? Obviously not; and still in common parlance we speak of the Glorious Revolution as one seeking to set up a constitutional government, and the stricter language of political science cannot deny that a constitution in our political sense was in the making in Britain at that time. To be sure, the Act of Settlement's guarantee of judicial independence was another very essential step. But the Glorious Revolution certainly aimed at setting up restraints on governmental action, and therefore at constitutionalizing the government. That only a fraction of the governed participated in the fray, does not alter this fact. Therefore "not too few" is a less ambiguous, if vaguer statement of the actual facts. But this numerical description is not all that we can offer regarding the makers of constitutions. In order to make the constitutional decision fundamental it is also necessary that it be participated in by some of those who are being governed as contrasted with those who do the governing. This differentiates it from the *coup d'état*. And finally, the decision must be reached after the mature deliberation of those who participate in the decision.

Participation of the governed.—The participation by some of those who are being governed, that is, the politically passive members of the community, does not necessarily mean democracy. It does mean, however, that an effort will be made to restrain governmental action. Therein lies the importance of the participation of these passive members. Any decision arrived at solely by the governing bodies is not likely to be directed towards defining methods of restraining governmental action. Cromwell realized this vaguely, and therefore persisted in his efforts toward securing parliamentary and popular approval. But since he was unwilling to allow restraints on his power in concrete instances, he found himself obliged to scrap one constitution after another. He could not shake off the idea, so characteristic of all absolutist governments, that opposition was rebellion.

Free speech and free assembly.—This autocratic attitude of confusing opposition with rebellion also prevents the mature deliberation of those who participate in the decision, our other essential criterion of a fundamental decision. Neither free speech nor free assembly are "natural rights," but they are necessary concomitants of constitutional decisions. For mature deliberation of an issue by any number of people who are to act collectively presupposes an exchange of views on the issues involved in the decision. If that opportunity is not available, nothing can be decided. This is the fundamental reason why plebiscites, so popular with dictators from Cromwell to the present day, have no political effect. Though they seem to offer an opportunity for collective approval of a government, their utility for that purpose is quite small. They carry little persuasive force in the community, because few of the participants feel any responsibility for the action taken.

The constituent power.—We are now ready to consider the group of human beings which we have broadly characterized in the last three paragraphs. No matter how large or small, it is a very decisive group which it is here proposed to call the constituent power. Political thinkers during the seventeenth and eighteenth century were deeply concerned with this power, and we owe to them a great deal of our elementary insight. A thorough discussion of their views belongs to a history of political theory, where it is commonly discussed under the heading "the right of revolution." And it is true that these early thinkers were preoccupied with the question of rights. A descriptive political science has no such concern; it does not ask whether people have a right to make a revolution, but what are the conditions under which they do make them. However, those writers in their efforts to vindicate a right of revolution, brought out with much learning what the conditions of revolutions were. Thus early Calvinist theorists pointed to the many revolutions recorded in the Old Testament as proof of the fact that God permitted and even commanded revolutions, an argument which the church had not altogether neglected in the Middle Ages. Later secular writers rested their case upon what they called natural reason. Of these Locke and Rousseau are perhaps outstanding. But we shall limit ourselves here to a brief quotation from the former.

Locke's view restated scientifically.—In his *Second Treatise of Civil Government* (¶ 149), the great English myth-maker remarks: "For no man, or society of men, having a power to deliver up their preservation, . . . to the absolute will and arbitrary dominion of another; whenever anyone shall go about to bring them into such a slavish condition, they will always have a right to preserve what they have not a power to part with; . . . And thus the community may be said in this respect to be always the supreme power, but not as considered under any form of government, because this power of the people can never take place till the government is dissolved." On the basis of our previous discussion, we should re-write this statement, as follows, in order to fit it into the hypothetical form of scientific thought: "For a considerable number of men having a tendency to maintain their freedom of decision . . . against the unrestrained and arbitrary decision of another (and these constituting the more intelligent and vital part of the community at large); whenever anyone shall go about to bring them into a constrained and dependent condition, the presumption is that they will try to escape from it even at considerable sacrifice; . . . and through this (more intelligent and vital) part of the community what may be called 'the constituent power' manifests itself, but not as considered *under* any government, because this power can never be exercised except to dissolve the established government." This transcription shows that

Locke's juridical statement, whatever its merits on legal and moral grounds, contains the kernel of two important scientific generalizations: (1) there tends to exist a residuary and unorganized power of resistance in the community which seeks to restrain the government, and (2) this constituent power can only come into play when the government fails to function. This second proposition is important in differentiating the constituent power from the constitutional amending power, for which provision is made in most modern constitutions (see below, Chap. IX). To be sure, the amending power is set up in the hope of anticipating a revolution by legal change, and therefore as an additional restraint upon the existing government. But should the amending power fail to work, the constituent power may emerge at the critical point. It is rather important to realize that the traditional doctrine of the "right of revolution" contains at least this kernel of scientifically valid generalization. Certain earlier writers on the subject, like Althusius, have, as a matter of fact, gone rather far in establishing revolution as a recurring matter of fact. The extended record of Jewish history as contained in the Old Testament had elicited their particular and lasting interest, as it seemed to show divine approval of such revolutionary efforts as were directed toward restraining the government in terms of a moral code. Still others, like Hotman and Buchanan, had likewise emphasized the historical fact of revolution as a valid part of their national history, whether French or Scotch. This earlier scientific interest in revolutions as manifestations of constituent power was obscured by the moralist turn which this problem was given by Locke, and more emphatically by Rousseau. But the more realistic analysis back of it continues to be the mainstay of the argument.

Conclusion.—In conclusion, it may be said that the constitution has, for modern political science, a very distinct meaning as the process by which governmental action is effectively restrained. In spite of the unfortunate fact that the word constitution has a variety of other meanings, biological, legal, philosophical, and what not, it seemed best to retain this traditional meaning. It would be less ambiguous, but also less meaningful, to speak of this process as the R-process. But as long as the word "constitution" is understood to refer to this process, the danger of ambiguity may be faced in order to retain the superior suggestive value of the customary expression. There is another reason for this way of putting the matter. The total complex of effective restraints which makes up the "constitution" of a given community will necessarily crystallize into more or less familiar word patterns, such as "legislative, executive, and judicial power," "states' rights," "due process," "freedom of speech," and so forth. These word patterns gradually become symbols of order, and thus the constitution as a political process emerges into the constitution as a political force. While this shows that, from even a political scientist's viewpoint, the word "constitution" has yet another meaning than that of a process restraining governmental action, namely, that of a political force maintaining an existing constitutional order (see below, Chap. X), we do not see therein an argument against retaining the word "constitution" for both, but on the contrary purposely brave a certain amount of confusion in order to demonstrate our belief that the traditional view is sound in that it allows a constitution as a political force to be perennially recreated by the constitution as a political process. But before this difficult phase of the "constitution" can be taken up, we must examine the constituent power somewhat further.

CHAPTER IX

THE CONSTITUENT POWER, THE AMENDING POWER, AND REVOLUTION

Introductory.—Revolutions are successful rebellions. If they have failed, their makers have with rare exceptions been executed for treason. Treason is commonly understood to be an attempt to overthrow the established order. The constituent power bears an intimate relation to revolution. To be sure, not all revolutions are made by a constituent power, as Locke and Rousseau tended to assume. For the constituent power is the power which seeks to establish a constitution. Many revolutions do nothing of the kind. We have been witnesses in our own day of a whole series of revolutions which sought to destroy a constitution rather than establish one. But every time the constituent power becomes active, a revolution (or at least a rebellion) will take place.

The plebiscite.—From our general discussion in the previous chapter it will be remembered that this power manifested itself through a not too inconsiderable group of individuals including some of the governed. After the preceding order has been overthrown, a measure of free speech and free assembly is necessary in order that the constituent power may work. The suppression of these two conditions thwarted the constituent power in Cromwell's time as well as in our own. National Socialist, Fascist, and Communist revolutionaries are united in their opposition to free speech. It is but natural, therefore, that no constitution should have been established in those countries which are ruled by these groups. But since the need for popular approval is still felt, these governments tend to employ the plebiscite as a substitute. They feel that a constituent power ought to have brought them into power, as its leaders, rather than their merely having usurped the absolute power of government. Therefore they seek the plebiscitary semblance of wide popular acclaim. Cromwell, the two Napoleons, Mussolini, Hitler,—they all have employed this technique.

Cromwell and the Puritan revolution.—Cromwell's *Instrument of Government* of 1653 provided in its Article XII that the officers supervising the elections to Parliament under this instrument should obtain from the electors a written acknowledgment "that the persons elected shall not have the power to alter the government as it is hereby settled in one single person and a Parliament." This provision contains the notion of an implied consent of the electorate, and a characteristic device for escaping the implications of an effective constituent power. Yet, no sooner had this Parliament assembled than it commenced an extensive debate on the constitution. This provoked Cromwell into making a speech (after locking up Parliament) to justify his demand that each member of Parliament sign a statement similar to the one just cited. In the course of this speech, the Lord Protector made it quite clear that he perceived a constitution to be a fundamental decision, and basically concerned with restraining arbitrariness. During the Long Parliament there had been, in his opinion, a definite drift toward parliamentary absolutism. "And so the liberties and interests and lives of people not judged by any certain known Laws and Power, but by an arbitrary Power; which is incident and necessary to Parliaments. By an arbitrary Power, I say: to make men's estates liable to confiscation, and their persons to imprisonment,—sometimes even by laws made after the fact committed; often by the Parliament's assuming to itself to give judgment both in capital and in criminal things, which in former times was not known to exercise such a judicature. . . ." For that reason he claimed the dissolution of the Long Parliament had been necessary. But Cromwell did not wish to take over the absolute power thus revoked. In bringing together the Little Parliament, popularly dubbed Barebones Parliament, he had another end in view which he himself claimed to be his greatest end, namely, "to lay down the power" which was in his hands "in which unlimited condition" he "did not desire to live a day." In other words, he wished them to draft a constitution. But they despaired of the task and decided "to deliver up unto the Lord-General (Cromwell) the powers we received from him." Upon the failure of these representatives to exercise the constituent power, the *Instrument of Government* was drawn up by some of Cromwell's supporters in the army and elections were called with the *proviso* cited in the beginning of this paragraph. After Cromwell's exhortation, most of the members signed the pledge not to propose, or give their consent "to alter the Government as it is settled in a Single Person and Parliament," yet immediately upon reconvening returned to constitutional controversies. Cromwell's admission that in every governmental charter "there must be something Fundamental, something like a *Magna Charta*, which should be standing, should be unalterable," and therefore in this "establishment there are some things which are Fundamental," others which "are Circumstantial," had left an avenue open for such a discussion of constitutional issues. To be sure, Cromwell had himself outlined three fundamentals of the *Instrument*, (1) "that Parliaments should not make themselves perpetual," (2) "Liberty of Conscience in Religion," (3) that the army "should be placed so equally that no one party neither in Parliament nor out of Parliament have the power of ordering it." Each one of these will readily be recognized to be a measure of restraining the government, and dividing its power between the executive and the legislative power. When Parliament kept on debating about the constitution, instead of attending to its constitutionally appointed task, Cromwell dissolved it, and thereafter governed as a military dictator,—a constituent power had not emerged in England, and Cromwell's rule collapsed with his death. The implied consent of the plebiscite of 1653 had remained a futile gesture.

Napoleonic plebiscite.—Cromwell's failure by no means deterred the two Napoleons from seeking to sanction their rule by a similar device. After the first Napoleon had staged his *coup d'état* (November, 1799), he proceeded to draft a constitution which centered all power in the first consul and submitted it to a plebiscite. Here, then, the consent was not implied, but explicitly asked for—and overwhelmingly given. The same thing happened again in 1802 when the consulate was bestowed upon Bonaparte for life. It is, however, important to realize that these "constitutions" contained no provisions for the restraint of the government, and were therefore no constitutions in the political sense which we have here employed. It is noteworthy that Louis Napoleon should also have had recourse to the plebiscite. After his *coup d'état* of December 2, 1851, the third Napoleon demanded from the people that they sanction his authority and that they delegate to him the necessary powers for making a constitution along the general lines of a proclamation he had issued. Again, the plebiscite was accepted by an immense majority, which is hardly surprising, in view of the wording of the plebiscite: "The French People wants to maintain the authority of Louis-Napoleon Bonaparte and delegates to him the necessary powers for making a constitution. . . ." The voter could either accept or reject this proposal, but was not given any positive alternative. Practically the same tactics prevailed about a year later when the imperial office was reëstablished under a plebiscite modelled on the precedent of the first Empire. The restraints established by these charters were quite weak, and even the more liberal Constitution of 1870, also submitted to popular plebiscite, was quite monarchical. That no true constituent power came into play through their adoption, was emphasized by a speaker who wished to see the constitutional laws of 1875 submitted to popular approval. On the 28th of January, 1875, M. Naquet said in the Assembly: "I believe that a constitution must be ratified by the whole people. By affirming that I merely return to the tradition of our great (revolutionary) assemblies; for the Constitution of 1793 and the Constitution of the Year III were submitted to direct ratification of the people. . . . We do not have to abandon this right merely because the Empire has abused the plebiscite, the right derived from an appeal to the people. . . . There is an immense difference between the imperial plebiscites which posed the question *a priori* (*ex post facto*) and made it one between some solution and pure negation, and an appeal to the people destined to ratify the charter voted by a national assembly after long and serious deliberations." In this concluding sentence, we find a clear recognition of the necessary ingredients of the constituent power, as we have here depicted it: not only participation of some of the governed, but also free speech and free assembly.

The plebiscites of contemporary dictators.—This point of free speech and assembly is essential in appraising the plebiscites of contemporary dictatorships. Hitler's plebiscite on his assumption of the presidential powers is as hollow a gesture as Napoleon's. Wholly different were the circumstances of the adoption of the Constitution of the United States. Here wide popular discussion, even heated controversy, preceded a vote on the Constitution, nor did an alternative government, the Confederation, cease to exist until the majority of the people had consented to the change. Likewise the Constitution of Switzerland of 1848 owes its existence to a true working of the constituent power. The parallel is interesting in that both these constitutions led to a federal government superseding a federation of governments.

Constituent and amending powers.—The rather pacific procedure which led to the adoption of the Constitution of the United States must not mislead us into thinking, however, that the constituent power can itself be brought "within the four corners of the constitution." To be sure, a constitution being by definition a technique (or a set of techniques) for the restraining of the government, acts of arbitrary and tyrannical violence are much less likely to occur under a constitutional government. Moreover, a wise constitution will provide for its own amendment in such a way as to forestall, as far as is humanly possible, revolutionary upheavals. That being the case, the constitutional amending power forms a vital part of most modern constitutions. Its value was, however, by no means realized at the outset. The several Cromwellian constitutions failed to contain any adequate provisions for their own amendment, and the French Revolution came around to a realization of the importance of amending provisions with much delay. In the nineteenth century constitutions were rarely made, however, without some thought to this problem. But no matter how elaborate the provisions for an amending power may be, they must never, from a political viewpoint, be assumed to have superseded the constituent power. The inner relation and the difference between the amending power and the constituent power is brought out with particular vividness by the constitutional history of Switzerland. In 1848 a new federal constitution superseded the federation of cantons which had broken down and given rise to a civil war in 1847. This federal constitution was adopted by a constituent assembly and submitted to the people of the several cantons for ratification, being accepted by a considerable majority. In 1874, this conservatively liberal constitution was entirely overhauled and democratized, but the draft failing to secure the necessary majority of cantonal ratifications as provided in the amending provisions of the constitution, it was remodelled and adopted in regular amending procedure in 1874. The constitutional amending authority proved sufficient to produce the necessary change. The constituent power manifested itself through the amending power; but that does not mean that it is identical with it; in fact even to say that it manifested itself through it is something of a misstatement. It would be more accurate to say that the group which might otherwise develop into the constituent power manifests itself through, acts through the amending power. For by the constituent power in the exact sense is to be understood the *de facto* residuary power of a not inconsiderable part of the community to change or replace an established order by a new constitution.

Constitutional change without amendment.—Curiously enough, England, whose constitution came into existence through the "Glorious Revolution" of 1688, has seen a profound change in her constitutional order take place without any explicit decision on the part of anybody. This fact merely goes to confirm our earlier statement that revolutions often take place without any constituent power crystallizing into action. The seemingly unrestrained power of Parliament, or of the oligarchy whose mouth-piece it was, was restrained without any explicit action to that effect by the evolution of the two large parties. This constitutional device, generally recognized today to have been of fundamental importance during the nineteenth century, is not based upon any explicit decision, and can therefore be considered only a rather weak restraint. The weakness of the constitution as a political process in England is offset by the strong traditionalism in that country. For tradition represents a powerful political force which will presently be examined (see next chapter).

Relation of the foregoing to amending process.—The British case raises, however, a very general problem. When one talks of a constitution as the fundamental decision regarding the political organization of a community, the impression is conveyed that all is settled once this decision has been made. The constitution is represented as absolute. But we know already that all restraints are matters of degree (see Chap. VIII, ¶7), and that the relativity of these restraints must not be lost sight of. What is more, even a carefully considered and widely discussed decision is subject to certain inherent limitations. Human language is anything but unequivocal. The working out of human relationships is difficult to forecast. The actual conditions of human society change. These three inherent limitations of all human decisions affect constitutions profoundly. Some of the subsequent amendments may be made through a supple amending power. But others will be made by those who govern, and they will be tacitly acquiesced in by those who are governed. They very often take the form of constitutional interpretation, not only by the courts, but by all departments of the government. The relative importance of such constitutional interpretation depends upon a number of factors, including the clarity of the constitutional document itself, and the nature of the formal amending process. If the process of formal amendment does not respond readily to any widely felt need for change, the change will be accomplished through interpretation. In the United States, where the formal process is rather cumbersome, many constitutional adjustments have taken place through such interpretation, and constitutional usages are numerous. Under the German Republic, which merely required a two-third majority of the two chambers of the legislature, constitutional amendments were frequent, and usages of the constitution were few and of minor importance. Again, the Swiss procedure of amending the constitution by popular referendum has lent itself rather readily to formal changes. In the period from 1893 to 1924 the referendum was used twenty-three times; eighteen of the proposed amendments were passed. In some of the American states where the process functions more smoothly than legislation (or, to put it another way, where determined minorities can more readily gather a popular than a legislative following) the constitutional amendment is employed for a great deal of legislation (see below, §13).

The American federal amending process.—The American federal amending power, while cumbersome, has turned out to be less of an impediment to change than was at one time assumed. In spite of the enormous impact of "interpretative" customs and usages, this American procedure deserves some attention, because its drafters had clearly grasped one conclusion of primary significance, namely, that certain amendments to a constitutional document are jeopardized, if the power of amending the document is vested in an officer or group of officers whose own power might conceivably be curtailed by such an amendment. Article V provides four methods for amending the constitutional document, thus making it impossible for either Congress or the state legislatures to block a constitutional amendment, and in keeping with this idea it has been decided by the Supreme Court that neither the President nor state governors have any veto power in this matter. In practice only one of the methods has usually been used so far, namely, that which requires the collaboration of Congress and the state legislatures. Amendments have originated in Congress, on the approval of two-thirds of both houses, and have been ratified by the legislatures in three-fourths of the states. But if Congress wished to avoid calling upon the state legislatures, it could insist upon special conventions in the states. If, on the other hand, a widespread movement for amending the Constitution got under way, and Congress would not respond to it, the legislatures of two-thirds of the states could demand that a national convention be called. Such a move was contemplated before the repeal of the eighteenth amendment; it has recently been advocated in connection with broad programs of constitutional reform. It will be noted that the American Constitution does not admit an initiative on the part of the "people," as does the Swiss constitution (though such a process has been suggested). Since no amendment has been added to the Swiss constitution by that process (nor to the German Republican constitution by a similar device), it may be doubted whether the loss is serious. At any rate, no one officer or group of officers has a monopoly of the amending power, as is the case wherever the amending of a constitution is vested in one legislature alone. It may, however, well be asked whether the process need be as elaborate as it is in the United States; this aspect of the matter has been subject to serious criticism. It is estimated that some 3000 amendments have been proposed in Congress. In 1912 Senator LaFollette and others gave vent to the resulting indignation by suggesting an amendment to the amending process permitting future amendments by a majority of both houses of Congress, to be ratified by a majority of the voters in a majority of the states. This suggestion failed. Since that time, several amendments have been passed. Particularly the repeal of Amendment XVIII has inclined people to feel that the constitutional amending process is probably sufficiently responsive to popular demands for change and progress.

Conditions under which formal amendment is necessary.— The rival processes of interpretation and formal amendment of a constitutional document are not, however, simple alternatives. In spite of the great changes which interpretation and practice may produce, certain specific changes may be quite impossible without a formal amendment. This is sometimes forgotten by those who would have us rely upon informal change. The American federal structure, the division of the country into states, could not be altered without a formal amendment, nor could the explicit distribution of functions. Thus intra-state commerce is a matter which the federal government cannot regulate, without first securing a formal amendment. Proportional representation, provided in Article 22 of the Weimar Constitution, could not be abandoned without formal amendment. In other words, matters about which the document itself is reasonably explicit, must be explicitly changed too. If the formal process is too elaborate, the constitutional structure may in the course of time be very seriously warped. As long as limitations of time and resources are not important, such warpings may cheerfully be endured. The years of effort and the millions of revenue lost in the struggle to put through the amendment allowing the federal government to levy graduated income taxes may fail to arouse the wealthy American nation; the Germans were not equally patient with the difficulties arising from their federal system after the war. Professor Burgess once put the matter rather forcefully, when he wrote: "When I reflect that, while our national conditions and relations have been requiring a gradual strengthening and extension of the powers of the central government, not a single step has been taken in this direction (Burgess was writing in 1890) through the process of amendment . . . , except as the result of civil war, I am bound to conclude that the organization of the sovereign power (read: amending power) within the constitution has failed. . . . When, in a democratic political society, the well-matured, long and deliberately formed will of the undoubted majority can be persistently and successfully thwarted, in the amendment of its organic law, by the will of the minority, there is just as much danger to the state from revolution and violence as there is from the caprice of the majority where the sovereignty (read: absolute power) of the bare majority is acknowledged." While Burgess' comparison is more than doubtful, he focuses attention upon the revolutionary implications of a situation in which the amending power fails to work in the direction of adjusting the constitutional document to altered needs. This is a problem which is quite generally admitted at present. But in addition, it is now realized by many that even a process of amendment which responds to the need for change, when widely felt, cannot completely protect the constitution against revolution. For revolution may be made by others than those who would constitute the constituent power. Just the same, the fact that all men must die does not dispose of arguments in favor of a doctor.

Holland, England, and France.—An interesting combination of the procedure of constitutional amendment by legislative enactment, and the necessary emphasis upon the fundamental importance of any such change is found in the Dutch constitution. This constitutional kingdom requires first a dissolution of the chamber and a new election, and then a new vote by a two-thirds majority. Through such a provision the amending power is vested in the representative legislature, and the new election insures the truly representative nature of the Parliament enacting the change. In making this arrangement, the Dutch have put into practice what Dicey wished to see adopted in England. The principle he advocated was "that no far-reaching changes in the governmental system should be made until the voters have had a chance to pass judgment upon the proposed amendment, at a general election" (Ogg). This has, indeed, at times been the case. Thus in 1832 the Liberal majority secured a mandate from the electorate to carry out electoral reform; but lacking a majority before, it could not have done otherwise. More significant is the instance when in 1910 the Liberal government possessing a stout majority in the Commons went to the electorate with a plan for reform of the House of Lords. But in contrast to this move, the enfranchisement of women and other changes in the electoral system were adopted in 1918 by a Parliament elected eight years before; similarly the Irish Free State was created in 1922 without consulting the voters. In republican France, no appeal to the people is required, either, for enacting a constitutional amendment. In keeping with traditional conceptions of parliamentary government (see below, Chap. XX) the two chambers, after separately accepting the proposal of a constitutional amendment from the cabinet, go to Versailles where in a joint meeting of the two chambers they proceed to ratify the amendment, thus marking the solemnity of the proceeding. This arrangement is a clever device for combining the recognition of a distinct amending power with the parliamentary system—a system under which the electorate has acquiesced in the complete exercise by the Parliament of the amending power.

Limitations on the amending power.—Where the constitutional amending power is vested in the legislature, limitations are usually imposed upon it. In France, an amendment of 1884 provided that the republican form of government should never be made the subject of a proposed revision. English constitutional lawyers have argued that Parliament cannot abolish itself, for that would mean binding its successors irrevocably. Even in the United States, the states are not supposed to be deprived of their equal representation in the Senate without their own consent. Whatever the ultimate validity of these provisions and arguments, they presage revolution. Poincaré, in arguing the binding character of the French inhibition just cited, insisted that "any revision which would have for its object the substitution of the monarchical system for the republic would be illegal and revolutionary." By thus forcing those who might constitute an emerging constituent power to have recourse to a revolution, such inhibitions would have the political effect of depriving the amending power of some part of what is its essential function, viz., to forestall the revolutionary emergence of the constituent power. That is the sound kernel of the objections raised to such provisions by those who insist that they are merely declaratory and cannot bind the "will of the people"—a remark repeatedly made in the French Chamber. But all we have so far discovered points in the direction of denying an identity between the "will of the people" and the constituent power. The "will of the people" has been too often a cloak for propagandizing gangs who were endeavouring to destroy the constitution and the constituent power. The Boulangist agitation in France is an interesting illustration. When considering such efforts, we see that such limitations also have the effect of thwarting revolutionary upheavals which are admittedly or secretly opposed to the maintenance of the constituent power. For as we have seen, revolutionary movements opposed to free speech and free assembly are quite frequent. They are politically possible in communities where the constituent power is atrophied for diverse reasons, and a determined gang is thus enabled to seize actual power and reorganize the government in its own interests and without consultation with the governed. But before we turn to the general problem of revolutions, we have to examine a bit further a distinction which Cromwell suggested in the speech quoted earlier when he pointed out to the Parliament that some things in a constitution are fundamental, while others are circumstantial.

Non-fundamental constitutional provisions.—A provision in the *Instrument of Government* had set aside £200,000 for the civil offices, that is, the administration—to pay the judges and other officials, to defray the charges of the council in sending their embassies, to support the governor-in-chief, and so forth, and this provision Cromwell called a circumstantial thing, "to be 'regulated' as occasion shall offer." He freely admitted that there were many such circumstantial things in the *Instrument* "which are not like the laws of the Medes and Persians" but a "matter of consideration between you and me." Any inspection of modern constitutions will reveal the justification of this view. Ordinary legislation within the confines of a "constitution" is particularly notorious in the state constitutions of the United States. The constitution of Oklahoma, Professor Holcombe tells us, contains eleven pages of legislation relating to the subject of corporations alone, besides much more ordinary legislation relating to homesteads and exemptions, banks and banking, insurance, the employment of children, and education. It forbids plural marriages, fixes the maximum rate of interest, abolishes the so-called fellow-servant doctrine and regulates the use of the contributory-negligence and assumption-of-risk doctrines as defenses in certain suits for damages, establishes the eight-hour day on public works and coal mines, and determines the test for the purity of kerosene oil. The tendency of which the constitution of Oklahoma is an extreme instance is, however, manifest elsewhere. The republican constitution of Germany abounded with constitutional legislation about railroads, schools, and other phases of community life. Now it is clearly unreasonable to place a provision like the one that Germany is a republic, or that all power emanates from the people (Article 1), on the same footing as the provision that all children graduating from normal school shall receive a copy of the constitution (Article 148). Similar contrasts, though perhaps not quite as extreme, can be found in the Constitution of the United States. Yet, nowhere has the amending power been organized in such a way as to take account of this difference. The simplest technique for coping with the difficulty would seem to be a provision that parts of the same constitutional document might be amended by different methods. A process requiring much deliberation and delay might be provided for the fundamental parts of the document, while constitutional provisions of a legislative nature could be amended by a simpler and more rapid mode. From the standpoint of a political science, considering the constitution a political process for restraining the government, this would seem a sound plan; the "fundamental" parts of the document would thereby be marked as the real constitution. Oklahoma and Virginia have attempted something of this order. It must be considered doubtful, however, whether their example will be widely emulated; the reasons for this difficulty result from the constitution also being a political force (see next chapter). Under the alternative scheme of leaving the amendment of the constitution to the legislature, as in England, reliance is placed upon public opinion for maintaining these fundamentals. The idea is that since revolutions turn upon these fundamentals, their emergence can not be prevented by a constitution anyway.

Limited and unlimited revolutions.—Trotzki's challenge that revolutions are the mad inspirations of history is, after all, not so very far from Cromwell's oft-repeated conviction that revolutions are the work of God. They both bear testimony to the fact that the great revolutions of our civilization touch the fundamentals of our way of life, and that their source was inspirational. Revolutionary leaders have conceived of themselves as instruments either of God or of nature. Eugen Rosenstock has developed the brilliant thesis that each of the great revolutions has been made by one of the great nations of Europe which in the course of its revolution has found its own basic form of life. This view is easily substantiated for the French and English Revolutions; it is more difficult to follow the argument in the case of the Reformation for Germany, and still more so in the case of the Papal Revolution through which the Italian people are alleged to have expressed themselves. Rosenstock has also undertaken to show that each of these "totalitarian" revolutions has in spite of its national aspect claimed to be a "world revolution" of which the authors expected that it would become the pattern of life for all of Europe. This phase of Rosenstock's theory is least apparent in the English Revolution; it would be hard to deny it of any of the others. Rosenstock has finally called attention to the widening group of active political "leaders" from the one pope, to the 100 princes of the Reformation, to the 3000-5000 gentry of England, to the 90,000 members of the bourgeoisie in France, to the million or more "proletarians" of the Russian Soviets, and the related fact that each of these comprehensive "revolutions" was in a measure directed against the immediately preceding revolution, because it had been made by the class whose rule it was now proposed should be overthrown. This brilliant and engaging synthesis of Hegelian, Comtian, and Marxist positions in terms of an autonomous group life is admittedly not a general theory of revolution in the simple sense of a change of government. When we find that Bolivia has suffered sixty-eight revolutions during the sixty-five years of her existence, we are forced to abandon Rosenstock's as well as Cromwell's and Trotzki's language. Aristotle already drew a distinction between revolutions which aimed at a change of government and others which merely substituted one person or group for another, but left the form of government intact. A survey of modern history obliges us to add the further distinction between revolutions affecting a change in a whole way of life, including religion, economics, and manners, as well as politics, and revolutions changing the form of government. Curiously enough, a revolution of this latter sort was going on right under the nose of Aristotle without his ever noticing it as such.

The same subject continued.—In France, a keen feeling for the difference between the Revolution of 1789 and the many revolutions which followed during the nineteenth century has crystallized into the expression *la grande revolution*, as an appropriate designation for the earlier event. If we examine this curious difference further, we find that it is not merely one of degree, but distinctly a difference of kind. For while all these revolutions are successful rebellions changing the government, if not in form, then at least in personnel, the "great" revolutions have a spiritual significance which the others lack. Though Cromwell listed freedom of conscience along with strictly governmental restraints upon parliamentary absolutism as a fundamental aspect of the *Instrument of Government*, this freedom of conscience in matters of religion, while operating as a restraint on the government, also represented a new spiritual conception which grew out of the Reformation. Likewise the Bill of Rights of man which appears in the American and French revolutionary constitutions represents a new spiritual departure in that it secularized and expanded the freedom of conscience. It thus gave political form to ideas which had germinated in the period of enlightenment. Finally, the socialist constitutions of post-war Europe, in setting forth the right to work, or even basing citizenship upon this quality of being a worker, as the constitution of the Soviet Union does, provided expression for the ideas which had taken root in the labor movement of the preceding generations. What these spiritual elements mean politically, will receive further attention in the next chapter when we take up the constitution as a political force. For the present, it is enough to conclude that revolutions may be limited to the political, governmental sphere, or they may be not so limited, and unfathomable, incalculable and incomprehensible to all but those who have been "seized by the spirit."

Impossibility of anticipating unlimited revolution through amending process.—The distinction between limited and unlimited revolutions has important consequences. While it is true that the latter must be of interest to the political scientist, because they affect governments profoundly, it is nevertheless quite important for him to realize that these unlimited revolutions transcend his science by reason of their material and spiritual ramifications. Limited revolutions afford a safer field for scientific inquiry. At the same time, the transcendental, meta-constitutional nature of the constituent power is nowhere so clearly seen as in these great spiritual upheavals. While it might be maintained that a wisely-drawn constitution would anticipate the revolutionary implications of the constituent power in matters of less than fundamental importance by so constructing the amending power that it would under sustained pressure yield to sweeping changes in the system of governmental restraints, it is difficult to see how even the most supple amending power could look into the future of man's creative evolution to the extent of anticipating wholly different ideas or a basically altered economy. That could probably only be accomplished by constructing the amending power so loosely as to expose the constitution to the danger of being overthrown in temporary emergencies (as has happened several times in Europe lately). Assuming, then, a more resistant amending power, the forces opposed to the "new spirit" are bound to appeal to the fundamentals of the "constitution" in their struggle to stem the rising tide of impending change. By doing so, they force the "new spirit" to attack and often to destroy the constitution. Sometimes, as in Germany after 1918, a new constitution will be built to take the place of the old. At other times, no constitution, but a government without restraint will attempt to realize the "new spirit" by force. An amending power broad enough completely to revamp as well as to amend the existing constitution is an extremely difficult, if not impossible, thing to construct. The Swiss, as we have already shown, accomplished a change approaching the fundamental in 1874. The English did it in 1832. Walter Lippmann has argued, in his *Method of Freedom*, that England and the Dominions, America, Switzerland, Holland, and the Scandinavian countries are in the process of revamping their governments so as to make room for the "socialist" right to work. It may well happen. Much undoubtedly depends upon the rapidity with which the demand for these changes develops and culminates. Much also depends upon the prevalence of that intelligent view which looks upon the constitution as a human creation subject to change, rather than as a divinely ordained thing of primordial perfection.

Hypotheses derived from Hitler's coming into power.—It is easy to exaggerate the dangers of change, as well as the dangers which spring from an amending process facilitating rather than preventing change. While it is undeniable that such a process might be used for destroying the constitution as a system of restraints altogether, it is not as likely as some writers would have us believe. There are people who might be tempted to cite the recent German events as evidence to the contrary. Did not the German parliament abdicate its own powers and hand them over to the chancellor? Might not Congress do likewise, if the amending power were vested in it? The answer is that the German parliament did not abdicate. In order to get parliament to do this, the Hitler government first purged it of many Socialists and all Communists. This purge terrorized many of the remaining deputies. It is significant that constitutional lawyers apologizing for the National Socialist government have themselves shown convincingly that the constitution of the Republic was not only violated, but actually abolished when a considerable group of deputies was excluded from parliament, and was therefore prevented from participating in the session of March 21, 1933, which voted to invest Hitler with absolute power. It was by revolutionary force, by a *coup d'état,* that Hitler came into power. But why should the Nazis first go through this "constitutional" ceremony, and then have their crown jurists claim it to be unconstitutional? Their reason for arguing thus, once the transition had been achieved, was to prove that the government was no longer bound by the constitution at all. Moreover, the Nazi masses longed to revel in the "revolutionary" spirit. The legal importance of it all lay in the fact that no provision of the constitution of 1919 could be cited against any measures or decrees of the government, no matter how arbitrary. On the strength of this "revolution," the constitution of 1919 had become "mere legislation."

Even though we recognize the element of forcible intervention, the German situation still bears testimony to the danger of vesting the amending power in parliament, particularly when such a parliament is only insufficiently restrained. Clearly, under a system of parliamentary absolutism, no constitution in the political sense would exist. Actually there existed in Germany, and still exists in England,

France, and other countries, the restraint which comes from a fairly independent judiciary. On the other hand, the restraint of a traditional two-party system was lacking. While it would be an exaggeration to describe the German situation as one of parliamentary absolutism, it rather closely approached the radical democracy which Rousseau had envisaged, with very extreme powers vested in a popular majority (nor was this surprising, since the makers of the Weimar Constitution were filled with Rousseau-istic ideas). The full significance of this set-up was hidden for a while by the multiple-party system. But the latent despotic powers of a popular majority were bound to appear as soon as such a majority could be built up. To the extent to which parliamentary absolutism must be recognized, Germany had no constitution in the political sense. Governmental powers were unrestrained. The constitutionally decisive reason for the failure of the Republic in Germany appears, therefore, to have been the weakness of the political constitution itself. Without an adequate system of restraints on governmental action, parliamentary absolutism yielded to dictatorship by the simple device of reducing the membership of parliament sufficiently to give the willing or unwilling partisans of change a safe majority. There is a great historical analogy for these developments. The events of the 21st of March, 1933, were nothing more nor less than a repetition of Pride's Purge, of December 6th, 1648. When the detained Presbyterian M.P.'s demanded of the officers: "By what Law, by what Law?" Hugh Peters, Cromwell's secretary, had to admit: "It is by the Law of Necessity; truly, by the Power of the Sword." We shall return to this question of necessity in our chapter on dictatorship (XIV). As far as the amending power and revolution are concerned, what these historical cases show is (1) that even the most flexible amending power cannot guarantee the constitution against revolution by those wishing to destroy not only the particular system of restraints, but all restraints; and (2) that a flexible amending power in fact facilitates a *coup d'état* (revolution from within) by a group desirous of destroying the constitution as a system of restraints upon governmental power; and (3) that a concentration of the amending power in time and space invites the application of violence in an effort to coerce the exercise of the amending power for the destruction of the constitution. It would follow from these hypotheses as a maxim of practical politics that constitutional limitations upon the amending power should not take the form of absolute prohibitions, but should provide for a greater diffusion of the power both by making it work slowly, and in separate localities. Thus the federal Constitution of the United States provides that no state shall be deprived of equal representation in the Senate without its own consent; if they should all consent, such representation could be abolished.

Aristotle's theory of revolutions.—The entire preceding discussion shows that the modern mind is and has been preoccupied with making suitable arrangements for change in a constitutional order. Change is viewed in an evolutionary sense, and is assumed to be moving in a certain direction which may be considered optimistically as progress or pessimistically as decline. In any event, change is taken for granted and revolution is deprecated, when it is deprecated, not because it is change, but because it is violent change. *Natura non facit saltum.* Revolution is unnatural, not change. Very different was the view of Aristotle. In the introductory chapter attention was called to this difference in the point of departure. Motion in modern physics is the natural state. Modern political science also is kinetic. But since Aristotle's theory of revolutions is still the only fully developed theory, it is fitting that we should examine it, before concluding this discussion. Aristotle described revolutions in terms of his fourfold method of stating a case (*αἴτιον*), namely to use modern expressions, the material and energetic conditions, the conceptual framework, and the end or objective. Stated simply, the material conditions of revolutions are found by Aristotle to root in the economic class structure, and more particularly in the division of the community between the poor and the rich. The energetic conditions are provided by the restless scheming of potential leaders who are seeking ascendancy. Certain indications are offered concerning their psychology. The conceptual framework for revolutions persists in the form of ever-conflicting ideas concerning the just share of each individual and group in the community. The end or objective of all revolutions is the complete seizure of power by the revolutionaries. This remarkably lucid and comprehensive theory of revolutions may be adequate for the political bodies with reference to whose experience it was framed, though no serious attempt has been made at such verification. It is at once apparent that the theory may not be adequate when we consider the great revolutionary upheavals of modern times, such as the French Revolution. For while the Aristotelian elements are present, other elements of a spiritual and all-inclusive sort have also been shown to loom large. Modern theories of revolutions in their turn have been attempting to focus attention upon these elements. Accepting change not only as the "natural" state of affairs, but as intrinsically necessary and desirable, they have often viewed revolutions as approaches to a progressively realizable millennium. And if not that, they have taken periodic adaptations of the political order to underlying social change as a necessary "adjustment." Aristotle, on the other hand, while admitting the fatal persistence of revolutions, viewed them as substituting one kind of maladjustment for another. He therefore tried to find the least unbalanced political order (in which the conceptual framework of revolutions would have smallest scope) and then to maintain the *status quo*. But in many passages he seems to lean toward the sceptical view that any political order persistently maintained is better than change. He was at least sufficiently interested in such a view to study the methods of maintaining various types of political order. What Aristotle had found out concerning the maintenance of tyranny, Machiavelli restated for the absolute prince.

Conclusion.—In conclusion it may be said that the phenomena of revolution, though vitally related to the constituent power, and therefore of decisive importance for an empirical theory of constitutions and constitutional government, have so far been only partially analyzed from the standpoint of modern political science. We know something, though far too little, about the working of plebiscites and amending processes. We have large-scale metaphysical interpretations of history asserting generalities concerning the implied political change. We have Aristotle's presumably empirical theory of revolutions in the Greek *polis*. But a welter of more or less detailed questions and facts present themselves with which we have not as yet effectively coped. Even after we discard "causes" and limit ourselves to the more modest inquiry into concomitant variations of interdependent variables, we are at the present moment only able to advance certain very tentative hypotheses, such as those stated at the end of ¶ 17. Some further light will be thrown on the subject of revolutions in the course of Chapter XIV and of the fourth part. One deviation from the Aristotelian view is fairly certain: when the revolution is carried out by the constituent power the end is not the seizure of complete power by the revolutionaries. The end being the making of a constitution, such revolutions aim at a separation of powers. To this problem we now must turn.

CHAPTER X

THE CONSTITUTION AS A POLITICAL FORCE

1. Introductory.—2. Bill of rights.—3. Such rights not natural but political.—4. Fundamental conflicts of principle.—5. Preambles.—6. Parties and public opinion.—7. Various writers characterized.—8. Two basic cleavages, cultural and economic divisions.—9. Autocratic imposition of unity.—10. Cultural disunity overcome: Switzerland.—11. German unanimity insufficient.—12. Attempted remedies and contrast with Great Britain.—13. Symbols and stereotypes.—14. Is all unanimity man-made?—15. Burke's and Lippmann's answer.

Introductory.—According to Rousseau, the most important of all laws "which is not graven on tablets of marble or brass, but on the hearts of the citizens" is embodied in what he calls "the real constitution." It "takes on every day new powers, when other laws decay or die out, restores or takes their place, keeps a whole people in the ways in which it was meant to go, and insensibly replaces authority by the force of habit." In this curious passage, reminiscent of Burke and other traditionalists, the great Swiss revolutionary is, according to his own words, "speaking of morality, of custom, above all of public opinion; a power unknown to political thinkers, on which none the less success in everything else depends." Since the days of Rousseau, political scientists have, however, been much occupied with this important power, although not infrequently neglecting its relation to custom and to the constitution. On the other hand, Professor Holcombe has stressed the connection when he said: "The fundamentals of state government are predetermined outside of the conventions by public opinion. . . . In so far as this is true, and written constitutional charters set forth the accepted moral standards, customs and public opinion, they themselves constitute a political force of great influence. In a sense this is obvious; for were it not so, there would be little sense in making constitutional charters.

Bills of rights.—The political force of the Constitution is particularly significant in connection with whatever restraints a bill of rights imposes upon governmental action. Clearly, such bills of rights differ materially from institutional safeguards of a separation of powers. If the President is given power to veto a bill passed by Congress, he is thereby enabled to restrain the action of Congress. This type of restraint, entrusted to a living human being, will be attended to by that trustee. It is a procedural restraint. But if it is provided that no person shall be deprived of his property without due process of law, that restraint depends directly upon the political force which the Constitution itself possesses. It is a substantive restraint. These substantive restraints embody a people's ways of life, transcending its strictly political philosophy.

Such rights not natural but political.—It is customary to look upon the bill of rights in any constitution as the instrumentality through which the arbitrary expansion of government is limited, and a sphere of "natural" rights of each individual is thus safeguarded against political interference. The idea that certain rights are natural rights has a long history. Whatever its grounds, it produces the impression that certain things, like private property, or freedom of assembly, have an existence and meaning quite apart from any government. Yet, in fact, all of them presuppose a government. It would therefore be more appropriate to call these rights social, or rather political. No more striking illustration of their political nature could be found than the fact that they are invariably limited to the citizen. Bills of rights express the dominant ideas concerning the relations between individual citizens and the government. But evidently they presuppose a working government for their enforcement. Take, as an example, the right of free assembly. The struggle against the authoritarian governments of the eighteenth century created the impression that interference with the free exercise of this right proceeded necessarily from the government. Closer scrutiny reveals that this impression is utterly untenable in the light of historical experience. If the community happens to be rent asunder by profound conflicts touching its customs and ways of life, such as are engendered by religious and social dissensions, more serious handicaps to freedom of assembly (and freedom of speech) arise from the interference of opposing groups with each other. To stick to modern illustrations, in Germany, first the Communists, and later the National Socialists, organized their followers in such a way as to make it physically dangerous, if not impossible, to allow them access to public assemblies. Large detachments of police, either mounted or on trucks, had to be scattered through Communist as well as Nazi demonstrations in order to beat off an attack by their opponents. What more telling proof of the need for governmental protection of these supposedly "natural" rights could be found than that? The Ku Klux Klan affords an American analogy.

Fundamental conflicts of principle.—If bills of rights express the ideas dominant in the community regarding the desirable relations between the government and individual citizens, such bills of rights must necessarily undergo considerable alterations when these dominant ideas change. For as new interests arise in the community they will clamor for recognition as soon as they become sufficiently weighty to arouse a sufficient group of people to rally to their support. As we have already pointed out (see Chap. IX, ¶8 ff.), difficult problems of adjustment arise in this connection which a well-constructed amending procedure may solve up to a certain point. Beyond that point revolution becomes inevitable, unless a compromise is found. And since compromises are well-nigh impossible between mutually conflicting fundamental positions, such compromises often assume a very peculiar form. Two mutually exclusive, conflicting clauses or formulæ may be inserted into the constitutional charter, each expressing the outlook of one group. The American federal Constitution contained very few if any such clauses until the enactment of Amendment XVIII. The courts could settle the conflicts with older rights which arose out of the enforcement of this amendment by maintaining the ancient principle that the later rule of law supersedes the earlier. There are, however, indications that Amendment XVIII was carried by an electorate which was only dimly aware of the implications of its principle and their effect upon the older rights, and that the movement for the repeal of this amendment gained momentum as these implications were becoming apparent. But what would be the attitude of a court or other official when the original constitutional charter embodied such compromises in the form of contradictory clauses? The German constitution of 1919 was drafted and enacted by what later became known as the Weimar Coalition, a conjunction of Liberals, Catholics, and Socialists. These parties had been united in their opposition to the monarchical government of pre-war Germany. But had they enough in common to draw up a constitutional bill of rights? Even a casual inspection of the second part of the Constitution of the German Republic would incline one to reply with an emphatic: No. These "Rights and Duties of Germans" contained liberal, Catholic, and socialist principles in a motley assortment. Such questions as church and state, the schools, and economic life reveal the indecision of the makers. Private property rights are declared to be inviolable, except where laws provide otherwise—which means that private property rights are not inviolable. The church was excluded from control of the schools, but a majority of the parents were given decisive influence—which meant that at least the Catholic Church would nevertheless control the schools wherever it predominated, and so forth. Nor is the German constitution singular in this respect. Many of the post-war European constitutions contain a mixture of liberal and socialist principles. It is the comparative unanimity of the American Constitutional Fathers in matters of general principle, all of them being more or less liberal in their outlook, which gives the American Constitution its great inner coherence. This coherence has unquestionably contributed to the permanence of the American Constitution. The one point on which there was fundamental cleavage was the federal issue which was settled by the Civil War. It is therefore not surprising that we should find the one clear example of dilatory compromise by contradictory clauses in this field. The national unity as expressed in the preamble stops before the several states' equal representation in the Senate which was declared unchangeable except by each state's consent.

Preambles.—Preambles of constitutional charters are of considerable weight as an indication of the public opinion to which a particular constitution owes its force. There is the well-known American preamble: "We, the People of the United States, in order to form a more perfect union, establish justice, insure domestic tranquillity, provide for the common defense, promote the general welfare and secure the blessings of liberty to ourselves and our posterity, do ordain and establish this constitution for the United States of America." It may be contrasted with the German Republican preamble: "The German people united in all its tribes and inspired by the determination to renew and strengthen their Reich in liberty and justice, to preserve peace at home and abroad, and to further social progress has given itself the following constitution." It will be seen that the stress laid upon peace and social progress is indicative of a more recent spirit, and one which would doubtless express itself forcefully in the preamble of any American Constitution written today. It is, therefore, often maintained that the *real* Constitution of the American people is no longer fully expressed in the written document. On the other hand, the preamble of the constitution of the Soviet Union sets forth ideas which are as yet quite generally rejected in the United States. Significantly, the constitutional laws of France have no preamble. Being adopted by people fundamentally at odds and quite convinced that their work would not last, the constitution embodied no substantive principles and no bill of rights. In recent years, however, the lasting success of the republican scheme has called forth a school of writers, ably led by M. Duguit, who maintain that the *Principes de Droit de l'Homme*, general principles of the rights of man, as framed in 1789, form an integral part of the French constitution of today. Insofar as these principles are liberal rather than socialist, M. Duguit's argument seeks to secure a constitutional sanction for the interests of those who are opposed to a socialist order of government. Such a sanction would be unnecessary, if opposition to socialism were part of the *real* constitution of France today. It is now time to turn to a further discussion of this *real* constitution of Rousseau, to custom and public opinion.

Parties and public opinion.—The greatest change in insight concerning this power of public opinion since the time of Rousseau has turned upon what we call the discovery of the political party (see below, Chaps. XVIII, XIX). The division of the people into more or less lasting groups which carry on the process of creating a public opinion has been found to be an essential feature of popular government. Rousseau obviously assumed this opinion to be one, but we incline to view it as divided into at least two. And yet, Rousseau remains in the right as far as the constitution is concerned. When Lord Balfour claimed that the English political system in order to work required a people fundamentally at one, he was reasserting Rousseau's conviction that there must be some binding elements of unity in outlook which constitute the *real* constitution. If a people should be fundamentally at odds, no constitution exists, and therefore no constitutional charter can be drafted. It was the basic mistake of nineteenth century political thought to assume that constitutional government could be brought into existence without regard to this sentiment.

Various writers characterized.—Lowell, Lippmann, and other writers on public opinion primarily drawing inferences from an observation of English-speaking countries have been concerned mainly with tracing the psychological and other aspects of divisions in opinion based upon a more or less tacit agreement as to fundamentals. Burke, de Maistre, and other writers reflecting upon the reaction to the fundamental challenge of the French Revolution were more concerned with the processes by which a certain measure of common agreement is reached and maintained. Marx, the Marxists, and their scholastic brethren in the United States, who expound the economic interpretation of events, have reversely been preoccupied with the forces which prevent any fundamental common agreement among basically opposed interests in the community. The shocking effect of these observations has in turn produced the Fascist reaction, shouting: "Shut your mouth!" ("Halt's Maul!"). Indeed, if parties are formed which are fundamentally opposed to each other all along the line, the simplest solution for the maintenance of the community is to suppress the voicing of opinions altogether. This was the solution of the Religious Peace of Augsburg (1555) when it ruled: "Cuius regio, ejus religio," that is, you have to confess the religion which the government of your country confesses. Since Germany did not possess a united government at the time, no one religion became dominant there. A fundamental division persisted.

Two basic cleavages, cultural and economic divisions.—Apart from the fundamental division which the equal or almost equal sway of two religions produces, there are two most formidable cleavages which are found to divide some modern nations, namely, the cultural and the social or economic groupings. This conclusion is suggested by the fact that people are willing to go to war and to die for a national culture or for the working class. If we accept this willingness as the final test of effective allegiance, any citizenship which is divided by such loyalties would seem to be distinctly heterogeneous. Next, of course, the relative size of these heterodox groups is of great importance. The significance of heterogeneity would be small for the constituent power, if the relation were nine to one; it would be very great, if it were one to one. The measuring underlying these ratios is, however, complicated by the qualitative differences discussed at the end of Chapter IX. A mere counting of heads, while a first step, will not be conclusive. However, it gives the investigator a point of departure. Countries like pre-war Austria or contemporary Czecho-Slovakia and Poland, which include large numbers of people who are sentimentally attached to other national cultures than that of the majority, or who even strive for complete independence, would seem to be so constituted that constitutional popular government can at best maintain no more than a very precarious existence. On the other hand, countries which, like Republican Germany, have a large organized Communist party are equally or perhaps even more unfit to establish such a system of government. The matter turns upon the non-existence of an effective constituent power and the consequent lack of a constitution real enough to become a political force. To repeat, modern popular constitutional government presupposes a nation fundamentally at one, whose customs and opinions will support the real constitution.

Autocratic imposition of unity.—The making of such culturally united nations has been a long and arduous process wherever it has been accomplished, as in England, France, Holland, Denmark, Sweden, and Norway. In the nature of the case, it had to be accomplished before the rise of the international labor movement superimposed a new element of dissension and disunity. For only then could the leaders of that movement be imbued with a sense of national loyalty sufficient to restrain them even after they had begun to admit a higher allegiance to the international labor community. In Italy and Germany, where national unity came after the rise of an international labor community had already commenced to take hold of its working class—if the publication of the *Communist Manifesto* (1847) may be taken as a date—these restraints remained insufficient. Consequently the intensification of nationalist emotionalism during and after the war led to a violent reaction against all popular constitutional government, calling itself Fascism here, National Socialism there. Both proceeded to attack ruthlessly the flourishing internationalist labor movement. They resuscitated the methods which were in vogue under the autocratic monarchies of England and France. This method, to be sure, started those countries on the road toward their unitary national culture, and culminated in two bloody revolutions in which the nations now united asserted their right to rule themselves. There is no great difficulty in placing Mussolini and Hitler in parallel to Cromwell and Napoleon. All reassert the national unity in an autocratic fashion after a period of confusion attendant upon a revolutionary outbreak of the constituent power. It is to be hoped that the German and the Italian people will emerge from the ordeal and evolve a popular constitutional government. Doubts may be entertained on account of the persistence of the international class conflict. The drift toward Russianism in the Soviet Union may, however, sap the Third International's strength to such an extent that Communist parties everywhere will return to the national fold.

Cultural disunity overcome: Switzerland.—There exists one popular constitutional government of great stability, though resting upon three very distinct national cultural groups: Switzerland. To aggravate the difficulty, each of these constituent elements of the Swiss people belongs to one of three most powerful national cultures on the Continent; French, German, and Italian are the three official languages of the little mountain republic. Nor are the Swiss linked by a common religion. It so happens, however, that these three distinct cultural groups are united by a long tradition of common political customs which through centuries separated them from the surrounding monarchical governments. The partly democratic, partly aristocratic member states, today called cantons, were uniformly republican and very proud of it. Protected to some extent by natural geographic conditions, and long surrounded by the halo of their startling victories over much more powerful princes (see Chap. IV, ¶8), the Swiss Confederation profited by peace and afforded an asylum to victims of the religious persecutions. Though each of its cultural groups stuck with tenacity to its own language, customs, and habits, none went far in attempting to proselytize the others. The leading French Swiss canton, Geneva, was kept away from France politically by its stern protestantism, and neither Germany nor Italy possessed a united national government to which their Swiss brethren could have rallied on the basis of common national sentiment. Thus a tradition of common political destiny welded the culturally divided cantons into a united whole. It is surely not just an accident that the most outspoken advocate of popular constitutional government, Jean-Jacques Rousseau, whose views exerted a more profound influence upon the minds of the French, as well as German and Italian, revolutionaries than any other, should have been a Swiss. As is well-known, his cradle stood in Geneva. In him a tradition crystallized and found theoretical expression which had been in the making for over three hundred years.

German unanimity insufficient.—Switzerland thus affords the most striking illustration of the weight of a common tradition rising from a joint past as the procreator of that *real* constitution which transforms a written charter into a political power of lasting importance. Burke, who was turned into a reactionary by the spectacle of the French Revolution, nevertheless restated Rousseau's doctrine of national unity as a necessary prerequisite of popular constitutional government. In his *Appeal from the New to the Old Whigs* he said: "The power of acting by a majority . . . must be grounded on two assumptions; first, that of an incorporation produced by unanimity; and secondly, an unanimous agreement that the act of a mere majority . . . shall pass with them and with others as the act of the whole." Now this unanimity at the start of an association or a group (what Burke calls an incorporation) must, in the case of so extensive and complex a group as that which constitutes the citizenship of a modern country, be built upon a fairly long period of living together under one government. Perhaps a hundred years should be considered a minimum. The failure to realize this sufficiently was one of the fatal errors of the German republican leaders. Modern Germany having only been united under one government for less than fifty years, the time was not ripe for overthrowing it without jeopardizing the underlying sentiment of unanimity and cohesion.

Attempted remedies and contrast with Great Britain.—It was not pusillanimity, as the radicals charged, when Friedrich Ebert sought to retain the monarchy, but a sound sense of the fragile foundation of German political tradition. That sense for the need of continuity found expression in the curious phrase of the preamble ". . . to renew and strengthen *their* Reich . . . ," as well as in a lengthy debate over the retention of the word *Reich* itself. There is a great contrast between the use of the word *Reich* in this preamble and the meaning given to it in the preamble of the imperial constitution of 1871. There it was said that "His Majesty the King of Prussia, . . . His Majesty the King of Bavaria, His Majesty . . . and so forth (enumerating all the ruling German princes and the governments of the free cities of Hamburg, Bremen, and Lübeck) . . . do conclude an everlasting union for the protection of the federal territory and of the rights valid therein, as well as for the furtherance of the welfare of the German people. This union shall bear the name of the German Reich and shall have the German constitution." In this preamble, then, the term *Reich* is nothing but the name for the union of monarchs ruling in Germany, who even insisted that the emperor be merely German Emperor and not Emperor of Germany. From the point of view of this preamble, then, those members of the republican constitutional convention were doubtless right who maintained that the term *Reich* referred to the monarchical past and should be eliminated in favor of the term

German Republic. Sounder councils prevailed, however. Instead of accepting this legal formalism, Friedrich Naumann and others urged that the word *Reich* was a symbol of German national unity, that it embodied much more than the Bismarckian preamble allowed one to infer, and should be retained. Professors Munro and Holcombe were very right in translating the word as commonwealth, thus suggesting the analogy to Cromwell's time and the idea of a nation united under its own government; for this is the meaning which the term had before the imperial constitution was written, and had reacquired or rather retained in the mind of the people. It was a stroke of genius when Lord Balfour, in search for a symbolic formula around which sentiments of underlying traditional unanimity could rally within the British Empire, hit upon the expression "British Commonwealth of Nations." For in the days of Cromwell, too, several nations had been united under a common weal.

Symbols and stereotypes.—Perhaps enough has been said on the subject of customs, traditions, and general opinion to illustrate the point that an underlying sentiment of unanimity is a necessary condition for making a constitutional charter a political force. Charters written without that sentiment behind it are scraps of paper, and the notion that popular constitutional governments can be set up with any hope of permanence by such a device is a sorry delusion. Its fundamental provisions must be "engraven on the hearts of the citizens" as Rousseau so poetically says. Something more may, however, be in place here regarding the outward manifestations of that sentiment of unanimity, because important lessons can be derived therefrom regarding the ways of retaining such unanimity. In recent years, the problem of symbols has received more general attention from political scientists than it used to. Professor Hayes' searching inquiries into the nature of nationalism has focused attention upon the important role which flags, national anthems, and the like play in rallying mass sentiment. Walter Lippmann has shown that the actions of the mass-man are largely determined by certain fixed notions which Lippmann has called stereotypes. These stereotypes elicit more or less predictable responses, and it is obvious that distinct appeals to the senses can be produced by certain combinations of colors, shapes, or sounds. All this is by no means totally new; for unless shrewd practical men had been aware of these effects, such symbols would not have been created. But what is new is a clear recognition of the bearing these psychological factors have upon the political manipulation of men. It is no longer possible for us to look upon traditions and customs as God-given or natural, as was done by Burke and many of his contemporaries and predecessors. We know that these traditions are created by men, that they can be manipulated, in short, that propaganda permeates our existence on every side.

Is all unanimity man-made?—It is readily apparent how this "disenchantment" of ideas and sentiments through exposure to the glaring searchlight of modern psychology, how this "debunking" of ideals once held to be sacrosanct as "natural rights," shatters the foundations of the unanimity which we have found to be an essential prerequisite of a constitutional order. If all ideas and ideals are merely shrewdly designed veils hiding special interests in their sparring for position, where is that underlying unanimity to come from which can give a constitution lasting force? Are modern communities bound to dissolve into a free-for-all in which the most ruthless will eventually win out by imposing their will, trampling popular constitutional government underfoot? Or are there traditions and customs which, though admittedly created by men, yet do represent habitual preferences and patterns of behavior in certain communities? These questions are more easily raised than answered at this stage of our inquiry. Only towards the end of the entire volume when we have considered the gamut of dictatorship, party politics, and the rest will a reasoned answer be possible.

Burke's and Lippmann's answer.—In the meantime, it may be worth while to cite one of Burke's most telling arguments of English traditionalism. In his *Reflections on the Revolution in France*, he argues as follows: ". . . from Magna Charta to the declaration of right, it has been the uniform policy of our constitution to claim and assert our liberties, as an *entailed inheritance* derived to us from our forefathers, and to be transmitted to our posterity; as an estate especially belonging to the people of this kingdom, without any reference whatever to any other more general or prior right. By this means our constitution preserves an unity in so great a diversity of its parts. We have an inheritable crown; an inheritable peerage; and a house of commons and a people inheriting privileges, franchises, and liberties, from a long line of ancestors." This view was expressed by a man who was by no means unaware of the power of propaganda. For in the same essay he speaks of the matter at length, particularly when discussing the alliance which in his opinion commercial wealth and the masses in France had concluded for the overthrow of the landed aristocracy. "Writers, especially when they act in a body, and with one direction, have great influence on the public mind; the alliance therefore of these writers with the monied interest (their connection with Turgot and almost all the peoples of the finance), had no small effect in removing the popular odium and envy which attended that species of wealth. These writers, like the propagators of all novelties, pretended to a great zeal for the poor, and the lower orders, whilst in their satires they rendered hateful, by every exaggeration, the faults of courts, of nobility, and of priesthood. They became a sort of demagogues. They served as a link to unite, in favor of one object, obnoxious wealth to restless and desperate poverty." There is clear realization here of willful influence upon public opinion, the clothing of interests by effective stereotypes, as Walter Lippmann has analyzed it. Is it surprising, then, that we find in Lippmann sentiments very much akin to those of Burke just above quoted? In his *Method of Freedom*, he writes: "It has been the fashion to try to discover the future of capitalism by studying countries where capitalism is primitive and the future of political institutions where liberty has no *traditions*. Yet one might as well go to Massachusetts to study the habits of the palm tree as go to Russia to learn about the prospects of modern capitalism or to Central Europe to learn about the evolution of modern representative government. It would seem reasonable to remember that in the English-speaking countries there are the oldest and most powerful of governments,—therefore, presumably an aptitude among the people for the art of governing." No matter what the scientific value of such statements, they are themselves expressions of the power of tradition, and thus of the constitution as a political force.

CHAPTER XI

THE SEPARATION OF POWERS

Introductory.—The entire history of government shows that substantive restraints embodying the opinion and customs of the community, their way of life, rest upon a tenuous foundation, unless reinforced and backed up by procedural restraints of one sort or another. True constitutional government does, in fact, never exist, unless procedural restraints are effectively established. Such restraints always involve some division of power; for evidently some considerable power must be vested in those who are expected to do the restraining. The modern, rational theory of separated powers with which we shall be primarily concerned in the following chapter is only a late and more scientific effort along lines well established in classical antiquity.

The theory of mixed government.—The Roman Republican constitution affords a particularly striking example of carefully divided powers. When Polybius came to analyze the Roman constitution in terms of the classification of forms of government evolved by Plato and Aristotle, he was baffled by the discovery that several forms were mixed together. He thereupon constructed his theory of mixed government which exerted a considerable influence down to modern times. In fact, English theorists in the seventeenth century evolved from it the theory of the separation of powers. This they were led to do by their preoccupation with law as valid generalization upon established matter of fact. The amazing harvest of discovery yielded by this approach in the fields of natural science is generally appreciated. It is less well realized that we owe to this approach also the modern theory of the separation of powers which forms so vital a part of modern constitutionalism. For, once political thinkers undertook to analyze political processes from a functional point of view, they discovered the distinctive features of certain basic functions or "powers."

Importance of institutional background.—In the definitive form which Locke gave it, it was an attempt to generalize the results of the struggle of the English Parliament for an equality of status with the Crown. As is usual in political theory, it was the product of a long evolution of political organization, and by looking primarily to theoretical precursors we mistake the theory for something largely divorced from practice. Nothing is further from the truth. English political thinkers would never have evolved the theory of the separation of powers from that of mixed government, if the institutional evolution in England had not pointed in that direction. Already in the fourteenth and fifteenth centuries, the governments of some of the great and almost independent cities, like Strassburg, had evolved a fairly subtle separation of powers between three councils, each charged with more or less distinct functions. But since the territorial governments which superseded these free cities tended to concentrate the powers in the prince and his council (see above, Chap. II), continental theorists only perceived the theory, when it came to them from England. It was then looked upon by the monarchical governments as a revolutionary principle.

England.—In England and Sweden, to return to our previous point of discussion, the development followed quite a different course, eminently favorable to the discovery of the doctrine. In England, the function of interpreting the law in a high court of Parliament was transformed by a very gradual process into the function of making the law. Early statutes were conceived of as stating what the old law was rather than as creating new law. From the time of Fortescue, who in the fifteenth century praised the rule of law as the outstanding feature of English government, this function of creating the law became increasingly important. The efforts of James I to challenge explicitly the supremacy of the law—in itself a reasonable challenge, since the law was rapidly becoming man-made legislation instead of eternal custom—gave rise to a violent opposition which claimed absolute parliamentary supremacy and divided the prerogative. The rapid succession of royal and parliamentary absolutism, Cromwellian dictatorship, and a return to royal absolutism, which marks the several phases of this struggle, impressed upon English minds the need for some harmonious balance between those who make the law and those who execute it. This harmony the Glorious Revolution of 1688 tried to achieve, and in the fashion of the age Locke's essay gave it the halo of general and eternal truth.

Cromwell's *Instrument of Government.*—Cromwell's *Instrument of Government* (1653) had, however, made a first attempt to distinguish and separate the executive and the legislative power. In Article XXIV, it provided "that all Bills agreed unto by parliament, shall be presented to the Lord Protector for his consent; and in case he shall not give his consent thereto within twenty days . . . that then . . . such Bills shall pass into and become laws, although he shall not have given his consent . . . ; provided such Bills contain nothing in them contrary to the matters contained in these presents (the constitution, Ed.)." Again, in Article XXX it was provided "that the raising of money . . . shall be by consent of parliament, and not otherwise. . . ." The great importance which Cromwell himself attached to these separate legislative powers can be gleaned from his speech on dissolving the Parliament elected under the *Instrument.* Cromwell, deeply disgusted at their debating constitutional issues instead of making laws and granting money, told them that they had wasted their time instead of attending to their duty, which was to make "those good and wholesome laws which the people expected" of them. His opening speech in which he had outlined the necessary legislation, much as the American chief executive does in his Inaugural Address, he had concluded by saying: "I have not spoken these things as one who assumes dominion over you; but as one who doth resolve to be a fellow-servant with you to the interest of these great affairs, and of the people of these Nations." When he finally dismissed them, after their injudicious palaver, he told them more explicitly that the government was limited and divided between a single person as chief executive and a Parliament. "This was thought most agreeable to the general sense of the Nation;—having had experience enough, by trial, of other conclusions; judging this most likely to avoid the extremes of Monarchy on the one hand, and of Democracy on the other; . . ." he exclaimed, thus showing the connection between the separation of powers and mixed government in the minds of practical politicians of the day. It did, however, never occur to Cromwell to provide for his own popular election, and so English constitutional development drifted back to hereditary monarchy as the method of determining the chief executive.

Locke's view.—Locke's view of the system is briefly this. He distinguishes the legislative power, that is, the power which makes general rules, from the executive and federative power. The latter is concerned with foreign affairs and security. But he does not at all attribute the legislative power to Parliament, and the executive and federative power to the king, as is often supposed. Rather he divided the legislative power itself, attributing it to the king in Parliament, as orthodox English constitutional law provided. This is also practically the system which we have just found to underlie the Cromwellian *Instrument of Government.* The difference lies solely in how the chief executive is created, a point not germane to the theory of the separation of powers proper. The division of authority between the king and Parliament with respect to the legislative power is not, however, balanced by an analogous division of authority in the executive and federative power. These are solely attributed to the king and his council. An explanation is given only in the case of the federative power which requires expedition and cannot be bound by general rules because it depends too much upon the changing international and internal situation (in case of civil war). Now, the division of authority and the separation of the executive and legislative powers is justified rather than explained by Locke on the well-known ground that it is necessary for the maintenance of liberty; liberty suffers when the same human beings make the laws and apply them. This view was canonized by Blackstone in his *Commentaries on the Laws of England* (1765) when he wrote: "In all tyrannical governments, the supreme magistracy, or the right both of *making* and *enforcing* the laws is vested in one and the same man, or one and the same body of men; and wherever these two powers are united together, there can be no public liberty."

Montesquieu's reinterpretation.—When Montesquieu came to rewrite Locke's doctrine, the Act of Settlement of 1700 had already, in paragraph three, undertaken to guarantee to English judges tenure during good behavior. He was, of course, equally concerned with liberty. Granting that as a starting point, Montesquieu himself was next primarily interested, as a result of the contemporary situation in

France, in the problem of how to secure or rather to maintain an independent status to judges (see above, Chap. VII, ¶13). What was therefore more natural for him than to rename Locke's executive power and to call it judicial power? The executive's function as described by Locke had been to execute the laws, anyway. This transformation of Locke's executive power was in the analysis of Montesquieu accompanied by another equally significant change, whereby Locke's federative power emerged as the executive power in Montesquieu. By emphasizing the importance of maintaining internal as compared to external peace, and by thus assimilating the police functions to the functions of defense and foreign policy, Montesquieu constructed the modern executive power. This executive power included also the prerogative which English lawyers had always carefully kept apart for special purposes. It will be seen that through these changes Montesquieu assimilated the core of modern government, bureaucracy, as it had developed on the Continent, to the English doctrine which had emphasized legislation or the power to make general rules. It is therefore not surprising that the theory had much wider appeal in the form which Montesquieu gave it. Men of affairs throughout Europe recognized in Montesquieu's executive power the type of government with which they had been familiar.

American problems.—It was of the greatest moment that these constructions happened also to fit the political experiences of most of the American colonies, where a governor, a distinct colonial legislature, and a fairly independent judiciary had come to constitute the essential organs of government. After the Declaration of Independence had severed the bonds with the mother country, a brief experiment with legislative supremacy in some of the states had led, moreover, to majority tyranny, and had thus made people ripe for an application of the celebrated theme. Nevertheless, in many of the state constitutions which contain an express statement of the doctrine, the older English emphasis upon the importance of general laws remained intact. The most famous and perhaps the most succinct statement of that doctrine is contained in the constitution of Massachusetts, which declares that the reason for the separation of powers into a legislative, executive, and judicial branch is to make sure that this will be "a government of laws and not of men." The federal Constitution, too, though abstaining from stating the doctrine, puts the legislative power first and therefore by implication foremost. And in spite of the silence of the Constitution regarding the doctrine, the Supreme Court has repeatedly called it a fundamental tenet. Many who today belittle the separation of powers seem unaware of the fact that their clamor for efficiency and expediency easily leads to dictatorship (see below, Chap. XIV) and therefore threatens the foundations of constitutional government, although the one party dictatorships in many countries ought to awaken them to a realization of where the fusion of power leads. The most important argument advanced against this point of view is derived from what is alleged to be the nature of parliamentary government in England. There an increasing fusion of executive and legislative powers does not seem to have destroyed the foundations of free government.

Fusion of powers in England.—Though the problems of parliamentary government will receive more careful treatment later on (see below, Chaps. XVI ff.), it is necessary to deal here in a general way with the fusion of the legislative and executive branches in England. The consequent relative absolutism has been endurable because of a constitutional safeguard which no one clearly envisaged until after Montesquieu's time: the regular alternation of two large parties in controlling this broad power. These parties are a traditional growth built upon human groupings, usually of long standing, in each local district; upon these the electoral system is based. It is in this connection that the aristocratic organization still retained by English society exerts its most profound influence upon the political life of the nation. And it is upon the absence of this traditional aristocratic basis of English parliamentary government that the failure of European systems presumably modelled after the English pattern is at least partly to be blamed. There the confusion of small parties fails to respond to the recurrent popular demand for clearly recognizable leadership. In some countries it thereby contributed to the development of one-party systems. Under the pressure of actual or trumped-up threats of communist dictatorship so freely advocated by the adepts of a proletarian revolution, the public at large accepted a complete fusion and concentration of powers without the constitutional custom of a recognized opposition as we know it in England. What is worse, the independence of the judiciary was swept away at the same time, though that part of the separation of powers has always been retained in England. Thus safeguards won by centuries of human sacrifice and bloodshed, on the Continent as well as in England and America, have been lost in the brief period of restlessness since the war.

The *Charte Constitutionnelle* of 1814.—For it is often forgotten that the constitutions of nineteenth century monarchies in Europe were in fact almost as much built upon a separation of powers as was the fundamental charter of the United States. These developments are the more interesting because they were accompanied by a deep-seated mistrust of the theory itself, which was supposed to be inextricably related to the rights of man and of popular government. This had actually been the case in the ill-fated constitution of 1791, in which the principle had made its debut in continental constitutional law. In Title III, which deals with the "Public Powers," it is provided that the legislative power is delegated to one national assembly, that the judicial power is delegated to judges, and that the executive power is delegated to the king in order to be exercised under his authority by ministers and other agents. But all these powers were said to be ultimately derived from the people. On the other hand, the *Charte Constitutionnelle* of Louis XVIII (1814) is built upon a separation of powers in fact and a denial of the separation of powers in theory. To quote the relevant passage: ". . . although all authority in France resides in the person of the king, our predecessors have not hesitated to alter the exercise thereof in accordance with the change of times . . . that only the supreme authority can give to institutions which it establishes the strength, permanence, and majesty with which it is itself invested; . . ." In these words the preamble of the Restoration Charter reasserts the doctrine of monarchical absolutism. But it should not be overlooked that the preamble speaks of authority rather than power. In the same spirit the charter is granted: "We have voluntarily and by the free exercise of our royal authority, accorded and do accord, grant and concede to our subjects, as well for us as for our ancestors forever, the constitutional charter which follows . . ." But when we come to the actual organization of the government, we find that the separation of powers—though not of authority—is recognized. Article 13 provides that to the king alone belongs the executive power; this is elaborated upon in Article 14 in strict consonance with Montesquieu's doctrine of the executive power. Article 15, on the other hand, vests the exercise of the legislative power in the king, the Chamber of Peers, and the Chamber of Deputies collectively. Finally, Article 58 makes the judges irremovable, although they are appointed by the king who, as Article 57 declares rhetorically, is the person from whom all justice emanates. These articles reveal a close analogy with the set-up in England after the Act of Settlement, but before the evolution of parliamentary cabinet government had commenced. Nor was it long before a similar evolution had begun in France, gradually reducing the king to a rather neutral and moderating role. The provisions of this charter soon became the model for a considerable number of other constitutions, such as those of Holland and Bavaria.

German constitutions.—In central Europe, however, the actual separation of powers was carried even further, while general declarations which seemed to maintain the absolute authority of the monarch were rigidly maintained. For here the separation of powers became in time the bulwark behind which the executive establishment directed or at least presided over by the monarch entrenched itself against the rising tide of legislative pretensions. Thus the constitution of Bavaria (1818) states in the preamble: "Maximilian Joseph, by God's Grace king of Bavaria . . . the present constitution is the work of our *free* and firm will, drawn up after mature and extensive consultation." Similarly, Title II, 1 provides that the king is the head of the government (state), unites in himself all rights of government (state power), and exercises these powers according to the provisions of this constitutional document *given by himself*. What is here asserted, namely a concentration and fusion of powers in the person of the king, is not borne out by the later provisions of the constitution, which confer the essential legislative and financial power upon the Estates' Assembly (Diet), set up a relatively independent judiciary with final jurisdiction even in constitutional matters, and finally bind the king by a solemn oath to this constitution. It will be noted that this document has nothing to say regarding the responsibility of ministers, a matter which was only regulated formally after the uprising in 1848 (as also in other German states and in Holland). We have here, then, a rather strict separation of powers between king, Estates, and judiciary. The examples of France and Bavaria have been selected as indicative of the general pattern of monarchical constitutionalism. It is important to recall this phase of European development, because the later struggles for a republican and democratic scheme have obscured the essential features of these systems which have much to recommend them to the student of politics who has become aware of the dangers of majority tyranny in absolute democracies.

Weakness of monarchical executive.—It is, however, important not to lose sight of their inherent weakness in maintaining a separation of powers intact; in spite of the grandiloquent proclamations of their preambles, the king usually lost control over the ministers through the ascent of Parliaments. Though at first glance the French king under the *Charte Constitutionnelle* seems to be considerably stronger than the President of the United States, he did not prove so in practice. That he shared in the legislative power to a wider extent tended to weaken his position rather than strengthen it. What is more important, his tenure based upon heredity proved inadequate when pitched against the popularly elected Parliament. The American President as leader of his party possesses resources of reserve strength which were utterly lacking to these constitutional monarchs. If they did not wish to submit to the dictation of Parliament, they had to assume absolute power once, and by a *coup d'état* break the constitution, as happened in Prussia under Bismarck in the period of conflict (1861 and following years). When, at that juncture, the Prussian Parliament sought to establish its sway, Bismarck retorted: "Prussia's kings have not yet fulfilled their mission. Prussian kingship is not yet ripe enough to form a purely ornamental trimming of the constitutional system, it is not yet ready to become a dead piece of machinery in the mechanism of parliamentary rule." For more than fifty years Germany, under the leadership of Prussia, held out against parliamentary government under a constitution which separated the powers much as they had been separated under the *Charte Constitutionnelle* and other monarchical constitutions. During this period the same drift toward parliamentary supremacy which had transformed the English and the French constitutions manifested itself in Germany, but before it could culminate, the World War broke loose, which defeated Germany and interrupted her constitutional evolution.

Sweden's unusual separation.—A rather unique development occurred in Sweden. There experience with parliamentary as well as royal absolutism during the seventeenth and eighteenth centuries led to the elaboration in 1809 of a constitutional system based upon a dualism of king and representative assembly which even the evolution of cabinet responsibility to Parliament did not abolish. In a sense, an administrative power became separated from the executive power. While the executive power of the crown is conducted according to the system of parliamentary responsibility, the great public services, like the Post Office, are conducted with considerable independence, "according to law." Their responsibility is enforced through judicial boards especially concerned with complaints against administrative action, and these complaints are facilitated by throwing all the files open to public inspection. In other words, if a Swedish citizen believes that he has been arbitrarily mistreated by an official, he can and frequently does request the permission to look over the files which deal with that particular matter. To buttress further the responsibility of these very independent administrative services, a solicitor-general, elected every year by Parliament, has the right to prosecute any employee who has failed to discharge his official functions properly. The duties, competence, and organization of these boards and offices being outlined by permanent instructions, issued by the executive, no considerable difficulties are encountered. There can be little doubt that without any theoretical recognition of the fact the American federal government tends in the same direction of differentiating between strictly executive and purely administrative functions.

The doctrine compounded of a theoretical and a practical part.—The foregoing discussion about differentiating between executive and administrative functions brings us once more to a discussion of the theory of separated powers. However, we shall not consider it any longer from the historical point of view, but shall ask ourselves instead what truth it contains from the scientific point of view here expounded. If the general doctrine is examined, it is found that it has an implicit double meaning. On the one hand, it contains a generalization, theory or hypothesis; on the other hand, it contains a practical suggestion, a proposal for the organization of government in the interest of individual liberty. For the doctrine declares that governmental powers can be separated into three categories: executive, legislative, and judicial; it also holds that the exercise of these same powers should be entrusted to three separate bodies or persons. In accordance with our general view of political science (see above, Chap. I), it behooves us to test the theory or hypothesis by the standard of scientific truth, in other words, by asking the question: Is this division of power valid? What are the grounds for it? The practical proposal, on the other hand, we should test by the standard of expediency, in other words by asking the question: Is the attribution of these powers as distinguished to different bodies essential for attaining the purpose of limiting the government in its relation to non-governmental spheres of community life? To an examination of these two questions we must now turn.

The theory of the three types of decision.—The idea that there are three major types of governmental power would seem to be a valid generalization and one in accord with human psychology as we know it. Without proving the point, it may be assumed that political theorists when speaking of power mean that a person or group possesses the ability to command. This ability to command involves the ability to decide, whenever there is a choice between several alternatives. Now such decisions are of two elementary types which might be illustrated by the following examples. A man seeing a hat lying about, may say to himself: "I will pick up that hat," a decision which is directed towards one particular instance. On doing so, he may continue by resolving: "I shall never allow hats to lie about," a decision which involves an indefinite number of instances. What has just been said regarding decisions, holds equally true regarding commands, of course. It is evident that if two basic types of deciding and of commanding can be distinguished, powers admit of a corresponding classification. Specific decisions and commands are the realm of the executive power, general decisions and commands the sphere of the legislative power. The latter is for that reason often called the rule-making power. Analogously, the executive power may be called measure-taking. As to the judicial power, it will now be apparent that it stands between the two; for it transforms a general into a specific decision. When a general command has been given, or a general decision made, that is, a rule has been established, there still remains the further decision involved in applying the rule. If I have resolved never to let any hat lie about, I may be obliged to decide whether a particular object, for example, a cap, is a hat and therefore falls under my general rule, or whether a hat, being placed on an anteroom table is "lying about." This kind of decision is related to the general decision in that it cannot arise without a rule having previously been established; it is related to the specific decision in that it is itself a specific decision. Evidently this kind of decision, and the judicial power which makes it, is more intellectual, less active than the other two. It does not involve a command, and that is why the courts' activities are described as decisions. This analysis also shows that most of the time we are our own judges; for whenever we decide to do or not to do something because the law demands or forbids it, we are applying that law by subsuming the particular situation with which we are confronted under the established legal rules. Ordinarily, it is only the doubtful and controversial points of law which are brought up before the courts. All this is more than obvious, once we look at it in this way, and yet those who incline to criticize the doctrine of the separation of powers have rarely shown any appreciation of this sound theoretical aspect of it. This is so, because the theoretical aspect is seldom clearly distinguished from the practical proposal of attributing these several powers to different bodies. To an examination of this proposal we must now turn.

The proposal of divided exercise.—Let us begin with correcting a false impression. It was never proposed that the exercise of all of each power be entrusted to one person or body. On the contrary, the doctrine of checks and balances requires that after the main exercise has been attributed to one person or body care should be taken to set up a minor participation of other persons or bodies. Budget and impeachment, judicial review and pardon are examples of this sort of check. Moreover, we have already seen that everywhere in Europe the separation of powers was in practice always and foremost a separation or division of the legislative power between the king and Parliament, and that this separation was clearly demanded by Locke, if not by Montesquieu. When seen in this light, there is nothing peculiarly impracticable about the practical proposal contained in the doctrine. Whether such division of power will, however, effectively restrain governmental action, as the doctrine maintains, depends upon other considerations as well.

Necessity for an effective party system.—It is often said that the reason the separation of powers has worked in the United States is due to the party leadership of the President. Through this party background of both executive and legislative functions the divided powers are said to have been re-integrated and brought together for fruitful action. Of course, whenever either house of Congress has a majority belonging to another party than the President's, this argument falls to the ground. This exception, which has so often been a fact that it is hardly possible to treat it as an exception, points to the really important consideration that an established two-party system is of decisive importance in maintaining a constitutional separation of powers intact. Wherever one-party rule establishes itself with any degree of permanence, as it did in England during the better part of the eighteenth century, and as it now prevails in some of the American states, the separation of powers is weakened too. It may actually fail to operate as an effective restraint upon governmental action. As a result, the government may drift in the direction of parliamentary supremacy, as it did in England. Or it may lead to one-man rule and dictatorship, as was the case in Germany or Louisiana. A single party at times contains sufficiently powerful factions to prevent such an outcome as, for example, in Wisconsin. But unless there exist well-organized opposing groups which can entrench themselves in the different departments of government as separated in their power by the Constitution, the probability is great that these departments will in course of time be merged and power concentrated in one or another of the several persons or bodies.

The need for a guardian or neutral power: the king.—Such entrenchment will, however, never afford real protection to the weaker of the two opponents, unless there is somewhere a fairly neutral arbiter. John Adams' view that a balance of powers in the constitution itself will be able to control the parties and thus keep them in check can no longer be accepted. To be sure, a carefully worked out balance of separated powers is a first step in the direction of controlling party ascendancy, but a mere mechanism can never defend itself against the lust for power of organized human beings. John Adams himself would consider the only alternative to be a monarchy and a standing army. But might it not be possible to combine the two devices and to make the monarch the neutral arbiter over and above a balance of separated powers? Benjamin Constant, in his famous *Reflections on Constitutions and Their Guarantees* (1814) proposed to do just that. If the three powers of Montesquieu interfere with each other, disturb each other, or impede each other, it is necessary to have a power which puts them back in their place. This conception of the royal as the neutral power is closely akin to the English prerogative which, in the words of Dicey, is "the residue of discretionary or arbitrary authority which at any time is legally left in the hands of the Crown." It is, therefore, the final security of the subject against the abuse by ministers, politicians, and others of their part therein. While it was difficult for the king to maintain this prerogative against a prime minister backed by a compact parliamentary majority, a new day is possibly dawning for it since the advent of the Labour party has led to minority cabinets. The new situation was forcefully illustrated by the reappointment of MacDonald as Prime Minister in 1931, after his Labour cabinet had resigned. Harold Laski has expressly claimed a breach of the constitution by the king on this occasion. In imperial affairs, likewise, the royal prerogative has emerged anew as the effective link between the parliaments at home and in the Dominions. It would, however, be contrary to fact to call the English king a guardian of the constitution. Whether he could, for example, effectively oppose an onslaught against the independence of judges may be doubted, though the fact that their appointment is part of the prerogative might help him in such struggle were it ever to arise.

The German president.—Under the Republican constitution of Germany, it was hoped by some that the president might become such a neutral arbiter and guardian of the constitution. His powers were typically those of a constitutional monarch, including the power of pardon, of appointing and dismissing the prime minister (chancellor), of appointing the civil servants, of being supreme commander of the army and other defense forces, of receiving ambassadors, and otherwise representing Germany in foreign affairs, and so forth. In the exercise of these powers, he was bound to the countersignature of his minister. But due to the confusion of parties, and the state of emergency which arose, the German president was pushed into assuming wider and wider powers of actual government. From a representative head of the government, he became its executive center. This process was hastened by the fact of his being a party man, elected by a majority of the people. If re-eligibility had been barred, he might have remained sufficiently neutral. At first Hindenburg, not dreaming of a second term, rose above parties and became detached from the factional discord. But as his advisers gradually persuaded him to seek re-election, overemphasizing his true constitutional position, he lost the neutrality which was hoped for and which would have been essential for a guardian of the constitution.

The Supreme Court of the United States.—The great improbability, if not impossibility, of securing a neutral watchdog for the constitutional restraints in any kind of elective officer or body was, however, clearly seen by Alexander Hamilton more than a hundred years before the German Republican constitution was drafted. In the *Federalist*, we are told: "Whoever considers attentively the different departments of power must perceive that, in a government in which they are separated from each other, the judiciary, from the nature of its functions, will always be the least dangerous to the political rights of the constitution; because it will be least in a capacity to annoy or injure them. . . . By a limited constitution I understand one which contains certain specified exceptions to the legislative authority; . . . Limitations can be preserved in no other way than through the medium of the courts of justice whose duty it must be to declare all acts contrary to the *manifest tenor* of the constitution *void*. . . ." This doctrine has led, as is well-known, to the doctrine of judicial review of the constitutionality of legislative acts in the United States. The problems raised by this doctrine are too intricate to pass over without further consideration, so the next chapter will be entirely devoted to them. Here it may suffice to call attention to the fact that the Supreme Court has, in the United States, been entrusted with that neutral power which we found to be a necessary condition for the maintenance of a separation of powers. Of course, no power is absolutely neutral, or it would not be any power at all. But the power of such a high court is not derived from a popular election, but from the cumulative respect and reverence which a civilized community entertains toward those whose function it is to uphold the law, and therefore order in the community.

Conclusion.—In short, the proposal that the making of rules and their application and the adjudication of controversies regarding the applicability of such rules should in the main be entrusted to different bodies is still pertinent. At any rate, these powers should be divided between several relatively independent bodies or persons. It may be wise to modify the three-fold scheme by the older English doctrine of the prerogative which would keep a separate body or person charged principally with the representative function and therefore with foreign relations as well. If so, the distinction between the executive and the administrative functions will have to be clarified and perhaps broadened by a recognition of the distinction between government and administration which the French Conseil d'Etat has taken such pains to elaborate. Such a recognition of a governmental (executive) function exercised in common by the legislative and the administrative branches would insure the degree of integration which must be maintained for the safety of the political order as a whole, without leading to a complete fusion of all powers. Anyway, against the prophets of a dictatorial concentration of power in one leader as the form of government of the twentieth century, the case for a separation of powers may be allowed to rest upon much broader grounds than are suggested by the limited doctrines of Locke and Montesquieu. Lack of historical sense prevents the prophets of absolutism from perceiving that their allegedly *new* form is a very ancient and primitive form: the tribe at war led by its chieftain amid the shouts of the multitude. At the same time, stripping the doctrine of its historical garb and showing its underlying scientific foundation may persuade political students of the more fortunate nations which have already achieved a measure of lasting order and unity and some balanced constitutional order that some scheme of separated powers may be evolved to fit the needs of an industrial society.

CHAPTER XII

JUDICIAL REVIEW OF LEGISLATIVE ACTS; THE GUARDIANSHIP OF THE CONSTITUTION

Introductory.—Hamilton's view that a high court of justice affords the best protection of a constitutional system, that is, a system imposing restraints upon governmental action, was a political restatement of the famous dictum of Justice Coke that "Magna Charta is such a fellow that he will have no sovereign." In the days of Coke, to be sure, it was the king in Parliament which seemed to threaten this "supremacy of the law." But in Hamilton's time the English Commons were progressing steadily in the direction of parliamentary supremacy, and it was therefore apparent to him and to many other Americans that what was needed were limitations upon the legislative authority, irrespective of whether it was being exercised by a prince or by an elective body. A "tyranny of the majority" had loomed up in some of the states, and the makers of the Constitution sought to restrain it. The development of this power of the courts to interpret the Constitution is closely related to the separation of powers, and signifies the most radical difference between English and American political techniques.

Coke's belief in a higher law.—It would, however, be false to assume the system of judicial review to be entirely novel. Coke and his fellow believers in the supremacy of law assigned a similar position to the courts in interpreting acts of Parliament according to the common law. His most signal conflicts with King James originated in his belief that the Court of Common Pleas and other high courts of England had the right to decide whether a certain act of Parliament was "legal" or not. In the famous case of Dr. Bonham he declared: "It appears in our books that in many cases the common law will control acts of parliament and sometimes adjudge them to be utterly void; for when an act of parliament is against common right or reason, or repugnant or impossible to be performed, the common law will control it and adjudge it to be void." However, his view as expressed in this opinion did not triumph in England, though lip service was given to it until the end of the eighteenth century. This was, however, just long enough to influence American juridical thought to the effect of substituting the Constitution as the fundamental law of the land for Coke's common law. In the course of a century and more of judicial "interpretation" of the Constitution, a great deal of common law has been worked into the American legal fabric.

The supremacy of Parliament.—In England, however, the supremacy of the law got merged with the supremacy of Parliament. English legal historians have perhaps been inclined to minimize unduly the importance of Coke's position. Certainly Cromwell was, as we have seen, deeply convinced of the need for some fundamental law limiting the power of Parliament. Even Bacon, Coke's opponent on the king's side, admitted that English law "is grounded on the law of nature." But this notion became a rather empty formula after the evolution of cabinet responsibility in the eighteenth century, as it also had been in the period of Tudor absolutism when the supremacy of the law first came to mean the supremacy of Parliament. That the lawyers in England never placed any considerable obstacle in the way of this development had, as is justly argued by Professor Holdsworth, very important consequences for the English constitution and English law. That the system has worked well for a long period of time, does not, however, prove its fundamental soundness. Nor has its success been as uninterrupted as is now sometimes assumed. For the American struggle for independence arose at least in part on the issue of taxation without representation. This question evidently turned upon one of those principles of a fundamental nature which Coke and his contemporaries sought to except from parliamentary legislation. As Professor McIlwain has convincingly shown, justifiable doubt could be entertained by conscientious men as to the constitutionality of these measures. To argue that the courts had not, in fact, disallowed any acts of Parliament (an assertion not wholly true, anyway), is merely to say that Parliament had stayed within its constitutional limits.

The problem of "arbitrary" legislation.—It is, however, hardly surprising that the framers of the American Constitution should have been particularly sensitive to the chances of arbitrary usurpations of power by a legislature. The magistral John Adams is full of thoughts on this subject, which were shared to a greater or less degree by his contemporaries. To these men, Hamilton's doctrine was most palatable, and Justice Marshall's famous decision of *Marbury v. Madison,* reasserting it, was equally so. American insight into this problem carried, however, little weight on the Continent, where people were, as Gneist observed, immensely concerned with securing bills of rights, but seemed to care little about securing sufficient legal guarantees for their enforcement. One striking exception which we have already mentioned is to be found in the constitution of the Kingdom of Württemberg. There it was provided in Article X of the constitution that a constitutional court (*Staatsgerichtshof*) should be entrusted with the guardianship of the constitution.

The constituent power recalled.—Before going further in our analysis of these questions, it seems desirable to recall what we found in examining the constituent power. The constituent power, we said in Chapter IX, is the power exercised in establishing a constitution, that is, the fundamental decision on revolutionary measures for the organization and limitation of a new government (see Chap. VIII, ¶ 11). From this constituent power must be clearly distinguished the amending power which changes an existing constitution in forms provided by the constitution itself. For the amending power is itself a constituted authority. In French constitutional law the expression *pouvoir constituant* is often used to describe the amending authority as well as the constituent power. We shall see below how this confusion contributes to the controversy over judicial review.

Workability of amending power a factor.—In Chapter IX we also saw that the relative smoothness with which the amending power functions greatly affects the relative importance of explicit amendments as compared to constitutional interpretation; and that such interpretation may take the form either of usages or judicial review or both. When the Supreme Court of the United States confirmed the pocket veto (1928), it sanctioned by judicial interpretation what had been an accepted usage, introduced by the President in dealing with part of his legislative functions. In the United States, no usage can be considered final, unless it has received this sanction of judicial interpretation. But many usages are practiced which have never received that sanction. Such usages are numerous and the judicial interpretation of the Constitution is of profound significance in the United States, because the process of amendment is rather cumbersome. In the France of the Third Republic where the process of amendment is rather easy, constitutional usages are less numerous and judicial review has not been accepted (see below, ¶ 18).

Simplicity of constitution.—The greater or less smoothness of the amending process is, however, not the only factor affecting the relative importance of constitutional interpretation. Another important element is the relative simplicity or complexity of a constitution. The American Constitution is more complex than the constitution of the Third French Republic; for it contains a federal system and a bill of rights. The German Republican constitution of 1919 was even more complex than the American Constitution; for its bill of rights was based upon conflicting political and social philosophies, liberal, Catholic, and socialist, and was therefore in many respects quite equivocal. If one provision of the constitution seemed to set up a separation of church and state, another forthwith by implication denied it (Articles 135, 136, 137, and 146). Which of the two was a court to enforce if a controversy came before it in which one of the litigants based his case upon one, the other upon its opposite? The development of the due process interpretation by the American courts since the adoption of Amendment XIV offers another striking illustration of the opportunity which equivocal provisions of a constitution provide for constitutional interpretation. Even more significant is the role of interpretation in connection with the whole welter of complex provisions through which the American Constitution attempts to settle the relation between the federal government and the states. The gamut of questions which arise here has been discussed before (see above, Chap. X, ¶ 4). Undoubtedly a certain measure of such difficulties and complexities are inherent in any constitution embodied in written documents.

Flexible versus rigid constitution.—These two factors, easy process of amendment and inherent complexity, together constitute what is often discussed as the relative flexibility or rigidity of a constitution. The argument is usually extended to include the English system of government, where no distinction is made between the legislative and the amending power, or to put it another way, where no fundamental distinction is admitted between constitutional and other law. Such a system seems more flexible than any other. But we have already seen that the traditional device of a two party system embodies an effective restraint, the more so when, as in Britain, the government in power is obliged to appeal to the electorate on any major issue. Such fundamental changes as would involve a repeal of, let us say, a principle established and set down in the Act of Settlement, like the tenure of judges during good behavior, could not be enacted by a government, unless it had fought and won an election on it. When in 1911 the Liberals wished to curtail the powers of the House of Lords, they had to carry the issue to the voters. From a political science point of view, therefore, the amending power is recognized in Britain to belong to the electorate, whatever the constitutional lawyers may say about it. Only a referendum will sanction constitutional change. But that means a bare majority of the electoral districts which may not even be a majority of the people (see below, Chap. XVII). It is, therefore, difficult to say whether the English or the French constitution is more flexible; probably the balance is about even. It follows that the French lawyers, who range the French constitution with the American and who then contrast it with the English, overemphasize the formal legal recognition in France of an amending power (*pouvoir constituant*) separate from the legislative power. Their discussion of the relative advantages and disadvantages of rigid and flexible constitutions will throw some further light on the question.

Relative advantage of flexibility.—The great and outstanding advantage of a flexible constitution is the smoothness with which it can be adapted to new conditions and altered conceptions in the community. This advantage is particularly apparent, of course, in times of rapid change. An oft-cited example is afforded by legislation regulating the conditions of labor under modern industrial conditions. In England the introduction of new rules prohibiting child labor proceeded apace and unincumbered by constitutional provisions regarding freedom of contract, and the same is, of course, true in

France. It is, however, obvious that such flexibility presupposes a nation steeped in traditions and by nature opposed to change, or the whole political structure will easily become the object of attack from restless and irresponsible groups. A most formidable illustration of the great dangers inherent in an easy amending process was brought out by the events of March 1933 in Germany. Here a bare majority of Nationalist and National Socialist deputies abused its legislative power to bar part of the opposition (the Communists) and then proceeded to "amend" the constitution by giving the government absolute power to change it. Such a procedure had never been sanctioned by even a majority of the electorate.

Relative advantage of rigid constitution.—The overthrow of the German constitution "from within" brings to light the great advantage of a rigid constitution. In fact, it would be better to call such a constitution firm, because the epithet "rigid" intentionally or accidentally prejudices the case. A firm constitution provides effective safeguards against what one might term mob militancy, or, with de Tocqueville, majority tyranny. It seems for that reason better adapted to a constitutional order which is not deeply rooted in tradition, as the English or Swiss constitutions are. This is particularly true where the people are deeply divided by religious, racial, or class conflicts. If, moreover, the form of government is new and untried, a firm constitution lifts it somewhat above the party struggle, while a soft and pliable charter would be tossed about by the more or less passing storms of popular discontent. While a firm constitution makes constitutional amendments more difficult, it obliges advocates of such changes to concentrate upon the essentials and to build up solid popular sentiment behind them. If such support has been secured, however, the changes will be swift and decisive. This conclusion is amply supported by the history of constitutional amendments in the United States.

Informal change.—What is equally important, constitutional change of more detailed provisions takes place without reference to a formal amendment, through the action (or inaction) of all departments of the government. The American pocket veto resulted, as we noted, from inaction on the part of the President; the Senate pressed for and the President conceded senatorial influence over appointments, known as the senatorial courtesy; the French Parliament, in 1924 and 1926, authorized the executive to modify by decree (*décret-lois*) existing laws, thus interpreting in a very controversial manner the provision of Article 1, § 1 of the constitutional law of February 25, 1875, which provided that the legislative power shall be exercised by two assemblies: the Chamber of Deputies and the Senate. Analogous steps have been taken in many other countries during times of crisis demanding prompt action. Our recent American steps in that direction are well-known. (See Chapter XIV for a discussion of such emergency government.) Equally important changes have been brought about through judicial interpretation. But the question we are here concerned with is primarily that of judicial review of legislative acts, viewed as a technique for preventing such "interpretations" from going beyond a reasonable point. By judicial review, in other words, the judicial sanction is denied to measures, even of the legislature composed of the representatives of the people, which according to the manifest meaning of the constitution are void. The crucial question, however, is that which inquires: "To whom is this meaning of the constitution manifest?" For it stands to reason that steps which are contrary to the constitution in the opinion of all men will hardly be taken except by those who exclaim with the afore-mentioned Senator: "To hell with the Constitution!" when the Constitution happens to come between them and one of their cherished dreams, for example, the virtue of the white women of South Carolina. There have been instances when such laws have been enacted, but they are few and far between, except in such travesties of a real constitution (as we have defined it) as those of the two Napoleons and Mussolini.

The nature of judicial review politically restated.—Concentrating entirely now upon the judicial review of laws, and leaving aside the review of executive and administrative measures, we are brought to conclude at once that the institution of judicial review substitutes the judgment of judges for the judgment of the elected representatives of the people, whenever doubt exists regarding the full meaning of a constitutional provision. It is *not* a question of the *manifest tenor*, as Marshall maintained, but on the contrary a question of the doubtful meaning of various constitutional provisions, or the actual lack of any provisions. Courts have been in the habit of obscuring the brutal truth of this statement by arguing about the "intention of the framers." But doubt usually has arisen where no intention was indicated in the debates. Take the case of the delegation of legislative powers to the executive department in France, for which there are many parallels in the United States. The sentence of the constitutional law which we have cited, that the legislative power shall be exercised by the Chamber and the Senate tells us nothing regarding this question of delegation. A court may argue (and has often argued) that there existed an old maxim of the Roman law that *potestas delegata non potest delegari,* that is, that a delegated power must not be delegated further. Since the legislative power, the argument runs on, is delegated by the constitution-making power to the legislature, the legislature cannot delegate it further. But were the framers of the constitution aware of this maxim of the Roman law? And has this maxim any application to a constitutionally delegated power, when it was originally evolved to maintain the hierarchy of Roman officials intact? These questions the courts do not ask, and do not answer, except by the cryptic statement that there is nothing to indicate that the framers did not intend it thus.

The German case.—The problem which we are now confronted with was thrown into especially clear relief under the German Republican constitution, because that constitution contained so many contradictory compromises (see above, Chap. X, ¶ 4). The first case in which the German Supreme Court claimed the right of judicial review of a legislative act sprang from just such a controversy. According to the constitution (Article 143) the right of private property was declared to be inviolable, except by law. Someone's private property rights had been infringed by a presidential decree (similar to the American emergency measures) promulgated under delegated legislative power. Was such a decree, being an exercise of delegated legislative power, a true law, in the understanding of the property clause of the constitution? The court said it was. For many different reasons it picked the more socialist of the two possible interpretations. But was that tendency of the court a persistent one? Far from it. A little later, the expropriation of the former German princes was provided in what the communist originators intended to be a legislative referendum. The government, opposed to the plan, turned to the Supreme Court for an advisory opinion. In this case, the court held that an act depriving specific individuals or families of their property was not a law; for according to Article 110 of the German constitution all Germans were declared equal before the law, and therefore a measure under which they were treated as unequal was said not to be a law. It followed, the court argued, that such an act of expropriation aimed at certain individuals was not a law, but a special measure. Since private property rights were guaranteed by the constitution, except were the law provided otherwise, such a special measure amounted to a change in the constitution, and therefore required constitutional majorities for its enactment. Here then the court took the side of the anti-socialist interpretation of the constitution. But there is an underlying idea which unites the two decisions; for in both of them the court was upholding the executive branch of the government. Since that was in keeping with German tradition, it really acted conservatively in both cases. With this finding we are squarely facing the truly political issue of judicial review.

Judges and propertied interests.—Those who, from Jefferson to LaFollette, have attacked judicial review have argued that judges are conservative folk, and that the judicial attitude of mind is ill-adapted to the solution of problems which require striking out along new paths. It has often been pointed out by more radical reformers that judges are, through their training and upbringing, closely linked with the propertied interests. This may have thrown them on the side of the revolutionary middle classes in the days of Coke, when these classes were battling the king and his feudal landowning aristocracy. But today it puts them with the big business interests opposed to the reforms desired by farmers and workers. Though exaggerated claims may often be advanced under this heading, it is difficult to deny that the charge is on the whole a correct one, though there are notable exceptions to the rule in this country as elsewhere. The situation is aggravated by yet another consideration which we must consider before we turn to the other side of the balance sheet.

The political aspect of precedent.—Judges whose primary function it is to settle controversies between contending private parties when they disagree about the meaning of the law (see above, Chap. VII), must in the nature of things be very careful to be consistent, lest the community feel themselves subjected to quite arbitrary rulings. All judicial systems are, therefore, careful in observing precedents at least within their jurisdiction. This in itself acts as a conservative force. It generates a habit of mind which turns to the past for guidance and counsel. What is more, any new departure must be supported by a good show of supporting reason, as in the case cited earlier in this chapter where the court argued from the legal maxim that a delegated power cannot be delegated. This technique of more or less public exposition of the reasons which led a court to decide as it did helps to settle the controversy by appealing to the *reason* of the losing litigant. It also serves the important legal and political function of holding the legal rules together so that they are something more than isolated bits, even if they do not, from a realistic point of view, constitute a perfect legal system. These two functions of legal reasoning are more or less impaired if judicial language becomes highly technical and incomprehensible to anybody but a trained lawyer. It will be found that the very great lawyer-judges, like Marshall, have usually been distinguished by a very lucid style. This lucidity may hide serious logical defects, but it serves the political functions just the same, as long as these defects are not discovered by any but the very astute minds, which are comparatively few. But on the other hand, there can be no question that this type of "reasoning" is not very helpful in dealing with distinctly *new* problems of a social or economic type. These require a scientific attitude of mind which is not authoritarian, but anti-authoritarian, which does not seek guidance from the past, but distrusts its judgment.

Disinterestedness and representative quality.—Yet the judicial and the scientific attitudes have one very important aspect in common, their "disinterestedness," or rather, their effort to be disinterested. It is admittedly easier to be detached when the issues are not of the human sphere, but an economist studying the incidents of a certain tax, and a judge deciding a case involving the conflict of interests between capital and labor must both strive to detach themselves from their own personal bias. This they can only do by realizing what that bias is presumably going to be. If they find themselves habitually on the side of capital, they must be particularly suspicious of any conclusion which seems to favor capital. To accomplish this feat is admittedly a great moral as well as intellectual achievement, and many, if not all, judges and scientists fail at times to live up to this standard. The extent to which they do so, and are believed to do so, profoundly affects their political role. The willing acceptance of judicial review in the United States has been due to the fact that the community has faith in the comparative disinterestedness of the judges composing it. This faith gave the Supreme Court a truly representative character, even though, or perhaps rather because it was not elective and therefore not so obviously partisan. In countries where the courts do not possess that representative quality they cannot readily assume the arbitral function of interpreting the constitution. But before we conclude this argument in applying it to the present situation, we must consider another aspect of the matter which is of no small weight in determining the political significance of judicial review.

Universality versus partisanship.—We have already had occasion to hint here and there at the problems of majority tyranny in a democracy. If a constitution is a technique for restraining the action of government, any community which allowed free reign to the majority, no matter what the issue, could not be called constitutional, no matter how democratic. The nineteenth century was prone, under the persuasive influence of thinkers like Rousseau, to assume the substantial identity between democracy and constitutional government. The warning voices of political thinkers like de Tocqueville and John Stuart Mill were not generally heeded. This was probably due in large part to an insufficient realization of the importance of parties in a democracy. When the case between a court and a legislature is put on the ground that one is elected by the people, and the other not, as is still done in most French and English textbooks, the case looks bad for the courts. The elected legislature appears to be "representative," the court "aristocratic." But once the legislature is viewed as divided into parties, its representative quality is seen to be of a very particular kind; for such majorities change, and the more universal aspects of community life may well be removed from its immediate effect. A court comprehending the highest legal talent in the community may, on the other hand, often be representative of the community's legal conscience in a very much more real and universal sense.

Siéyès' constitutional jury.—But why should the ordinary courts be entrusted with this particular duty? Would it not be more in keeping with all angles of the problem if a separate body were set up to handle these thorny questions? The great French revolutionary politician, Abbé Siéyès, thought so, and accordingly expounded the idea of a constitutional jury in his famous speech before the Convention on the 2nd of Thermidor of the year III. The distinction between the amending power and the legislative power requires, he held, a guardian of the constitution. But this guardian cannot be the judicial power; it must be a special political representative body. "I demand," he said, "a jury of the constitution . . . or constitutional jury. This jury must be a real body of representatives which I demand should have the special mission (function) of judging all protests against any infringement of the constitution. . . . If you wish to give a safeguard to the constitution, a salutary curb which keeps each representative action within the limits of its special function, then establish a constitutional jury!" This idea of a constitutional jury was, in a way, realized in the form of the *Senat Conservateur* of the year VIII which was supposed to be the guardian of the constitution. But of course these functions remained on paper under the autocratic rule of the first Napoleon. A similar Senate reappeared in France under the third Napoleon; for in the constitution of 1852 it was provided that the Senate should be "the guardian of the fundamental charter and of the public liberties" (Article 26). Its practical fate was not very different from that of the first Senate.

Post-war European constitutional tribunals.—After the war, however, this idea of a special body charged with safeguarding the constitution gained much adherence in countries engaged in establishing new constitutions. In Republican Austria, Germany, and Czechoslovakia, special courts were set up under the constitutions to examine the constitutionality of legislation. But in most cases these courts were really advisory bodies, as in Austria, or restricted to controversies between governments, as in Austria and Germany. The European "public corporation" offered, however, an entering wedge for extending the jurisdiction of these courts. Thus in Germany, parties were admitted as litigants before the Court of State in contesting an election procedure, and elections in certain states were actually held null and void because the election procedure did not correspond with the requirements of the national constitution (see below). In Czechoslovakia, the constitutional tribunal has, in fact, been striving to achieve the position of the American Supreme Court by admitting individual litigants, but the issue remains controversial. The functions of these bodies, then, while charged with guarding the constitution, are not to be confused with judicial review. Nor are plans like that of Switzerland which provide for judicial settlement of conflicts between cantonal legislation and the federal and cantonal constitutions, which are also found in Germany, even under the Empire, to be confused with true judicial review. Are such bodies to be preferred to judicial review in the true sense, that is, the power of *all* courts to inquire into the validity of national statutes under a constitution? Siéyès, in affirming this proposition, rested his case upon the idea that such a body would be political and representative. The American practice of judicial review, in denying the proposition, brings out that the courts are, on the whole, unpolitical, and yet representative. Looked at from the point of view of the political scientist, it would appear that the judicial courts which a new constitutional order inherits from the past, are the residuary legatees of a great deal of power over the minds of the community, commanding much traditional respect and loyalty. French and German authorities opposing judicial review in their countries have rightly insisted that "in order to attribute to the courts so delicate and important a role, it is necessary above all else that the judiciary possess a very high authority: it is necessary that the people have a profound confidence in its wisdom and its professional and scientific standard." But even if this be accepted, there arises at once the objection that such function, when attributed to the courts, will in time undermine their standing, will politicize them.

Fundamental cleavages in the nation undermine representative quality of judiciary and thereby political utility of judicial safeguards for constitution.—This argument was urged with particular emphasis after the war in Germany, where political passion ran very high. It is undeniable that such a danger exists, and that much wisdom and self-restraint on the part of the court is needed in order to escape from its damaging consequences. But of course, the more deeply the community's respect for the courts is rooted, the less dangerous it is for such courts to assume the arbitral function of ultimate constitutional interpretation, particularly if an amending process of proven utility offers hope to the discontented that they may alter provisions which irk them. In post-war Germany, the courts did not enjoy such an unqualified respect. Nor do they in the rest of Europe, wherever the Marxist labor movement is strong. For according to Karl Marx' class war doctrine, the courts are nothing but camouflaged exponents of the so-called bourgeois class aiding their class in the exploitation of the toiling masses. In other words, they dispense class justice, instead of mass justice (see above, ¶ 13). It is evident that whenever such opinions have wide currency and this will be true where a Marxist labor movement assumes leadership of a large part of the electorate, as in Germany general confidence in the "disinterestedness" of the judiciary will be greatly reduced. If courts in such a country are called upon to decide cases which involve the "interpretation" of constitutional provisions, which may be partly socialist and partly not, the ensuing controversies will further undermine their position, no matter which way they decide. If, moreover, many of the judges are held over from a previous regime, and kept because of the principle of judicial tenure during good behavior, the loyalty of the courts to the new government may also become suspect, as was unquestionably the case in post-war Germany. We have mentioned the economic class conflicts first among the conditions depriving courts of their representative quality, because they happen to be in the foreground of popular attention today, and appear wherever modern industrialism prevails. But other basic cleavages can have the same disruptive result. Thus national minorities will rarely accept the decision of a court manned by the majority as rendering "disinterested" justice. They will always suspect a national judge of partisanship. Therefore again a supreme court could not hope to be the effective guardian of a constitution which undertook to guarantee minority rights, as in Rumania, or Germany. None but an international tribunal or a mixed arbitral body containing members of their own nationality will be able to satisfy such a national minority. In other words, the actual disunity of the political community in fundamental respects cannot be bridged by even the most liberal-looking constitutional provisions and seemingly stringent judicial safeguards.

A traditional judiciary can to some extent escape from this dilemma.—Both these examples, but more particularly the economic class division, indicate that the political scientist is really confronted with a problem quite distinct from that outlined by Hamilton in the *Federalist.* There the emphasis is all on which of the three powers will be least likely to extend its authority on its own initiative. Hamilton's conclusion has stood the test of a century, and there is not much actual fact which would oblige us to question it today. Hamilton, of course, in the fashion of his day, did not stop long to consider the function of parties under popular government. Yet, it is well known that the contest between the executive and the judicial power did not commence until the issue of partisanship was injected under Jefferson and Marshall. At that time, it was to some extent a matter of economic group interests, as everybody realizes today. Marshall was an exponent of eastern business and manufacturing interests, while Jefferson fought for the southern and western farmer. However, the issues and the conflict were kept in bounds by their common acceptance of an America which they saw as a whole. But when such group interests crystallize into dogmatic and mutually exclusive positions, and if, moreover, the courts are believed to be all on one side, the matter becomes rather different. This, to be sure, is not true in America at the present time. Still, the court is believed to be divided (as, of course, it actually is) into progressives and conservatives, and their respective balance is a matter of public controversy and great political pressure, as it used to be before the Civil War in connection with pro- and anti-slavery members. Obviously, under such conditions the confidence of the community in the court is considerably shaken. A wise court with a sound tradition will seek to check that decline in public esteem by avoiding extreme positions on the most controversial issues, but this is not always possible. In so far as it does, it ceases to perform the function of being guardian of the constitution, since it accepts the "interpretation" of the legislature. It might be argued that therein lies the main advantage of judicial review: that it can weigh such considerations in the balance, and decide without fearing for itself any too immediate popular reaction. There is the other aspect, characteristic of all real power: the legislature will try to avoid enacting measures which are too palpably beyond any conceivable "interpretation" of the existing constitution.

Conclusion.—In conclusion, it may be said that the political technique of judicial review can be employed only where considerable confidence in the integrity of the courts is generally entertained by the people at large. On the other hand, no "constitutional jury" other than such a judiciary will be sufficiently neutral and detached to exercise the functions of a guardian of the constitution effectively. Therefore we must conclude that, in the absence of a constitution deeply rooted in tradition such as exists in England, France, Switzerland, Sweden, the non-existence of such a judiciary will prevent the establishment of a constitution in the political sense of a set of techniques for restraining the actions of government. For a constitution presupposes an actual community, a people fundamentally united.

CHAPTER XIII

FEDERALISM AND THE TERRITORIAL DIVISION OF POWER

Introductory.—The rise of modern constitutional government has been accompanied by an increasing number of federal schemes. The United States, Switzerland, Germany, Canada, Australia, and the Union of South Africa, Brazil, the Soviet Union, Austria, and finally the British Commonwealth of Nations have evolved a governmental structure known as federalism. The earlier ones brought forth their federalism out of a preceding federation. The later federal schemes were set up as a concomitant of centrifugal forces. Considering the territory and population of the countries just mentioned, it is undeniable that federalism constitutes an important phase of modern government. A realistic study of the political nature of these federal schemes has, however, been delayed by an exceptional amount of formalistic, juristic battling over words. Having first posited that all states possess an indivisible sovereign, jurists have strained human ingenuity to discover such a sovereign in a federal state. But, as a wit remarked later, even the incredible learning of a German scholar could not find something which was not there. The following discussion will not be concerned with these controversies about sovereignty and the state. Instead, it will discuss federalism as the territorial form of dividing political powers under a constitution.

Federalism in terms of a pattern of objectives.—From a pragmatic viewpoint, an effectively centralized government, a decentralized government, a federal government, a federation, confederation or league of governments, an alliance, an alignment, a system of "independent" governments, and finally completely "independent" governments (such as those of Rome and China in the time of Cæsar), all these could be represented as differences of degree in the relation of government to the territory affected by it, between two extremes, complete unity and complete distinctness. However, a predominant amount of interest has centered upon the point at which we pass from a federal government to a federation or league of governments, for it seems to be at this point that we pass from unity (no matter how organized) to multiplicity. But this is an optical illusion resulting from a monistic conception of government. In actual reality, even the most effectively centralized government possesses marked diversity, composed as it necessarily is of a considerable group of human beings with diverse interests, objectives, and so forth. From such a standpoint, a federal government appears to be as hard to distinguish from a federation of governments by any clear line of demarcation, as it is to distinguish it, at times, from a thoroughly decentralized government. Nevertheless, the focal points are distinct, and federalism (comprising both) undoubtedly appears as the form of political organization suited to groups or communities which have partly general and common objectives, traditions, and interests, and partly particular or conflicting objectives, whenever these divergences follow a territorial pattern. Now, whether it will be *one* federal government, or a federation of governments may sometimes be difficult to determine. But the distinction would seem to be related to the relative balance of these patterns of objectives. In this respect governments are similar to other groups which may form a federation or unite and merge under a federal organization. In all these cases, regarding territorial governments and functional organizations of all kinds, the same observation is made: When the particular objectives are sufficiently strong and compact to hold together the territorial (or functional) subdivisions of the more comprehensive group, sustaining them as or molding them into autonomous groups, then a federation is the adequate political pattern. On the other hand, the federal organization is indicated when conflicting objectives (interests, purposes) are not as yet, or are no longer sufficiently strong to sustain autonomous groups. The contrast between the federal and the federational type of organization must not blind us, therefore, to the intimate relation between them. For they are both organizational patterns evolved in response to a (varying) combination of common and general, and particular and sometimes conflicting objectives. This is most clearly seen, when we do not limit either conception to governmental organizations. In fact, both federations of groups and federally organized groups are found in all fields of human activity. The American Federation of Labor, the Federal Council of Churches in America, the National Union of German Industry, the International Federation of Cities, or the Second International, all these and many others are genuine federations of groups, held together by common objectives, but composed of distinct and autonomous entities. A truly comprehensive analysis of federation should undoubtedly comprehend all these groups. But since we are concerned in these pages with modern government, we will limit ourselves to federations formed among governments, and to the federal form of government as we find it in the United States.

Federations and leagues, a comparative view.—Historically speaking, federal governments evolved out of federations. It was so in the United States. It had been so in Switzerland and in the Netherlands. In view of this, it seems reasonable to inspect the organizational features of federations, if we wish to progress along pragmatic lines, in our analysis of federalism. If we study the early city leagues, like the Achæan League, the Hanse, and the Suabian City League, or if we study the Swiss Union and the Dutch Union, or if we study the American Confederation, the German Confederation, and finally the League of Nations, we always find three elements of organization: (1) an assembly of representatives of the constituent members making and mantaining a charter (treaty = [Latin] *foedus*); (2) an executive organ of some sort, set up by the members, carrying out the decisions of the assembly of representatives; (3) an arbitral or judicial body interpreting the charter in its bearings upon the relation between particular members of the federation and the federation itself, as well as upon the relation between two or more particular members of the federation; such arbitral procedure is ordinarily supposed to eliminate the recourse to arms between members. Now what were the common objectives of these federations? They were different for different federations, but there was always (with the possible exception of the League of Nations) the objective of resisting some outside pressure to which all the members were alike exposed (see Chap. IV).

The common objective of many federations.—This common desire to resist outside pressure is obvious in the case of the city leagues. Likewise the Swiss Union was formed in order to resist the feudalizing and later the centralizing inclinations of the Dukes of Austria and of Burgundy. From the thirteenth to the sixteenth century these tendencies were dominant. From then on, outside pressure tended to disappear, and the Union tended to disintegrate, though the neighboring monarchical and "absolutist" governments remained sufficiently threatening to prevent a final dissolution. The invasion by revolutionary French forces, and the forcible establishment of a rather centralized Helvetian Republic (1798) served to remind the Swiss of the precariousness of their existence, and the federation set up at the end of the Napoleonic wars was not as loose as the preceding federation. Ultimately, after the forces of dissension had once more sought to reassert the complete autonomy of the constituent cantons in the abortive War of Secession (*Sonderbundskrieg,* 1847), the federation became a federal state under the constitution of 1848. Perhaps even more striking, and certainly as dramatic, is the case of the United Dutch Provinces which for decades after 1555 waged an apparently hopeless war against the most powerful government of the day, the Spanish monarchy, because that government attempted to force Catholicism upon them. But unlike the Swiss cantons, the Dutch Provinces eventually merged under a unitary government, although the Dutch upper chamber preserves to this day the remnants of the country's federational past. It is hardly necessary to elaborate upon the outside pressure in response to which the American Confederation was formed. Here, however, common (economic) objectives so completely overshadowed other considerations that the federational structure soon gave way to a federal government. Not so in Germany. Though the economic forces might have been expected to produce a similar result, the several principalities with their well-integrated administrative organizations under monarchical leadership proved themselves more stubborn preservers of local autonomy; they provided conflicting objectives of more enduring tenacity than the newly formed state governments in the United States. But eventually they, too, were welded into a federal whole, although one beset by innumerable difficulties arising from an historically conditioned complexity. The common objective here was not only to resist the recurrent aggressions of neighboring nations, but the entire complex of cultural aspirations which modern nationalism has proclaimed as the God-given objective of a people having a common speech.

The question of economic forces.—Nationalism, then, is an internal as well as an external force, providing common objectives for a group of autonomous units. Another such force is economic. This force, rather than nationalism, has been shown to have stood at the cradle of American development. In Switzerland it was important, too. And in Germany it was surely not wholly lacking. It is common knowledge that many people pinned their hope for the success of a League of Nations upon similar world economic interests which, it was felt, would balance the nationalistic forces of regional antagonism. Today, greater scepticism prevails in that regard. It is, at any rate, interesting to note that where the prevalence of such common objectives associated with internal forces can be observed, federations tend to emerge as federal structures; a genuine union with a government for the whole seems to emanate. This certainly was the situation in the United States, in Switzerland and in Germany. Perhaps this accounts for their different development, which contrasts so markedly with earlier federations, such as the city leagues; it was their history and the application of it to these emerging federal unions which misled Freeman into his mistaken generalizations about federalism as such. The outbreak of the Civil War certainly offered him a seemingly convincing point of departure. But before we enter into a further consideration of such federal structures and the political implications of their constitutional framework, we shall have to examine the three elements of organization which we find in all federations and their historical forms as far as we know them. It will be best to begin with the representative assembly, its nature and its functions.

Organizational aspects of federation: (1) participation through a representative assembly.—All the federations of which we know have had some kind of representative assembly. The Achæan League as well as the Hanse, the Swiss Confederation, and the United Provinces, all held periodic gatherings of one or more days duration, in the course of which they settled broad questions of policy, involving war and peace. There was, however, often a curious lack of formal regularity about these assemblies. The gatherings of the Hanse contained, so Gierke tells us, now the representatives of some towns, and now those of some others. The leading cities, Lübeck and Hamburg, seem always to have been on hand; whatever the attendance, the decisions of the gathering bound the whole federation. Altogether, the organization of the Hanse League seems to have been very loose; the exchequer arrangements were quite indefinite; the executive leadership of Lübeck very much of the "muddling along" variety. The Rhenish City League, on the other hand, sprang into life in 1254 with a well-worked-out organization; but it did not last. Is there some deeper meaning in this curious contrast? It is certainly striking that the Swiss Federation—of all the territorial conglomerations the one which endured—also is distinguished by a vague set-up which only very gradually reached a distinctive federational pattern. However, even the earliest agreement, the Perpetual League of the three forest cantons, concluded in 1291 that they might "better defend themselves and their own," provided for recurrent consultation, and the settlement of dissension by an arbitral body of representatives. After 1353, there were fairly regular meetings or diets composed of representatives from the several members of the league, but no real executive was established during the entire lifetime of the old federation, down to 1798. Civil war occurred repeatedly, for example, 1442-1450 and again in 1531; the latter was engendered by the religious dissensions of the Reformation period, and ever afterward Switzerland remained internally divided by these fundamental antagonisms. Nevertheless, the federation lasted, and in the course of the nineteenth century the rising forces of integration produced a federal union in 1848. All federations have organized similar representative assemblies, and it would be tedious to describe them one by one. It will be enough to bring out one point which all these assemblies have in common, the equal representation of the members of the league. To be sure, there are occasional slight exceptions to this rule, as when the very powerful city of Ulm is given two votes in the Suabian City League. But even such deviations do not alter the fundamental truth that equality of the federated units is one of the keys to federational organization. The minimum effect of such equality is that each member has at least one vote. But often it goes much further. The rational foundation for such an arrangement is easy to perceive, as long as the actual differences between the federated units are not too great. It is certainly interesting that the same had been true, as far as we know, of the Achæan and the Ætolian Leagues of ancient Greece. The explanation offered for this equality is that if the smaller units had not been given equality, they would have been apt to break away. This had been the experience of the Hellenic League, in which the smaller cities felt themselves to be discriminated against and consequently tended to rebel. In contrast, the Achæan and the Ætolian Leagues hoped to create a centripetal force on the part of all the cities by basing their federations squarely on the cities as units. The reason underlying this decision is probably of general validity. But there is another reason. These leagues were mainly the result of external pressure; the federal movement resulted from a generally felt need. The Hellenic League, on the other hand, was created by the superior strength and leadership of Macedon; the dominant government therefore sought to preserve its position, as did Prussia in our own day. Such organizations should, perhaps, be distinguished altogether from real federations as crypto-leagues. It is interesting how this problem reappears in the League of Nations today (see also ¶ 8 below).

(2) **The common executive.**—Besides the federative assembly, there is the common executive. In federations whose sole objective is defense against common enemies, this executive will be of a military type. It was so in the Achæan and Ætolian Leagues, but the military commander was supported by a treasurer and general secretary. In early modern times, the complexity was great. In the Swiss federation, arrangements for even rudimentary military coöperation were made in terms of rules binding upon the member communities, rather than by setting up a unified command. Such unity as the recurrent warfare of the fourteenth and the fifteenth centuries entailed was brought about by *ad hoc* arrangements under the leadership of individual member governments; it is truly extraordinary how much action, not only defensive, but soon distinctly offensive in nature, was possible on the part of so vaguely organized a body. The Hanseatic League was almost as haphazard in providing for unity at the center. Here the common objectives were not only military, but commercial; yet skillful and unpretentious leadership on the part of Lübeck seems to have provided for the federation's need of executive direction. There was, however, a common treasury kept by Lübeck, and one gains the impression that Lübeck's leadership was to some extent justified in the eyes of the lesser confederates by

her willingness to make up the deficits. The United Provinces, on the other hand, set up a distinct federal executive at the outset. Although they were formally called to office by the representative Estates General, the able and skillful management of common affairs by the consecutive members of the house of Nassau and Orange soon gave their governorship a halo resembling that of the surrounding European monarchs. Well into the seventeenth century, however, their position was that of a federal executive, a highest magistrate, as it was so ably depicted in the political system of Johannes Althusius (Althaus). Under such a system, the executive is expected to carry out the decisions of the representatives of the federated governments, particularly in the field of foreign affairs, to maintain an effective military organization with the fiscal resources placed at his disposal, and in general to safeguard the common objectives of the federation.

(3) Judicial or arbitral set-up.—The final, and in some respects perhaps the most crucial feature of all genuine federations is the erection of some kind of arbitral machinery to prevent the outbreak of internal dissension. This phase of a federation is today recognized by all in the League of Nations. The Council's functions in this respect are numerous; "the importance attached to this function by the framers of the Covenant is shown by the fact that no less than seven articles of the twenty-six in that Constitution—numbers 10, 11, 12, 13, 15, 16, and 17—are concerned with the mediatory, arbitral, or punitive actions which the Council may take in behalf of the preservation of international peace." (Morley.) At the same time, the League of Nations' activity in this sphere has been complicated by the fact that the League is supposed not only to preserve peace amongst its members, but also to safeguard world peace. Since countries outside the League are actually, though not perhaps formally, beyond its jurisdiction, its arbitral activities have suffered from a certain confusion of objectives. Yet, on the other hand, the development of international judicial machinery has to some extent preceded the League. If we go back to earlier and less comprehensive federations, we find that some kind of judicial or arbitral bodies are always provided for the settlement of (a) disputes between the federated members, (b) disputes between a member and the federation. All these scattered experiences do not indicate any very clear trend. The means of coercion range all the way from diplomatic pressure through fines to actual war; in the Hanseatic League the extreme measure seems to have been exclusion from the League, called *Verhansung*, a measure which carried with it a boycott by all the members of the League. In view of the fact that the League comprised a very large portion of the trading towns of Northern Europe, such a boycott spelled disaster. At first it was largely used to enforce compliance with the decisions of the representative assemblies; later on it was used for the purpose of maintaining an aristocratic constitutional order in the cities; in the fourteenth century the League thus forced the city of Braunschweig to abolish its craft-guild government. After the maintenance of existing constitutions had been made a fundamental principle of the federation, in 1418, any internal change within the member-cities was apt to develop into a dispute between the member and the federation. Yet, while it is always formally possible to turn the arbitral powers of a federation toward the enforcement of such "constitutional uniformity," it is not in keeping with the facts to claim that such uniformity, or homogeneity, is a necessary concomitant of a federation, as has sometimes been done. The Swiss Federation contained all sorts of governments, ranging from the extreme democracies of the forest cantons to the arbitrary oligarchy of the city of Bern. The Achæan League, to cite another example, also abstained from going beyond the prohibition of tyranny. "This (prohibition of tyranny) was doubtless," says Ferguson, "a requirement of the federal laws, which, consisting of treaties . . . and of general enactments . . . bound the citizens of the individual cities no less than the local laws which they themselves passed. Otherwise the city-states were at liberty to adopt whatever form of government they chose." Turning the inherently necessary arbitral function to the task of enforcing "constitutional uniformity" may well be, as Gierke claims for the Hanse, an indication of coming collapse. At the same time, the constitutional provision of such homogeneity as we know it in the United States undoubtedly removes many aggravating problems with which arbitral bodies of a federation might not otherwise be able to deal. No attentive student of the League of Nations can fail to appreciate the cogency of that conclusion which was expounded by Immanuel Kant when he maintained that such a league presupposed that all government would become republican, i.e., popular. But whatever the weight one wishes to assign these advantages, constitutional uniformity is not essential to federation in general, or to the exercise of arbitral functions in particular. While in earlier days arbitral functions were often exercised by the federal assembly or by the federal executive (in minor disputes), even then there often appeared a distinct judicial organization. Thus the Rhenish City League of 1254 had an elaborate judicial set-up. The same was true of the United Provinces later. But these arbitral bodies usually recognized the autonomy of the members by providing that a representative from each of the contestants should participate in the arbitration of the dispute. Disputes between a particular member and the federation as a whole were even here settled by action of the representative assembly. It was, in other words, never so much a question of protecting the member against the whole, as holding the whole federation together and overcoming the unwillingness of the members to conform.

A pragmatic view of federal governments.—If we now turn from federations to the so-called federal states, that is, countries where the constitutional order divides power between a central and various local governments, we find that such a government is characterized simply by the fact that it resembles a confederation in respect to one or more of its organizational features; that is all. Nor is this very surprising in the case of those federal structures which have supplanted a preceding federation, as was the case in the United States, in Switzerland, and in Germany. The fact that such constitutional charters declare the local units "sovereign," does not need to disturb the political scientist; we have in such declarations simply a verbal concession to those who might oppose the establishment of the union—a concession to which nothing real corresponds (if ever anything real corresponds to the word "sovereignty" after the passing of the monarchical governments of the seventeenth and eighteenth centuries). In reality, once "we, the people . . ." or some equivalent person has constituted itself as the constituent power and made a constitution for the whole, from which the territorial subdivisions can no longer secede, we do not have a federation of governments, but one single government, even if it is federative in pattern, and its powers consequently divided between a central (national) government and local (state) governments. This fact may be contested by legalists, but it will actually manifest itself in coercive measures preventing secession, such as occurred in the *Sonderbundskrieg* in Switzerland, the Civil War in the United States, or the executions against Bavaria and Saxony under the Weimar Republic. The contrast with, let us say, the League of Nations, or the Pan-American Union is obvious. To show the way in which organizational features of a federation may be embedded in a constitutional order constitutes the pragmatic "theory" of federalism. It is of sufficient interest to warrant analysis of a few of the leading examples in the following paragraphs. In each case we shall have to inquire: (1) Is there a representative assembly legislating (and amending the constitution, if the latter is recognized as distinct) in which the local governments are represented as if they were equal, or nearly so; (2) do the local units as such have a part in selecting the executive or in conducting the executive work for the whole; (3) is there a judicial body or bodies for the settlement of disputes between local government units and the central government, and so forth. Let us first take up the representative assembly in the United States, Switzerland, and in Germany under the Empire and the Weimar Republic.

Federal representative assemblies: the problem of equality in the United States and Switzerland.—All three, the United States, Switzerland, and Germany, provided for participation of the component units in the formation of general policy and legislation for the whole commonwealth. Each has organized a scheme of representation for the whole which is a compromise between a federational scheme, in which the representative assembly is exclusively composed of representatives of the component units, and a unitary scheme in which national representation is based upon numerically equal subdivisions of the whole. Thus the Congress of the United States has the Senate and the House of Representatives to which correspond the Swiss Council of Estates as contrasted to the National Council, and again the German Federal Council as contrasted with the Reich Diet (*Reichstag*) under the Empire, the former of which was transformed into the Reich Council under the Republican constitution of 1919. This sort of compromise, dividing as it does the legislative power, provides a rather effective constitutional restraint, and one which appears reasonable.[1] It is, however, important to keep in mind the mounting criticism which has in recent years been levelled at the American Senate as "unrepresentative" of the people. What this means is that the federational equality of the component units within a federal structure conflicts with the "democratic" equality of the citizens within the federal whole and a consequent potential distortion of popular majorities. Thus, each voter of Nevada has one hundred and thirty-five times as much voting strength in the Senate

[1] Below we shall consider the desirability of such an arrangement in terms of the constitution as a political process. See para. 19.

as has each voter of New York, because Nevada has 77,000 inhabitants, and New York has 10,385,000.[1] Similarly, there are eighteen states with less than 1,000,000 inhabitants giving them (with an equal population) more than ten times the representation of New York state in the Senate. In certain matters over which the Senate has a large measure of control such as foreign or agricultural policy this difference may be of grave consequence, because region is arrayed against region. Certain writers, like W. Y. Elliott, have therefore argued that a maintenance of a federal scheme in the United States will require a consolidating and regrouping of the component units. "The states as at present geographically constituted have lost all reality as economic units. Even as rough boundaries of cultural unity and traditional loyalties, there are few of them that possess enough vitality to resist the inevitable march toward federal centralization." This view is hotly contested by some people, and not only states' righters; those strongly in favor of centralization feel, too, that such larger component units would be objectionable, because they would throw greater obstacles in the path of central authorities. Whatever the merits or demerits of such a change, the United States would still retain a federational representative assembly composed in part of representatives of the component units. In view of this fact, it may be well to consider whether the divergencies are not being exaggerated when we compare Nevada with New York. After all, Nevada and New York together contain less than ten per cent of the population of the United States. While the differences between the next two members, at both ends, Wyoming with 194,800 and Pennsylvania with 8,720,000, are still far apart, each voter in the former has only forty-five times the voting strength of the voter in the latter. If we list all the states in order of their population, we find that, with the exception of Nevada on one end and Pennsylvania and New York on the other, they constitute a series, few elements of which are more than 20 per cent apart, and the mean difference between them is roughly 12 per cent. In other words, they approximate a statistical continuum. (See table, page 187.)

Under such conditions, any ten consecutive states can be grouped together, and the voting weight of the inhabitants in each state will not deviate greatly from the mean voting weight of these ten states.

[1] These figures are based on the Census of 1920. The voting ratio as calculated on the basis of inhabitants is slightly distorted in favor of Nevada, since the families are smaller in Nevada, 3.5 as against 4 persons per family in New York.

Wyoming	is	151 %	greater than	Nevada
Delaware	is	14 %	" "	Wyoming
Arizona	is	49 %	" "	Delaware
Vermont	is	5 %	" "	Arizona
New Mexico	is	2 %	" "	Vermont
Idaho	is	19 %	" "	New Mexico
D. C.	is	2 %	" "	Idaho
New Hampshire	is	1 %	" "	D. C.
Utah	is	1 %	" "	New Hampshire
Montana	is	22 %	" "	Utah
Rhode Island	is	10 %	" "	Montana
South Dakota	is	5 %	" "	Rhode Island
North Dakota	is	2 %	" "	South Dakota
Maine	is	19 %	" "	North Dakota
Oregon	is	2 %	" "	Maine
Florida	is	24 %	" "	Oregon
Nebraska	is	34 %	" "	Florida
Washington	is	5 %	" "	Nebraska
Connecticut	is	2 %	" "	Washington
Maryland	is	5 %	" "	Connecticut
West Virginia	is	1 %	" "	Maryland
South Carolina	is	15 %	" "	West Virginia
Arkansas	is	4 %	" "	South Carolina
Kansas	is	1 %	" "	Arkansas
Mississippi	is	1 %	" "	Kansas
Louisiana	is	.4%	" "	Mississippi
Oklahoma	is	13 %	" "	Louisiana
Virginia	is	14 %	" "	Oklahoma
Tennessee	is	1 %	" "	Virginia
Alabama	is	5 %	" "	Tennessee
Minnesota	is	2 %	" "	Alabama
Iowa	is	.7%	" "	Minnesota
Kentucky	is	.6%	" "	Iowa
North Carolina	is	6 %	" "	Kentucky
Wisconsin	is	3 %	" "	North Carolina
Georgia	is	10 %	" "	Wisconsin
Indiana	is	1 %	" "	Georgia
New Jersey	is	7 %	" "	Indiana
Missouri	is	8 %	" "	New Jersey
California	is	.7%	" "	Missouri
Michigan	is	7 %	" "	California
Massachusetts	is	5 %	" "	Michigan
Texas	is	21 %	" "	Massachusetts
Ohio	is	23 %	" "	Texas
Illinois	is	13 %	" "	Ohio
Pennsylvania	is	34 %	" "	Illinois
New York	is	19 %	" "	Pennsylvania

Also the regional groupings average up, as is shown by the regional groupings in the Statistical Abstract of the United States.[1] The

[1] The same would be true of the regions which Professor Elliott wishes to consolidate into regional commonwealth. When taken as such groups, they already have a voting strength in the Senate much more nearly equal than the individual votes by states.

division called "Mountain" with eight states, and therefore sixteen votes, has only 3,336,000 inhabitants, whereas New England, with 7,400,000 inhabitants, contains only six states giving her twelve votes, but that difference is not too serious. On the whole, equal representation in the Senate appears still reasonable, because the total picture reveals very gradual increases in the size of states, and a resulting relatively low deviation at the centre where the 30 states containing more than 50 per cent of the population of the United States do not deviate more than 89.7 per cent from their mean voting weight. On the whole, equal representation in the Senate is not so absurd as is claimed at times, and does not seem to require an immediate overhauling of the whole machinery.

The Swiss have likewise provided strict equality of the component units, called cantons, in their Council of Estates. Further concessions are made to their federational past by leaving the election and tenure of these representatives (two for each canton, and one for each half-canton) to the cantons themselves. As Professor Brooks remarks, the Council of Estates, or States as he prefers to say, "was designed in a peculiar sense to represent the cantons. Consequently it was felt that the latter should be left to decide everything possible regarding the make-up of this body." Unlike the Senate of the United States, the Swiss States' Council is on an even keel with the popular National Council, as far as functions are concerned; it has neither more nor less. Once the members are elected, they are, however, no longer dependent upon the cantons; legally, they cannot be instructed regarding their vote. Actually, there is between them and their electors the usual interplay of forces. In most cantons today, the members of the States' Council are elected by the people; but in some of them election is still by the cantonal representative assembly. In recent years, the principle of equal representation has been attacked, and efforts have been made from time to time to introduce a system which would take account of the differences in population. For in Switzerland, too, the differences between the weight of votes is quite striking. A citizen in the canton of Uri with 23,000 inhabitants has thirty times as much influence upon federal legislation through the States' Council as has a citizen of the canton of Bern with 690,249. However, no such efforts have thus far been successful. In spite of these divergencies, Swiss cantons are roughly like American states in that they can be arranged in a series in which no two consecutive elements differ excessively from each other. Their population figures, too, form a fair statistical continuum.

The German case.—Not so in Germany. Here the state of Prussia contained, according to the 1925 census, roughly three-fifths of the population of the whole country, with the next largest state, Bavaria, containing less than one-fifth of the population of Prussia, and the smallest state, Schaumburg-Lippe, 24,000, or one sixteen-hundredth of that of Prussia. Under such conditions, a mechanical application of the principle of equal representation was entirely out of the question. As a result, the imperial constitution sought a compromise solution which was largely followed by the Republican constitution of 1919. This compromise still recognized the minimum of equality among the component units by giving each state at least one vote in the Federal Council; it also recognized equality by reducing the difference between Prussia and the other states; nevertheless it differentiated between the states by assigning them markedly different voting strength in the Federal Council. One might therefore at first sight be inclined to feel that the nature of this council is un-federal: the provision of Article 61 of the Weimar constitution that there shall be one vote for each seven hundred thousand inhabitants certainly violates the principle of state equality. The two qualifying provisions that (1) no state shall be represented by more than two-fifths of all the votes (which equals two-thirds of the remaining votes), and that (2) every state shall have at least one vote are, however, derived from the principle of state equality. The further provision which divided the Prussian votes between the state government and the thirteen provinces gave additional scope to the equalitarian idea. We therefore had the following distribution:

Pop.[1]	State	Vote[2]	Pop.	State	Vote
38,791	Prussia	26	674	Mecklenburg-Schwerin	1
	State Govt.	13	545	Oldenburg	1
	Provinces	13	501	Brunswick	1
7,477	Bavaria	11	351	Anhalt	1
4,992	Saxony	7	338	Bremen	1
2,580	Württemberg	4	163	Lippe	1
2,312	Baden	3	127	Lübeck	1
1,609	Thuringia	2	110	Mecklenburg-Strelitz	1
1,347	Hesse	2	24	Schaumburg-Lippe	1
1,152	Hamburg	2			

[1] Figures in thousands, according to census of 1925.

[2] Figures for 1928. Before 1928 there existed a separate state of Waldeck which had one vote for 28,000 inhabitants; after its incorporation Prussia could not have more than twenty-six votes (two-thirds of forty votes).

It will be seen from these figures that about 1,437,000 inhabitants of Prussia are represented by one vote in the Council, while about 24,000 inhabitants of Schaumburg-Lippe are represented by another. Therefore the representation of Schaumburg-Lippe is about sixty times as large as that of Prussia. Leaving, however, Schaumburg-Lippe and Prussia out of account, we find the next widest margin, between Mecklenburg-Strelitz and Bavaria, to be still almost one to seven. Such inequalities are a striking testimony of the persistence of a considerable measure of equality of the members. This conclusion is strengthened, if we go beyond the rather formal question of how many votes each member state has in the Council and ask (1) who creates these representatives, and (2) how do they vote.[1] In answer to the first question we find that state governments were represented by members of their cabinets. A glance at the list of members shows that the leading members of each state cabinet were delegates (*Bevollmächtigte*) of their respective governments; each delegation to the Council was headed by the Prime Minister. It would, of course, be absurd to suppose that these men were constantly in session at Berlin. They could not devote their time to it any more than the Governors of American states. Were the Federal and later the National (Reich) Council meeting only once in a while for a short time? Not at all; the very opposite was the truth. These councils were practically permanent. The diminution in the power of the Council under the Republic did not lead to a diminution of its business. How, then, was the dilemma solved? By appointing deputy delegates. These deputy delegates were not substitutes for the regular delegates; they were themselves direct delegates of states, besides whom personal substitutes were allowed. A surprisingly large number of such deputy delegates existed, often several for each regular delegate. Who were these deputy delegates? They were usually permanent officials of the respective ministries who handled certain Council business as part of their regular routine. Prussia, whose capital—Berlin—was also the national capital, found herself in an especially advantageous position. Her officials merely had to take a taxi to attend the Council meetings. The other larger states, like Bavaria, maintained as head of their delegation a permanent resident minister who was in general charge of business in the Council. These

[1] It will facilitate the task of answering these questions, if we first consider them in their application to all the states except Prussia, and then treat Prussia separately.

officials were, historically speaking, remnants of former times when the delegations from Prussia, Bavaria, and the other "sovereign states" had met as a Council of Ambassadors at Frankfurt. Under the Council procedure, these ministers became an integral part of the constitutional fabric; when other delegates and deputy delegates were absent, they would cast all the votes for the state they represented. This leads us to a summary answer of our second question: how did delegates in the Council vote? They always voted *en bloc,* in other words the delegation of each state cast its vote as a whole, as they do in the electoral college in the United States. This was possible, because the delegations were definitely instructed, and ready to act on their instructions, since they were composed of members of the administrative hierarchy in the several states. What is even more important is the fact that most of the business of these Councils was transacted in their standing committees. It seems quite natural that a group of administrative officials had no great inclination to avail themselves of plenary debates; the more intimate discussion in committees composed of "experts" like themselves was more in keeping with their methods of work. There were eleven such committees: (1) Foreign Affairs, (2) Economic Affairs, (3) Internal Administration (including police), (4) Communciations, (5) Budgets and accounts, (6) Taxes and customs, (7) Justice, (8) The Constitution and Procedure in the Council, (9) National Defense, (10) Maritime Affairs, (11) Execution of the Peace Treaty. Now, in these committees Prussia, Bavaria, Saxony, and Württemberg each had one vote. Baden had one in all but that on Maritime Affairs, where her seat was given to Hamburg. The rest of the membership of these committees (usually there were nine members) was scattered among the other members according to their interests. Under the Republic the meetings of these committees were presided over by a national cabinet minister, or a high official of his ministry in his stead, usually the Minister of the Interior; even before the war running this Council had already become one of the important functions of the Ministry of the Interior (then of Prussia). Not being a member of the Council, the presiding officer under the Republic never had a vote. The discussion so far has shown that membership in the committees went to the states, not to individual delegates (as in the United States Senate). This practice, in accord with the general principles of organization governing the Council, on the one hand strengthened its federalistic quality and probably more than balanced the infringement entailed by sacrificing complete equality. On the other hand, it facilitated the practice of the states of sending officials who were specialists in particular fields of legislation and administration to attend meetings of particular committees when certain bills were pending. In this connection it is worth noting that the Council's committees did in a measure correspond to the ministerial organization of the several governments. Obviously this kind of conciliar organization of the representation of the member governments under the German constitutions is essentially modelled after the procedure of an international congress, or a federational assembly: the delegates vote by states, they act according to instructions, they are members of the administrative branch of the several governments. Seen in the large, it appears to have been an endeavour to integrate the several administrative centers which the member governments had built up in the centuries before Germany had a national government. As such it is functionally related to the German scheme of leaving much of the execution of federal legislation to the state governments, a question which brings us to our second question. But before we enter into it, we must, for the sake of real understanding, supplement the foregoing with a description of the special arrangements made for Prussia under the Republic.

The Prussian anomaly.—It will be remembered that the Prussian delegation was omitted from consideration because of the provincial delegates. This curious plan of splitting the Prussian delegation under the Weimar constitution resulted from a desire to destroy Prussian domination of the Council. In pre-war Germany, Prussia had been able to manipulate the work of the Council; for although she did not have an absolute majority, the number of her votes (then seventeen) was large enough for most practical purposes. They were, in the first place, sufficient to block amendments to the constitution. Certain crucial legislative matters like those touching the army, the navy, and taxation were also subject to a veto power given to Prussia. A vigorous policy of securing the collaboration of the very small states bordering on Prussia, or completely surrounded by her, actually turned this "equality" of the smallest units into a method of enhancing the predominance of Prussia; the prince of Waldeck went so far as to surrender the government of his principality entirely to Prussia. It was this peculiar set-up which might tempt one to describe the German Empire as a crypto-federalism. Whatever it was, the political power of Prussia had aroused deep antagonism, and Hugo

Preuss' first draft of a republican constitution had provided for the break-up of Prussia into several parts small enough to place them on a fairly even footing with the other states. But this plan encountered unsurmountable opposition. Its national centralizing implications were suspect in Bavaria and elsewhere among federalists, its decentralizing, federalizing implications for the large part of Germany which was comprised within Prussia provoked the advocates of an unitary Reich. Many who did not care for the old Prussia, looked upon it, nevertheless, as the iron clasp by which Germany might hold together under the separatist strain of post-war developments, particularly in the Rhineland. Preuss' radical scheme thus blocked, the constitutional provisions actually adopted were a compromise. In order to destroy Prussian domination in the Council, not only was her representation limited to two-fifths of the whole membership, as we have seen, but the provinces, thirteen in all, were given half of the representatives, or one each. Thus the Prussian government could instruct only thirteen of the sixty-six votes in the Council, or only two more than Bavaria. The other thirteen were chosen by the provincial councils, a body elected by the people of the province, and not part of the central administration, as they had formerly been. The provincial delegates thus resembled members of the American Senate before direct election was introduced. As a consequence, we find them to be farmers, professional men, and the like, rather than high government officials. The Prussian government tried to hold these provincial delegates in line, but it was frequently unsuccessful. This is not surprising. The provincial delegate was elected shortly after the election of the provincial council which sent him; he could not be recalled. When the council went out of office, he did too. Inasmuch as the elections in the provinces came at different times, the provincial delegates came and went in a rather irregular fashion. Nor could they readily be instructed. That is, there was no effective way of making the instruction binding upon the delegate. As a result of these circumstances, the provincial delegates voted against the Prussian delegation as well as against each other. There was no voting *en bloc* any longer. Thus on July 14, 1921, and often thereafter, the elected members voted against the appointed ones. A memorandum of the Minister of the Interior took it for granted that some of the provincial delegates would vote with Bavaria against Prussia. Statistics also show continued irregularity. Between 1921 and 1928 (when reforms were being discussed) Prussia's government had the support of all the provincial delegates only forty-eight times, out of a total of two hundred and fifty-seven roll calls. In sixty-three roll calls Prussia had only the same number of votes as Bavaria or less. Moreover, the possibility of threatening independent action affected the decisions of the Prussian government, and obliged it to make concessions. Partisan considerations also played a role, and gradually became serious. A careful analysis of these situations has not been made. The truth of the matter was that the arrangements for the provincial delegates were based upon ideas derived from predominantly legislative bodies, such as the United States Senate; they were therefore not in consonance with the conciliar structure as a whole, tied in as that was with the administrative branch. But the most paradoxical consequence of these complicated arrangements was the political result. In the Empire, Prussia had been the conservative stumbling block of progress. Under the Republic, Prussia had one of the most progressive governments, the so-called Weimar coalition (see below, Chap. XIX) remaining in power practically the entire time, until it was forcibly and illegally ousted in July 1932. Splitting off the provincial delegates thus crippled the republican efforts of Prussia; the conservative or rather reactionary elements in some of the provinces could combine with their partisans in Bavaria and elsewhere. It is another one of the striking illustrations of how men fail to appreciate the indirect effects of changes in political organization. All in all, however, the provision of these provincial delegates did not alter the federal character of the Reich Council. By injecting a measure of federalism into Prussia, it rather strengthened federalism. But the weakened position of the Council under the Republic counteracted that gain. It is better to postpone a more detailed consideration of the problems concerning the relation of the Reich Council and the Reich Diet to the chapter on Parliaments (see below, Chap. XXI). Whatever its power, the retention of the council type was probably a mistake. We may say that the chamber type of federal representative assembly seems to be better adapted to popular governments, because it responds more readily to the party system without which popular government cannot be successfully operated. In fact, the council system of German federalism was a very peculiar device for integrating autonomous administrative systems—strictly analogous to the Council of the League of Nations and other outright federations. For that function the council type of representative assembly is better adapted than the chamber type, and it is worth noting that the conception of the American Senate, as revealed through the debates of the constitutional convention of 1787, was rather conciliar. It was through a slow process of gradual adaptation that the Senate evolved into its modern form; the lack of any elaborate administrative set-up in the states and the parallel emergence of a system of the same two parties in Congress and the state legislatures no doubt greatly aided this process.

The distribution of functions: a matter of expediency.—If the composition of these federal representative assemblies thus startles the student by a wealth of heterogeneous forms, the distribution of their functions is even more complex. Many federal constitutions contain long catalogues of what the federal legislature may do; for example, the American Constitution is relatively simple as compared to the German Republican constitution. It goes without saying that such divisions of the competencies must and will vary according to time and space. Economic and social life, the military and geographical factors, all will play their role in determining the particular assortment. From a political standpoint, no distinctive generalization or principle has been derived. It is a question of more or less on both accounts, with a general implication that if the functions of the central government are increasing at the expense of those of the local governments, a tendency or trend toward transforming the federal into a unitary government is likely to be present. Lawyers have made a great deal of the difference between a central government with powers specifically delegated to it, such as that of the United States, Switzerland, and Germany, as compared to the Canadian set-up with powers specifically delegated to the provinces. The existence of residuary powers has even been held to constitute the decisive test of "statehood" for the component units. In reality, such residuary powers are a delusion, if the powers or functions delegated to the central government are practically all-embracing, as they were in Republican Germany; broad delegated powers would mean more "local government" in actual practice than such a "residue" of "genuine self-determination." For in either case, the only guaranty for whatever distribution of functions there is, delegated or residuary, is the constitution which determines the governmental structure as a whole. And for that reason the really decisive question as far as functions are concerned is this: Do the local units, states, cantons, *Länder*, provinces, dominions, or whatever you call them, actually participate as such in the process of amending and altering the constitution, either through their representatives in the federal representative assembly or directly or both? To this thorny question we must now turn.

Participation of the component units in the amending power.—Every federal system of government we have examined provides for the participation of the local units in the amending power. The particular provisions in the American and Swiss Constitutions we have described in an earlier chapter (IX, ¶ 9), when we discussed the general problems of this power and its relation to the constituent power (IX, particularly ¶¶ 6-8, and 12). Here as in Switzerland and Germany, the provisions for a constitutional amendment developed quite organically from those of a preceding federational compact. In fact, we probably could trace a clear realization of the importance of and a practical procedure for the amending process to the federational origin of these constitutions. Certainly before the adoption of the Constitution of the United States the need for adequate amending provisions was not distinctly perceived (see above p. 117). On the other hand, the various federations of an earlier time all had faced this issue of changing their league charters, usually through the action of instructed delegates. The United States and Switzerland, it will be recalled, both provided for participation of the local units as such in the amending process. In both countries, the component states' representatives in the federal representative assembly as well as the component states themselves must assent by qualified majorities. In the United States the local legislatures or special conventions have to "ratify" the amendment as proposed by the Congress; in Switzerland amendments proposed by the federal legislature (or by a popular initiative) must like ordinary laws be ratified by a majority of the cantons, as well as by a majority of the voters at large. To be sure, disagreements sufficiently wide to make popular majority and cantonal majorities vote opposite are rare (among the thirty-two amendments noted by Brooks there was only one such disagreement), but this is hardly surprising since the federal representative assembly already represents the two majorities. In Germany, both under the Empire and under the Republic, no direct participation of the territories (*Länder*) or their electorates was required. This was natural enough under the Empire, since constitutional amendments had to be adopted by the Federal Council, which was composed of direct representatives of the several monarchs, as behoved an "eternal union" of princes. Under the Republic, however, this omission was the more noteworthy in view of the weakened position of the National Council. As we have seen, this Council had lost much of its representative quality. Nevertheless, two-thirds of its votes had to be cast in favor of constitutional amendments, and if it refused thus to "ratify" the amendments proposed by the Diet, they were supposed to be submitted to a popular referendum. This latter procedure was never actually invoked; but it shows that ultimately constitutional amendments could be put through without the consent of even an ordinary simple majority of the states. The realization of this fact presumably affected the attitude of the Council when confronted with constitutional amendments, according to the rule of anticipated reactions (see Chap. I, ¶ 17). The rudimentary proportions to which the component units were thus reduced in the German Republic's constitutional amending process suggest the possibility that this federal structure might in the course of time have completely disappeared. This is particularly arguable in view of the famous Article 18, according to which a component unit could be broken up or entirely transferred. Although known under the title of *Lex Antiborussica*, this article actually permitted Waldeck to vote its total absorption into Prussia, while the attempts to reëstablish an independent Hanover or to set up an independent Upper Silesia failed. When the Republic collapsed, several other small territories were considering the possibility of following the example of Waldeck. Whatever the future might have brought, the amending power under the Weimar constitution was certainly not federalistically organized. Whether on account of this fact one wishes to assert that Germany had ceased to be a "federal state" is a matter of definitions; certain it is that her governmental and constitutional structure was federal in many other respects. In contrast to the vanishing German federalism, the emergent federal structure of the British Commonwealth (see below, ¶ 16) shows this typically federal participation of the component units, England and the Dominions, in the determination of the constitutional order through the Imperial Conference, whose acts must be implemented by acts of the several Parliaments. This form of evolving constitutional uniformity is quite in keeping with the British tradition of drawing no clear distinction between constitutional and other legal rules. If the British constitution proper was allowed to evolve as a congeries of rules, regulations, and customs, it is natural that the Commonwealth should follow in these footsteps. Yet, attentive students of this development have been able to point out a distinctive pattern of Commonwealth-Empire relationships which partake of the "constitutional" order. Its federational type has engendered considerable controversy among the sovereignty-hunters, and various incompatible conclusions have been drawn. It would serve no useful purpose to survey these here. It will be interesting to watch, however, whether the British will not gradually be diverted from their older tradition of treating constitutional rules on a par with ordinary legislation. For the rise of constitutions embodied in a single document has had one of its most powerful stimulants in the needs of federal governmental structures. In setting up fairly permanent adjustments between the central and the local governments, such documents have served a most useful purpose in the political life of peoples as closely akin to the English as the Americans and the Swiss, not to speak of several Dominions who themselves are part of the Commonwealth.

Federal executives.—Our second organizational feature of a federation was found, it will be remembered, in the executive-administrative sphere. The local units as such either have a part in selecting the federal executive or in conducting the executive work for the whole or both. Our federal structures in the United States, Switzerland, Germany, and the Dominions all satisfy this criterion. To be sure, in none of them (except the German Empire) have the local units more than fragments of the power of selecting the federal executive. Thus in the United States, we may say that voting by states in the electoral college is a partial recognition of the states; for the President is not elected by a majority of the whole people (as under the German Republic) but by a majority of state majorities. Another fragment of state participation is the constitutional right of the Senate to advise on and consent to presidential appointments. Out of this has grown the rather important tradition of "senatorial courtesy." It is a kind of liberum veto, and means no more than this: that while the Senate will not suggest particular nominations, it expects that the President, in naming certain local office-holders will choose persons satisfactory to the Senator or Senators of the President's political party from the state in which the offices are located, or from which the appointees come. "The strength of the pack is the wolf, and the strength of the wolf is the pack." Particularly through the latter, but also through the former, particularistic considerations are given a considerable weight in making national decisions. The President's desire to hold certain states in line for renomination affects his policies, as well as his appointments, and the Senate's regional sensibilities insure to the citizens of all the states a certain measure of "opportunity." It is difficult to assess the relative advantages and disadvantages of these practices. In Switzerland, the president and the executive council are elected by the lower house of the legislature, but the existence of the local units plays some role in the tradition that the two large cantons of Bern and Zürich should be represented on the council, and that the remainder should be evenly distributed among the other cantons. This means primarily that the French and Italian cantons get at least one or two members. Finally, in Germany, under the Republic, there was hardly any such participation, since the President was elected by the nation at large, and no patronage system in terms of the several states could be imposed by the weak Reich Council. On the other hand, and perhaps partly to balance this, the states in Germany had a particularly large part in conducting the executive and administrative work for the federal government. Under the Republic as well as under the Empire, the member states were administering a good part of federal legislation, though there was a gradual increase in national administrative organization. This arrangement was in marked contrast to the situation in the United States and other federal structures; the existence of a large and highly efficient administrative organization in Prussia, covering three-fifths of the Reich's population and centered at Berlin, undoubtedly had a great deal to do with it. Now under the Empire, the supervision of this executive and administrative activity, though briefly provided for in the constitution, never became much of a practical issue. The Republic, on the other hand, undertook to put teeth into supervision. Under a somewhat broader, though quite controversial, constitutional grant of power (Article 15) the central government could and did send delegates to the states to inspect the execution of Reich law. These delegates or commissioners did not have executive or administrative authority themselves; they merely could ask questions, look into files, hear testimony. If they found something wrong, it was up to the central government to address a complaint to the government of the state. But what if the government of the state paid no attention? In such cases, the central government was given the authority to enforce its view, under Article 48, though the state government could appeal the matter to the Court of State. This "execution" was by no means a paper rule, but came into play time and again, against Saxony, Thuringia, and finally against Prussia in the summer of 1932. This formidable power, part of which corresponded to the presidential emergency powers in the United States, rendered the supervisory powers of the central government fairly effective, and commissioners appeared time and again to break down local nullification. But the arrangement cannot, on the whole, be judged very satisfactory. A detailed examination of these conflicts shows that they invariably arose when different parties controlled the central and local governments. In the earlier cases of Saxony and Thuringia, the central government was opposed to the radicalism of the local governments, and these provisions provided a convenient pretext for proceeding against them. Later on, in the case of Bavaria, reactionary tendencies provoked the conflict. The complications between Thuringia and the central government in 1931 were engendered by the Nazis' entry into the Thuringian government. Finally, and most seriously, the conflict between Prussia and the Reich which led to the deposition of the Prussian government in July 1932, was brought about by the unwillingness of the Prussian government to follow the reaction which was in full swing in the central government under von Papen. This was frankly stated in the arguments before the Court of State, as well as in the daily press. Though such an interpretation of the constitution was violently attacked by the lawyers for the state of Prussia and others, and though the Court later held that Prussia had not violated any of its obligations or duties, the Commissioner who had displaced the Prussian government remained in office; the German federal structure had collapsed. The central government had displaced the state government in all but name.

The constitutional judiciary.—The controversies discussed at the end of the last paragraph have obliged us to refer several times to a German judicial body, thus showing that the third organization feature of a federation was also present here. In this function, the Imperial Federal Council was replaced by the Court of State, organized especially for the purpose of dealing with these controversies between the central government and the states, and between the several states, as well as with other constitutional issues. Practically every one of the conflicts was brought before the Court by the respective state government. On the whole, the Court showed a decided disposition to give the central government the benefit of the doubt. In the Prussian case, however, the Court was obliged to decide in part against the central government. Unfortunately, by straddling the issue, the Court managed to discredit itself with both sides of the controversy. We find such a judicial body for the settlement of disputes between the central and local authorities in all the other federal systems. This is well-known in the United States. Here the Supreme Court has not followed a consistent course, as between the central and the local governments. Under Marshall, the Court was nationally minded and several of his most famous decisions, like *McCulloch v. Maryland* and *Gibbons v. Ogden*, asserted doctrines which favored the central government. Later on, the Court in the course of the slavery controversy, shifted toward a "states' rights" position which culminated in the ill-starred Dred Scott decision. After the Civil War, the Court returned to its earlier outlook. There was prevalent a feeling that the war had settled all questions in favor of the central government. The doubtful logic of this sentiment has recently become manifest by the court's swing back to a states' rights viewpoint. But whatever the merits of detailed issues under dispute, the notion of judicial settlement of such disputes between local and central authorities remains as a clear indication of the federal nature of the American governmental structure. This is likewise the case in Switzerland, and it is noteworthy that provisions, similar to the German provisions, about the administration of federal legislation by the cantons have not resulted in similar complications. This is probably due to the fact that the cantons have been less sharply divided by partisan issues (neither Communism nor Fascism assuming serious proportions), and that the central government has practiced marked moderation in employing force, relying rather upon persuasion and other kinds of pressure. But there have been different situations, as we noted above. In all these governmental set-ups we observe then that an arbitral or judicial method for the settling of constitutional controversies affecting the federal structure is provided. In the preceding chapter we have shown the general importance of such provisions, because they tie in with, and thereby strengthen, the whole constitutional system. In the British Commonwealth of Nations we find that such constitutional controversies go before the Judicial Committee of the Privy Council and the new Commonwealth Tribunal. The former interprets the several Dominion constitutions in relation to the law of the mother country, the latter settles justiciable disputes between the governments of the British Commonwealth. It is not a permanent court, but rather it provides the framework for the arbitral settlement of each dispute; its use is discretionary with the disputants and membership is determined anew in each case, the number of arbitrators being five. Students of the British Commonwealth consider this set-up another step in the direction of organizing a confederate Crown for the whole Commonwealth, because it keeps the Dominions from appealing to the Permanent Court of International Justice or to the League. Here we have the emergence of institutional patterns of federalism in a governmental structure subject to marked forces of decentralization and local autonomy in certain areas. This process is of considerable interest, because it contradicts an assumption often made in nineteenth century discussions about federalism and the federal state, namely, that the federal state is nothing but a half-way house toward a unitary state with an orthodox "sovereign." This assumption is due perhaps to the unquestioning acceptance of nationalism as a permanent factor. Actually, even in these terms the manifest trend in Austria-Hungary might have cautioned a realistic observer. At any rate, we may ask today whether the emergence of such institutional patterns of a federal structure justifies us in considering the congeries of governments comprised under the term British Empire (including the British Commonwealth of Nations) as together constituting a federal government. To this problem we now turn.

The problem raised by the British Commonwealth of Nations.—Certainly the British Empire as a whole is best described as a federal structure of government. In asserting this, one runs counter to the prevailing opinion. We may discard the arguments of those who center their attention upon sovereignty, though in their learned efforts they have set forth many important items of detailed constitutional behavior which must be included in any analysis. But even realistic students have argued that the Commonwealth, at least, is a federation of "independent states" rather than a federal state. Only a common military establishment has held them together, they say. This "only" is, however, a most fundamental qualification. Security and the military establishment are, as we have seen, at the very core of modern government. What shall we say of the German Empire, then, in which Bavaria actually had its separate army? Did it not possess a common federal structure of government? And how is it that this "league of independent states" is at the same time a part of the British Empire? To be sure, the Dominions have also separate military establishments and they possess some separate diplomatic representatives, in the League of Nations, at Washington and so on. But did not France have a separate minister at Munich? Did that make Germany a "league of independent states"? As we have shown, every common federal structure of government, every federal state—to use the old phraseology—leaves a great many functions to the local units. In fact, most of these federal structures indicate the sphere of the central government as one of delegated powers, with the residuary powers left to the local governments. What particular functions these are appears to be purely a matter of expediency. In the British Empire, Great Britain, which might be called the central government of the Commonwealth of Nations, while it assuredly is also the local government of one of its component units, handles (by agreement through Imperial Conferences, acting as representative assemblies) naval, and to a considerable extent other military affairs, aided by the Imperial Defense Committee. It also handles Colonies and Dependencies, and a considerable part of foreign policy, the local units merely retaining a rather dubious veto power. This veto power is dubious in the light of what is known about the conduct of modern diplomacy (see above, Chap. V). The difference between this sort of arrangement and a "league" or "federation" can readily be seen, when we compare the actual set-up in such organizations and find that *not a single one* shows a common military establishment. This is well-known in the case of the League of Nations. But the same is true of the German Federation and the Swiss Federation, not to speak of earlier leagues. A common military establishment, if of any military significance as compared to the military establishment of the local units, indicates the existence of a common government. Another decisive pragmatic test is secession. The existence of a federation is indicated only if secession by one or more of the federated governments is looked upon as part of the accepted order of things and does actually occur. The League of Nations, the Swiss Federation, and the Hanse, as well as many other historic confederations (or federations, or leagues) of actually separate governments have recognized the withdrawal of membership. Not so the British Empire—though it has been claimed by the Irish Free State as a "right," just as it used to be by John Calhoun and his friends for the states composing the American Union. That such a claim should be advanced, deserves the attention of political observers; but it should not be confounded with the general acceptance of withdrawal as part and parcel of the governmental set-up. If that common government, as a matter of fact, possesses the organizational features of a federation as it has been outlined in previous paragraphs, its structure is federal. Therefore, the British Empire is federal today. It has a representative assembly in which the local governments, Great Britain and the Dominions, are recognized as equal in law. This representative assembly is evolving the constitution for the whole Empire (in the larger sense), and is collaborating with certain offices, like the Foreign Office, which are being conducted by Great Britain for the whole (just as Prussia conducted the foreign policy for the German Empire). This collaboration takes the form of "consultation" which is acclaimed as the magic formula for strengthening the bonds between the several Dominions and Great Britain. As far as the executive branch is concerned, we find that the local units indeed share in its conduct. For since 1904 an Imperial Defense Committee uniting in a rather informal way various cabinet members in Great Britain and the Dominions, as well as other officials, around a permanent secretariat, has taken a definite hand in military questions, though in a purely advisory way. During the war its functions were greatly expanded, and it became a "War Council" coördinating the war machine of Great Britain, and keeping elaborate records. In the words of Lord Balfour, the Committee of Imperial Defense provides "a continuing instrument of consultation within and without the Government Departments, the ministers responsible to the British Parliament, and, when they desire it, the ministers responsible to the Dominion Parliaments. But nowhere and under no conditions can it modify or limit parliamentary control or ministerial responsibility." As far as this latter problem is concerned, the British have developed the same device which was so popular with seventeenth century monarchs in central Europe: a common crown dealing with each local Parliament separately. The dualism in the Hapsburg Empire down to the World War was a survival. Of course, the impersonal nature of the "crown" and its complete dependence upon the several Parliaments through parliamentary responsibility of its ministers makes such "personal union" much more precarious now than it was in the past. Federal governmental structures are, however, always somewhat precarious. The greatest measure of local autonomy does not transform a common government—the confederate crown, as it has been called for the British Empire—into a federation of governments. To come to our third criterion, there is finally, as we have already seen, a judicial body, the Commonwealth Tribunal (as well as the Judicial Committee of the Privy Council). In other words, we are forced to the conclusion that the British Empire today is governed by a federal structure of authorities which, although like all federal structures it shows the impact of the particular historical forces which shaped it, shows the general characteristics of such a structure as an integral part of a *common* government covering in its various ramifications the whole Empire. And inasmuch as this Empire was at one time not so very far removed from a unitary government, it is also the most striking modern illustration of a government becoming federalized. To the trend from federation through federalism to unity, emphasized in the nineteenth century, we must add the opposite trend from unity toward federalism, as indeed a more extended view of history should have maintained right along.

Federalism versus decentralization.—As long as unitary government is thought of as centralized government, there is no great difficulty in distinguishing between it and a federal structure. But what if the unitary government should be decentralized, as it has been in England or Prussia? In fact, in the latter there appeared after the war a State Council organized somewhat like the United States Senate, which gave Prussia at least one element of a federal structure (thus placing her on a level with the Netherlands, which also have an upper house of that type). Are there no distinctions between such a decentralized government and a federal one, as one distinguished scholar has recently asserted? Is it merely a matter of "the territorial composition of the state"? Can "no issues different in kind" be raised in regard to one or the other? The preceding discussion ought to have shown that the answer to these questions is in the negative, and not only in terms of "the time-honored divisions of Federalism and Local Government." The difference is precisely this, that federalism affords a constitutional sanction to the territorial division of governmental powers, the change of which is beyond the reach of the central government. Of decentralized England it can be said that "the British system is nevertheless dominated by the idea that all legislative power is presumed to lie in the first instance in the king in Parliament and all executive power in the Crown—a twofold constitutional principle which represents the very apotheosis of centralization." But even if elements of decentralization should be supported by a constitutional sanction, as they are in many American states, and as perhaps local government was in England at one time —for we must not forget that the English Parliament changes the constitution as well as legislates—we do not have federalism, unless the local units are represented as such in the representative assembly which changes the constitution (and legislates), and unless these units' powers are safeguarded by adequate arrangements for a constitutional judiciary. This contrast is strictly pragmatic, and enables one at any time to determine whether a particular governmental structure is federal or decentralized.

Conclusions: strength and weakness of federal structures of government.—The foregoing shows that federalism is intimately related to modern constitutionalism, as indeed is suggested by its rise alongside of it. There is nothing in the distinction between federalism and decentralization which would imply an inherent superiority of one over the other; their advantages and disadvantages can only be contrasted in terms of the peculiar conditions of the time and place under which a particular government is supposed to operate. If one reflects upon the whole array of human experience with federalism, he is led to the conclusion that it is essentially a part of modern constitutionalism. A federal governmental structure provides a regional, as distinguished from a functional, division of powers. Such a division operates as a rather effective restraint upon the exercise of governmental powers. Indeed, in many situations it is more likely to be effective than a functional division, for this, as we have seen, can be more readily overcome by the extra-constitutional activities of an effective party organization. In other words, what federalism does is to mobilize actually operative local powers in support of the constitution as a political process, and to protect them through the constitution as a political force. Localized groupings are thus treated in a manner analogous in some respects to the treatment of the individual citizen, to whom a sphere of relative independence is likewise guaranteed. Furthermore, the rather fortuitous advantage of providing an opportunity for limited experimentation in one or more of the component units deserves mention. However, this latter consideration points toward the primordial weakness of federal structures of government. It is the difficulty of adjusting such a relatively rigid scheme to the shifting exigencies of a dynamic industrial society. Under modern conditions areas of friction are bound to develop where technological change radically alters the conditions under which government has to be conducted. If competencies are divided between the central government and the local governments, as they are in the United States, governmental functions may emerge, which can only be performed by one of these units, and for which no constitutional provision has yet been made. Recent developments in the United States, as for example, in the case of the Agricultural Adjustment Administration, have focused public attention upon this problem. The Court, by insisting upon the constitutional inability of the central (federal) government to do what the local (state) governments could not in fact do, is creating a midnight zone utterly beyond governmental action. Such a state of affairs naturally is fraught with dangers. The particular difficulties in the United States are at present believed to be solvable by delegating specific functions to the state governments and making the central government one of residuary powers, but it would be a mistake to assume that the problem would thereby be solved permanently. There would presently appear situations in which the local (state) governments alone could as a matter of fact act, and yet, under the new constitutional arrangement, only the federal government, with its residuary powers, would be constitutionally able to act. In other words, the rigidities which arise from a division of powers are inherent in the federal scheme and are the price which has to be paid for the advantages set forth above. In this the spatial division of powers does not differ from the functional division. In both cases a measure of inefficiency is the price we have to pay for the measure of freedom which such constitutional restraints afford us.

CHAPTER XIV

CONSTITUTIONAL DICTATORSHIP AND EMERGENCY POWERS

Introductory.—In three preceding chapters various means have been discussed for the establishment and maintenance of effective restraints upon the exercise of governmental powers. Their common characteristic was the division of powers between several individuals and groups of individuals. Thus the concentration of powers characteristic of modern government in the making was broken up in the course of a long struggle, popularly known as the progress of liberalism. Since the earlier monarchical governments replaced, as we have seen, the medieval constitutional order (characterized itself by an elaborate scheme of divided powers), the development may, however, be more appropriately depicted as a great pendular swing between the two poles of divided and concentrated powers. Furthermore, this swing is by no means uniform in its direction, but there are many oscillations (see, for example, Chap. II, ¶2). Now the great ground-swell of the rising concentration of powers under the earlier monarchs was engendered, it will be remembered, by the exigencies of religious upheavals, of increasing and technically more formidable warfare, and of the industrial revolution accompanying them (see Chap. II). The violence and constant recurrence of these emergencies during the latter half of the sixteenth and throughout the seventeenth century made it possible for certain gifted individuals to break down the medieval division of powers to a very large extent, and to concentrate these powers in their own hands. Due to the military and administrative requirements of the emergencies the princes who had been charged with military and administrative powers in medieval society were rather advantageously placed for a successful usurpation of this kind. It would, however, be very erroneous to assume that this transformation was in any way sudden. The process was, as we have seen at various points, an exceedingly gradual one. What technique the princes employed in their efforts to consummate their ambitions will be shown presently. A peculiar interest attaches to this subject on account of the present trend toward concentrated powers. Again the necessity for such concentration arises, we are told, from the emergencies with which we are confronted: the conflict between classes in our industrial society and the exigencies of modern mass warfare. Are our constitutional governments likely to be able to cope with these situations of unprecedented magnitude and gravity? Many answer no, and turn toward dictatorship as their solution. Now every modern constitution has recognized the problems of temporary emergencies and has sought to provide for a temporary concentration of powers to be used in overcoming such emergencies. In common law countries (England, United States), this is done on the basis of martial rule, in civil law countries through the state of siege. Constitutional dictatorship is the term we shall use to designate all such techniques for the temporary concentration of powers.

The commissioner.—Similar techniques were recognized by the medieval constitutional order, but the princes ultimately succeeded in transforming them into instruments for the destruction of medieval constitutionalism itself. How was this result accomplished? Essentially through the institution of extraordinary commissioners or *commissarii* whom they, following the papal precedent, appointed out of the fullness of their authority (*plenitudo potestatis*). For it was held to be part of the royal prerogative to determine when an exceptional situation required exceptional measures. Thus in place of the regular officials with legally, if not constitutionally, defined spheres of jurisdiction, there appear specially appointed delegates of the king who, on the basis of a special instruction, are called upon to handle particular situations. Thus we find commissioners authorized to inspect markets, to requisition food and other support for the army, to carry on negotiations, and so forth. Perhaps the most celebrated historical form of such commissioners are the intendants whom Henry IV of France employed to such a remarkable degree. They then aided him materially in securing the revenue which enabled him to dispense with the Estates. But even before Henry IV the institution of commissioners had been developed by the French crown. A striking chapter in Bodin's treatise on the state is devoted to a discussion of the legal and practical aspects of such commissioners (he himself occasionally acted in this capacity). In this chapter, Bodin clearly distinguished the commissioner from the regular official. Since the latter's activities were created by express and public law, his office was more or less permanent, and the official had a sort of right to his office. On the other hand the commissioner, owing his right to act to a royal ordinance, exercised only a temporary function, and had therefore no right to his office, but was completely dependent upon his master. Therefore the commissioner's activities were narrowly circumscribed by his instructions, while the official used a certain amount of discretion. This latter observation obviously held true only if the tenor of the instructions was narrow. If, however, the prince saw fit to make the instructions very comprehensive, for example, in requesting a certain commissioner to employ all necessary means for quelling a rebellion, then such a commissioner with a commission unlimited as to the means he saw fit to use was very likely to suspend existing laws and rights on a considerable scale. It is at this point that the analogy between these commissioners and the office of the dictator becomes apparent.

The (Roman) constitutional dictatorship.—Bodin himself placed the Roman dictator in line with the commissioners of his time. For he too was appointed for a given task like that of concluding a war or suppressing a rebellion, and as soon as his commission was carried out his office similarly came to an end. In fact, however, the Roman dictator could with any show of reason be compared only to a commissioner with very extensive powers; for he became the chief executive of the Roman Republic for the period of his appointment, whereas the commissioners of Bodin's time and later were usually agents of a king who remained the chief executive and who employed them for more or less limited tasks. Perhaps the nearest approach to a Roman dictator can be found in the Imperial General Wallenstein who during certain periods of the Thirty Years' War wielded comprehensive authority. But even he never replaced the imperial office. It is, however, worthy of comment that the Estates, no less than the kings, appointed commissioners wherever the circumstances seemed to require it. It is in this light that the career of Cromwell must be studied. But as the story of Cromwell shows, when compared with that of the many royal commissioners, such commissioned dictatorial powers are much more readily recalled by a monarch than by a large assembly. Particularly if a true emergency exists, the individual who commands the forces fighting this emergency is difficult to dislodge. This was no less true of the Cromwellian and Napoleonic dictatorships, than it had been of that of Sulla and Cæsar. In all these cases the effective command of the army was of decisive importance. But we are not here concerned with the transition from a temporary to a permanent concentration of powers (see below, ¶ 14 and Chap. XXV), but with the temporary concentration of powers for emergency purposes. The Roman example is significant, because for several centuries dictatorship there remained a bulwark for the Republican government, and did not lead to any usurpation of powers. The conditions of this state of affairs seem to have been essentially four. In the first place the appointment of the dictator took place according to precise constitutional forms. Secondly, the dictator himself could not at his discretion declare the state of emergency. The dictatorship occurred, thirdly, always in defense of the existing constitutional order, never with a view to changing it (as under Cæsar). And a fourth condition of great importance was a strict time limit imposed upon the dictator for the fulfillment of his task, never to exceed six months. Obviously, all these conditions are themselves dependent upon the constitutional order, and can therefore be properly called constitutional limitations. Now the commissioners of the monarchical governments were, on the contrary, personal servants of the king in whose hands power was being concentrated. Their object was, therefore, not so much the maintenance of a constitutional order, but of order as such. Their purpose was conceived in technical terms, and evaluated in terms of the reason of state (see Chap. XV, ¶5). It is thus quite apparent that from a political, as compared to the legal, standpoint constitutional dictatorship is the very antithesis of such commissionerships (or commissioned dictatorship, as they have been called). Nothing shows this more clearly than the fact that when these commissioners become permanent, they form the core of the monarchical bureaucracy, whereas when the constitutional dictatorship becomes permanent, it becomes unconstitutional and leads to the perversion and eventual overthrow of the constitutional order. A concentration of powers has replaced the division which previously reigned.

The same, contrasted with the commissioner.—It is, therefore, quite inadmissible to place the modern constitutional provisions for martial law and the state of siege into a parallel with the commissioners of old, as has sometimes been done. As so often in the history of political institutions, a legal continuity hides a fundamental transition in political function. For it is undeniable that both martial rule in common law lands and the state of siege on the Continent of Europe are derived in part from institutions similar to the commissionership. Yet, like the Roman Republican dictatorship, martial rule, emergency powers, and the state of siege are all conceived in terms of maintaining a constitutional system rather than destroying it (until they are perverted into a usurpation of concentrated powers). To be sure, the apologist of absolutism would insist that the kinship of the two institutions lay precisely in the fact that both were extraordinary means for maintaining "the state." But the word "state" is itself a propaganda tool of the absolutist. From the standpoint of political science, interested in the incidents of power, two instrumentalities, one of which aids the concentration of power, while the other prevents it, are quite distinct. The distinction, therefore, is not between commissioned and non-commissioned (sovereign) dictatorship, but between constitutional and unconstitutional (unrestrained) dictatorship. The modern forms of constitutional dictatorship are martial rule, the state of siege, and constitutional emergency powers. The first is found in England, the Dominions and in the United States, the second is found in France, in Germany before 1918, and in many other continental countries, and the third is characteristic of the American federal government and the German Republic, among others.

Martial rule.—As we have already mentioned, the differentiation between martial rule and the state of siege is essentially related to the difference between a common and a civil law system. The concept of a martial rule is understandable only in terms of the rule of law which it replaces. Where this rule of law is taken to be the core of the legal system, because it alone guarantees a calculable stability of legal relationships, an emergency is essentially a condition of things which threatens the continued maintenance of this rule of law. The most decisive evidence of such a disturbance would be the fact that the courts are closed and can no longer perform their function. This the American Supreme Court held to be the condition for the application of martial law.[1] Similarly, Judge Mackintosh once said[2] that when it is impossible for courts of law to sit or to enforce the execution of the judgments, then it becomes necessary to find some rude substitute for them and to employ for that purpose the military which is the only remaining force in the community. But on the whole, the English courts have not been quite so strict, and the American courts may also deviate from this older precedent today. The important point is that ultimately the judiciary are the arbiters who determine whether or not the actions taken by executive organs are in fact necessary. On the other hand, there is no limit beyond which the authorities exercising such constitutional dictatorship may not go, if they can afterward convince the court of the necessity of their action. It is hard to say much more about it, for the law of martial rule is very vague and ill-defined by a maze of conflicting precedents. Nor is there any clearly defined measure by which the initiation of such a system of martial rule is clearly indicated. Although it is customary for the executive "to declare martial law" before initiating extraordinary measures, this declaration does not entail any very definite consequences. It may be a mere threat. It may presage the most extreme measures, violating all the customary constitutional limitations upon governmental powers. Whatever measures are taken, they must be defensible in terms of the nature of the emergency, which arose from the onslaught of hostile forces against the customary rule of law.

State of siege.—Very different is the state of siege. Here a specific declaration by the legislature or the head of the government or both is required by law, or even by the constitution (preferably). Thus the French constitution of 1815 (*Acte additionnel*) requires that the declaration of the state of siege take the form of a law. What is perhaps more important, the state of siege is defined in terms of a suspension of certain enumerated individual rights, more particularly the right to be tried in an ordinary court, the right to free speech and to free assembly. It is at this point that the contrast to common law practice can be most clearly seen, and it is indeed of decisive importance in civil war situations. Whereas the executive and/or the legislature have the final word as to whether an emer-

[1] *Ex parte Milligan*, 4 Wall. 2 [1866].

[2] Clode, Charles M., *The Administration of Justice under Military and Martial Law* (1872), p. 165.

gency situation has arisen, the courts have this function under the common law. Politically speaking, this means that a political authority, an admittedly partisan organ, has the ultimate authority in continental jurisdictions, whereas a neutral authority, or at least one which presumably tries to be a non-partisan organ, has the last word in Anglo-American jurisdictions. At the same time, continental countries seem to see the emergency in an effective threat against public safety and order, whereas in common law countries it is a matter of the suspension of the rule of law. In practice the two states of fact may largely coincide; but the concept of public safety and order focuses attention upon the political system, or "the state." On the other hand, the rule of law seems preoccupied with the safety of the private individual. In other words, we are led to perceive a most important shift of emphasis, and this difference is undoubtedly responsible for the inclination of common lawyers to look upon the state of siege as a wicked institution, traceable to the heritage of the Continent's monarchical past.

Constitutional emergency powers.—In reality, this distinction between martial rule and the state of siege as related to common law and civil law hides a profound cleavage between England and the United States. This cleavage is of such importance that it makes one question the significance of the difference between common and civil law as far as this matter of emergency government is concerned. The point is that the unfettered legislative authority of Parliament and its cabinet gives a partisan majority ultimate control in Great Britain. Thus the Defense of the Realm Act (1914), while furnishing no clue as to the political implications in a civil war situation, showed that the English judiciary, unlike the American, has no ultimate authority in this matter. For only American courts can question the authority of executive as well as legislative organs in the exercise of their discretion. It is for this reason that constitutional emergency powers in the strict sense of the American Constitution must be distinguished from the law of martial rule as well as from the state of siege. Such constitutional emergency powers may be vested in the executive and the legislature (the American Congress can suspend *habeas corpus*), but whether these powers were exercised according to the Constitution, still remains for the judiciary interpreting the Constitution to say. As we have already mentioned, the Supreme Court of the United States found that as long as the courts were still open and able to function, such a state of emergency did *not* exist.[1] The denial of *habeas corpus* was consequently revoked. The German constitution of 1919 made a step in the same direction, but the traditional pusillanimity of the courts merely facilitated the destruction of the constitution through the abuse of executive power.

The flaws in the Weimar constitution.—The German constitution provided (Article 48) that if public safety and order are materially disturbed or endangered, the president may take the necessary measures to restore public safety and order and, if necessary, to intervene by force of arms. This power of the president was checked, however, by the right of Parliament to demand the revocation of any or all such measures. This check was in fact rather ineffectual on account of the president's power to dissolve the Parliament. The power of dissolution had, therefore, the fatal result of leaving the president largely in control of a very extensive emergency power. Now an emergency is a state of fact. Under the continental judicial tradition a court has no right to inquire into a state of fact, once it is alleged by the government. Therefore no judicial check, such as that in the United States, could be brought into play. If the German courts had had a more independent tradition, it is conceivable that the Supreme Court might have challenged this procedural inhibition to inquire into states of fact when constitutional issues were involved. As guardian of the constitution (see Chap. XII) the court could have expanded the budding doctrine of the legally relevant fact. But such was not the case. This concentration of emergency powers in the hands of the president had fatal consequences. In the summer of 1930 it entailed the calling of an election which brought a very large group of extremists into the legislature. In the succeeding two years, it enabled Dr. Brüning to stay in power without adequate parliamentary support, through the threat of dissolution. After his dismissal in the spring of 1932, the invocation of the emergency power of the president led to a series of ever more dubious dissolutions and consequent elections, according to the notorious remark of the ill-fated General Schleicher: "Let them vote, until they pop off." By these events the existing constitutional order, the parliamentary regime, was being discredited without being actually in operation. Thus the unchecked emergency powers of the German president, though supposed to be created for the maintenance of the constitution, were actually used for its destruction.

Modern constitutional limitations inadequate; (a) the ap-

[1] *Ex Parte Milligan,* 4 Wall. 2 (1866).

pointment of a dictator.—If we now ask ourselves to what extent the four criteria of a constitutional dictatorship outlined above (see ¶ 3) are realized in the various provisions for martial rule, the state of siege, and constitutional emergency powers, we have a test by which to evaluate these arrangements. This test may afford us some clue as to the relative value of these several arrangements. At the same time, such testing will reveal a considerable amount of similarity between the three forms of constitutional dictatorship. As to the first criterion, it must be admitted that only constitutional emergency powers regularly fulfill the condition laid down by it, to wit, that the appointment of the dictator take place according to precise constitutional forms. In England where the application of martial rule occurs at the discretion of a cabinet supported by a legally and constitutionally unlimited majority in the House of Commons, the appointment of the dictator may be said to be thus defined, but it is a pretty vague definition at that. In France where the state of siege is defined by the laws of August 9, 1848, and of April 3, 1878, it is provided that it shall be declared by legislative enactment, and when the legislature is not in session, by executive decree, later to be confirmed by the legislature. Here again an aggressive majority in the legislature could, by changing the existing laws, alter the provisions for the appointment of a dictator *ad hoc*. Although it is traditional under parliamentary government that the cabinet assume dictatorial functions, as happened in the case of Poincaré's dictatorship of 1926 for the stabilization of the French currency, grave consequences may follow from a parliamentary majority's using this traditional power for the purpose of forestalling the emergence of incipient opposition forces. Yet, with the intensification of social strife this possibility cannot be brushed aside. It is the fact that the constitution is at the mercy of the parliamentary majority which weakens, if it does not actually destroy, the dependability of the state of siege or mere martial rule as a technique of constitutional dictatorship. Only a constitutional order like that of the United States measures up to the first criterion with precise constitutional provisions concerning the appointment of a dictator when it provides, in Article I, Section 8: "Congress shall have power . . . (15) to provide for calling forth the militia, to execute the Laws of the Union, suppress Insurrections, and repel Invasions." But it so happens that the particular constitutional provisions are so worded as to omit the naming of a distinct dictator. This brings us to the second point.

Same subject; (b) the determination of an emergency.—Martial rule in England, the state of siege in France, and the constitutional emergency powers in the United States all seem to square with the second criterion, according to which the dictator himself must not be vested with discretionary powers for declaring or calling off the state of emergency. This implies that he must not be self-appointed. Now the American Congress, the English, or the French Parliament do indeed appoint someone else, and so seem to be in accord with the test. But this seeming accord is purely formal. For since these legislatures (the English and French always, the American a large part of the time) are led by the executive leaders whom their majority supports, the executive dictators are really self-appointed. This is no less true of Franklin D. Roosevelt than it was of Poincaré. And although parliamentary majorities may and do disintegrate—in which case genuine checks result—from the viewpoint of power analysis the disquieting feature of these arrangements is that the parliamentary majority initiating the dictatorship actually derives increased powers therefrom, at the expense of the minority whom they may be combating. The American Civil War situation is a doleful illustration of this interrelation. To make the point more practically applicable to present-day controversies: if the second Roosevelt had had to abdicate his presidential powers in asking Congress to appoint a temporary dictator to deal with the emergency which he claimed to exist, he would possibly have been more doubtful about it. And if it had been his function to determine the end of the crisis for the purpose of resuming his presidential powers, the end of the crisis might have come sooner. Such statements as these may sound partisan and biased, but they are not meant to be so; the same thing would hold true for any other man occupying the presidential office with a solid majority of partisans in Congress. What is, in this respect, true of the United States, is, of course, *a fortiori* true of England and France, not to speak of Republican Germany. We must, therefore, conclude that the present systems of constitutional dictatorship in the leading countries do not accord with our second criterion. Whether their constitutional orders will, therefore, be perverted into governments with concentrated powers, as happened in Germany, would seem to depend upon the extent to which recurrent crises will entail the employment of presumably temporary emergency powers.

Same subject; (c) the defense of the constitution itself.—The third criterion which demands that the temporary concentration of powers be employed for defending the existing constitutional order, and not for changing it, has so far been fulfilled. It is, however, very disquieting that no explicit provisions safeguard the employment of martial rule, and the state of siege in this regard. The purely military background of both institutions, and the consequent preoccupation with the technical problem of producing a certain effect are inimical to adequate consideration of this problem. On the battlefield victory is an ascertainable technical goal and victory once achieved the emergency evidently has passed. But in social and economic crises the matter is not so obvious and the tendency of partisans to identify their particular solution with the only solution is extremely strong. Hence measures of extreme violence, like let us say the forcible destruction of all labor unions, may appear to be a necessary condition of social pacification to one group, while the forcible expropriation of all private industries may seem equally unavoidable to the other. It may be said that at such a point a constitutional order becomes impossible. But whether that be true or not, it is undeniable that neither martial rule nor the state of siege under a parliamentary regime offers any safeguards against their abuse by violent partisans in a civil war situation, so that these modern attempts at constitutional dictatorship are liable to be the first step in the destruction of an existing constitutional order. Constitutional emergency powers, on the other hand, are not exposed to the same objection. For here the arbitral position of the courts in determining the *constitutional* exercise of all governmental powers can to some extent be brought into play in order to insure that the dictatorial powers be confined to defending the existing constitution. The United States Supreme Court gave striking illustrations of that fact in interfering with the atrocities of the reconstruction period. They show signs of acting likewise at the present time. But unless the judiciary or some other magistrate can thus be brought into play, the situation is likely to get out of hand. Thus the constitutional emergency powers wielded by the German president and cabinet under the Weimar constitution, unchecked by a constitutional judiciary, were very adroit in concentrating powers in their hands over ever longer periods of time, claiming an emergency which no longer was considered in the light of maintaining a constitutional order, but rather in that of the particular partisan views which they happened to entertain. Emergency powers which were supposed to support a constitutional dictatorship changed into concentrated powers directed towards the destruction of the constitution. We must conclude, therefore, that the attempts of modern constitutional systems to organize a temporary concentration of powers for dealing with an emergency fail in large measure to fulfill the requirements suggested by our third criterion for a constitutional dictatorship.

Same subject; (d) the precise time limit.—The last criterion, namely, the imposition of a strict time limit during which concentrated powers can be exercised, is not rigidly fulfilled by any modern constitutional order. To be sure, there is supposed to be an implication of such a time limit in the provision of a legislative check upon the exercise of these powers. Various constitutions and laws provide for the immediate reporting of any measures taken by the dictatorial executive, and for their revocation if the legislature should demand it. But by such provisions this criterion merges with the second one, which would withdraw from the dictator the discretion of determining the end as well as the beginning of the emergency. It was shown with regard to these provisions that in view of parliamentary dependence upon executive leadership (cabinet system) no real check is provided against the arbitrary abuse of this discretionary power. At any rate, such a procedural rule cannot be said to take the place of a fixed limitation of time such as that which was imposed by the Roman Republican constitution. It may be true that the six months there provided were suggested by the usual extent of a military campaign. Whatever the particular period of time, a constitutionally fixed time limit is a vastly different thing from any check which with proper manipulation is capable of indefinite extension. It is a curious thing that modern constitutional systems have never faced this problem squarely, though with the vagueness surrounding so-called social crises and emergencies it would be most important. Even a constitution so deeply permeated by a distrust of power as the American Constitution fails to insist upon some such limit.

Emphasis upon the general rules may explain these inadequacies.—We must conclude, therefore, that all in all the quasi-dictatorial provisions of modern constitutional systems, be they martial rule, state of siege, or constitutional emergency powers, fail to conform to any exacting standard derived from the political implications of even a temporary concentration of powers. Consequently, we must further conclude that all these systems are liable to be transformed into absolutist schemes, if the conditions become at all favorable to it, unless radical changes are made to tighten these provisions. It goes without saying that even such provisions are merely technical improvements, and that no constitutional order can maintain itself which is not supported by the loyal enthusiasm of its citizens. It may, however, be justifiable to ask why modern constitutions so uniformly neglect this problem of constitutional limitations. No exhaustive answer can be given. But it may well be that the emphasis upon legislation as the real core of governmental action is responsible for this. From Rousseau to the present time, martial rule, the state of siege, and constitutional emergency powers have been taken to be largely limited to executive action. Indeed, they have been looked upon as extensions of this "power." At the same time, the doctrine of the central importance of rule-making was retained, and all such emergency powers as were wielded by executives could only be used to suspend the laws but not to alter them. To be sure, extensive delegation of legislative powers has occurred in France, in Germany, and elsewhere. In the United States, such delegations have recently once more been held unconstitutional. In terms of the prevailing opinion, however, such delegations could be permitted, because the elected assembly, the "legislature," remained as the guardian of legislation; it could revoke any rules it did not like. And wherever legislation and constitutional rules were identified, the same body appeared also as the guardian of the constitution. The more strictly executive or administrative phases of the process apparently did not seem to matter in comparison. The notorious power of the Roman dictator over life and death (of an individual) might not be equalled on account of *habeas corpus*, but a boundless extension of administrative competence would be accepted, although it might entail the life of thousands or even millions. What such a doctrinaire approach to the problem overlooks is the potential cumulation of such practices into a fixed pattern. Orthodox tradition looked upon the whole process as merely temporarily enlarging executive power; in terms of the distribution of power the process appears as a rapid concentration of power in the hands of a ruling oligarchy, represented by an individual capable of effectively dramatizing its position (see below, Chap. XXV). The traditional (and legalistic) attitude appears to be that an emergency is an undesirable state of fact (rebellion, crisis). A specific technical solution must be found. The phrase "state of siege" is indicative of this attitude. The siege must be lifted; that is all. An executive officer is seen in analogy to a military commander; he must take command and accomplish the desirable end.

This done, nothing really fundamental has happened; things have returned to their usual state. The rule of law having been reëstablished, everything is precisely where it was before. Such a view now appears absurd. In terms of power analysis the temporary concentration of powers cannot be dissolved again unless residuary power is left somewhere for that purpose. Even if one accepted the view that general rules are of central importance, he would observe that. Recurrent measures crystallize into rules, and under appropriate conditions a continuous state of emergency arises. It is curious that the later nineteenth century should have failed to revise its notions on this score in spite of the spectacle of the actions of Napoleon III and of Bismarck right before their eyes. The general optimism prevented a searching consideration of deeper springs of action in such situations. Rigid constitutional limitations such as the one suggested by the present analysis will not save a constitutional regime which prevents the realization of what is considered just by the community. But they will add a most powerful brake which in the day of crisis may be decisive in bringing the skidding constitutional order back into its groove, while the necessary adjustments are made in the distribution of power according to the believed-in standard of justice.

The pattern of transition from constitutional to unconstitutional dictatorship.—The details of the transition from a constitutional government to an unconstitutional one may not yet be known. But the broad outlines of the process are distinctly discernible. The constitutional government is weak. It lacks the support of tradition. The division of power under the constitution is faulty, resulting in too much friction or in too much authority for weak groups in the community. It contains channels for the manifestation of mass emotions, however. Typical tools of radical democracy, such as general elections or referendum machinery (plebiscitary apparatus) are available under it. The dissatisfied groups throw their strength in this direction. They thrust forward one or more leaders who are able under the constitution to secure positions of power, and thus legitimate authority. They buttress intransigeant demands for broader channels of mass emotionalism by appeals to the tenets of radical democracy. In the meantime their mass supporters carry on guerilla warfare against all opponents, thus creating a civil war situation. The attendant disorder and the eventual anarchy stir the indifferent elements in the community into action. The tension rises. More disorder, clashes between groups of citizens, murders, burnings follow. Dictatorial methods for the maintenance of the constitutional order, indeed any order, appear inevitable. The resulting constitutional dictatorship lacks drive, because of the instability of the constitutional morale. Complete faith in this morale would alone justify measures of ruthless violence. This problem of "justification" is politically of crucial importance, because as the latent civil war develops, the decisive question is which side the army will take. In Russia the army was revolutionized through the war; the decision of the Kerenski government to continue the war was its fatal error. In Italy the army remained neutral, which was enough to give Mussolini the upper hand. In Germany the army refused to march against Hitler, as it looked upon the nationalism of the masses as the most effective support for the desired re-armament and re-militarization. In Poland, the army always supported Pilsudski, their own general. Likewise in Jugoslavia, the army supported *their* supreme commander, the king. That the army should have been willing to support their celebrated general, the first Napoleon, seems hardly surprising. It is more surprising to find that quite a little opposition to the plebiscites extending the power of Napoleon I (see below, Chap. XXV, ¶ 2), came from the army. Under the third Napoleon, the army again sided with the threatened bourgeoisie. Bismarck's assumption of dictatorial powers in Prussia in 1862 was caused by the needs of the army; there could be no question of its loyal support. Recent developments in Spain leave the question in suspense; the Spanish armed forces are split and are thus deprived of any decisive influence. If one turns to South America, coup after coup through which unstable constitutional regimes give way to periodically re-appearing dictatorships turns upon the support of the armed forces. It appears, in other words, that the division of powers under constitutional government cannot forestall the concentration of powers, when it merely neutralizes the armed forces. They must be as positively attached to the constitutional order as to any other political order. It is here that the problem of constitutional morale meets its crucial test; the failure to perceive this problem spells eventual disaster. Neither Locke nor Rousseau saw this problem clearly, and the entire constitutional doctrine was equivocal about this matter. But the Swiss people have always been keenly aware of it, and their views have had a measure of resonance in the United States. Curiously enough, the keenest exposition of the problem in theory is offered by none other than Machiavelli. In his *Discourses on Livy,* as well as in his other works, he always returns to the *militia* as the central theme. In doing so, he rationalizes the historical conceptions of Livy.

Conclusion.—In view of the permanent stabilization of dictatorial (tyrannical) regimes for extended periods of history, such as Hellenistic Greece, Augustan Rome, Renaissance Italy, and monarchical absolutism, it is not impossible that "the pattern of dictatorship with its submission to authority, its entrenchment of the powerful economic interests, its gaudy adornments, its system of status, its intolerance, will invest with a deep security a new age of despots." Certain it is that the provisions of modern constitutions for the establishment of temporary constitutional dictatorship and the practice of constitutional governments in "neutralizing" the armed forces seem woefully inadequate in times of crisis. Whether effective changes can be brought about in the light of all this experience is a question beyond the judgment of the scientist. He can merely exhort: *Videant consules, ne respublica detrimentum capiat.*

CHAPTER XV

RESPONSIBILITY AND ITS ENFORCEMENT

Introductory: electoral as distinguished from other types of responsibility.—We have seen that the constitution is essentially an instrument through which the arbitrary power of government is restrained. Those generations which fought for a constitution in their effort to restrain the concentrated power of monarchical governments tended, therefore, to identify restraint with rendering the government responsible. It thus became customary to consider government according to a constitution responsible government. To be sure, people remained perfectly aware in practice of the decisive importance of impelling action as well as restraining it, and the sound traditions of English politics are nowhere more clearly apparent than in the development and maintenance of clear-cut cabinet responsibility (see below Chap. XX). But even in England the growing complexity of modern government and administration has engendered the organization of a permanent civil service of large proportions whose responsibility cannot be enforced through changes in cabinets, except on lines of broad general policy. Generally speaking, the political problem of responsibility has been obscured by preoccupation with the electoral techniques for securing responsible conduct. This means that the discussion has been arbitrarily limited to the question of "hiring and firing."

The *Myers Case*.—It is in keeping with this general preoccupation with dismissal as a technique for enforcing responsible conduct that the Supreme Court of the United States, in its celebrated decision of the *Myers Case*, proceeded essentially on the assumption that the power of removal was a necessary part of making officials responsible to the President. For that reason, the court held, the President must have unlimited power of removal in order to retain responsibility for the administration of his office. This view is entirely wrong, and the learned judges could easily have discovered the unsoundness of their view, if they had examined administrative experience elsewhere; for in many constitutional democratic countries of Europe with highly efficient administrative services practically all the officials are appointed on life tenure. The power of dismissal is, in other words, only one of several techniques for making official conduct responsible. In fact, dismissal is not even a particularly effective method for producing responsible conduct, but has many disadvantages and shortcomings, which ought to be considered for purposes of comparing the removal power with other means or techniques for producing responsibility. Again, the problem of how to produce responsible conduct cannot be considered without reference to the nature of the activities which are being carried on. Evidently, the Supreme Court would be prepared to grant that its own conduct is "responsible" without anyone having an unchecked power of removal. Recently, the Supreme Court itself seems to have partially recognized its mistake in the *Myers Case* when it ruled in the *Humphreys Case* that Congress could lay down for officers possessing quasi-legislative or judicial functions such qualifications as it saw fit. In case of controversy, such qualifications would, of course, be interpreted by the courts, thus further extending the judicial power into the administrative field. This raises, however, other difficulties in connection with administrative justice which will be discussed below (see ¶ 15). At any rate, it should now be apparent that these questions are of such fundamental importance for constitutional government, from the standpoint of political science, that we must go beyond the accepted notions, which are much too limited.

Religious responsibility.—In terms of a broad historical perspective, we find that responsible conduct of power-holders has been enforced not only through secular, political, administrative, or judicial sanctions, but through religious sanctions as well. In fact, if the mere bulk of political experience is considered, it would seem that such religious responsibility has been much more significant than any of the others. The medieval constitutionalism which we discussed above (see Chap. VIII, 9) was largely built upon that sanction. When a certain religious spirit prevails in a community (and it does not inherently matter what particular religion it is), the possibilities of producing responsible conduct in terms of that religious ethic are on the whole more promising than any of the secular devices. Since responsibility presupposes logically a set of norms or standards in terms of which conduct can be evaluated (and even the will of the people amounts to that), the actual prevalence of a believed-in set of such norms makes responsibility of conduct almost automatic, as long as the faith lasts. It would be exceedingly instructive to show the workings of Chinese bureaucracy in these terms, but even our own civilization has relied upon religious sanctions for long periods. As might be expected, there exist two primary forms corresponding to the two primary patterns of Christian ethics, the Catholic and the Protestant. Yet they have much in common. Under both creeds, the person who is supposed to be made responsible for his acts is made responsible for his acts to God. In practice this means, of course, responsibility to the church. Perhaps the most extraordinary figure embodying the effectiveness of this faith is the Holy Roman Emperor, Henry III, founder of Bamberg Cathedral, and the only emperor who has been canonized by the church. He took the view that the imperial office was as holy as the papal one, and that he as emperor should therefore live in virtual celibacy, his successor to be chosen according to merit. By thus voluntarily spiritualizing his conduct, Henry almost completely obliterated ecclesiastical influence. For lesser men, however, such an escape was impractical, and the ensuing controversies have re-echoed through European history from the Emperor Henry IV down to Bismarck's *Kulturkampf* and the Third Republic's agitation over laicism, not to speak of Hitler's constant difficulties. But if the Catholic Church's independent and highly effective political organization entailed never-ending conflicts with the secular authorities, and a corresponding decline of the religious ethic upon which its power was reared, the dependence of some protestant churches (Lutheran and Anglican) upon the secular prince himself (who became its head) weakened its position as an effective enforcer of responsible conduct. In fact, as epitomized in the career of Archbishop Laud, there appeared an unmistakable tendency within the clergy to extoll the princely position for the sake of ecclesiastical preferment. It would, however, be quite erroneous to assume that because of this possible dependence there was no responsibility in Protestant lands. As long as the faith was vigorous, an appeal on the basis of conscience proved a very powerful restraint, readily discoverable in the records of the council proceedings of any Protestant country in that period.

Its breakdown.—We have seen that religious responsibility is conceived in terms of a divinely ordained or inspired faith which compels conduct in conformity with the ethical standard which that faith implies. Evidently, therefore, the way to escape from this type of responsibility is to emancipate oneself from the religious faith itself. It is well-known that mediaeval constitutionalism completely broke down in Renaissance Italy when religion declined. A most savage period of tyrannical abuse of power ensued. A very similar development took place in Protestant domains when the princes began to set aside the religious faith itself. Thus Frederick the Great got rid of the restraining influence of his clergy by becoming frankly atheist. It is, however, a characteristic feature of religious ethics to outlast the faith in its dogmatic foundations. As a consequence, Frederick's celebrated *Anti-Machiavel* in which he expounded the motto of enlightened Christian despotism, "I am the first servant of my state," in opposition to the Florentine political philosopher's utterly un-Christian views, is thoroughly permeated by his forefathers' Protestant ethic. We have already seen how the royal administrative service animated by this spirit took over the restraining functions of the clergy, and evolved an attitude which is aptly paraphrased by the rhyme: "Unser König hat es gut, wenn er unsern Willen tut." (Our king has a good time, provided he follows our orders.) Anyway, the wave of constitutionalism imposing secular restraints was just then beginning to rise, and therefore the tyrannical abuse of power could never assume the dimensions which it reached in Renaissance Italy.

Reason of state.—Whenever the enforcement of religious responsibility is not almost automatic, it entails an insoluble conflict between secular rulers and priests (or, to use the earlier terminology, between church and state), and thus involves peculiar pitfalls for the official who seeks to be guided by it. There are bound to occur situations in which the ethical norm conflicts with the exigencies of the conduct of government. The government which follows the norm succumbs to its rival which disregarded it. To have observed and described this fact with corrosive frankness is the glory of Machiavelli. His attempt to escape from the dilemma by idealizing power (the state) has earned him the condemnation of all Christian people. It is no accident that a Catholic priest, Botero, attempted to fit this view into the prevailing Christian pattern of thought by constructing the idea of a *ratio status*, a special governmental rationality which is at the bottom of the doctrine of the two moralities. In a previous chapter we have seen the working of this doctrine in the practical implications of Cromwellian and latter-day dictatorships. Although reason of state has not been recognized in Anglo-American political thought, the fundamental category of purposive or objective rationality in political behavior has gradually emerged in political science in the United States, accompanied, however, by a studied avoidance of Machiavelli's glorification of political action or the state. This leaves the question of a conflict between rational needs and a prevailing ethical norm obscure. And yet, whatever else may be said regarding the matter, "responsible" conduct of government is a phrase without precise meaning, unless a decision is made between the ultimate validity of ethical norms on the one hand and of practical exigencies on the other. An occasional leader of exceptional strength may fall back upon the Cromwellian method which was so aptly stigmatized by Lilburne when he said that Cromwell called God to record, even while he struck you under the fifth rib, but most rulers are not likely to succeed with such techniques. There are some beautiful passages in Stephen Vincent Benét's *John Brown's Body* where Abraham Lincoln ponders over this question. "What is God's will? They come to me and talk about God's will in righteous deputations and platoons, Day after day, laymen and ministers. . . . And yet, if it is probable that God Should, and so very clearly, state His will to others, on a point of my own duty, It might be thought He would reveal it me Directly, more especially as I So earnestly desire to know His will. The will of God prevails. No doubt, no doubt— Yet, in great contests, each side claims to act In strict accordance with the will of God. Both may, one must be wrong. . . ." If reason of state as an idea indicates the attempt of human minds, the Christian mind, to grasp the meaning of deviations from an ethical standard, the only way in which it could be done was to make the particular government itself a divine institution. It was thus that government by divine law became the divine right of kings in the seventeenth century.

Political responsibility.—Important though religion has been as an instrument for enforcing responsibility, modern government has been on the whole obliged to seek other means for accomplishing this end, because of the deterioration of religion itself. In fact, modern government can in some respects be interpreted essentially as an effort to produce responsible conduct of public affairs without religious sanctions. The idea of toleration implies an indifference toward the absolute standards which a religious sanction presupposes. In the place of such standards mutually accepted interests (public interests, so-called) are taken as guide-posts for official action. A person holding an office acts, then, in accordance with the will of another person or body of persons—that is, political responsibility is conceived in terms of a relationship between human beings. There are two basic types of such responsibility and relationship. One is the authoritarian and the other is the parliamentary or electoral form of responsibility. But in either case responsibility is measured in terms of service to interests determined by the will of another. This circumstance invests political responsibility with a distinctly rational quality; the interests can be and often are argued about, and the services which lead to their realization are thus rendered rational or at least capable of rationalization. To be sure, comprehensive notions, such as that of a "national interest," are not particularly definite, and the conduct of officials in terms of them is therefore only vaguely rationalized, as Charles Beard has so lucidly shown with regard to the United States. Such notions possess rather the nature of a believed-in standard or value, and this is not at all surprising in view of the fact that nationalism has developed into a sort of substitute for religion. In fact, C. J. H. Hayes has gone so far as to place nationalism right in line with Christianity as a *bona fide* form of religion, and contemporary events in Europe seem to support that view. But whether a real religion or a substitute, nationalism tinges a concept such as national interest with an irrational, awesome hue. How are we to solve this problem of holding the several interests together and giving them a common direction, of integrating them into a more or less consistent whole? How, in other words, can the discordant private interests be converted into a common public interest? Frederick the Great answered: "I am the first servant of my state" and thereby implied that his will determined what interests constituted part of the public interest. Mussolini and Hitler are similarly minded. Orthodox democracy attempts to substitute the will of the people. But how is the will of this somewhat vague unity, the people, to be found? This question lies at the core of electoral responsibility. Let us hear what Edmund Burke, the classical expounder of parliamentary conceptions, has to say on this score.

Burke's views on mandatory instructions.—In a celebrated speech to his electors at Bristol, Burke enunciated the idealistic conception of parliamentary responsibility thus: "My worthy colleague (his opponent for the seat) says, his will ought to be subservient to yours. If that be all, the thing is innocent. If government were a matter of will upon any side, yours, without question, ought to be superior. But government and legislation are matters of reason and judgment, and not of inclination; and what sort of reason is that, in which the determination precedes the discussion; in which one set of men deliberate, and another decide . . . ? To deliver an opinion is the right of all men; that of constituents is a weighty and respectable opinion, which a representative ought always to rejoice to hear; and which he ought always most seriously to consider. But *authoritative* instructions; *mandates* issued, which the member is bound blindly and explicitly to obey, to vote and to argue for, though contrary to the clearest conviction of his judgment and conscience; these are things utterly unknown to the laws of this land, and which arise from a fundamental mistake of the whole order and tenor of our constitution. Parliament is not a *congress* of ambassadors from different and hostile interests; which interests each must maintain, as an agent and advocate, against other agents and advocates; but parliament is a *deliberative* assembly of *one* nation, with *one* interest, that of the whole; where not local purposes, not local prejudices ought to guide, but the general good. . . ." And pushing the matter one step further and into the realm of religion once more, Burke pointed out: "Certainly, gentlemen, it ought to be the happiness and glory of a representative, to live in the strictest union, the closest correspondence, and the most unreserved communication with his constituents. Their wishes ought to have great weight with him; their opinion high respect; their business unremitted attention. . . . But his unbiased opinion, his mature judgment, his enlightened conscience, he ought not to sacrifice to you, to any man, or to any set of men living. These he does not derive from your pleasure; no, nor from the law and the constitution. They are a trust from Providence, for the abuse of which he is deeply answerable."[1]

[1] *Works,* Boston, 1839, Vol. II, pp. 12 f.

The sceptical position.— The crux of this type of political responsibility, then, is the conflict of various interests and their possible relation to a more comprehensive public interest. Ideally conceived, of course, a special mandate cannot be admitted, since it would make the members of representative assemblies into mandatories for special interests. In the United States, to be sure, the members of the Senate, at any rate, are actually supposed to be mandatories for local interests, and the Senate *is* supposed to be a congress of ambassadors, and this has naturally had its effect upon the House as well. What is more, the whole people of the United States, through electing the President of the country, are represented by the chief executive, who thus has an immense advantage over Congress as an effective claimant for the role of representing the public, the national interest. But even the classical English doctrine, as found in Burke, may be inquired into by a politically-minded, a rationally-minded person, who would say: "Who decides whether you, Edmund Burke, have carried out this trust from Providence?" To which Burke could answer: "The electors of Bristol!" "Very well," his cross-examiner would continue, "what about de Jouvenel's well-known squib about Parliament, that after having become a deputy, one need have but one essential preoccupation, to remain a deputy? Will it not be true that unless a representative does obey the mandates and instructions of his electorate, or of groups of them, he will fail of reëlection?" Such sceptical thoughts are now the common property of most people who consider electoral responsibility; for the actual behavior of most elected representatives belies the lofty sentiments of Edmund Burke. Even in Burke's own day, many a listener to his speech must have chuckled inwardly as he reflected upon the complete subservience of most members of Parliament to the great aristocratic landowners, who did not even have to issue instructions, so assiduously did "their" members study their every wish before each vote in Parliament (see below, XXI, ¶ 7). As realistic students of political behavior we must, therefore, conclude that Burke's doctrine of reason and conscience as applied to electoral responsibility is as untenable a rationalization as was the sanctification of government by those who sought to bridge the gap between an ethical standard founded upon religion and the exigencies of political life, as embodied in the notion of a reason of state.

A truly realistic approach recognizes the conflict of interests as real.—Yet, if we recognize the difficulties raised by the conflict of interests under any conceivable scheme of electoral responsibility, it does not follow that we have to surrender to the corroding scepticism of writers like de Jouvenel, Kent, or the contemporary Fascists. Indeed the *political* problem of responsibility would not exist, if these conflicts of interest did not intrude themselves. As we have seen at the outset, it is of the essence of political life to cope with conflicts, and to discover ever new syntheses as new situations arise. Now, the realization of such political responsibility in its electoral form has many ramifications, and actually constitutes the core of the third part of this volume. It is therefore only necessary here to carry somewhat further the discussion of how to enforce political responsibility in its authoritarian form when religious sanctions are lacking. For the authoritarian form is very important in connection with bureaucracy (that is, administrative services) even where fundamental lines of policy are determined by a representative assembly and an elected chief executive. For such an elected executive head of the government confronts practically the same questions in seeking to secure responsible conduct on the part of his subordinates as does an hereditary monarch. The fact that the base lines of his policies are determined by popular preferences, rather than his own, does in no wise alter the need for coördinating the administrative execution of these policies. Furthermore, the popular preferences are likely to coincide with his own purposes, since he was elected on account of his vigorous advocacy of them. Conflicts between popular and personal preferences are, therefore, usually matters of detail rather than of fundamental direction.

Five ways of enforcing responsibility of the authoritarian type.—On account of the preoccupation with electoral forms of responsibility, there has been a tendency in Anglo-Saxon countries to narrow the possibilities of enforcing responsibility in an authoritarian set-up down to the power of hiring and firing, appointment and removal. At the outset, we criticized the Supreme Court of the United States for having accepted former President Taft's view that the President would have to have the power to fire any and all administrative officials of the federal government, if he were to be held responsible for the administration. We suggested that a comparative evaluation of experience in other countries would have produced a different view. What are these experiences and what do they suggest? It seems that one can distinguish five types of measures which influence the actual realization of the authoritarian political responsibility such as one would want to secure in a functioning administrative set-up. First, there are the promotional measures. These are based on the psychology of encouragement. Second, there are the disciplinary measures which are based on the psychology of discouragement. Third, there are financial measures of control and audit of expenditure, based on the rule of anticipated reactions. Fourth, there are the judicial measures based upon civil and criminal law. Such judicial measures are necessary concomitants of a legalized order and constitutional government, and have also been unduly emphasized in English-speaking countries. Fifth, there are critical standards in terms of objective achievement. This fifth method of enforcing responsible conduct which is becoming increasingly important at present has for a long time been the almost exclusive technique in the judicial branch of the government (except where judges are elective), and yet it has received wholly inadequate attention. It is in some respects akin to religious responsibility; for the standards of science are taken as absolutes. More regarding that matter later.

The promotional methods: promotion.—The promotional measures which are based upon the psychology of encouragement consist essentially of five things, promotions themselves, salary increases, titles, orders, and decorations. A considerable amount of responsibility can be secured from officials by a judicious employment of all of these; but most of these possibilities have been badly neglected in the United States. Lately, the Commission of Inquiry on Public Service Personnel Problems, in a notable report, insisted upon the decisive importance of promotion when it wrote:

"There can be no career service in government, or anywhere else, without promotion. The creation of promotion opportunities, however, is not easy to bring about, especially in large organizations, because the top officials with the power to appoint and promote may not know the younger subordinates or have any contact with their work. . . . A regularly organized system of promotion, maintained by the chief executives through a properly established personnel office, thus performs three indispensable services: first, it makes the service attractive to promising young men who will not enter an employment which is known not to give the opportunity of advancement based on proved merit; second, it results in an energetic staff by displacing the stagnant atmosphere of a stationary service; and, third, it brings to the top positions men who combine energy with knowledge of public administration, rather than partisans, amateurs, or men, with or without energy, who do not know the public service.

From the standpoint, therefore, of the establishment and maintenance of a career service, the promotion system is indispensable."

The educated young man of ambition who enters the civil service of England, France, or Germany is driven by competition with his equals to exert himself to the utmost in discharging his duties. To strengthen further the impetus toward self-exertion, the British have developed a system of annually certifying that service has been satisfactory as a condition for promotion as well as for salary increases. The United States forms a woeful contrast to this situation. Here it is difficult to get young people of ambition and ability to enter the government service, except as a stop-gap, because there is no clear road to promotion. Nor does the person who exerts himself to conduct his office responsibly find himself rewarded by promotion. It is a curious thing that in a country in which the lure of promotion is generally recognized by business leaders as of decisive importance in managing a large-scale organization efficiently, the need of a career in government has been overlooked. To be sure, one should avoid making a fetish out of the career element in enforcing responsibility. The over-stimulation of ambition may lead to very undesirable practices. Students of the problem of promotion have sometimes tended to neglect its dangers, and to make it a panacea for all ills. What must particularly be guarded against are schemes which seek to provide for a certainty of promotion. If a career in government service is taken to mean that, all the value of promotional opportunities in stimulating responsibility are lost. What you need in order to get responsible work is the possibility of promotion, not the certainty of it. Those who are unwilling to gamble with themselves are not, as President Lowell used to say, safe as a gamble for anyone else.

Promotional measures continued: titles.—Closely related to promotion are titles. If the greater responsibility of a higher office is to be publicly recognized and honored, an appropriate title has to be provided for such an office. Since much valuable ambition is generated by the desire for honor, it is almost absurd to fail to make use of the opportunities which human nature offers in this realm. It is sometimes asserted that America's tradition is opposed to the use of titles. In fact, courts, universities, and the defense forces, three very important branches of the national life, employ them extensively, and it is very startling to notice the use of such titles as that of colonel in the National Guard even in strictly private business relationships. The extension of this habit to governmental positions is clearly indicated by the facts. All that is necessary is that the community awake to the tremendous power wielded by the high-placed officeholder. If you can get a conception of certain offices as honorific in their very names you are securing a powerful impetus for responsible government service. Yet much that is most valuable in this sphere is beyond human control. Titles seem to follow something which corresponds to Gresham's law in economics—their value seems to decrease with the increase of the numbers acquiring them. The history of titles shows that you can never recoup a deteriorated title. The only possible method is to impose a still higher rank. The German *Geheimrat* is an amusing illustration. Eventually the point was reached when it was said that a professor or an administrator of the higher class could not escape becoming a *Geheimrat* unless he committed a crime. Yet, at one time, the word *Geheime Rat*, that is, Privy Councillor, was merely the description of an office, that of advising the king confidentially, and there were very few of these councillors. Gradually, more and more people desired to be able to claim that office, and therefore it passed from being a description of a job into being a title, because the kings took advantage of this common desire to be honored. It follows that any effort to create titles must be guided by what people desire as an honor. Nothing would be more silly than to imagine that one day Frederick the Great or Louis XIV called his officials into his office and said: "Now, boys, let us set up some titles in order to increase the efficiency of the service." Every one of the honorific titles in European administrative set-ups is the result of a very slow historical growth in the course of which a functional distinction became transformed into a titular one.

Promotional measures continued: orders and decorations.—Orders and decorations, on the other hand, can be created, and have been created. Therefore, if the growth of titles does not proceed fast enough you can establish honors through orders and decorations. However, there are here other considerable limitations. For the honor which is attached to such orders and decorations is great only if there is a general belief in the traditional significance of the person who establishes the order. If a king sets it up in a monarchical country, the decoration has that quality, but if the President of the United States does it, it does not necessarily have the same effect. For the President is a party man. This point is well illustrated by the story of congressional decorations. Honorary degrees by universities also have a very limited appeal, particularly because of the abuse made of it by various institutions in search of funds. Quite naturally; for orders and decorations are likewise subject to the law that the value of a thing is enhanced by its rarity. The French *Légion d'Honneur* is a case in point; when on reading in the paper about a friend's receiving that decoration I ventured to congratulate him at lunch the following day, he grinned wrily and remarked: "You know, in polite circles that 'honor' is no longer mentioned." And to be sure I noticed that he did not wear the little red ribbon in his button hole.

Disciplinary measures.—Besides these promotional measures, disciplinary measures based on the psychology of fear have always loomed large in the efforts to enforce responsibility in authoritarian set-ups. In fact, many persons would try to persuade us that only the harshest disciplinary measure, dismissal, affords an effective technique for enforcing responsible conduct of officials. That this view is erroneous we have already shown. That disciplinary measures are, nevertheless, an important weapon in the armory of the enforcer of responsibility must be admitted. But before the extreme penalty of dismissal or removal is applied, six other measures are available, each of them a valuable tool and effective within limits. They are reprimand, fine, temporary suspension, reduction of salary, and transfer to another, presumably less attractive, post. To neglect all these and focus exclusive attention upon removal is like trying to set up a criminal law with capital punishment as the sole penalty. According to administrative experience elsewhere, removal should only be used when all the other disciplinary measures have failed; it should, in other words, be recognized as the extreme penalty for the worst offenses, and it should never be used except on the basis of an established judicial procedure. Here, in fact, lies the core of the administrative law which we have discussed above (see Chap. VII, 12). Preferably, all these disciplinary measures should be imposed only after a hearing. In other words, instead of arguing about whether or not the President should have the arbitrary power of removal, it would be more useful to organize a judicial procedure for the imposing of a whole series of disciplinary measures, all of which would to some extent contribute toward administrative responsibility, especially if their imposition were carefully guaranteed against abuse by ill-advised superiors. Particularly when promotion depends upon service records, the entry of such a penalty upon the record effectively lessens the chances of promotion, even in case of a simple reprimand. I have listened in German administrative offices to long arguments as to whether a particular official should be reprimanded for a certain action, and the seriousness of so deciding was fully realized. All those present at the hearing seemed to appreciate the fact that the reprimand was an important tool in enforcing responsible conduct.

Fiscal measures.—Time-honored and yet often not sufficiently appreciated are the fiscal techniques for securing responsible conduct of administrative business. They are essentially three: forecasting the expenditures through an appropriate budget, controlling the payments when they are being made in order to insure their consonance with the budget, auditing the accounts afterward. In terms of the administrative organization itself, these controls are partly internal and partly external. Budgeting is both internal and external. The drawing up of the budget, with which the President with the assistance of the Bureau of the Budget is charged in the United States, while in England it is the Treasury, and in other countries the Ministry of Finance, is internally done by administrative officials. The approving of this budget, on the other hand, is external and entrusted to Parliaments (see below, Chap. XXII, ¶7). The controlling of the payments as made is internal in Europe, where the Treasury or Ministries of Finance have ultimate control, though in England the Comptroller and Auditor-General has some part in the matter. In the United States, on the other hand, the Comptroller-General as an independent "legislative" officer has complete control (short of court review), an arrangement which has led to very serious friction. Auditing, finally, is external everywhere with highly judicialized techniques being preferred on the Continent (*Cour des Comptes* in France, *Reichsrechnungshof* in Germany), executive work in England (Comptroller- and Auditor-General), as also in the United States (Comptroller-General). But everywhere parliamentary supervision, either of the judicial or executive officials, implements this machinery, by some sort of committee on accounts, wherever there is parliamentary government. Probably the preference of continental countries for a judicial set-up in the audit field is due to traditions derived from their monarchical past. Some sort of independent body, like the *Oberrechnungskammer*, established by Frederick William of Prussia as early as 1711, or the *Cour des Comptes*, established by Napoleon, is essential for the maintenance of financial integrity, even (or rather particularly) in an authoritarian administrative set-up. These bodies continued to develop into courts, because under the separation of powers as practiced by monarchical constitutional governments (see above, Chap. XI, ¶9) judicial safeguards of administrative integrity were most palatable to these governments; they looked upon them as acceptable alternatives of parliamentary supervision. When, later on, Parliaments were able to extend their jurisdiction, they found these independent bodies quite acceptable as aides in discharging their supervisory function. From this circumstance, as well as from the general theory of the separation of powers, it might be argued that the United States would be well advised to follow the pattern of a judicialized procedure for the auditing, and such a change has indeed been advocated. The present fusion of controlling and auditing functions in one "independent officer" certainly has not produced results which argue for the continuance of such an arrangement. Hence if a Court of Accounts were set up, the controlling function could then be put back under the administrative direction of the Treasury Department, where it belongs. Whatever the general framework of government, these several techniques have been found invaluable aids in securing financial responsibility. Politically speaking, they operate largely in accordance with the rule of anticipated reactions. It is, as in all such cases, futile to offer elaborate statistics as to what items have been disallowed, or what misdemeanors have been detected. They are, taken individually, important enough. But a much larger result is due to the fact that administrative officials who know that their expenditures have to be approved, and that they will be audited, are much more careful in their financial conduct. Anyone who has had practical contact with spending departments of the government will testify to that fact.

Judicial measures.—The preceding discussion of promotional, disciplinary and fiscal measures has sketched a wide variety of techniques for making the conduct of governmental officials more responsible. But most of these measures presuppose a willingness at the top to employ them when necessary. Suspicion, first of the king, and later of party bosses, has inclined the majority of people in Anglo-Saxon lands to look for outside controls. The judiciary provides the most obvious and ancient technique for this purpose. Judicial measures for rendering official conduct more responsible are, therefore, of great importance. Modern conceptions of the rule of law demand that all officials be subject to civil and criminal law. Whatever exceptions may be necessary regarding certain actions taken in the course of official duties, it goes without saying that no civilized community will suffer its government personnel to steal, cheat, or rape with impunity, though occasional relapses into that kind of barbarism seem indicated by certain recent developments. But such checks upon personal misconduct of officials can only take care of a minor part of the task of enforcing responsibility. Even if it be admitted that such judicial measures make an official responsible for doing something which should not have been done, they certainly do not provide any safeguards against the failure to do what should be done. Since administrative action is largely positive and an administrative agency must primarily be interested in "getting something done," judicial measures are rather narrowly limited in their applicability to governmental responsibility. What is more, the admission just made for the sake of argument cannot be accepted in fact. Many things which officials should not do are beyond the reach of the judiciary. Take, for example, offensive and overbearing conduct toward the public. This is certainly a bureaucratic vice of widest occurrence. Yet courts cannot deal with it at all, or rarely will the offense reach the point of extremity where the offended citizen could sue for tort. Again consider the case of slothful red tape or even deliberate lying. The damage to individuals may be very great, but nothing can be accomplished through the courts. An instance of that sort came to my attention recently. A subaltern clerk in an American Consulate rejected an invitation from an American citizen to a foreign relative (which is required as evidence of a *bona fide* visit), claiming it was not properly executed, and requested a duly sworn invitation instead. She added that the visa could not be issued, unless the duly executed form were in the hands of the consul four weeks before the intended departure. But there were only five weeks left, and consequently it was impossible for the alien to secure such an invitation within the time limit stipulated by the official. However, inquiry at the State Department revealed that no such rule existed; was there any judicial remedy for the improper and irresponsible conduct of the clerk concerned?

Governmental versus personal liability.—Not only are courts largely unable to bring about official action, and partly unable to prevent irresponsible conduct, but they are furthermore hampered, in the United States, by the ancient rule that "the king can do no wrong." This rule means that the government cannot be held liable for acts committed by an official in the course of duty. Damage suits against officials must, therefore, always establish that the official acted *ultra vires.* If the court finds that he acted *ultra vires,* the claim of the individual has to be enforced against the individual officer. It is evident that in many cases the individual officer is totally unable to pay the claim. If, on the other hand, the court finds that the official did not act *ultra vires,* then the damaged party is dependent upon the grace of a "sovereign legislature" for adequate compensation. The disadvantages of this situation are, however, by no means limited to the "public" which may sustain damages. Inasmuch as it exposes the official to constant danger of a ruinous suit for personal damages, it makes him over-cautious and thus irresponsible from the point of view of a vigorous pursuit of his duties. The recognition of this exceedingly unsatisfactory state of affairs has led legislative bodies to provide specifically for the responsibility of certain large-scale government enterprises in the case of torts committed by any of its officials. Certain municipalities have recognized their obligation for damage done by their fire departments, and more recently the federal government has provided similarly in the case of the T.V.A. It is indeed as evident as anything can be that the government should take the same responsibility for any large scale service enterprise which it manages as would be provided for if that enterprise were privately owned and operated. If it is to the community's benefit to undertake such tasks, the community and not the damaged individual should bear the losses involved in its operation. Actual experience in local government bodies where a certain amount of that type of corporate liability is allowed tends to show that objectively responsible conduct in terms of the particular service can be secured by internal measures such as we have sketched earlier in this chapter.

The same subject illustrated with reference to responsibility. —To put the matter positively, it appears that relieving the officer of the government from this type of personal liability has the great advantage of placing the responsibility where it belongs. If, let us say, a man lying asleep on his porch is accidentally shot by a policeman, the important point is not whether the policeman acted according to his legally defined duties. Even if he did not, it might be a gross injustice to burden him with the liability as long as he believed that shooting was the only effective means of handling the situation. If an American citizen is seriously damaged without due process of law by an officer of the government trying to maintain law and order or what not, he is entitled to just compensation. This compensation should come from the party responsible for the damage, namely, the American government and the American people as a whole. It is then up to the government to determine whether its officials acted responsibly or not, and to collect, in the latter case, what they can from the official, or to punish him according to established disciplinary procedure. This, broadly speaking, is the practice in continental European jurisdictions, and all the facts point toward the conclusion that responsibility is more effectively enforced by such provision. In fact, only such a plan will insure that a government service wielding vast powers of control, supervision, and regulation in every phase of the public's activities will not deteriorate into an irresponsible bureaucracy, now irremediably damaging private individuals in executing "laws" however bad, now timorously shirking from responsible action because of the absence of unequivocal "legal" authority. The problem of how to "judicialize" such a responsibility, how to organize courts which would specialize in adjudicating controversies arising out of administrative action is a grave one. We have treated it in broad outline when dealing with the judiciary as a governmental technique (see above, Chap. VII).

Measures based upon an objective standard.—It remains to inquire into what we called measures based upon an objective standard of performance as a possible technique for insuring responsible conduct. Perhaps the most ancient instance of the application of such an objective standard is found in the judiciary itself. As we pointed out when discussing the judiciary in relation to the bar (see Chap. VII, ¶ 8), judicial decisions are relatively responsible, because judges have to account for their action in terms of a somewhat rationalized and previously established set of rules. Any deviation from these rules on the part of a judge will be subjected to extensive scrutiny by his colleagues and what is known as the legal profession. The judges' sensitivity to criticism of their brethren off the bench, their feeling of responsibility toward that wide fraternal community, is a typical illustration of the kind of objective standard of performance with which we are here concerned (for greater elaboration regarding the judiciary see above, Chap. VII). It has only recently been observed that administrative officials seeking to apply scientific standards similarly have to account for their action in terms of a somewhat rationalized and previously established set of *hypotheses* or *rules.* Any deviation from these hypotheses will be subjected to thorough scrutiny by their colleagues in what is known as "the fellowship of science." If an official in the Bureau of Standards, let us say, should make regulations which would show lack of acquaintance with the essential knowledge in his field, he would be criticized so strenuously by fellow-engineers that his authority would presently vanish. There are, of course, here as well as in the judicial field, wide areas where doubt and controversy prevail. With regard to those activities, indecision or arbitrary selection among possible alternative solutions remains unavoidable. But it should be evident that even in these cases the necessity for justifying the choice will impose enough responsibility upon the official to make him wary of changing his conduct in a similar matter without weighty evidence. Thus a certain amount of regularity and predictability is secured.

Conclusion.—Almost all the preceding considerations of possible techniques for securing responsible conduct on the part of governmental officials depend for their most efficacious operation upon the condition that the government's service is being looked upon as a life career by those engaged in it. Officials are obviously more likely to pursue the government's tasks with a view to the general interest for which the service has been established when they are not forced to cultivate outside relationships to take care of them when they are removed from their public post. Even if contemporary governments do not go as far as princes in the seventeenth and eighteenth centuries, who would not permit anyone to leave the service after having received the necessary apprentice training, certain glaring abuses have obliged the United States Treasury to frown upon anyone who has been in the Treasury's revenue service acting as councillor for private individuals or firms in their tax dealings with the government. The real remedy is, of course, the provision of a satisfactory career prospect within the service. It is thus seen that ultimately the promotional measures are the decisive ones in guaranteeing a responsible government service, whereas "rotation in office" based on the Jacksonian slogan of ubiquitous aptitude for government service renders the service irresponsible in a high degree. The notion that an effective partisan orator or organizer qualifies himself for responsible work in, let us say, the revenue service because "he represents the will of the people" is largely discredited. We realize today, owing to the teachings of modern psychology if not to those of common sense, that there is no such thing as a specific "will of the people" with regard to the technicalities of revenue collection or any other "objective" function. All the people want is good execution of this function.

Consequently responsibility to the people does not require partisans of a particular general outlook, whether republican or democrat, conservative, progressive, or socialist, but it does require specialists who know their job and will, therefore, effectively execute the general rules decided upon by executive or legislative leadership in accordance with popular preferences. Fortunately, people aware of such "objective" standards and sensitive therefore to objective responsibility within a given function are often glad to be relieved of the obligation of making decisions where no objective standards are available. The very passion for objectivity and impartiality which renders them judicially or scientifically minded, makes them shrink from any rash and arbitrary decision. They are delighted to leave that task to the "people" or their elected representatives, with the aside: "Fools rush in where angels fear to tread." For it is the peculiar conceit of such specialists not to realize that *some* decision often has to be made. To the representatives of the people, both executive and legislative, falls the difficult task of making these decisions, or guiding the electorate in making them. The ensuing electoral responsibility, however, is so completely intertwined with the problems of representation that we cannot as yet fruitfully carry the discussion beyond the general sketch offered in paragraphs 6, 7, and 8 above. Admittedly the primary objective of parliamentary forms of government was and is to make the conduct of government responsible as well as responsive. But only after studying its workings will we be able to determine the extent and the conditions of the realization of this objective.

Part III

THE POLITICS OF CONSTITUTIONAL SYSTEMS

CHAPTER XVI

GENERAL PROBLEMS OF REPRESENTATION

1. *Introductory: representation as a method of securing responsible conduct.*—2. *Representation in Rousseau.*—3. *Representation in Hobbes.* —4. *The dual nature of representation.*—5. *Monistic constructions are false.*—6. *The scope of representation.*—7. *Electoral methods are not essential.*—8. *Why legislation is emphasized in representation.*—9. *The views of Hooker, Locke, and Rousseau on the importance of laws.*—10. *Fiscal matters.*—11. *The general problem of restraint as the link between a representative scheme and constitutional government.*—12. *Reasons for the late appearance of representative bodies and their importance.*

Introductory: representation as a method of securing responsible conduct.—In discussing responsibility and its enforcement, we pointed out that one of its most important forms was electoral responsibility. From a political standpoint, efficacy in securing responsible government must be considered the decisive element in all the various schemes of representation. In strongly religious epochs the notion that the king represents God on earth may be the most powerful impulse toward making him and his officials responsible. But when that faith declines, the most arbitrary tyranny may and often does grow out of such a scheme of representation. As was said before, modern government can in some respects be interpreted as an effort to produce without religious sanctions the responsible conduct of public affairs. The idea of toleration implies indifference toward those absolute standards upon which a religious sanction is built. In the place of such standards mutually accepted interests (public interests, so-called) become the basis for evaluating official action (see Chap. XV, ¶ 6). But who is the final judge as to the concordance of governmental action and the public interest? The orthodox answer is the public. In our large modern countries the public cannot foregather in the market place, like the Athenian citizens of old. Hence the only possible method of securing adequate controls is some scheme by which a small selected group of citizens acts for the whole body. Such action is representative. Since interests are relatively rational, and have to be coördinated by argument and discussion, a rational method for discovering such a representative group had to be evolved. In our modern world, direct general election has been generally accepted as the most rational method, though this view is by no means conclusively proven. Courts, for example, are manned by a different method, which may be more rational, and probably is more effective. This selection is based upon a relatively objective standard of technical competence. It could be argued that legislatures should be similarly selected. Their representative quality would not necessarily disappear; it might in fact be heightened. Burke, in his previously quoted discussion of parliamentary representation (see Chap. XV, ¶ 7) insisted that even the elected representative must conceive of himself as a guardian of national interests. Parliament, he said, was not a congress of ambassadors from different and hostile interests, but a deliberative assembly from *one* nation, with *one* interest, that of the whole; these representatives ought to be guided not by local purposes, but by the general good. Such an idealist conception of members of Parliament and congressmen evokes the ridicule of moralists and cynics alike; whatever Parliament ought to be, it surely is a congress of ambassadors from different and hostile interests, they would maintain. A change in the process of selecting them might be a constitutional reform of the most desirable consequences, the advantages being akin to those commonly believed to distinguish the appointive as compared with the elective judge. Such a reform need not affect the representative character of such a legislature, provided the standards of selection are themselves constitutionally defined. But whatever the possibilities of such future developments, our present purpose is to study and describe the techniques for securing representatives by election, and the relative success and failure in securing responsible conduct of public affairs through such techniques.

Representation in Rousseau.—In Anglo-Saxon minds the idea of representative government is firmly linked to that of democracy. It is, therefore, worth noting that Jean-Jacques Rousseau, the most ardent and influential expounder of democratic ideas, utterly rejects representation as contrary to the very essence of modern government. In his *Social Contract* he asserts that as soon as public affairs cease to be the primary occupation of the citizen, the state is bound to perish. If it is a question of going to battle, the citizens prefer to pay mercenaries and stay home themselves. If it is a matter of going into the assembly, they appoint deputies and stay at home. From indolence and by money they have soldiers to tyrannize the fatherland and representatives to sell it for profit. Therefore sovereignty cannot be represented, and for the same reason for which it cannot be surrendered: it rests upon the general will. The deputies of the people are, therefore, not its representatives, but merely its commissaries; they cannot give a definitive decision. Every law which the people have not approved is null and void; it is no law at all. It is obvious from these remarks that Rousseau was misled by giving too much weight to the experience of the ancients. Where the active citizenry had been able to foregather in the market place, as in Athens or Rome, their failure to do so did indeed spell disaster to the commonwealth; in modern communities the tendency of the citizen to neglect his voting privileges is the parallel development. If Rousseau were correct it would, in fact, make it impossible to organize responsible popular government in our modern countries with their millions of people. Nor is there any reason for denying in the governmental sphere what is a common occurrence in private life. For we know a considerable number of situations in which an individual or a corporation appoints an agent to attend to some business. Where many people have the same right or interest, it is often absolutely necessary for them to agree upon one person to represent them, lest their interest be neglected for want of unity in urging it. Since agents, curators, mandatories, and so forth, are a common type of human relationship recognized by every more highly developed legal system, there is no apparent reason why this sort of relationship should be unavailable or immoral in the conduct of government. It may, however, be conjectured that Rousseau's violent hostility to any kind of representative scheme was possibly in part engendered by the fact that his great antagonist Hobbes gave it such a prominent place in his political system. Moreover, the small self-governing cantons of his native Switzerland provided a living model for active participation of the citizenry which persists to this day. Following this historical precedent, Switzerland has taken the lead in developing the popular referendum and initiative as a technique of modern government (see below, Chap. XXV).

Representation in Hobbes.—It seems strange to us now that representation should at one time have been one of the most important ideas brought forth in the defense of absolutism. No writer offers a more striking illustration than Thomas Hobbes. Hobbes' entire conception of the state or even of a community rests upon the idea of representation. According to him, "A Multitude of men, are made *One* Person, when they are by one man, or one Person, Represented. . . . For it is the *Unity* of the Representer, not the *Unity* of the Represented, that maketh the Person *One*. . . . *Unity,* cannot otherwise be understood in Multitude."[1] Political writers in more recent times have often paid too little attention to the crucial significance of this notion when considering Hobbes' idea of the state. His notorious doctrine of the governmental compact, according to which every man covenants with every other man to make one man or assembly of men their representative, is rooted in this conviction that the unity of the state can in no other way be understood. And why can it not be understood? an unsuspecting student of politics might ask the philosopher of Malmesbury. Because each individual composing the multitude is a being utterly apart, like a particle of matter, moving through time and space in search of "power after power unto death." Therefore, only the superimposition of one such individual over all others can bring unity and order out of multitude and chaos. It is quite evident that such a point of view was eminently fitted to an age in which monarchical absolutism blossomed. It serves to show, at the same time, that the modern idea of representation is different, indeed. For by also avoiding the mysticism of Rousseau's general will, the modern conception is built upon the idea that the many specific interests in the community—local, professional, commercial, and social, to mention only the more important divisions—can by argument and discussion be coördinated and compromised, by public scrutiny and criticism be scaled down to become compatible if not identical with the public interest, that is, the interest of the community as a whole. It is the task of the popular representatives thus to coördinate and criticize. The necessary unity does not logically follow from the unity of the representer, as Hobbes would have it, but must be created and constantly re-created through a political process of great complexity, the most important constituents of which are parliamentary action and elections. Since both involve multitudes of persons, those with relatively similar interests form parties, that is, groups of people with common interests and ideals. Therefore parties are a third item of great importance in any discussion of representation. But before we turn to these matters,

[1] *Leviathan,* Chap. XVI.

in Chapters XVII, XVIII, and XIX, it is necessary to determine the scope of representation in terms of political science generally.

The dual nature of representation.—Historically speaking, representative assemblies developed in most European countries in the course of the later Middle Ages as an important part of the medieval constitutional order. Very often the three "estates" were composed of nobility, clergy, and the merchants of the cities (the burgesses). But the greatest variations existed in this respect. The most important of these assemblies is undoubtedly the English Parliament, where the higher nobility were joined with the higher clergy in the "Lords Spiritual and Temporal," while the knights together with the burgesses constituted the Commons. The reasons for this and most of the other variations are very controversial, and therefore scientific inquiry must content itself with noting the fact that in one way or another the more important groups in the community —sometimes rather rashly referred to nowadays as "classes"—were represented in assemblies called together by the king or his minister for the purpose of securing their consent to extraordinary taxes or levies. This was necessary, because the undeveloped state of central administrative systems and the absence of effective means of coercion (see above, Part I, and particularly Chap. IV) rendered the collection of such levies impossible without local coöperation. Quite naturally, these representatives when gathered together undertook to bargain for their consent to such grants of money; they presented complaints and petitions, which the crown had to heed, in order to secure what they wanted. These, then, were not national representatives but agents of local powers acting under special instructions or mandates. This was true, however, only as long as they acted separately. When the king and the two houses of Parliament acted together, after having settled their differences and reached a compromise, they were taken to represent the whole body politic. This is of decisive importance. In the same way, they were supposed to represent the entire body politic of the realm of England when acting as a high court (and that was supposed to be their most solemn function in the days of Edward Coke). This body of historical fact shows us clearly that it is quite inadmissible to draw a hard and fast line between agents with definite instructions or mandates and representatives empowered to attend to a general task. An elected body may and usually will be both a set of agents from different interests, and a representative group determining the common interest. Therefore, to return to our previously quoted statement from Burke, Parliament is both: a deliberative assembly from *one* nation, with *one* interest, that of the whole, as well as a congress of ambassadors from different and hostile interests.

Monistic constructions are false.—Older definitions of representation have tried to escape from this dualism, which lies deeply embedded in the political reality of representative schemes. But the logical faculty of political thinkers made them look for some unitary focus. Thus Hobbes with his general theory of man as a machine propelled by irrational drives to make rational efforts toward their achievement would "define" representative action as any action which actually served to realize the goals established by such human drives. To illustrate: the preservation of order by a monocrat, be he ever so tyrannical, is truly representative of the people simply because the desire for order is known to be a basic drive resulting from man's primordial fear of his fellows. It is evident that quite apart from the psychological aspect of this position, such a "definition" is much too broad and arbitrarily neglects the recurrent conflict of interests and values, not only between groups, but within the individual himself. These objections hold also of the contemporary Fascist and National Socialist doctrines, as well as of the Communist claim to represent the proletariat. Such self-appointed guardians of allegedly apparent interests, whether proletarian or nationalist, are ultimately forced into seeking some kind of religious or inspirational sanction for their asserted insight into objective needs, whether the inspirational guide be called Marx, Mussolini, or Hitler. The cult which grows up around such individuals places them into parallel with the demi-gods of old, and thus political representation has been transformed into religious representation once more. On the other hand, Rousseau with his emphasis upon will, by which admittedly he meant something akin to natural reason, could acknowledge as representatives only mandatories fulfilling instructions. If they deviated from these instructions these mandatories or agents necessarily abused the function for which they were called. He omitted from consideration the possibility of reaching a conclusion through deliberation which would be a true compromise in the sense of being in the interest of all, although all acting together could not possibly have arrived at it.

The scope of representation.—If then, we avoid these extremes, born as they are of logical rather than factual considerations—if not of political prejudice—we find that the scope of political representation can well be indicated by adopting Robert von Mohl's unpretentious definition. Representation then would be the process through which the influence which the entire citizenry or a part of them have upon governmental action is exercised on their behalf by a smaller number among them, with binding effect upon those represented. Some aspects of this definition deserve further comment. It is advisedly a matter of influence rather than participation or control, since representation is necessitated by the large number of citizens. Such a large body of people is not very likely to participate in or effectively to control governmental action. It is secondly by no means an accident that "governmental action" in general is spoken of, rather than any particular part of these activities such as legislation. The reasons legislation has figured so prominently in representative schemes is discussed below (see ¶ 8). But there is no reason why other governmental activities might not also be subjected to popular influence, a thought hardly worth mentioning in the United States today, but until recently often advanced by political thinkers. By admitting, further, that influence of a part of the citizenry, as well as the whole, may be represented, we escape the absurdities which would result from our denying a representative quality to the American Senate. Furthermore, the representation of the whole people is, historically speaking, a very recent development, whereas group representation is an ancient thing.

Electoral methods are not essential.—In addition to these elaborations of one definition, it should be pointed out that we have omitted any reference to election as an essential feature of representative bodies. It was stated at the outset that elections are merely one possible method for securing representatives; but its peculiar worth is by no means proven by its wide acceptance in the modern world. It may well be that more recent experiences will lead to a reversal and a corresponding limitation of the use of electoral methods. Apart from the method of selection on the basis of objective achievements, which at the present time is to some extent employed in the selection of judicial officers, there is the older method of having the officials of constituent corporate bodies be *ex officio* members of a larger representative body. This method is employed for the Fascist Council of Corporations, but no truly representative body results on account of the control which the government possesses over the corporate constituents. In other words, since these corporations are dependent upon the government, they cannot be said to possess influence upon it. It is also employed by the League of Nations, where the foreign ministers of the various nations are usually members of the assembly or the council or both. This form of representation also characterizes various economic councils, such as the French and the Czechoslovak Council. The defunct German Economic Council was similarly organized. Another method of considerable historical significance is inheritance of the office. The English House of Lords is an important illustration, and the upper houses modelled after it could be cited as further cases in point. And even if we admit the broad applicability of electoral methods, we must beware of identifying such methods with equalitarian principles. If the election is envisaged as a method for securing people adequate for representative purposes, it by no means follows that all those whose interests are to be represented should participate in the selection as such. This equalitarian prejudice has brought representative institutions to the brink of disaster, if it has not actually destroyed them. In the light of these experiences, we may readily admit that such feeble limitations as that every voter must be able to read and write are indeed indicated by the nature of the tasks which representatives are called upon to fulfill, and we may in course of time witness a considerable extension of such qualifications for the electorate. It should be remembered in this connection that thoughtful men in the days of Burke and John Adams saw property qualifications to a considerable extent justified by the greater education which such men were apt to possess, and while the social conflicts of our day would rule out any such arbitrary qualifications, we might in time evolve other and more equitable means of weighing the capacity of the voter. No such constitutional provisions would in and of themselves render a representative scheme less representative, as the equalitarian impulse may lead us to suppose.

Why legislation is emphasized in representation.—How can we explain that legislation came to be considered the peculiar province of representative bodies, of popularly elected bodies, when in fact medieval representatives had little or no concern with legislation? Ever since the sixteenth century, legislation was believed to be the most striking manifestation of political, or of governmental power. Legislation entailed the making of rules binding upon the whole community. Bodin had maintained that this power was the peculiar characteristic of a state. As we have seen before, the medieval notion of law as eternal custom, as something already there and merely to be found by learned men, was giving way to a realization that laws are man-made, that they are essentially decisions as to what ought to be rather than as to what is. In reality, the shift was of course merely one in emphasis. The High Court of Parliament had changed the law in the process of finding it, and so had the other courts of the realm. But even the great Coke had still insisted upon the "higher law" as a standard and criterion by which to evaluate parliamentary enactments (see above, Chap. VII, ¶2 ff.). He saw it as fixed and immutable, the peculiar and precious heritage of every Englishman, an embodiment of the principles upon which his life was built. This relation of general rules to principles, religious, moral, and otherwise, was the other pillar upon which men's preoccupation with laws and legislation as a manifestation of governmental power rested. You cannot force human beings in matters of principle, is the underlying idea. A specific act of government may be justified in terms of a specific emergency, but no general rule ever can. This leads us to the important if elementary consideration that the making of a rule presupposes that there is a series of events which have certain aspects in common. In other words, there must be a "normal" situation. This means that time is available for deliberation to determine what had best be done regarding such a situation. Now representative, deliberative bodies require time, obviously, and therefore legislation seems to be peculiarly fitted for such bodies. This very important truth has recently been carried to a logical *reductio ad absurdum* by linking parliamentary deliberation to the romantic passion for everlasting conversation, an idea which is as glittering as it is paradoxical. For parliamentary deliberation is entirely focused upon, and organized with a view toward action, the enactment of a general rule. The history and practice of parliamentary procedure proves this beyond doubt. But it is action which requires careful preparation in the coördination of conflicting viewpoints prevailing among the people. Insistence upon a certain amount of agreement among elected representatives seemed in part justified by the ability any considerable group of people in a given community possesses effectively to resist the enforcement of rules which they do not, or which they cannot, approve. The failure to perceive this underlies the Fascists' contempt for elected representatives as valuable guides in the enactment of permanent legislation. Their emphasis upon the desirability of unity in a community does not solve the problems which arise from the diversity of actual viewpoints. Like Bodin and Hobbes, both heathens to the core, they assert that the unity of legislative decisions is more important than the substance of what is being decided. When the conflict of norms in a given community becomes insoluble, when therefore the several groups have no common ground upon which to reach an effective compromise, the arbitrary superimposition of one possible solution is the only alternative to civil war or complete dissolution. Communists and Fascists both maintain that such is the case at the present time, and they both proceed to impose their particular norms. Once one grants their premise—and one has to when their factions grow to any considerable size—he cannot escape from their conclusion, unless he is prepared to adopt an equally radical position (as the *monarchomachs* did in the sixteenth century) and deny the rights of citizenship to Communists and Fascists (as conservative opinion in the United States tends to do). Such a stand is based upon the intrinsically sound conviction that a political community under popular government cannot endure where basic and indissoluble conflicts of principle prevail. That is why legislation is of such crucial importance and the peculiar province of representative bodies.

The views of Hooker, Locke and Rousseau on the importance of laws.—To show the strong sentiment regarding the importance of laws and of legislation (as the process of making such laws), it may be well to cite here the three leading constitutional theorists, Hooker, Locke and Rousseau. Rousseau describes the fundamental nature of a republic in terms of law: "I therefore give the name 'Republic' to every State that is governed by laws, no matter what the form of its administration may be: for only in such a case does the public interest govern, and the *res publica* rank as a *reality*. Every legitimate government is republican; what government is I will explain later on." Locke's discussion of the forms of a commonwealth is based on the conception of law as the essence of a commonwealth: ". . . for the form of government depending upon the placing the supreme power, which is the legislative, it being impossible to conceive that an inferior power should prescribe to a superior, or any but the supreme make laws, according as the power of making laws is placed, such is the form of the commonwealth." And Hooker concludes his first book of *The Laws of Ecclesiastical Polity* thus: ". . . of Law there can be no less acknowledged, than that her seat is the bosom of God, her voice the harmony of the world: all things in heaven and earth do her homage, the very least as feeling her care, and the greatest as not exempted from her power: both Angels and men and creatures of what condition soever, though each in different sort and manner, yet all with uniform consent, admiring her as the mother of their peace and joy."

Fiscal matters.—This preoccupation with law and legislation must not blind us to the fact that representative bodies are not usually limited to that activity. At the very outset, representative institutions were generated, as we have seen, by the ability of nobles, clergy, and townsfolk to resist the royal tax collectors, to defend their ancient right of being asked for their consent to new or exceptional levies. In this case, the influence which one part of the citizenry, the nobles, and then another, the burgesses, actually possessed entailed representative institutions for the exercise of that influence. The purely negative power of resistance could thus be converted into the positive power of affecting the conduct of government through petitions, complaints, and so forth. But this celebrated "power of the purse" has remained one of the cherished activities of parliamentary bodies, although the English Parliament has delegated all detailed control to the cabinet. Closely related to this power is the power to determine the expenditures of the government. In the beginning the two were joined; Parliament granted specific levies for specific tasks. Today, the expenditures of the government are, under a representative scheme, fixed through an annual budget. Since many of these expenditures are the direct outgrowth of legislation, however, the lines of distinction cannot be clearly drawn. A final aspect of fiscal influence exercised through representative bodies in civilized countries is the accounting control usually carried out by some kind of independent officer or "court" directly responsible to the popularly elected body, such as the Comptroller-General in the United States, or the *Cour des Comptes* in France (see above, Chap. XV, ¶ 15). Their relation to the representative bodies is rather formal.

The general problem of restraint as the link between a representative scheme and constitutional government.—Rather than carry forward an enumeration of representative assemblies, which would anticipate later topics, it seems better to turn to the general problem of restraint. In our discussion both of the separation of powers and of federalism we showed that the problem of restraint is indissolubly connected with the problem of dividing governmental power. Such a division can take several different forms, of which the most important are the functional separation of powers, in the classical sense, and the territorial subdivision through some sort of federalism. For both purposes, representation is of vital importance. Distinct divisions of the electorate, created and maintained under a constitution, offer the opportunity for selecting distinct sets of representatives between whom the several functions of government may be divided. Historically, the most important aspect of this arrangement in England was the division of the legislative power between king, lords, and commons, and the separation of the judicial power from all of them. But the most decisive forward march of democratic representation coupled with careful divisions of governmental power occurred in the United States. Here the application of divided representation of the whole and its parts made it possible to escape from the dangers of majority tyranny which seemed to be implied in such a thorough democratization, and the federal organization must therefore be considered an essential part of representative constitutional government in this country. Similar are the arrangements under the constitutional order of Switzerland where traditional Swiss elements are brilliantly blended with lessons derived from the experience of the United States. As compared to these schemes, the French and English systems must be considered decidedly unstable. While it is quite possible that the remarkable political traditions in one or both of these countries may succeed in imposing upon the central government the moderation which a scheme of concentrated powers does not force upon them, we cannot afford to treat lightly the acute observation of Professor Barthélemy who commented upon the parliamentary regime in France in this sense: "If a parliamentary regime is bad for a centralized administration, a centralized administration is equally bad for a parliamentary regime." In order to appreciate the full significance of this observation, it is of course necessary to keep in mind that the parliamentary regime is *par excellence* for French thought a constitutional order based on a functional separation of powers which in the United States is pictured as a presidential regime. In either case, a constitutional safeguard for local powers, which is the essence of federalism, as we have seen, is part and parcel of such a scheme.

Reasons for the late appearance of representative bodies and their importance.—It has often been said that representative schemes are of rather recent origin; they certainly were not found, as Montesquieu asserted, in the forests of ancient Germanic tribes. They arose as part of the medieval constitutional order when that order assumed proportions which forbade any direct action. In the first place, the unitary organization of Western Christendom through the Catholic Church necessitated representative assemblies, the great councils, in which all the Christian people were believed to be present. It was natural to apply the same idea to the representation of monasteries and cathedral chapters within a secular feudal order. And when the cities and towns reached a place in the sun in the course of the thirteenth century, and had to be reckoned with as centers of wealth and power, a further extension of corporate representation of these municipalities was clearly indicated. Was it a matter of peculiar genius or of pure accident that Simon de Montfort, in calling the Parliament of 1265, issued a summons to the knights of each shire, as well as to the burgesses? It has been suggested that the exigencies of the English crown, hard pressed by unruly and powerful barons, gave the minister of Edward I this idea as a matter of electoral strategy. At any rate, the shires were corporate entities, capable of representation by analogy to the towns. Apparently in all these cases the corporate spirit of solidarity was sufficiently developed to render the group willing to exercise its influence through agents or representative persons. This the whole preceding discussion has implied as a necessary corollary of representation. Where personal attendance is practically impossible, and the result is considered more important than personal participation and insured by corporate solidarity, that condition will be fulfilled. Now in classical antiquity neither was personal attendance impossible in the small city states, nor was the result considered more important than personal participation. In fact the prevalence of slavery afforded the citizenry the position of a small leisure class who immensely enjoyed the daily gossip in the market place. But this insistence upon personal participation became fatal, whenever such a city-state reached larger proportions. The attempts at solving this problem through a federal organization foundered upon the inability of the ancients to work out a representative scheme. Ingenious as were the arrangements of the Romans for their Latin Federation, they could not get away from the idea of embodying the citizenry of each city in the Roman citizenry, with the result of swelling its numbers so unduly that eventually they had to abandon this practice altogether. As we have seen when discussing federalism, its embodiment in an effective political order has to await the completion of a representative scheme under which the whole people as well as the people of each component state can be given a certain influence upon the federal affairs, and a firm and uniform federal authority can thus be established. Through participation in the representative bodies of the federal union the justifiable demand for influence and control is being satisfied and the states are thus protected against total obliteration. From such a point of view logrolling is not a purely vicious practice, but one which secures a certain protection for local interests. This being the case, the federal administration can be given more power and independence, and under certain conditions it may be directed by a few or even a single person, as in the United States. Such an organization is greatly superior to a congress of ambassadors, such as characterized the federations of old, and has been revived in the League of Nations. What is perhaps the most interesting development of all is the drift of the British Empire toward a federal structure. Although the Imperial Conferences have been only intermittently called, the whole evolution of the Empire toward a federative Commonwealth is perhaps the most striking achievement of the process of representation in the modern world. It gives one hope that the higher aspiration of a representative federal government of all nations may also eventually come to fruition.

CHAPTER XVII

ELECTORAL SYSTEMS IN THEORY AND PRACTICE

Introductory: the problem.—Tom, Dick, and Harry trotting to the voting booth enact the most distinctive process of modern politics. There have been kings, revolutions, constitutions, and vast bureaucracies since time immemorial, but the mass voter is something quite recent. To Aristotle democracy (polity) meant that the vital decisions were made by the assembly of the whole citizenry in the market place. To us it means that the whole citizenry goes and elects representatives, after having read about their platforms in the newspapers, listened to them in a meeting or over the radio. We have seen in our discussion of representation (see above, Chap. XVI, ¶7) that these elections are not an essential feature of representation, although it is popularly so assumed. Elections are merely one possible method for securing representatives, and perhaps not even the most efficacious method. Nor must we jump to the conclusion that all those whose interests are to be represented should participate in the selection as such. A considerable number of people are quite obviously disqualified to select a modern legislator, let us say. To admit that obvious truth, does by no means imply a plea for government by intellectuals. On the contrary, the real backbone of an elective system are the cautious steadfast men and women of common sense who can see the forest rather than the trees. It is one of the recurrent errors of the Fascist and Communist critics of representative government to make light of the sound sense of the average citizen. Thus the critical evaluation of electoral methods which democratic enthusiasts have too long neglected has in our days become the favorite hunting ground for those who would overthrow representative constitutional government altogether. Therefore such a comparative estimate must now be one of the most urgent concerns of the political scientist, as well as the practical reformer.

The English system in historical perspective.—Parliamentary government in England rested for a long time upon a strictly traditional system of elections. It had grown out of the corporational basis of early Parliaments. Until the Reform Act of 1832, it abounded with the most extreme situations. Districts which had once been populous centers, and therefore entitled to separate representation in Parliament, retained this representation after all just claims had gone. One such "rotten borough" actually had been swept away by the sea. On the other hand, thriving cities had grown up in the industrial north of England which had no member in Parliament at all. The series of parliamentary reforms during the nineteenth century undertook to cope with this problem, and at first sought to employ the expedient of giving several representatives to one district. This system lasted down to 1884-1885, when the single-member constituency came into general use. Since that time, elections in England are held on the basis of what is known as the system of plurality, that is, relative majority. This means that the candidate who secures the largest number of votes (but not necessarily an absolute majority) wins the seat. At the same time, the elections are now secret, whereas formerly they were public, and took place by a showing of hands. As a result, polling was an occasion for much brawling and merrymaking. "Rivers of beer were set flowing; bribes were openly offered and accepted; organized bands of 'bludgeon-men' went about intimidating and coercing electors; non-voters thrust themselves joyously into the fray; political convictions were expressed in terms of rotten apples and dead cats; heads were broken and a generally riotous time was had by all" (Ogg). Yet there is much to be said for an open election. As John Stuart Mill pointed out, the right to vote is a public trust, and should therefore be exercised in such a fashion as to give the public a chance to see how it is used. What is more, under proper conditions of free assembly, it develops in the citizenry that most desirable quality of civic courage which does not shrink from standing up for one's convictions. Unfortunately, modern economic pressures have introduced a new element into the situation which obliges us to forego these advantages in order not to deprive a large body of citizens of their "right of suffrage." Since 1885 then, England has adopted secret balloting under a system of single-member constituencies. The purpose of these constituencies is to elect a Parliament which in turn will be ready to support a cabinet, which in turn is to govern the land. In other words, the English electoral system is clearly directed towards the goal of dividing each constituency and thus all England into two halves, the majority to govern, and the minority to criticize. This may mean permanent voicelessness for a man who belongs to a perpetual minority, like a Democrat in Vermont, or a Republican in Alabama. As Walter Bagehot told his readers many years ago: "I have myself had a vote for an agricultural county for twenty years, and I am a Liberal; but two Tories have always been returned, and all my life will be returned. As matters now stand, my vote is of no use. But if I could combine with 1,000 other Liberals in that and other Conservative counties, we might choose a Liberal member."

Proportional representation.—The foregoing statement sounds like a criticism of the existing English electoral system; in fact it constituted part of a reasoned defense of that system against those who had just brought forward the plan known as proportional representation. To be sure, Thomas Hare's scheme, first expounded in 1857 in a pamphlet entitled *The Machinery of Representation* (more fully developed in 1859 in his *Treatise on the Election of Representatives, Parliamentary and Municipal*) cannot claim to be the first exposition of the idea of proportional representation. The idea appeared in the French National Convention in 1793, without leading to action. It was further elaborated by the mathematician Gergonne (1820), and developed independently by an English schoolmaster, Thomas Wright Hill, whose son took it to Australia (1839). At about the same time, in 1842, the idea gained a foothold in Switzerland when Victor Considérant proposed a proportional representation system to the Council of Geneva (*De la Sincérité du Gouvernement, Lettre à Mss les Membres du Grand Conseil . . . de Genève*—repr. 1892). Two years later Thomas Gilpin published a pamphlet *On the Representation of Minorities of Electors to Act with the Majority in Elected Assemblies* (1844), setting forth another plan for proportional representation. Finally another twelve years later the Danish minister of finance, Carl Andrae, worked out a system resembling the Australian plan, but using ballots. The following year Hare published his tract. From this rapid survey, it can be seen that proportional representation was "in the air." The underlying idea of all the various systems is to secure a representative assembly reflecting with more or less mathematical exactness the various divisions in the electorate. Why should such divisions be reflected? They should be "represented"! The voice of minorities should be heard! Justice requires that no votes be lost, that the Bagehots be able to get together and send a representative to Parliament. A man of the eminence of John Stuart Mill extolled the virtues of the scheme in his *Considerations on Representative Government* and called it one of "the very greatest improvements yet made in the theory and practice of government." Yet all these arguments show that proportional representation shifts the basic meaning of representation. In determining the scope of representation we saw (Chap. XVI, 6) that it referred to the citizenry as a whole, not to the divisions among them. Representation meant the exercise of their influence through a smaller number acting in their behalf. Proportional representation, on the other hand, looks upon the divisions in the electorate as the entities to be represented; in the last analysis it looks upon the individual as the representable element or unit. Thus proportional representation reveals itself as a distinct manifestation of that extreme individualism which made its appearance in the course of the nineteenth century. It therefore ran afoul of the firmly embedded communal tradition of the British people, and has not been able to make substantial headway in that country, which more than any other, with the possible exception of the United States, has contributed to the development of representative institutions. It may be well to recall the traditional view at this point once more, as set forth by Blackstone: "Every member (of Parliament), though chosen by one particular district, when elected and returned serves for the whole realm. For the end of his coming thither is not particular, but general; not barely to advantage his constituents, but the *common*wealth; . . . And therefore he is not bound to consult with or take the advice of his constituents upon any particular point, unless he himself thinks it proper or prudent to do so." This traditional view was more fully developed by Bagehot, in his *English Constitution*, and it has remained the crucial point of rebuttal of the proportionalists. His classical discussion deserves, therefore, a brief summary here.

Bagehot's view of it: the functional approach.—Bagehot considers it the fundamental difference that election by a majority entailed compulsory constituencies, whereas proportional representation allowed voluntary constituencies. A constituency being the group or segment of voters who are entitled to send a member to Parliament, this is indeed the basic point, although the language of proportionalists often obscures it. To put Bagehot's point another way, all proportional schemes say to the electorate: if so and so many among you can agree upon a candidate[1] that candidate shall be elected, whereas the majority system says: so and so many among you shall constitute an electoral district or part of the whole people and whomever the largest number among you elect, shall be one of the members of Parliament. As Bagehot pointed out, the temptations of the idea of a voluntary constituency are very plain. "Under the compulsory form of constituency the votes of the minorities are thrown away. In the city of London now, there are many Tories, but all the members are Whigs; every London Tory, therefore, is by law and principle misrepresented: his city sends to Parliament not the member whom he wished to have, but the member he wished *not* to have. But upon the voluntary system the London Tories, who are far more than 1,000 in number, may combine; they may make a constituency and return a member. In many existing constituencies the disfranchisement of the minorities is hopeless and chronic." "Again, this plan gets rid of all our difficulties as to the size of constituencies." "Again, the admirers of a great man could make a worthy constituency for him." Yet Bagehot saw defects in the scheme which overbalanced and outweighed these merits. Essentially, under the voluntary system, so-called central party organizations would acquire an overweening influence. "The crisis of politics would be not the election of the member, but the making the constituency. . . . The result of this . . . would be the return of party men mainly. The member-makers would look, not for independence, but for sub-

[1] The required number varies greatly. The following list will give an idea:

Austria	39,500
Belgium	40,000
Bulgaria	20,000
Czechoslovakia	45,400
Denmark	22,500
Finland	17,125
Germany	127,000
Ireland	20,000
Netherlands	70,800
Norway	17,650
Poland	61,200
Sweden	26,100
Switzerland	20,000

servience—and they could hardly be blamed for so doing. They are agents for the Liberal party; and, as such, they should be guided by what they take to be the wishes of their principal. The mass of the Liberal party wishes measure A, measure B, measure C. The managers of the registration—the skilled manipulators—are busy men. They would say: 'Sir, here is your card; if you want to get into Parliament on our side, you must go for that card; it was drawn up by Mr. Lloyd; he used to be engaged on railways, but since they passed this new voting plan, we get him to attend to us; it is a sound card; stick to that and you will be right.' Upon this (in theory) voluntary plan, you would get together a set of members bound hard and fast with party bands and fetters infinitely tighter than any members now. . . . The full force of this cannot be appreciated except by referring to the former proof that the mass of a parliament ought to be men of moderate sentiments, or they will elect an immoderate ministry, and enact violent laws. But upon the plan suggested, the House would be made up of party politicians selected by a party committee and pledged to party violence, and of characteristic, and therefore immoderate representatives, for every 'ism' in all England. Instead of a deliberative assembly of moderate and judicious men, we should have a various compound of all sorts of violence. The voluntary plan, therefore, when tried in this easy form, is inconsistent with the extrinsic independence as well as with the inherent moderation of a parliament—two of the conditions which, as we have seen, are essential to the bare possibility of parliamentary government." It seemed desirable to quote these memorable phrases at such length, because they have always remained dominant in England, in spite of persistent agitation for proportional representation over the last fifty years. What is more, they foretell in the most extraordinary manner the experiences which we have been able to observe where such systems have been put into force. On the other hand, these arguments do, of course, by no means exhaust the problem, particularly since they are applicable only to a parliamentary government, and possess cogency only when the divisions or cleavages of the people have not as yet reached such an intensity that any electoral system would be abandoned which did not give these warring groups adequate representation in national affairs.

Gerrymandering (electoral geometry).—Besides the representation of important minorities, proportional representation seemed to Bagehot to possess the merit of getting rid of the difficulties as to the size of constituencies. As long as the population shifts, periodic readjustments of the size of electoral districts are necessary, if gross injustices such as the rotten boroughs are to be avoided. In the United States, that problem is a familiar one through the recurrent struggle over reapportionment. In recent years a somewhat agitated controversy has been raging among statistical scholars regarding the "just" method of such reapportionment. It is this difficulty which affords many of the illustrations of those who argue for proportional representation. But, of course, unequal electoral districts are not of the essence of the system of plurality elections. At the same time, it must be conceded (at least from the standpoint of the scientific observer) that this system does, *usually,* show considerable maladjustments in the size of electoral districts. What is worse, under adverse conditions of unscrupulous party politics, it lends itself to the practice of gerrymandering, so-called after a former Governor of Massachusetts who perceived the potentialities of affecting the electoral result by manipulating the geography of the constituencies. Since all a party needs to gain a seat is a small majority (or in three-cornered fights a mere plurality) of votes, you can draw the boundaries of your electoral districts in such a way as to crowd large percentages of your party opponents into a few districts, and then divide the rest in such a way as to give yourself a majority. What you are thus doing is merely artificially creating conditions which resemble those which arise in course of time through the shifts in population. To give a concrete illustration: suppose you had an area which had to elect ten representatives for 100,000 voters. These voters are divided between party A and party B in such a way that party A is adhered to by most of the city-dwellers, whereas party B is counting most of the farmers as its partisans. There are three cities in the territory, one of 20,000 voters and two of 15,000 voters. If party A were in power and undertook to gerrymander this territory, they would want to get about 7,000 of their supporters into seven districts, thus giving them a clear majority in the representative body. They would do this by constructing mixed country and city districts, leaving the rest of the voters in solid agricultural areas. But the managers of party B also would want, if they were in power, to construct mixed districts, but in such a way as to leave some strictly urban districts. The two pictures would compare thus:

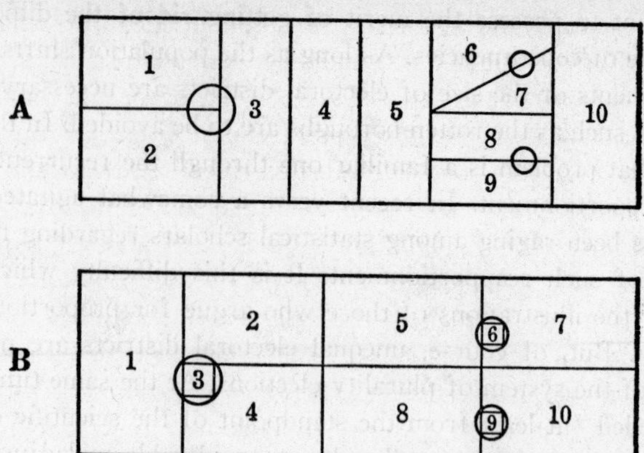

The districts under the gerrymander of A would be:

(1)	A	7,000	B	3,000		(6)	A	7,500	B	2,500
(2)	A	6,500	B	3,500		(7)	A	7,500	B	2,500
(3)	A	6,500	B	3,500		(8)	A	7,500	B	2,500
(4)	A	0	B	10,000		(9)	A	7,500	B	2,500
(5)	A	0	B	10,000		(10)	A	0	B	10,000

The districts under the gerrymander of B would be instead:

(1)	A	3,500	B	6,500		(6)	A	10,000	B	0
(2)	A	3,250	B	6,750		(7)	A	2,500	B	7,500
(3)	A	10,000	B	0		(8)	A	2,500	B	7,500
(4)	A	3,250	B	6,750		(9)	A	10,000	B	0
(5)	A	2,500	B	7,500		(10)	A	2,500	B	7,500

These samples illustrate in a typical fashion how the same *total* electorate may give entirely the opposite result, if divided along opposite lines. Many American states show the most extraordinary shapes for electoral districts, shapes which are much more exotic than the salamander to which the gerrymander was supposed to be related. But even if party managers do not stoop to such tactics, where moderation is indicated by the possibility of a popular reaction against such unscrupulous manipulation, it would be too much to hope for from human nature to expect party managers to change electoral districts when the social forces have produced effects akin to our example but quite independent of any manipulation. Precisely this was the situation in England throughout a large part of the nineteenth century; it also was the situation in the German Empire before 1914. But whereas the English reforms undertook to redistrict the country, and eventually in 1885 divided the whole realm into a fairly even number of single-member constituencies, probably because the more conservative Liberals, like Bagehot, could not see eye to eye with proportional representation, the German Social Democrats who had advocated proportional representation before the war, because they had been the main sufferers, stuck to their conviction after the revolution of 1918, and adopted a thoroughgoing system of proportional representation in spite of the fact that it would have been to their distinct advantage as a party to redistrict the country and hold elections in single-member constituencies. But before we turn to these matters of practical experience we ought to develop more fully the idea of proportional representation in its specific form.

The different functions of proportional systems.—Unquestionably, Bagehot put his finger upon the fundamental objection, from a political viewpoint. But he did not perhaps formulate it in the most persuasive fashion. For in terms of our previous discussion, and in terms of the accepted focal interests of modern political science, it is more important that a majority system of elections force the voter to *decide* between two or more alternatives, than that the constituency be compulsory. In reality, both these observations are of course derived from the same set of facts, but the need of a decision is paramount, when the representative body has over and above everything else the function of providing the government which is to hold office as long as the representative body is willing to support it. Since the time of Bagehot this is admitted to be the most important function of the English Parliament; indeed this is the very meaning of parliamentary government. For a long time this function was obscured by the older doctrine of a separation of powers, particularly since it prevailed in the United States. Parliament was looked upon as a legislative assembly. But while this function is quite important, it is not *as* important as the executive management of the whole state. And the influence of the whole electorate upon this executive management as exercised by their representatives must become focalized into a few clear alternatives. For as Lowell has so clearly shown, large numbers of people cannot decide between any but two or three very simple alternatives. It is, however, by no means a foregone conclusion that the function of the representative assembly should be a decision as to who shall govern. Not only in the United States, but in Switzerland and in pre-war Germany the main function of the representative assembly was legislation. Now legislation, particularly modern economic and social legislation, touches the everyday interests of all citizens, and the divisions of interest between them are more or less permanent. It cannot, for example, reasonably be expected that the employer and capitalist would be persuaded to hand all profits over to his workers, nor can we hope that the workers will readily yield to those who would bid them to grow fat on the joy of work, and be content with long hours at starvation wages. Legislation touching these and many similar issues between the various groups in the community must be framed as an acceptable compromise in which all relevant views are voiced with a vigor approximately comparable to their actual strength in the community. A representative assembly, then, whose primary function is the framing of such legislation would greatly benefit from a well-thought-out system which would bring into it the various groups in the community in rough proportion at least to their strength. This object proportional representation hopes to realize. But as was apparent before, proportional representation is by no means a uniform proposition. In fact the number of possible variations is quite large. A thorough discussion of all of them is both impossible and unnecessary. No matter what the variations in detail, the fundamental principle is always the same: to secure a representative assembly reflecting with more or less mathematical exactness the various divisions in the electorate. Now, there are two predominant ways of achieving that purpose, the single transferable vote advocated by Thomas Hare, and the list system of proportional representation widely used in Europe. The first scheme gives the voter leave to indicate first, second, and third choice (and more if there are more candidates in the district). Thus the voter continues to choose between individual candidates. The second scheme, on the other hand, asks the voter to choose between lists of candidates which contain as many names as there are representatives to be chosen. Rather than enter into an abstract discussion of these schemes, it seems better to study them in the particular forms which they have been given in various countries. For even though these practical plans are often combinations of the two basic types, they will offer an opportunity for an understanding of both. The most radical applications of the list system of proportional representation may be found in the German Republic, whereas the single transferable vote is being tried in Ireland (Free State). More or less mixed plans are being used in Belgium, Denmark, Netherlands,

Norway, Sweden, and Switzerland (among others). Let us turn now to an examination of these various systems. We shall begin with some of the last mentioned, since they have been longest in operation.

Practical application in Belgium and The Netherlands.—The oldest system of proportional representation for national elections is to be found in Belgium. Here the voter has to choose one of the several party lists, but at the same time he is entitled to indicate his preferences within the list. The list itself is made up by the party, and if the voter is satisfied with this order, he merely votes for the list as is by making a cross at the top. If, however, he should desire to see some other order, he can also put a cross beside the name whom he prefers. To give an example: In the elections of 1910 the Catholic list in the district of Brussels which was to elect twenty-one representatives received 97,358 votes for its list, and 31,794 votes for individual candidates on the list (preferences). By adding these two figures, we get what is known as the electoral number (*chiffre electoral*). In order to find out how many seats a party gets, and which ones of their candidates get them, the number of votes which will be necessary, known as the electoral divisor (*diviseur electoral*), is determined by a method invented by Professor d'Hondt.[1] In this case it was 13,720. Their total vote being 129,152, the Catholics got nine seats. The man at the top of the list, Nerincx, had received only 741 preferences; he therefore had to be given 12,979 additional votes given to the list without preference, in order to reach the electoral divisor. For according to this system, each candidate is entitled to whatever votes without preference are left to make up his full electoral divisor, going down the list. Therefore the decisive test for the preferential ballots comes toward the end of the list, as can be clearly seen in our example. After Nerincx' seat had been filled, we get the picture on page 272. It is apparent that only a few individual preferences were expressed for the first candidates on the list, because their election was certain. The real agitation was over de Coster and Colfs, and Colfs won, because of the large number of preferences expressed on his behalf. Wouvermans received the ninth seat, without reaching the electoral divisor, because he had the next highest number of votes, and the list was en-

[1] Professor d'Hondt's method is to divide the electoral number successively by 1, 2, 3, 4, and so forth, and to list the quotients until you come to one which most nearly corresponds to the figure you get by dividing the total vote by the number of seats. See for further detail Hoag and Hallet, *Proportional Representation.*

	Individual Ballots	List Ballots	
2. de Lantsheere	670	13,050	13,720
3. Vanderlinden	364	13,356	13,720
4. Renkin	1,835	11,885	13,720
5. Carton de Wiart	1,357	12,363	13,720
6. Theodor	1,601	12,119	13,720
7. de Buc	2,780	10,940	13,720
8. Wouvermans	1,497	10,666	12,163
9. de Coster	6,869	—	6,869
10. Colfs	13,980	—	13,980
		97,358	

titled to nine seats. This example shows clearly how right Bagehot was when he asserted that the real battle (the crisis of politics, as he called it) would be fought over the constituencies, or, to put it another way, the electoral group being Catholic, anyway, the decision of this part of the electorate was over the question of which candidate might best represent them. We might say, for this reason, that the preferential ballot added to the list ballot under the Belgian plan gives the voters something corresponding to the American primary. But since such influence of the electorate comes only at the very end of the list, the central party bosses have the lion's share in determining the outcome of the elections.[1] It is noteworthy, that under this system of proportional representation, a remarkable stability of party strength has given the strongest party, the Catholics, long periods of undisputed leadership. While it cannot be denied that a certain amount of uneasiness was felt regarding this rigidity of party lines before the war, the broadening of the electorate since the war has, by ending the numerical predominance of the Catholics, laid the ghost of permanent Catholic domination. In its place, Belgium has experienced marked ministerial instability which is beginning to undermine the long-felt satisfaction with proportional representation in that country. Very similar in its conception to the Belgian system is the Dutch electoral plan which was adopted in 1917 after very extensive deliberations and inquiries over many years. In the Netherlands, however, the entire country was constituted as one single electoral district. The voter does not express a separate preference for the list and the candidate, but is asked to vote for a candidate on a list, and this vote is at the same time a vote for the list. After omitting here the complications arising from the fact that several lists

[1] Since 1919 certain further complications have been introduced to allow for the combination of lists over several districts, which we omit here, as they contribute nothing to our discussion.

may be combined by their parties into a group, we can distinguish essentially two steps in determining the outcome of such an election: (1) dividing the seats among the several lists, and (2) dividing the seats given to each list among the several candidates. The first step is taken as follows. The actual ballots cast for all parties are added together and divided by the number of seats in Parliament, which is one hundred. This quotient is the general electoral divisor. By dividing the number of votes each party has received by this divisor, you get the number of seats to which each party is entitled. But since some seats remain unassigned (because the divisor does not divide evenly into the number of votes cast for the several lists), these are assigned on the basis of the largest surpluses. The details do not matter here. Now in order to take the second step and divide the seats attributed to a list among the several candidates on the list, you have to find a second divisor, the list divisor, which is found by dividing the number of ballots cast for the list by the number of seats. Those candidates which have received as many as or more votes than this divisor are elected. Their surplus votes are transferred to the other candidates on the list in the order in which they appear on the list. Here, then, the power of the central party directorate reappears again, but as subsidiary to the preferences of the voters. Here is an illustration, found in the Dutch Royal Commission's Report:

A list received four seats, the several candidates had votes as follows:

J. van der Horst	800
M. Meijs	600
G. van Loon	125
C. de Lange	75
P. Kooij	250
J. de Vries	150

The divisor of the list is

$$\frac{\text{Vote}}{\text{Seats}} = \frac{2000}{4} = 500$$

The divisor being 500, the first two candidates are elected. Their surplus of 400 is divided between van Loon, who gets 375 and is elected, and de Lange. Although de Lange only gets 25, which gives him 100 votes in all, the last seat goes to him, because none of the remaining candidates having reached 251 (one more than half the divisor) the seat goes to the next on the list. This Dutch system also has led to a remarkable stability of party strength, and, on the whole, public opinion is quite satisfied. It is noteworthy that Holland as well as Belgium is ruled by parliamentary government. To be sure, when proportional representation was first introduced into the Dutch kingdom, it seemed to call forth a marked increase in the number of parties: fifty-three instead of thirty-two parties appealed to the electorate, and sixteen as against nine were successful. But in 1925 the number dropped back to thirty-two and eleven respectively. At present there are 15 parties represented among the one hundred Dutch deputies. It should not be surprising, if the very fact that parliamentary government renders small parties ineffectual should hold the tendency toward a multiplication of parties in check. This expectation is the more justified in view of the experience of Belgium, where in spite of the long duration of proportional representation, we find essentially only three great parties, the Catholics, the Socialists, and the Liberals, which stand for the three dominant creeds as well as the three dominant economic divisions of the country. To these has been added the Flemish Independence Party which since the war agitates for the racially and linguistically distinct Flemish minority. When we come to our general conclusion, we shall suggest what permits these countries to combine effectively parliamentary government and proportional representation.

In Norway, Sweden, Denmark.—The three Scandinavian kingdoms, Sweden, Norway, and Denmark, also combine parliamentary government with proportional representation. Their systems are each different from the other, but both Sweden and Norway have list systems, whereas Denmark has tried to work out a complicated plan of combining single-member constituencies with proportional representation. Without entering into the details of these arrangements, it is necessary to characterize briefly these three systems (to which the Finnish is related, being in point of adoption the first of all). Whereas the order of the candidates as determined by the central party directorate has considerable weight in the elections of Belgium and Holland, the voter has the sole voice in the matter of which candidate comes first in Sweden and Norway. In order to accomplish this end, the country is divided into definite districts, with fixed number of seats attributed to each of them. The range in the size of the districts is greater in Sweden than in Norway, one district having only three seats and one as many as sixteen. In Norway they vary from three to eight. The districts of Norway are fixed in the constitution, a problem of principle which, as we shall see, is of the greatest significance. The voter can put on his ballot as many as five more names than there are deputies to be selected in his district. He can pick these names from various lists, and he may even add the names of persons not named in any official list. By numbering them, he can indicate the order in which he prefers them. The method of determining who has been elected is complex, but it is simplified by the fact that the voters do not avail themselves of the extensive freedom which the electoral system bestows upon them. In the election from 1921-1927 the candidates have always been elected in the order in which the party proposed their election. In the district of the city of Oslo, only 559 out of a total of 900,851 votes were irregular. The Swedish system is similar, but instead of allowing the voter only to combine candidates of several parties, it provides for the running of a candidate for several parties. There is also the possibility that within a party a certain faction will indicate its particular candidates, once more a device which gives the voter rights somewhat akin to those conferred by the American primary. There are considerable variations in the extent to which the voters of the several parties exercise their own judgment in the matter of individual preferences. While the social-democratic electorate (labor) are very loyal, the conservative and liberal groups are more ready to bolt from party headquarters. In spite of these elements of flexibility, the Swedish electoral system has been considerably criticized in recent years, and occasional voices have been heard which demand the return to some kind of single-member constituency. The main point of attack has been the power of central party bosses and the lack of connection between the voter and the elected representatives. However, neither in Sweden nor in Norway does there seem to be any inclination to abandon proportional representation, and the same thing is true of Denmark. To be sure, Denmark has worked out a peculiar plan according to which the voter elects representatives in single-member constituencies with certain complicated provisions for the transfer of his vote to adjacent constituencies combined into districts. Finally, thirty-one seats are distributed nationally on the basis of the proportional vote for each party. The main objection to the Danish system is its complexity; but it does not seem to perturb the Danes, who are operating parliamentary government under its ægis with considerable success; whatever difficulties were encountered in connection with forming a workable ministry were not attributed to proportional representation. We must now turn to a case where proportional representation is part of a non-parliamentary constitutional order, Switzerland.

In Switzerland.—Not only is Switzerland without a parliamentary executive, but she also has a federal government. In other words, her constitutional order resembles that of the United States more nearly than any of the governments we have so far considered. It is hardly surprising that proportional representation first made its appearance in some of the cantons (the Swiss name for the units composing the federal union), notably the canton of Geneva. Elections to the lower house of the federal legislature did not become proportionalized until 1919 and experience with this system is therefore rather limited. The Swiss system is another variant of the list system, made more flexible by giving the voter entire freedom in making up his list, as in Norway and Sweden, and adding the opportunity of voting twice for the same candidate. The practical working of the plan had best be illustrated by an example, taken from the elections of 1928 in the canton of Zurich. There were 132,656 ballots turned in, containing a total of 3,502,211 votes; for there were twenty-seven seats in this district. In order to find the number of votes which will elect one candidate, you divide the total number of votes by the number of seats plus one and then add one, thus: $\frac{3,502,211}{27+1} = 125,078 + 1 = 125,079$; this is the electoral quotient. By this figure you divide the number of votes each party received, to wit:

	Votes	Seats
Democrats	399,968	3
Peasants	634,764	5
Liberals	609,874	4
Communists	120,550	—
Protestants	123,421	—
Socialists	1,327,330	10
Social Christians	254,307	2
Social Indep. Prot.	31,997	—

This would have been the preliminary distribution of seats, leaving three seats to be assigned, if the non-Socialist parties had not formed a combined list; but since they did, their total vote which was 2,022,334 must be divided by the electoral quotient, and thus the combined list receives sixteen seats (as against the fourteen they would get separately). Since the Socialists had received ten seats, one seat remains. In order to determine who gets this seat, the number of votes of each party is divided by the number of seats assigned to it before plus one, thus:

Combined list $\frac{2,022,334}{16+1} = 118,960$

Socialists $\frac{1,327,330}{10+1} = 120,666$

Communists $\frac{120,550}{0+1} = 120,550$

Therefore the Socialists receive the seat, because they have the highest quotient. Now the division of the several seats assigned to the combined list of non-Socialists is proceeded with according to the same method, namely by dividing the votes for each list by the list quotient. Thus we get three seats for the Democrats, five for the Peasants, five for the Liberals, one for the Protestants, and two for the Social Christians. By this method, then, an almost mathematical representation of the existing views in the community is achieved. The considerable division of parties under this system cannot, however, endanger the conduct of the executive government, since the Swiss Executive Council does not feel obliged to resign, if the vote in the legislature is adverse to its recommendations. Instead, it sets to work in the preparation of a measure more in keeping with the wishes of the representatives. To be sure, it cannot be denied that certain splits, like that between the Liberal and the Peasants' party (the latter having formerly constituted part of the former) were helped, if they were not engendered, by the proportional system (the Peasants' party has only one member in the Federal Upper House elected on a plurality system). Yet the possibility of finding majorities for legislative measures as one goes along makes such a divided representative assembly a satisfactory institution for the carrying out of their one essential function, that of legislation.

In the Irish Free State.—Whereas Switzerland is on the whole a country famous for its moderation in politics, the Irish Free State is noted for the violence of its political partisanship. Yet, proportional representation seems to have taken root there without much friction. Indeed, it is claimed that the very intensity of political animosities necessitated a proportional scheme, because the lack of unity might have led the party defeated by an ordinary plural system to resort to violence. Be that as it may, the Irish Free State has adopted the single transferable vote system of proportional representation which the British Proportional Representation Society has so long been advocating. It resembles in some respects the Danish system, and while it is perhaps too much to say that this system allows a greater amount of free choice than any other proportional system, it certainly gives the voter a very large freedom of choice. The names of all the candidates in an electoral district having been printed together alphabetically on the ballot, the voter is asked to put figures before each name indicating his order of preference. Each voter has only one vote, but if a candidate should receive more than his share of first choices, the second choices of his ballots are distributed among the other candidates to see which then gets the highest number. Practically every county is constituted as an electoral district. Since the counties differ in size, they send from three to nine members to Parliament. The several parties nominate their candidates, usually residents of the county. In 1927, Galway with nine seats nominated twenty-two candidates in all. Although the parties may instruct their followers as to which candidate to put first, they usually content themselves with urging their voters to vote for the men on their list—or so it is asserted. At any rate, the voters can do as they please. This may have important political consequences, as in the election of 1922, when the two factions of Sinn Fein—those who favored the treaty with England and those who did not—had put forward a combined list. The voters, by indicating a preference for those candidates which were known to favor the treaty, provided the government with the necessary backing for this contested step. In order to see clearly how this system of the single transferable vote works out, it will again be well to analyze an example. Suppose an electoral district has eight seats and 80,000 voters participate. If a candidate received 10,000 votes, he would automatically be elected. Ordinarily, however, the votes will be either more or less. Suppose one of the candidates got 20,000 votes. Then 10,000 of his votes must be distributed among the second choices. In order to do this, the election official must redistribute all these ballots. He finds that P got 10,000 of these votes, Q got 5,000, and R also 5,000. Each of these candidates is entitled to one-half of these, because the other half is needed for A himself. If one of them had enough first choices to reach the full quota with these second choices, he would be elected. After all surplus votes have thus been distributed among the second choices, there may still remain some unfilled seats. In this case, the candidate with the lowest vote will be declared defeated, and his votes will be added to the votes of the candidates appearing as the second choice. As soon as one of these candidates receives a full quota, he is declared elected. This process is continued until the seats are filled.

Thus all the seats are filled according to the sequence of preferences of the entire electorate. In the county of Dublin, in the election of June, 1927, the distribution of votes and seats was as follows:

Parties	First Choices	Seats
Government..................	22,685	3
Fianna Fail..................	16,012	2
Independents..................	15,989	2
Labor..................	9,623	1
National Ligue..................	3,844	0
Sinn Fein..................	1,937	0
	70,090	8

For the whole Irish Free State the results were similarly proportional; about 7,500 votes elected a candidate. It is widely believed that this system has had a stabilizing influence upon the conduct of affairs in Ireland. The relative stability of party strength under this plan has prevented the extreme oscillations in the policy of the government which a new country with such passionate partisanship might otherwise have experienced. Since the necessary minimum quota of votes cannot readily be reached by groups which are too small to command solid support in at least one district, the number of parties is not exceptionally large. To be sure, two small parties, the Labor party and the Farmer party, would scarcely have any representation. Their existence has, however, had a somewhat moderating influence upon Ireland's relation with England, since these parties have held the balance for considerable periods between the friends and the enemies of the treaty with England, and while they have sold their support for concessions to the special groups which they represent, they have nevertheless exerted a wholesome effect. It would perhaps have been fatal if these "marginal voters" had shifted back and forth between the two major parties, thus bringing about rather extreme changes in the course of official policy. But the experience is still too short to consider the evidence conclusive regarding the compatibility of proportional representation and parliamentary government in the Irish Free State.

In the German Republic: the list system (unalterable party tickets).—From the Irish Free State we must finally turn to the ill-fated German Republic of 1919, where proportional representation according to the list system was carried to its logical conclusion, and by some is held largely responsible for the collapse of the Republic. In contrast to the small or dependent states which we have so far considered, Germany was, even after the World War, a large power with a complicated foreign policy of its own. She had had, before the war, a majority system somewhat less radical in its operation than the English plurality system; its greatest shortcoming was a wholly obsolete districting of the country which gave the agricultural conservative elements an undeserved preponderance, based as it was upon the distribution of the population in 1864. The main sufferers under this system had been the Social Democrats who would have had more than twice their representatives between 1887 and 1912, whereas the Conservatives would have had only about 70 per cent of what they actually had. It was therefore natural that the Social Democrats should have been ardent advocates of proportional representation, and so they proceeded to apply that system after coming into power in 1918. But having given only cursory thought to the problems involved, and being greatly rushed by what seemed at the time to be more important problems, they proceeded to adopt a rigid list system for determining the relative strength of parties. This method seemed to them free from serious objections also on account of their vigorous party discipline, which looked upon the individual member of parliament only as a soldier in an army fighting for labor's interests. The German system is rather simple in its conception. The country was divided into thirty-five electoral districts. Each party prepared a list of candidates for these districts, the larger parties usually containing as many candidates as there were seats to be filled in the district. For each 60,000 votes this ticket received, one of its candidates was elected, and exactly in the order in which they appeared on the ticket. The voter could make no changes, as in many of the other countries where proportional representation is used. He really voted for a party, rather than a candidate. Consequently, if in a certain district, 100,000 votes had been cast for, let us say, the Communist party, that party would get one seat. But what happened to the remaining 40,000 votes? They were transferred to another list, put up for several such districts, forming a union of districts, and if any remained, they were further transferred to a national list. The purpose of the national tickets was to make use of all the left-over votes, so that "no lamb may be lost." There was another idea back of this notion: that it would make it possible for national leaders to return to parliament without undergoing the exertion and sordidness of an election campaign. This idea did not prove to be correct to any considerable extent; rather these lists provided safe berths for the party managers and wire-pullers behind the scene. Since it was permitted to put a candidate on several lists, men who fought in contested districts also had their names put on the national list for safety's sake. It is apparent that such a system, particularly in a large country like Germany, placed a premium upon the formation of separate parties, so that even a leader and prophet of some crankish cult, like Haeusser, could attempt to secure the necessary 60,000 votes. But his successful campaign led to an amendment of the election laws which provided that no party could get more seats through the national ticket than it had secured on the several local tickets. This somewhat curbed the smallest groups. Thus a small party with the sole objective of having the losses from inflation made up by the government, calling itself magnificently the Party for the Rights of the People, received 271,931 votes but no seat in the election of 1930. Previous to the change, they would have gotten four seats. But even with this limitation, a party, once it commanded sufficient local support, could make itself felt. As a result, the German parliament became one of the most multi-colored representative assemblies ever seen, and in course of time the formation of cabinets became practically impossible. It may be well to give the figures for one of the later parliaments, like that created by the elections of May 20, 1928. In order to show the influence of the proportional system upon the

Parties	Seats	Plurality	Majority
Social Democrats	153 (125)[1]	225	8
Nationalists	73 (60)	37	5
Catholics	62 (51)	88	23
Bavarian Catholics	16 (13)	26	14
People's party	45 (37)	2	
Communists	54 (44)	12	1
Commercialists	23 (19)	—	—
Agriculturists	3 (2)	4	1
Social Christians	10 (8)	1	—
Hanoverians	3 (2)	3	—
Peasants	8 (7)	2	1
Democrats	25 (20)	—	—
National Socialist	12 (10)	—	—
Saxon Peasants	2 (1)	—	—
People's Rights' party	2 (1)	—	—
	491 (400)	400	43

[1] In order to facilitate calculations, the actual figures are transcribed proportionally, on the basis of a total of 400 candidates. These figures are given in parentheses. This table is taken from Johannes Schauff's "Die parteipolitische Struktur Deutschlands" in *Neues Wahlrecht*, 1929, pp. 149-151.

increase of small splinter parties, we add certain comparative figures. (See table on preceding page.) These do not, of course, give the full picture, because the absence of a proportional scheme would further strengthen the actual drift toward the larger parties. This tabulation shows with striking force that all but four or five parties would have disappeared from German politics, if a plurality system had been adopted. Besides, the Communists, who made it so difficult for the Socialists to govern, would have been kept within very narrow limits, and radical extremists, like the National Socialists, would never have gotten a chance. Thus this aspect of the German proportional system alone may be said to have greatly complicated the conduct of government. It will, however, be well to examine the arguments advanced against the system in greater detail in a separate paragraph.

Criticism of German system.—The German system was, during its entire lifetime, subjected to searching criticism by both theorists and practitioners. How much this system contributed to the breakdown of German constitutional government has recently been stated with striking candor by a thoroughgoing student of this entire controversy. He goes so far as to assert that proportional representation was a necessary condition of the German catastrophe. Maintaining that democracy can reconcile liberty with authority only by subjecting the minority to the will of the majority, he finds that "certain fundamental tendencies are created by proportional representation which make this compromise impossible, replacing it by that kind of constitutional deadlock which is the ideal preparation for dictatorship." The expression, proportional representation, here refers of course only to the list system as used in Germany; and as there are indications that the political incidents of this system are quite distinct from those of other schemes, it is hazardous to generalize concerning proportional representation. But what were these "certain fundamental tendencies?" Perhaps most important was the fact that the list system not only stratified existing party organizations, but created new ones. On a rough guess, we are told, it was eight times as easy to found a new party under the German system as under a majority system. What is more, the parties under such a list system, where the lists are controlled by the party bosses, are very different from those which a majority system engenders. The German experience essentially bore out the predictions of Bagehot (see above, ¶ 4) as to the rigidity of party lines and the disregard for the marginal voter; it showed further that the political consequence of that emphasis upon regularity, dogmatism, and creed was the rise of radical extremist parties. Hence the homogeneity which parliamentary government needs is not only not created, but actually destroyed. Yet, curiously enough, this emphasis upon dogmatism did not banish the impact of special interest groups. On the contrary, each moderate party tended to become identified with some particular one of these interests, and some interests actually organized parties of their own, as did the real estate interests when they founded the Economic Party of the German Middle Classes. The result of such a combination of entrenched interests on the one hand and radical dogmatism on the other was a recurrent deadlock when it came to making up a cabinet. There never was any clear "decision" at the polls in terms of which a cabinet could be set up. Presidential compromise cabinets and intrigues behind the scenes to maneuver them followed. To make matters worse, the rising predominance of radical extremists threatened any such compromise cabinet with constant defeat, but never was such defeat followed by the extremists' assuming power and responsibility in turn (see below, Chap. XX).

The disregard of the marginal voter was only an especially unfortunate instance of the general disregard for the voter. Internally, in their relations between members and leaders, the parties ceased altogether to be democratic. The overweening position of the party bosses was further enhanced by the size of the electoral districts under the list system. These, in Germany, numbered about 2,000,000, which made personal contacts impossible. While a small constituency depends upon the cooperation of local volunteers for much of the work, the large German constituencies allowed the party to pay a permanent secretary and to become quite independent of genuine membership cooperation. Unlike the man who seeks election, such party functionaries remained unknown to the electorate, and dissatisfied groups in the party following were unable to make themselves heard.

This oligarchic and bureaucratic trend naturally also moulded the relations between the rank and file of the representatives and the top men. Having no personal backing in the electorate, they had to look toward the party boss for support. Such boss rule is of course found everywhere, but the German list system greatly aggravated this evil. The result was a painful change in party leadership.

Where seats are personally contested under an electoral system, a man seeking election must be able to fight. This brings forward men of the "leader" type. Under the German list system with its emphasis upon party regularity, a man seeking election had to conform; this brought forward the bureaucratic type. In the German parliament there were many excellent specialists on technical matters, but leaders were decidedly lacking. What made matters worse was the premium such an arrangement placed upon older men. Young men found it surprisingly difficult to break into the ranks of all but the most radical parties. "The ideal of democracy was defended by white-haired old men, and it became almost impossible not to regard democracy as a thing of the past." It did not help things that every party had to try to placate as many specific interest groups as possible by providing places for their representatives on the party list. Even when such "experts" were not outright corrupt, they were apt to confuse the interest of their group with the public interest. Once more, this was not a novel condition, but one which the list system forwarded to an unprecedented extent. Although many more detailed demonstrations of the evil workings of the list system of proportional representation could be given, it ought to be quite clear from this summary that it greatly increased certain defects in the democratic process. The central objection, however, is one which Rudolf Smend insisted upon in a celebrated essay in which he argued that the election under this system (Smend, in fact, claimed it for all proportional systems) ceases to be a creative political process in which vital political decisions are made. Since the election is the central political process of democracy, democracy is thus destroyed. "The parties fight of course for the votes even under a proportional system, but only for the individual votes, rather than for the total result of a majority of the electorate. Thus a very distinctive creative political element is lost; for the voter is much more deeply concerned where he is confronted by defeat or victory to which he makes a vital contribution. . . . The voters . . . do not fight each other with a view to determining the political will of a given constituency which would be a truly political result. . . ." It is clear that Smend is harking back to the original arguments of Bagehot (¶ 4). Unhappily, these aspects of the list system were not clearly perceived in 1919. Only a very small group of men under the able leadership of Friedrich Naumann had grasped the fundamental issue involved. Consequently the discussions in the constitutional convention were quite inadequate, and Friedrich Naumann's warning, "The result of proportional elections is the impossibility of parliamentary government; parliamentary government and proportionalism exclude each other!" remained unheeded.

Defense of proportionalism.—It must, however, be admitted that there remained to the end certain convinced adherents of proportionalism in all parties who were not motivated by any narrow partisan points of view. The case for proportional representation was put essentially on the ground that one should beware of blaming the proportional system for every flaw in the German Republic, because a system allowing free preferences on the part of the electorate should have been substituted for the system of fixed lists, or unalterable tickets. In short, it was claimed that most of the objections are eliminated by abandoning unalterable tickets. These objections could not, therefore, be considered arguments against proportionalism itself. This is not true of the rise of the interest groups. But as far as these groups are concerned, it must be admitted by all students of English and American politics that they appear also under majority systems of representation. In fact, their influence has been used to argue for the adoption of proportionalism. Besides, even where such interests do not actually lead to the organization of parties, they often influence party politics to an inordinate extent, as Professor Holcombe has shown (see below, Chap. XIX). Proportionalism merely brings these groups out into the open. As to the minor economic groups, they would not be able to gain ascendancy even under proportionalism, if proportionalism is so constructed as to necessitate a certain amount of local support and voters' preference, as was shown by an analysis of most of the proportional systems in the small European countries. Now as to the fundamental argument of Professor Smend, which at bottom is identical with the argument of Bagehot and others, we had better turn to a more elaborate consideration in the form of concluding remarks.

Conclusion.—Whatever the merits of other schemes of proportional representation, the proportional scheme which makes the whole country one constituency and bases its proportionality upon votes for unalterable party tickets has been found wanting and utterly incompatible with parliamentary government. As to systems which allow the voter all necessary freedom to choose between individual candidates, the case is not so clear. In the first place, it must be admitted that in a non-parliamentary system such as that of

Switzerland, a proportional system allowing the voter freedom of choice, and requiring a considerable amount of local support is desirable as a technique for securing popular representation. For here the main concern of the representative body is legislation, and therefore a multiple-party system does not seem to entail serious difficulties, while the adequate representation of all important groups in the community is in many respects desirable, particularly when social and racial differences are marked. In the second place, it cannot be denied that under conditions of marked and fixed political diversity in the community proportional representation may be the only system acceptable to the larger minorities. The decisive question here would be how permanent these minorities are. Racial and social minorities frequently have this important quality which distinguishes them from traditional English and American party support: they are quite permanent yet can never hope to grow into a majority. Where such minorities exist, and have reached a state of self-consciousness, the people are no longer "fundamentally at one," to use again Lord Balfour's famous phrase. They therefore need an electoral system which assumes diversity rather than unity. But it must be urged that such countries should not adopt parliamentary government of a thoroughgoing variety. In answer to those who would point to the governments of Belgium, The Netherlands, Sweden, Norway, Denmark, and finally Ireland, we would answer that in the first place none of these countries are powers of the first magnitude. But three of them have a marked foreign policy, and this foreign policy is protected by a very large measure of dependence upon greater powers which gives even these countries a certain never-questioned solidarity in the field of foreign affairs: there are no possible alternatives! Thus Belgium *must* rely upon England for maintenance of her neutrality, Sweden *must* guard herself against Russia by all available means, Holland *must* guard herself against England and Germany by a policy of strict neutrality between them. (See below, Chap XXII, for greater detail in this matter.) But apart from this strong tendency toward neutrality, and the consequent solidarity of all in the matter of foreign policy (internationalism is, in these smaller countries, not a doctrine exclusively cherished by the Socialists!), there are special factors to be considered in these several lands. In Belgium, Holland, Sweden, Norway, and Denmark monarchy has survived in a form more nearly resembling older constitutional forms than is true in England. While these governments are parliamentary, in the sense that they must find support in parliament, the royal head of the government still exerts a marked influence in the selection of the candidates, and his moderating tendency is often apparent. Only recently, the dignified Queen of the Netherlands said, and said rightly: "This country stands for sanity." It is obvious that the very smallness of these countries allows for an intimacy between court and parliament which would be hard to maintain in larger countries. What is perhaps even more important, it is notable that Holland and Sweden, who in many ways have the most distinctive foreign policy, have developed traditions in the administrative field which effectively neutralize a large part of the executive establishment and thus limit parliament largely to the legislative function, as in Switzerland under a separation of powers (see above, Chap. XI, ¶ 13 for details). This is well illustrated by the recent experience of Sweden, which was governed for several years by a cabinet (the Ekman ministry) composed of members of the smallest party in Parliament which by striking a middle course effectively secured majorities for its legislative program as it went along. Finally Ireland is in the first place still a dependent political unit as one of the Dominions in the British Commonwealth of Nations, her foreign policy, while to some extent independent, is as yet indistinct, and where it is distinct, resembles that of the countries just discussed, and on top of it all so central an issue of general policy divides the whole Irish electorate that even the proportional scheme has engendered the organization of what is essentially a two-party system. All this goes to show that the prevalent English and American opinion against proportional representation, while practically sound, cannot support the proposition that parliamentary government and proportional representation are incompatible. There are many special conditions under which they are quite compatible. But it must also be said that the proportional representation enthusiast, who would argue from the relative success of proportionalism in these countries that its speedy introduction into Great Britain, France, and the United States is indicated, goes similarly wrong. As we have pointed out, special conditions prevail in each of these countries which make the elections to a representative assembly something different from a fundamental decision of the electorate concerning who shall govern the country for the time being. Nor are the aggravating problems of foreign policy of such all-permeating significance. But it must also be said that, of all these great powers, the United States is most readily adapted to proportional representation. This evidently is due to the constitutional order being built upon a separation of powers scheme. But it also means that the President as chief executive must forever be elected by a simple plurality. Since the whole country constitutes one constituency for this election, the tendency of the parties to stick together for this all-important test of electoral strength would probably act as a powerful deterrent to the development of minor parties beyond the large amount of party irregularity already present. It must, therefore, be admitted that a proportional system would probably be a workable substitute for the present plan, if a large section of the public desired it. If introduced, it would unquestionably hasten the development of a stronger emphasis upon matters of principle, whether this came about by the gradual rise of a Socialist party, or by an effective re-grouping of existing party allegiances with a progressive and a conservative opposed to each other. The significance of such parties of principle as compared to parties built upon patronage is, however, a problem transcending the present chapter (see below, Chap. XVIII). Concluding upon the basis of the data so far discussed, we can say that electoral systems cannot be considered and evaluated in absolute terms, but must be studied with reference to the whole constitutional order, as well as the social and other conditions of the country concerned. No popular government can escape from the necessity of working out a system adapted to its peculiar needs.

CHAPTER XVIII

POLITICAL PARTIES: GENERAL PROBLEMS

Introductory.—Parties are undoubtedly one of the more important phases of popular and particularly of parliamentary government. It is now generally agreed that they are indispensable features of democracy. Yet, one hundred and fifty years ago, their place and function was generally unknown. At the founding of the United States, the "people" were looked upon as capable of acting as a unit. Washington, as everyone knows, warned in his farewell address against "factions." Later historians have mockingly remarked that Washington was inclined to look upon efforts to disturb Federalist rule as "factionalism." This is true except that Washington did not know "Federalists" as a party; what came to be the platform of the Federalists was to him still the one sound, patriotic, American policy to which there did not exist any equally possible alternative. To be sure, in England in the course of the eighteenth century the idea of parties as a part of the governmental scheme had been dawning on the minds of the most acute observers; but Bolingbroke's persuasive arguments against such a plan, his readiness to identify it with "corruption" and to extol the ideal of a patriot king still held sway over many minds. Curiously enough, the American colonists were revolting at the same time against this corruption in Parliament and against the tyranny of the king who tried to cope with it. To understand this paradox, one should recall that George III had been emulating the technique of Walpole and the Whigs by building up a royalist faction of henchmen in Parliament. He was, in other words, tarred with the same brush. But his underlying ambition was to become such a patriot king as Bolingbroke had depicted. He was going to rule according to the original scheme of the constitution as an independent chief executive. But by organizing a party, he acknowledged their place and function in the constitutional order; no wonder that the party outlived him and his personal ambitions.

Party origins and the cabinet system.—Historically speaking, the English cabinet's parliamentary responsibility arose out of the party struggle; it is generally agreed that the evolution of the two institutions is inseparably intertwined. It is therefore rather difficult to discuss the development of one without the other. But since the Whigs and Tories of the last years of Charles II's reign are admittedly the prototype of the modern English party system, it must be conceded that the parties antedate the cabinet system. We may say, as we did in the previous chapter, that the single-member constituency with plurality elections is peculiarly adapted to the two-party system under responsible parliamentary government, because it forces the electorate to make up its mind between two clear-cut alternatives. But we must remember that the plurality vote and the resulting sharpness of party division preceded the cabinet system the functioning of which it later insured. Now the reason why the responsibility of the cabinet to Parliament (the cabinet system) was engendered by the party strife is that each party in its effort to buttress its position, but more particularly the Whig party under Walpole and Pelham (1715-1760), sought to secure for itself a solid majority in Parliament, thus facilitating the realization of all policies for which the coöperation of Parliament was necessary. This Walpole proceeded to do by a carefully worked out system which to contemporaries and moderns alike can appear only in the light of corruption. Wraxall tells us in his memoirs that the government under Pelham handed each of their partisans in Parliament from five hundred to eight hundred pounds at the end of a session, the amount varying according to the services rendered. These payments were official enough to be entered on a record kept in the Treasury. More recent investigations have been able to show that the Whigs at that time had worked out a very elaborate system of governmental favors, ranging from direct payments to voter and member of Parliament, through patronage, to the various favors available in foreign trade and the privileged trading companies. All this is well known enough, since it was so intimately bound up with the struggle for independence waged by the American colonies a few years later. What is less readily seen is the lesson which this story teaches, namely that the English two-party system is rooted in a traditional struggle for spoils between two distinctly aristocratic factions or divisions of the (aristocratically controlled) electorate. In fact, Walpole once remarked that he and Lord Townshend constituted the "firm" to which the king had entrusted the country's government.

A two-party system grows out of one party.—It would, however, not be generally conceded today that the long Whig rule under Walpole was the true origin of the English parties. Historians have for a long time argued about this problem and while some have, with Sir Erskine May, dated party growth back to the Puritans under Elizabeth, others, like Lord Macaulay, have refused to admit anything worthy of the name prior to the Roundheads and the Cavaliers of the Long Parliament. The truth lies in between. Some of these differences in opinion are traceable to different conceptions as to what constitutes a party. Obviously, the more one stresses organizational features, the later one will have to put "party origins." Of course, when party is taken to mean something akin to faction, the partisans of the Red and the White Rose in the fourteenth and fifteenth centuries were members of a "party." But since these factions of nobles were baldly striving to seat their head on the throne, no question of principle entered in. On the other hand, the Puritans under Queen Elizabeth lacked all effective organization, and they hardly attempted to control Parliament (without parliamentary responsibility, such control was not particularly important). They had deep-seated convictions, to be sure; but many of these beliefs transcended the strictly political sphere. Under James I, however, the Puritans took on something of the quality of a party which developed into the Roundheads of the Long Parliament. While the Puritans did not explicitly claim it, they really sought the control of the government. Or, to put it another way, they sought to escape from the control which the king had hitherto exercised over the government. The system of patronage and corruption which the Tudors had developed for the purpose of keeping Parliament in line is too well known to require recounting here. (It was essentially this Tudor system which George III attempted to revive.) What matters to us is that the Puritan party developed as an opposition to the government as such, and more particularly to so-called royal prerogative (see above, Chap. XI). This remained so down to the Long Parliament period when the Puritans themselves gained ascendancy. Then they in turn claimed an exclusive control, eventually calling forth the Cromwellian dictatorship. This party was not recognized as a legitimate undertaking; the government belabored them by calling them rebels, and they returned the compliment by denouncing the crown as tyrants. It was only after these violent revolutionary experiments with one-party rule had proven abortive that the English people settled down to a mutual acceptance of each other's political viewpoint. Thus we could say that a two-party system develops out of a one-party predominance. Only after the resulting civil war has shown a people the danger of party violence does the two-party system with its complete dependence upon a certain amount of toleration become acceptable to the group at large.

Ideal and material objectives.—The English evolution suggests another hypothesis to the student of politics, and that is that parties in order to live and function must be compounded of ideal and material purposes or objectives. A lasting party must and will have an interest both in certain ideas concerning law and government and an interest in securing the power of government and all that goes with it in the form of patronage and the rest. In other words, the distinction between patronage parties and parties of principle, which is so popular among writers on politics in Europe, is untenable. There is no such thing as a party which lacks either of these elements completely. Moreover, this is a distinction of which one should be particularly wary from a practical viewpoint; it is one of the most common tricks of demagogues to contrast the ideal aspirations of their own group with the actual performance of their opponents. At the same time, it is one of the most telling indicators of a country's lack of political education to let itself be beguiled by such claims. The experience which follows will invariably belie such promises of a government of pure virtue. But it is equally deplorable, and very short-sighted, to engage oneself in undiscriminating denunciations of parties as such. "Parties are inevitable," Lord Bryce justly said, "no free large country has been without them." But of course the most ferocious detractors of parties would in conceding this claim insist that for that reason popular government must go. There is, we are told, always much corruption and patronage connected with party government. This cannot be denied by anyone who studies the historical records attentively. But what can be denied is that this tendency toward corruption and patronage is in any way peculiar to party government. Authoritarian regimes do not differ in that respect; they, too, are never entirely free from corruption and nepotism, and in periods of decay are notoriously honey-combed with both. The real difference is that the dirty laundry of popular regimes is washed in public, whereas under authoritarian rule it is washed behind the scenes or—not at all. For that reason, it is justifiable to describe any type of authoritarian regime as essentially a one-party government. This means that the control which comes from alternation with the other party is lacking. Why the probability of greater purity in the conduct of the government should thereby be insured is very difficult to see. The authoritarian regime which strives for the good of the country all of its own volition is to be found only in the blue skies of the philosophers. A realistic political science can state with some confidence that all parties strive for a combination of ideal and material objectives. What is more, every observation on the actual working of government points toward the conclusion that the ideal objectives are forced upon parties by their struggle for gaining control of the government. It is a platitude of practical politics that the outs are invariably more emphatic in their advocacy of principles than the ins. Therefore authoritarian (one-party) regimes are apt to be more corrupt and venal than two or more party set-ups. So-called "historical" instances pointing supposedly in the opposite direction, like the Prussian monarchy under Frederick William I and Frederick the Great, turn out upon closer investigation to have been subject to very special conditions which account for the relatively small amount of corruption *in spite* of the authoritarian nature of the regime. Frederick William I was fired with a passionate ambition to clean up the vast corruption which had prevailed under his spendthrift father and at the same time to overcome the large remnants of feudal dispersion and corruption which disunited and weakened his scattered domains. Frederick the Great was engaged in very extensive foreign warfare which necessitated as high an efficiency as was attainable in his administrative staff, and the later phases of his reign were filled with an unceasing effort to rebuild and consolidate his exhausted kingdom. But as soon as he was gone, a process of large-scale corruption set in and brought this authoritarian government to the brink of complete disaster, during the Napoleonic wars. All this suggests the conclusion that corruption is even more characteristic of authoritarian than of popular government.

Material interests and majority rule.—The admission of the fact that all organized parties strive for material as well as ideal objectives should not, however, blind us to the fact that considerable differences exist between parties in this respect. Continental European observers have often commented upon the relatively large role which material objectives seem to play in the history of English and American parties. This is undoubtedly in part due to the fact that the parties in these countries have had a real prize for which to fight, namely the actual control of the government, whereas in many of the continental countries, but particularly in Germany, the limited power of the representative body has tended to keep a considerable section of the public and the parties speaking for them on the outside of actual government, and consequently emphatic in their advocacy of ideal purposes. Both Liberal and Socialist parties were deeply affected by this, as will be shown in greater detail later. Furthermore, all evidence seems to point toward the conclusion that the larger the party, the more pronounced are its material interests. Professor Holcombe has shown this quite convincingly for American parties, which throughout their history have been sensitive to the broad economic interests of various sections of the country. It is evident that a party in order to hold together a rather heterogeneous following (and any party aspiring to an actual majority must do that) will shun a decided stand on questions of principle, while at the same time making concessions to a variety of theoretically perhaps incompatible interests. By such a policy the party manager may gain the adherence of sufficiently large groups to lead his banner to victory. Socialism affords a rather striking illustration for this observation. Theoretically, socialism is based upon the idea that the interests of employers and employees are incompatible, and that capitalism must be destroyed and supplanted by state or government control. Practically, the interests of workingmen are in higher wages, lower hours, better working conditions generally, in unemployment and old-age insurance, and so forth. These material interests are precisely those which an American politician will quite readily support, if workingmen's support is essential for his being reëlected, whereas he probably would only with horror contemplate the possibility of becoming a "Socialist." Of course, both Republicans and Democrats expound a long series of "principles" in their official platforms, but most of these principles are so vague as to turn out, on closer inspection, to be almost identical for both parties. As a result, the material interests, including patronage, remain as the real cement of parties, wherever the system of election by plurality prevails—and as we have seen in the previous chapter this is made one of the points of attack upon this system by the proportionalists. We will see a little later, however, that a rather vital difference between the several kinds of material interests must be admitted. For the moment, let us admit that material interests are of vital significance to parties seeking an actual majority.

Hatschek's law regarding English party development.—The preponderance of material objectives in large party organization has led Julius Hatschek to suggest a rule regarding English party development which may have more general significance. He finds that this development follows a definite course. First, a party with a distinct and coherent program comes into power. This program is used up in the process of realizing it. The party then breaks up into divisions. This disintegration offers to another party, irrespective of whether it has evolved a distinct and realizable program or not, the chance of concentrating and unifying its forces; then that party gains ascendancy. After a while, this party is subject to the same process of disintegration. This means that once party organizations have come into existence, the existence of a realizable program is no longer necessary. A party can not only continue to live, but may be able to displace the other party in the government, merely because its organization under a powerful leader is more effective than is that of the other party. The party lives by the strength of its organization, and therefore the organization is the main thing, the program a side issue. This fact was already noted by Hume, who in his *Essay on Parties* remarked: "Nothing is more usual than to see parties which have begun upon a real difference continue even after that difference is lost." Putting it simply, and in analogy to the hypothesis discussed in the previous paragraph, one may propose the hypothesis that the older the party, the more pronounced its material interests. Hatschek believed this to be a peculiarity of English party life, but if he had considered American parties, he would unquestionably have concluded that the situation was much the same here. And we shall furthermore see that the same trend occurs in other countries and under very different conditions of party life.

Parties secure power for their leaders.—We have now found that parties live independently of their programs, although programs are vital at their inception. We also have seen that parties pursue material as well as ideal objectives. A third observation of real significance is that parties strive to secure power for their leader or leaders, rather than themselves. For only through such leaders can the body of the party membership hope to secure the material and ideal advantages which they seek. This does not, of course, preclude the possibility that the leaders may cheat them; under certain conditions it invites such a conduct. Thus MacDonald in 1931 unquestionably betrayed the trust which his Labour followers had put into him—whatever his motives may have been. This inevitable preponderance of the leader is the result of the same forces which produce monocratic leadership; for the party is almost constantly in the position of a nation at war. The unceasing struggle either to maintain or to gain ascendancy in the government provides that pressure from which we saw monocratic or at least strictly hierarchical leadership to result. It is, therefore, impossible to agree with Hatschek that this dominance of the leaders is something peculiarly English; wherever a party is seeking actual control of the government, such hierarchical structure is bound to develop and maintain itself. Starting from a large body of careful observations, Robert Michels showed that (in keeping with the hypothesis just stated) parties advocating democracy and equality are just as prone to be authoritarian and boss-controlled as authoritarian parties. Michels' particular interests centered around the German Socialist party which showed this hierarchical, bureaucratic trend in a very marked degree. It was with acute insight that the leader of German Social Democracy was often jokingly referred to in international socialist congresses as "Kaiser Bebel." In fact, the authority of his position corresponded much more nearly to the popular conception of a *Kaiser* than that of the German Emperor. But there is nothing particularly shameful about it, as the innocent reader of Michels' study might be led to infer. Nor yet can this trend be in any way explained by the bureaucratic tradition of Germany. The Socialists were violently opposed to this tradition. It was the difficulty of their position and the resulting intensity of their party warfare which necessitated such strictly hierarchical organization. In order to dispel any blue-print notions to the contrary, the essential identity of the situation in England may be indicated by a citation from the memoirs of an English parliamentarian under the younger Pitt: "I was never present at any debate I could avoid, or absent from any division [that is, vote] I could get at. I have heard many arguments which convinced my judgment, but never one which changed my vote. I never voted but once according to my opinion, and that was the worst vote I ever gave. I found that the only way to be quiet in Parliament was always to vote with the ministers." That many of the contemporary lamentations about the decline of Parliament lose much of their force when considered in the light of such statements (and they could be many times multiplied) will be shown more specifically later (see Chapter XXII). What matters here is that monocratic, or at least oligarchic, leadership is inherent in party organization, because parties are fighting groups.

A definition of party.—We are now, I believe, ready to pull together our several hypotheses into a "definition" of a party, since definitions are implied hypotheses. We may say that a party is a group of human beings, stably organized for the purpose of securing or maintaining the control of a corporate body by its leaders, on the assumption that such control will give to members of the party ideal and material benefits and advantages. A *political* party under this definition would be a group operating to secure control of a government, state, or country as contrasted with, for example, a church party. This definition, while developed from earlier ones, differs from them in two important respects. In the first place, we speak of *control* of a corporate body, rather than power within it, because the latter way of putting the definition would make a group of men founding a newspaper a party, since they surely seek to secure power within a state. On the other hand, Max Weber used to emphasize the fact that parties rested upon "formally free recruiting," i.e., that they allowed anyone to join up. Weber introduced this criterion to differentiate parties from aristocratic factions and the like. But since it is never practical for political science to deviate markedly from common usage, and since we are nowadays accustomed to speak of the Communist party in Russia, the Fascist party in Italy, and so forth, it is no longer possible to insist upon that criterion of free admission. But inasmuch as Weber was getting at a very important distinction here, we may say that parties either will allow free recruiting, and then may be called open parties, or they will not, and then are closed. Closed parties constitute the organized following of an authoritarian group which has gained complete control of a government, but feels the need for large-scale popular support. If differences of opinion and clashes of loyalty occur in such a following, they cannot under such a government lead to the formation of new parties, and therefore result in factional strife. Such factionalism is, of course, violently denounced by the preponderant group, and may be forcefully suppressed, as was done by Hitler in the course of the so-called *Purge* of June 1934. But these denunciations bring us back to our starting point, when, in the days of Cromwell, if not of Washington, parties generally were decried as factions. An effort to distinguish parties from factions in terms of the above definition seems in order, therefore, as a conclusion to this general discussion of parties.

Conclusion: parties and factions.—It is very common among political writers, after defining a political party, to remark that their definition historically fits many contending groups, such as the patricians and plebeians of ancient Rome, the Guelfs and Ghibellines of the Middle Ages, and so forth, but to add that such groups had perhaps better be called factions. Such vagueness is quite undesirable. If a definition does not distinguish a party from a faction, we must either hold the two to be identical in fact, or alter the definition so as to distinguish them. If we adopt the former view—for which much can be said—it might be added that a faction is a party we do not like. A faction, then, would be identical in objective factual content with party, but viewed from the subjectively different standpoint of the opponent. Such verbal differentiations are quite frequent in the political sphere, as we saw when discussing bureaucracy and administration. But it will be seen, on reconsidering our definition, that it contains elements which suggest a clear-cut distinction between party and faction. In the first place the requirement of stable organization is a distinguishing feature of a party. In the second place, the ideal benefits of which our definition speaks are, as we know from previous discussion, related to principles or ideals believed in and pursued as desirable objectives for the corporate body as a whole. It may often be difficult in actuality to determine whether a stably organized group pursues such objectives, if there is no recognition of free speech by the group in power. But eventually, after a certain lapse of time, it will almost always be possible to answer this question one way or the other. Thus both the historical examples cited above must be admitted to have pursued such objectives. What gives them the character of factions is rather the absence of stable organization; for a group with scattered leadership, such as the Ghibellines, cannot be said to possess a stable organization.

CHAPTER XIX

POLITICAL PARTIES: A PANORAMA OF THEIR COMPARATIVE DEVELOPMENT IN EUROPE

Introductory: Lowell's description of psychic dispositions.—In the concluding chapter of his *Public Opinion in War and Peace*, A. Lawrence Lowell presents an essay on the changes in the disposition of men which will help us in painting the comparative panorama of European party politics. It will reveal the large measure of similarity between the party systems of various countries. Discarding an old classification of people into those desiring liberty and progress on one side and the defense of the established order on the other, Lowell suggests that people be divided into the contented and the discontented, and those who are sanguine or not about possible changes. By combining any two of these traits, one finds four groups of people: those who are discontented with present conditions and sanguine about improvement, the radicals; those who are contented and sanguine, the liberals; those who are contented, but not hopeful of improvement, the conservatives; and finally those who are not content with existing conditions and at the same time see no prospect of better things to come, the reactionaries. A graphic representation of these divisions can be given thus:

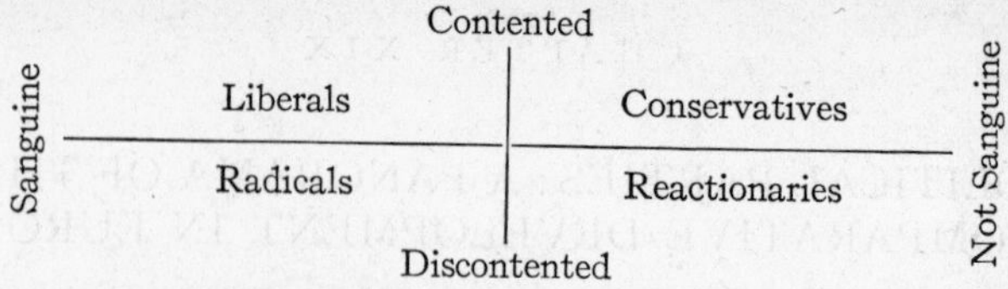

Then in considering the change from one of these dispositions to another, Lowell, following Röhmer, speaks of the tendency of men to run the cycle from radical to reactionary as they grow old. In the same connection he points out the rarity of persons changing from one disposition to another diagonally opposed, the reason being that two basic changes would be involved, that from content to discontent, and from sanguinity to despondency, a combination which is not very likely to occur at the same time. Now, the combination and relative prevalence of these four dispositions is a matter of great importance concerning the politics (and the party structure) of various countries. For they determine both the stability of the order and the probability of change. If the people at large are represented as enclosed in a circle, four diagrams can be used to illustrate the results:

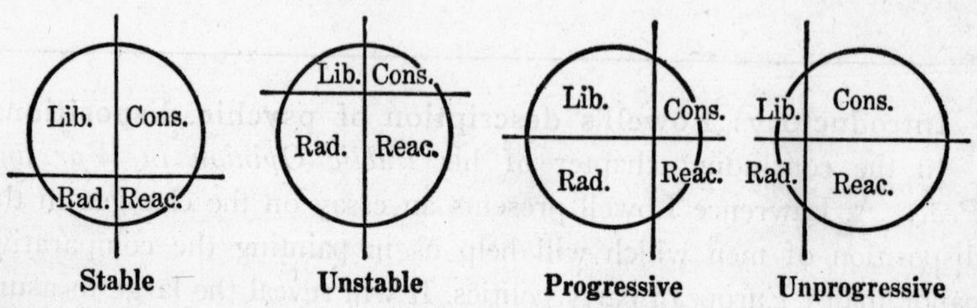

Lowell believes that the first diagram represents the situation in England from the reform of the House of Commons in 1832 to the World War, while the second is characteristic of France from the fall of Napoleon until the stabilization of the Third Republic in 1889 (defeat of Boulanger). The second diagram is also strikingly true of the German situation since 1918, and particularly since 1930. While these observations regarding popular dispositions will aid us greatly in untangling the party developments in Europe, it would be quite wrong to identify political parties with such dispositions. As we shall see, some very important parties are built upon racial and religious cleavages.

The social substratum.—Racial and religious cleavages, as well as class groupings of one sort or another, suggest that it is not possible to analyze party systems with reference to psychological dispositions and attitudes alone. In fact, a comparative survey of actual political systems, both past and present, seems to lead to the conclusion that party cleavages built exclusively upon such dispositions are the exception rather than the rule. They presuppose a very homogeneous social substratum so that the electorate is on the whole "fundamentally at one," as Balfour once put it, and therefore "can safely afford to bicker." It follows that the description of party systems really presupposes a thorough knowledge of the various layers of the social substratum as well as a comprehension of possible emotional dispositions. Political scientists are just beginning to work out this background. In his justly celebrated *Political Panorama of the West of France* André Siegfried studied the problem in a limited region, district by district, seeking to discover interrelations between social and political party change. But a clear correlation does not exist. The area which Professor Siegfried investigated is relatively static and conservative anyway. But even under conditions of highly dynamic flux, such as those of post-war Germany, the rise of a party like the National Socialists cannot be accounted for in terms of any equivalent change in the social substratum. On the other hand, in pre-war Germany, the shift in population is reflected in the rise of the Socialist party. In 1870 over 50 per cent of Germany was rural; in 1914 less than 30 per cent lived in the country. This organization continued after the war, and the leaders of German socialism thought their party's post-war continuance and growth assured by this as well as other factors. But National Socialism proceeded to crush these hopes by splitting the following of the Socialists wide open, detaching almost completely the artisans from the workers. By similarly breaking up the bourgeois alliance which had coalesced in opposition to the Socialists' ascendancy, and detaching from the parties composing this alliance the small farmers and the lower commercial groups, shopkeepers, white collar employees, officials, and so forth, the Nazis secured a following which believed in a pink socialism and a red-hot nationalism, a mixture better suited to the predispositions of these groups of people than either the anti-nationalism of the Socialists, or the anti-socialism of the bourgeois parties of various shades. But while this party *change* cannot be explained in terms of a *change* in the social substratum, even these rather cursory remarks show how essential an understanding of this substratum is for the understanding of party growth. It is, however, not practicable to offer such a descriptive analysis here, nor is it perhaps necessary. Fortunately, the nations with which we are here concerned are from this point of view very much alike and can be treated as if they had the same social structure. They all possess a large degree of industrial civilization organized in national patterns. Their traditional mode of religious faith is Christian. Their social organization has, in the past, been built upon private property. These are all elementary data which are fairly well known to every student of party set-ups.

The policy of the government as a factor in the development of parties.—If the social conformation of European nations shows such considerable similarity, why should the two-party system have taken hold in England and nowhere else? What conditions favoring its development in England were absent in all these other countries? We have already found the plurality system of elections and the development of a cabinet system to have been important contributing factors. Another very important condition is the *early* development of the parties. Escaping the religious division (and the consequent development of a Catholic party) on account of the overwhelmingly Protestant nature of the country, buttressed as it was by the fact that Catholics were deprived of political privileges until well into the nineteenth century, England could evolve the fundamental and simple division of conservatives and liberals (with some reactionaries and radicals thrown in on each side) during the course of two centuries of more or less undisturbed domestic peace. She could therefore enter into the era of the industrial revolution with that pattern firmly established. What is more, the radical tendencies engendered by this industrial revolution for a long time found an acceptable voice in the traditional Liberal party and only the twentieth century has witnessed the rise of a distinct Labour party. This party, after two decades of growth, shows all signs of superseding the Liberal party as the party of progress. On the Continent conditions were vastly different. After the restoration in France, a major cleavage existed between Republicans, in favor of the principles of 1789, and those opposed to these principles on various grounds. But the French restoration ministers, unlike the Stuarts, never attempted to organize a party of the crown, for they knew that such a party was apt to call forth an opposition which would eventually establish parliamentary supremacy. So the tactics of Louis XVIII and Louis Philippe followed the maxim: divide and rule so as to avoid the consolidation of parties. Thus a multiple party system established itself in France, the total situation remaining markedly unstable, as the revolutions of 1830 and 1848, the Second Empire and its overthrow in 1870 clearly show. By the time the Third Republic had firmly settled itself, the Socialists had got under way as a factor to be reckoned with. Since socialism assumes a fundamental cleavage in the electorate, class antagonism between capitalists and workers, the party divisions of the electorate assumed the proportions of a permanent disruption of the people into mutually exclusive and lastingly hostile interests. In Germany the development took a different course, but the result was the same. Here the Socialists could consolidate their position even more definitely, before a cabinet system supported by parliamentary majorities was set up by the constitution of 1919. Since the Reich was created by Prussian leadership, the Prussian development before 1871 was indicative. There Bismarck, instead of seeking majority support for the government's policies, openly flouted the parliamentary opposition. After his internal and external victories, he made no attempt to collaborate with the party most ready to support him—the National Liberals—but sought to secure his majorities as he needed them. When the Socialists, as a result, were forging ahead rapidly as the party of progress, he attempted to suppress them by force; the failure of these efforts toward the end of Bismarck's career brought the Socialists back into parliament as a firmly entrenched party proclaiming the Marxist doctrine of inevitable class warfare. Disunity thereafter became the earmark of German representative bodies. The sly scheme of building a compact alliance of bourgeois parties around imperialist policies topped by the big navy program failed in a doubly disastrous way; on the one hand, it brought the alienation from England and the consequent catastrophe of the World War, on the other hand, it drove the masses into the arms of the Socialists as the only true advocates of progress and popular government. These two sketches show that party development is affected not only by the dispositions of men, and the social substratum of the community, but also by the policy of the government in the period preceding and initiating parliamentary, representative government. Does this mean that we are confronted by situations totally at variance with each other in the several countries? Evidently not. In spite of a number of variations, there remains much similarity in the party formations of all the European nations. And while the two-party system, so-called, has its distinct advantages from the standpoint of parliamentary responsibility, we should not deceive ourselves in overestimating either its importance or its permanence. After all, the two large English parties have frequently been divided into warring groups; such groups have often caused the downfall of the government. Besides, even in England since the Reform of 1832, two parties have been the exception rather than the rule. The Peelites, the Radicals, the Liberal Unionists, the Irish Nationalists, and the Labour Party have followed each other as third parties, and it would, in the light of all the facts, be more appropriate to describe the English as a two-and-one-half-party system. If each of these parties is recognizably divided into a radical and a moderate group —and such is unquestionably the case—we can count six "parties," and more than six real parties are not found in other European countries, either. We really have everywhere a shading from blue to red, with a separate blotch of color such as the Irish green or the Catholic black set off by itself; how the lines are drawn in setting off the shades from each other, remains a somewhat arbitrary matter.

Liberal parties, first phase: their relation to conservatism.— In England, as well as in most other European countries, you find liberal as well as conservative parties. As we have seen before, there was *one* party in the English Parliament between 1600 and 1641, the party of opposition to the royal prerogative. A similar party developed toward the end of Charles II's reign, when Shaftesbury organized the "Green Ribbon Club," the nucleus of the Whig party organization. This "Country" party, as it was called in contrast to the "Court" party, was animated by hostility to the crown's subservience to France and its tendency to favor the Catholics. Foreign policy and religion, both rooted in strong national sentiments, therefore provided its main arguments, though it is now generally held that the economic interests of the rising mercantile classes also were a powerful cement. That the rights of Parliament should have become another central tenet is only natural under the circumstances; the king being supposedly beyond reach, any effective opposition had to seek a strengthening of Parliament. If we remember that opposition to Catholicism was already to some extent opposition to orthodoxy, that the banner of toleration had been raised, and that deism and atheism had made their appearance, we are justified in saying that all tenets of orthodox liberalism except the doctrine of free competition were already implied in Whig doctrine, and the transition to the nineteenth century Liberal party was by no means such a break with the past as has occasionally been assumed in our time. The tenets of the Tory party were implied in the viewpoint of the Whigs; they constituted essentially a reaffirmation of the traditional mode of life and thought. Thus as against toleration, parliamentary rights, and mercantile interests, they stood up for the Church of England, the royal prerogative, and landed interests. This was the party of squires and parsons, and like all conservative parties ever since, it was essentially concerned with maintaining the existing order. This very natural tendency is the reason for the wide diversity of form which conservatism takes in different countries and at different times. It is essentially compounded of the groups who happen to be the *beati possidentes,* and therefore want to keep things as they are. A conservative in pre-war Germany was a monarchist, a conservative in the United States is a constitutionalist, and a conservative in contemporary Russia is a Stalinist. It is evident from this observation why there should have been no real conservative party in post-war Germany; there were only a very few people who wanted to keep things as they were. But in most countries and at most times there are enough such people to constitute a sizeable group in the community, and these are then and there the conservatives. It is for this reason really unnecessary to discuss especially the conservative parties from a programmatic viewpoint. By reversing the positions taken by the leading party advocating change it is always easy to derive the position and the interests back of the respective conservative parties or groups. This is curiously illustrated by the history of English Toryism in the eighteenth century. The Whigs having put over the Hanoverian succession, and thereafter ruling England for decades under Walpole and Pelham, drifted so markedly into the position of the government, that the Tories lifted the banner of "reform." They did so, as we have seen, in the rather ineffectual manner of demanding that the "corruption" of the Whigs be remedied. Thus, even though the Tories insisted upon the rights of Parliament, they never adopted a position frankly demanding the change of existing institutions. As a result, the growing forces of public sentiment in favor of parliamentary reform tended to associate themselves with the Whig party, and by carrying their viewpoint to triumph in the great enactments of 1832 (see next paragraph) they transformed the Whig into the Liberal party. This was probably not unrelated to the fact that at bottom the mercantile interests had continued their association with the Whigs. For the great centers of industry and commerce were woefully discriminated against by the then existing electoral districts (see above, XVII). A redistribution of parliamentary seats would greatly increase, so it seemed, the representation of these mercantile interests. The Tories could hardly be expected to foster such a scheme. But as a matter of fact, another problem was steadily coming to the fore, and by the time the Parliamentary Reform Act had become law, the Liberal party was beginning to face a dilemma touching the very foundations upon which its ideology was built. That was the social problem. Before entering upon this second phase of the evolution of Liberal parties, it may be mentioned in passing that nowhere except in Sweden had a party made its appearance which as closely resembled the later Liberals as the English Whigs. In France, Prussia, and the Hapsburg Dominions absolutist monarchy reigned supreme, and whatever enlightenment found expression in governmental policy did so through the benevolent despots ruling these lands. Frederick the Great, Joseph II, and Louis XVI were all profoundly influenced by certain basic tenets of liberal philosophy, such as toleration and the furtherance of trade and industry, but no parties corresponded to or supported these monarchical policies.

Liberal parties, second phase: the dissolvent of social reform.—After the French Revolution and the Napoleonic wars, liberal parties appeared in almost all countries of Europe. Often in collaboration with Free Masonry and other "enlightened" currents of the times, they advocated policies in the representative assemblies which bear a close resemblance to the major policies of the Whigs. In France, men like Benjamin Constant undertook to combat clericalism, royalism, and the landed interests, and when their opposition proved of no avail, staged another coup which, in 1830, placed a bourgeois king on the throne. The notorious words of this king, Louis-Philippe, "Enrich yourselves," embody the doctrine of progressive industrialism which these dominant commercial classes preached to the "people." A similar situation prevailed elsewhere. In England the mercantile interests back of the Whigs had gradually, during the eighteenth century, become articulate. Their faith in individual initiative was closely linked with the desire to see the fetters removed which hindered the expansion of industrialism. These ties, often referred to as feudal by writers of the time, but in fact of much later growth, and in part the result of the stagnation of the artisan craft guilds, in part consequent upon the monarchical efforts to develop various manufacturing and other economic activities (see above, Chap. VI), had undoubtedly at the time inhibiting effects upon the teeming energies of industrialism. Change pointed in the direction of doing away with all such restrictions, and the Liberals were voicing this demand. But at the same time, new problems began to make their appearance which were closely related to this selfsame expansion of industrialism, the problems of the worker in industry. These problems called for effective restrictions rather than freedom. As a consequence, the English Liberals, faced by an insistent wing of so-called Radicals, found themselves obliged to enact legislation aiming at the reform of factory and laboring conditions. So apparent were the needs for change in this respect during the thirties of the last century that even a certain group of imaginative Conservatives, like the young Disraeli, sought to capture this field of reform and thus to push the Liberals out of the position of fostering the interests of the working man. But they were unable to detach the trade union leader from the radical wing of the Liberal party. It is, nevertheless, interesting that Bismarck should have made a similar effort in his struggle with the Socialists. But since Bismarck cannot readily be classed as either a liberal or a conservative, he perhaps merely illustrates personally the dilemma into which continental Liberals had already drifted before the middle of the nineteenth century. Unlike English Liberals, they found themselves confronted with the necessity of neglecting social reforms in their efforts to push forward the fight for constitutional representative government. Consequently those who believed social reform more important, or at any rate more urgent, than parliamentary government, began to organize new parties, Workers', Labor, or Socialist parties, whose early aspirations culminated in the *Communist Manifesto*. We shall presently go further into that matter. What matters here is that continental Liberals could not absorb the new forces as readily as their English colleagues. We have here a striking illustration of the importance of an already existing organization, like the English Whigs, seeking to win the support of as many concrete material interests as it possibly can. But in the end, the English Liberals have proved to be as unable as their continental brethren to assimilate the interests of labor. The almost heroic intellectual efforts of thinkers from Bentham through John Stuart Mill to Hobhouse to interpret the various restrictions which a program of social reform entailed as part of real "liberty" have not been able to alter the fact that the dominant groups, to whose advantage a minimum of such restrictions undoubtedly redounds, have drifted away from the Liberal and into the Conservative party, while those seeking a realization of a maximum of such restrictions have found a program unencumbered by "bourgeois" subtleties more inspiring and have therefore flocked to the Labour party. Perhaps it could be argued that the Liberal party might have become the Social Reform party, if its leaders had shown sufficient suppleness to abandon early enough the liberal political philosophy of as little government as possible. It is more sensible to admit that this is too much to ask; for while the transition from whiggism to liberalism was a gradual one, and implied no clear-cut rejection of one of the major tenets previously held, such a turnabout would have been necessary to pass from liberalism to socialism. From this viewpoint, then, the rise of parties of social reform, replacing the liberal parties, or pushing them into the position of conservative parties, appears inevitable. Nor is it difficult to understand why it should have happened much earlier on the Continent than in England. Since continental liberalism had not inherited any effective party organizations, nor any secure claim to recurrent participation in the government, it found itself readily rivalled by groups proclaiming radical social reform programs. Not so the English Liberals. They, as we have seen, received the Whig legacy. It is quite possible that this long delay, in the course of which the Liberal party may be said to have acted as an incubator for the insurgent forces of socialism, has had the important effect of "liberalizing" the new elements sufficiently for these groups to preserve what remains of value in the older liberal creed. We shall deal with the question further when we come to treat of the socialist parties. Before that we must consider another factor which helped to decompose liberal parties everywhere: nationalism.

Liberal parties, third phase: the blind alley of nationalism. —We saw at the start that the English Whigs were animated by national sentiments from the very outset. Likewise, the French Liberals of the revolutionary period, like Mirabeau, objected to the monarchy partly on the ground that it endangered the national existence. Siéyès went further and actually identified the Third Estate with the nation. Again, under the Restoration monarchy the Liberals were aggravated by the king's dependence upon foreign support, and it was indeed difficult to deny that Louis XVIII ruled by the grace of Metternich and Castlereagh, rather than by that of God. Humiliations in the field of foreign policy contributed their share to the overthrows of 1830, 1848, and in 1870 actual defeat on the battlefield destroyed Napoleon III. The Liberal elements under Gambetta, who succeeded Napoleon, were naturally animated by passionate patriotism. As a result, the Liberals of the Third French Republic have remained rather outspoken nationalists to this day. But if the French Revolution proclaimed nationalism, the reaction abroad was not very slow in meeting the challenge. In England Whigs and Tories alike thundered against the atrocities of the hereditary enemy; this is hardly surprising when one remembers that the wholesale executions of noble families touched the very foundations of sentiment in aristocratic England. To be sure, radical societies took up the revolutionary doctrines, but the public at large did not follow suit, and general patriotic agitation did not subside until the Napoleonic Empire had been downed. This injection of fervent nationalism the English Liberals have never entirely outlived. When the issue of Irish Home Rule raised another problem of vital import, the decision of Gladstone to make this issue a part of Liberal party policy induced a good many of the nationalist elements under the leadership of Chamberlain to break away, calling themselves Liberal Unionists. They were eventually absorbed by the Conservatives. When, in 1905, the Liberal party came back into power with a very large majority, the nationalists and imperialists had, however, once more gained the upper hand, as the appointments of Sir Edward Grey and Lord Haldane to the Foreign Office and the War Office showed. Haldane himself has told the impressive story of this Liberal clique's ascendancy, and their determination to seek another show-down if the party should be unwilling to put them into power. Thus there remained, in spite of very strong international sentiments in large groups of the Liberal following, an effective union of liberalism and nationalist imperialism, as far as the actual policy of the party was concerned. And yet, as the cleavage between leaders and part of the followers in this and earlier periods shows, there was something anomalous in this position. Doctrinaire writers on liberalism are interesting in their desire to minimize the significance of this factor. And yet, certain manifestations of expansive nationalism, particularly imperialism, are much more specifically liberal than conservative, as the Whig foreign policy from Pitt to Palmerston shows. The tendency of Conservatives to assume the imperialist position, particularly since Disraeli, is to be understood only if we see it as part of the Conservative party's trend to assume in fact the liberal position. This nationalist and imperialist implication of liberalism is quite understandable, once we consider the material interests of the mercantile classes which constituted such a large part of its following during its earlier growth. It is these classes which profited by the colossal colonial empire which afforded markets as well as raw material resources. It is these classes, again, which were most embarrassed by the rise of any potential rival of truly competitive powers, such as the Napoleonic or the Bismarckian Empires. On the other hand, the laboring classes which throughout the nineteenth century were inclined to support the radical wing of the Liberal party, and the leaders of this wing, animated by radically rationalistic and humanitarian views, had a strong predilection for peace and international solidarity. By wishing to make the Liberal the "Little England" party, they voiced the sentiments of large groups of this progressive electorate. After the Midlothian campaign in 1880, during which Gladstone violently attacked the methods of British imperialism in the Near East, and after the adoption of the Home Rule platform in 1886, the situation changed. The remaining nationalist and imperialist elements in the Liberal party leadership decided to keep the *arcana imperii* of foreign and colonial policy out of popular discussion. Later under Grey the whole gamut of imperialist foreign policy became veiled in mystery, and the outer appearance of Liberal strength was being maintained by the leaders at the cost of deceiving their own following. As a student of politics could have predicted, the Liberal party was, in the long run, bound to be destroyed by such practices. If leading liberal historians admit today that a full and frank statement of Grey's policy would have led to the downfall of the ministry—an argument which has been advanced to excuse the failure to do so—they imply by such an admission that the conflict between nationalist and internationalist elements in the Liberal party had become irremediable. Such tactics of equivocation will never solve the dilemmas of a party's ideal objectives. An attempt to do so has the most disastrous consequences, not only for the party itself, but for all the institutions which its power affects by such a fraud. The World War and the speedy eclipse of the Liberal party afterward are only the most portentous results of this devious double-dealing. It was not only understandable but inevitable that such men of character as Trevelyan should quit the Liberal and join the Labour party.

The same subject: Germany.—If the English Liberal party was rent asunder by the explosives of modern nationalism and imperialism, it can hardly surprise us if the same development can be observed in Germany and Italy. For here at the beginning of the nineteenth century, the central goal of a nationally minded people, national unification, had not been achieved. Therefore, when liberalism got under way after the French Revolution, it adopted the founding of a free national government as a central tenet. In Germany, this meant first of all the throwing off of Napoleon's foreign yoke, and after that was accomplished, opposition to the petty monarchical governments dividing Germany into many parts; in Italy where a good part of the nation lived under foreign Austrian dominion or within the Papal State, the remainder in small tyrannies controlled by the Hapsburgs, Liberals had to make opposition to the imperial rule of the Hapsburgs and to the international ambitions of the Papal State. Since the Hapsburg Empire actively supported the petty German princes (nationalism was bound to disrupt the Empire, as it actually did later), German and Italian Liberals had one common enemy: Metternich, who ruled supreme in Austria until 1848. Since Metternich upheld the ideas of monarchical absolutism, this opposition had to assume quite conservative forms; but in adapting itself to the exigencies of the situation, the Liberal parties in these countries were finding themselves in a hopeless dilemma, created by the conflict of two primary, yet often incompatible objectives. Nothing illustrates this dilemma more strikingly than the ill-fated German National Parliament of 1848-1849. This assembly of brilliant and well-intentioned leaders foundered because it was confronted with the task of at once uniting and liberalizing the governments of Germany. Since unification remained the uppermost concern of the majority of Germans, their failure to achieve it produced a set-back from which German liberalism never recovered. When afterwards the methods of military force employed by Bismarck succeeded where the parliamentary methods of German Liberal parties had failed, it embued large numbers of Germans with a lasting anti-liberal bias. The National Liberals consequently occupied the unenviable position of the dog which, while wagging its tail at the master is being kicked about without mercy. Until the end, Bismarck treated them with studied contempt; yet they were the only group to raise their voices in protest against the veteran statesman's abrupt dismissal. Having learned nothing from past experience, these National Liberals, as they called themselves, later felt obliged to support the nationalist and imperialist policy of William II's chancellors, while another group calling themselves Progressives challenged this tradition and sought under the able leadership of Friedrich Naumann to discover new paths for a more international outlook. But this division of Liberal party strength, which was none too considerable anyway, contributed its share to the puny role which this party was forced to play. After the World War and the collapse of the Empire, this fatal division continued. The Democrats, successors to the Progressives, collaborated with the Socialists in building a republican government, while the so-called People's party, which had taken over the legacy of the National Liberals, joined forces with the reactionaries, the German Nationalists, until the actual governmental experience of Gustav Stresemann led this able statesman after 1923 to seek leftist connections, in order to support his international policies. The superhuman efforts of Stresemann to hold together the coalition backing his policy were in a sense necessitated by the earlier failure of German liberalism to find a solution for the dilemma which nationalism had posited. But perhaps there was no solution; at any rate, the decomposition of German Liberal parties was almost complete, before they ever had a chance to show what they might have done for the country.

The same subject: Italy.—In Italy the development was rather different than in Germany. Here nationalist liberalism triumphed completely under the brilliant leadership of Mazzini and Cavour and solved constructively the twofold problems of national unity and free constitutional government. Nowhere has the Liberal party had a more successful or a more brilliant record. What then can account for the complete eclipse of Italian liberalism? The Fascists who have destroyed the Italian Liberal parties came to the fore as an opposition to the Socialists and Communists. The rise of these latter was inevitable, once the problems of social reform became distinct. The industrialization of Italy brought them to a head in that country as elsewhere. Mazzini's early dream of combining liberalism and socialism did not come true any more than that of his English friends in the radical wing of the Liberal party. The Italian Labor Movement soon was carried away, first by the anarchism of Bakunin, and later by Marx' doctrine of the class war. But this anticipates developments which belong in our next paragraphs, in which the rise of socialism as the effective opposition will be traced. In conclusion, the three phases in the evolution of Liberal parties may be summarized once more. In its first phase, the Liberal party forms an aggressive opposition to the traditional monarchical government, in England from 1680 down into the nineteenth century, on the Continent since the French Revolution and more explicitly since the Napoleonic Wars. In its second phase, the Liberal party attempts to cope with the social problems raised by the industrialization, but inasmuch as the more radical Socialist elements are becoming the effective opposition, the Liberal party begins to adopt a defensive attitude, and in so far as it does, it becomes conservative. In its third phase, the Liberal party gets embroiled in the conflicts engendered by the rising nationalism everywhere, without being able to offer a clear-cut answer in terms of its own tenets, and therefore breaks up into nationalist and internationalist factions. The acute crisis of the second phase is reached when socialism triumphs or at least supersedes liberalism as the main opposition, while the acute crisis of the third phase culminates in the Fascist dictatorship exterminating the Liberal along with all other parties, except their own.

Socialist parties before the war.—If the story of Liberal parties begins with England and ends with Germany, the situation is reversed when we come to socialism. The reasons for this situation are implicit in the history of Liberal parties. It seems at first sight as if the strength of the Liberal party in each country between 1848 and 1914 stood in inverse proportion to the growth of an organized Socialist party. Where the Liberal party did not fulfill the function of an effective opposition, the Socialists pushed forward to take their place. But of course the Liberals also were not an effective opposition where they more or less dominated the government, as in Italy. This destroys the validity of the impression first gained; if the Liberal party is very strong, the Socialists also grow rapidly. This seems to suggest that the growth of the Socialist parties is dependent upon whether they represent the most clear-cut alternative to the party in power. Whether this party is Conservative or Liberal does not seem to matter. This fact is explainable in terms of our second hypothesis, according to which a party requires for its growth valid ideal as well as material objectives. What were these ideals of the Socialist parties? They addressed themselves to the solution of the social problems raised by industrialism, proclaiming them more important than any other matter within the purview of politics. Religion, foreign policy, constitutional government, all these can wait until the pressing needs of industrial society have been successfully met. The great dogmatic thinkers of this new creed, like Karl Marx, theoretically justified this subordination of all other issues to the social problem by trying to prove that the problems of religion, foreign policy, or government were all rooted in the social problem, were in reality an outgrowth of the conflict of social classes. The state was proclaimed to be an instrument for the exploitation of one class by another. Such a position would naturally find its most ardent supporters among the groups who suffered most from the industrial system, the factory workers. Both in France and Germany (as well as in other continental countries), the first beginnings of parties with programs taking some or all of these positions got under way in the thirties of the last century. However, in Germany the organizations of journeymen under Weitling and others became the incubators of socialist thought, whereas in France original thought along socialist lines had been growing in intellectualist circles. This earlier theoretical interest in socialism laid a foundation for the factiousness of French socialism. The resulting situation was rendered more complicated by the fact that several of these thinkers, notably Fourier and Proudhon, were anarchists. The German movement, on the other hand, was primarily practical and concerned with the needs of the workers. But neither in France nor in Germany do we, as yet, find durable organizations. To be sure, the Revolution of 1848 brought a certain number of socialist leaders to the fore. In France three such men participated in the provisional government following the February Revolution. Their insistence upon the social problem helped to frighten the bourgeoisie into later accepting the dictatorship of Napoleon III. In Germany, where they had some voice in the liberal Frankfort Parliament and in the Prussian revolutionary assembly, the Socialists were not as yet strong enough to do more than weaken, as in France, the liberal cause in the eyes of the propertied classes. It was only after the reaction to these revolutionary upheavals had spent itself that genuine parties of socialist outlook got under way, in the early sixties in Germany, in the late seventies in France. Ferdinand Lassalle was the man who, in 1863, founded the General German Workingmen's Association, the first organized German Labor party. It was out of this party that the German Social Democratic party developed. Until German unification was accomplished, the German Socialists were much divided by the question as to whether to include or exclude the Hapsburg Empire in a united Germany, a question which mattered greatly to German workers, since their party from the beginning expected the solution of the social question from the state. The political philosophy of Hegel, that quaint mixture of ideas derived from Rousseau, the Greek city state and Prussian bureaucracy, animated Lassalle even more than Karl Marx. Although the latter's materialist ideas gradually permeated the German Socialist party, Lassalle's idealist and nationalist ideas always retained a certain influence among German Socialists. In France, although orthodox Marxism remained a minority, state action similarly occupied the foreground of attention among Socialists. During the German siege of Paris in 1871, the most radical elements of the movement, together with a group of bourgeois Radicals, seized power and tried to organize popular resistance to the enemy by instituting a communist regime. The inevitable collapse of this ill-considered move cast a shadow over French socialism, and prevented party organization until 1876, when Jean-Joseph Barberet got together a National Labor Congress which endorsed his mild reformist program for trade unions stressing technical education, the creation of employment bureaus, the establishment of coöperative bureaus and mutual aid. But as early as 1879 leadership had passed to the revolutionary elements led by Jules Guesde. At the Congress of Marseilles in that year he declared that the collectivization of all the instruments of production should be pursued by all available means. This radical collectivist position was associated with a deep distrust of any kind of collaboration with existing bourgeois parties, insisting that the only possible way to realize their goal was a social revolution. Guesde was admittedly and dogmatically Marxist and remained so to the end of his life. The struggle between his followers and those who, like Paul Brousse, believed in the possibility of such coöperation (therefore called *possibilistes*) continued throughout the party's pre-war life. When Millerand entered the cabinet of Waldeck-Rousseau (1899), the party split wide open over the issue of whether or not ministerial participation of a Socialist could be condoned, but reunion was effected in 1905. These internecine struggles were part of another peculiarity of the French Socialist party, its continuous controversies with the trade unions. Unlike trade unions in other countries, the trade unions in France were the more radical elements of the socialist movement. Jules Guesde's influence was most securely anchored here. With France a parliamentary republic, it was natural that members of the political party should be tempted by participation in the government, particularly those sitting in parliament. But the trade union elements, made suspicious by the repeated "treason of intellectuals" who had used the workers' support as a stepping stone for a political career, followed those who, like Guesde, preached revolution of the proletariat as the only means of seizing power permanently preliminary to inaugurating an all-round collectivism. Thus it may be said that the Socialist party did not really seek power within, but rather the overthrow of, the existing government. In terms of our definition, we have to conclude that the French Socialist party sought power, then, within the corporate body of France, rather than within the Third Republic. There was, however, another group of people organized as a powerful party seeking to realize certain measures of social reform, the Radical Socialists. This party, in spite of its name, is not socialist in any strict sense of the word. It is radically progressive and democratic, and is widely supported by the small shopkeepers, artisans, and farmers. Since industry has and is still playing a minor role in France, this party until lately has continued to hold its own against the Socialist party, which is really the party of the industrial workers. However, so strong is the impact of the forces behind the Radical Socialist party that the French Socialist party, in contrast to its German equivalents, has sought and in some measure found a bridge to small farmers and artisans. This is essentially the work of Jean Jaurès whose brilliant leadership in and out of Parliament came to an untimely end by assassination at the outbreak of the World War. Jaurès deduced his socialism from democratic ideas. The socialization of capitalist property he held to follow logically from democratic equality. As a result, the property worked by one's own hands, such as the workshop of the artisan and the farm of the smaller peasantry are beyond collectivization and will be preserved in the social democracy which is dawning. This kind of stand is radically at variance with orthodox Marxist views. Consequently it could have no place in Germany. For the German Social Democratic party was professedly Marxist, although after the Congress of Gotha (1875) the democratic, reformist "interpretation" of Marx became dominant in guiding the political conduct of the party. The rapid growth of the party (1871: 102,000 votes; 1874: 352,000; 1877: 493,000) created consternation among the conservative elements, just the same, and when in 1878 two attempts were made upon the life of the aged Emperor, William I, Bismarck secured the passage of the so-called "Laws against Socialists" under which the government could prohibit associations which through social-democratic, socialist, or communist tendencies seemed to aim at the overthrow of the existing political and social order; it could also prohibit papers and books advocating these views. Moreover, the government could declare the state of emergency (see above, Chap. XIV) which would allow it to deport socialist agitators. The penalties under this law were very high, the possibilities for arbitrary action considerable. These laws were in existence until 1890 and they have influenced the development of the German Social Democratic party deeply. However, opinions vary considerably as to the nature of the influence. Liberal writers have felt that it thwarted the party's natural development towards a constructive attitude. Furthermore, these writers feel that it strengthened the revolutionary drift in the party councils. To be sure, at a congress held in Switzerland in 1880, the party decided to abandon strict legality. In spite of such evidence, socialist radicals have repeatedly pointed out that these laws prevented effective criticism from below, thus strengthening boss rule and bureaucracy in the party. As the leaders grew old, this stratification of the party opened the doors wide to reformist tendencies of the small bourgeoisie. Such writers emphasize also that the re-interpretation of Karl Marx in an evolutionary sense by Karl Kautsky and others occurred in this period. It is perhaps a significant bit of detail that Karl Marx's scathing criticism of the program of Gotha was withheld by the party leaders until 1891. Whatever the merits of these observations—and there probably is a certain measure of truth in both of them—the progress of the German Socialist party was delayed only temporarily by Bismarck's measures. After their inglorious abandonment, the growth of the party resumed its rapid progress. In the election of 1890 they secured 1,427,300 votes, in 1903, 3,010,800, and in 1912 they reached 4,250,400, thus being the largest party in the German Parliament, a position which they retained until the advent of Hitler in 1933. As remarked before, the Social Democrats were *the* party of effective opposition and social reform. They, too, like their French brethren, sought a fundamental change in the form of government, being avowed republicans and anti-federalists; before the outbreak of the World War, they could justly entertain the hope of capturing an actual majority and of then forcing the adoption of parliamentary government. No one can tell whether these hopes would have been shattered, as were those of the Prussian Liberals in the sixties, by the government adopting a dictatorship such as that which Bismarck had assumed in the earlier conflict (see above, Chap. XIV, ¶ 15). If such a conflict was looming, its outbreak was forestalled by the World War. Voices have been heard from time to time which have explained the German government's readiness to enter the war as offering a way out of the impending social conflict; this view has been even more emphatically set forth for Austria-Hungary and Russia. That there were people in influential quarters who consoled themselves over the outbreak of the war with the new integration of the masses and the revival of patriotism cannot be doubted; how far their views can be taken to explain the position of the governments is a difficult question which we do not need to answer here. It is beyond controversy that the policies of parties and governments in pre-war Germany were profoundly affected by the rise of the Social Democratic party that has just been described.

Particularly the British Labor party.—Very special problems are connected with the rise of the English Labor party. It has been pointed out before that the English Liberal party throughout the nineteenth century was successful in absorbing the elements interested in radical social reform. Particularly after Karl Marx's abortive efforts to organize a *Workingmen's International* (1866 and after) and the ill-fated experiment of the Paris Commune which Marx had had endorsed by the *International* (1871), English trade union leaders remained attached to the Liberal party. They strengthened the Liberals' "radical" wing, though from a Socialist viewpoint their attitude was obviously very "conservative." But English liberalism could only with subtle dialectics manage to foster such more advanced social reform programs. Such dialectic did not appeal to the laboring masses. It also seemed pale when subjected to the searchlight of radical analysis, such as the theorists of the Independent Labor party (organized 1893) and of the Fabian Society (organized 1884) were inclined to focus upon the liberal doctrines. The Fabians, emulating the tactics of *Fabius Cunctator* after the battle of *Cannae*, admittedly wished to go slowly; they resembled the French *possibilistes* in their belief in democratic, parliamentary government. But they perceived the central aims of social reform to be incompatible with the policies of a party directly descending from Manchesterian free-competition liberalism. Constant contact with continental Socialists, many of them the leaders of powerful parliamentary parties, concerting through a revived (*Second*) *International* for the pacific parliamentary conquest of power in other highly industrialized countries, strengthened the theoretical conviction of this group that England must have a Labor party too. The most prominent persons in this group were Ramsay MacDonald, Sidney and Beatrice Webb, Bernard Shaw, H. G. Wells. Their outlook was not dogmatically Marxist, but rather akin to that of Jean-Jaurès sketched above. In the pre-war period, although they did not found the Independent Labor party, they succeeded in permeating this party with their views. The party began to play a role, particularly in local government. But in Parliament, the group was not strong enough to pursue a very independent course. In the election of 1905 they won twenty-nine seats, in the two elections of 1910, forty and forty-two respectively. They generally supported the Liberal party, though in debates on foreign policy they tended to assume a strongly critical attitude toward the imperialist clique. During the war, Arthur Henderson and the more patriotic trade union members supported the government, and "Uncle Arthur" actually entered the cabinet where he remained until the quarrel between the government and the trade union-socialist groups over the question of the Stockholm Conference in 1917. But the radical group, notably Ramsay MacDonald, steadfastly refused to collaborate. (Perhaps this episode provides the explanation for MacDonald's later conduct, so bitterly condemned by his former Socialist friends: MacDonald appears to be an uncompromising champion of *peace* in all its forms; his national government would then seem an ill-considered attempt at transcending the class struggle.) They thus provided the ferment which later led to the break between Henderson and the government. These episodes indicate, in all their complexity, the ideal and practical conflict between national and international labor interests which have become the touchstone of socialism in the post-war period.

Socialism during the war and the beginnings of communism; the stumbling block of national allegiance.—Like the English, the French government during the war attempted to secure Socialist support, as did the German Imperial government also. The gloomy spectre of the murdered Jaurès combined with the imminence of national catastrophe, as symbolized by the invasion of France, to persuade even very radical French Socialists to support the *Tricolore.*

Not many of them did it, however, in such poor taste as Gustave Hervé who, having harassed French Socialists before the war with his pacifist extremism (he advocated the general strike at the outbreak of a war), re-baptized his newspaper, *La Guerre Sociale,* as *La Victoire,* and joined the front rank of extreme chauvinists. Most of the Socialists sadly persuaded themselves that the bourgeois Republic's fight had to be supported, because it was, after all, France that was being invaded, and their friends, the German Socialists, seemed ready to support what appeared to them rank imperialist aggression. There were, however, some stout souls in France as in England, men and women who took their lead not from what others did, but from what they themselves believed in. The same was true in Germany. The majority of Social Democrats, confronted with the imperial oratory of: "I know no more parties, I know only Germans" (August 4, 1914) remembered that they were Germans first, and Socialists and pacifists afterwards, and voted war credits. For in Germany it was, "of course," no question of entering the cabinet. But the matter of war credits was crucial. So was service in the army. But there were others, a small minority, with Liebknecht at their head, who saw things in another light. Avowed Marxists, they did not care about the destruction of the bourgeois government. The German people would remain. The spectre of Russian Czardom did not frighten them. Lenin and Trotzki would finish that in course of time. On all fronts, the battle of an uncompromising struggle must be waged against the established authorities, their prestige undermined at home and abroad, their power destroyed. To the men fighting this battle, it did not matter much who lost the war. Whoever it was would see the triumph of Marxist socialism, the dictatorship of the proletariat and the establishment of the classless society. These fervent views could not be squelched by throwing Liebknecht and his friends into jail; no indeed, there were others to carry on the struggle. It was this group of small minority leaders in France, in Germany, in Russia, in Italy who came together during the World War in secret conclave in Switzerland to agree upon a common strategy for the overthrow of the capitalism which had brought on this terrible slaughter. Zimmerwald (1915) and Kienthal (1916) are the two hamlets which provided old barns for these sparks of world revolution. For the break between majority and minority Socialists in France, in Germany, and other continental countries marks the birth—or if one accepts their own ideology, the *re*-birth—of militantly internationalist communism such as Karl Marx had dreamed of in the days of the First International. Bourderon, Cachin, and their friends in France, Liebknecht, Rosa Luxemburg and those who after their death carried on in Germany, and above all Lenin and Trotzki were the nucleus around which the Third International eventually emerged. But the process of disintegration of the united front of industrial labor which had been built up before the war was a slow one. The turning point came with the Russian Revolution and the Stockholm Conference in 1917. Originally this conference was to unite Socialists of all shades of opinion in an effort to stop the war. It was born of the ideas of Kienthal and Zimmerwald now spreading rapidly through the war-weary ranks of labor throughout Europe. But the allied governments professed to see in it a plot of "Prussian" socialism, a super-Machiavellian move of Imperial Germany. Gompers, a life-long foe of socialism, obligingly provided the entering wedge by refusing to have American labor represented at the conference. England, France, and Italy refused passports. The urgent request of the more moderate Russian Socialists to allow the conference to take place proved of no avail. Henderson, sent to Russia to investigate, came back a supporter of the Russian viewpoint; his advice was disregarded; he quit the cabinet; the war went on; the radical Bolsheviks in Russia gained the upper hand with their cry of "Bread and Peace." It is not too much to say that these fatal blunders of the allied governments materially contributed to the victory of militant communism. May they be exonerated, because Karl Marx would have said that they were bound to commit these blunders? Whatever stand one takes on this issue (involving as it does the metaphysics of determinism), he cannot escape the conclusion that the World War, as the most terrific catastrophe of Western civilization within recent times, acted as the incubator of communism as it is known today; not a theory, but a stern reality challenging the fundamentals of the modern political order in word if not in deed, centering around an International permanently located in Moscow, the capital of one of the world's great empires. Here is a profound contrast to the pre-war internationalism of Socialist parties, consisting largely of periodical conventions meeting in different cities of Europe (Brussels, Amsterdam, Copenhagen, Stuttgart) and discussing resolutions which might express the sentiment of Socialists throughout the world. Their practical work has been taken over by the International Labor Office in

Geneva, while the Third International carries on a militant policy of stirring up revolutionary unrest wherever their representatives are active. In this work it is backed by the vast physical power of the Communist party which stands behind the Soviet government, though the government of the Soviet Union, as distinguished from the Communist party, has recurrently washed its hands of this business.

Socialist parties in power: Germany.—The collapse of the central empires carried the moderate Socialist parties into power along a considerable front. Before the fall of 1918 the Socialists had already taken over the government in Sweden under the able and restrained leadership of Hjalmar Branting. The German "revolution" of November 1918, initiated as it was by the radical and communist elements, miscarried; the moderate Social Democrats were able to maintain themselves in power with the quietly effective support of what was left of the German army. The frightened bourgeois element came to their support also. The Social Democrats, while holding the communist uprisings at bay, thus could combine with left wing reformist groups and the Catholic Center party to form the "Weimar Coalition." For the constitutional convention had been convened at Weimar, in a half-hearted attempt to rally to its support the spirit of Goethe and Schiller, at the same time removing the convention from the pressure of the street fighting which was going on in Berlin. Similar activities were being carried on all over Europe, in Austria, in the several succession states, in Poland. Everywhere moderate socialism proceeded to establish lengthy constitutions embodying mild provisions which looked toward the realization of a socialized community, but establishing them only with much caution and after constant consultation with the existing administrative staffs, their experts and specialists. These measures, many of which are being adopted or pushed in the United States today without much general discussion of socialism, seemed rather pale in comparison with the red hot dictatorship of the proletariat which was being forged in Russia. Throughout the post-war years the Social Democrats were harassed by their Communist opponents for being traitors to the workers' cause, and ridiculed for their pusillanimity and readiness to compromise with the "bourgeoisie." Unfortunately, a certain measure of patronage and corruption crept into governmental activities along with this extension of party control. Even if one discards the exaggerated claims of their late detractors, the detached observer is obliged to recognize certain undeniable facts, like the recurrent scandals about municipal finance. Sklarek, Kutisker, and other such names are the blots on the escutcheon of socialist and generally leftist government in Germany. Nor is the story very different in other lands. There is nothing surprising about these events; moral indignation was often the greatest in quarters where the actual practices were no better when power came to them in turn. Nevertheless, German and other socialism had, before the war, fed upon just such moral indignation, and when they were found embroiled in the same methods, their moral position was greatly weakened. The Communists and later the National Socialists saw to this. In ever-repeated harangues the workers were reminded of the various "failures" of the Socialists, their failure to nationalize even the key-industries (railroads had been governmentally owned and operated in these countries before the war), their failure to tax big business, their failure to bring about real peace in the international sphere, and so forth. The tendency of parties to espouse lofty rectitude in matters of principle while out of office, which was noted in the general discussion, worked in this instance with particular vehemence, because the Marxist movement is cast in strongly dogmatic terms, anyway. It was not very long before the Socialists lost control of the government. Having instituted proportional representation (see Chap. XVII, ¶ 11), they lost in the elections to the Communists as well as the Leftist bourgeois forces. Their recurrent participation in the government on a coalition basis (in Prussia during the entire period from 1919 to 1932) obliged them increasingly to seek protection of their interests with the aid of the accepted methods of parliamentary politics: compromise in principle, compensation in the shape of offices for the party bureaucracy. In Germany as well as in other countries this state of affairs produced a stratification of the party itself. The old leaders, most of them pre-war products, monopolized the party caucus and the conventions, forced the party to move according to the tactical considerations of coalition needs, backed by the older workers who had grown cautious and disillusioned in the service of the party. Recurrent movements among the younger elements to stage an overthrow of this hierarchy met with defeat; the brilliant group of "Young Socialists" could not secure enough influence to inject new vigor into the general outlook of the party. In the foreign relations field, for example, the party pursued a policy of national reconstruction, but kept on talking as if they were of the same mind as Moscow; no effort to reconstruct party ideology in terms of the new reality succeeded. This duplicity in word and deed served as a constant basis of attack, the Communists denouncing the actual policy as one betraying the German worker to Western "Big Capitalism," the Nazis railing at the old Marxist ideology of internationalism as an irrefutable proof of the unpatriotic attitude of social democracy. On the whole, it must be said that the party possessed many good men who did their best to remodel Germany along lines which would have given her a decent popular, if not a socialist, government, and who proved competent administrators when confronted with specific tasks. But the party lacked really brilliant leadership. Not a single genuinely great man appeared amongst them. Friedrich Ebert, the Republic's first president, comes nearest genuine stature as a statesman, and both Loebe and Severing were men of high moral calibre, but Social Democracy has not provided the names which shine in the annals of post-war German politics. The absence of really prominent leaders is a rather difficult thing to explain; it seems highly improbable that the human material was not there in view of the large size of the party. One encountered men with the making of really remarkable leaders, but they were thwarted by the bureaucratic machinery of this highly organized party. The power of the organization, developed in pre-war days in response to the difficult position in which the party found itself under the imperial government, proved its undoing in the later stage. This evil was, however, not limited to the German party.

The same subject: France and England.—In France and England, whose governments emerged victorious from the war, the course of development has been rather different from that in Central Europe. After their severe defeat in the Khaki elections of 1919 the British Labor party staged a brilliant come-back on December 6, 1923 when they were returned as the second largest party in Parliament, though without a majority. They then decided to take over the government with the support of the Liberals in Parliament. The wisdom of this decision, which was in keeping with English parliamentary traditions, no doubt, may be questioned in the light of later developments. As Asquith observed: "You cannot achieve legislation on an heroic scale . . . when you are in a permanent minority in this House . . . and when, in consequence of that, you are denuded of . . . the power of taking the time of the House, moving the Closure, and of regulating its proceedings in accordance with your wishes." The weakness of such a minority government was strikingly illustrated by the troubles of the Labor party in 1924. "The present Government again and again have said that they stand in a peculiar position because they do not command a majority in this House." It was particularly unfortunate for the Labor party to take over the government under such conditions, because under their elaborate platform they were pledged to extensive social reforms which were violently opposed by Liberals and Conservatives alike. The very essence of their party life was bound up in these reforms, like the nationalization of the coal industry, for example. But the Labor party fell because of their Russian policy. It was a matter of course that the Labor party should seek the recognition of the Soviet Union and the establishment of effective trade relations with this socialist republic. In the matter of recognition, they were supported by the Liberals, but difficulties soon developed. What was worse, the cautious course indicated by their difficult position in Parliament (192 Laborites with the (uncertain) support of 159 Liberals, against 258 Conservatives) engendered internal conflicts. In a different context, and in different form, we have here the same pattern as in Central Europe, and more particularly in Germany after the war. To be sure, the radical wing did not split off into a Communist party, or rather that party remained very small, on account of the single member constituency (see Chap. XVII, ¶ 2). But the insurgent left-wing Laborites were able to force the dropping of one governmental measure, the prosecution of Campbell, a Communist writer, and the adoption of another measure, the signing of the Russian Trade Treaty. Here as in Germany the very rigidity of party principles characteristic of Socialist parties enhances the probability of break-ups. When the regular party has only a minority behind it, its ability to deal with disaffected individuals or groups within its own ranks is greatly lessened. The Zinoviev letter incident, while probably intrinsically a fraud, made such an effective appeal, because the controversies within the Labor party about their relations to the Communists had created a state of profound agitation among the general public. The mere suggestion that certain labor groups had received money from Moscow, as the letter was alleged to prove, sufficed to crystallize this state of mind. Curiously enough, the British Labor party, or at least its leaders, seem to have learned little or nothing from these experiences. When, after the elections of 1929, they were returned with a following slightly larger than the Conservatives (Labor 288, Conservatives 260, Liberals 59, Independents 8) they again decided to return to the seat of power, this time with the compelling argument that the losses of the Conservatives had largely been their gain, and that parliamentary comity pointed to their taking over the government. From the viewpoint of the detached student of politics, it would seem that even more than in 1924, the kinship was between Liberals and Conservatives (as the coalition of 1931 was to prove later). The government's difficulties began at once with the debate on the Address to the Throne. Stanley Baldwin, as leader of the opposition, pointed out: "The Government is a minority Government and, therefore, the House of Commons as a whole has its rights. . . . Nevertheless," he added, "it is . . . essential for the Empire, that we face the world as a united Parliament." At once, the government found itself thwarted in its desire to secure the procedural aids which precedence for the government's business afford (see Chap. XXII, ¶ 3). Only after a very lengthy debate, could it get the Address to the Throne through, and in the divisions it had to rely now on support from the Liberals, now on that from the Conservatives. Without going into the tortuous history of the Labor party's ministerial fortunes, it may summarily be stated that the same process as in 1924 took place. Cautious governmental maneuvering aroused a spirit of defiant opposition in the more radical circles of the party. This insurgent attitude was intensified by the economic difficulties centering around the maintenance of the pound and the unemployment insurance which was sapping the financial strength of the country with ever-mounting payments to be made. The great debate on the Unemployment Insurance Bill No. 3, in July 1931, foreshadowed the conflicts which brought about the disintegration of the cabinet, its resignation, and the disastrous defeat of the party in the ensuing elections (after the government of national coalition had been formed by MacDonald). Having declared that increased taxation was impracticable, the government, through this Unemployment Insurance Bill, sought to cut benefits. In attempting to do so, it encountered much opposition from its own party, not from its parliamentary opposition, the Conservatives and Liberals. This state of affairs was untenable from the party's point of view; it is fair to say that this debate already showed the party's decomposition. The British Labor party has not yet recovered from the shock of this internal conflict and subsequent electoral defeat, though it should be noted that its loss in votes is much less considerable than the number of parliamentary seats would indicate. This is due to the vagaries of simple majority elections. At the same time, the party leadership as well as its following has been radicalized. Their program as it stands today is even less realizable without an absolute majority in Parliament than were the earlier ones. The party has at last seen the lesson of experience, and while no formal votes have been adopted it may well be doubted whether it will once more accept the responsibilities of forming a government without having a real majority. In France, the Socialists have stood aloof. Under the leadership of Léon Blum, they have refused to enter into coalition with bourgeois governments, although they lent considerable support to the Herriot ministry in 1924, particularly to its policy of reconciliation with Germany. French Socialists have long debated the question of coalition. Millerand's entry into the cabinet of Waldeck-Rousseau in the early 1900's actually provoked a break in the party which was only healed in 1905. A resolution forbidding a Socialist to become a minister was adopted. Small groups calling themselves Socialists, such as Aristide Briand and his following, have pursued a different course. (And, of course, the Radical Socialists who are hardly Socialists, and certainly not radical ones, have been participating in the government right along.) This policy the orthodox Socialists have maintained since the war. Only since the election in the spring of 1936 have they abandoned it, have, in fact, taken over the government recently, and seem to be confronting precisely the same troubles against which their German and English comrades before them battled in vain. Hindered by coalition and compromise with bourgeois liberals, harassed by radical agitation and communist opposition, they are hard put to it to maintain governmental prestige. But the situation they are confronting contains one rather novel factor—the factor which brought them into the government in the first place. It is the threat of Fascism. In France, military dictatorship as an alternative to mass insurgency is not a new thing. The Napoleonic tradition is there ready to be re-awakened. But the future is opaque, and it is not our task to forecast it.

Socialism in Austria.—A rather unique situation developed in Austria. Here socialism after the war remained a compact party, pledged to the revolutionary principles of orthodox Marxism. At the same time, the able leaders of Austrian Marxism refused to associate themselves with the Communist Third International. They decided to play their own little fiddle, and their ventures into international action were dubbed the 2½ International. Within the small rump of

German-speaking Austria which was left over after the disintegration of the Hapsburg Empire the Socialists at first had a clear majority and could establish a thoroughly social democratic constitution to suit themselves. Hans Kelsen played a prominent part in this work. But no constitution could have halted the economic collapse resulting from the dismemberment of Vienna's economic *Hinterland*, and the Socialists had to bear the brunt of the blame and rapidly lost their hold upon the government, except in Vienna. In this large and beautiful city and its many industrial suburbs the Socialist power was solidly anchored in the industrial masses. There consequently developed a rather clear-cut antagonism between the progressive, socialist metropolis and the conservative, Catholic countryside. The Alpine peasant, orthodox and patriotic, was the backbone of the other great party, the Christian Social party. Under the skillful leadership of a Catholic clergyman, Dr. Seipel, this party succeeded in monopolizing the opposition to the Socialists, and the issues were so clear-cut that almost a two-party system developed, in spite of proportional representation (see above, Chap. XVII). The Socialists, opposed to federalism and ready to join the German sister republic at the first opportunity, could not enter into any coalition with left wing bourgeois elements, because there were hardly any such coalitionists available. Going into the opposition soon after the inflation, they were able to purge themselves, and return to principles and orthodoxy. Otto Bauer's superior ability as a political and intellectual leader staved off any considerable left-wing radicalism. Eventually, when the indignation of the masses over the economic troubles of the depression threatened the Christian Social party under Dollfuss, popularly dubbed Milli-Metternich, with electoral defeat, the latter proceeded to suppress the Socialists (July-August 1933), egged on by his Fascist and legitimist associate Prince von Starhemberg. But the Austrian Socialists were determined not to let themselves be pushed aside like their ill-fated German comrades in Prussia. They prepared for another coup to dislodge their Catholic adversaries, by force if necessary. Dollfuss thereupon proceeded to break their resistance and in unexpectedly brutal proceedings had the army attack and partially destroy the modern workers' quarters, jail and shoot the leaders, including Vienna's able Socialist burgomaster, Karl Seitz; he then promulgated another "constitution" which forever barred such popular elections as might have displaced him. But as it is written, "Who sows wind, will reap storm," Dollfuss was murdered in the course of an insurrection staged by Austrian followers of Hitler who had hoped to conquer the government.

Catholic parties, particularly in France.—The Austrian Republic has been dominated for some time by a Catholic party. This party is not a unique thing in Europe, though its power and influence are. In many countries, particularly those with proportional representation, Catholic parties play an important role. It is, therefore, necessary briefly to examine their background and compare their position in various lands. Like the socialism back of various parties of workers, Catholicism is an elaborate creed, a philosophy of life, and transcends all national boundaries. Indeed, as everyone knows, Catholicism has an international organization of mighty traditions, older and more tradition-bound than any of the governments of present-day Europe. It looms in our modern world from an age when no national governments were in existence; the latter learned from the church many of their most essential techniques, as was shown in the discussion of bureaucracy, diplomacy, and other topics. Those who are strongly attached to this creed are almost bound to carry their convictions into politics. But whereas in the United States the impact of Catholicism upon politics has been local and indirect, the peculiar conditions of European politics have led to the formation of Catholic parties, particularly where the Catholics have constituted a numerous minority, or a bare majority. The formation of parties upon the foundation of the Catholic faith is conceivable in two ways, ideally speaking. Since the Catholic faith espouses an active ethic, it maintains a very definite belief about the end of all government as an aid toward man's ultimate end: the salvation of his soul. But there is also the more practical proposition of fighting for greater freedom and independence of the church whenever the government attempts to interfere. In either case, the Catholic parties appear as the mainstay of a comprehensive program of opposition to Marxist materialism, at least to their own followers. From this point of view, it is no longer a question of independence of the church from the government, but of protection for the government by the church. To these ideological objectives are joined, as in all parties, the concrete advantages to be derived from securing adequate or favored treatment for faithful members of the church. But the historical origins of Catholic parties in Europe are sometimes more clearly related to one or another of these objectives. In France, the aggressive hostility of the revolutionary government and its interference in church affairs (by secularizing church property and by attempting to separate the clergy from Rome) called forth political activity of the Catholics which accrued to the support of the first Napoleon and the restored Bourbons as well. The new Catholic view found brilliant expression in de Maistre's *Du Pape*. He argued that Catholics must rally to the leadership of the Pope now that the governments were becoming anti-clerical. Gradually, these battle-lines as drawn during the revolutionary period became transformed in the course of the nineteenth century into a bitter hostility between liberalism and radicalism on one side and Catholicism on the other. Four great encyclical letters by Leo XIII present the issue comprehensively: *Diuturnum* (1881), which deals with the nature of political power, *Immortale Dei* (1885), which deals with the nature of the state, *Rerum Novarum* (1891), which deals with the social problems, and *Sapientiae Christianae* (1890), which deals with the duties of citizens. The mixed trends of French politics during the greater part of the nineteenth century prevented the crystallization of a compact Catholic party, though Catholicism is a constant issue between various party groups. When the *Affaire Dreyfus* had thoroughly aroused the French public and re-kindled a spirit of republican enthusiasm, a group of Catholic politicians sought to compromise with certain tenets of liberalism and founded the *Action Liberale Populaire*, a rather conservative group with a mildly reformist program, the three R.P.'s: *Représentation Proportionnelle, Représentation Professionnelle,* and *Répartition Proportionnelle des Crédits Scolaires*. The issues of the *Affaire Dreyfus* also created, or rather revived, a militant form of reactionary conservatism, the royalist and Catholic *Action Française* which has flourished intellectually, if not politically, for the last thirty years under the brilliant leadership of Charles Maurras and Léon Daudet. But this group was condemned by the church in 1926 and can, therefore, hardly be considered a Catholic party. Minor groups on the left further illustrate the lack of unity in French Catholicism under the Third Republic.

The same subject: Germany and other countries.—Very different has been the role of political Catholicism in Germany. Here the original impetus was provided by a struggle against the monarchs. In Catholic countries, like Bavaria, the government had seized all church property, and in return had guaranteed the church an income. In Protestant monarchies, like Prussia, the government had undertaken to foster such progressive measures as mixed marriages, which the church opposed. In either case, the inevitable conflicts with the government could be influenced in favor of the church if her interests were represented in the elected assemblies. The transformation of clerical representatives in diets of the estates, where they had constituted one estate[1] into a parliamentary party was a gradual one in these German principalities. Even at best the church could not hope to achieve a position rivalling that of former days (in the England of Henry VIII the "lords spiritual" outnumbered the temporal lords) except under unusual circumstances such as those in Austria after the war. But even a minority group could achieve results by compromising on other issues. This primary interest in certain issues touching the position of the church explains the shifting position of the Catholic parties. Under the constitutional monarchies they were prepared to support the throne in exchange for concessions in matters of authority over the schools and similar concerns. In Republican Germany after the war they were equally ready to collaborate with democracy in the interest of the same vital issues. Throughout the nineteenth century the central objective of these Catholic parties remained the same: to free the church and certain areas of social life which she considered vital from as much interference by the government as possible. In the earlier period, their constant argument was that the Catholic Church is the best bulwark against revolution; but she can fulfill this function only if she is left in charge of education, family life, and so on. Napoleon the First set the pattern for the sort of relationship between church and state characteristic of the nineteenth century by concluding his concordat with the Holy See in 1801. Bavaria and other South German governments followed later. By thus concluding "international" agreements with various governments, the church reasserted its independent position and the fact that the church is not a governmental institution and never should be one. The priests are, therefore, never civil servants, even though they receive their salary from the government. This they do only because the property of the church was secularized by force, i.e., confiscated. By way of compensation, the governments at the same time expressly accepted the obligation of supplying the wants of the church. Besides these questions of mixed finance, by far the most important practical aspect of clerical

[1] A survival of this type of feudal representation is found in the British House of Lords where the Church of England, or rather its bishops, still has twenty-six seats.

politics is the conservation of clerical influence in the schools of all grades, whether through separate parochial schools or direct influence upon public schools. All these interests were paramount, and the Catholics acted accordingly. If the Catholic parties in various South German principalities had been ready to collaborate with the monarchs, another group of Catholics succeeded in organizing a Catholic Club within the revolutionary Constitutional Convention at Frankfurt in 1848 with the express purpose of defending the political rights of the Catholic Church. Under the able leadership of Radowitz and Reichensperger this Club succeeded in securing the support of the Catholic masses as almost all trends of political attitude were represented with the moderate elements prevailing; all were united in the effort to secure an independent position for the church through a federal organization of the dreamed-of popular *Reich.* When these dreams faded, the local clubs became important starting points for further political activity. Though Catholic party activity flared up in 1852 in Prussia in opposition to constitutional violations of the government, still it might have died away for lack of any real issues, as it did in France, had not Bismarck ventured forth into his ill-fated *Kulturkampf*. Around the issues of this struggle Catholic politicians were able to organize a lasting party organization in the eighteen seventies. The party of the Center, so-called because their seats were in the center of the assembly, had been reorganized in 1870. Catholics had, through the exclusion of Austria, become a minority. Their hope of a Germany federally united under Austrian leadership had been destroyed. At the same time, the recently declared infallibility of the Pope had complicated the relationship between the Catholic Church and the governments, since it raised anew the issue of allegiance. The unification of Italy and the consequent destruction of the Papal State making the Pope a voluntary "prisoner in the Vatican," had added further complications, particularly for Prussia, since Bismarck had supported the Italian unification. Unhappily, some of the non-German subjects within the Empire happened to be Catholics, like the Poles in the East and the French in the West. The Catholic clergy shared the feelings of these national minorities. It favored the use of their mother tongue in schools and churches. Some French bishops, whose dioceses included territory which had passed from France to Germany, fanned the flames by unwise decrees. The newly formed Catholic party naturally became the mouthpiece of these various sentiments. Being the second largest party, with fifty-seven seats in the newly elected *Reichstag,* it proceeded to demand intervention of the Reich in favor of the Pope's right to stay in Rome and to retain the city as his worldly dominion. To help the minorities, it demanded the inclusion of the Prussian bill of rights in the imperial constitution. The Bavarian particularist elements, hostile to the Prussian leadership, allied themselves with the party. Under the skillful tactical leadership of Windthorst, the Catholic party became the most effective opposition to Bismarck's government. This only changed in the nineties when, because of the rapid increase of the Social Democrats, a rapprochement between the various bourgeois groups seemed indicated. The appointment of Prince Hohenlohe-Schillingsfürst, who was a Catholic and an experienced parliamentarian, as Chancellor, cemented this reconciliation of the Center party with the Empire. But the Catholics retained their rather independent position, often making opposition on particular issues, like the treatment of Alsace-Lorraine, freed themselves more and more from strictly clerical influences, and through the powerful Christian Trade Unions maintained a strong connection with the labor movement and other left wing tendencies. During the World War these elements in the Catholic party gained the upper hand. The appointment of the Catholic Count Hertling to the chancellorship was an indication of the growing influence of the party. The radical group under Erzberger took a prominent part in forcing the peace resolution of the spring of 1917, at the same time persuading the Pope to make his several overtures for a negotiated peace. It was, therefore, quite natural for these left-wing Catholics to play a prominent role in the reshaping of Germany after the war. Through Erzberger, the party became inextricably connected with the Versailles settlement. The Nazi agitation against the "stab in the back" always was in part directed against the Center party. Erzberger, by disposition an optimistic tactician rather than a statesman, had firmly expected Wilson's Fourteen Points to prevail. When they did not, he nevertheless was among the most ardent advocates of accepting the peace as dictated at Versailles. In the meantime, the party had helped to draft the Republican constitution. At that time, many non-Catholics looked upon the Center party as their salvation from outright state-socialism such as was expected from the Social Democrats. It is undoubtedly due to this Catholic influence that the German constitution embodied so many contradictory provisions on various phases of national life, such as religion, the school, property and so on (see above, Chap. X, ¶4). As the reaction against this progressive national charter set in, the Center party gradually drifted to the right. At first in Bavaria, whose Catholic group split off from the Center party as the Bavarian People's party, and later on elsewhere, the drift of the Catholic majority was toward a reassertion of authoritarian ideas. Wirth, Marx, Brüning, and von Papen, successive Catholic chancellors under the Weimar Republic in the period of reconstruction before the Ruhr invasion, the period after Ruhr and inflation, the great depression, and the eve of Nazidom, respectively, mark the phases of this shift. At the same time, the Center party proved its suppleness by continuing a member of the Weimar coalition of leftist groups in Prussia throughout the entire period, with the unique result that when von Papen attempted to expel the Prussian government in the summer of 1932, he was proceeding against his own former party colleagues. The fruit of this policy (unprincipled from the standpoint of parliamentary traditions) was a position of unique influence for certain Catholic parliamentarians, like Dr. Schreiber, who effectively assumed the role of bringing together the rival administrators of the Reich and Prussia. More specifically, the Center party was able to induce the Prussian government under democratic leadership to conclude a concordat with the church, a startling achievement in view of the anti-clerical, even anti-religious bond of the other members of the coalition. When the National Socialists came into power, the Catholic party was obliged "voluntarily" to disband along with the rest. This fate aroused mingled feelings. In the eyes of a good many observers, the Center party had been the curse of the German Republic; others took precisely the opposite view that German parliamentarism would never have worked had it not been for the moderating influence of the Catholic party. Such wholesale explanations explain very little, but they serve to emphasize the complexity of the impact which the existence of this "parliament within the parliament" had upon the structure of the German party system. Similar problems have arisen elsewhere. Other European countries with solidly organized Catholic parties are Switzerland, Belgium, the Netherlands, and Austria. As noted before, the presence of a solid Catholic minority has served to emphasize the need for proportional representation in the former three countries (see above, Chap. XVII). In Switzerland, Catholicism and conservatism have always gone hand in hand, and the Catholics have never quite recovered from the loss of prestige which the ill-starred war of separation (*Sonderbundskrieg,* see above, Chap. XIII, ¶ 3) inflicted upon them. In Belgium, the Catholic party has always been associated with conservatism, too, but the greater number of Catholics in that country gave the Belgian Catholics for a long time an almost uninterrupted control of the government. In the Netherlands, on the other hand, the Catholics adroitly used their position as an intermediary, and under the leadership of Dr. Nolens grew in power to such an extent that in the late twenties one could encounter repeatedly the comment that things happen in Holland *Nolens, volens.* In Austria, as has been remarked, the Christian Social party after the war was able to secure a predominance similar to that in Belgium. Under the Hapsburg monarchy, Austria had been the protector of the church; under the Republic, the church became the protector of Austria. The international position of Catholicism was shrewdly used by Seipel and Dollfuss. Curiously enough, the Christian Social party increasingly assumed a stand hostile to unification with the German Republic, though such unification (*Anschluss*) was often opposed in Protestant parts of Germany on the ground that it would give the Catholics too strong a position. The reason is obvious, when one considers that the predominant position of Catholicism in Austria proper would be endangered at the same time that Catholicism would be strengthened in Germany as a whole. But the best argument against advocating the *Anschluss* in the eyes of Seipel and his brethren was a good one: that the *Anschluss* was not practical politics. As they were the party in power that argument was decisive. Add to it that such unification seemed to close the door to the Hapsburgs' return and the Catholic party's position is clear enough. For the Christian Social party was conceived in terms of social conservatism, if not reaction. Its pre-war leader, Lueger, was one of the spiritual fathers of Hitler's social philosophy, as Hitler himself has shown in his autobiography. This spiritual kinship between social conservatism and Fascism, as well as Nazism, is also operative in Italy. To be sure, the Catholic party of the Popolari was rather dedicated to reconciling Catholicism and social reform; its leader, Don Sturzo, was exerting an increasing influence in the days preceding the Fascist March on Rome. But when Mussolini had firmly entrenched himself, the Catholic Church preferred to conclude a concordat with him, and to request Don Sturzo to go into exile. Mussolini's concordat bears a close resemblance to Napoleon's. The anti-clerical elements in the Fascist party are violently opposed to it. But it gave to Mussolini the support of the church, and to the church the support of Mussolini. At last the Italian government had recognized the international position of the church, and the territorial existence of the Vatican, concessions which perhaps no Catholic party could have wrangled out of more liberal and popular governments.

Bonapartism, Fascism, National Socialism.—Throughout Europe, the Catholic, or Christian, opposition to socialism could not be effective wherever the underlying religious faith had been shattered, even though the opposition itself were firmly rooted in property and other interests. If the tradition of self-reliance, of self-government, of self-restraint is weak in these masses, and if they therefore demand or rather yearn for authoritative leadership, the nation offers itself as another goddess. Around this golden calf the Fascist masses of Europe are dancing today. There was much precedent for that. The French Revolution, though enthroning the goddess "Reason," had already shown a decided penchant for the rival goddess "Nation." Many thinkers see the birthplace of modern nationalism here. Reason having become discredited by the Terror, Napoleon led the French armies to victory after victory for the greater glory of *La Nation*. Carlton J. H. Hayes has emphasized the profound conflict between the religions of nationalism and Christianity. Bonapartism, Fascism, National Socialism: three forms of the same nationalist religion, each born of the terror of the middle classes at seeing their security threatened by the masses. In the ancient world, the challenge of Christianity was directed against the tribal multiplicity of gods, each protecting his or her particular city. In contemporary civilization, the challenge of Fascism is directed against the Catholicity of a Christian faith transcending all national loyalties. Communism, cherishing the ideal of a mankind composed of workers and united by an international bureaucracy of supermen, attempts to substitute a millennial hope of all-round material prosperity for the transcendental faith in eternal salvation of the soul which the Christian churches espouse. The terrified small property owners, farmers, peasants, shopkeepers, craftsmen, white collar employees, professional men, and their like, unwilling to become mere "workers" under an international bureaucracy, yet unable to maintain a faith in Christian views, return to the tribal fetishes which once dominated the minds of men. The parties dedicated to these views are as intransigent as the Communists, and as ready to wage a war to end all war as ever Wilson was; only this time it is civil war. It is the fighting answer to a fighting challenge. In saying this, we do not wish to imply any belief in the Fascist myth about the impending Communist revolution which animated their March on Rome on September 29, 1922. Even less do we propose any faith in the Nazi myth that the German Parliament building was fired by Communists on February 27, 1933. In either case, the particular events to which the myth has attached itself are irrelevant; in fact their very insignificance testifies to their symbolic importance. If the Fascist masses had not been ready to believe anything of the Communists, they would surely never have believed these improbable tales. Fascism as well as National Socialism are post-war products, but both have their roots in the party controversies of the past. In spite of certain differences which are at present often emphasized by admirers, and sometimes by detractors, they are fundamentally alike. In their social philosophy they resemble the trust-busters in the United States, the Radical Socialists in France. They are for maintaining property, but hate big business. For faith in democracy, however, they have substituted faith in the leadership of one man. In this they resemble the Communists, although originally the latter emphasized the party rather than the leader. In practice, Lenin and Stalin have come to occupy a position much like that of Hitler and Mussolini. It must, however, not be forgotten that the Fascist leaders made their "program" themselves and to order, whereas the Communist masters continue to acknowledge the writings of Marx as their inspirational source. This willingness to follow a "Bible" introduces a measure of argument into the party councils. Orthodoxy remains a controversial matter. A man like Trotzki going about in other countries denouncing the doctrines and actions of Stalin as not thoroughly Marxist is hard to envisage for Fascism. From the standpoint of the student of party development the details of Fascist party activity and development are not very important. The frequent emphasis upon the discipline of these parties is rather misplaced. The discipline of the German Nazis hardly rivalled that of their Socialist and Communist antagonists. The apparent external regimentation may hide a considerable amount of internal dissension. In Germany particularly, where the Nazi party was slowly built up under the Republic from 1921 onward, the organization is honeycombed with factionalism. Labor battles with business interests, farmers fight both, the doctrinaires of race purity are scorned by the groups interested in economic welfare, and so forth. This is only a natural result of the party's willingness to appeal to everybody on his own terms: farmers were promised higher prices for their produce, while workers were offered a lower cost of living at better wages; yet the employing group were cheered by expectations of seeing the trade unions destroyed. While debtors heard the "slavery of interest" denounced, creditors discovered a silver lining in the proposed return to good, old-fashioned German honesty. All this sort of straddling of real issues is familiar enough in the United States, where party managers have always been obliged to placate many factions and interests in order to hold a majority together. In Germany it was startling, since the more limited appeal of parties had allowed a sharper focusing of issues. The Nazis were rewarded by eventually becoming the largest German party, before coming into power. It is noteworthy that they rallied to their many-colored banner more followers than any German party ever did in the history of German party development. And while they were in the opposition, the self-contradictions in their appeals could not readily be revealed, except to the thoughtful. And after all, any one group or interest had at least a betting chance of coming out on top in the end, when the party had taken over the power. At the same time, it can readily be seen that Hitler, with his entourage, could not possibly be expected to take over power unless he could hold it secure from criticism for a long time; for these contradictory promises were otherwise bound to lead to his very speedy downfall, the more so since he did not even possess a simple majority. Hitler would have been, as so many politicians before him, the captive of his own rhetoric. By indoctrinating the mass of his followers with the belief that parliamentary machinery is useless or worse, he protected himself while turning radical democratic ideology inside out. For if the majority of the people were willing to sanction such a procedure who could question it from a democratic standpoint? Locke and others had written that the people would not and could not surrender their self-determination; if they did, he and his liberal followers simply were wrong. Actually, the German Nazis never secured a majority, as they might not now if a free election could be held in Germany. But this is not the place for discussing the party as it has functioned since the violent destruction of the constitutional order in Germany in March 1933. The techniques of direct popular action will be taken up below.

For the same reason, there is not much to add about the Fascists or the followers of Pilsudski in Poland. In both cases the parties were rather small and insignificant until their respective leaders assumed the headship of their governments (*il capo del governo*). Mussolini and Pilsudski share a Socialist past which gives them a better comprehension of the social conflicts of our day. Both men were deeply dyed in the color of nationalism, however; Pilsudski as a revolutionary military leader, Mussolini as a result of his controversy with the strongly internationalist and pacifist Italian Socialists during the war. Like Hitler, Mussolini and Pilsudski were able to appeal to unsatisfied nationalist emotions after the war, and on a strongly personal basis to build up a following resembling in social and economic structure the Nazi following. Mussolini has publicly declared that the Italian peasants have always been the most loyal supporters of his regime; this is equally true of Pilsudski and Hitler. If socialism is the ideological weapon of the labor movement, Fascism in its various forms serves the same purpose for the farmers' movement. In these central European countries the peasants constitute as large a minority as the workers, if not larger. It is a group which has never before been really awake to its political power. In Germany as well as Italy the peasants uncomprehendingly supported the interests of the large estate owners, or were divided between the several bourgeois parties, none of which gave them a feeling of solidarity. Whether their hopes have been realized is, of course, another matter. It must, however, be noted that the violent anti-semitism of the Nazis and their friends in Poland has its deepest roots in this rural population. Much of the trading in rural communities being done by Jews, the Jews were not held in any higher esteem than cattle dealers and their ilk have ever anywhere been held by the farmer. His antagonism could readily be made the point of departure for a campaign to blame the Jews for everything. As a wit remarked: "The Germans beat up the Jews, because they cannot beat up the French." The bewildered frustration of post-war politics, accompanied as it was by constant international humiliations, cried for a *Prügelknabe*, some group to blame for it all. The Nazis seized this demagogic opportunity—or rather their own predilections made them stumble upon it. In Italy the same has not happened. The reason is not, as apologists of Fascism would have us believe, any innate superiority in the strictly Fascist creed, but simply the fact that the Jews in Italy offer no such golden opportunity for baiting. That the inherent need for such opportunities is the same, the Ethiopian campaign proved beyond doubt. Nazi apologists have in turn pointed with pride to the fact that their leader has not attempted to subdue Ethiopia. Such specious claims obscure the essential fact that tribal religion invariably carries with it a ruthless readiness for war against any outsiders, whether they are physically located within the boundaries of the country or beyond them. No more need be said at this point concerning the development of these parties of militant self-assertion, except that their ideology as well as their practice brings us back to the situation as it prevailed in Renaissance Florence. The party which identifies itself with the government, with the state, and with the country is, after all, once more the *il stato* of Machiavelli's writings. For *il stato* literally meant the party of the Medicis who, as princes of Florence, became the prototype of the absolute rulers of Europe who surrounded their power with the mystery of the *State*.

Conclusion.—Throughout the preceding discussion the intermingling of ideal and material objectives in the development of parties has been quite evident. The mercantile battling the landed interests, the workers the businessmen, the farmers the city-dwellers—we observe a constant procession of thesis and antithesis, the latter always posing as a new synthesis which it actually fails to be. Party development, more than any other sphere of political life, displays a dynamic evolution. There is here no final rest, as in the Hegelian metaphysics with its ultimate synthesis, nor any harmonious swing of the pendulum so often alleged as a "law of politics," but constant change in one direction or another, with never a return to the starting point. The great panorama of the history of modern parties is a reflection of the secular evolution of modern society in the mirror provided by the elected assemblies of modern constitutional governments. The psychic dispositions so lucidly portrayed by Mr. Lowell are ever present, but they attach themselves to different ideologies expressive of different configurations of interest. One hundred and fifty years ago, the theory of absolute democracy reached its abstract perfection in the glittering generalizations of Jean-Jacques Rousseau. The great French Revolution, as well as the dictatorship of the first Napoleon, is anticipated in its brilliant passages about the unlimited power of the sovereign majority, whether expressed directly or through a divinely inspired law-giver. Not a word about parties occurs in this piercing tract. No wonder that Communism,

Fascism, National Socialism, as well as Bonapartism, should have felt satisfied when assured approximate majority support. They are all children of the democratic age. They are all drunk with the will of the people. Nations whose familiarity with the working of constitutional government was largely academic and theoretical, whose thinking was confused on the difference between constitutional government and absolute democracy have surrendered themselves to the leadership of one man or a few who claimed such divine inspiration. The longing for unity has issued into a make-believe unity of one party identifying itself with the whole people. "All good Germans are National Socialists," cries Adolf Hitler; "All good men are Communists," echoes back Stalin. The plurality of parties, though generally admitted by political observers to be an essential feature of working constitutional government, has not found its apologist. Yet if parties are organized for securing power within a group, is not that very fact objective proof of the need for several parties? To deny this proposition, we would have to assert that men when holding all the power concentrated in their hands are never likely to abuse it. The political experience of mankind points in the opposite direction. In order to prove the superiority of one party, people have argued against innumerable parties. But are not two parties better than one or three? Neither monism, nor pluralism, but dualism corresponds to the harmonious equilibrium. To permit this equilibrium enough flexibility to move with the change in the evolution of society is the touchstone of an effective constitutional order.

CHAPTER XX

CABINET SYSTEMS

1. Introductory.—2. Classification of cabinets.—3. Internal organization. 4. The English cabinet.—5. The French cabinet.—6. The German cabinet.—7. The Swiss cabinet.—8. The American cabinet.—9. Conclusion: the representative position of cabinets.

Introductory.—Cabinets are older than Parliaments. Princes surrounded themselves with councils or cabinets for the direction of their bureaucracies as soon as central administrative systems arose. In fact, these bodies, composed of leading administrative officials, are the very core of such centralized systems. It is therefore no wonder that the cabinet tends to occupy a somewhat independent position and is not ordinarily, as the phrase used to go, "an executive committee of Parliament." If this were ever true in England, it surely was not true for a very long time, but only during the short period after the Reform Act and before massive party organizations arose in the late seventies. A certain measure of dependence upon Parliament, in other words, must not deceive one into considering the cabinet as an errand boy of a parliamentary majority, unless there is definite factual evidence to support such a contention.

Classification of cabinets.—In the light of the foregoing remarks we can attempt a rough classification of cabinet systems. Cabinets may possess a very high degree of independence from such a representative assembly, like that of England before the time of Walpole, or of the United States at present, or of other governments molded upon the American pattern (for example, a number of the American states). On the other hand, cabinets may be completely dependent upon Parliament, as they are in France and other governments modelled after the French pattern, such as pre-Fascist Italy. Finally, we may find cabinets occupying a somewhat intermediary position, as they do in England, where the Prime Minister's leadership of the dominant party gives them a very considerable measure of independence without freeing them altogether from considerations of parliamentary politics. A different sort of intermediary position was occupied by the cabinets under the Weimar constitution, where a popularly elected president with considerable powers could restrain parliamentary influence, particularly in view of the earlier German tradition of complete independence, which continued to dominate the thought of the army and the bureaucracy. Still different is the situation in Switzerland, where a cabinet, known as the Federal Council, has secured a measure of independence by restricting itself voluntarily to administrative problems, accepting in the realm of legislation the final verdict of the representative body. From this survey it can be seen that the question of parliamentary responsibility of cabinets issues into any number of different patterns of interdependence between cabinet and Parliament.

Internal organization.—There is need for a broad comparative analysis of cabinets in terms of their internal organization. Generally speaking, a cabinet may either be subject to leadership by a single individual or it may be a collegial group of equals. The first pattern, which may be called monocratic, is found in the United States, England, and the Dominions. In these countries the head of the cabinet is at the same time the leader of the party upon whose support the cabinet depends. The collegial cabinet is found in France. Here each of the several members of the cabinet figures as the leader of one of the groups which together constitute the parliamentary support of the cabinet. This polyarchic type, as we may call it, is also found in Switzerland, where the members of the cabinet are not, however, necessarily leaders of groups or parties, but merely representatives of such groups with high administrative qualifications who are thus delegated to the Federal Council. Governments following the French pattern, as far as the general relationships between Parliament and cabinet are concerned, are apt to have this collegial type of cabinet. We find it in pre-Fascist Italy as well as in a number of the smaller countries of Europe. In this matter of internal organization of cabinets we also find intermediary types, that is, types which oscillate between many leaders and one. Such a situation is found in Germany, for example. Here the rise of an effective leader such as Stresemann or Brüning might for a time create a situation approximating the English arrangement. But the many parties would at other times, in the absence of such a leader, necessitate a strictly collegial cabinet. To illustrate these possibilities, it will be necessary to describe several cabinet systems in somewhat greater detail. We have selected the English, French, German, American, and Swiss systems for this purpose.

The English cabinet.—Historically speaking, the English cabinet developed as a committee of the Privy Council. It does not, as is sometimes assumed, comprise all the officials responsible to Parliament, but only the more important among them, including the heads of the principal departments. There are the First Lord of the Treasury, the Chancellor of the Exchequer, and the First Lord of the Admiralty, as well as the Lord President of the Council and the Lord Privy Seal. In recent decades the cabinet has usually had around twenty members, more or less. They are selected by the Prime Minister according to considerations of party expediency. Various factions within the party as well as personal considerations and administrative necessities enter in. In view of this fact it is hardly appropriate to call the Prime Minister *primus inter pares*, as is so often done. While it would be inappropriate to call his cabinet colleagues his subordinates, it is clear that no individual could remain in the cabinet contrary to the Prime Minister's desire. Perhaps the most adequate statement would be that the Prime Minister is the superior of each individual member of the cabinet but not of the whole cabinet taken together. The actual relationships are necessarily fluid since they rest upon the extent and effectiveness of the Prime Minister's party leadership. For it is this party leadership rather than the leadership in the House of Commons which is of decisive importance. Nevertheless, the party leader is elected by a caucus composed of the members of Parliament in the respective parties supplemented by a few outstanding leaders from the outside. For this reason as well as others it is not practicable to make too rigid a distinction between the cabinet's parliamentary majority and its following outside Parliament. As Lowell has put it, "the governmental machinery is one of wheels within wheels; the outside ring consisting of the party that has a majority in the House of Commons; the next ring being the ministry, which contains the men who are most active within that party; and the smallest of all being the cabinet, containing the real leaders or chiefs. By this means is secured that unity of party action which depends upon placing the directing power in the hands of a body small enough to agree, and influential enough to control." Formally speaking, of course, the cabinet is responsible to Parliament. Apart from the legal responsibility of the entire ministry, this means that the members of the cabinet, both collectively and individually, are affected by certain actions of Parliament, which by convention oblige them either to resign or to dissolve Parliament and to call a general election. These actions of Parliament are three. Parliament may pass a vote of "want of confidence." Such a vote would indicate disapproval of the general policy of the cabinet and is therefore unusual. This is also true of the vote of censure, by which the Parliament may criticize the cabinet or one of its members. More usual is the defeat of a measure which the cabinet has sponsored and refuses to abandon. Substantially identical with this is the case in which Parliament insists upon a measure along lines which the cabinet opposes. Now any one of these steps could be taken by Parliament only if a certain number of the supporters of the government had become sufficiently dissatisfied to vote with the opposition party. A development of this sort presupposes a considerable measure of confusion concerning a certain issue. This was the case with the Irish question which frequently provided the occasion for cabinet changes in the later nineteenth century. In the period immediately before and since the war cabinet changes have come about rather by the initiative of the cabinet itself, when it decided to appeal to the people in a general election, as it did in 1910, 1918, 1923, 1932, and 1935. At other times a reconstruction of the cabinet has been undertaken in order to anticipate an adverse decision, as in 1905, 1915, and 1932, or by Parliament's statutory period coming to a close at the end of five years. The compactness of party organizations has, in other words, brought about a gradual transition from a parliamentary to an electoral responsibility. To put it another way, the cabinet governs Great Britain today with the advice and consent of Parliament. Serious difficulties have arisen through the rather considerable size of the cabinet. Twenty or more persons form a somewhat unwieldy body for the purposes of collective action. The recurrent demand before the war for a much smaller directing body led to the emergence of a small, informal group of five during the war. Under Lloyd George's active and energetic leadership this group took upon itself the making of the most important decisions, but the large amount of criticism which this arrangement engendered led to its abandonment after the war. Lloyd George's memoirs show, however, the great value which this instrumentality possessed in his eyes during the emergency. Therefore it may become an important precedent for similar occasions. The English cabinet owes another important innovation to the war; that is the cabinet secretariat. It was a peculiarity of the English cabinet not to keep any records of its meetings. A considerable amount of confusion and uncertainty resulted. A member of the cabinet would go ahead on the assumption that something had been decided in a meeting, only to have it repudiated later by his colleagues. This very inconvenient and extraordinary practice is no longer prevalent. The cabinet secretariat, under changed regulations, keeps a record of all cabinet meetings, communicates important decisions not only to cabinet members but also to other ministers, prepares agenda and the materials for cabinet meetings, and in many other ways attends to a type of administrative detail which in other systems has for a long time been attended to for cabinets along lines established by the earlier administrative councils. The existence of this secretariat has facilitated the tendency of the cabinet to work through committees as is indicated by its size. These committees, of course, have no authority to make a final decision but only to report and recommend. The committee sittings ordinarily may be, and often are, attended by ministers who are not in the cabinet. The most extraordinary committee development is the Committee of Imperial Defense, which is not technically a committee of the cabinet at all, but, since it consists of the Prime Minister as chairman, the political and technical heads of the defense services, the Chancellor of the Exchequer, and the Secretaries of State for Foreign Affairs, the Colonies, and India, as well as representatives of the Dominions, it is an important endeavour to develop an imperial executive besides the British cabinet, which in its functions is limited to the Empire outside of the so-called Commonwealth of Nations (see above, Chap. XIII, ¶17). Apart from these committees the whole cabinet meets quite regularly once or twice a week while Parliament is in session. In critical times meetings may, however, multiply. These meetings are quite informal and frequently of a rather conversational order. Such is the nature of the British cabinet which has been variously described as the "keystone of the political arch" or the "pivot around which the whole political machinery revolves." It is undoubtedly true that the cabinet is today the core of the English government. As the exponent of the majority party it directs the affairs of the country until that party support disintegrates. It does not merely execute and administer, as people who think in American terms are apt to assume. It also decides upon, drafts, sponsors, and puts through Parliament new legislation, and takes full initiative in all fiscal and budgetary matters.

The French cabinet.—The French cabinet occupies a very different position. It could not possibly be described as the core of the government. To be sure, one authority claims that it too tends to become the center of gravity in the parliamentary system, but as such it certainly does not radiate energy and activity. It is quite significant that writers speak of it as "the ministries," thus emphasizing the ministers' separate and individual roles. So realistic and perspicacious a commentator as Robert de Jouvenel in *La République des Camarades* discusses "ministres et ministères" without referring to a collective cabinet at all. In discussing the ministers, he merely describes how an individual parliamentarian is put into a ministerial position and how this minister copes with the permanent administrative services, how he is surrounded by his personal and private secretarial staff (called in French *le cabinet*), and how he tries to get through his administrative functions without either previous knowledge or opportunity to acquire it while he is in office. "To administer," says this witty commentator, "is to appoint officials whom one does not know to positions of which one is ignorant, in other words to distribute promotions and decorations in the midst of solicitations, recriminations, and threats." There is also, of course, the all-engrossing task of keeping on good terms with Parliament, and more particularly, with one's own parliamentary group. In view of this it seems more appropriate to look upon the French cabinet as a group of individuals whose task it is to act as liaison between the dominant parliamentary group and the permanent administrative staffs in the various ministries. Of course there are very considerable differences due to personality here as in England; for example, Delcassé managed to occupy a position of very great independence as Minister of Foreign Affairs between 1897 and 1905 and to conduct a policy which was largely unknown to the parliamentary group supporting the ministries to which he belonged. Similarly, Ministers of War have been able to maintain a position of great independence. It has justly been said that the amount of change to which French cabinets are subject is more apparent than real. Particularly the ministries of War and Marine show a decidedly more stable personnel. The statistical picture in the fifty-four cabinets between August 31, 1871, and March 22, 1913, is twenty-eight Ministers of Foreign Affairs thirty-two of the Navy, thirty-three of War, thirty-seven of Justice, and thirty-nine of the Interior. The same was true after the war. In the period from November 16, 1917 to July 23, 1926 we find that in fifteen cabinets there were seven Ministers of Foreign Affairs, eight of War, nine of the Navy, ten of the Interior, ten of Finance, and eleven of Justice. Correspondingly, we find some individuals holding parliamentary positions a great many times, one, in fact, twenty times. To put it another way, by taking all the cabinets from 1871 to 1930 we find that of a total of 1026 cabinet positions, 482, or almost half, were held by sixty individuals serving from five to twenty times. In the light of these figures, M. Barthélemy's remarks are worthy of attention. "The French democracy has been heavily blamed for its extreme fickleness and the reckless way in which its chambers have consumed one ministry after another. It has been described as a frenzied rush of cabinets across the political stage from one wing to the other. These criticisms, though perhaps justified to a certain extent by certain periods in the history of the Third Republic, are for the most part greatly exaggerated and the conclusions drawn from certain well-established facts are not always well-founded." He then gives a good many illustrations of the fact that ministers have often outlasted several ministries, continuing as ministers without interruption. This is quite natural in a situation where the cabinet is a collegial body and where the position of each minister is to some extent dependent upon his individual support in Parliament. The number of available individuals is limited, and certain groups can only be held in line by including the man whom they are willing to follow. In spite of this dependence of the ministry upon constant parliamentary support, French constitutional writers are much more inclined to emphasize the separation of powers than are Englishmen. They still take seriously to some extent the classical doctrine of politics according to which the parliamentary system as established by the constitution of 1875 depends upon a balance of power with Parliament on one side and the president on the other. This doctrine, which sees the cabinet as the link between the representative body and the chief executive, contains no description of the French reality at all. For, elected by Parliament and without the power of dissolution, the French president possesses no independent authority to match the power of Parliament. On the other hand, a certain difficulty arises from the fact that the cabinet depends not only on the confidence of the Chamber of Deputies but on that of the Senate as well. Attempts to shake off the dual control of the Senate have occasionally been successful. Inasmuch as the composition of the Senate and the Chamber are often at variance, the forming of a cabinet is greatly complicated, at times producing well-nigh insuperable difficulties. This has been true, for example, in recent years. The situation is saved only by the looseness and fluidity of the groups in both Houses. If strongly organized parties or blocs came into existence, a complete stalemate might result. Of course the disjointedness of the cabinet also helps, since it facilitates the dropping of individual ministers who have lost the confidence of either house. All this may seem very curious unless one remembers that the paramount concern of the men who developed this system was to control the permanent administrative staff. Just as the dislike of the French public found expression in the epithet "bureaucracy," so the long-established dominance of this centralized bureaucracy has been the main target of the popular movement in the nineteenth century. M. Barthélemy voices this French viewpoint when he writes that a change of ministers is very desirable because the minister is actually the controller of the bureaucracy. For that reason he feels that the minister must not have the spirit of a bureaucrat, which he undoubtedly would have if he remained in office for very long periods. His vigilance must constantly be kept on the alert for parliamentary control and the threat of removal. He is not a technical expert, but rather the political superintendent of a stable and specialized bureaucracy. For that reason he feels that a certain instability of ministers is rather advantageous than not. The aim is to obtain a balance.

The German cabinet.—It is not surprising that the makers of the Weimar constitution, animated by a similar dislike for the bureaucratic tradition, looked with a certain measure of sympathy upon the French cabinet system. They, too, felt that their ministry was to be the political supervisor of a permanent bureaucracy. The more thoughtful ones among them could not help but feel that the French system, with its polyarchic diversity in the cabinet, responded more nearly to the needs of Germany with her many parties. Like France and unlike England, she faced the task of building up a parliamentary tradition in terms of the free professions, particularly those of law and journalism, since a republican order could not hope to command the allegiance of the aristocracy, which formed the backbone of the English parliamentary and cabinet personnel. On the other hand, the instability of French politics appeared in such an unfavorable light that arguments like the one set forth in the famous essay of Redslob,

Parliamentary Government, True and False, made a deep impression. Consequently, the German Republican constitution provided for popular election of the president, thus giving the chief executive a plebiscitary foundation (see below, Chap. XVIII). The resulting balance did not last, and this popularly elected president became a mighty factor in the destruction of the whole parliamentary system. Due to the double dependence of the cabinet upon the president on the one hand and the Reichstag on the other, both popularly elected representatives of the entire German people, it oscillated, as we said before, between different arrangements as far as its external relations were concerned, and these oscillations in turn profoundly affected its internal structure. Unlike the unstable groups in the French Parliament, the several German parties were highly organized (see above, Chap. XVIII). Unlike the English, none of these German parties ever commanded a majority. Since the constitution explicitly demanded (Article 54) that the Chancellor and his ministers need the confidence of the Reichstag and that they must resign individually as well as collectively if the Reichstag withdraws its confidence, the president adopted the method of asking a certain parliamentary leader to form a cabinet and only to appoint him Chancellor after he had succeeded. This practice, which is also found in France, had the unfortunate consequence of calling to the attention of the public the bickering which is involved in forming a cabinet. At first this method centered in negotiations between the parties for the formation of a coalition. Gradually, however, and partly as a result of the increasing economic difficulties, there emerged the idea that the cabinet must not only possess the requisite parliamentary majority but must also contain all those who otherwise might disturb the government by extraparliamentary means. Thus a third dependence, that upon broad popular support, was recognized. Until 1923 cabinets were formed by the parties whenever they could get together, and when they could not, the initiative of the president sufficed to bring about a coalition with sufficient support to carry on. After 1923 cabinets were regularly supported by a minority in the center, and made constant efforts to broaden the base of support. Since these efforts came to naught, there emerged after 1926 an increasing inclination to have the cabinet organized by presidential initiative and then have it seek the support of Parliament as it went along. Through this development the central idea of parliamentary government, namely, majority support, was abandoned. It was an endeavour to return to the German tradition of an independent government of administrators in terms of three slogans: "government of the middle way," "cabinet of personalities," and "government above parties." The most serious difficulty resulting from such an arrangement was the ever present danger that the two radical wings of the House which were thus excluded from the cabinet would combine in a vote of non-confidence without having any intention of combining to form a new government. This happened, for example, to the second Marx cabinet, which was overthrown by the combined vote of the Nationalists and Social Democrats. It was therefore argued that the real intention of the second sentence of Article 54 was not and never could have been to make it possible for obstructionist groups of radically opposed views to get together for the mere purpose of destroying a government without any intention of forming a new one. From this premise it was further argued that a vote of non-confidence could not have the effect provided for in the constitution if the vote of non-confidence is an act of pure obstruction. This rather strained interpretation was not generally accepted for a time, but it underlay a considerable part of the parliamentary maneuvering of Brüning, and even those who objected to the interpretation conceded that it would be desirable to amend Article 54 so as to require the vote of non-confidence to be sustained by a uniform set of reasons. This, it was felt, would make it difficult for radically opposed parties to get together on such a vote. Whatever the potentialities, Dr. Brüning always retained the idea that the cabinet must command the support of a parliamentary majority. How right he was is apparent from the hopeless impasse which resulted when the ministries of von Papen and von Schleicher, which followed his, attempted to conduct business without such a majority. It has often been felt that such a presidential cabinet system was bound to arise in Germany on account of the multiplicity of parties, but it has been cogently argued that this is not really true. Not the number of parties but their relationship to the electorate matters. Fundamentally, the German parties were so definitely linked with economic groups in the community that their leaders, when united in a cabinet, could not command a sufficiently representative position (see above, Chap. XVI), as long as they were believed to be the creatures of these parties. Only the president, as the representative of the entire people, could give them this broader appeal. The complexities of the external dependence of German cabinets were reflected in their internal relationships. While parties were themselves taking the initiative and bringing about ministerial coalitions their delegates in the cabinet tended to occupy relatively independent positions in spite of the express recognition in the constitution that the Chancellor is the head of the cabinet. Later on, when the president became decisive in forming cabinets, particularly that of Brüning, we find effective monocratic leadership by the Chancellor closely resembling the situation in England in this respect. In this connection it is important to remember that the Prussian tradition and the German Imperial practice which were to some extent related, had a profound effect upon the relations within the cabinet under the Republic. Ever since Frederick the Great the Prussian kings had been convinced that the maintenance of royal power required their preventing the rise of a strong Prime Minister. Consequently the Prussian ministers had been very independent in their respective departments and the Prime Minister merely the presiding officer. That system Bismarck had found very aggravating, and consequently, in the Reich government which he constructed he saw to it that the heads of departments were placed in strict dependence upon him as Chancellor. But after his death lesser men found the task too exacting, and since no cabinet traditions had developed under Bismarck, the Reich cabinet tended to return to the Prussian pattern. A great deal of the pre-war confusion in German policy—for example, the dangerous conflict between naval and foreign policy—is vitally related to this lack of coherence in the cabinet. Undoubtedly the innate centrifugal tendency of post-war coalition ministries was greatly aided by this traditional lack of coöperation. The fierce struggle between the permanent civil servants, proverbially a source of considerable difficulty, commenced to feed upon party conflicts. The permanent officials rapidly learned how to manipulate the party dissensions in the Reichstag. As in so many other matters, so in the cabinet system also, the Weimar constitution combined too many discordant elements and was drafted with too little realistic consideration for the traditions of German politics and administration. If, instead of the popularly elected president, who, in spite of his national majority, was looked upon as a partisan, the system had been built around an hereditary monarch, it is possible that it would have worked as well as the constitutional parliamentary monarchies of Holland and the Scandinavian countries are working, for in all of them the party systems are very similar to that in Germany. There are many parties and they are fairly well organized and clearly connected with economic interest groups. On the whole, it is probably true that a cabinet system directly dependent upon parliamentary support is very hard to combine with a republican organization of government. France has been unique in making a success of this combination, but the profound difficulties in recent years suggest caution in placing too much confidence in the precedent it established. Moreover, France has not had to battle with the complications arising from a federal set-up (see above, Chap. XIII, ¶ 15). For a federal republican set-up, the Swiss and American types would appear to be much more suitable. It is indeed surprising that the makers of the Weimar constitution did not follow either of these patterns more closely.

The Swiss cabinet.—The Swiss collegial cabinet shares with the French system the tradition of polyarchic independence of the several ministers as department heads. But in spite of the fact that they are elected by the legislative assembly, they constitute a permanent and powerful executive, for this system differs completely from the French and other systems as a result of the tradition of not resigning when defeated on any policy in the representative assembly. The ministers simply go back to work out a new legislative proposal more in keeping with parliamentary views or they abandon the particular policy altogether. Professor Brooks has called this type of cabinet system "government by commission," and there is indeed some similarity between the relationship of, let us say, the Interstate Commerce Commission to Congress and the Swiss Federal Council to the Swiss legislature. The origin of this unique system must be sought in the Swiss cantons, which are organized on this pattern. But the adoption of this traditional cantonal organization by the federal government was greatly aided by the profound suspicion with which the constitution makers of 1848 looked upon anything resembling monarchy. It was a conscious decision by which they rejected the American plan of a popularly elected president. Although this Federal Executive Council is elected by a joint session of both houses of the legislature (see below, Chap. XXI), after an election, and although the terms of the councillors are three years, it has become the recognized custom, to which there are very few exceptions, to reëlect members as long as they are willing to serve. Consequently, members of the council usually serve many terms. Professor Brooks cites cases where members have served continuously for thirty-two, twenty-seven, and twenty-five years. When one considers that it is now habitual to elect to the Federal Executive Council only men who have served for a considerable period in the representative assemblies, the National Council, and the Council of States, and that many have previously served either in the cantonal representative bodies or in administrative or judicial posts, it is clear that the Swiss Executive Council is composed of men thoroughly seasoned in the art of politics and administration. This Federal Executive Council is presided over by a president who is elected by the Federal Assembly each year. It would, however, be a great mistake to assume that this president has any powers over the council besides presiding over it. His function is relative; his bureau acts as a sort of secretariat for the council as a whole; he is, in other words, unlike the English Prime Minister, a real *primus inter pares*. As such, his office is an honor and involves a certain measure of representative functions particularly in foreign affairs. While the several members of the Federal Council are therefore on an equal footing with each other and the president, who is, of course, an active member of the Council and quite often in charge of the Department of Foreign Affairs, they do act collectively on certain issues of general importance. In the words of the Swiss constitution, the Federal Council is the "supreme directive and executive authority of the union." This general provision is implemented by another which gives a detailed list of particular functions. The significance of the latter is, however, largely in terms of the federal distribution of power, for it indicates clearly that the council has the same functions in the administrative field which the assembly has in the legislative field. Besides, the council has to supervise whatever administration of federal legislation is entrusted to the cantonal authorities. Of all this work the council has to make detailed reports to the Federal Assembly. These reports are the subject of extended discussion, and as a result the assembly may address specific demands, known as postulates, to the federal councillors. What is more, a resolution to back such a postulate is unconditionally obligatory for the council. It is clear that such a system makes the executive a genuine administrative executor of the decisions of the representative assembly. It would, however, be very unrealistic to allow oneself to be blinded by these constitutional provisions. After all, the members of the Federal Executive Council are leading politicians, often actually party leaders. When this party leadership is supplemented by the special knowledge which they possess as heads of the administrative departments, their word must necessarily carry a great deal of weight. Although the range within which patronage pressure can be brought to bear in Switzerland is very narrow, people have often claimed that it helps to consolidate the council's leadership. Professor Fleiner has said that the continuous expansion of federal functions and of federal administrative authority has given the members of the Federal Council such a secure position that the council has become more and more independent of the assembly and has extended its influence upon it. This is perhaps more significantly expressed in the fact that the Executive Council is not based upon a party majority in the representative bodies. Naturally, since councillors are continually reëlected, the party composition of the council must vary considerably from that of the legislature. At the same time, members of the council are elected from parties radically opposed to each other. Consequently the Swiss council is not like a coalition ministry in France or Germany. On the contrary, it traditionally includes representatives of all the important parties, even those which are in general opposition to the government's policies. From the point of view of those who are accustomed to think in terms either of single party support or of an effective coalition, it may seem difficult to imagine such a plan. The deliberate emphasis on the administrative aspects of its work may save the council from some of the pitfalls of such an arrangement. Nevertheless, very sharp differences of opinion are bound to develop from time to time, and occasionally a member of the council will arise to oppose the proposal of a colleague before the legislature. Since ultimately the legislature can and will decide the issue, the necessary unity is imposed upon the council from without. Under these circumstances the council will in a great many matters follow the decision of its member who has the particular matter in charge. Since Switzerland has developed an admirable civil service, many decisions are thus effectively neutralized and judicialized. This tendency has been enhanced since the war when it was decided to refer certain matters directly to the permanent administrative staff. Significantly, in all such matters appeal is allowed to an administrative court, thus further emphasizing the judicial controls. After much hesitation this administrative court was organized in 1928 as part of the Federal Court. It may be well, in conclusion, to quote an estimate of the Swiss executive which, written many years ago, would still seem to be correct: "Apart from all criticism and suggestions for reform, however, it is generally conceded that the Swiss executive has developed high efficiency within the limits of its powers and opportunities. In the opinion of two well-known English students 'the members of the Federal Council yield to no other government in Europe in devotion to their country, in incessant hard work for a poor salary, and in thorough honesty and incorruptibility. A diplomatist who knew them well and appreciated their good qualities aptly remarked that they reminded him of a characteristic industry of their own country, that of watch-making. For, having to deal with very minute and intricate affairs, their attention is unremittingly engaged by the most delicate mechanism of government, by the wheels within wheels of federal and cantonal attributes, by the most careful balancing of relations between contending sects and churches and by endeavors to preserve the proper counterpoise between two (French and German), not to say three (the third being Italian) nationalities.' "

The American cabinet.—Very different is the position of the cabinet in the United States. Whereas the president of Switzerland is merely the chairman of the Executive Council, in America the cabinet consists of the heads of departments, who are merely the subordinates of the President. The President is not a member of the cabinet; the cabinet is his. In a sense, it occupies the position which *le cabinet*, the private secretariat, fills in helping a French minister to attend to his job. Lord Bryce once observed that "there is in the government of the United States no such thing as a cabinet in the English sense of the term." In *that sense*, he is right. Why, then, bother to consider the American cabinet in this discussion at all? Because there is no particular reason for accepting the English sense of the term as the only one. In fact, the American cabinet system provides us with the most striking type of a strictly monocratic organization, of leadership concentrated in a single person such as existed in European monarchies during the age of absolutism. The position of the American President is modelled upon the pattern of Louis XIV, *le roi soleil.* But this position rests upon his party leadership, and the sphere of his authority is rigidly circumscribed and restricted (see above, Chap. XI, ¶7). Though the President is formally entirely free to choose his ministers as he sees fit, the exigencies of his dependence upon party support tie his hands. Often, the choice falls upon men to whom the President owes his election—indeed, pre-election deals are not infrequent in order to build up the necessary support for the nomination or to secure the funds with which to carry on the campaign. If the party following of the President is rent by factions, it will often be necessary for him to include leaders of the several contending groups so that their support may be gained and maintained. Lincoln's appointment of Seward and Chase in 1860 would be an historical example to which Wilson's appointment of Bryan, or the second Roosevelt's choice of Farley might furnish less laudable parallels, not to mention the deals of Harding or Coolidge. Men appointed under such conditions are difficult to dislodge. It is unrealistic to look upon them as merely the administrative subordinates of the President. Today, at any rate, they are of vital importance to him in his national representative function. It is only through them that he can associate with himself a number of representatives of the different social forces which make up the support of his political party. Under the second Roosevelt, Roper "represents" the business man, Wallace, perhaps a bit less effectively, the farmer, while Morgenthau appears an ingenious combination of the two. Labor has its representation through Miss Perkins and others, and so it should be. Similarly, allowance must be made for regional interests and claims. The President must take into account personalities which have become associated with broad groupings in the electorate, if he is to be a representative of the nation. This system illustrates in a particularly striking way the interrelation and interaction of the two aspects of representation. Not only an elected body, but even a single elected individual will, through his associates, be both a representative in terms of the common interest and an agent for different interests (see Chap. XVI, ¶4). While the difference between a collegial cabinet such as the Swiss, and monocratic leadership as we find it in the United States, is very great, the distinction should not be made absolute. Through both systems the decisive social forces will secure a share of the government's power. The share may vary, as the balance of social forces shifts, but no considerable group can be excluded for any length of time without the government's loosing its representative position, and thereby its power through consent. Now it is obvious that the American President's independent representative position rests upon constitutional provisions. His virtually direct popular election, his fixed term of four years,[1] his sole responsibility for the executive and admin-

[1] The legal right of Congress to remove the President by impeachment cannot be considered a strong weapon, since it has rarely been tried and never successfully.

istrative direction of national affairs, make him the head of the government in a somewhat more real sense than the British king, the French or the Swiss president. But undoubtedly, direct popular election is the really decisive factor in a democratic age, when election above all else is accepted as proof of legitimacy in the exercise of power (see Chap. XVI). The question often asked whether the people vote for the President or for the party is a false alternative; they vote for both, or at least think they do. It is inescapable that under such conditions, where the President and his cabinet are viewed as the representatives of the common national interest and the representatives of various social groups, respectively, a good deal of the most important policy will be determined by discussions not of the cabinet collectively, but of the President with individual cabinet members. Sometimes, of course, an important piece of legislation, particularly when it touches several departments, will be discussed in the cabinet. But votes are seldom taken on such matters, and they are considered mere expressions of opinion. There is a well-known story told about President Lincoln who concluded a discussion in the cabinet during which everyone had taken sides against him by remarking: "Seven nays, one aye, the ayes have it." This story might have been told of the Great Elector (see Chap. III, ¶2-3); but unless the President's policy turned out to be sound, his disregard of his cabinet's viewpoint might spell disaster for his party and cause his defeat at the next election. It is, therefore, true only in a limited sense that "the cabinet is merely the kind of organization which the President wishes to make of it and is his own council in a very peculiar sense," as Charles A. Beard claims. As everywhere in politics, so here too formally independent positions may in fact be tied down to very definite prescriptions dictated by prudence and tradition. The American President's position offers, in this respect, a useful guide to the understanding of Hitler's real place in the present German government. He is not the entirely independent individual master he is pictured as in contemporary description, but constantly has his eye on his following. For he must hold together enough of it to counterbalance the violent antagonism which his extreme measures have engendered (see Chap. XXV, ¶ 10). On the other hand, the fact that there is no definite time limit to his tenure of office, nor any restriction on the scope of his power (there is not even any body which could impeach him for the commission of criminal acts) deprives his following, and more particularly his cabinet colleagues, of all formal occasions for exerting their pressure, such as arise for American politicians when a presidential term is nearing its end or a congressional majority is required. In short, the American President and his cabinet are a working group of administrators, dependent upon popular support through a party which may, and often will, also control the Congress. During the recent emergency, this body was implemented by a larger National Emergency Council which included the heads of various new organizations such as the NRA, the NHA, and so forth. Whether this organization will acquire any permanent significance remains to be seen. Similar organizations created during the World War did not survive. There have also been recurrent "kitchen-cabinets," ephemeral informal and small groups of advisers whom various Presidents have employed; but these have not thus far been institutionalized. Having once been invested with his monocratic powers, no President is likely to distribute this power to others, and if a particular President should, out of indolence or altruism, move in that direction, his successor is apt to redress the balance on assuming office. The concentrated powers of the American President are a part of the pattern of constitutional relationships established by the separation of powers; they are endurable only because that pattern provides other restraints through limiting the concentrated powers themselves (see Chap. XI, ¶7). It is another method of coping with the problem which in the opinion of Lord Bryce (and many another liberal thinker) is the greatest which confronts free peoples: how to enable the citizens at large to conduct or control the executive business of the state. The full contrast between the American "independent" executive and the parliamentary "responsibility" in European governments will not become apparent, however, until we can consider the much-discussed power of dissolution possessed by the English and other executives.

Conclusion: the representative position of cabinets.—Our comparative discussion of cabinet systems has shown us that the internal as well as the external relations of cabinets affect the representative position and consequently its place in the governmental structure as a whole. To be specific, the greater dependence of the cabinet upon Parliament lowers its representative position, while the prestige and representative glamor of the executive are heightened by more effective monocratic leadership. As a consequence, the countries we have inspected in some detail may be ranged in the following order as far as the representative position of their executive establishments are concerned: the United States, England, Germany (Weimar), France, Switzerland. Perhaps the Weimar Republic should be ranged with England after Dr. Brüning assumed the Chancellorship. It may not be amiss to call attention to the curious fact that this sequence stands in inverse relation to the sequence in which these countries would have to be arranged if we considered the strength and rationalization of their administrative system and their civil service. Does this imply that there is a negative correlation between the representative function of the leaders of the executive branch and the technical efficiency and competence of its permanent staff? Does it mean that executive establishments are aided in fulfilling their administrative roles by being insulated against the virus of politics?

CHAPTER XXI

PARLIAMENTS AS REPRESENTATIVE ASSEMBLIES

Introductory.—Parliaments have until recently been the institututional core of modern representative government. At present the executive, particularly when representing a majority party, is forging ahead and is tending to become the heart of representation, as was shown in the last chapter. Parliaments held the center of the stage until the World War for a whole congeries of reasons. History made Parliament the elected representative and as election came to be looked upon as the primary basis of representative qualifications, the position of Parliaments was enhanced. The emphasis upon legislation as a man-made body of rules (see above, Chap. XVI, ¶¶ 8 and 9) helped to strengthen Parliaments, because their public deliberations were peculiarly well adapted to the legislative processes. Finally, the doctrine of the separation and balance of powers, particularly as applied to constitutional monarchies (see Chap. XI, ¶ 10), strengthened the claim of Parliaments to be the representatives of the people, as offering a counterpoise to the Crown. In England, France, and Germany, as well as in many other European countries, the emergence of so-called parliamentary government in the course of the nineteenth century placed the Crown or its agents in actual dependence upon the parliamentary majorities if it was not eventually altogether supplanted by Parliament, as happened in both France and Germany. The United States and Switzerland, on the other hand, adopted constitutional provisions which prevented such direct dependence. Yet it is difficult to appraise correctly the effect which such provisions have upon the inner working of parliamentary bodies; it seems that the effect is less marked than one might be led to expect by considering that parliamentary activity is directed into quite different channels. But an effect there is; the contrast in the position of the Speakers in the Commons and in the House of Representatives is perhaps the most striking illustration (see below, ¶¶ 8 and 9).

Representation as integration.—Traditionally, legislation is considered the peculiar province of representative assemblies (see above, Chap. XVI, ¶8). Following the classical doctrine of separation of powers, representative assemblies are in fact referred to as the legislature, although it is always at once conceded that these assemblies do not have exclusive control over legislation nor are they concerned only with legislation. Nevertheless, legislation is traditionally looked upon as their permanent function. Such a view is legal rather than political. Politically speaking, the function of making laws is nowadays, at least, as much carried on by the central bureaucracy which drafts all important bills in England, France, Germany, and other European countries, and to an increasing extent in the United States. The next most important role in the law-making process should perhaps be assigned to the special interest groups such as the American Federation of Labor or the Chamber of Commerce, who often initiate proposals for new legislation. The United States Chamber of Commerce has been particularly ingenious in developing a referendum for this purpose. The political function of representative assemblies today is not so much the initiation of legislation as the discussion and coördination of proposed legislation and the carrying on of the popular education and propaganda which is involved in that function. Parliaments and parliamentarians appear as integrating agencies through which the plans of the central bureaucracy and the claims of the various interest groups are expounded to the larger public with a view to discovering a suitable balance. There can be little doubt that this educational function is highly significant. Without such coördinating guidance the average citizen is unable to comprehend the pros and cons of pending proposals. He is equally unable to appreciate the implications and significance of new legislation. The evil consequences of the lack of such contact between the government and the citizen is very apparent in Nazi Germany. A great many measures of the government, which may intrinsically be necessary, meet with sullen indifference, if not hostility, from the people merely because they are not understood. Occasional rhetorical outbursts on the part of a few leaders are not sufficient. It is true that under the preceding parliamentary regime the German public, unaccustomed to the heated discussion of issues of public policy by contending parties, developed at first a strong sense of insecurity and frustration, particularly since the peculiar difficulties resulting from the lost war did not allow those counselling moderation to prevail. Both Stresemann and Brüning, not to mention others, were sincerely devoted to a political philosophy of self restraint, but the indignation engendered by post-war misery overtook them, since there were others who did not hesitate to exploit these sentiments for building up a political following.

The importance of party structure for the work of Parliaments.—The organization and structure of Parliaments is profoundly affected by party organization. A two-party system divides the House into two more or less equal parts. A multiple-party system may, following the French tradition, range from conservatism to radicalism. Again, it may, as befell in the post-war German Parliament, possess a cluster of moderate groups at the center, surrounded by groups of radical extremists who might be either reactionary or revolutionary or both. The seating arrangements in Parliaments sometimes are, and perhaps always should be, expressive of the innate structure and relationship of the groups contained in it. Thus, if the conservatives sit on the right side of the House and the radicals on the left, as was the case in the French Constituent Assembly and has been the case in France ever since, it is possible to speak of the "right" or "left" in a symbolic sense. It is a tribute to the force of French ideas that these expressions are now used in countries like England and the United States where no such seating arrangement is actually found. For the English House of Commons is divided into two halves facing each other. One half is supposed to be occupied by the party supporting the government, the other half by His Majesty's Opposition. In the American Congress, both Senate and House, the representatives are scattered all over according to seniority and personal preference. No architectural plan was worked out to correspond to the actual relation of groups in the German Parliament. The imperial Parliament had been built to resemble the French Chamber of Deputies, except that the government sat in front, facing the House. This building was retained by the Republic;

deputies ranged from the Nazis at the extreme right to the Communists at the extreme left side of the House. The appropriate structure for the German Parliament would have been an amphitheatre with the government in the center and the moderate supporting groups sitting on the benches surrounding it, the regular opposition which might be prepared to take over the government somewhat higher up, and the extremists in the top rows furthest away from the government. Such an architecture would be the true expression of the idea underlying proportional representation, by which the German and a number of other continental party systems have been given their present form (see Chap. XVII, ¶ 3).

Social composition of membership.—Even more important, perhaps, than the party system and the physical structure of Parliament resulting from it is its social composition. There can be little doubt that the aristocratic backbone of the English Parliament which persisted throughout the nineteenth century was of great importance in giving to the English Parliament a certain homogeneity of outlook and a code of "gentlemanly" conduct which materially affected its mode of procedure. What is more, the willingness of the English aristocracy to absorb new members who distinguished themselves in public affairs added a powerful social sanction to whatever conventional restraints were suggested by such a code. In France and Germany, where Parliaments arose in opposition not only to the monarchy but also to the exclusive hereditary aristocracy which supported it, professional men, particularly lawyers and to a lesser degree journalists, predominated at the outset. However, in more recent times, the peculiar feature of French Parliaments has been the large number of farmers (and estate owners) relatively speaking, with a fairly even distribution between other professional groups. The two outstanding features of post-war German Parliaments were the numerous representatives of economic interest groups (the so-called *syndics,* lawyers for trade associations, and the trade union officials) and the surprisingly large number of bureaucrats contained in them; there were between one hundred and one hundred and fifty outright governmental officials. Their entrance into Parliament had been facilitated by the constitutional provision which allowed them to attend Parliament irrespective of their administrative duties. There were, secondly, a considerable number of permanent party officials. Finally, there were the permanent secretaries of various trade associations, chambers of commerce, industrial cartels, and trade unions. Not only in the German, but in all these Parliaments, there has been a steady increase of members who formerly were workers. It is, however, important to remember that almost all these so-called workers are, unlike the traditional farmer in American representative assemblies, not men who come directly from the factory, but men who have risen through the trade union bureaucracy and are therefore actually trade association officials when they go into Parliament. This and other developments have contributed toward a gradual increase in the heterogeneity of parliaments. This social heterogeneity has increased friction and complicated the course of parliamentary procedure.

General problems of procedure.—Procedure, which is intrinsically a very technical subject, is nevertheless in its broad outlines directly related to the workings of the Parliament within the total context. Josef Redlich, in his celebrated treatise on the history of parliamentary procedure, has done more than anyone else to show this vital relationship. For our present purposes the earlier period can be omitted, in the course of which, prior to the reign of Elizabeth, the fundamental procedural device of legislation by bill rather than by petition had been worked out. The later development can be roughly divided into three periods. During the period when Parliament was engaged in its struggle to curb the Crown, it was essentially a question of preventing the exertion of undue influence by the Crown's ministers over the deliberations of the House. Perhaps the most important achievement of this period was the establishment of each member's full right as an individual participant in the debates and decisions. It is to this period also that we owe the gradual separation of the Speaker's office from the Crown, as well as the development of separate readings, and the provisions insuring the opposition a fair share of the time of the House, the famous protection of the minority. This development was carried forward in the second period, when, after 1688, the House was divided by the two more or less well-defined aristocratic factions who governed the country rather oligarchically, particularly after the accession of Walpole. In this period, by the consistent refinement of various technicalities, the great conservative speaker, Arthur Onslow, and his colleagues thoroughly developed the institution of His Majesty's Opposition. Among the technicalities may be mentioned the employment of the committee of the whole for the debate on all bills, the use of the same form for all budgetary questions, and the many different techniques which make it possible to bring up any subject at any time. All these and many other provisions were meant to encourage the participation of members in the debate, which was often lacking, and since the whole Parliament was an instrument for the maintenance of an English aristocratic government, there was not much inclination on the part of the opposition to use its power for purposes of obstruction, nor did the majority care to do violence to the minority. Considering this, Redlich believes that the period from 1688 to 1832 could almost be called the golden age of the English Parliament. Oligarchic rule evolved parliamentary responsibility. During the period after the Reform Act and down to the late seventies, when the Irish obstruction began, Parliament faced very different problems. The House of Commons was then the real core of the governmental system, as Bagehot showed in his famous treatise. Two fairly evenly matched groups were pitted against each other in the House under the very able leadership of such men as Palmerston, Disraeli, and Gladstone. As industrial, social, and imperial problems multiplied, the great procedural reforms were concerned with expediting necessary business and preventing debate from being merely the occasion for the display of brilliant rhetoric. To this period, therefore, we owe the rules of debate and the elaborate system of interpellations and questioning. After the Irish obstruction arose, it became increasingly apparent, in the period from 1880 to the World War, that the ministry was dependent not so much upon parliamentary, as upon electoral support. In other words, as party organization and the caucus supplanted parliamentary control, the dominant question of procedure became how to insure to the government, that is, to the majority party, efficient control of the business of Parliament. To this period, therefore, we owe the development of closure and various other techniques for regimenting parliamentary discussion. The reaction to this tendency, which was in part stimulated by the confused developments during and after the World War, has been a demand for the curbing of this overweening governmental control. This controversy also involves the problem of committees. Partly through observation of conditions in the United States and France, the development of standing committees has gotten under way and these committees are constantly becoming more important (see below, Chap. XXII). But as yet their influence does not extend very far toward the control of the ministry. "The union of all political power in the hands of the House of Commons and the simultaneous transfer of this concentrated living force to a cabinet drawn exclusively from Parliament are the dominant features of the modern development of public law and politics in England. . . . The very completeness of its power, which, if we disregard technicalities, may be said to comprise the whole administration of domestic and foreign affairs, has compelled the House of Commons to abdicate the exercise of almost all its authority in favor of its executive committee, the ministry." This summary by Professor Redlich written in 1905 still aptly delineates the result of the developments we have just sketched.

The House of Lords and second chambers.—In the preceding paragraph, the emphasis has almost imperceptibly shifted from Parliament as a whole, comprising Lords and Commons, to the House of Commons by itself. In fact, since the Parliament Act of 1911 the question of whether or not there is a place for the continued existence of the House of Lords within the modern constitutional machinery has never ceased to command popular interest. The Conservatives favor its retention, it might be suspected, while many Liberals and the Labor party demand its radical change or abolition. This view is partly the result of partisan considerations: the House of Lords with its six hundred odd peers has always contained an overwhelming Conservative majority. In spite of the very wide use made by the Liberal party after 1905 of the Crown's prerogative to create peers, there were in 1914 only one hundred and sixteen Liberal peers out of a total membership of over six hundred. This development may be dated from 1886, when Gladstone split the Liberal party over the issue of Home Rule for Ireland; a great many members of rank and position went over to the Conservatives as "unionists." Today, with the Labor party providing His Majesty's Opposition, the situation is even more marked. The whole problem revolves around the question of representativeness. From the standpoint of electoral majorities, the House of Lords is merely an anachronism; "it represents," as one wit has remarked, "nobody but itself, and therefore enjoys the full confidence of its constituents." But we know that representation is not necessarily brought about by an election, a simple counting of heads (see above, Chap. XVI, ¶¶ 4, 6, 7). It may be based upon objective achievement, and a variety of other believed-in qualifications, such as birth or the possession of property. Such qualifications may be wholly illusory. As a matter of fact, as Benjamin Franklin once remarked, to pick legislators on the basis of heredity is just as sensible as to pick professors of mathematics in that fashion. But elections by electoral majorities may be equally unproductive of representatives, as we have seen in our survey of electoral methods (see Chap. XVII). If it be true that the House of Lords is more concerned with the interests of landed property and the established church than those of other groups, it would not conclude the argument about their representative value, unless it were shown that these groups are no longer of great significance. It is for this reason that failure attended Lord Wemyss' proposal to make the House of Lords something of real significance; his ideas found no favor with the Bryce Committee, which instead brought forth a complicated scheme of indirect representation. But such a scheme at least faced the Socialist attack as it was pressed by the Webbs: "Its [the House of Lords] decisions are vitiated by its composition—it is the worst representative assembly ever created, in that it contains absolutely no members of the manual working class; none of the great classes of shopkeepers, clerks and teachers; none of the half of all the citizens who are of the female sex; and practically none of religious nonconformity, of art, science, or literature." Other voices have arisen to suggest that the House of Lords be based upon proportional representation. Perhaps the most imaginative proposal in view of the federalization of the Empire (see above, Chap. XIII, ¶18) was that of "turning the Second Chamber to good account for the purpose of including in it persons who might be qualified both to express the views of the Self-Governing Dominions and other parts of the British Overseas possessions, and to join with full knowledge in discussing questions affecting them," as the Bryce Report put it. But the Bryce Committee did not feel free to enter into a consideration of these possibilities. They were outside the scope of its points of reference. Since 1917, the independence of the Dominions has progressed so far as to make such plans quite dubious. All such proposals of change assume that a second chamber is intrinsically worth while and desirable. Although English discussions have never been much concerned with the significance of such a body, as affording the basis for a different and balancing scheme of representation (such as is set up under a federal system, where one house "represents" the majority of the whole people, the other the majority of the component units), the value of such a house as a check upon the other has rarely been overlooked. And in turn, it is precisely this check upon the popularly elected majority which has brought forth the most virulent attacks. The *Labour Speakers' Handbook* declares

(1923): "Abolish the Second Chamber altogether; any second chamber would be a reactionary body. . . ." This is obviously merely practical politics; a second chamber composed in large part of the representatives of organized labor would evidently not be. But Labor's view is in the tradition of Benthamite radicalism, pure and unadulterated; a second chamber, Bentham regarded as "needless, useless, worse than useless." His objection is strictly logical, coherent, unequivocal. Since the end of government is "the greatest happiness of the greatest number," a legislative assembly should be based on universal suffrage. There is no room for a second chamber. If it represents the general interest, it is useless; if it represents only a particular interest, it is bad. If the first chamber has not produced the proper kind of legislation, the right check is to turn it out (or to improve it), but not to establish a second chamber. This argument apparently holds only as long as one accepts Bentham's rational view of human beings, and is willing to discard the time factor. Otherwise it might happen, as it did happen in France in 1851, or in Germany in 1933, and even in England under Cromwell, that "it is too late" for any turning out. Of late, another line of argument has become popular. It claims that a second chamber buttresses genuine democracy against the pressure of special interest groups and party bosses by an appeal to the electorate. This has indeed been the function of the House of Lords, the Senate of France and the German National Council, but whether one could justify the maintenance of a second chamber on such slender grounds is a matter of judgment on which reasonable men seem to differ. But since this whole gamut of questions really is related to the problems of the separation of powers and checks and balances, it should be referred back to our earlier discussion of these problems (see Chaps. XI and XII). As far as representation is concerned, it is all a question of who should be represented in the particular community. If persistent subdivisions entitled to separate representation are contained in it, or if certain interests are recognized as of paramount importance from a governmental viewpoint, two or even three chambers may be indicated. It is undeniably true that such multiplicity raises grave complications, but these may in part be offset by the gain in providing for a reasonable and convincing division of powers, thus aiding the maintenance of a constitutional order.

Bentham's views, their influence and results.—His unqualified rationalism not only led Bentham to demand the abolition of second chambers, but it also made him sponsor views on parliamentary procedure. These constitute, in the opinion of leading authorities, the only attempt at theoretical clarification of the immense mass of procedural detail which is found in the practice of representative assemblies throughout the world. They are also worth considering on account of the wide influence they have exerted on the Continent, if not in England. The first impact of his ideas came through his brief sketch of the English procedure which he furnished Mirabeau as a model for the procedure of the French constituent assembly in 1789. But more important was the effect of his *An Essay on Political Tactics* (1816). This treatise undertook to fit the mass of detailed rules of procedure, particularly of the English Parliament, into a rational pattern; as a result, it greatly enhanced the general appeal of English procedure. Through its Genevese editor, Dumont, it entered Switzerland. It also exerted a profound influence upon the French Parliaments of the Restoration, and through them down to the present day. It also helped to shape the procedure of the German National Assembly in 1848, and from there its influence spread over central Europe while the French procedure was molding Belgian and later Italian and other parliamentary practices. The central purpose of the rules of procedure, according to Bentham, is to produce a majority and thus to discover the true will of the assembly. That the proceedings should be public, is now generally conceded. Bentham offers a number of reasons: (1) to constrain the members of the assembly to perform their duty, (2) to secure the confidence of the people, and their assent to the measures of the assembly, (3) to enable the governors to know the wishes of the governed, (4) to enable the electors to act intelligently in elections, (5) to provide the assembly with the means of profiting by the information of the public, (6) to give amusement. The objections seemed to Bentham to resolve themselves into one, namely, that "the public is incompetent to judge of the proceedings of a political assembly." This objection he will not allow, because the public will judge, whether informed or not, because it desires to do so. If they were willing to forego judging because incompetent, they would be not common men, but philosophers. Omitting reference to those who do not judge at all, he argues further that those who judge anyway will judge ill upon incomplete information; they will, according to Bentham, judge better when fully informed. To deny them such information is to say: "You are incapable of judging, because you are ignorant; and you shall remain ignorant, that you may be incapable of judging." This argument would be conclusive, if men were rational; overstating a good case, it has suffered from the hands of Fascist and Communist expounders of irrational human nature. In order to maintain Bentham's view, re-statement of his position, taking full account of man's irrational behavior, must be attempted. We shall return to this problem when considering the problems raised by the growth of committees in modern representative assemblies (see below, ¶14). For the time being, let us remember that Bentham's arguments prevailed and that publicity of parliamentary proceedings was instituted everywhere in the course of the nineteenth century, in England as well as on the Continent. At the time of Bentham, this was nowhere the case, and his insistence upon publicity cannot therefore be called a rationalization of English practice. In fact, we find Bentham expressing himself very critically: "How singular 'soever it may be thus to see the deputies of the people withdrawing themselves with so much hauteur from the observation of their constituents . . ."; the public even in England did not particularly care. The Reform Act and the attendant popularization of the House of Commons changed all that in a generation. But at the time of Bentham's writing the House of Commons was not really composed of the deputies of the people. It was an aristocratic *junta* which stood back of both Houses of Parliament. Nevertheless, they were deliberative assemblies. As such, the particular object of its tactics was to obviate the inconveniences to which a political assembly is exposed in the exercise of its functions. Bentham saw these functions essentially as decisions about legislation (see above, Chap. XVI, ¶¶ 8 and 9). He consequently lists as inconveniences inaction, useless decision, indecision, delays, surprise and precipitation, fluctuation, quarrels, falsehoods, decisions which are defective in form, and others which are defective in substance. Ultimately, all these "inconveniences" come down to two: not reaching a good decision, when it might have been reached, or reaching a bad decision. Who is to judge what decisions are good? This question did not concern Bentham; he simply answers that good decisions are those which promote the greatest happiness of society. Such a reply recommends itself by its simplicity, rather than its adequacy. Yet Bentham's view of procedure aroused considerable enthusiasm when it was first expounded. English radicalism, with its faith in the rational nature of man, took it to be the final word. The more sophisticated, almost Machiavellian debating primer of W. G. ("Single Speech") Hamilton was condemned as "the wickedest book in the English language." Its failure to consider the general good earned it the most outspoken condemnation by Bentham himself. Yet intrinsically, Bentham's own *Tactics* does not lack a touch of Machiavellian preoccupation with pure *technics*. The main shortcomings of Bentham's work result not so much from the general ethical purpose which he posits, as from the neglect of certain factors in the real situation. In England, these omissions were perhaps not very serious, since the reader could supply them from his own experience. But wherever Bentham's theories were taken as realistic guides, as was the case among Liberals on the Continent, the effect was serious and has contributed its share to the breakdown of parliamentary politics. It was only toward the end of the last century that these fatal omissions were clearly perceived by such more realistic scholars as Josef Redlich. In considering it the main business of deliberative assemblies to make laws, Bentham had failed to recognize that it was as much a matter of fighting the opposition party. Indeed he recognized the necessity of parties; but at the same time he viewed with indignation Hamilton's notion that "Parliament [is] a sort of gaming-house; members on the two sides of each house the players; the property of the people . . . the stakes played for; . . . what course will be most for the advantage of the universal interest, a question never looked at, never taken into account. . . ." He knew the fact, then, but he condemned it. Despising party strife in its extreme form, he would give as little consideration to it as possible in developing a theory of procedure. Thus falling into the opposite extreme of neglecting the real value (the general interest) which attaches to securing effective party support, he failed to perceive the significance of cabinet responsibility to Parliament which was just then emerging. Debating laws *and* supporting the government, not debating laws *or* supporting the government would seem to have provided the right approach to the problem. The fact that Parliament became capable of overthrowing a cabinet is a fact so well-known as not to deserve mention were it not for the consequence that in response to this potential crisis, the cabinet has since Bentham's time brought about the most decided governmental leadership in debate, by effecting sweeping changes in parliamentary procedure. Techniques, such as closure, for limiting parliamentary debate, are at least in part the outcome of this governmental leadership. In addition to minimizing the procedural significance of party struggle and governmental leadership, Bentham also completely misjudged the possibility as well as the probability of organized obstruction. In many benign sentences, scattered through his *Tactics* and too long to quote here, he expressed his doubt as to such methods ever gaining a foothold. He considered them self-defeating. A permanent minority like the Irish Nationalists lay beyond the confines of his experience. Yet, parliamentary procedure everywhere has to some extent been affected by organized obstruction; the filibusters of small minorities in the American Senate are perhaps the best known, but the Irish Nationalists developed great skill in availing themselves of every conceivable procedural advantage. All such tactics have undoubtedly contributed much toward discrediting Parliaments, the most striking illustration being found in the vivid description of the impressions Adolf Hitler gained when watching the proceedings of the Austrian Imperial Diet. But the writings and reminiscences of politicians of an anti-parliamentary outlook in Italy, France, and other countries are equally filled with such observations. Bentham could not conceive of a Parliament willfully discrediting itself, because he never considered that popular forces might arise which would be utterly out of sympathy with deliberate assemblies. Through one of the paradoxes so frequent in institutional history, his radical views mightily contributed toward the adoption of unrealistically rationalist procedure in countries where parliamentary government has since been overthrown. He prevented parliamentarians from considering the problems of procedure in terms of the party system. Julius Hatschek has noted a considerable number of minor absurdities which crept into parliamentary practice in France, Germany, and elsewhere, because procedures well-adapted to the English two-party system as it existed in England in the time of Bentham were slavishly adopted in countries with very different conditions, a multiple-party system, permanent national minorities, and class-conscious groups. The resulting conditions in Parliaments naturally approached anarchy.

Presiding officers: (1) the English Speaker.—If the effectiveness of a procedure is to be measured by results, perhaps the most important question is how to provide adequate leadership for a legislative program. In the United States such leadership is provided by the Speaker or the floor leader as presiding officers, with the aid of the Committee on Rules. Other deliberative assemblies, in following the theories of Bentham, adopted the idea of a neutral presiding officer, forgetting that in England such legislative leadership is provided for by the government. Curiously enough, at the time of Bentham's writing, the strictly neutral position of the Speaker in the House of Commons had not yet been realized. Bentham merely anticipated developments. But his very success in forecasting the English evolution bolstered his authority elsewhere. Consequently, Josef Redlich could rightly conclude his discussion of the speakership with Bentham's dramatic statement. "Throughout the whole business, the grand problem is to obtain, in its most genuine purity, the real and enlightened will of the assembly. The solution of this problem is the end, that ought everywhere to be had in view. To this end, everything that concerns the president, ought of course to be subservient.—The duty and art of the president of a political assembly is the duty and art of the accoucheur: *ars obstetrix animarum,* . . . —to assist nature and not to force her—to soothe upon occasion the pangs of parturition;—to produce in the shortest time the genuine offspring, but never to stifle it, much less to substitute a changeling in its room. It is only in so far as it may be conformable to the will of the assembly, that the will of this officer can as such have any claim to regard. . . . Any influence whatever that he possesses over the acts of the assembly, is just so much power taken from the assembly and thrown into the lap of this single individual." This statement is not a descriptive generalization; it is a norm realized in the British House of Commons, but only because actual leadership comes from the cabinet (and not from the "real will of the assembly" as Bentham would have us believe). Where the peculiar conditions of British cabinet leadership do not prevail, the presiding officer cannot assume, and does not assume, such a neutral role; if he tries to, the result is chaos. It is quite significant that the neutrality of the Speaker in England develops right along with such cabinet leadership. The first great example of a neutral speaker, Arthur Onslow (1727-1761), falls into the period of Robert Walpole's and his successors' power and influence. Before his time, the speaker had been oscillating between being an instrument of the Crown (More, Coke, Finch, Sir John Trevor) and the spokesman of the parliamentary party (Lenthal and others). Stubbs has shown how Sir Thomas More directed the House of Commons according to the directions of Wolsey. Of Coke's subservience (in great contrast to his later views) we have a graphic account, too. In the words of Redlich: "There can be no doubt that the absolutist domination of parliament by Henry VIII and his successors found its main support in the position of the speaker as a servant of the crown and as a representative of the crown's interests." In other words, as long as the British constitution was built upon the medieval separation of powers between king and the Houses of Parliament effective leadership in the House of Commons had to come from the Speaker (just as in the House of Lords it had to come from the Lord Chancellor). In this period, the Speaker also usually held a position under the Crown, as, for instance, Sir Edward Coke, who was Solicitor General. Such a situation would have been unendurable, once the government (the cabinet) became a party government. Once the majority in the House of Commons supported the cabinet, there was an urgent need and a profound reason for developing the speakership as a judicial office mediating between the majority party and the opposing minority. Just as the judiciary itself in the course of the eighteenth century became independent of the party struggles and removed from the influence of both Crown and Parliament, so also this "moderator" and judge presiding over parliamentary proceedings became neutral and more and more effectively insulated against partisan influences. His decisions are "rulings," they "apply" the precedents of parliamentary law and custom according to legal logic, and whatever discretionary authority he possesses closely resembles the type of authority of a judge, and is derived from a skillful use of existing precedents. More particularly since the reform of Parliament, this independent judicial position of the Speaker has been recognized. Not only inside of Parliament, but outside of it as well, he must observe the strictest neutrality. According to prevailing practice he is not opposed in his own district and makes no speeches nor even visits his former party club. He has an official residence, and is on all sides surrounded by the repressive pomp of royalty. His salary is £5000, and on his retirement he is made a peer and given a liberal pension. In every respect he resembles the highest judicial officer in the land. On account of this elevated position, reinforced by many ceremonial details inside of Parliament and out, the Speaker is enabled to maintain that high order of efficiency and dignity which characterizes the proceedings of Parliament. He can, with the aid of the Sergeant-at-Arms and the Metropolitan Police, arrest any person, whether a member of Parliament or not, and deliver him into jail. There is no appeal against his decisions. This plenary power contrasts strongly with the helplessness of the president of the French *Chambre* or the German *Reichstag* whose ultimate weapon, suspension of the sitting, is precisely the aim of obstructionist groups. Inside Parliament, all speeches are addressed to the Speaker, and his direction of the debate and other proceedings is absolute. F. A. Ogg justly cites Speaker Lowther's humorous remark: "The Chair, like the Pope, is infallible." If Parliament was once a court (see above, VII ¶ 2), today it is a court that presides over Parliament, and that one-man court is as absolute, as final in its decisions as any in the realm. Only through such a device, does the British constitution manage to combine great dispatch of business of all kinds, legislative, budgetary, and so forth, embodying the policy of the majority party, with an adequate protection of the minority's opportunities to speak and express their vigorous criticism, even when it is as small a minority as it was between 1931 and 1935 when the National coalition had 556 votes and the combined opposition only 59, a situation reminiscent of that after 1905 when the Liberals including Labor and Irish Nationalists had 510 as against the Conservatives 156. In this task the Speaker is mightily aided by the peculiar nature of English parliamentary law. His function is best understood in analogy to that of the judge. "Just as the immense, and many-meshed net of the common law binds the judge a thousand times in his decisions, but also offers him a thousand times the opportunity to develop the law through the employment of the stored-up precedents, and to create new law, in just the same way the Speaker faces the parliamentary law and customs. Here too vast fields extend beyond the limited line of positive norms, the vast field of parliamentary practice developed through hundreds of years as it is recorded in the proceedings." To develop new law is the highest function of the English Speaker. This state of affairs must not blind one, however, to the fact that ultimately Parliament itself is the sole judge of its procedure. By making a positive rule, it can sweep away whatever precedent may have grown up. Parliamentary supremacy is not subject to judicial fetters in this area any more than in other fields of legislation. No law behind the law can be appealed to.

(2) **The American Speaker.**—Very different is the situation in the United States and in the several states of the Union, as far as the position of the presiding officer in the deliberative assemblies is concerned. The tendency has been just the reverse of that forecast by Bentham. Everyone knows that party leadership in the House of Representatives at least is provided from the chair, whether occupied by the Speaker or by the floor leader as chairman of the Com-

mittee on Rules. Allusion has already been made to the underlying major factor explaining this complete difference. James Bryce, in *The American Commonwealth,* pointed out, "A deliberative assembly is, after all, only a crowd of men; and the more intelligent a crowd is, so much more numerous are its volitions; so much greater the difficulty of agreement. Like other crowds, a legislature must be led and ruled. Its merit lies not in the independence of its members, but in the reflex action of its opinion upon the leaders, in its willingness to defer to them in minor matters, reserving disobedience for the issues in which some great principle overrides both the obligation of deference to established authority and the respect due to special knowledge." Another writer elaborated this in saying that he wanted "a centralized, responsible authority, like the Cabinet of the British Government or of Canada, which will determine what laws are to be considered, and cast aside without mercy the mass of trivial and irrelevant bills that now discredit our legislative records. . . ." The presiding officers in American legislatures have often attempted to fulfill such a function. It was the explicit purpose of Speaker Carlisle, who considered it the duty of the Speaker to have a legislative policy and "to take every means in his power to secure its accomplishment." That view was continued and carried forward by his successors, Reed and Crisp. Each in his turn at the end of the last century made his particular contribution toward strengthening the power of the speakership, until at last in 1909-1910 revolt rose against their system as personified by Speaker Cannon. Robert Luce rightly observes that the epithet "Cannonism" was rather undeserved, as Cannon merely carried on what others had done before. It is curious that Carlisle himself, after having done so much to strengthen the power of the Speaker, should have attacked the system upon leaving the chair. He felt it to be an inevitable scourge. "Under any system of rules that can be devised, the presiding officer in a body so numerous as the House of Representatives will necessarily have more power than ought to be entrusted to any man in this country." Numbers alone hardly suffice as an explanation; for the British House of Commons is much larger. It is a question of the confusion resulting from lack of effective party leadership. Reed, his successor, gave an effective rationalization: "The object of a parliamentary body is action, and not stoppage of action. Hence, if any member or set of members undertakes to oppose the orderly progress of business even by the use of the ordinarily recognized parliamentary motions, it is the right of the majority to refuse to have these motions entertained and to cause the public business to proceed. Primarily, the organ of the house is the man elected to the speakership; it is his duty in a clear case, recognizing the situation, to endeavor to carry out the wishes and desires of the majority of the body which he represents." Here it is frankly stated that "leadership" is the central task of the Speaker. Several devices, such as the absolute discretion as to whom to recognize, pre-arranged schedules for the debate and what should be taken up therein, extensive control over committee vacancies (Robert Luce emphasizes the fact that this control was often overstated), all these contributed their share to the indignation which in 1910 led to the overthrow of the Speaker. A coalition of the Democrats, then in opposition, with insurgent (progressive) Republicans took away from the presiding officer much of his discretionary power; they enlarged the Rules Committee, provided that it should be elected (by the two caucuses in the ratio of six to four) and deprived the Speaker of a seat on it. A little later, it was further provided that all committees should be elected by the House. "Amid cheers for 'the fall of the Czar' and the end of 'despotism,'" C. A. Beard tells us, "a dissipation of leadership was effected." Yet, as Beard shrewdly remarks, this revolution did not destroy leadership. Concentration of power has remained. However, there is a certain distribution: leadership shifts about between the Speaker, the Rules Committee, the Chairman of Ways and Means, the floor leader and the "steering committee" of the majority party. The resulting uncertainties have raised anew the demand for more effective leadership; in certain quarters the President is favored as the effective leader in Congress. Powers such as that of dissolution, the item veto in the budget, and so forth, are favored as desirable modifications to bring about such a change. If such presidential leadership were to become a reality, the Speaker of the American Congress could travel the road of the English Speaker, retire from active political leadership and provide an impartial umpire or moderator for the House. Such was his position at the outset, but as long as measures vitally important to the majority party were delayed or even defeated by opposition tactics, the Speaker in conjunction with one or more of the other directing forces would be obliged to assume a measure of leadership. Such is his political function within the American set-up, and what is true of the Federal Congress is largely true of the states as well, though the Speaker in Massachusetts, for instance, is much more nearly an impartial moderator than the Speaker in other legislatures.

The chief whip.—When James Bryce wrote his celebrated volume about *The American Commonwealth,* he commented extensively upon the lack of any recognized leaders in either the Senate or the House. How can such a statement be squared with the previous discussion? Was Bryce unaware of the existence of the Speaker, the Committee on Rules, and so on? Had he never heard of the floor leader at all? Curiously enough, Bryce himself calls the Speaker "almost the leader" of the House; the importance of the floor leader he tended to overlook. As is so often the case, the foreign observer, by looking for the institutions familiar in his own country, failed to notice the comparable importance of others because of the difficulty of ascertaining the functional nature of the different device. The American Congress (and the same is true of American state legislatures) carries on most of its work in committees (see below, Chap. XXII, ¶ 5), and the votes in the whole House mostly ratify the committee reports. Nor does the position of the majority party in the House depend upon any particular vote. Only during the last few days of the session do conditions requiring something like the English parliamentary strategy prevail, and for these few days it is relatively easy for the caucus to keep members in hand. What Bryce was admittedly looking for was the "whip." It is desirable for a complete understanding of the contrast between the English Parliament and the American legislatures as representative assemblies to know what these whips are. Bryce considered them a "vital, yet even in England little appreciated, part of the machinery of constitutional government." The term, taken from the hunting field—whipper-in!—denotes the men aiding the government in Parliament. The government party in the House of Commons appoints certain of its members as officials, nominally, whose real function it is to direct the party forces of the majority. The chief whip is the First (Patronage) Secretary of the Treasury, the others are mostly Junior Lords of the Treasury. Viscount Gladstone, chief whip himself from 1899 to 1905, claims that the office of the government whip originated about 1836 (note that this is after the Reform Act) though surely the practice can be traced to Burke's days, and that the whip became ex-officio patronage Secretary of the Treasury in or about 1845. This means that he keeps his machine running by handing out jobs (less important today), titles and orders (still quite important), and other favors. Under the direction of the cabinet, the chief whip, with the help of the assistant whips, lays out the plans for the parliamentary session, prepares a schedule, determines what opposition leaders are proposing to do, tries to arrange a fair distribution of work and keeps the cabinet informed of important developments in the party. He may also smooth out difficulties between several leaders. Lloyd George, for example, has claimed that the rift between him and Asquith would not have developed, if the Liberal whip had not died and thus deprived the party of a skillful moderator. We are also told by Bryce that "a ministerial whip is further bound to 'keep a house,' that is, to secure that when government business is being considered there shall always be a quorum of members present, and of course also to keep a majority. . . . Without the constant presence and activity of the ministerial whip the wheels of government could not go on for a day, *because the ministry would be exposed to the risk of casual defeats*. . . . Similarly the Opposition . . . finds it necessary to have their whip or whips because it is only thus that they can act as a party. . . ." From these remarks it should be clear that the institution of the whip is completely bound up with the position of the English House of Commons as the supporter and critic of the cabinet. Not only the government, but the opposition party as well has its whips. Gladstone has shown that in fact the role of the government whip and the opposition whip are quite far apart. The opposition chief whip, according to Gladstone, is more interested in work outside the House of Commons to prepare for victory in the next election. He collaborates with the party agent in giving financial assistance to candidates, in recommending and discovering suitable candidates, and in keeping local organizations in running order, and so on. Robert Luce has pointed out that "most American legislators would strongly resent any such control" and furthermore that the power of American whips as they have functioned since 1900 is much more limited, and that "all we want and ask of them is that they shall incite members to be on hand at moments of party importance." And indeed, if any person resembles the English government party's whip, it would much more nearly be the representative of the President, such as the Postmaster General under many administrations, who is officially concerned with patronage.

Procedure and parties.—So far, our discussion of the relation of procedure and parties has been mainly concerned with pointing out the effects of the party (and electoral) systems upon procedure. It is, however, a question of interaction, and one may ask what effect a certain procedure has upon parties. We have already, in several connections, referred to the famous protection of the minority under English parliamentary procedure. Authorities are agreed that the several devices provided for this purpose greatly aided the Irish Nationalists in developing their party organization. In France, the practice, only recently abandoned, of providing for the election of the all-important committees (see next chapter) by arbitrary divisions of the Chamber, the so-called *bureaux*, checked the development of real parties by emphasizing the individual member of parliament. In Germany, when the system of proportional representation adopted under the Weimar Republic (see above, Chap. XVII, ¶11) produced too many small "splinter parties," a rule was introduced according to which only parties represented by a certain number of deputies could claim seats on the committees. This was done in order to discourage the election of representatives of such small parties by making it impossible for such representatives to accomplish anything. In the United States Senate, the loose procedure providing for closure only in extreme emergencies has, as Lindsay Rogers has shown, greatly aided the maintenance of "independents" and other opposition groups. In England, many new and vexing questions arose in the post-war period when the Labor party tried to carry on the government as a minority party with the "support" of the Liberals. It has been shown that the procedure in the House of Commons has in more recent times been developed in response to the system of a cabinet responsible to the House of Commons through its majority party support. This procedure proved very ill-adapted to the needs of a minority government, and it may well be questioned whether the Labor party was wise in accepting the commission without insisting upon sweeping changes in the procedure. The difficulties became quite apparent during the very first debate on the Address to the Throne in 1929. The Labor government could not get preference for government bills, being opposed on this vital issue by Conservatives and Liberals alike. It is conceivable that it might have made this very issue a question of confidence; for here was the test as to Liberal "support." While a Conservative attempt to force a commitment on the protective tariff was defeated with the aid of the Liberals, a Liberal effort to secure the repeal of the Home Rule for Scotland Bill (passed by the preceding Conservative government) was defeated with the support of the Conservatives. In other words, the Labor government was at the very outset shorn of real "leadership," such as Bryce had claimed existed in the House of Commons, because it did not command a majority. English procedure, developed for a two-party system, was unfit for the new situation (for which the procedure of, let us say, the Swedish *Riksdag* is much preferable). As a consequence, procedural handicaps prevented the Labor government from doing any real work and measurably discredited it with the people; whether the party can recover the damage it suffered remains to be seen. The present radicalization of part of the British Labor party, and the manifest hostility of many of its members toward the parliamentary system are indirect results of these conditions.

Majority and minority; the problem of consent and constraint.—The impact of procedure upon parties is merely an institutionalized expression of the relation which exists between the problems of procedure and constitutional government. Rules of parliamentary procedure appear as restraints upon the exercise of power which the majority accepts as readily as the minority. Intrinsically, the majority could change the rules to give it complete ascendancy (as happened in Stuart and Cromwellian times); actually, such a change is out of the question, as long as you accept the other party as your partner in a contest which requires the participation of both—in the long run. In the United States, the constitutionally fixed recurrence of elections at stated intervals obliges the contestants to look beyond temporary advantage. In England, the periodic "appeal to the country" seems practically as inevitable, though a parliamentary majority could presumably change that as well as anything else in the constitution. But of course, the protection of the minority does not extend really to the point where procedural means are used for the purpose of destroying the possibility of parliamentary work. Filibustering and various other devices resembling the boycott, when carried beyond a certain point, become attacks against the constitutional order as such. The power of the minority, as well as the power of the majority, can be abused and needs to be restrained. This limitation was exceeded by the policy of obstruction of the Irish Nationalists in England, of the various subject nationalities in Austria before the World War, and of the Communists and Fascists in continental parliaments after the war. The Irish as well as their continental brethren denied the constitutional order under which they lived, and therefore the right to exist of the Parliament to which they belonged. These developments have shown that the parliamentary system of modern constitutional government rests ultimately to some extent upon certain tacitly accepted conventions. Josef Redlich's treatise was devoted to unfolding this aspect in great detail. From the vantage point of English (and Austrian) experience before the war he emphasized what has become so painfully apparent since that time: that the acceptance of such conventions depends upon the fundamental agreement amongst the people concerning their whole political order. "Parties of such intransigence that they reject the political order (*Staatsverband*) as such, which demand the subjection of this order to the Church, or which want to destroy the whole social order, parties, finally, which are rooted in a principle as deep as religious conscience, namely the principle of nationalism, such parties are in irreconcilable conflict with these conventions upon which parliamentarism rests. . . ." And Redlich continued: "Where political antagonisms of such force appear, that they destroy the political allegiance of the individual, because his political philosophy is rooted in still deeper and firmer political convictions, like his religious feelings, his national consciousness, or (in the future) his desire for social and economic equality, there the primary foundation of parliamentary government, the convention back of the majority principle, loses its moral force. With it the principle of the protection of the minority also loses its support." These prophetic words, written in 1905, not only foreshadow the doom of the Hapsburg Empire; they also indicate the point at which government by consent faces its most severe test.

The representativeness of representative assemblies: quantitative approach.—We have so far considered parliaments as representative assemblies in terms of certain institutional devices and social conditions which these parliaments have developed in the past. It is, however, possible to study the representativeness of elected representatives and the behavior of such groups in terms of the statistical picture which their votes offer to the investigator. Stuart Rice has made a very interesting attempt along these lines. He analyzed the votes in selected American representative bodies in the hope of throwing light upon two moot points regarding such bodies. It is often assumed that a legislator is representative, because voters tend to select men of their own "kind" to office, even though similarity in kind may be based on the voter's "identification" of himself with the social, economic, or intellectual attributes of the officeholder. Related to this is the second notion that such a legislator is representative, because he responds to legislative issues on the whole in about the same manner as would his fellow group members in the constituency. In order to verify these assumptions or hypotheses, Rice undertook to correlate the "progressiveness" of Minnesota legislators with the "progressiveness" of their districts. The *indications* were that such a relation did exist, although the coefficient of correlation was no higher "than could be reasonably expected." This tested the first assumption; other experiments along similar lines would have to be carried on, however, before much weight could be attached to any conclusion. More particularly would it be necessary to construct tests referring to particular legislative issues rather than a complex such as progressiveness. In terms of our prior hypothesis (see above, ¶ 2) it may be found that the assumptions should rather be that a legislator is representative, because he effectively correlates with existing notions legislative issues brought forward by special interest groups and is successful in selecting those for attention which, through education and propaganda, he can "put across" to his fellow group members in the constituency. In other words, he is a specialist in diagnosing group opinion in his constituency, and knows just how far to go in order to strike a balance between the pressure from various special groups and the resistance (passive pressure) from the group as a whole. Now as to the first point, that voters tend to select men of their own "kind," Rice selected as the social factor the representative's *nationality*. He had already explicitly excluded as possible factors wealth, legal and political training, and possibly education generally. In order to determine the influence of nationality, that is, to find an answer to the question of whether voters tend to select as representatives persons of their own nationality, Rice studied the members of both houses of the legislature in Minnesota and Wisconsin for several years. They were selected, he tells us, on the basis of availability, personal familiarity with these states, and an arrangement of legislative districts generally conforming to county lines (which is the unit used by the census). Over a hundred of these legislators were born in foreign countries. A quotient which Rice called "the ratio of nationality excess" was calculated for each district in terms of his representative to determine whether there was a higher percentage of that nationality in the district than in the state at large. He found that there existed "a well marked disposition on the part of foreign-born voters to elect men of their own nationality to the legislature." While this is probably true, the data examined do not justify so explicit a conclusion, but rather the more modest one that there existed a well-marked disposition on the part of districts with an excess of voters of a certain nationality to elect a representative from that nationality; for as to who voted no data were examined at all. It must be remembered that where such an excess existed, a greater probability existed that men from that nationality would be available for election to a representative assembly as for anything else. It would be highly desirable, if many more such explorations could be undertaken, to trace out the extent to which and the conditions under which the assumption from which Rice started is correct. Comparative and historical material of a less quantitative, though sufficiently definite, sort suggests that under different social and political conditions the impact of nationality is much more pronounced than would appear from Rice's analysis. In Switzerland, for example, it is a matter of course that the French cantons elect French representatives, the Italian cantons Italian representatives, and the German cantons German. Of course, in most of these cantons there would appear a high "ratio of nationality excess." Again, in pre-war Germany, the Poles elected Polish representatives. Czechoslovakia offers another interesting political arena of a similar sort, where the antipathy of nationalities toward each other is at times so profound as to make election of a representative of the other nationality utterly inconceivable. Germans, Slovaks, Hungarians, Ruthenians—all these struggle against the Czechs and against each other with such intensity that the nationality issue is of paramount significance, whereas in Minnesota and Wisconsin it is a minor factor. Again, Czechoslovakia and Switzerland have proportional representation, which favors the separate representation of distinctive groups; thus in Czechoslovakia you find German, as well as Slovak and Czech, Socialists. Various factors may, in other words, carry different weight, depending upon the electoral system. Here would be a "political" condition, as contrasted with the previous "social" condition, affecting the weight of the nationality factor. What is true of the nationality factor is, of course, equally true of the factor of "class," for example. All this goes to show that the first assumption of Rice should, perhaps, also be restated for purposes of further inquiry. In keeping with our general analysis of representation, it might be better to say that a person is representative, because voters tend to reject men who do not possess certain traits which correspond to dominant objectives and prejudices of the voters themselves. These traits could probably be arranged in an order of relative weight, such ratings presumably being subject to variations under differing social and political conditions. It is doubtful whether the distinction between rational and irrational objectives, interests, prejudices, and so forth, would serve any useful purpose in this connection. Rational interests, such as a trade union's interest in higher wages, may take precedence over any irrational prejudice against a representative of a foreign nationality, or vice versa. Whatever the further conclusions, Stuart Rice has opened up a rich field of enquiry bearing upon the representativeness of representative groups. Perhaps further study will show that the preoccupations and prejudices of the voters today are themselves the force which is undermining the representative faculty of a numerous deliberative assembly, as contrasted with an individual or a small group girded for action without public deliberation.

Conclusion and summary.—The particular importance of deliberation in the work of numerous bodies of elected representatives is a matter of such complexity as to deserve treatment in a separate chapter (See Chap. XXII). Pending the final conclusions which will become possible after that analysis has been completed, it remains at the end of the present chapter to retrace the path which has so far been travelled. After pointing out that in the course of the nineteenth century parliamentary assemblies had become the core of modern representative government, we showed that their prime function is not so much the initiation of legislation (in the sense of making laws) as it is the discussion and coördination of proposed legislation, and the carrying on of popular education and propaganda on behalf of those proposals which have been adopted, or in the opinion of the representatives should be adopted. Parliaments and parliamentarians, it was said, appear as integrating agencies through which the plans of the central bureaucracy and the claims of the various interest groups are expounded to the public, with a view to discovering a suitable balance. It was shown how important party structure is for the inner workings of such bodies, and the role which the social composition of members plays in their work. Procedure, though a highly technical subject, appeared in its broader phases to be closely linked up with what place representative bodies occupy in the constitutional order. The problem of second chambers was shown to be intimately related to the structure of the community, and to whether any permanent subdivisions requiring separate representation existed within it. Bentham's arguments against it were built upon the idea of a prevailingly homogeneous community. Such rationalist simplification of actual complexities pervades Bentham's unique endeavour at constructing a theory of parliamentary tactics. This system is today of significance primarily because of the profound and rather unwholesome influence which it exerted on the countries which undertook to model a constitutional order after the English pattern. It is claimed that it materially contributed to the failure of various parliamentary regimes. England and the Dominions as well as the United States were not swayed by the logical brilliance of Bentham's deductions. While the development followed his demands, as far as the English speakership was concerned, it did so for different reasons and in a different way. The Speaker in the House of Commons did not combine leadership with impartiality, as Bentham had required, but abandoned leadership in favor of neutrality, while the leadership in legislation was assumed by the cabinet. In the United States, under the constitutionally safeguarded separation of powers, the Speaker of the House of Representatives abandoned neutrality in favor of leadership, and even though he today divides such leadership with several others, he still plays a decisive and partisan role. Similar conditions exist in most of the state legislatures. In the British Dominions which have adopted parliamentary cabinet systems of government the Speaker has assumed the neutral position of his English colleague. The English cabinet's legislative leadership has been cemented by the development of the office of the whip, and even the opposition has found it expedient to coördinate its activities through such whips. While, broadly speaking, the party system has decisive effects upon parliamentary procedure, the latter often reacts back upon the parties. To the extent to which procedural rules become fixed, they can and do mold party development. They can thus become powerful tools in the hands of a majority, or a combination of larger groups. Ultimately, rules of parliamentary procedure appear, therefore, as restraints upon the exercise of power by a "sovereign" body of representatives. They are the heel of Achilles, the soft spot of the modern constitutional system. Redlich's recognition of the relation between these "conventions" and the future of constitutional government as a whole, while now more generally recognized, then constituted a profound prophecy. All such institutional studies of past practices require, it is submitted, implementation by statistical analysis of present practices as manifested in the voting behavior of representative groups under the most varied conditions, socially, economically, politically. Only a few pioneering efforts along such lines have been made, notably by Stuart Rice. They seem to suggest that the general assumptions underlying the present study, concerning representation and the function of elected bodies of representatives within the modern constitutional order, are in keeping with the facts. But much further inquiry is indicated.

CHAPTER XXII

PARLIAMENTS AS DELIBERATIVE ASSEMBLIES

Deliberation and representation contrasted.—Modern parliaments not only represent the "will" of the people, they also deliberate. Their political function is a double one: as representatives they integrate the community through periodic appeals, based upon a continuous process of education and propaganda; as a deliberative body they endeavour to solve concrete problems of communal activity: to do or not to do, that is the question. While the two functions are closely intertwined, they may, from the standpoint of political science, usefully be distinguished, as the present chapter will attempt to show. Parliament, it will be seen, deliberates upon many questions and decides many issues upon which it does not and could not consult the "will" of the people, nor does it attempt to develop such a will by education and propaganda. On all such occasions, publicity is unnecessary, often even undesirable. Procedural devices have been developed to guard the confidential nature of such deliberations. Lest it be thought that all such proceedings are contrary to the "spirit" of parliamentary institutions—a view widely popular with their detractors—let it be remembered that there was a time when the deliberations of the "mother of parliaments" were entirely withheld from public view. In the age of Dr. Johnson, no person with as much as a pencil was allowed within the halls of Parliament. An anecdote told of Johnson well illustrates this point. In a tavern, friends were discussing the quality of parliamentary oratory when one amongst their number recited verbatim a speech of the elder Pitt as an example of beautiful English diction. Upon turning to Johnson to hear his opinion, they were told that he himself composed that speech while working for a London paper, basing it upon a brief report by one of the attendants in Parliament! Only in the last quarter of the eighteenth century were reporters allowed, and regular publication of the debates followed. For a time the peculiar conditions of English electoral politics made possible a continuation of the deliberative function of Parliament in the full daylight of publicity, but under the impact of democratic forces Parliament in England gradually ceased to be a deliberative body; at the end of the century critics began to describe it as a "voting machine." It became, in the words of Finer, purely a "will-organization," and ceased to be a "thought-organization." How the English Parliament has undergone, and how it and other Parliaments have tried to escape, this transformation, will be the central topic of this chapter. Here closure and committees are the two battle-cries. For the rest, it will be shown that fiscal and administrative supervision by a Parliament are entirely dependent upon the fact that it continues to be a deliberative body. Technical as these matters may seem, they are vitally related to the future of parliamentary institutions.

Speech and debate.—Speech is the essence of parliamentary activity, it is the very life blood of Parliament's corporate body politic. But just as blood has to flow through well encased channels in order to fulfill its salutary function, so speech has to be circumscribed and regulated in Parliament. Not the Tohu-bohu of a multitude of voices, but the balanced and ordered procedure of speech and reply, of argument and of debate is "speech" within Parliament. The privilege of the "freedom of speech" is not an absolute privilege of the individual member, it is the relative freedom compatible with the freedom of others. In the words of the Marquess of Hartington, when discussing closure in the House of Commons in 1882: ". . . the privilege of speech is a privilege which the House permits to be exercised for its own instruction, for its own information, in order to form its own opinion, and . . . not a personal privilege to be used irrespective of the convenience and the efficiency of the House. . . ." He could, in the same vein, insist that the business before the House, and nothing but the business before the House, determined the rules and limitations of debate. When all relevant arguments have been advanced, it ought to come to an end. But who is to say when this is the case? Modern English and American practice has given the say to the majority party. This naturally raises the problem of constraint of the minority.

But "filibustering," "talking against time," and similar practices in turn raise the problem of constraint of the majority. As in other political arenas, so in parliaments a certain measure of constraint is inherent in the situation. Effective political engineering needs to be directed toward achieving a minimum of such constraint, just as mechanical engineering aims at a minimum of friction in constructing a machine. The eighteenth century was occupied with the development of rules guarding against the restraining of private members; in the period of the Irish obstruction it became a matter of guarding against the restraint placed upon the majority by a recalcitrant minority. The latest problems raised by the fact that there may be no majority party have hardly been faced, except by academic discussions. But throughout these different phases certain iron-clad rules have persisted which crystallized so early that their beginnings are obscure. Without wishing to go here into the many technicalities which the rules of debate in the House of Commons and other parliaments contain, it may be well to recall certain general practices which are of decisive importance. In order that there may be a debate a definite proposal, called a motion, must ordinarily be before the House. Whatever anyone may say ought to be and ordinarily is germane to the subject matter of this motion. At any rate, no new motion can be introduced, until the old one is disposed of. After those who wish to speak have each had their opportunity to do so, "the question is put" and a vote is taken. A proposal, a discussion of the proposal, a decision regarding the proposal—these are the iron-clad stages of an orderly parliamentary transaction. It is evident that speech is the essence of it.

Closure.—Even an ordered debate has to come to an end at some time. This fact has engendered certain rules from the very beginning. Short of the presiding officer "putting the question," the classical form for achieving this purpose of terminating the debate is motions for adjournment. There were essentially three, adjournment to another day (fixed adjournment), adjournment without naming another day (indefinite adjournment), adjournment until after something else has been done, such as securing certain necessary information (relative adjournment). Each one of these motions became a tool in the hands of a determined obstruction. For as on each of them a vote (division) would have to be taken, and as these votes consumed a great deal of time, much delay could thus be effected. In other words, motions for adjournment could be employed much as the roll calls are being used in American legislatures. These motions for adjournment, as well as the inevitable extension of debate in a very numerous House of Commons, produced in course of time a demand for procedural devices which might be effective in expediting business. In France and in the United States such devices have had a longer history, but even in England the Speaker has for a long time had the right of bringing the debate to an end by putting the question. This sort of closure was not, however, regularly used unless and until everybody appeared to have had a fair hearing. Only the crisis brought on by the obstruction of the Irish Nationalists in 1881 induced the then Speaker, Brand (later Viscount Hampden), to discard the ancient restraint and to bring a debate which had lasted forty-one hours to an end by putting the question. He explained his procedure in a short statement:

> The Motion for leave to bring in the Protection of Person and Property (Ireland) Bill has now been under discussion for above five days. The present sitting, having commenced on Monday last, at Four o'clock, has continued until this Wednesday morning, a period of forty-one hours, the House having been frequently occupied with discussions upon repeated dilatory Motions for Adjournment. However prolonged and tedious these discussions, the Motions have been supported by small minorities, in opposition to the general sense of the House.
>
> A crisis has thus arisen which demands the prompt interposition of the Chair, and of the House. The usual rules have proved powerless to ensure orderly and effective Debate. An important measure, recommended in Her Majesty's Speech nearly a month since, and declared to be urgent, in the interests of the State, by a decisive majority, is being arrested by the action of an inconsiderable minority, the Members of which have resorted to those modes of "Obstruction," which have been recognized by the House as a Parliamentary offence.
>
> The dignity, the credit, and the authority of this House are seriously threatened, and it is necessary that they should be vindicated. Under the operation of the accustomed rules and methods of procedure, the Legislative powers of the House are paralysed. A new and exceptional course is imperatively demanded; and I am satisfied that I shall best carry out the will of the House, and may rely upon its support, if I decline to call upon any more Members to speak, and at once proceed to put the question from the Chair. I feel assured that the House will be prepared to exercise all its powers in giving effect to these proceedings.
>
> Future measures for ensuring orderly Debate I must leave to the judgment of the House. But I may add that it will be necessary either for the House itself to assume more effectual control over its Debates, or to entrust greater authority to the Chair.

The action of Speaker Brand had been taken with the understanding that the government (Gladstone) would at once proceed to alter the procedure in the House of Commons. This was done and, amended by minor innovations later, closure was introduced into the House of Commons, so that any member of the House may, with the support of one hundred members, move that the question be put. In the train of these reforms, even more coercive forms for limiting the debate were soon adopted, the so-called guillotine, and the closure by compartments. The former provides that after a set time, the question is brought to a vote, no matter what the state of the discussion; the latter, that a bill may be divided into sections (items), and a certain amount of time, agreed to beforehand, allotted to the discussion of each of these sections. Finally, in 1911 the so-called Kangaroo type of closure was added, which permits the presiding officer to declare which of a number of amendments proposed shall be debated. When impartially employed, this type of closure can be highly beneficial. Yet, it discourages active participation by members of the House. What is equally serious, it undermines the belief in the deliberations of the Parliament. If measures of the highest importance can be put through without even a word of debate, the deliberative function of such assemblies becomes a farce. This in turn weakens their representative position. To quote Finer again, it makes parliaments will-organizations, rather than thought organizations. In terms of our own analysis, it deprives parliaments of their national representative position, and places them in the position of representatives of a party. But it must be remembered that the obstructionist tactics which engendered closure and such tools are themselves expressions of the fact that the community is rent by violent conflicts—conflicts which obstruct the maintenance of community and consequently of its representation, anyway. One way of escaping from the difficulties involved in such social cleavages is to reduce the representative importance of a parliament. This is manifestly the case under the American Constitution. Here federalism and the separation of powers make Congress just one cog, though an important one, in the whole set-up of representative organs, with the result that the burden of national representation does not fall only on Congress (as it almost does on the House of Commons). The impact of the (absolutist) ideas of sovereignty, and the consequent hankering after unitary representative decisions (see above, Chap. XXI) are correspondingly weakened. Even the markedly partisan exercise of the closure rules in the American legislature is more readily endured, as this assembly is not at all taken as the sole national representative. Speaker Reed, who has done as much as any man to strengthen the control of the majority over the debates in Congress, voiced sentiments much like those of the Marquess of Hartington, cited above, when he said that the purpose of a parliamentary body was action and not the stoppage of action. Hence he felt that if anybody undertook to obstruct the orderly progress of business even by regular and permitted means, it is right for the majority to refuse to have such motions entertained and to cause the public business to proceed. He and his successors were instrumental in bringing about the implied majority control by making it possible to discard motions, by forbidding speeches exceeding one hour except by unanimous consent, by allowing motions for putting the "previous question," and by placing the power of arranging legislative business at the discretion of the Committee on Rules, controlled by the majority. Since the American Senate admits closure only on the basis of a special vote by a qualified majority, measures fostered by the majority party (or opposed by it) will more readily meet an adverse vote in the Senate. From this fact, Lindsay Rogers has rather persuasively argued that "with responsibility divided and confused, the check which is on occasion exerted by senatorial obstructionists is of great value. . . . Only the American Senate can act as a 'teaching apparatus' or bring about a 'catastrophe' of obstruction. . . . The Senate can help the country to form opinions and by its eternal vigilance . . . act as the 'real balance-wheel' of the Constitution." The absence of closure in the Senate, which many people so bitterly resent does not prevent a reasonable amount of business from being attended to; but of course the Senate of the United States is a relatively very small body. If a measure is opposed with real spirit by even a limited minority, it had better be abandoned, Rogers argues. Such a view is difficult to accept as regards the Senate's power in foreign affairs; it seems to lead to inaction. It is also questionable in matters where social reform is urgent (lynching!), yet can be prevented by an interested minority. The anarchic potentialities of the *liberum veto* lurk in the background of such unlimited debate. (Rogers also argues the value of having no closure for controlling the executive, a question which is dealt with below in ¶ 9). Closure, when applied with proper discretion is to be viewed as a safeguard of the deliberative functions of parliaments. When deliberation is allowed to deteriorate into a circus by reading purely extraneous literary productions, like *Childe Harold* or the *Pilgrim's Progress*, into the record, it damages the deliberative as well as the representative function of parliaments.

Parliamentary committees, England.—Since the pressure is undeniably great in the English as in other parliaments, critics of the system of closure have been looking for relief in other directions. As a consequence, they have advocated an expansion of the standing committee system in the House of Commons. This system is of rather recent origin, though it possesses historical roots. It grew out of the procedural reforms in the eighties. The arrangements have been fluctuating considerably, as to both number and size of committees. The late appearance and the still rather limited scope of these committees is a peculiarity of the English House of Commons. Redlich has pointed out that the Commons could so long avoid a practice which had become very widely accepted elsewhere because of the procedural device of turning from the formal proceedings to what is known as the Committee of the Whole House. This committee is simply the House with relaxed rules of procedure; members may, for example, speak several times on the same matter. This committee has its greatest utility in the field of financial and budgetary functions (see below, ¶ 7). These functions, when referred to smaller permanent committees as in Congress, the Chamber of Deputies, or the Reichstag, constitute the real strength of the committee structure. In England, where the whole House deliberates upon these matters in Committee of the Whole House, the demand for permanent committees arose in connection with the increase in all kinds of legislation in the second half of the nineteenth century, and the increasing complexity and technicality of this legislation. At present there are five such committees, designated by the letters A, B, C, and D, with a fifth committee devoted to Scottish affairs. Each has thirty to fifty members, with the possibility of adding up to fifteen specially interested members. The chairmen of these committees are members of the majority, supporting the government, and the business of the committees is definitely and decisively directed by the government. While formally these committees are allowed considerable scope in amending bills referred to them, they are in fact quite restricted. In the words of Finer: "Though the members in Committee are said by some to be freer from party alignment than members in the House, they are not much, if at all, freer, since the Minister in charge exacts the support of members of his party, of whom a majority are upon the Committee." Yet the same writer also reports that "it is universally admitted that they [the committees] do good work: considerable emphasis being placed upon the fact that they vote after hearing the arguments (this is unusual in the House) and that the Government is prepared to make concessions as the argument goes." Such concessions are of course in matters of technical detail; for the broad scope of the bill has been settled before it is referred to the committee. English parliamentary committees are supposed to aid and do aid Parliament in these matters of detail; very important bills are often reserved for consideration by the Committee of the Whole House. The committee's work is, of course, scrutinized by the whole House in what is known as the Report Stage; the tendency of the House to employ this discussion for doing over the work of the committee led to a rule that the discussion must stay within the ground staked out by the committee's recommendations. The theory (and to a large extent the practice) of the English standing committees is perhaps most succinctly summarized by a quotation from Sir Courtenay Ilbert, at one time Clerk of the House, which runs as follows: "It proceeds on the view that when the general principle of a bill has been affirmed, a reasonable chance ought to be afforded of having its provisions discussed, that this chance is improved by sending a bill to a Standing Committee, that, as a general rule, discussion in a Standing Committee is more business-like and effective than discussion in a Committee of the Whole House, and that the time of the House is saved by dividing the House into compartments for discussing the details of legislative measures." In keeping with these general arguments, writers like Ramsay Muir advocate an extension of the committee system to improve the opportunities of members of the House to participate in the deliberative function of the House. In considering his views, it must be remembered that Muir looks forward to recurrent minority governments, particularly if proportional representation, which he strongly favors, is adopted. Even without proportional representation, the post-war situation suggests the recurrence of governments such as the first and second Labor government supported as they were by only a minority party. Under such conditions, Muir argues, a system of six standing committees, each concerned with the activities of one of the great "spending departments," would have most salutary effects. In order to avoid a dispersion of ministerial responsibility, he would make the minister of the department the chairman of the committee with the right to rule out questions of policy. Such committees, he feels, could not only aid in considering bills, but they could also maintain a continuous review of the work of the departments with which they are concerned (equipped as they would be with full powers of investigation), and secondly, they could receive the estimates of these departments as soon as they were ready, go through them and draw up a Report for the House when it came to consider these estimates. The questions of administrative and fiscal control and supervision which these observations raise, will be more fully considered below (see ¶¶ 7 and 8). But in the strictly legislative (rule-making) field, there would also emerge another significant function, namely the scrutinizing of all the orders and regulations issued by departments under statutory delegation, that is, the delegated legislation which Muir calls "the legislative powers of the bureaucracy." These and similar proposals palpably call to mind American and French practices; yet Muir is emphatic in asserting that "neither the American nor the French system is suitable for transplantation" to England. "We do not wish," Muir says, "to see small committees, independent of and unrelated to the responsible Ministers of the Departments, wielding so high a degree of irresponsible power as the committees of the American House of Representatives do." He is equally unwilling "to see the responsibility of the Cabinet for the general policy of the country so seriously undermined as it is in France." But although Muir (as most other Englishmen) does not wish to copy alien institutions, he admits that the experience of France and the United States has a lesson to teach.

Same subject; United States.—The extensive development of committees in American legislatures, though connected by a thin thread with early English beginnings, which "waned under the deadening influence of the cabinet system," commenced after 1800. There were committees in Virginia and elsewhere, and the experience of the former undoubtedly influenced the Constitutional Convention. Only in that colony had the committees started the modern American practice of framing and amending bills. Special (select) committees were, to be sure, common in England and all the colonies for the work on particular bills, but in Virginia, as throughout the United States today, they were standing committees. In spite of considerable arguments to the contrary, it seems best to follow Robert Luce's judgment that "this process has been a matter of convenience, a natural development of orderly system, not begun with any deliberate purpose. . . ." Congress, constitutionally separated from and therefore not subject to executive leadership, was soon confronted with the executive function of drafting new legislation (see above, Chap. XXI, ¶ 9), of supervising the administration of such legislation (see below, ¶ 9), and of considering the expenditures involved in all such legislation. For these functions another method of procedure had to be adopted than the general debate, increasingly cumbrous in an ever more numerous assembly. Whenever a large group of men find themselves in such a situation, they are apt to resort to some form of committee for the preparation of decisions requiring attention to detail. As Luce remarks, this procedure is so obvious that it hardly would require comment, if the committee system in American (and French) representative assemblies were not constantly subjected to a barrage of criticism. And it is true that such committees are at variance with the representative function of parliaments. But, as was pointed out before, it greatly enhances the capacity of parliaments for deliberation. Those who cry out against the secrecy of committee proceedings (see below, ¶ 11) forget what every experienced parliamentarian would tell them: "No man is the same in private and in public. The more numerous the observers and auditors, the less the frankness, sincerity, confidence. Universal experience tells us that in all manner of conference and deliberation, we reach results more speedily and satisfactorily if those persons directly involved are alone." It has been shown that the English Parliament at the time when it was a deliberative body, closely guarded the privacy of its proceedings. Thus the baneful effect of "talking to the galleries" was eliminated. There is little room in a committee meeting for oratory. Such businesslike procedure became essential in connection with the legislative and fiscal autonomy of Congress. While at first the committees "were looked upon as merely organs to investigate some fact, and to digest and arrange the detail of a complicated subject," they have in the course of time become the active, directing centers of congressional life. Bills originate with members occupying a powerful position on the committee to which the bill is bound to be referred, the advice of committeemen is sought by administrators who thus anticipate the discussion of increased budgets, representatives of various interest groups are in constant contact with the members of the congressional committee charged with supervising the governmental activity which most closely touches their daily affairs—railroad representatives trail members of committees on Interstate Commerce labor representatives pursue those concerned with labor, educators, patriots, farmers, women, all join in the fray (see Chap. XXIV). In the United States Congress, where bills are at once referred to some committee without any previous discussion by the whole House or Senate (and the same is true of many state legislatures) many bills are killed in committee. This pigeonholing of measures has naturally and persistently aroused the ire of some part or other of the public (whoever happened to favor the bill); in contrasting the situation with that prevailing in England, these critics forget that such bills could not even get introduced into the House of Commons. It is reported that during the five Congresses preceding 1926, 29,332 bills and resolutions were introduced into the United States Senate, of which 3,113 were passed, and during the same period 82,632 such bills and resolutions were introduced into the House of which 2,931 in all were passed. This is only a little more than 10 per cent in the Senate, and only about 3.5 per cent in the House. Since no distinction is made here between public and private bills, as is done in England, it is difficult to compare these figures with those concerning the House of Commons, but every writer on English parliamentary practices remarks upon the difficulty of getting any bill discussed which is not a "government bill." In the United States, the majority party will, if it is the party of the President, push "administration measures" whether advocated by a presidential "Message to Congress" or introduced by a Senator or Congressman favorable to the administration. But in either case, immediate reference to a committee merely insures it attention and possibly retention of its major "policy," but innumerable changes of real importance are bound to be made. The now ignominiously buried NRA typically evolved out of a presidential message as a result of compromising the pressure of organized business and organized labor, one securing the infringement of the anti-trust laws, the other the sanctioning of collective bargaining. In their effort to crystallize the policy which they are to recommend to Congress, these committees hold hearings. These hearings, being sometimes public and sometimes private, have also been subjected to a considerable amount of criticism. The length to which they have gone in their efforts to compel witnesses to appear and testify has been denounced as congressional autocracy, and the extent of the power of Congress in this respect is highly controversial, with the Supreme Court acting as a final authority. Since the investigation of past performance and the determination of possible lines of change and reform are closely interwoven, this usual distinction is more significant legally than politically. Private hearings before congressional committees have been defended on the ground that witnesses can then more readily be induced to communicate confidential information. Certain it is that this is true at times. Yet Massachusetts, with her tradition of uniformly public hearings, has not been greatly handicapped. Whichever practice is better, hearings either public or private are an integral part of committee work. Considering the active leadership which emanates from the committees in American legislatures, naturally the question as to who selects them is of vital significance. Beneath the surface differences of selection by the Speaker, by a committee appointed for this purpose (as in England), or by the whole House, selection by the parties prevails today in practically all legislatures. Speaker Reed, in the heyday of the power of that office, remarked that if he was a Czar, the power he had was held on sufferance of the majority of his party. Committee appointments entrusted to him reflected necessarily the preferences of his party colleagues. The questionable effects of the Speaker's power were mostly observable in his appointments of members of the minority party. It was here that tyrannical, unrestrained power could be exercised, and not in the appointment of his own party colleagues. He might, and he often did appoint strong minority members to committees overcharged with routine business in order to keep them away from an important policy determining committee. Since the change of 1911 (see above, Chap. XXI, ¶ 9), the party caucus, directly or indirectly, controls the membership of committees, as it long had in the Senate. From this it follows that what the change really did was to extend party control to the minority party members of the several committees, and although the new arrangement has at times produced greater difficulties, and there are those who would suggest going back to the old plan, party control of both minority and majority members of the committees seems more in keeping with effective deliberation. In this respect, then, American and English practice are today much more nearly alike, for the Committee of Selection in the House of Commons, to which the naming of members for committees is entrusted, is subject to strict party control, both as to majority and minority. It remains to say a few words concerning the number of such committees. Apart from select committees, there were forty-four committees in the House at the beginning of the seventy-third Congress, and thirty-three committees in the Senate at the same time (1933). These committees ranged in membership from two to thirty-five in the House and from three to twenty-three in the Senate. The average important House committee has around twenty. Contrasting these figures with those in England, we find congressional committees to be more numerous, but smaller in size. This difference the different nature of their work readily explains. Accepting the complexity of modern legislation as inherent in the industrial society in which we live, we have only one remedy for the multiplication of committees in our legislatures, and that is to permit administrative bodies and officials to extend the range of delegated legislation as has been done in England, to allow them unrestrained and uncontrolled power in administering this trust within the limits imposed by intermittent appeals to the electorate, and to forego any effective scrutiny of expenditures by others than the leading members of the majority party. This (English) method of handling the problem has found so many well-informed detractors where it is practiced today that its desirability may be seriously doubted. The strength of the English Parliament lies in the broad integrating value of its debates upon issues of general policy, the strength of the American legislature in its deliberations upon specific legislative proposals and administrative activities. Whether a combination of the two could be effected, as some reformers on both sides of the water seem to hope, it is difficult to say. The two functions of representation and deliberation do not seem entirely compatible with each other as long as such a combination remains a hope rather than a reality.

Same subject; France.—The French Parliament comes nearer effectively combining English and American practices than many students of these problems appreciate. This fact is perhaps not entirely unrelated to the previously described central position which the French Parliament occupies in the whole scheme of things (see above, Chap. XX, ¶ 5). French parliamentary government is almost government by Parliament, not merely government under the more or less effective supervision of Parliament. This applies, of course, only to the Third Republic. Before that time, French government had been, with minor interruptions, administrative government, subject to a varying amount of parliamentary control, and indeed very little of it under the two Napoleons. In this period, select special committees were the usual procedure. Curiously enough, it took the French Parliament just about the same twenty odd years that it had taken the American Congress to evolve its system of committees. To be sure, permanent committees had been appointed in the revolutionary assemblies, notably the "convention," and these committees undertook the task of government and administration. The experience with these committees, among which the Committee of Public Safety was the most notorious, brought on a violent reaction. The fusion of power which they effected and the resulting dictatorship led the Directory to forbid the formation of such committees by express constitutional prohibition. Reflecting the horror felt for the "Terror," such committees remained taboo until almost the end of the nineteenth century. Since that time they have emerged as perhaps the most distinctive feature of French parliamentarism. The French committee system, like the American, is based upon the parties in the Chamber. Since 1909 the several parties have been represented on the committees according to their numerical strength in the House. The parties or groups, as they are called, make up their own panel, and through their leaders these panels are combined and presented to the Chamber for formal approval. Ordinarily, therefore, the coalition supporting the cabinet will have a majority in the committees when it has a majority in the Chamber (for important exceptions see below, ¶ 8). In view of the decisive role the committees play in all matters requiring the action of the Chamber or touching the relation of the Chamber to the ministries, this arrangement is, of course, highly desirable, nay even indispensable for effective work. As in the United States, so in France bills, whether coming from the government (when they are called *projets de loi*), or from a particular deputy (when they are called *propositions de loi*), as well as other matters coming before the house, are nowadays at once referred to the appropriate committee. The Chamber eventually considers the bill as reported out of committee, rather than the government's bill. The government can and often does re-introduce provisions which have been changed in committee, acting through a deputy or directly proposing its amendments to the bill as reported. The leadership which the committee, through its reporter, assumes in dealing with bills or with the budgets of the various ministries is clearly indicated by the seating of the committee in the house, for in France these committees are placed in front of the house right next to the ministerial bench. Barthélemy is justified in pointing to this seating arrangement as characteristic of the French representative system, as it profoundly distinguishes it from English parliamentarism. Parliamentary work is directed not only by the government, but by the committees as well. Nevertheless, the committees are, at least in matters concerning legislation, supposed to confine themselves to preparing the decision of the Chamber; this supposition is accurate in regard to bills which actually come before the Chamber, but it is not true concerning bills which are buried in committee, for they are so buried, because the committee decided that they did not deserve their attention. Outside the field of legislation, for example in the realm of administrative supervision, the committees handle many matters without ever referring them to the Chamber. The powerful Foreign Affairs Committee attends to many issues which never come before the Chamber. In these fields, the committees are acting for the Chamber rather than preparing its work. What is more, the Chamber tends so much to be guided by the advice received from its committees that the rule of anticipated reactions would suggest that ministries, particularly in more technical fields, are much guided by the known views of committee members in drafting any legislation. In the jargon of French politics, this art is called "to play the committees" (*jouer les commissions*), an expression supposedly invented by Briand. Barthélemy gives an interesting instance which occurred in connection with the granting of a governmental subsidy to the French Line *(Compagnie Generale Transatlantique)*. Such subsidies are a ticklish business for any administration to handle because of the possible implications of graft, and yet the French Line employs so many people, and means so much to the prestige of France throughout the world that action of some sort seemed indicated. Under these circumstances, four ministers, MM. Pierre Laval, Flandin, Pietri, and de Chappedelaine, went before the Committee of Finance and the Committee of Merchant Marine to set forth their plans. Barthélemy believes that the purpose was fourfold: (1) to show Parliament their regard; (2) to test the drifts of parliamentary opinion; (3) to prepare the bills required by the situation and acceptable to Parliament; (4) to make the committees share the responsibility for taking the initiative in this matter. By thus preparing the ground in the committees, these ministers presumably facilitated the later passage of the bills. Since the direction of the Chamber's work comes from the committees as much as from the government, such a getting-together seems entirely natural. This intimate collaboration between administrative officials and deputies is further facilitated by the French practice of having the committees appoint reporters so that the committees do not necessarily communicate with the Chamber through their chairmen. Rather, the committee members divide this reporting between themselves, usually quite amicably. It is customary to request a report from one of the members on any matter before the committee, and then to appoint that member reporter of the bill to the Chamber, if his report is, on the whole, acceptable to the committee majority. Very often, the sponsor of a certain bill will in turn be asked to report that bill to the committee, if he is a member of it. As a consequence, the reporter of a government bill is by implication collaborating with the government. While deputies ordinarily try to report important bills, there are occasions when the unpopularity of a necessary measure produces a general flight. These reports are written, they are often very elaborate, they are printed and distributed to members after having been introduced into the Chamber, and are published as *Parliamentary Documents,* of which they constitute the bulk. On the whole, the reporter is pretty free, as is the committee, to decide when to bring in his report, and efforts to impel deputies to come forth with their reports within a given time have remained a dead letter. In fact, a deputy may hold out the report as bait to the government in order to exact a concession. Where it is difficult to assign a matter to any one committee, the assignment will be made in principal to one, and other committees will be asked for advisory reports, which have at times been more important than the principal report. As the committee system has more and more deeply entrenched itself in French parliamentary politics, the committees have developed a formidable initiative in matters of general policy. When, in December 1932, M. Herriot wished to secure the Chamber's consent to a token debt payment to the United States, he found himself blocked by the two hostile committees on finance and foreign affairs; they listened to M. Herriot, adopted a joint resolution opposed to payments which the Chamber passed, 357 against 37, and thus forced the resignation of Herriot's cabinet. Barthélemy remarks that such a role would have been unimaginable for the committees to play thirty years earlier. The joint leadership of committee and cabinet in the French Parliament is recognized in many rules of procedure; the chairman of the committee and the reporter of the particular bill must be heard at any time, irrespective of the list of speakers; when the previous question is moved, the right to speak is limited to the mover, one member opposed, a speaker for the government, and a speaker for the committee in charge, and so forth. Only by moving the question of confidence can the government reassert its authority in a clash with the committee. When one listens to a debate in the Chamber, discussion flies back and forth between the government bench and the committee bench a good part of the time. The committee as well as the government can demand additional meetings (ordinarily the French Chamber meets Tuesday, Thursday, and Friday). But many minor propositions are accepted by the Chamber without any discussion, or very little of it, merely on the authority of the committee's work. As a result, there has developed in France in recent years a procedural device known as "vote without debate." Matters which some committee or the government considers urgent, are put upon the calendar with the provision that "there be no debate." If thirty deputies demand a debate, it automatically goes off the calendar. If one deputy wishes to comment, he may do so in writing, and the committee will then submit a supplementary report in which it attempts to answer the particular member. He can repeat this process twice more; but after that only thirty members can prevent a vote without debate. This technique substitutes written discourse for public debate where only small objections exist. But such a procedure manifestly lends itself to abuse, since many deputies do not take the trouble of reading the order of the day with care. It shows once more what Barthélemy pertly summarizes in the statement: "To the Chamber, the votes, to the committee, all the discussion." The deliberative function of the French Parliament has to a considerable extent been transferred to the permanent committees. It is small wonder, therefore, that voices have been raised which would dispense with amendments in plenary session altogether, provided the committee in charge of the matter has acted by a two-thirds majority. But since the French committees are strictly confidential, even the proportional composition of these committees, representing as they do all groups in the Chamber, will not silence the fierce opposition which such frank recognition of the dwindling deliberative function of the whole house still encounters.

Fiscal and budgetary control.—There is one field of parliamentary activity in which the value of the committee system has been quite generally recognized, and that is the field of financial and more particularly of budgetary control. At the same time, the committees dealing with these matters are generally looked upon as the most important ones in the system. In the United States the Chairmen of the Committees of Ways and Means and of Appropriations have traditionally been considered second only to the Speaker of the House. In Britain, on the other hand, expenditures (estimates) and revenues (ways and means) are traditionally handled by the whole House, sitting as Committee of the Whole, which means in practice merely a simplified procedure. Now since it is a fixed custom that the Commons must not increase items of expenditure, and since the cabinet would (and at times does) make any reduction in such expenditures a question of confidence, the discussions in the Commons have completely changed their nature. No detailed deliberation is devoted to the expenditures of the government; formal motions, for example, to reduce the salary of the Secretary of Foreign Affairs are made the occasion for a discussion of general policy. Thus this procedure produces publicity, rather than deliberation. And this publicity is not of much value, because of the way in which the government keeps its accounts. But, as Ramsay Muir has pointed out, "Even if the accounts of the Departments were presented in the clearest form, the exercise of any effective control over their working must be impossible, so long as the House of Commons pursues its present methods of dealing with the Estimates. As a rule, twenty days in the parliamentary year are devoted to the Estimates of a score of Departments, some of which spend tens of millions of pounds, and have enormous staffs performing very varied functions." A parliamentary committee which studied the working of this system reported in 1918 that "there has not been a single instance in the last twenty-five years when the House of Commons, by its own direct action, has reduced, on financial grounds, any estimate submitted to it. . . . So far as the direct effective control of proposals for expenditure is concerned, it would be true to say that if the estimates were never presented and the Committee of Supply never set up, there would be no noticeable difference. Indeed as large part of the estimates are formally passed, year after year under the closure at the end of the session without even the appearance of discussion; while every estimate, whether closured or not, emerges from the Parliamentary process in precisely the same shape as it entered it, yet it cannot be contended that there is never an occasion in any year, or under any head, on which proposals for expenditure could with advantage be reviewed and amended." In order to remedy this situation, the parliamentary committee recommended the setting up of several Standing Committees on Estimates, and other authorities have followed it in urging such a change. The actual Standing Committee on Estimates which was organized afterwards did not have the powers demanded by the Select Committee, namely to recommend the reduction or elimination of items which did not affect policy, to hear evidence of the administrative departments, and to secure the advice of accountancy experts. Nor was their work (backed by the power of the Commons when sitting as a Committee on Supply) extended to the point of disallowing minor budget items contrary to the wishes of the cabinet without such action becoming a question of confidence. It is clear that apart from this last provision, relating to the cabinet's right to demand a favorable vote or resign, these recommendations envisage a procedure modelled upon the American plan. Whether they can be fitted into the English pattern of government by a cabinet responsible to Parliament appears arguable. French experience would suggest an affirmative answer, particularly since it is borne out by experience in such constitutional monarchies as Belgium, the Netherlands, and Sweden. It is, of course, not only a question of parliamentary committees. Indeed, American experience with such committees was rather deplorable as long as authority for making the appropriations was widely scattered among different committees and numerous appropriation bills. But these difficulties have now in a large measure been remedied by the Budget and Accounting Act (1921). Since that important enactment, the federal government has a comprehensive budget prepared by the Bureau of the Budget and presented to Congress by the President; this budget is then considered in conformity to its great divisions, corresponding to the organization of the government, and embodied in a series of related appropriation acts. Under the procedure which at present prevails in the American Congress, all appropriations have to be reported by the Committee on Appropriations, which deliberates upon them after a preliminary survey by its subcommittees corresponding to the various administrative departments. Whenever legislation is enacted which entails appropriations, such appropriations have to be passed upon by the Committee on Appropriations as well as by the committee concerned with that particular type of legislation. The reason is that such appropriations must be considered in relation to all other appropriations. Such a procedure naturally entails many delays, and by contrast English procedure is praised for its dispatch. There is nothing startling about this contrast; it is merely a special example of the technical efficiency of power when it is fully concentrated. W. F. Willoughby has rightly pointed out that such concentration of power is at variance with the American governmental system. Moreover, he feels that the evils which were associated with legislative determination of appropriations in the past have been largely due, not so much to the possession by the legislature of such power over appropriations, as to the lack of any definite and comprehensive program such as is now provided by the annual budget message of the President. It was, in other words, a question of redressing the distribution of power over appropriations so as to produce a clear division between the function of formulating a comprehensive program, which properly belongs to the administrative head of the government, and the function of deliberating upon this program and readjusting it in terms of an emerging compromise over major policies of the major party, a function which properly belongs to Congress. As already remarked, it is, however, significant that even countries with executive establishments dependent upon parliamentary support, such as that of France, have developed committees specially charged with the supervision and control of governmental finances. In fact, these countries which adopted parliamentary government under the influence of the ancient slogan about the power of the purse have been inclined to look upon such committees as the very core of parliamentary prerogative.

The French finance committee.—The French Committees on Finances (*Commission des Finances*) in both the Chamber and Senate occupy a very central position in the parliamentary system of that country. In recent years, a great deal of the criticism of the parliamentary system has been focused on these all-powerful committees, and the role they have played in connection with the budgetary and financial difficulties. As Joseph Barthélemy has pointed out in his remarkable study of the committees in the Chamber, even the physical facilities at the disposal of these committees, from a separate room in the building to special stationery, symbolize the preëminence of these bodies. They are the queens among parliamentary committees. Curiously enough, these committees seem often to be the center of parliamentary opposition to the government, in spite of the system of proportional representation which would lead one to assume that the majority supporting the government in the Chamber and the Senate is reproduced in the Finance Committee. Barthélemy has given an acute analysis of this situation. The leading position of the presidents and reporters of all committees (as discussed above, ¶ 6), but more particularly the Finance Committee, alters the situation considerably, because these obviously cannot be elected on a proportional basis. It could, of course, be provided, that such presidencies and reports be in the hands of members of the majority, as is in fact the case in the United States, but in France the chairmen (presidents) of committees often acquire a quasi-permanent position. Thus M. Malvy has been the president of the Finance Committee for seven years, no matter what the majority supporting the government. When, in 1932, M. Tardieu was Prime Minister (President of the Council), he meant to govern with a center-right coalition in the Chamber, but the Finance Committee was presided over and its views represented before the Chamber by two members of the left, MM. Malvy and Lamoureux. It is hard to disagree with Barthélemy when he remarks: "The committees which ought to play the game of the majority in confidence with the government become the centers of intrigue against the majority, and of maneuvres against the government." What is more, the fluidity of French parliamentary groups often brings it about that a member delegated to a committee by such a group, but belonging to one of its wings, does not follow the majority of this group in relation to the government. Barthélemy goes so far as to comment, "Under the French system the best of the majority are in the government, while the best of the opposition are in the Finance Committee." Yet, it would be fallacious to assume, as is sometimes done, that the chairman and the reporter exceed the finance minister in power; if the finance minister is a man capable of real leadership, he readily prevails, as the examples of Léon Say, Rouvier, Caillaux, Cheron, and Germain-Martin can prove. If, in turn, one of these able and skilled finance experts becomes later the head of the Finance Committee of either house, he is apt to be predominant. This has been the case of M. Joseph Caillaux in recent years, whose commanding position has recurrently obliged ministers to retrench their stand. The events of the last few years should, however, not be taken as very typical; the world economic depression has brought in its train in France as everywhere else novel problems of unprecedented magnitude, particularly in connection with unemployment. Here social philosophies fiercely clash, and the progressive leaders in the Finance Committee have been inclined to look upon the situation in a different light than the more conservative majorities in the Chamber, which desired a reduction in taxes, and maintenance of the stability of the currency. Barthélemy whose heart is with the latter groups strongly criticizes the conduct of the work of the Chamber Committee, while the work of the Senate Committee he views with favor, though it raises many of the same procedural questions. It is necessary, though exceedingly difficult, to detach these questions from one's preferences in matters of legislation and appropriations. In keeping with the general practice of the French Parliament, the budget comes before the whole House in the form which the Finance Committee gave it. It is hardly surprising that this should recently have led to the Finance Committee's attempt to substitute its own budget for that proposed by the ministry, and finally to report a compromise between the two. The French have always retained a single budget law, the *loi des finances,* which is reported by the general reporter, in addition to a series of separate budgets for important services, each reported by a separate reporter. Barthélemy lists thirty-four such separate budgets for 1933. The general report on the finance bill undertakes to coördinate these separate budgets. While originally undertaken with a view to the sound purpose of more effective scrutiny of the government's budget proposals, this division of labor has gradually led to a deplorable lack of coördination. The separate reports are not the result of any discussion and deliberation of the committee, but the work of the particular reporter. Since such reports have come to be looked upon as rungs in the ladder toward a ministerial post, they have gradually grown in bulk, until now some of these reports are huge quarto volumes. M. Archimbaud, who has reported the budget for the colonies since 1921, recently brought in a document numbering 450 pages. Another member, a reporter for public education, undertook to discuss the state of poetry in the twentieth century. It is obvious that such reports have no ascertainable relation to the work of the committee, and if it held one hundred and thirty sessions in 1932-1933, they were devoted to the general framework of the budget. Whether such a division of labor is undesirable is hard to say. After all, the general budget is most deserving of thorough discussion, and the special reports constitute, without a doubt, a mine of detailed information on the conduct of French administration, in spite of occasional *extravaganzas.* Cases are quite frequent where dangerous administrative abuses have been attacked in such reports and later remedied. To restrain such criticism, administrative officials exert themselves considerably to accommodate the reporter, to furnish him all the information he asks for, and to win him as a collaborator who might speak for the administrative needs in the Chamber—a process not unknown in the United States. Such tendencies are naturally enhanced by a member's reporting the same budget year after year; they lead to a *camaraderie* of the specialists in the administration and in Parliament, both rather permanently concerned in the particular affairs, maintaining a certain solidarity against the minister, the Parliament at large, and the public. But this situation should not be so overstated that the reporter appears as the man in control. For, after all, there remain considerable executive functions entirely beyond his reach, and his budgetary report is only a small part of his parliamentary and representative activities. Nothing shows this more clearly than the appearance, in recent years, of technical advisers to the Finance Committee (as well as certain other committees) who are permanent officials. It was mentioned before that proposals for the reform of financial procedure in the House of Commons envisaged such expert advice. The French Chamber Finance Committee employs six at present (1933). As in the United States Congress the Appropriations Committee, so in the French Chamber the Finance Committee has jurisdiction concerning all matters involving expenditures. The proposed creation of a separate committee on financial legislation has so far not materialized. Although, strictly speaking, the committee should not concern itself with anything but the financial aspects, it is inevitably drawn into a consideration of the relative merits of various bills, since a discussion of their financial merits is inseparably linked with at least a consideration of their importance. The French practice of advisory as well as basic reports, noted above, facilitates such consideration by the Finance Committee. Nevertheless, the burden of work is enormous, with the result that discussion in the committee is cut short by tactical considerations, and considerable delays are occasioned. These seem particularly unfortunate when they prevent parliamentary deliberation from being effective. Contrary to the rules which provide distribution of the budget report well in advance, the committee often asks the Chamber to consider matters on which no report has become available, or has just been distributed a few hours before. This evil is aggravated by the practice of legislative riders in the general budget law. In recent years, this committee has also commenced to unseat ministries by refusing consent to important measures (see above, p. 404). This tendency is closely related to the previously noted inclination of this committee to substitute its own budget for that of the government, as has already been frankly admitted on the floor of the Chamber. If such a tendency became dominant, the ministry of finance might just as well be abolished. Actually, there can be very little doubt that all the deliberation on financial matters has passed from the Chamber (and the Senate) to their respective committees, if not already beyond. At one point, Barthélemy goes so far as to exclaim: "The leftist group (in the committee) deliberates, the committee decides, the government follows." Just the same, he does not wish to abolish the committee, as others do. He rightly remarks that after all the committee is a mirror, even if a broken mirror, of the Chamber, that a measure of unanimity in the people would express itself readily enough through such a committee, and that the committee merely reflects the confusion prevailing in the Parliament as a whole. It also seems that the lack of really effective leadership on the part of the government has given a great impetus to the Finance Committee's strength. Recent governments have apparently been very slow in submitting budgets, particularly the general *loi des finances*. But are not these troubles at least in part the result of too much divided responsibility? If one reads the many discussions on this subject in France today, he definitely gains the impression that everybody is blaming everybody else for the troublous times in the hope that the accused will try to do something to better them. The problem of the Finance Committee cannot be separated, one may agree with Barthélemy, from the whole problem of parliamentary government, and, one might add, of constitutional government. It is a question of devising a procedure which will insure a competent decision after a sufficiently mature deliberation. Competence can be contributed primarily by the permanent administrative staff, deliberation and supervision by a limited group of people representing the major divisions in the community, decision by a large representative assembly. The French as well as the American system contains all the major elements of a sound solution, but their working is encumbered by a series of minor maladjustments. One does not abandon an automobile, because it will not move under too heavy a load; it is a matter of either building a larger car, or dividing the load between two or three. The problem of the French Committee seems to be very much of that order.

Administrative control.—The discussion of the last two paragraphs has shown how intimately the problem of administrative control and supervision is bound up with the fiscal problem. It is nevertheless distinct. Both in the United States and in France (as well as in many other countries), the committee system, quite apart from the question of appropriations, is an essential tool of Parliament in controlling the administration. It is natural, therefore, that voices should have arisen in England demanding a similar system of standing committees to restrain the "bureaucracy." In an earlier part of this volume (see Chap. XV) it has been shown that many techniques exist for making officials responsible for their conduct. Under modern conditions, parliamentary supervision has had a very strong appeal. Here were persons well acquainted with the particular matter in hand through their legislative activity; why should not they see to it that these (and all other) laws be faithfully executed? It is hard to deny the good sense of such a plan, and particularly in the earlier phases of the movement for constitutional government such control seemed wholly beneficial. The deep-seated suspicion with which the average man in France and the United States viewed the "bureaucracy" served as a powerful drive toward the establishment of such control mechanisms. But as the century wore on, and parties began to appear more and more distinctly behind the imaginary outline of a united people represented by one single Parliament, it was discovered that such control by Parliament and parliamentary committees was, after all, control by parliamentarians. Such a system of control offered to these individuals and the party groups behind them opportunities of pressure which could be turned to quite different account than the protection of the public's interest against administrators. The evils of patronage, corruption in connection with governmental contracts, nepotism, and so forth, made their appearance. Parliamentary control soon began to look like parliamentary tyranny. Factionalism was introduced into the administrative services, with many an influential parliamentarian having a group of henchmen in various ministries who looked to him for promotion in return for assistance offered him in the promotion of various more or less legitimate interests. The difficulty lies in part in the intangible quality of such control. Unlike the preparation of a bill or a budget, we have here conversations, questions, a certain atmosphere of either hostile criticism or collegial collaboration—all matters which are subject to a good deal of manipulation and diplomacy. This setting is further emphasized by the lack of publicity (in many cases) which raises very fundamental problems (see ¶ 11). In spite of all these troublesome complications, detailed parliamentary control seems essential if the administrative services are to be held in check. Reliance cannot safely be placed upon control of the cabinet at the top alone. There are many minor abuses and irregularities which certainly do not justify the ousting of a cabinet. Such developments can readily be reported to the plenary session, and thus given adequate publicity. What is more, the existence of such a watchdog puts the officials on their guard. They will readily anticipate the reaction of a parliamentary committee. It might, of course, be argued that an entirely separate body of quasi-judicial persons should be entrusted with this task, so as to forestall the development of the various forms of collusion of which mention has been made. But such a procedure would further complicate an already top-heavy structure, and it would deprive the members of legislatures of a most valuable school in which to learn about the difficulties of administering a certain body of laws. Nor is it apparent why such a group should not be likewise subject to the temptations which at present beguile legislators. The great value of all such control is readily apparent to any student of contemporary dictatorships, which are frequently accused of corruption (see below, Chap. XXV, ¶¶ 10, 11). This is often merely the result of inadequate supervision as there is no one around to do the supervising. If one studies the fierce techniques the Prussian kings adopted in order to cope with this evil—techniques which did not outlast in effectiveness the reigns of their institutors, Frederick William I and Frederick the Great—he appreciates even more distinctly the difficulties which lie hidden here. Yet effective and reasonably efficient administration is of paramount value in modern life, and hence parliamentary work might be justified on that score alone. In order to exercise this function of administrative control, parliamentary committees have gradually evolved a large number of practices, such as hearings for taking evidence from officials as well as private persons, or direct inspection of the service (often involving the much contested right to look into the files). In France one also finds the reporter system for the purpose of securing information. Through these procedures the many highly technical and complicated activities of modern governmental administration are brought up for discussion in a small circle of fairly well-informed men and women. Points of controversy can be thrashed out and a better understanding reached of the manifold activities of a modern administration. It is, for that reason, understandable that ministers have occasionally seen fit to resign after they encountered a hostile reception in the particular parliamentary committee, as happened to Briand in 1922, and to Loucheur in 1925. In each case, the committee merely served as an indicator of the drift of parliamentary opinion, and allowed the minister to gauge and anticipate the parliamentary reaction. If, on the other hand, the committee should be inclined to take a course at variance with the sentiment of the house, it is always possible and highly probable that the minister will appeal the matter. The whole range of activities of committees involved in carrying out their supervision of administrative activities remains, however, geared to the legislative and deliberative function of parliaments; it is remote from the representative function. In the United States, where the cabinet and through it administrative officials do not depend upon the confidence of the assembly, Congress has developed the system of investigating committees to look into and in due course to make public whatever abuses it or one of its committees may believe to exist. The impending threat of such an investigating committee fulfills somewhat the same role which the threat of a scandal involving the support of the cabinet entails in England. It brings to the attention of the public, preferably preceding an election, matters which will discredit the "ins." Such committees are naturally most likely to be appointed when the President has lost his majority in one of the Houses of Congress. In England, Royal Commissions of Inquiry are looked upon in a somewhat similar light, but since they are appointed by the Crown, that is, the government in power, they are more likely to look into areas of social controversy than into the administrative services themselves.

Control of foreign affairs.—A distinct set of problems is found in the realm of foreign affairs. The English Parliament has been very slow to enter into this field which was for a long time looked upon as a "prerogative" of the Crown. To be sure, the clash over the Bulgarian atrocities between the humanitarian principles of Gladstonian liberalism and Disraeli's skillful diplomacy afforded Gladstone the major plank for his famous Midlothian campaign, though the policy of collaboration with the Turk was blandly continued after he entered office. The shock of thus seeing problems of imperial concern carried before the multitude and building popular appeal upon it served as a considerable lesson to the British Foreign Office; henceforth they carefully guarded their secrets against Parliament. This system culminated in the complex situation preceding the World War (see above Chap. XIX, ¶ 6), when fear of the parliamentary reaction induced Sir Edward Grey to pursue a more secret policy than had been followed for a century. France also carefully avoided parliamentary control of foreign affairs; the two parliamentary committees on the subject were beginning to build up a measure of surveillance, but remained highly secretive themselves. Since the United States did not bother about evolving an active foreign policy, but merely drifted along with the aid of a few "policies," such as were supposedly contained in the "Monroe Doctrine" and the principle of the "Open Door in China," sporadic attempts by Presidents and Secretaries of State did not invite any measure of effective control. Hence not until after the World War do we find anywhere a vigorous parliamentary participation in Foreign Affairs. The general disaster of the World War, the establishment of the League of Nations, the general outburst of democratic and pacific enthusiasm, all aided in lending color to various efforts to realize the promise which had been held out by Wilson's point (one of the ill-fated fourteen) about the abolition of secret diplomacy, and the substitution of "open covenants openly arrived at." As a technical device, the French and American system of a special committee made a strong appeal. In England it was ardently advocated by the Union of Democratic Foreign Policy, in Germany a special article of the constitution was devoted to the establishment of a standing committee on foreign affairs, in Holland, in Sweden, in Norway, in Czechoslovakia, everywhere standing committees on foreign affairs were set up. The French committees in both the Senate and the Chamber became more vocal. But if the idea had at first been that parliamentary control would aid in making international relations smoother, the activities of the United States Senate Foreign Relations Committee in connection with the Peace Treaty and the League Covenant therein contained might have given a suitable warning. It was soon discovered that everywhere parliaments and their committees were inclined to outdo their ministers in insisting upon national "interest" and national "honor." The nationalist reaction first entrenched itself in Germany in the Foreign Affairs Committee of the Reichstag, membership in which gave to the deputies the air of "being in the know." In the French Parliament, nationalist elements likewise managed to dominate the scene in the plenary sessions as well as in the committees, and the more conciliatory policy of Briand met its first as well as its last serious defeat in these committees. Even in small and pacific Netherlands the able Foreign Minister van Karnebeek was forced out by Parliament, because he had made a conciliatory treaty with the Belgian government concerning the Scheldt which supposedly violated national "interests." Another almost insuperable difficulty appeared as a result of large Communist parties in many of these parliaments which, on the basis of the proportional principle, had a right to seats on these committees. They recurrently raised suspicions of collaborating with Moscow (the government of the Soviet Union, as well as the Third International) and were therefore felt not to be entitled to any confidential information. Sometimes this difficulty was met by forming a more informal inner circle of members of the committee who received the really confidential information. But whatever the attempted solution, nothing could make more evident the deep fissures that were running through modern nations across the well-nigh unbridgeable gulfs which separate these nations from each other. At times, an observer might be tempted bitterly to remark that the only covenants openly to be arrived at are declarations of war. Experience renders doubtful the utility of parliamentary deliberation in the field of foreign affairs. Perhaps it is time to return to the notion of the makers of the American Constitution of a small representative council of long tenure, such as the Senate was originally meant to be.

The problem of publicity.—The parliamentary control of foreign affairs squarely raises the issue of publicity. It is a question which has much bearing upon the whole system of parliamentary committees. Committee meetings are secret, either wholly or in part, and many of the most serious attacks are levelled at this feature of the system. How central the issue may be considered, is suggested by the work of Bentham, who opens his classical *Essay on Political Tactics* with a discussion of publicity. "Before entering into the detail of the operations of the assembly, let us place at the head of its regulations the fittest law for securing the public confidence, and causing it constantly to advance towards the end of its institution. This law is that of publicity." Clearly, committees as ordinarily constituted violate this law thoroughly, except perhaps committees on foreign affairs, for Bentham would allow three exceptions to the law, one of which are situations where it would favor the projects of an enemy. It is, therefore, quite natural that the committee system should have been attacked on this score. Many prominent students of politics including Woodrow Wilson have unqualifiedly condemned the secrecy of committee deliberations. Robert Luce, after citing from Wilson's writings, asserts on the contrary that "the complete justification of privacy is that its absence would enure to the injury of the public business." He adduces the privacy of cabinet meetings in England and America, as well as the relations between doctor and patient, clergyman and parishioner, lawyer and client. It may be doubted whether such arguments meet the core of Wilson's objections to secrecy. "Legislation, as we nowadays conduct it, is not conducted in the open. It is not thrashed out in open debate upon the floors of our assemblies. It is, on the contrary, framed, digested, and concluded in committee rooms. It is in committee rooms that legislation not desired by the interests dies. . . . There is not enough debate of it in the open house, in most cases, to disclose the real meaning of the proposals made. . . . There is not any legitimate privacy about matters of government. Government must, if it is to be pure and correct in its processes, be absolutely public in everything that affects it." The last phrases are evidently an overstatement, but the objections to the secrecy of the deliberative process of legislation are not met by merely pointing out such exaggeration. No one has stated more forcefully the arguments in favor of making all deliberative transactions public than did Jeremy Bentham. It has been mentioned before (see above, ¶ 1) that at the time Bentham considered the subject, the English Parliament was just emerging from its previous practice of carefully guarding the secrecy of parliamentary proceedings. Bentham himself, in surveying "the state of things in England," noted the contrast between the as yet unaltered rules designed to insure strict secrecy and the actual practice: "It is to these fortunate crimes that England is indebted for her escape from an aristocratic government resembling that of Venice." What, then, are the arguments Bentham advances on behalf of complete publicity of parliamentary proceedings? The first purpose is "to constrain the members of the assembly to perform their duty," the second "to secure the confidence of the people, and their assent to the measures of the legislature," the third "to enable the governors to know the wishes of the governed," the fourth "to enable the electors to act from knowledge," the fifth "to amuse the public." Now it will be readily seen that all these objectives relate to the representative, rather than the deliberative function of elected assemblies. The failure to differentiate between these two functions leads and has led thinkers in the past to argue for or against privacy and secrecy. But if the question be posited in terms of the double function of elected assemblies, it will become apparent that a measure of privacy is indicated by the nature of the deliberative function, while it is inimical to the representative function. Robert Luce undoubtedly voices the experience of many conscientious representatives when he writes: "When a man thinks his words are to be repeated, he has an eye to the ultimate consumer. Instead of talking solely to those who are to make the immediate decision, he frequently talks with remote effects in mind. This would turn a public committee conference into a sparring spectacle for personal or party advantage." But, of course, elected assemblies should have an eye to the ultimate consumer, Bentham would reply. The conflict of ideas cannot, therefore, be resolved, except in terms of an explicit recognition of the double function of elected assemblies and the consequent need for differentiating their techniques accordingly. A measure of privacy for deliberations should be provided, and the committee system provides that opportunity. But the ultimate value of publicity should likewise be recognized, and public debates, either of the whole house or some of its committees, be provided for. This is in fact what we found elected assemblies to be striving for. The American Congress, the English Parliament, the French Parliament, all provide for public debates as well as private (secret) deliberations. In England parliamentary procedure proper recognizes such privacy most sparingly, but all descriptive accounts of the English system point to one conclusion: the compactness of English party organization permits all essential deliberations to be carried on among party leaders outside of Parliament proper, the "ins" in the clubs and the cabinet, the "outs" in the clubs alone. Elsewhere, party organization being less authoritarian and the leadership less effective, much deliberation and the compromise which results from it is carried on in the committees.

A glimpse at the caucus.—In the United States the problem of the "secret" party conclave is not unknown, either. In fact, a great deal of controversy has surrounded the development of the caucus in the American Congress. It is significant, and in keeping with British experience, that the caucus should always have made its appearance in conjunction with strong presidential leadership, such as that of Jefferson and Wilson. But Luce asserts that the caucus is rather insignificant in American state legislatures, and more particularly in Massachusetts it has not been employed. In the United States Senate it does not play a significant role either, according to Luce, and the same fact is attested to by the absence of even the word from L. Rogers' index to his volume on the Senate. Perhaps this weakness of the caucus in the Senate is directly related to the weakness of presidential leadership in the Senate. The caucus was somewhat strengthened in the House through the revolt against the Speaker in 1909-1910 (see above, Chap. XXI, ¶ 9), but on the whole the privacy of committee proceedings in Congress has made the caucus a preliminary rather than a decisive stage. If genuine deliberation could no longer take place in these committees, the caucus might conceivably become increasingly the forum where actual deliberations would take place. Deliberation with its need for privacy will retreat to party conclaves, if the regular legislatures do not provide suitable opportunities for the thrashing out of questions involving much technical detail. The Senate has several times debated this subject, and in the course of these debates it has been stated that caucuses have rarely, if ever, undertaken to bind members to any particular action; their main power lies in the part they play in filling committee memberships and other such personnel questions, and in their ironing out dissensions over policy matters bearing upon party fortunes, particularly as they are related to presidential elections. These are matters of great political importance which do not come before committees, nor could they be considered in the presence of the opposition party. It is not readily apparent how national party organizations could be held together without some effort at concerted action of their national representatives. What is detrimental to the prestige of parliamentary institutions is the tendency of parliamentarians nonchalantly to allow the committees to take complete direction. The pressure of the mass of modern activity is, after all, the main explanation of that tendency. Each member of the assembly is so busy as the member of one or more of its committees that he would just as soon forget about the rest. All over the world committee work has been crowding out general debate in open session. And what time committee work would not take, the ever-increasing electorate with ever more efficient means of communication would absorb. The thousands of letters, telegrams, and telephone calls which many American Senators get at certain crucial moments are merely the peaks of this ever-rising curve of public business. Is it a fever curve? When the substance of our activities is mounting, we become indifferent to procedure; a very busy man is apt to be less polite than a man of leisure. All this is widely admitted; reports on parliamentary procedure in the United States, in England, and elsewhere are full of such observations. Impatient men are ready to pronounce the breakdown of the system. In order to get efficiency, they would scrap all publicity and revert to the complete secrecy of bureaucratic direction. Russia, Italy, Germany have gone that way. In terms of Bentham's five objectives of publicity very widespread governmental propaganda is proposed to realize the second of these objectives, a limited, though quite numerous party following acting as the voice of the people is to realize the third, parades and the like are to amuse the public, modern masses being less intellectual, more emotional. The first and fourth objectives have disappeared with the disappearance of the elected assemblies themselves.

Conclusion.—But perhaps the sword of propaganda is made of lead, the party following disintegrates as dissenters are done away with (Trotzki, Roehm, and so forth) and becomes mute, and parades turn out to be less amusing in the long run than parliamentary debates (since parades are always the same, whereas the argument varies). If experience should thus prove that the dictatorial alternatives to public debates in representative, deliberative assemblies are weak and temporary substitutes, and that the resulting actions and decisions are more frequently wrong than when they are the outcome of public deliberations (and it is our contention that the facts and observations of political science point that way), renewed efforts will probably be made in those countries which have abandoned them to organize them anew. Certain reports allege that such efforts are already under way in the Soviet Union. Whether that be true or not, the existing remnants of public deliberation, such as party congresses and popular plebiscites, are intrinsically capable of such development, of course. But neither the "Parliaments" of Cromwell, nor the revolutionary assemblies of France were, speaking merely of the past, capable of such a transformation. Nor were the assemblies which replaced them at once designed to meet the standards of Bentham. Whatever the drift in those countries (see below, Chap. XXV, 13), it would seem that some of the more mature parliamentary bodies are evolving toward a fairly equilibrated balance between their representative and their deliberative functions and the techniques required for the realization of both. Change should be directed toward a further development along these lines, with a greater measure of privacy indicated for the British, and greater measure of publicity for the American and French Parliaments. If at least adequate records could be kept for the committees dealing with financial matters, which would be open for study by the public (which nowadays means interested groups and scholars) after a suitable length of time, say six months, and a larger amount of open debate be provided for, in case of disagreement within the committee, much would be gained. If, furthermore, certain specially qualified persons could be admitted upon special request after, perhaps, swearing not to publish what they had heard, a suitable corrective of present abuses might thus be provided.

Whether these or other such changes be thought desirable roads of reform, the analysis of experience up to date has, it is hoped, shown that the representative and the deliberative functions of elected assemblies are fairly distinct, and that such assemblies are responding to real needs when they differentiate their techniques accordingly. If men could deliberate without thinking of the reactions of those who are to elect or rather reëlect them, such differentiation would be unnecessary.

CHAPTER XXIII

THE PRESS AS THE FOURTH ESTATE IN THE REPRESENTATIVE SCHEME

1. *Introductory.*—2. *The beginnings of the press as an instrument of opposition, particularly in England down to the end of the eighteenth century.*—3. *Toward an "independent" press: England.*—4. *France: the press as an agent of revolution.*—5. *The problems of the American law of libel: no restraint.*—6. *The political effects of a commercialized press.*—7. *The forces behind the mass press.*—8. *A comparative survey of the nature of the modern press in certain leading countries.*—9. *The English press.*—10. *The American press.*—11. *The French press.*—12. *The German press under Empire and Republic.*—13. *Press under contemporary dictatorships and propaganda.*—14. *Governmental control and censorship.*—15. *Conclusion: judicial restraints.*

Introductory.—When we speak of "the people," which is back of parliaments, we may think of a vague mass of unassorted individuals, but from the point of view of the member of parliament this public is represented by two readily identifiable and already institutionalized sets, the press and the interest groups. Of these, the press, in all its shades, represents opinion to such an extent that as a forum for the discussion of public questions it has entirely outstripped parliaments. It is significant that for some time parliamentary debates have not found their way into the press as they used to. The London *Times* is perhaps unique in giving at least very extensive extracts from parliamentary debates. In the United States speeches of individual Senators and Representatives, and in France and other countries the discourses of ministers, are fully reported. But the debates as such do not mold public opinion. According to Charles A. Beard, when President Hoover insisted that Congress give him the right to raise or lower tariff rates, his appeal appeared on the first page of the newspapers, but arguments made in the Senate against his demand, speeches of the highest quality and understanding, based upon careful study of the circumstances, received relatively little consideration. In fact, the most searching of all these counterblasts received almost no attention at all. This is, as we have seen, due partly to the increasingly representative position of the President. But when considering the press in its relation to government, we come to appreciate that the shift in representative quality is at least in part traceable to the much greater "news value" of the President. There is only one President, whereas there are many Senators and Representatives. Consequently, from the news reporter's point of view any slight move on the part of the President is worthy of attention. In spite of the profound impact of the newspapers and the press in general upon government and politics, political science has tended to neglect the press. Some years ago Walter Lippmann called attention to the fact that political science, as expounded to future business men, lawyers, public officials, and citizens at large, paid little or no attention to the sources of popular information. The will of the people was treated as if unrelated to the information available; news gathering was not considered a part of the political process. Actually the emergence of constitutional government, and in particular the crystallization of the systems of popular representation as we know them, are inextricably interwoven with the growth of the modern press. Without it constitutional government is unimaginable. Thomas Jefferson dramatized this view by saying that if he were confronted with the choice of having a government and no newspapers or newspapers and no government, he would have no hesitation in preferring the newspapers; as an ardent believer in restraining the government, he realized that it could not be done without independent newspapers. The press remains, of course, subject to governmental regulations of varying scope. Such regulations may help to fit the papers into the institutional pattern as well as into the economic organization and physical environment of the community. The size of the United States, for example, produces a press markedly different from that of England. The literary preoccupations of the continental press are not unconnected with the governmental censorship to which that press has been subjected for long periods of time. In spite of these contrasts, there is a considerable measure of uniformity. This has been enhanced in recent decades by the levelling impact of technical processes, such as the telegraph, and the general impact of modern economic forces implied in large scale production. All in all, the press is an important concomitant of political processes in modern times, and we must trace its development and describe its present status. But in doing so we must not forget that we are dealing only with a part of the press, which contains many other elements. A recent inquiry at Harvard showed that a majority of undergraduates were taking the Boston *American,* a Hearst organ. Someone, disturbed by the political implications of this discovery, inquired into the reasons for their doing so. It was found that in the opinion of the students the Boston *American* had the best comic strips, and, as for the rest, they did not care.

The beginnings of the press as an instrument of opposition, particularly in England down to the end of the eighteenth century.—The medieval constitutional order passed away before the powers divided under it could avail themselves of the new opportunities which the press offered. The tremendous outburst of pamphlet literature, of which the writings of Martin Luther stand as the most lasting monument, heralded the coming of the press. Even more important were the regular "news letters" which had made their appearance still earlier. In the course of the sixteenth century these became more and more elaborate. Wealthy merchants particularly, like the Fuggers of Augsburg, organized a regular service. Printed periodical publications containing news reports and opinions did not get under way until the seventeenth century. In 1609 two printed weeklies made their appearance, one in Augsburg and another in Strassburg, probably the oldest regular periodicals. Soon after, another one appeared in Leipzig. While these were independent commercial enterprises, in England and later in France the governments, which at that time maintained a strict control over all printed matter, usually had their hand in it. The weekly news started in England, and in 1622 was devoted to what purported to be foreign news. "The transition from the spasmodic series of reports from abroad published before 1622 . . . to the not altogether regular issues of the newspaper is easy and natural. At the start it had nothing in common with what we understand by a newspaper today except the fact that it was a continuous enterprise." Thus Shaaber summarizes the beginnings of the newspaper. Nine years later, in 1631, the first French newspaper, called the *Gazette*, was started at the instigation of Richelieu, who granted it a monopoly in the distribution of news. Since he was able to control this paper, he was subjecting the entire process of distributing news to governmental supervision. In a sense, this system has continued, not only in France, but in other large European countries, down to the present day. The great news agencies, the Agence Havas in France, Wolff's Telegraphenbureau in Germany, and Stefani in Italy have, unlike the Associated Press in the United States and the Reuter Agency in England, always been subject to governmental supervision, rather than under the influence of the commercial groups controlling the enterprise (see below, ¶ 4). The first genuine challenge to the system of governmental direction occurred in the course of the English Civil War. It is natural that during that period when Parliament and the Crown were fighting for supremacy, the parliamentary party should demand freedom of the press along with other instruments of popular opposition. Yet when the Puritans came into power they in turn commenced to oppress the opposition, and Parliament repeatedly enacted measures for the suppression of what seemed to it objectionable publications. Still, Milton's ardent appeal for liberty and the unsatisfactory experience which the official licenser reported at the end of one year (1649) led to a certain leniency. Cromwell, to be sure, could not suffer an independent press, but his natural tendency was in that direction. After the Restoration, suppression once more became the order of the day. Charles II adopted the policy of Richelieu, and licensed the publishing of an official newspaper by L'Estrange, the *London Gazette*. This same gentleman also acted as censor and prosecutor of unlicensed publications. Nevertheless the Whigs continued to publish, particularly after 1679 when the licensing law was repealed. James II, on his accession, attempted a revival of rigid censorship, but the developments overtook him. After the Glorious Revolution the publishing of newspapers became more general. A series of Intelligencers made their appearance. Partisanship availed itself to an ever-increasing degree of the opportunity the press offered, particularly as the public acquired the taste for constant news. The literary talents of Addison, Swift, Bolingbroke, and Steele were all placed at the disposal of this rising tide of journalistic effort. The opposition party in particular derived considerable benefit from the constant agitation in the daily press. Yet all these Intelligencers, Journals, and the like lacked the institutionalized security which the modern press commands. The lack of representative opposition and of power of the press during the entire eighteenth century is indicated by their not being allowed to report parliamentary debates. Privacy of debate was still considered the privilege of the aristocracy which was directing public affairs.

Toward an "independent" press: England.—The press in England during the eighteenth and the first half of the nineteenth century was essentially partisan. There can be little doubt that it helped materially in holding a parliamentary opposition together. It was in this period that the reporting of news was merged with interpretation and opinion in one paper, and to these were added literary and other items. It was natural that this should have been so, for it helped to secure readers who might be indifferent to the political controversies. During this entire period, however, and down to 1855, the so-called stamp tax handicapped those who might want to start new papers. It thus made it easier for the governing classes to regulate the contents of the press. Since the party controversies in England flowed in more or less established channels this handicap was not seriously objected to until the time of the French Revolution. But after English radicalism got under way, a movement, it will be remembered, which was directed against the aristocratic nature of English politics in general, the restrictions imposed by the stamp tax as well as by the libel law and the import duties on paper (abolished in 1861) were seriously attacked. And in spite of these restrictions, radicalism was able to carry forward its struggle for the reform of Parliament, that is, the electoral system, considerably aided by the press. After all, the financial restrictions could be overcome by sufficient zeal. The libel law which during the Napoleonic era had been interpreted to mean that to criticize the ills of the electoral system was "to utter seditious words against the matchless constitution" could not well be used against the revelations of outright scandal and corruption, nor could it cope with the fervent pen of an artist like Charles Dickens (after 1836) who was a trained journalist. It is therefore not surprising to find that Cobden's famous struggle against the tariff on grain (1838-1846) was already completely fought outside Parliament and through the press. Nor is it any cause for wonder that in the decades which followed the restrictions were removed one after the other. After 1860 the press entered upon its new career and commenced to rival Parliament as a platform of political discussion.

France: the press as an agent of revolution.—In France, where governmental restrictions persisted up to the Revolution and were revived by Napoleon, the opposition nevertheless availed itself of the press, which was largely subterranean, as is the opposition press in Germany today. On the whole, the periodic upheavals in France during the nineteenth century were accompanied by extensive changes in the position of the press, which on its side took a considerable part in the bringing about of these changes. The revolution of 1830, for example, is generally believed to have been maneuvered by a group of newspaper editors. At the critical moment, according to Artz, in

July 1830, the journalists met first. This is not surprising, since the first of the oppressive ordinances that the government had decided upon forbade any publication without governmental authorization. The opposition journalists asked Thiers to draw up a protest. In it he announced: "The legal regime has ended, that of force has begun. Obedience ceases to be a duty. We shall try to publish our journals without asking for the authorization which is imposed upon us. It is for France to judge how far resistance should go." The statement was signed by forty-three journalists and appeared in *Le Temps* and in Thiers' *National* on July 26th. This is perhaps the most dramatic occasion upon which journalism opposed a government. Here the press took over the function which was fulfilled by Parliament in England during the Commonwealth or by the Third Estate in France later. It was the first time that the fourth estate emerged as politically decisive. In the course of the latter half of the nineteenth century this has become so generally accepted a fact that it seems unimaginable for a political opposition to survive without developing an extensive press of its own.

The problems of the American law of libel: no restraint.— Such a development could, of course, not have taken place without considerable changes in the legal framework. Freedom of the press has been looked upon as perhaps one of the most essential features of political bills of right and there is no democratic constitution which does not expressly provide for it. American politics have been carried on without any material restrictions upon the conduct of the press, except the common law of libel. There is, then, no statutory inhibition. As a result, when the British Foreign Office made its survey of press laws throughout the world, it reported that it could find none in the United States. Actually there are some state laws dealing with particular matters affecting moral standards, and the federal government does something along similar lines through its control of the postal service. But by and large the legal restraints under which the press of the United States operates are covered by the common law of libel. This holds the press responsible civilly and criminally for defamation of character. How very limited that restraint is may be gauged from a report that one of the most sensational of tabloid newspapers paid $5,000 in all on account of libel suits totalling $7,000,000 in claims. Nevertheless the liability for libel does make the press wary in dealing with private citizens and corporations. This is not the case when they report governmental affairs. For protection of the press from prosecution for libel in reporting and commenting on governmental performance is connected with the peculiar nature of the common law of libel which demands that the party bringing suit show that damage has been done to it. Moreover, a suit for libel, on the precedent of Zenger's case, requires of the plaintiff that proof be brought to show that the alleged statements are untrue, proof which it is often impractical for governmental agencies to undertake. In Zenger's case the issue was clear, for he was put in jail for printing reports about the government, the truth of which nobody denied, but on its precedent papers nowadays frequently print news the falsehood of which nobody doubts. It is a question, in part at least, of where the burden of proof shall fall. In the eighteenth century all that the government had to do was to allege that the statements were libellous, and all that it had to prove was that they had been printed by the person being prosecuted. The interest of the government was the sole consideration. It was unhesitatingly identified with the public interest. Such an arrangement is manifestly unacceptable from a democratic point of view, but whether the exactly opposite arrangement of leaving the determination of what is in the public interest to privately controlled business enterprises is the solution to the problem may be seriously doubted. Probably D. M. Keezer is right in saying that those who led the struggle for freedom of the press would probably have lost much of their enthusiasm if they could have foreseen this outcome.

The political effects of a commercialized press.—The question of irresponsible comment and slanting of the news has raised a general problem of economic versus partisan and political control. It is a problem which is confronting democracy in all the more highly industrialized nations. The tendency for advertising to go to the papers with the largest circulation combined with the mechanical developments of the last fifty years have converted a large part of the great metropolitan press into a few huge corporations linking already powerful and highly organized papers in an extensive chain. Such is the case in the United States with the Hearst, Scripps-Howard, and other organizations. Such is likewise the story of the Northcliffe, Rothermere, Inveresk, and other trusts in England. The Hugenberg concern offers a German parallel. Only France, of the large countries, has retained a more divided press, though François Coty also commenced to build a chain of rabidly nationalist papers. It is perhaps no accident that these great corporate enterprises tend to deteriorate the quality of the news and to throw their weight to the support of jingoistic nationalism (though the Scripps-Howard chain must here be excepted). At any rate, even if one concedes that the masters of these undertakings are not the scheming and satanic plotters that they are sometimes depicted to be, the problem remains as to how to cope with organizations that look upon the process of opinion formation, so essential to the conduct of democratic government, as secondary to that of making money. The accepted American doctrine of the difference between facts presented in the news and opinions expressed on the editorial page is too superficial to require comment. It is obviously a situation arising from very powerful underlying trends which may be quite indirect and unrelated.

The forces behind the mass press.—What are some of these phenomena to be considered here which seem definitely related to the rise of the mass press suggested by the names of Hearst, Pulitzer, and Northcliffe? Certain technical developments since the American Civil War, such as the conversion of wood pulp into news print, the invention of the linotype machine, and many others, cheapened the cost of production. At the same time the spread of popular education constantly expanded the available reading public, and the rapid increase in population did the rest. We find that between 1850 and 1900 the number of daily newspaper publishing establishments, as classified by the United States Census Bureau, increased from 254 to more than 2000. At the same time the circulation of their publications increased from 750,000 to 15,000,000 per day. Between 1900 and 1910 both figures continued to rise, but the increase in establishments was much less than that in circulation, namely from 2,226 to 2,600 and from 15,000,000 to 24,000,000 per day. After this the number of papers actually began to decline, and by 1920 had fallen to 2,441. This decline continued, and in 1930 there were 2,293 such papers in the United States. In the same period circulation rose to 42,000,000. These figures suggest something of the enormous transition that was taking place. Pulitzer, Hearst, and Harmsworth, afterward Lord Northcliffe, are simply individuals who rode the crest of the wave. They were essentially skillful and unprincipled business men who perceived the possibilities of cheapening the wares which journalism had to offer, both from a material and cultural point of view, and in making a profit from the broad market. Sensationalism gained an ever more extended hold upon the press in this period. Scandal and corruption in the government were as acceptable as any other untoward developments. The implications of the profound cynicism thus engendered in the masses did not worry these master showmen of the press. They did, however, markedly alter the configuration of modern politics. Of course these popularizers of journalistic goods did not completely displace the older and more established papers. Their inventions and discoveries were bound to spread as they were being initiated by competitors. Eventually after the war so-called tabloids actually outdid Hearst and his brethren. In order fully to appreciate this mass press one must compare it to the older and more traditional patterns of the press of the leading countries.

A comparative survey of the nature of the modern press in certain leading countries.—In any comparison of the press in relation to the government in the various leading industrial nations one must keep in mind the differences between these countries, as far as the place occupied by the government in the whole political process is concerned. But it would be misleading to cast the analysis into a rigid pattern of "national" types. The comparison of governmental systems should not obscure other similarities and differences. Thus the labor press in all these countries bears a marked resemblance in its tendency to focus interest upon trade union activities, a perfectly natural thing to do. As was said before, there are also marked differences which have only an indirect relation to the governmental structure, such as the geographical configuration of the country. Nevertheless, a brief survey of the press in terms of governmental structure may be helpful. In America, where the government is federally divided and where a major political interest is focused on the contest between two large political parties of somewhat similar outlook, the press tends to be politically neutral, and much of its interest is centered upon local matters. England's centralized government, contested for by radically opposed parties (Conservative and Labor) and conscious of its imperial tasks, tends to make the press vigorously partisan and much concerned with affairs in distant lands. Moreover, the possibility of distributing a paper overnight all over the country makes it possible to serve certain groups, such as finance or labor, by a paper distributed from a single center, like the London *Times* or the *Herald*. In France, where parliament is supreme and divided into many contending groups, the editorship of a moderately successful paper is one of the safest careers leading into politics, and many prominent politicians, like Clemenceau or the brothers Sarraut, have been editors. It is not likely that such men will give up their independent control. Consequently the French press is divided into many individual enterprises. At the same time, the dominant position of Paris in the country's politics offers the same opportunity for distribution of a paper from a single center and gives the Parisian press national scope. Germany, as long as it had constitutional government, was federally divided, with its politics involving a contest of a number of highly organized parties. Here the press again tended to be strictly partisan, but with many different organs, to serve the different parties, available to the reader seeking a cross section of the opinion of various groups. There were also significant papers in different parts of the country. A number of other European countries have a similar party structure possessing an analogous press. After this rapid comparative survey, it may be well to consider each of these systems in somewhat greater detail.

The English press.—English politics today revolve around two primary poles, the leader of the majority party, who is Prime Minister and who directs the government, and public opinion which criticizes and in a measure controls this government. Such public opinion develops influence and maintains it through many different channels, but the strongest position here is occupied by the press. In spite of the vast extent of the sphere of personal contact through the radio, the printed word remains the most widely scattered influence. Particularly since the eighties of the last century, when the curtailment of parliamentary debates began, the press has become the most effective critic of the government. In spite of all the emphasis upon mere reporting of the news, the selection of items is of such importance that it is, from a political viewpoint, decisive. So-called slanting of the news, which may take the form of continued emphasis or merely passing notice as well as many others, makes the newspaper a "view"-paper. Perhaps the most important technique of slanting the news is the tactics of appropriate headlines. What is particularly interesting in England is the dovetailing of this general newspaper technique with the work of Parliament. The method of questions (see above, Chap. XXII, ¶ 2) would be utterly ineffective today if it were not for the potential interest that the press might take. Parliament itself can only in rare instances commence a debate, but a newspaper can work up a question by giving it appropriate attention through editorials, related news items, letters to the editor, and so on. In spite of the vigorously partisan nature of most of the English press, a tradition of fairness toward the party adversary has been maintained. Speeches of opposition leaders are faithfully reported. Deliberate lying is frowned upon. In return the government is inclined to treat the papers with respect, even to take them into its confidence. This was true at least until the World War. Since that time the rise of the Northcliffe and Beaverbrook press has somewhat deteriorated this tradition. Situations like that which arose between the Northcliffe press and Lloyd George in 1921, the attitude of the *Daily Mail* and others in connection with the Zinoviev letter incident in 1924, and the atmosphere which developed at the time of the forming of the National coalition in the late summer and fall of 1931 show a degree of bitterness and unfairness such as has not been witnessed in England since the agitation over the Reform Bill. These events have focused attention upon the fact that the newspapers are, after all, privately owned and capitalized enterprises. When confronted with the policies of the Labor party it is difficult for them to maintain the degree of neutrality which they could maintain toward parties which never questioned the foundation of their own existence. Also, as long as the country's electorate was divided between Conservatives and Liberals there was some positive advantage, from the point of view of party management, in not having the papers too closely tied with the parties. Thus, while the *Times* might be Conservative, the *Daily News* Liberal, and the *Manchester Guardian* radical, their editorial staffs developed personalities of their own which gave to each paper a more distinctive flavor than the broadly conceived party platforms under a two-party system would indicate. This situation was helped, of course, by the fact that in England, as elsewhere in the nineteenth century, these and many other leading newspapers were owned by families injecting a personal element and tradition into the policy of the paper. Through the papers these families were permanent factors in the politics of the land. The family of John Walter who had founded the *Times* in 1785, the Taylor Scotts who have owned the *Manchester Guardian* since 1821, the Roundtrees and Cadburys with their *Daily News,* all possessed a directing influence in their respective party councils. Under such conditions, and when we remember that one or the other of these parties would actually conduct the government, it is quite natural that England should not possess a governmentally controlled press. It does not need and could not have such a press, since whichever party was in power would have the necessary publicity channels.

The aristocratic tradition of the country with its governmentally controlled orders, titles, and so forth, insures a noiseless collaboration which is in many ways more effective than any official press organ of the government could be. The *Times* offers perhaps the best concrete illustration. It has been particularly remarkable in the extent to which it has been able to participate in the conduct of foreign affairs. Since the days of its great editor, John Delane, the *Times* has been a factor of independent importance. While usually collaborating with the Foreign Office, it has often profoundly influenced its policy. In every important capital of the world the *Times* has correspondents of its own, very well paid, sometimes rivalling the position of the Ambassador as a representative of English policy. As in foreign policy, so in many other matters, the *Times* would have the leading specialists as contributors. One very striking instance of great political importance was the position occupied by Colonel Repington, who acted as a highly confidential go-between for the Foreign Office, the army, and the French Embassy in the difficult negotiations concerning the military collaboration between England and France in 1906 and later. Since the war the *Manchester Guardian* has made considerable strides toward fulfilling a role, somewhat similar to that of the *Times* for the more radical elements in the country. Though not in any sense an official Labor organ, the *Manchester Guardian* has drifted sufficiently far left to occupy such a position. Yet as far as foreign affairs are concerned, it is more than probable that the lack of effective support in the press has had a good deal to do with the difficulty the Labor party has experienced when in office, particularly since the Northcliffe and other papers of the mass press have not hesitated to carry on rather violent campaigns, of which the Zinoviev incident is the most disagreeable example. While no other papers can be compared with the *Times* as far as power and influence are concerned, it may be well to mention some of the more important ones. On the Conservative side there are *The Daily Telegraph* and the *Morning Post*. The former caters to the higher middle class, the latter to the aristocracy and Society. On the Liberal side there is Lloyd George's *Daily Chronicle* which is democratic and popular, and on the Imperial Whig side of the Liberal tradition, the *News-Chronicle*. While all these papers rest upon the foundation of private capital and are in the last analysis business enterprises, the Labor party has recurrently endeavored to develop an organ of its own, the *Daily Herald*. This paper had, as long as it was a party organ, a very hard time competing with the powerful journalistic appeals of the mass press. Today the *Herald* is one of the most widely read papers in England. Yet the gradual conquest of newspapers by profit-seeking capitalists has led to an increasing emphasis upon magazines and reviews as the true focal point of opinion, at least among the educated classes. The Liberal *Edinburgh Review,* started in 1802, and the Conservative *Quarterly Review,* founded in 1809, have set a tradition of high achievement and represent the most effective efforts at long range influence in politics. Although most of these magazines are again identified with some political party or group, they are not in any sense dependent upon them. On the Conservative side we have the *Spectator,* the *Saturday Review* (now violently Imperialist) the *Outlook,* and J. L. Garvin's *Observer.* On the Liberal side the *Nation* used to be of great significance. It is now merged with the Fabian publication, the *New Statesman.* The *Labour Leader* was a more radical Labor organ. It has now become *The New Leader.* Somewhat more remote from party politics and therefore perhaps even more influential are the Conservative *Fortnightly Review* and *Nineteenth Century,* the Liberal *Edinburgh* and *Contemporary Review* and the *Review of Reviews.* Besides these the strictly economic journals, *Economist* and *Statist* must also be mentioned.

The American press.—In America—to summarize well-known material for purposes of contrast—the press is far removed from the government, and rarely if ever connected with party politics. Nor does it have the same intimate personal relations with the parties which we find in England. Much more definitely the American press has been guided by the business considerations of securing large circulation. Since many readers are not very vitally interested in party politics and only quadrennially, in connection with presidential elections, care to hear much about it, the adoption of a partisan viewpoint would deprive the paper of a good deal of its circulation. It is natural, therefore, that the American press should be independent of party politics. Papers like the *New York Times* will not even allow the party organization to have special editions of the paper made because it might give the paper a black eye. It is widely believed, however, that the American press has exchanged the dependence upon parties for the dependence upon capitalistic influences which might be exerted either through ownership or through advertising. It is difficult to get adequate factual information upon which to base a judgment concerning this question. Since advertising depends upon circulation and circulation depends upon reader interest, it is obviously not possible for a newspaper to heed the wishes of advertisers beyond the point where reader interest would be lost. On the other hand, reader interest is a somewhat intangible matter, leaving a fairly wide margin of discretion to the editorial office. Adolph S. Ochs, the long-time owner of the *Times,* rightly remarked that the more readers a paper has, the more independent it is of any advertiser. But this consideration does not apply to problems where all advertisers feel more or less the same way about an issue. The Commission of Inquiry of the Interchurch Movement, investigating the steel strike of 1919 felt that "it is inconceivable that the public which relied upon the Pittsburgh newspapers could, by any human method of reading newspapers and allowing both for exaggeration due to bias and inaccuracy due to haste, have understood either the causes of the steel strike or the significance of its incidents." It is widely felt that similar situations are frequent where the conflict between capital and labor is involved. On the other hand, newspapers often give very complete accounts of developments which the owners of the papers do not like at all, and it is for that reason difficult to draw any definite conclusions. Newspapers as business enterprises are torn between the desire to utilize fully the sensational quality of this struggle and the owners' and advertisers' desire to have it settled in favor of the capitalist interests. The outcome of this conflict of motives is naturally uncertain. All this would seem to show that the American press is rather far apart from political life. Actually, it plays a more decisive role, but this role is not one of leadership and guidance such as we find in Britain. It is rather that of voicing the reactions of particular groups of interest or of the public at large which reads the papers. Newspaper editors in the United States share with other folks the desire to climb on the winning band wagon. What has been said of the newspapers is equally true of magazines except the small group of weekly and monthly journals which are devoted to voicing the opinions of those who are opposed to the present order of things. Unlike the English magazines, a great many American journals seem quite indifferent to government and politics and for that reason do not interest us here. Only recently, in connection with the supposed challenge to the capitalist order by the Roosevelt regime, have magazines like the *Saturday Evening*

Post commenced to show a strictly partisan outlook. This is an important development in view of the enormously wide distribution of these journals. While most of their contents are in the form of stories and similarly neutral material, it is possible to inject clandestinely a certain measure of partisanship. This has actually been a noticeable trend; whether it is merely a passing phase or the harbinger of a complete reshovelling of party alignments remains to be seen. There can be little question that if the American party structure corresponded to the division between Conservatives and Progressives, as it at present most certainly does not, American magazine journalism and perhaps even newspaper journalism would take on a much more vital relationship to politics, and, to the extent to which the division between Progressives and Conservatives is the true political division of the country, that is already the case. Whatever the outcome of the present developments, there can be no doubt that such magazines as the *New Republic,* the *Nation,* and, more recently, the *New Masses,* as well as the in some ways more neutral *Survey* and *Living Age,* represent a vital body of political opinion in the United States whose influence and significance seems to be in inverse proportion to its numbers. To these magazines of longer standing may be added a whole flock of journals of more recent origin representing various shades of radicalism, such as the *American Review,* which is agrarian and anti-democratic, the *Commonweal,* which is progressive and Catholic, and a good many others.

The French press.—In France, where the editorship of a paper large or small is one of the safest careers leading into politics, the link between the press and the government is not through parties or groups, but through personalities. For that reason the French press in its relation to politics is very difficult to describe adequately. There is a great deal of change going on all the time. Ordinarily speaking, the French newspaper world can be divided into five distinct groups. There are five great commercial dailies published in Paris which resemble American newspapers in their permanent interest in circulation. Then there are three celebrated dailies of long tradition which seem not to care for circulation at all. The third group of Parisian papers, perhaps the most truly French in having no counterpart elsewhere, are papers which represent little except the political outlook of their editors and their personal following inside and outside Paris. Next follows a group of very sucessful regional papers of great circulation which are distinctive in their partisanship. Finally there is the large number of small provincial dailies which are often subservient to a particular individual or interest. They are completely dependent upon the commercial news services. Omitting the last group from our detailed consideration (for such papers seem to exist in all the countries we are considering, and without having much significance except in their bulk), it may be well to characterize in a few bold strokes some representative papers of the other types. The "Big Five," composing the first group and sold all over France, are *Le Petit Parisien, Le Journal, Le Matin, Le Petit Journal,* and *L'Echo de Paris.* The first of these is supposed to have a circulation of 1,700,000, the others 1,000,000, 800,000, 600,000, and 200,000 respectively. While they resemble each other in many ways, the first four in particular, being rather neutral and tending to side with the government in power, are used by the government for informing the public. To these may be added *L'Intransigeant,* with a circulation of 450,000. In none of these papers are the editors much in evidence, though M. Bunau-Varilla, the director of *Le Matin,* is reputed to have said of his administrative chair, "This seat is worth three thrones." Although he was doubtless correct in thus suggesting the great power which is connected with the control of one of these papers, not much attention of the reader is drawn to this control, which works clandestinely, as it does in the American press. The three exclusive papers of the second group, not much interested in popular appeal, are *Le Journal des Débats* (1789), the oldest daily paper of France, *Le Figaro* (1826), and *Le Temps* (1861). As Mr. Hayes has pointed out, "They are the patricians of the press, reflecting those qualities of French civilization which Frenchmen consider as their contribution to modern culture: elegance and purity of style, well balanced judgment, delicately tempered wit." The balance of the judgment and the temper of the wit would, indeed, as Hayes implies, seem more apparent to a conservative Frenchman than to persons of different political opinions. As far as foreign policy is concerned, *Le Temps* occupies a position somewhat similar to that of the *Times* in England. Very distinct from these commercialized and institutionalized papers are the very highly flavored personal organs of the third group. *L'Action Française* is the mouthpiece of the violently royalist and brilliantly literary Charles Maurras and Léon Daudet. Similarly *L'Homme Libre,* founded in 1913 by Clemenceau, provided a platform for that remarkable leader. *L'Humanité* voices the opinions of the French Communists under the able direction of Marcel Cachin. A more moderate Socialist tone is found in Léon Blum's *Le Populaire.* Others could be added to this list, particularly the significant new arrival, *La République.* These observations may suffice to give an idea of the personal papers. Now as to the provincial press. Though Paris and the Parisian press still enjoy a leading place, a number of regional papers have occupied a position of great influence, particularly since the war. Of these, *La Dépêche de Toulouse,* the leading journalistic expression of French progressivism (Radical Socialism), is perhaps the most noteworthy, though *Le Nouvelliste de Lyons* (Catholic and Conservative) with a circulation of 230,000, *La Petite Gironde,* and *Le Petit Marseillais* (Nationalist) with a circulation of 300,000, *Le Progrès de Lyons* (Nationalist) with a circulation of 250,000, and half a dozen others ought to be added. All of these papers are compounded of front page stuff dealing with national politics and foreign affairs, and made up in Paris, with local material added in various provincial editorial offices filling the inside pages. Due to modern means of rapid communication these papers have cut down very considerably the circulation of the Paris dailies. *La Dépêche de Toulouse* is the leading one among these regional dailies because, calling itself *"Le Journal de la Démocratie,"* it is the most influential organ of radical thought. Its director, Maurice Sarraut, has been president of the Radical Socialist party, and practically all the members of the party who have participated in governments of the left, as well as many of the leading intellectuals, have contributed to its pages. There are eighteen daily editions published in various towns in southern and central France, covering about one third of the country. Besides these daily newspapers France has of course, just as other countries, a very considerable body of magazines and journals. As might be expected, the personalist trend of French political life finds an even more effective outlet in these magazines than in the daily papers. They cover all shades of opinion from the extreme right to the Communist left. Carleton J. H. Hayes, or rather Miss Vera Mikol, has listed and annotated one hundred and eight such periodicals which are of importance because of their wide circulation or their representative quality.

The German press under Empire and Republic.—Unlike England and France, and in this respect resembling the United States, Germany possessed under both Empire and Republic a distinctly regional press, composed of many papers, owned, operated, and edited in different regional centers rather than in Berlin. The press paralleled, in other words, the federal structure of the Reich. In practically every one of the federal divisions of the Reich there was an important newspaper (or several) which was leading in that locality. It is indeed significant that the most widely known paper, internationally, was the *Frankfurter Zeitung* (1856) with a dominant position in the Southwest. As the paper of the Liberal Progressive bourgeoisie it achieved a national leadership, never really rivalled by either the *Vossische Zeitung* (1604) or the *Berliner Tageblatt,* both Berlin papers of a similar outlook. The fact that the *Frankfurter Zeitung* succeeded, through able editorial direction, in establishing itself as the semi-official organ in international matters was not perhaps entirely unrelated to the low esteem in which the German monarchy was held abroad; for the *Frankfurter Zeitung* was anti-monarchial, Republican in its sympathies. Another such regional paper of somewhat more Conservative, yet Liberal views was the *Kölnische Zeitung* (1802), leading newspaper of the Rhineland, along with the Catholic *Germania.* Bavaria voiced its Conservative or rather reactionary views through the *Münchener Neueste Nachrichten* (1847), displacing the older and Liberal *München-Augsburger Abendzeitung* (1609), which under the Empire had rivalled the *Frankfurter Zeitung* in Bavaria. The Hanseatic cities in the North expounded their interests and overseas views through the *Hamburger Fremdenblatt* (1828) and the more Liberal *Hamburger Nachrichten* (before 1813). As will be noted from some of these figures, it was a characteristic of the German press that many of its leading organs were a hundred and more years old, as was the federal structure of the country. They, in fact, embodied the tenacious traditionalism of Germany's regional culture. The efforts of the Prussian and later of the Imperial German government to build up for themselves governmental press organs like the *Norddeutsche Allgemeine Zeitung* which could be relied upon to voice the official views, were not effective. In this connection it may be worth passing notice that the *Kreuzzeitung* (1848), the most outspoken Conservative daily of Berlin, was under the Empire almost as irritating to the government as the *Frankfurter Zeitung.* This paper came into its own only after the election of Hindenburg to the presidency of the Republic; for its primary reason for existence was that the old gentleman read this paper, and it alone.

The traditional and regionally rooted press which we have so far described could not, of course, remain unaffected by the rise of industrialism and the massing of readers in urban centers. Nor could the modern technological achievements fail to give rise to new developments in Germany as elsewhere. The Northcliffe press, the Coty chain, and the Hearst trust found a parallel in Germany in the *Hugenberg Konzern.* This post-war product, a very extensive chain of Berlin and local papers, formerly of the colorless type *(Generalanzeiger),* was built upon very much the same idea as its parallels in other lands: exploitation of sensationalism and nationalism for profit and (as a by-product) for the maintenance of the existing economic set-up. Its leading Berlin organ was the *Berliner Lokalanzeiger.* The peculiar economic structure of this press giant rested upon the dictatorial power of Hugenberg himself, and the practice, fixed in the by-laws, of reinvesting all profits in the enterprise. By extending control not only to magazines, but to advertising (the leading German advertising agency was owned by this trust) and to the movies (the leading German cinema corporation, the UFA, was also Hugenberg's) Hugenberg succeeded in obtaining a formidable stranglehold which is widely believed to be responsible for the undermining of the Republic, particularly in the provinces, and outside the effective trade union organization, which controlled German labor. The formidable influence of Hugenberg's business enabled him to oust the conservative leader, Count Westarp, and assume leadership of the German Nationalist party himself (see Chap. XIX).

This brings our survey to the third distinctive aspect of the German press, its partisanship. A number of the leading newspapers, and obviously the Hugenberg trust, were not only partisan, as are the English papers, but actually party organs. The older, more independent papers we have discussed all drifted into definite connections with a party even under the Empire. Thus the *Frankfurter Zeitung* was close to the Progressives, known under the Republic as the Democrats; so was the *Vossische Zeitung* and the *Berliner Tageblatt.* The *Kölnische Zeitung* was National Liberal, that is, after the war, an organ of the People's party; the same may be said of Stresemann's *Der Tag* and of Stinnes' *Deutsche Allgemeine Zeitung* (successor to the *Norddeutsche* mentioned above). *Germania* was, as already stated, the exponent of the Catholic Center party (its more conservative wing), while Hugenberg's papers expounded the views of the German Nationalist party. Wherever we look, we find the strongest affiliations between party and press. To these papers must now be added the *Vorwärts* (and many similar papers in smaller towns) which was the official party gazette of the Social Democrats. While the relations between that paper and various groups in the party were at times the occasion for violent controversy, the actual control of the party bosses was complete, for they could, on the basis of their financial control, oust obstreperous editors, as happened in 1905. When the Communists split off from the Socialists after the war, they in turn founded and maintained a party organ, *Die Rote Fahne* (The Red Flag). It was therefore quite in keeping with the German tradition that the National Socialists should proceed to found their own party organs, of which *Der Völkische Beobachter*, edited in Munich, and *Der Angriff*, edited in Berlin, were the outstanding ones, followed by a whole crop of *Beobachters* and *Angriffs* in the various regions. Such a strictly partisan press naturally tended to take a rather unrestrained view of governmental measures, and thus in turn heightened the violence of party conflicts and the general confusion of the electorate. The many well-organized and well-defined parties (see above, Chap. XVII, ¶ 11) each with its particular *Weltanschauung,* offered all shades of opinion so that partisan papers could avoid being flat. The party views were sufficiently specific, in other words, to serve as a basis for effective journalism. At the same time, they drove to despair the intelligent non-partisan citizen who was unable to provide himself with a newspaper that would strive for a measure of objectivity and restraint without being flatly commercial. The difficulties of men like Stresemann and Brüning, who sought a broader national appeal, were greatly enhanced by the lack of any neutral press organs which might echo their broadly conceived views and help them to build up a non-partisan following.

The lively partisanship of the German newspapers, their large number, their traditional interest in literature, art, and science and their tendency to open their columns to scholars, novelists, and writers held the development of political journals and magazines somewhat in check. Their outlook was sufficiently specific and focused to supply the need which magazines like the *Nation* and the *New Republic* fulfill in the United States. There are exceptions to this situation. Among the Socialists and Communists, where the press was boss-ridden, magazines offered an outlet for more independent thought, and we find *Die Gesellschaft, Die Weltbühne, Sozialistische Monatshefte* and various others. The many different shades of political Catholicism had always sought outlets through magazines, and under the Republic *Hochland* became a striking representative of progressive Catholic youth. Staid and dignified official conservatism of the academic sort spoke and speaks through the *Preussische Jahrbücher* (1858). *Süddeutsche Monatshefte* added the voice of rampant nationalism, as it flourished in Bavaria after the war. But on the whole, in this respect also, Germany resembled the United States, in that newspapers rather than magazines were the leading channels of political journalism.

Press under contemporary dictatorships and propaganda.—It is well-known that most of this rich regional and partisan journalism of Imperial and Republican Germany has fallen upon evil days under Hitler. No area, except the universities, shows more strikingly the profound difference between the monarchical constitutional order of pre-war days and the present one-party autocracy. As in Communist Russia and in Fascist Italy, so in National Socialist Germany, the freedom of the press is gone. Goebbels, at one time editor of *Der Angriff*, knows through his own experience the skillful use which can be made by political journalism of the freedom of the press. Like Mussolini, who himself had been the editor of Socialist papers, Goebbels knows the potential power of the fourth estate. Consequently, the law to which the press is subject in Germany, as in Italy and Russia, is conceived in terms of propaganda. It is not merely a question of censorship, but following the example set during the World War, a constant stream of governmental news material is poured into the press of these countries with a view to holding public opinion in line. It is a system of primitive simplicity to maintain a certain amount of consent without permitting any public discussion. In this area, at least, Fascism and National Socialism are very much alike. The enforcement of discipline amongst journalists is accomplished by requiring every writer in a newspaper to be enrolled in an association which is controlled by the government; without such enrollment no person can be a member of a paper's staff. In other words, each newspaperman is held in line by the threat of losing his job—a formidable thing in a country as overcrowded and bureaucratized as Germany is; being barred from his professional work means starvation for the victim and his family. None but the martyr-saints will fail to anticipate the reactions of the Ministry of Propaganda. To be sure, the "Chamber of Culture" to which the journalists belong, is not technically a subdivision of the ministry, but the actual control is complete. How all-embracing the hug of this boa constrictor is may be gleaned from the further observation that the Chamber of Culture also includes the associations of writers, broadcasters, actors, musicians, and so forth, whether they are employees or independent artists. It is clear that no avenue of escape is left. Besides this formidable machinery for enforcing general "discipline," special standards have been set up for editorial behavior. No one unacceptable to the Propaganda Ministry can be an editor. To remain acceptable, an editor must "withhold from publication everything which (1) confuses selfish with common interests in a manner misleading to the public; (2) can weaken the strength of the German people nationally or internationally, the German nation's will toward unity, German defensive capacity, German culture or German business, or may hurt the religious feelings of others; (3) is offensive to the honor and dignity of a German; (4) illegally injures the honor or the well-being of another person, hurts his reputation, or makes him ridiculous or contemptible; (5) is for other reasons indecent." This list of "standards" is a veritable hodge-podge of ideals shared by newspaper folk throughout the world, equivocal generalities, and invitations to a callous disregard of truth. Very similar regulations prevail in Italy under the Statute of the National Fascist Union of Journalists. The attitude of the rulers of this kind of press has been well stated by Dr. Joseph Goebbels: "Since we National Socialists are convinced that we are right, we cannot tolerate anybody who contends that he is right. For if he, too, is right, he must be a National Socialist, or if he is not a National Socialist, then he simply is not right." The paradox of this pedantic tirade provoked the bitterly sarcastic commentary: "The real will of the people claims precedence over the will of the people." Criticism is silenced under dictatorship. However, under Fascism and national socialism it is not merely a matter of silencing possible critics, but of making them extol the virtues of their new masters, or, to use a familiar American expression, of making them eat their own words. The situation in Russia is somewhat different. Here the disappearance of private ownership has swept away all but Communist press organs. The Communist press consists of governmental newssheets, pure and simple. Whether that gives the Communist party a "positive and constructive power in the shaping of the press" as distinguished from the restrictive power of Fascist governments is more than doubtful. After all, the Fascist parties also have their own papers, and no particularly constructive note can be found. All this press, whether Communist or Fascist, is constructive from the partisan point of view in that it forwards the spread of the party's creed. It may, however, be noted in passing that the Communist press has been gaining enormously, owing in part to the rapid disappearance of illiteracy. In 1932 there were in the Soviet Union 2,230 newspapers printed either every day, every three days or every five days with a total circulation of 33,000,000, whereas in 1913 there were 859 newspapers with a circulation of about 2,500,000. Such comparisons are, of course, not available for the vociferous propagandists of the Third Reich. On the contrary, newspapers seem to be losing ground as the sceptical reader turns away from them in disgust. Hundreds of papers have died out, and the circulation figures of even the militant party organs have declined. One hears that the *Angriff* lost almost half its readers, its circulation going from 94,000 in December 1933 to 54,000 a year later. The *Völkische Beobachter* has fared somewhat better; its circulation has touched figures approaching a million daily, but that is perhaps in part due to the fact that its editor has remained, whereas *Angriff* lost its leading man, Dr. Goebbels, to the Propaganda Ministry. What was there left to attack anyway? The great Russian Communist organs, *Pravda* (for the Communist party) and *Izvestia* (for the Soviet government), each with a circulation of 2,000,000 copies daily, have a more intellectual role to fulfill. It is their task to interpret the developments of the day in terms of the elaborate Communist theory which underlies the whole institutional framework of Communist Russia. Their vigorous competition is cast in this pattern of dogmatic orthodoxy. Efforts of the Nazi press to do likewise with reference to the Twenty-five Points of the party's program are doomed by the self-contradictory content of the party program, and its consequent dogmatic weakness. Present indications are that these rigid systems of control of the press defeat themselves, that a saturation point is reached beyond which news offered through such propagandistic channels is no longer accepted by the reader. Such a reaction was even noticeable in the United States after the war. It is, therefore, hardly surprising to hear reports nowadays of tendencies among newspaper readers in countries like Germany not only not to believe what is reported in the papers, but actually to believe the opposite, or at any rate constantly to be on the lookout for the "nigger in the woodpile." Such a tendency on the part of the readers may be assisted by hostile editors through the practice of the gentle Chinese art of innuendo. This is nicely illustrated by a news report which appeared in 1933 in some formerly Jewish-owned papers: "We hear with considerable indignation that Baer is reported to have said before his bout with Schmeling that every sock he would land on the jaw of his opponent would be in retribution for the injustice done his people." This was the only form in which Baer's remarks could have been reported.

Governmental control and censorship.—The Fascist (and Communist) reactions undoubtedly have called attention to the problems of the press as represented by the old slogan of liberty versus license. There can be little doubt that a press largely hostile to the present popular trend in favor of governmental restraints, and consequently oblivious to what is believed by many to be the public interest, raises very serious difficulties in a democratic age. Even if the extreme claims of Rousseauistic champions of the majority are discarded, there is no doubt that constitutional government can not look with indifference upon the present state of affairs. In times of manifest emergency such as the World War, all governments had recourse to censorship. Where the danger was small and popular fervor considerable, as in the United States, such censorship did not have to be carried very far. In England and France, where opposition to the war developed almost immediately after the outbreak of hostilities and gradually became more and more insistent, censorship was applied with considerable rigidity, perhaps more so in France than in England. Long white columns in many French papers attested to the effectiveness of the working of this machine. Clemenceau, who chafed under these restrictions, published his paper *L'Homme Libre* under the significant new title *L'Homme Enchainé* after the censor had deleted one of his editorials. But while censorship may be used for a brief period such as the World War, it is highly unsatisfactory as a control mechanism, even though it be admitted that the question is not between a controlled and an uncontrolled press. Outright administrative control, particularly in matters of public policy, defeats itself because it undermines the confidence of the public. In due course of time it would be inevitable that the same results would follow such administrative interference on the part of a constitutional government as have followed in dictatorial regimes. The problem of force and consent has to be faced. Now European governments have attempted to cope with this situation by developing monopolies of news agencies which are in turn subjected to governmental influence. *L'Agence Havas* affords the most striking and well worked out scheme, for Havas not only controls the ordinary channels of news communication but also possesses a virtual monopoly in the advertising agency field. In Germany, Wolff's *Telegrafenbüreau* fulfilled a similar function under the Republic, as under the Empire. Both these powerful news agencies were in effect subsidized by their governments. Reuter's, the British agency, had, to be sure, never taken such financial aid from the government, but as Will Irwin and many another experienced newsman will attest, it held intimate relations with the Foreign Office and other governmental agencies, following the old tradition. Now in this matter of news agencies, America again shows a marked contrast in that the Associated Press, the United Press and the other leading news services of the United States were organized and operated as corporations for private profit. Governmental subsidies would be utterly unthinkable in the American set-up. But again the question turns not upon control or no control, but upon that of who controls, particularly when questions touching the foundations of capitalist enterprise make their appearance. It is significant that radical groups in the United States have tried to cope with this problem by organizing separate services such as the International News Service. For obvious financial reasons they have not been much of a success. These problems of the control of channels of communication, and particularly those of the news, are positing themselves at the present time with particular vividness in the sphere of the radio and the newsreel. Everywhere the public is awakening to the fact that we are not settling the political problems which are involved in these situations by merely insisting that the government do not interfere. In fact, those groups which oppose the present order of things are emphatic in their demand for precisely such government interference. From the standpoint of the political observer, both arguments are misleading, one because it treats private capital as a neutral control, the other because it treats the government as a neutral control. Whether we think of the newsreel, the radio, or the press, in every instance we are facing the same set of problems in contemporary constitutional systems. How can we prevent the exclusive control of these channels of communication and therefore of public opinion, by any one of the contending groups?

Conclusion: judicial restraints.—Constitutional government rests upon the provision of effective restraints on the exercise of institutionalized power. The press of today is thoroughly institutionalized in its corporate structure, and yet we talk about it in terms simply of individual liberty. We realize its representative position, particularly in such cases as *The Times* (London), *Le Temps,* or *Frankfurter Zeitung,* yet we have not evolved any effective technique for coping with the problems involved. To be sure, an attempt has been made in England to nationalize *The Times* by making it a trust akin to the great universities. But this endeavor does not face the most pressing problem of all: economic versus governmental control. It is not the task of the present volume to suggest concrete practical measures in this any more than in any other field of political activity. It may, however, be permissible to indicate certain contemporary trends and to comment upon them in conclusion. The method which most readily suggests itself for constitutionally restraining the fourth estate is "censorship." But as we have just pointed out, censorship carries with it all the handicaps of administrative interference. The experiences during the World War and under dictatorial regimes since that time do not encourage further experimentation. Censorship in particular fields, as it is practiced in many American states, is almost as unqualified a failure. One alternative remedy would be the time-honored battle-cry against trusts and monopolies. You could try to withdraw the legal foundation of the large-scale modern newspaper by appropriate changes in corporation law, perhaps. But the technical exigencies of modern news-gathering render that method exceedingly doubtful, even if it could be enacted. The most promising avenue of approach lies through subjecting the process of news-dissemination to judicial restraints. We have seen (Chap. XII, above) that the most effective guardianship of individual liberty is achieved by entrusting a high court with the function of rendering an "interpreting" judgment concerning the meaning of constitutional clauses whenever a private party wishes to question the interpretation of another authority, such as Congress or the President. May it not also be possible to "judicialize" the press procedure by outlawing certain types of sensationalist disregard for the truth and then leaving it to aggrieved parties to bring their complaints before a court-like body which would consider the evidence? Walter Lippmann, in his *Liberty and the News,* has put this matter so judiciously that no better conclusion for the present chapter could be found than to quote his own words:

> We need, first, to know what can be done with the existing news-structure, in order to correct its grosser evils. How far is it useful to go in fixing personal responsibility for the truthfulness of news? Much further, I am inclined to think, than we have ever gone. We ought to know the names of the whole staff of every periodical. While it is not necessary, or even desirable, that each article should be signed, each article should be documented, and false documentation should be illegal. An item of news should always state whether it is received from one of the great news-agencies, or from a reporter, or from a press bureau. Particular emphasis should be put on marking news supplied by press bureaus, whether they are labeled "Geneva," or "Stockholm," or "El Paso." One wonders next whether anything can be devised to meet that great evil of the press, the lie which, once under way, can never be tracked down. The more scrupulous papers will, of course, print a retraction when they have unintentionally injured someone; but the retraction rarely compensates the victim. The law of libel is a clumsy and expensive instrument, and rather useless to private individuals or weak organizations because of the gentlemen's agreement which obtains in the newspaper world. After all, the remedy for libel is not money damages, but an undoing of the injury. Would it be possible then to establish courts of honor in which publishers should be compelled to meet their accusers and, if found guilty of misrepresentation, ordered to publish the correction in the particular form and with the prominence specified by the court? I do not know. Such courts might prove to be a great nuisance, consuming time and energy and attention, and offering too free a field for individuals with a persecution mania.
>
> Perhaps a procedure could be devised which would eliminate most of these inconveniences. Certainly it would be a great gain if the accountability of publishers could be increased. They exercise more power over the individual than is healthy, as everybody knows who has watched the yellow press snooping at keyholes and invading the privacy of helpless men and women. Even more important than this is the utterly reckless power of the press in dealing with news vitally affecting the friendship of peoples. In a Court of Honor, possible perhaps only in Utopia, voluntary associations working for decent relations with other peoples might hale the jingo and the subtle propagandist before a tribunal, to prove the reasonable truth of his assertion or endure the humiliation of publishing prominently a finding against his character.
>
> This whole subject is immensely difficult, and full of traps. It would be well worth an intensive investigation by a group of publishers, lawyers, and students of public affairs. Because in some form or other the next generation will attempt to bring the publishing business under greater social control. There is everywhere an increasingly angry disillusionment about the press, a growing sense of being baffled and misled; and wise

publishers will not pooh-pooh these omens. They might well note the history of prohibition, where a failure to work out a programme of temperance brought about an undiscriminating taboo. The regulation of the publishing business is a subtle and elusive matter, and only by an early and sympathetic effort to deal with great evils can the more sensible minds retain their control. If publishers and authors themselves do not face the facts and attempt to deal with them, some day Congress, in a fit of temper, egged on by an outraged public opinion, will operate on the press with an ax. For somehow the community must find a way of making the men who publish news accept responsibility for an honest effort not to misrepresent the facts.

CHAPTER XXIV

INTEREST GROUPS AND THE RELATION OF GOVERNMENT TO MODERN INDUSTRIAL LIFE

1. *Introductory: the deterioration of political representatives in terms of the general interest.*—2. *General interest and special interests.*—3. *American lobbies.*—4. *Chambers of Commerce and similar semi-official bodies in France, Germany, and other countries.*—5. *The Russian Revolution and the trade unions, particularly in Germany.*—6. *The German National Economic Council.*—7. *The Fascist "corporate state."*—8. *National Socialist "estates."*—9. *Communist councils.*—10. *Guild socialism.*—11. *Pressure groups in the United States today.*—12. *Conclusion.*

Introductory: the deterioration of political representatives in terms of the general interest.—As was pointed out at the beginning of the last chapter, interest and pressure groups are the living "public" apart from the press. Such groups were viewed with moral indignation and alarm by the last generation. They were held up to scorn by muckrakers and sane students of politics alike. They were the sinister force gnawing at the foundations of modern democracy, of representative government, and the word "lobby" supposedly comprehended a whole congeries of abuses, corruption, fraud, and the like. There was (and is) more than a kernel of truth in these assertions. The activity of these "interests" has manifestly weakened the belief in *popular* government by undermining the faith in a united *people*. Wilson's attack upon congressional government, and its committee system (see above, Chap. XXII, ¶ 5) was built around the allegations about the power which interest groups had arrogated unto themselves. "It is in committee rooms that legislation not desired by the interests dies. It is in committee rooms that legislation desired by the interests is framed and brought forth." Even earlier, a searching appendix to Bryce's *American Commonwealth* was devoted to the "lobbies." While in the United States and in the British Dominions, as well as England, the "interests" worked and pressed upon each party, in countries with a multiple-party system the interests often associated themselves to a greater or lesser degree with particular parties (see above, Chap. XIX). The rise of Socialism and of Socialist parties identified with the industrial workers' interest considerably hastened this process, or at least the general recognition of it. As parties thus became identified with special interests, or members of representative assemblies yielded to special interests, and thus appeared as their tools (or could be claimed so to appear), the representative quality of these assemblies declined. When, in the depths of the crisis of German democracy a German minister asked, "Shall we forever remain a collection of special interest groups, rather than become a united people?" he was voicing a doubt regarding representative government which had waxed strong in the minds of intellectuals. The corresponding feeling of disappointment was at the same time turning the masses to Fascism and Communism as possible ways out. The ill this German minister was crying out against was not only troubling Germany, as so many Germans believed. Marxists of various shades had been indoctrinating the masses throughout Europe with the theory of "the economic determination" of human activity. Royalists and reactionaries had preached with wit and passion that the Third Republic was honeycombed with the corruption of big business. The United States, as we saw before, was reverberating from time to time with the revelations of the dark machinations of interest groups, and the high protective tariffs stood as a lasting memorial to the logrolling proclivities of Congress, to remind anyone who had eyes to see or ears to hear the message. It was (and is) natural that plans should have made their appearance for legalizing these pressures and influences, for coördinating them with and fitting them into the regular framework of government. In France, economic advisory councils representing the "interests" had come down from the days of the "estates" and the mercantilist efforts of Henry IV. In Germany, Bismarck had tried to bring together the representatives of capital and labor through an Economic Council but had failed, since parliamentarians feared that he wished to balance the popular forces as represented in the *Reichstag*. After the war, such councils appeared everywhere as part of the new constitutions. At the same time, Soviet Russia erected a conciliar structure of government. Fascism and National Socialism have followed with comprehensive corporative set-ups. These corporative structures are supposed to replace the older representative scheme; whereas the post-war economic councils are intended to function as a complement rather than a substitute. Are these movements expressing a rapid stratification of our modern industrial society? Are these organs capable of effective operation, of fulfilling the deliberative function which once fell to elected assemblies? To a consideration of these questions of contemporary politics this chapter is devoted.

General interest and special interests.—In discussing representation, it was shown how Burke formulated the classical norm of a representative's task: to consider issues and to decide them in terms of the general interest. A reminder of how far from a description of actual reality such a view was at the time of Burke may be had in an autobiographical remark of his contemporary, "One-Speech" Hamilton. Before retiring from parliamentary life, he wrote his patron, who had requested his continuance, that he might consider the request, if he were permitted to vote according to his own convictions. The permission was not granted! Apart from the reality, the difficulty with Burke's view is that most politicians (that is, human beings) are quite positive that they are "considering the general interest" even when they are following very special interests; for it is usually possible to rationalize the special interest as an essential part of the general interest. Thus the welfare of, let us say, the shipping industry is of paramount importance to the English people, and therefore its continued existence "a matter of general interest." The same can and will be said of the workers, the farmers, the doctors, either in whole or in part, and always with some show of truth. It seems, therefore, that the "general interest" is similar to Rousseau's "general will"; a metaphysical entity, a yardstick of indefinite length with no inches or feet marked on it. Considered in such broad terms, the general interest is obscure, remains undefinable. And yet there is a difference. It is a question of more or less. The interest of farmer C. J. Friedrich is different from the interest of the farmers of Windham County, or the American dairy farmers. Again, the interest of these groups of farmers is different from the interest of all American farmers. In other words, some interests are more general than others. A true and ideal "American" representative would therefore consider the interests to be most important which all Americans have in common and which are therefore most "general." It is obvious that no such person is likely to exist. The earlier analysis of electoral systems undertook to indicate the limitations. But while the norm of such an "ideal" representative cannot serve any useful purpose in describing reality, it can help us in determining the representativeness of particular parts of the government. The American President would seem to be "more representative" than any individual member of the House or the Senate, but the Senate and the House, when acting with large bi-partisan majorities, would be "more representative" than the President (who is necessarily of one party). In certain realms, for similar reasons, the Supreme Court is "more representative" than either Congress or President. It has been shown before what the political importance of representative quality is (see above, Chap. XVI). It remains here to add the obvious remark that the narrower the special interest is, the lower is the representative quality of those whose actions are directed toward its realization. And an interest is narrow or broad depending upon the number of human beings whose interest is identified with it. The most general interest is the interest of widest application, conceivably comprising all humanity. The great appeal of the Marxist view lies partly in its claim to universality, at least as far as all workers of the world are concerned. The same is true of peace and pacific endeavors. At the same time, interests of very general application are frequently lacking in intensity of appeal to the interested party.[1] They are for that reason of rather remote interest to the man seeking reëlection to Congress or any other such elected assembly. He must, necessarily, be more concerned with the fortunes of the local soap factory, the needs of the farmers in his district, or whatever may be indicated by the particular social pattern of the community in which he is being elected. Such a state of affairs is less perturbing from the viewpoint of modern political science than from that of the stand-pat democratic doctrinaire. The more general interest is recognized as a compound of many less general interests, and by bringing spokesmen for these various interests together, such a compound may emerge, if the working conditions are right. Faulty electoral methods, outworn procedures for deliberation and action, and unrestrained license of the press may, however, bring about conditions under which the less general interests become so hardened, and so violently pitched against each other that no working compromise can result. Then the complex mechanism will stall and

[1] The fervor of the advocate of such interests cannot be argued to invalidate this conclusion; for such fervor is engendered by other impulses than the "interest" of the advocate himself—except in so far as he may sense the immense potential power to be derived from the effective realization of a universal interest.

eventually break down. Such breakdown is not, however, the result of special interests dividing the community, or of the advocacy of such views by elected representatives (as the Fascists and Communists allege); but rather the result of the particular maladjustments which prevented compromise between these interests.

American lobbies.—Whatever the reasons, it is a fact that the pressure of special interest groups manifested itself in an organized form quite early in the United States. The large size of the country, the legislative initiative assumed by Congress, the comprehensive vagueness of party programs all contributed to a development which brought interested citizens together in the support of legislation or in opposition to legislation which was of special interest to them. The farmers' organizations, seeking governmental control or at least supervision of the railroads are one striking illustration. The number of such organizations and the interests they represent have more recently become so impressive that they are nationally recognized. Broad surveys of the whole range of activities, as well as searching and detailed studies of particular activities, have appeared in the course of the last decade, analyzing the rise of this "assistant government," as it has aptly been called. Since the administrative departments have been taking a greater part in legislation, and since they have been vested with ever more discretion in administering them, they also have become the target of the pressure of these interest groups. E. P. Herring, the leading writer on this subject, has listed the following as of outstanding importance: the Chamber of Commerce of the United States, the National Association of Manufacturers, the Anti-Saloon League, the American Farm Bureau Federation, the National Education Association, the American Federation of Labor, the National League of Women Voters, the American Legion, the American Publishers' Conference, the Board of Temperance, Prohibition and Public Morals of the Methodist Episcopal Church, the railway brotherhoods, the Association of Railway Executives, the Federal Council of Churches, the Association against Prohibition, the Women's Christian Temperance Union, the National Grange, and a dozen or more strong trade associations, such as those of the woolgrowers, and coal, oil, lumber, meat packing, and sugar interests. Probably the organizations concerned with prohibition are somewhat less important today than at the time of Herring's study, but on the whole the picture is similar. It is a far cry from these large, publicly conducted organizations to the scheming and usually corrupt methods of the early lobbyist, looking for land-grants and similar concessions. Every one of the modern organizations more or less persuasively identifies itself with the public or the national interest. "The American Federation of Labor talks of working for 'labor and the people.' 'Its accomplishments have benefited all the people, for the trade union movement is as deep and wide as human life.' The Chamber of Commerce of the United States takes the position that 'what is good for the business is good for the country.' The Farm Bureau Federation states that 'in reviving and invigorating American farm life, we are regenerating and preserving the nation.' Similar statements may be encountered in the literature of others of these associations." These statements are not untrue, but they hardly describe the purpose for which these organizations were created. The nature of interest, however, is such that in the long run the subjective purpose pales into insignificance beside the objective reality in which various less general interests merge into the more general interests of the more comprehensive community. There are today hundreds of such organizations, voicing the "will of the people" in one field or another. To the older institutions, more particularly Congress, falls the difficult task of weighing these pressures and effecting the necessary compromise.

Chambers of Commerce and similar semi-official bodies in France, Germany, and other countries.—In Europe the development has been somewhat more askew. There exist, of course, in practically all the more industrialized countries organizations constituting the exact counterpart of the American scene (with the exception of the prohibition lobbies). But while some of these organizations have for a long time been more or less officially recognized—the Chambers of Commerce constituting in France and other countries semi-public authorities—and others have played a conspicuous role in politics, notably the trade unions, still others, particularly in the field of reform and similar interests, have lacked the financial backing for effective organizational activity. In England, to be sure, certain reform movements played an altogether decisive part in the parliamentary history of the nineteenth century. Such great names as Bentham, Cobden, and John Stuart Mill are definitely associated with these activities. But ultimately all these movements played their game in Parliament, rather than upon it, and associated themselves with parties or founded them, rather than standing aloof, distributing praise and blame as the modern American organizations do. These movements thus became readily coördinated with the existing governmental machinery, raising no such problems as are at present confronting constituted governments in the United States, in England, and in France. In France, special interest groups likewise forged ahead into the Parliament and the government. Certain trade associations, like the Chambers of Commerce, were given official status, others fostering patriotism and similar purposes were actually promoted by the government. The same tendency was even more markedly observable in Germany, where the Navy League and the Colonial Society, to mention only two, were operating with the blessings of the respective ministries. At the same time in all these countries the industrial workers, organized in great unions, were helping to build Labor or Socialist, and, after the war, Communist parties, rather than attempting to "play" the existing party system. From their vantage point the activities of a Samuel Gompers trying to work through "bourgeois" parties appeared naïve, if no worse. Yet, it may be doubted whether the doctrinaire spectacles of such observers did not blind them to ironclad realities of the American political scene.

The Russian Revolution and the trade unions, particularly in Germany.—In Imperial Russia the hamstrung representative assembly, the Duma, afforded no outlet for the activity of a radical party leader, nor did the trade unions, which were outlawed. To be sure, these workers' organizations were sporadically and clandestinely attempted, but usually their initiators ended up in Siberia, if they were not shot. The daily contact of factory workers nevertheless afforded an opportunity for skeleton organization. Councils or soviets composed of these more radical elements in the factories (and in the army) offered themselves, therefore, as the most readily available means of organized support after the revolution. The Communist party, politically speaking, is an organization bringing these elements together in a Pan-Russian and comprehensive group. Therefore, if later all the councils are found in the hands of the Communists, there is nothing startling about that. The soviets are the organic foundation of Communist party activity (see below, ¶10). But as is so often the case, what was an inherent necessity in one political arena is carried by doctrinaires into another where it has no such place. Thus we find that the revolutionaries in Germany and other parts of central Europe who were partisans of the Russian revolution set up councils of workers and soldiers. But here they ran afoul of the well-established and highly disciplined Socialist trade unions and the bureaucracy of the Social Democratic party securely backed by its following. The Workers' and Soldiers' Councils consequently failed to have any functional value. The great congress of such councils convened at Berlin in December 1918 was readily dominated by men connected with the older hierarchies, and refused to foster the erection of a soviet or conciliar Republic. When, thereupon, the radical followers of Liebknecht, calling themselves Spartacists and Communists, went into the streets and began to barricade themselves, civil war broke loose. The radicals were bloodily suppressed, since the Soldiers' Councils were unable to prevent the support of the moderates by the remnants of the imperial army. Since social democracy had been effectively organized for years, there was no real value in the councils. Very soon after their first appearance, Hugo Preuss had formulated the fundamental objections to this sort of hidden dictatorship, in a famous article. "In the old bureaucratic state," he wrote, "the citizens had little to say; in the present state he has no say at all; at this moment more than ever before the people as a whole are nothing but the object of a government which is set above them by inscrutable council. The only difference is that it rests its authority not upon God's grace, but upon the equally obscure people's grace. . . . Not classes and groups, not parties and estates in isolated opposition, but only the entire German people represented by a democratically elected National Constitutional Convention can create a truly popular government." Such thoughts made a great appeal to the more moderate elements (which did not cherish the thought of a fate similar to that of the Mensheviks in Russia), backed as they were at this time by a large number of the bourgeoisie who were prepared to give support to whoever seemed ready to prevent real revolutionary violence. For the highly educated German middle classes did not only think of Russian developments; they also had before their minds the course of the French Revolution, which they had learned to detest from their childhood. This revolution, as well as the Commune of 1871, had shown what absolute power concentrated in the hands of self-appointed councils meant. Theoretically, of course, these councils had been subject to recall at any time, as was in keeping with Rousseau's ideas of direct democracy. But how could such recall be effected when anyone advocating it was subject to the wrath of the councilmen? Direct popular action is a myth in such a context (see below, Chap. XXV). The masses of German workers as well as the middle class (insofar as they actively participated in political life at this time) would have none of such concentrated power in anybody's hands. In fact, the general attitude toward councils became so hostile that the efforts of radical elements to work such a structure into the proposed constitution met with defeat. A compromise provision was appended to the document as its last article to bring to an end a new armed uprising which had been raging in Berlin in March 1919. This National Economic Council with its never completed substructure of regional, district, and factory councils had, however, ceased to be a National Workers' Council. It placed all groups in the economic life of the country on an equal footing, or attempted to do so, thus realizing a highly conservative set of ideas for functional or professional representation. Catholic parties had long advocated such a return to medieval, static forms of representation (see above, Chap. XIX, ¶ 15). As mentioned before, even Bismarck had evolved such a plan after the adoption of his tariff system in 1879. As a first step, he organized a Prussian Economic Council in 1880 which, however, met only three times. A bill for a similar council for the nation failed of acceptance because the *Reichstag* remained suspicious of the project. But the idea never died. During the war, plans appeared for remodelling the Prussian House of Lords on a functional basis. In France, the idea of advisory councils was very old, dating back to Henry IV in the beginning of the seventeenth century; it remained significant throughout the mercantilist period. The semi-public nature of Chambers of Commerce was in part the result of their functioning in such an advisory capacity; toward the end of the nineteenth century Chambers of Agriculture had followed suit. Before the war, the demand for similar Chambers of Labor had appeared as a complement to this conservative type of organization; such Chambers were to give trade unions semi-official sanction. Into this pattern of a gradual integration, or at least coördination, of the government with the organizations pervading all walks of economic life, the National Economic Council of the German Republic fitted quite naturally, and after the first exaggerated expectations had given way to a more reasonable estimate of its role, a measure of success was insured.

The German National Economic Council.—In discussing the German National Economic Council as organized under Article 165 of the constitution, it needs to be remarked at the outset that it was not wholly unique. Similar organizations with similar powers are found throughout the world today. France organized such a council in 1925; other countries which have them are Japan, Czechoslovakia,

Poland, Spain, Mexico, and Jugo-Slavia. Some of these countries are, to be sure, on the verge of dictatorship, and as we shall see presently, in Italy and Germany functional representation has been brought forth as a decisive innovation and propagandized as the idea of the corporate or "corporative state" (see below, ¶¶7 and 8). Furthermore councils like the French one are rather technical advisory bodies than working parts of the constitutional order, like the German council; yet this distinction while perhaps legally significant need not be taken too seriously, from a political science viewpoint. At any rate, the German council (now merged into the National Socialist endeavors to create a corporative set-up) well illustrates the possibilities and the limitations of such councils as parts of a constitutional order. Its history having, for the present at least, come to an end, one may speak with a measure of conclusiveness about its experience. As the working of such a council within the total framework of a rather complicated constitutional machinery was felt to be somewhat uncertain, a provisional council was organized in 1920. This provisional council was never replaced by a permanent one, although a bill for its establishment was under consideration when the Hitler forces came into power. But even this provisional council was an independent part of the German constitutional order, and its relative success is indicated by the fact that the pending bill for the permanent council measurably increased the powers of this body by proposing to give it the power of initiating legislation. What were the functions of the provisional council, how was it composed, and how did it work? The functions of the council were concentrated in the fields of business regulation, social welfare and finance. It played a part in both the legislative and the administrative fields. The government was obliged to submit to the council legislation dealing with such matters, and it submitted the reports of the council to the *Reichstag* and the *Reichsrat* together with its own memoranda. In the administrative field, the council was called upon in many laws to nominate representatives on various technical boards in the field of economic regulation, labor, and so forth. On the whole it is believed that the council made substantial contributions in these activities. It goes without saying that it slowed up the process of such legislation, and consequently voices were heard in Parliament and among permanent administrators which denounced the council as an unnecessary encumbrance. It was claimed that the various interest groups organized in the council proceeded to press their claims again when the bill came up in the Parliament for decision, after having already tried to exert their influence when the bill was being drafted by the administrators. But on the whole, the body could be made to work within the parliamentary system. More serious problems arise when one turns to the question of its composition. It was generally agreed that the provisional council was too large, and this was due to the fact that every pressure group tried to secure as many seats as possible. What indeed is the relative importance of various activities within the whole economic life of the nation? It is clear that a certain measure of arbitrariness is unavoidable. The provisional council was composed as follows: there were six groups, so-called, Agriculture and Forestry with sixty-eight representatives, Gardening and Fisheries with six, Industry with sixty-eight, Commerce, Banking and Insurance with forty-four, Transportation, Communication, and Public Enterprises with thirty-four, and Handicrafts with thirty-six. To these were added thirty representatives of the Consumers (for example, German Association of Housewives with four representatives), sixteen representatives of the officials and the free professions and twenty-four members appointed by the government. This makes a total of three hundred and forty-six members. In the first six groups employers and employees were jointly represented, each nominating half of the members. In practice, this hitching together of capital and labor did not work. The labor members of the various groups all collaborated, being directed by the united German trade union organization, and thus established what became known as a division (*Abteilung*) to which the division of the employers corresponded, supplemented by the others as a third division. We thus find eventually three divisions (or Estates), capital, labor, and groups not identified with either. The pending bill had recognized this development and proposed to assign membership in the council on the basis of these divisions. Thus in Division I, the various great organizations of industry, commerce, agriculture, and so on, were each to name their representatives, while all the members of Division II were to be nominated by the General German Union of Trade Unions (*Allgemeiner Deutscher Gewerkschaftsbund*). Actually this had been the situation even in the provisional council. The original hope of effectively integrating employers and employees had not materialized. The government in order to break the deadlock which would result from the opposition of these two groups, particularly in social questions, fell back upon the third division, composed of consumers, officials, free professions, and appointees of the federal government and the state governments (through the National Council—see above, Chap. XIII, ¶11). This development was viewed with much alarm by certain writers who saw in it a victory of the professional politicians over the idea of true economic representation. The gradual ascendancy of the divisions over the groups brings us to the inner working of the council. In fact, the procedure of the council itself provided the entering wedge. For after a first outburst of enthusiasm when the great captains of industry like Hugo Stinnes participated in the deliberations of the council, the plenary sessions atrophied. After 1924 no more plenary sessions were held at all. All the work of the council shifted to the committees. Three of these committees were of leading importance, corresponding to the three main fields of council activity, one dealing with business regulation (*wirtschaftspolitisch*), another with social reform (*sozialpolitisch*), and the third with financial matters. The government voluntarily granted them an advisory supervision of ordinances and decrees as well as participation in legislation. Now the members of these committees were designated by three divisions of the council, each naming an equal number. Under the provisional council, the chairmanship of these committees was entrusted to members of the permanent civil service designated by the respective ministries (Economic Affairs, Labor, Finance), but the draft changed this and had the committees elect their own chairmen. As the business of the council had developed, the major committees were really to all intents and purposes the council. Working through numerous subcommittees and temporary committees, they received the drafts of the bills directly from the government, the steering committee, composed equally of members from the three divisions, acting merely as an intermediary. It is obvious from what has been said that the German Provisional National Economic Council, as it functioned under the Republic served essentially to coördinate the manifold organizations which modern economic life has brought into existence and to legalize or constitutionalize their participation in legislation and administration. In Czechoslovakia, where a similar council is at work, the experience with it is very much like that in Germany. Such councils can undoubtedly fulfill a useful function under modern conditions, and proposals for the organization of a similar body in the United States deserve serious attention. Not only France, in 1925, but England in 1930, created economic advisory councils. It is as yet difficult to say whether such more restricted bodies, attached to the cabinet itself, are preferable. In the United States, where legislation is primarily the work of Congress, and where the greatest pressure of organized groups is brought there, an independent body along the lines of Central European experiments would more nearly correspond to the needs of coördinating with the existing machinery these groups and their interest in economic, social and financial legislation.

The Fascist "corporate state."—It was remarked before that the German National Economic Council was merged in the legislation for giving a "corporate" structure to supposedly popular representation in Germany as in Italy under Fascism. This trend has aroused so much interest that a brief discussion of it seems indicated here, the more so since its advocates represent it as an alternative to the older electoral systems. Considering all available accounts, one finds a three-fold division of economic activities, as under the German council, as well as several groups such as agriculture, industry, and so forth. The three-fold division is that of employers, employees, and others (consumers, professional people, and so forth). These divisions and groupings are composed of various organizations. Each activity is recognized by the government through one organization only. Though the officers of some of these organizations are "elected," they practically all owe their offices to the government which either directly appoints them, or maneuvres their election through effective pressure. A measure of autonomy is, perhaps, preserved by some of the organizations of large business interests, banks, and so forth. But essentially the government and the party behind the government are using the "corporate" or rather associational structure of modern economic life for the purpose of coördination and control. Associations which before the advent of the Fascists maintained a vigorous life of their own, particularly in the labor field, are now all fascistized. In the conflicts between Fascist trade unions and Fascist employers' associations the government renders the final decisions. It inclines now to the one side and now to the other, as the exigencies of general policy seem to suggest, but on the whole the workers, being the weaker party of the two, come out at the short end. Fascist mythmakers look upon this set-up of bureaucratized associations as a first step in the direction of complete pacification in the industrial realm, when workers, employers, and consumers will be united in real "corporations"; but there are no signs, except official speeches and writings, to indicate any such trend, or to allow one to discern the "second step" in this evolution. As the ablest analyst of the system has remarked: "the term 'corporative' has been used, if not invented, to rouse a sense of wonder in the people, to keep them guessing, to provoke inquiry, and to contrive, out of the sheer mystification of an unusual word, at once to hide the compulsion on which the Dictatorship finally depends and to suggest that a miraculous work of universal benevolence is in the course of performance. . . . The 'corporate state' is a tool of propaganda." To this an Italian scholar of high repute, although an avowed enemy of Fascism, has rightly added: "From 1926 to 1935 the sole reality in Italian political life was the dictatorship of a man and his party. But side by side with this reality a new myth had grown to gigantic proportions—the myth of the 'corporative state.'" Not to grant Mussolini's propaganda efforts any greater space than they deserve the discussion of this governmentalization of all associational life may herewith be terminated. Its dynamics in no wise differ from the ordinary problems of bureaucracy as previously discussed.

National Socialist "estates."—In Germany, where the tradition of looking upon the government as the cure-all is very strong, the development under Hitler has been along lines very similar to those in Italy, though accompanied by a different verbiage. Here the mythmakers are talking about professional estates (*Berufsstände*) or guilds. Actually, the organizations functioning in conjunction with the National Socialist government and administration have little in common with the late medieval estates except the name. For whereas the estates proper were autonomous bodies and the mainstay of the medieval constitutional order (see above, Chap. IV), the Nazi estates are prolongations of the governmental bureaucracy just like the syndicates, federations, and "corporations" of Fascism. There is the National Economic Chamber, with regional chambers below it, composed of chambers of industry, of commerce, and of handicraft. There is the National Estate of Agriculture (*Reichsnährstand,* sometimes translated German Food Estate) composed of all the organizations of agriculture and allied businesses. There is the German Labor Front (*Deutsche Arbeitsfront*) composed presumably of all working Germans (the present figure of claimed membership is 23,000,000). There is finally the National Culture Chamber (*Reichskulturkammer*) composed of all the "free" professions, doctors, writers, artists, and so forth. Each one of these "estates" is hitched up with one of the ministries, Economics, Agriculture, Labor, and Propaganda respectively. Thus final coördination can come only through the Führer, Adolf Hitler, as boss of the several ministers in his cabinet. But in the meantime, each one of these estates may, by itself, undertake to reach out as far as possible and to gather as many Germans into its fold as will "join." Thus individuals and firms may belong both to the Chamber of Agriculture, and the National Economic Chamber. Again, they may combine allegiance to the National Economic Chamber and the German Labor Front. This depends entirely upon the nature of their business or activity. The German Labor Front, for example, is very keen about gathering into its fold employers as well as employees—as a symbol of industrial pacification and community. There exist, however, at the base of the industrial system in every factory so-called shop communities (*Werkgemeinschaften*) in which the employer is, according to law, the "leader" and the workers the "followers." After the destruction of the German Socialist and Christian trade unions, the National Socialists had to cast the relations of capital and labor into new forms. The recreational and fraternal activities of the trade unions, as well as the representation of the "labor interest" in the formulation of national policies was taken over by the German Labor Front; the determination of wages, working hours, and other practical questions were turned over to the individual employer as "leader" in his factory or place of business, but under the constant supervision of the government. Watchdogs, the Trustees of Labor, were created under the Ministry of Labor to settle any disputes. Such disputes are brought before them by "confidential councils" established in each factory. The members of these councils are annually proposed by the employer-leader and either accepted or rejected by the worker-following. It is said that about twenty per cent of these councils as proposed are rejected by the worker-following. In all such cases the Trustee of Labor for the district (thirteen in all) steps in and appoints a council. It is obvious that such a system of compulsory arbitration favors the employer as the stronger party in any dispute, and on the whole tends to keep wages, hours of work, and all the other conditions more or less stable. With constantly rising prices, such as have prevailed in Germany, the "real" wage of labor will constantly decline, as indeed it has under this set-up. The efforts of the German Labor Front to inject itself into this mechanism and thus to strengthen labor's position have had only rather limited success. The Front does, however, play a certain role in disputes. In order fully to appreciate the measure of constraint which this comprehensive coördination (*Gleichschaltung*) of all associational life implies, it is necessary to look at it from below rather than from above. With the "leadership principle" prevailing throughout this hierarchy (which one readily recognizes as the third criterion of bureaucracy, as described above, III, ¶ 7) any person who incurs the displeasure of his superiors at any point in this vast network of interrelated organizations is practically facing starvation. A worker fired from a factory, for example, will find it exceedingly hard to secure a place elsewhere; his "Labor Passport" immediately tells any prospective employer of his past. If he is talented, and might like to earn his living by writing, he is blocked because enrollment under the National Culture Chamber will be denied him. If he should be willing to begin anew in some handicraft, he will find himself blocked because of the compulsory guild under the National Chamber of Handicrafts, a part of the National Economic Chamber (as we have seen). But unemployment relief will also be denied him because of his status. The prospect of such a pariah status might well deter even a stout soul from offering effective opposition. And what is true of a worker would be equally true of a professional man, or in fact of anybody who does not enjoy unearned income from capital. Unfortunately the person provided with such an income is the most vulnerable of all potential oppositionists; for the confiscation of all his property for "treason" is easily possible through judgment of a regular court. It will be seen, therefore, that the second rule of anticipated reactions would justify us in concluding that even a few cases of opposition prove the existence of very widespread dissatisfaction (see next chapter, ¶10). Inasmuch as the *raison d'être* for this whole system of regimentation is the establishment of social peace (elimination of the class struggle), the existence of such dissatisfaction is decisive. It condemns the centralized governmental direction of associational life as unsatisfactory, and as offering no solution to the problem of the relation of capital and labor in particular and of various economic groups in general. Even in terms of the National Socialist focus of attention upon preparedness, and the gearing of the national economy for "the supreme task of war," this bureaucratized set-up is defective; for rapid disintegration of mass support will spell disaster under modern conditions of warfare.

Communist councils.—It was shown above how the Russian Revolution and its conciliar structure influenced the thought of German Radicals and thus indirectly prepared the ground for the National Economic Council which sought to integrate autonomous associations, whether of manufacturers, farmers, or workers, with the government in its various activities of legislation and administration. How did the Russian institutions themselves develop? Do they offer the solution which Fascist and National Socialist experiments seem to miss? The conciliar structure of the Soviet Union is the core of the whole system. From factory and village soviets or councils through county, district, and regional councils to the All Russian Congress (itself a vast council of over two thousand members, convened once a year) the structure rises by which the Communist party controls the community in all its phases of economic life. Just as in the German shop communities, the members of the incoming soviet are proposed by the executive officer of the council next higher up in the ladder. But these councils of workers are the only organizations recognized by the Soviet Union. It must be remembered that Russia under the imperial government did not possess any such rich associational life as other countries. Trade unions were outlawed. On the other hand, what organizations of employers and agriculturists there were could not have any place in a classless society as envisaged by the Communist doctrine. Only workers' organizations could be recognized, and they remained weak from the outset, being limited to recreational and fraternal activities. Thus the officialdom of the Soviet Union, united in the Communist party, actually constitutes a reigning bureaucracy, or, if you prefer, a hierocracy (government by priests). The problem of the relation between capital and labor in industry is "solved" by confiscating all capital, putting a bureaucracy in charge of its central administration, depriving the workers of direct participation in this administration, allowing them merely to protest against their own wages and working conditions, but consoling them by claiming effectively that it is all done on their behalf and for their ultimate benefit, and by maintaining effective social equality between the official bureaucracy and the other and dependent workers. The scheme is even more paternalistic and autocratic than the Fascist and National Socialist schemes, inasmuch as under these latter regimes at least certain powerful groups of business men maintain a measure of independence from the government, partly through the aid of the army. As in Italy and Germany, the non-Communist individual is practically at the mercy of the officials. Therefore, once more the second rule of anticipated reactions entitles us to conclude that even opposition on a limited scale indicates a very large measure of non-support of the government, if not of actual constraint. In fact, such opposition is occurring all the time, and even under the most favorable circumstances. The publications meant for circulation amongst the officials, like *Vlast Sovietov,* are full of incidents illustrating this desperate and stubborn resistance. In meetings for the election of factory and village councils (soviets) the majority will defy the local party boss even by a public showing of hands. Recent endeavors on the part of the Soviet government to introduce a greater measure of "freedom" into the system of "elections" may alter this situation, but they are claimed by many to have been instituted merely for purposes of foreign propaganda (the Fascists and National Socialists also make a great deal of their "elections"). Ideology and myths aside, it may therefore be doubted whether the Communist procedure of a self-appointed bureaucracy of "Marxists" administering the country's capital in the name of "working class," but at their expense, is a solution of the problem of the relation of social classes and economic groups under modern industrial conditions, either. Granting the rather imposing achievements of the Soviet government in industrializing Russia during the past fifteen years, one is nevertheless compelled to conclude that the manifold groupings of modern industrial life have been held in check only by setting up a rigid grouping of the people into a governing elite of Communist bureaucrats and politicians (or statesmen, after they die), and a mass of passive followers, exploited to a very high degree for the purpose of enhancing the future industrial power of Russia, that is the self-same Communist elite. To what account this elite will ultimately turn this gigantic power it is hard to say. But as foreign conquest and personal aggrandizement have been the common uses to which power has been put when uncontrolled and undivided, it is quite probable that both of them will play a role in the future evolution of the Soviet Union. Certain it is that whatever representative quality the Russian conciliar structure possesses is utterly obscure.

Guild socialism.—To these modern attempts at solving the problem of the relation of capital and labor, which is essentially the problem of power in distributing the return of mechanized industry, there must be added a brief discussion of a purely theoretical solution, guild socialism. The guild Socialists, as Socialists, demand the elimination of the capitalist. All industries are to be managed by "guilds." Taking the medieval handicraft organization as their pattern, they envisage factory guilds, combined into regional and national guilds for each trade through representatives elected by the members. Along with these trade guilds (which adherents of this view expect to develop out of the trade unions, but which are to include managers, experts, and so forth) there would be coöperative associations of consumers, service guilds of the professional groups, particularly an education guild and a health guild, as well as bodies controlling the public utilities, rounded out by an agricultural guild. Independent producers would also exist, both in agriculture and industry, who might not join any national guild. These several guilds and associations would together constitute directing bodies, locally, regionally, and nationally—the communes. These communes would exercise integrating functions, and act in judicial, legislative, and financial matters. They would have executive officers to attend to what administration there was. Inasmuch as every adult would participate actively in one guild and one consumers' coöperative anyway, it will be seen that guild socialism is a plan for thorough-going democracy in industry. All controversies are expected to be settled by agreement between the guilds, coming together in a commune, and thus the greatest amount of freedom would be insured. We have, therefore, in guild socialism a doctrine which combines features of the economic councils with features of the Soviet system—and also Fascism. Like the National Economic Council, it allows democratic determination from below in all the organizations entering into the scheme. Like Soviet communism, it recognizes only workers and consumers, but no employers—as the economic councils and Fascism do. Unlike all of these, it believes in strong local autonomy, and settlement of disputes by "agreement." It is at this point that Communists and Fascists alike would argue the breakdown of the system. To the Fascist argument the guildsman would, of course, reply that such agreement could only come about among organizations such as the guilds and coöperatives, composed of working people, but never between them and employer-capitalists whose interests are entirely at odds. To the Communist (State Socialist) argument they would reply that such agreement would perhaps be difficult where a central directing group like the Communists in Russia was bent upon great changes at the expense of the worker-consumer, such as are involved in the industrialization of the vast territory of the Union, but that it would be easy if no such task requiring large "savings" for capital account were envisaged, that is, in a highly industrialized country with a fairly stable organization. Indeed the development in England, and in the Scandinavian kingdoms (as well as in Germany before Hitler) points in this direction.

The successful development of municipal utility control and of powerful consumers' coöperative societies fits into the guild socialist pattern. To a certain extent these coöperative societies reach over into the producers' field (the English coöperative societies own dozens of plants). But on the other hand, the experience with producers' coöperative associations does not permit any very optimistic expectations of the factory guilds. The guild Socialists hope, however, that a society entirely operated in the pattern which they envisage would not encounter these difficulties. Although the National Guilds League ceased to exist in 1925, it is believed that the guild Socialists have profoundly influenced English socialism in the direction of group autonomy, as against governmental action.

Pressure groups in the United States today.—It is a rather far cry from the theories of the guild Socialists to the position of professional groups and associations in the United States today. To be sure, all such associations are democratically organized. Control over them is, at least according to the by-laws, exercised by the rank and file in the various organizations. This democratic pattern is recognized by the Chamber of Commerce just as much as by the American Federation of Labor. But none of the labor unions, and only a few of the professional associations, like the American Bar Association, are actually in control of their trades. Others, like the American Association of University Professors, occupy an intermediary position with their members exercising a varying, but rarely decisive influence in the colleges and universities of the country. Still others, like the associations of school teachers, have as a rule no such control at all. All these occupational and professional groups have as one of their primary functions the representing of the interest of the particular group for which they speak. As pressure groups before legislatures and administrative bureaus, they watch over whatever governmental policies would affect their members. The extent of such activity is, of course, affected by the measure to which the government has adopted any policies, and it therefore varies greatly; on the whole, it has been increasing in the last few decades. At the present time, their activity has become generally recognized as part of the contemporary process of politics (see above, ¶ 3). The same is true in England and France. Indeed, the National Recovery Administration undertook to coördinate the American economy on a vast scale with the help of these organizations. This experiment, even though it failed, stands as a significant monument to the rise of organized interest groups and their potential claim of participating in the government in an active and legal way. In fact, even though the NRA has been abandoned, similar coördinated structures in special fields continue to form part and parcel of the governmental pattern of the United States today. Thus the regulation of the oil industry under the Department of the Interior is modelled on a plan very similar to the NRA. Another very striking instance of the merger between occupational interest groups and governmental agencies is presented by the county agents. These are officials who are connected in an administrative-executive way with all three levels of the American government, federal, state, and local, as well as with the Farm Bureau Federation, one of the three great farmers' organizations. The United States Department of Agriculture, the extension services of the schools of agriculture in the state universities, the counties and the farmers individually through affiliation with the local Farm Bureau, all contribute toward the maintenance of the administrative work which this official and his staff carry on. In the labor field, similar developments are in the making through the Labor Relations Board of the federal government and cognate agencies in the states. In Massachusetts, for example, definite coördination has been worked out through administrative measures. All this goes to show that occupational groups are beginning to play a role in the American governmental process, just as they have been doing in other highly industrialized countries. Perhaps this approach is more promising than the one comprised under the formula of "legalizing the lobby." It is not so much a question of giving a legal status to these pressure groups as it is a matter of transforming them from mere pressure groups in their relation to the government and the general public into groups taking an active part and a measure of responsibility in the conduct of modern administration.

Conclusion.—In conclusion, it may be said that the relation of government to modern industrial life, and more particularly the question of the relation of employers and employees, of capital and labor, is generally felt to be the touchstone of contemporary political orders. The genuine representative significance of all organizations arising in connection with men's activities within the total context of modern industrial life has become sufficiently apparent to make it necessary to reckon with them as pretenders to the throne of government. Where the interests are sharply divided, due to a variety of different circumstances, certain of these groups have proceeded to take over the government and to revolutionize it in such a way as to suit their particular needs and conceptions. Such efforts have been accompanied by dictatorial methods—relapses into crude techniques of government which violate the fundamental premises of constitutional limitations. In order to overcome the one-sidedness of their representative basis, they have at times had recourse to the primitive device of seeking popular acclaim through general plebiscites (see next chapter). At other times, they have sought to extirpate the groups which they did not represent. Whether either of these methods is permanently successful remains to be seen. Constitutional governments of the established kind have seen a widespread movement for the participation of all kinds of occupational and professional groups in the administration of that part of national life in which they happen to be particularly concerned. But wherever we turn, functional representative devices are forging ahead as decisive elements in any representative scheme under modern industrial conditions.

CHAPTER XXV

DIRECT POPULAR ACTION

1. Objections to elected representatives: Rousseau.—2. The Napoleonic plebiscites.—3. The referendum and initiative: Switzerland.—4. Same subject: United States.—5. Direct popular action and the general problem of representation; Lowell's view.—6. The "will of the people" in the international field: plebiscites before the war.—7. Same subject: after the war.—8. Referendum and initiative in the German Republic.—9. The nationalist implications of direct popular action: the referendum on the Young Plan.—10. The plebiscite under the Nazi dictatorship.—11. The Fascist plebiscites.—12. The contrast of the Soviet Union.—13. Conclusion.

Objections to elected representatives: Rousseau.—The decline in the representative quality of representative assemblies which resulted from the rise of the modern press and of the interest groups has brought in its train an ever widening demand for direct popular action. This demand first manifested itself in the movement for popular referendum which had been incorporated in the Swiss constitution of 1874 and spread rapidly through the United States after the turn of the century. In Switzerland, direct popular action had remained the traditional form of political activity in some of the small rural cantons, and the modern referendum was essentially an adaptation of these methods to more numerous electoral bodies. Leaving the institutional analysis to a later paragraph, it may well be recalled at this point that the great apostle of democracy, Jean-Jacques Rousseau, had strenuously objected to the employment of representative assemblies for the purpose of enacting legislation; he felt that all such assemblies tend to pervert the genuine expression of the "general will" and to transform a democracy into an aristocracy (see above, Chap. XVI, ¶ 2). Though the complexities of Rousseau's doctrine of the general will cannot detain us here, we may say that we are inclined to understand the general will as referring to an objective thing, like the general interest, rather than the subjective element of will. Indeed, the metaphysical rationalism of Rousseau finds nowhere more striking expression than in the interpretation of will which his doctrine of the general will involves. For in order to make plausible this identification of will and interest or purpose, the public as a group must be interpreted as an organism, living and acting and deciding for itself. The vote of the majority of the individuals composing this group is an indication of what the will of the group, the general will, is or may be; but it is not itself the general will. Even so, it can be such an indication only if each individual as he votes asks himself: "What do *we* want?" rather than: "What do I want?"; for in the latter case you merely get a sum of individual wills. It was suggested above that it is very curious that Rousseau should have rejected the idea of representation; for it may be argued that elected representatives, being of a somewhat higher order than the average man in the street, would more often be inclined to ask the right question. The easiest explanation of Rousseau's animosity to representative assemblies is derived from his observations in Switzerland, where the aristocratic government of Geneva contrasted strongly with the simple democracy of the rural cantons. Indeed, his attempt to resuscitate the older democratic forms in his essay on the government of Geneva (for which he was exiled) stands as a vivid reminder of his intense interest in these contrasts. It is, therefore, not too much to say that these general ideas of radical and direct democracy, and the gradual spread of the referendum as an instrument of practical democracy in the second half of the nineteenth century are parallel developments mutually intensifying each other.

The Napoleonic plebiscites.—The French Revolution brought forth a curious application (or so it seemed to the actors on the revolutionary stage) of Rousseau's views when the Committee on Public Safety claimed to act on behalf of the general public because the members were subject to recall by the public at large. Unhappily, it remained quite obscure how this public was supposed to swing into action, since every opponent of the Committee landed promptly on the guillotine. Such a condition could not long be endured; but the efforts toward returning to a constitutional order ended in the ascendancy of Napoleon Bonaparte, who in turn claimed to be the executor of the general will, on behalf of the people, thus fulfilling the role of the (divine) legislator whom Rousseau had envisaged as a necessary corrective of human frailty in large political bodies. Napoleon, however, who in his youth had been deeply attached to the doctrines of Rousseau, and had rendered a measure of lip service to them all his life, went further than the Committee on Public Safety had done. At certain crucial moments in his career, such as his election to remain first consul for his entire lifetime, and his assumption of the position of Emperor, he called for popular plebiscites which would indicate what the public thought about these changes. Such was the theory. In practice, open registers facilitated a large measure of coercion, and the percentages of favorable votes were correspondingly high. In the first of these plebiscites it was found, on August 2, 1802, that 3,568,885 Frenchmen had voted "yes," and only 8,374 "no" on the proposal of making Napoleon consul for life. In spite of local frauds, these figures are generally believed to be accurate. Of course, the prefects and military officials undoubtedly exerted extensive pressure, but on the whole this result was due to Napoleon's victories and the reëstablishment of the church. The second plebiscite produced similar results. Assent to the establishment of an hereditary empire was given by 3,372,329 voters, while only 2,569 objected. In this case we know of a certain amount of manipulation, even by Napoleon himself, and the number of abstaining objectors may have been appreciably larger. There was also a great deal of local fraud. Voters who could not write were summarily reported by the authorities, and no real vote ever took place. A good many cases of actual intimidation are known. To proclaim such popular votes an indication of Rousseau's general will was a sordid sham, or a bad joke. When the third Napoleon executed his coup d'état in 1851, he at once revived the practice of his illustrious uncle and ordered a plebiscite to be held on the question of whether the French people approved of his action. They did. On the 31st of December, 1851, an electoral commission could report to the new dictator that 7,439,216 people had voted in the affirmative, and 640,737 in the negative. This dissent of about 7 per cent of the voting citizens considerably exceeds the opposition under the first Napoleon. The technique of open registers was discarded when loud protests were raised against it, but almost the same results were achieved by supplying only an insufficient number of ballots with "no" printed on them so that those who wished to object were obliged to write out their votes, which made them readily recognizable. It is now generally believed that the vote as reported is fairly accurate; nor is the difference between it and the vote given to Napoleon at the time of his election to the presidency (1848) so large as to imply the extensive use of force. A later plebiscite instituted to accept the elevation of Napoleon to Emperor yielded similar results, though the actual percentage of negative votes was smaller. There were 7,824,189 votes for, and 253,145 against the empire, or only about 3 per cent negative. But the abstentions are reported as amounting to 2,062,789. In certain parts of France, like the Vendée and the Rhône Valley, they ran to 40 per cent and over. But just the same, Napoleon had gained further adherents and could claim solid popular support. When, in the course of the evolution of the empire toward a measure of liberalism, a limited parliamentary regime was to be instituted in 1870, the proposed constitutional change was again submitted to a plebiscite. This time the outcome was more equivocal, particularly since the electorate had come to look upon the vote in terms rather of endorsing the government of Napoleon, than in terms of the proposed liberalization. Particularly in the cities this plebiscite revealed massive opposition. This opposition came, of course, to a considerable extent also from those followers of Napoleon who believed in the thoroughly authoritarian and dictatorial conduct of the government. Indeed, on the night of the plebiscite, when the first returns were coming in, things looked very black; for in Paris and the Seine department there were 138,000 "yes" votes, 184,000 "no" votes, 83,000 abstentions, and about 10,000 invalid votes. But the rural population solidly supported the Napoleonic dictatorship. For the whole of France there were 7,358,786 affirmative votes, and 1,571,939 negative ones, with about 2,000,000 abstentions and invalid votes. It will be seen that the latter remained about the same, but that about 20 per cent of the voters at this juncture turned out against the empire. The government did not attach too much importance to this trend. Yet within a year the empire had collapsed and its inner hollowness been revealed.

The referendum and initiative: Switzerland.—In Switzerland, direct popular action was put to a very different use. The radically democratic elements fostered it as a curb on the ruling Liberals. After a rapid spread of the movement in the cantons during the sixties, the referendum (and the initiative) were embodied in the constitution in 1874. Without going into detail, it may be said that such action was organized according to ancient traditions as a restraint upon the governmental agencies established under the constitution. To consult the majority of the people at large, as well as the majority of the people as divided into cantons, was made obligatory in all matters affecting the constitution itself. Moreover, with sufficient backing any matter could be embodied in the constitution through popular initiative with subsequent referendum. Both methods have been extensively used since that time and a considerate judgment is possible today. There can be no question that these methods of direct popular action as used in Switzerland are working fairly satisfactorily. It has been rightly remarked that in Switzerland the popular votes have tended to be on the conservative side, but in certain matters of social reform they have tended to favor progressive measures, such as the referendum on compulsory insurance for workingmen (1891), or the law for the purchase of railroads by the government (1900). Whenever such measures tended unduly to enhance the power of the central government, they have, however, been rejected, as happened to the constitutional amendment to extend the power of the federal government to uniform legislation on trades (1894), or the constitutional amendment for direct federal taxation (1918). The workings of this obligatory referendum on the constitutional amendments proposed by the federal legislature are simple. On the whole, the referenda have been positive. From 1874-1933 thirty-seven amendments were passed by the legislature, and only seven were rejected. There were fewer rejected between 1896 and 1919 (one in sixteen) than between 1874 and 1895 (four in ten), but since the war, from 1920 to 1933, this tendency has been slightly reversed (two in twelve). It is difficult to say what the reasons for these fluctuations may be. This obligatory referendum procedure is, as noted above, implemented by a constitutional initiative according to which 50,000 voters can demand a constitutional amendment. It has been said that this method acts as a spur in the flanks of the legislative steed, while the obligatory referendum is a bit in the mouth. As in riding, the spurs are used less frequently than the bit. At the same time, this method finds favor with the voters less often than does the obligatory referendum, even though the percentage voting is rather higher. The fact of the matter is that the initiative proceedings are employed for highly controversial subjects such as the right to work and the duty of the government to provide work (1894), or the recent estate tax (1922). With the present method dating from 1891, there have been twenty-four such initiative proposals, and of these eighteen have been rejected, down to 1932. Economic and social measures have been most frequent, in both initiative and obligatory referenda. After an initial period of extreme proposals, the measures put forward under the initiative procedure have on the whole been moderately progressive. They have helped in the process of democratic popular education; they have given the

Swiss people a feeling that the constitution is theirs for the making and unmaking. Similar methods prevail throughout the majority of the cantons. The federal constitution requires cantonal constitutions to be submitted to popular referendum. Initiative also is found in many of them. The problem of the constitutional amending power, always a thorny question in connection with constitutions (see above, Chap. IX, ¶ 6), has here found a significant solution. Direct popular action is, however, not limited to constitutional amendments. The constitution also provides for a referendum on important legislative measures, if eight cantons or 30,000 voters demand it. It is reported that of three hundred and thirty laws and resolutions which might have been subjected to such a referendum, thirty-five were actually so tested down to 1922, and of them nineteen failed of acceptance. These were not necessarily the most important measures, but rather the ones which had aroused popular interest. While the federal government does not recognize a corresponding right to initiate legislation, this is provided for in many of the cantonal constitutions and is extensively used. The percentage of the voters whose signatures are required varies between 3.09 per cent in Basel Stadt to 12.77 per cent in Schwyz. In the federal realm where the actual numbers are fixed as 30,000 and 50,000 the percentage has varied from about 12.5 per cent in 1848 to 6.1 per cent in 1910 (for initiative petitions). During the same period, the participation in these forms of direct popular action has been changing, downward in the case of compulsory referenda, upward in the case of initiative and optional referenda.

Year	Obl. Ref.	Opt. Ref.	Initiative	Elections
1871–1880..........	76.3	58.2	60.0	—
1881–1890..........	50.0	60.9	—	57.5
1891–1900..........	48.2	60.4	57.5	54.0
1901–1910..........	42.9	61.0	50.9	55.0
1911–1922..........	40.8	66.1	55.7	60.0
1923–1933..........	61.3	70.3	63.0	76.3

These figures are in keeping with what one would expect. Optional referenda and initiative proceedings are extensively propagandized beforehand in connection with the collection of the necessary signatures for the petition, while the obligatory referenda come from the legislature with the official approval which tends to insure them success at the hands of the electorate. The most competent writer on Switzerland in the United States, Professor Brooks, has summarized the whole experience in the following phrases: "Direct legislation in

Switzerland has not realized all the extravagant anticipations of its friends. But on the other hand it has completely falsified the dismal prophecies of chaos and revolution uttered by the conservatives of an earlier period. It has become a vital and freely functioning part of the Swiss political organism." The recurrent refusal of the general electorate to sanction constitutional and legislative measures designed to benefit particular groups suggests the referendum as an integrating mechanism, where the representative bodies may be inclined to yield to the pressure of particular interest groups. This does not, however, always work. When the law for the reduction of the salaries of civil servants was submitted to a popular vote, at the request of the unions of civil servants, it was defeated (1933), though by a narrow majority. We cannot close this discussion without brief mention of a post-war extension of the referendum system in Switzerland—that is, the addition, in 1921, of a constitutional provision to the effect that treaties with foreign powers must be, when requested, submitted to a referendum, if they are concluded for over fifteen years. The demand for this change originated in the popular dissatisfaction over the "Gotthard Treaty" of 1913, which limited the control of Switzerland over railroad rates between Germany and Italy. There can be little question that this provision is a logical consequence of the idea that the popular referendum expresses the ultimate decision. Even before the enactment of this provision the referendum had been used in connection with the entry of Switzerland into the League of Nations (1920). Indeed, this entry was accepted by a very narrow majority of 56.3 per cent of those voting, with 77.5 per cent of those entitled to vote participating in this momentous decision. A later treaty, the so-called *Zonenabkommen,* which was to settle the long-drawn-out controversy between France and Switzerland concerning their boundary adjustments, also was rejected by the electorate. Whether this decision was a wise one, and augurs well for the application of direct popular action in the field of international affairs is very questionable. The percentages against the proposal were very high in many cantons, but significantly they were lowest in the cantons most immediately affected, Freiburg and Waadt actually having a majority in favor, and Geneva almost so (48.9 per cent).

Same subject: United States.—The constitutional referendum migrated from the United States, where it was first employed in Massachusetts (1788) and again in connection with the ratification of the federal constitution, through France to Switzerland. But while it disappeared in the United States for almost a hundred years, it was developed and extended into the legislative field, as we have seen. To it was added the initiative in both constitutional and ordinary legislation, and toward the end of the century these various methods for direct popular action returned to the United States, there to sweep through the several states, beginning with Oregon in 1904. On the whole, the experience has been the same as in Switzerland; neither the ardent hopes of its first expounders nor the dire apprehensions of its opponents have materialized. Both referendum and initiative have become recognized parts of the American political machinery. But whereas Switzerland has developed them extensively in the national realm, the United States have so far limited them to the states. To be sure, at least one of the methods for constitutional amendment is a form of indirect popular referendum, but since it has not been used, it need not concern us here. We find, in the several states, and in many different forms and combinations, referendum, both compulsory and optional, and initiative, the latter two applicable to legislation as well as constitutional amendment. Compulsory referenda are the most frequently used of these methods. One is told that during the ten years from 1899 to 1908, 472 constitutional questions were submitted to the electorates of forty-three states, and from 1919 to 1925 over 600 such measures were thus voted upon. The optional referendum (also called popular referendum) has been put to the test between 1906 (in Oregon) and 1925 173 times in sixteen states. Finally, the initiative has been brought into play during the same period 440 times, but of these 120 times in Oregon. A few states with highly developed interest in direct popular action, such as Oregon and California, contribute a considerable part of the total sum. As in Switzerland, we find that the optional referendum and the initiative elicit a higher percentage of voter-interest than the compulsory referendum. Regarding the latter, the figures are very discouraging, rising only in a few localities above 50 per cent of the vote for Governor, for example. The figures in the last paragraph show that voter-interest in Switzerland is higher than that. This is undoubtedly in large measure attributable to the peculiar nature of American state constitutions. The mass of legislative detail included in many of them, when combined with the compulsory referendum, necessitates the submission of a large number of trivial and uninteresting matters to the electorate. Optional referenda and initiated votes usually reach as respectable a percentage as 75 per cent of the vote cast for governor, though this percentage is materially below the Swiss figures. While these procedures seem to arouse a larger amount of public interest, it cannot be said that the measures brought before the electorate are, on the whole, either foolish or extreme, nor does the action of the electorate itself seem irrational. As in Switzerland, there is a higher mortality amongst optional referenda and initiated proposals, more than half being rejected, but it is rare that measures are either proposed or passed which have not also been proposed or passed by some state legislature. One difficulty with ordinary legislative referenda is that they might be employed by special interest groups for the purpose of delaying the enactment of necessary, and sometimes even of urgent legislation. States have tried to cope with this situation by excepting emergency legislation from the operation of the optional referendum. The difficulty is that no agreement exists as to what constitutes an emergency (see above, Chap. XIV). Under the optional referendum and the initiative, the desire of the voters is ordinarily registered in the form of a certain percentage of voters subscribing to a list under a petition. Upon investigation it is found that these signatures rarely indicate any real urge on the part of the signer. Yet it is hard to see how the popular demand should otherwise be indicated. The trouble which results from this arrangement is found in the premium it places upon such petitions as find favor with financially potent groups. It may, however, be pointed out that other groups, like trade unions, command a sufficiently numerous following to secure signatures without any appreciable outlay of money, and the social reform initiatives in this country as well as in Switzerland bear witness to this observation. Inasmuch as one of the greatest advantages of direct popular action is felt to flow from the educational stimulus which results from the attendant agitation, official literature on the subject of referenda has in certain states been provided by the government, giving, in the case of California, the arguments pro and con. It seems that such arrangements materially increase the voters' interest. These instrumentalities for direct popular action are not perfect mechanisms. Only an inveterate Rousseauist could survey the experience to date and still maintain that they provide a panacea for the difficulties of popular government. The electorate is quite liable to abuse its power, and checks necessarily have to be put upon it. Inasmuch as all the forms of direct action have been developed in the states, they are subject to the constitutional limitations of the federal constitution which the Supreme Court enforces. Occasional tendencies to invade the sphere of private rights or to neglect the rights of minorities (racial and others) have thus been checked. The danger of the electorate's inclining to expand its own power has generally been adduced against the use of the initiative in the field of constitutional amendment (where it is used under the Swiss federal constitution). But one must agree with A. N. Holcombe that "there can be no doubt that the referendum is now permanently established among the political institutions of the states. There is little question of abandoning it," this authority continues. "The only questions concerning which there are still serious differences of opinion relate to the form in which, and the conditions under which, it shall be used." What is even more important, according to the rule of anticipated reactions, it is undoubtedly true that "the best effects of the popular initiative should be found, in the long run, not in the legislation placed by its use directly upon the statute books, but rather in the improvement of the legislation placed there by the legislatures."

Direct popular action and the general problem of representation.—The political problems created by the spread of the several methods of direct popular action have received a certain measure of attention. Their tendency to corrupt the people, and to weaken the representative assemblies has been urged time and again. A. L. Lowell has considered these questions. The low percentage of voters participating in many of these decisions has raised the problem of the trustworthiness of the result, and in the case of the compulsory referenda in the United States with their very low percentages, this trustworthiness has been widely questioned. Cases can readily be cited where the electorate reversed itself in short order. The possible delays involved in referendum procedure serve as another point of attack. It is unquestionably the most important question, however, just how direct popular action fits into the general pattern of representation. It has generally been assumed that there is a conflict between representation and direct popular action, and those who, unlike Rousseau, consider representative government in a favorable light tend to question direct popular action. It may, however, be asked whether such direct popular action does not itself possess representative quality. Not merely that it is exercised by the electorate on behalf of the people, though that is a point worth remembering. But rather that the electorate itself is represented by those who are participating in the vote. We have seen above that the voting in these referenda is rather limited. Now it will be recalled that our definition of representation (from Mohl) held that representation would be the process through which the influence which the entire citizenry or a part of them have upon governmental action is exercised on their behalf by a smaller number among them, with binding effect upon those represented as well as those participating in the decision. It is evident that the voters participating in a referendum stand in precisely such a relationship to the total electorate and the people at large as the concept of representation implies. The real difference between direct popular action and the action of legislatures and other "representatives" lies in the field of deliberation. The voters cannot assemble and discuss matters. But under modern conditions it may be doubted whether this difference is not more apparent than real. A constant meeting of minds is made possible through newspapers and other journalistic media. All questions of general public interest stir up discussion and argument. The big shot makes speeches which are reported in full columns, average Mr. Citizen writes a "Letter to the Editor." But both participate in the deliberation. What is more, many vital issues are thrashed out within the organized interest groups. The referendum within the United States Chamber of Commerce is a striking illustration. The representatives of these interest groups in turn participate in the public discussions, through speeches, articles, and other communications. The day to day history of any referendum reveals the wide extent of actual discussion which goes into such a decision. And after all, the discussion in deliberative assemblies is not as unrelated to these forces as earlier views tended to imply. We have seen how party, press, and interest groups are influencing what is being said in the halls of legislatures, if they do not actually dictate it. In other words, our modern means of communication have set up a context within which representative action by a much larger part of the electorate than formerly has become practicable. It remains to remark in this connection that the contrast between England, as the classical country of representative government, and countries like the United States and Switzerland must not be overstressed. After all, whenever an English election turns upon a hotly debated issue, as it did in 1923, 1924, 1931, and so forth, it amounts in practice to a popular referendum. This has often been pointed out and acute students have related this emergence of the general electorate alongside the cabinet as a primary aspect of the decline of Parliament (see above, 345). Whether it is actually caused by these developments, may well be doubted, however; the two go hand in hand as parallel changes in connection with the changes in the underlying social and technical pattern of life. If looked upon in this perspective, direct popular action requires subjection to effective constitutional controls. That subject was touched upon in the previous paragraph. In the United States, the most important check results from the federal dispersion of direct popular action. In Switzerland, the constitutional initiative opens up a practically unfettered realm for the exercise of unlimited power, but so far the Swiss voters have shown great restraint in extending their own influence. It may, however, be different in countries with a less firmly rooted tradition of political democracy, or rent more violently by the controversies of contemporary social conflict. Even in Switzerland, the introduction of direct action into the field of foreign affairs is a matter of some concern; in a larger country with a real foreign policy such a step might be disastrous (see below, ¶ 9).

The "will of the people" in the international field: plebiscites before the war.—Ever since the French Revolution direct popular action has also played a role in international affairs. Referenda concerning the territorial status of controversial areas have been held from time to time. The doctrine of popular sovereignty as expounded by the French revolutionaries following Rousseau logically led to the idea of national self-determination. At the same time, it proved a potent instrument in furthering the expansive aims of the Revolution in its later phases. In Avignon, in Savoy, in Nice, as well as in Belgium and the Palatinate, Mulhouse, and Geneva, plebiscites were held to determine whether the voters favored the attachment of their territory to France. The methods were fairly constitutional at first, but gradually became more constraining. Military occupations preceded and accompanied the popular votes, and pressure was exerted everywhere. As may be surmised, the monarchical reaction had very little use for this method of consulting the people, and no plebiscites were consequently held until after 1848. Cavour extensively relied upon them in his efforts to unify Italy, declaring that "the dukes, the archdukes, and the grand dukes will be found buried under the pile of ballots deposited in the electoral urns." And so they were. In all the Italian principalities the popular referenda went strongly in favor of unification. With the emergence of Bismarckian statesmanship the plebiscite suffered another eclipse. The consolidation of national states throughout Europe did not offer promising opportunities, except in areas where the existing powers would not even contemplate such a method. Obviously, the plebiscite might well have exploded the Hapsburg Empire by the end of the nineteenth century, if it had been offered to the subject nationalities. Even more portentous were its potentialities in the colonial sphere. The nascent "nationalism" in India and elsewhere might well have adopted the plebiscite as a promising weapon of combat, had it been allowed to do so. After all, had not the American colonies broken away by precisely this method? What was the Declaration of Independence but just such a plebiscite? It is not to be wondered at that the age of imperialism would have none of so dangerous a technique. Nevertheless, isolated instances occurred. After the forcible separation of Norway from Sweden, in 1905, the latter insisted upon holding a plebiscite, thus, it would seem, demanding an insult to top the injury, in view of the overwhelming sentiment expressed in favor of such a separation. All these instances suggest that the technique of direct popular voting seems relatively well adapted to the settlement of territorial controversies. The two major difficulties arise in connection with (1) the adequate policing of such votes, in order to prevent intimidation of the voters, and (2) the agreement, beforehand, upon appropriate methods for interpreting the results of the plebiscite, in order to prevent the controversy from being more troublesome after the plebiscite has been held. But both these problems, while they appeared in the plebiscites before the World War, can more readily be studied in connection with the plebiscites held since that time, a subject to which we now turn.

Same subject: after the war.—The principle of the self-determination of nations which Wilson had made part of his peace program led to the most extensive application of the method of plebiscites, although Wilson himself was not very favorable toward this particular technique for settling boundary problems. While he enunciated the general idea that "national aspirations must be respected," and furthermore that "peoples and provinces are not to be bartered about from sovereignty to sovereignty as if they were mere chattels and pawns in a game . . ." (February 11, 1918), he apparently became convinced, by the time the peace was to be made, that popular votes were unsatisfactory. It was the possibility of sanctioning secession which loomed in the minds of many Americans. After all, what would have happened if such a doctrine had been preached and accepted before the outbreak of the Civil War? And what about the clamor for Philippine independence? Once more the anarchistic potentialities of radical democracy appeared and they made Wilson and his advisers recoil. But there were so many points in the territorial settlement of Europe which seemed beyond the scope of any rational compromise that the exigencies of practical politics resulted in the provision for a considerable number of such votes. At the very outset, the Danes came forward with the demand for a plebiscite in Northern Schleswig, such as was supposed to have been held in 1867, but had been discarded by Bismarck. This plebiscite led to a division of the territory between Denmark and Germany. Held under the supervision of allied troops, it has been attacked by Germans as unfair; yet it was probably the most acceptable plebiscite held under the peace treaty, with the possible exception of the plebiscite in the Saar. Many of the more important plebiscites were written into the treaty as a compromise between the Allies themselves. Thus the plebiscites in East Prussia and in Upper Silesia resulted from the insistence of the English that the non-German character of these territories should be ascertained. Again, the plebiscite in the Saar valley was the compromise secured by France when she was forced to relinquish her claims upon the left bank of the Rhine, which were being resolutely opposed by the English and Americans. Now in all these post-war plebiscites the voting was more or less effectively supervised by police forces controlled by other governments than those involved in the decision of the plebiscite. The troops and the higher officials of both contesting parties were removed. It is, perhaps, unfortunate that such policing could not at once have been undertaken by neutrals as the Germans repeatedly had demanded. Particularly in the case of the Upper Silesian plebiscite, this failure of really neutral police supervision had the result of discrediting the outcome of the plebiscite. But as we shall see later, it was really not so much the vote which caused trouble in that case as it was the interpretation of the vote. Even though the Allies, and particularly France, could hardly be called neutrals in a vote between Germany and Poland, immediately after the war, a more adequate military force could have prevented the worst abuses, and suppressed the fierce civil war (Polish Insurrection) which developed out of the plebiscite. It must certainly be said that methods of neutralization such as were employed in the Saar valley plebiscite which was held under the auspices of the League of Nations are much more satisfactory. Furthermore, adequate arrangements for the interpretation of the vote would seem as important as the neutralization of the contested territory. Undoubtedly the most acceptable plan is one whereby it is definitely agreed beforehand just how the outcome of the vote is going to be applied. For obviously a great difference may be implied in treating the territory as a whole, or dividing it into various parts. The latter method obviously lends itself to extensive "gerrymandering." It was undoubtedly one of the best features of the Schleswig

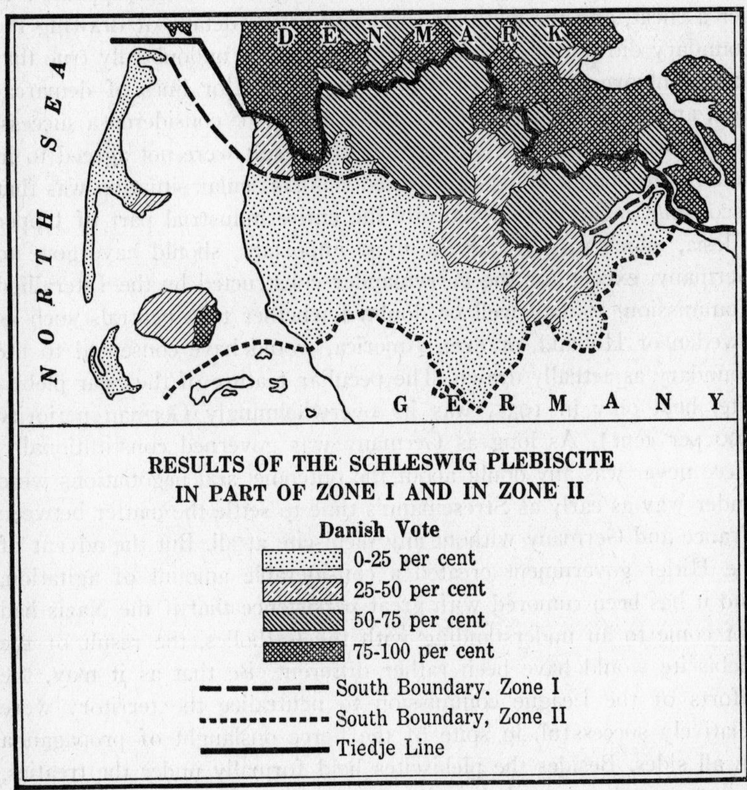

RESULTS OF THE SCHLESWIG PLEBISCITE IN PART OF ZONE I AND IN ZONE II

plebiscite that here the division of the territory was made beforehand, and embodied as part of the vital conditions. Nothing illustrates, perhaps, as well as the following sketch what can thus be accomplished. By skillfully dividing the Schleswig area, a Danish majority could be secured in the upper zone (I), whereas if the territory had been taken as a whole, the majority of the votes being for Germany, it would all have gone to Germany. But fortunately, this method of division had previously been agreed to by Germany, so that no controversy could afterwards result from it. Different was the case of Upper Silesia. Here too, as the following graph shows, the whole territory went for Germany by about 65 per cent, but it was quite feasible to divide it and cut off a part which would have a Polish majority. This was actually done, but unfortunately no adequate agreement had been reached beforehand concerning any such zoning. Consequently Germany has been smarting under what appeared to her a cheat, and the methods employed in the details of drawing the boundary did not alleviate this sentiment. It is undoubtedly true that little controversy can exist concerning the major lines of demarcation, and yet the plebiscite as a whole cannot be considered a success, because the methods of interpreting the result were not agreed to in detail beforehand. What aggravated this particular situation was that according to the vote, practically the entire industrial part of Upper Silesia, which was by far the most important, should have gone to Germany, except for the gerrymander constructed by the Interallied Commission. It may well be doubted whether true neutrals such as Sweden or Holland, or even America, would have consented to the boundary as actually drawn. The peculiar feature of the Saar plebiscite, held only in 1935, was its overwhelmingly German majority (90 per cent). As long as Germany was governed constitutionally, there never was any doubt about the outcome, and negotiations were under way as early as Stresemann's time to settle the matter between France and Germany without any plebiscite at all. But the advent of the Hitler government created a considerable amount of agitation, and it has been rumored with great persistence that if the Nazis had not come to an understanding with the Catholics, the result of the plebiscite would have been rather different. Be that as it may, the efforts of the League commission to neutralize the territory were relatively successful, in spite of the fierce onslaught of propaganda on all sides. Besides the plebiscites held formally under the treaties, there were also some informal ones, like the votes in two Austrian provinces, the Tyrol and Salzburg, demanding unification with Germany, but these came to nothing. They lacked entirely any attempt at neutralization, nor did any agreement exist as to their purpose. They were essentially popular demonstrations, voicing a certain sentiment. It seems clear from all that has been said that the plebiscite as a technique for settling boundary disputes holds distinct possibilities in a democratic age. The leading American authority on the subject is right in saying that the plebiscite is not to be considered a

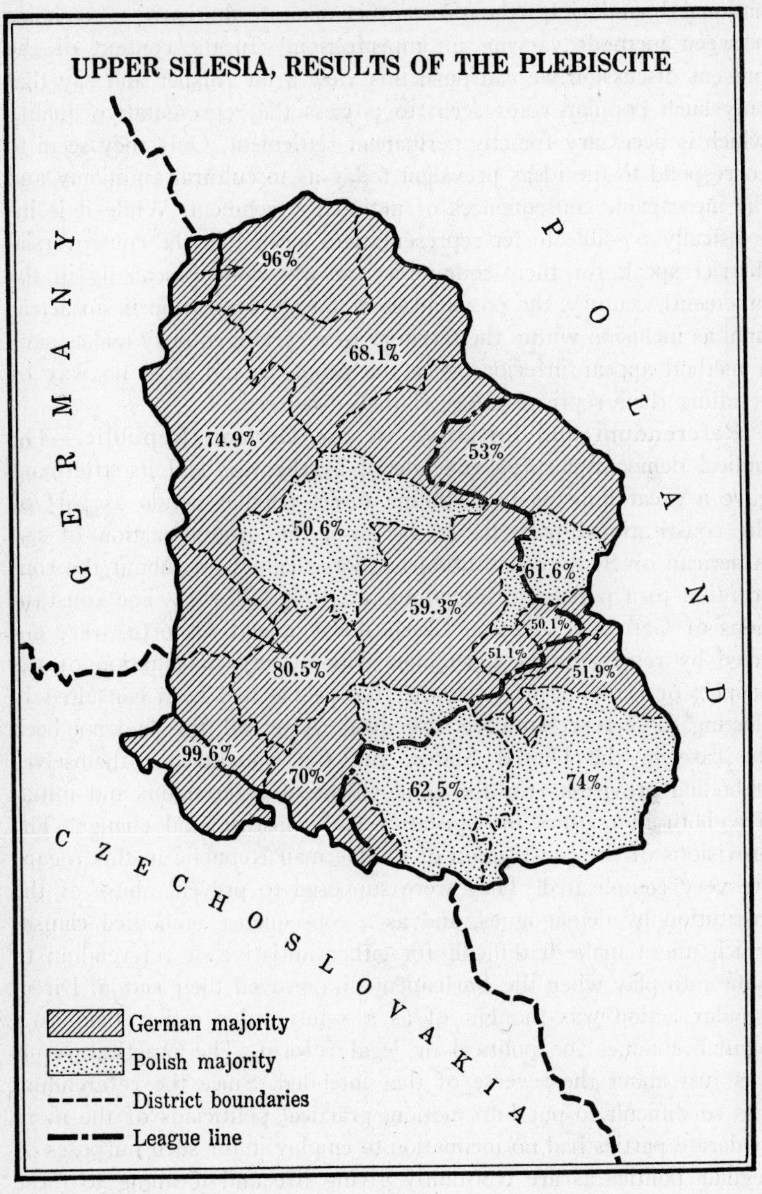
UPPER SILESIA, RESULTS OF THE PLEBISCITE
GERMANY
POLAND
CZECHOSLOVAKIA
96%
68.1%
74.9%
53%
50.6%
61.6%
59.3%
50.1%
51.1%
80.5%
51.9%
99.6%
70%
62.5%
74%
German majority
Polish majority
District boundaries
League line

perfect tool, but since there is no perfect method of establishing national boundaries, "the problem is one of alternatives, a choice between methods varying in imperfection." In the context of the present discussion we can push this view a bit further and say that only such popular votes seem to possess the representative quality which is necessary for any permanent settlement. Only they seem to correspond to the ideas prevalent today as to cultural autonomy and the inescapable consequences of national attachment. While it is intrinsically possible to let representatives elected in the controversial district speak for their community, as was done repeatedly in the nineteenth century, the possibilities of misrepresentation in an act as final as inclusion within the territory of a certain country makes such a method appear inferior, since the people would have no way of recalling their representatives if they disagreed.

Referendum and initiative in the German Republic.—The radical democratic surge engendered by the war and its aftermath gave a great impetus to including direct popular action as part of the constitutional pattern. To be sure, the original action of the American or Swiss constitution builders, namely to submit the constitution to a popular referendum, was not followed. The constitutions of Germany, Austria, Czechoslovakia, and so forth, were enacted by representative assemblies without any consultation of the people; or rather it was felt that the people had been consulted in electing those representative assemblies. After all, this had not been the case in the United States. But the constitutions themselves embodied provisions for the employment of referendum and initiative, both in matters of legislative and constitutional change. The provisions of the constitution of the German Republic in this regard are very complicated. They were supposed to prevent abuse of the institution by demagogues, and as a consequence embodied clauses which might make it difficult for either initiative or referendum to come into play when the Parliament disapproved their action. Direct popular action was thought of as a safety valve rather than as a regular channel for political or legal reform. The practical result was just about the reverse of that intended. Since the referendum was so difficult to put into motion, practical politicians of the more moderate parties had no inclination to employ it for such purposes of regular politics as are constantly giving life and meaning to these forms of direct popular action in Switzerland or the United States. Indeed it may be said that a certain bureaucratic tendency among

German party bosses (see above, Chap. XVII, ¶ 12) made them shy away from methods which might stir up their party following. No such scruples bothered the radical elements, the Communists and the Nazis. Of the three referenda actually brought to some test, the referendum enacting the expropriation of the princes was initiated by the Communists, and although the Social Democrats supported it, willy-nilly, they were unable to prevail upon the Communists to adopt a formula which might have secured it the necessary popular support (June 20, 1926). The following referendum (1928), calling upon the people to rule that no battleships should be built by the German government, was again initiated by the Communists. The third referendum was initiated by the die-hard wing of the Nationalists and the "Steel Helmet," the leading veterans' organization. It called for renunciation of the so-called war-guilt clause of the Treaty of Versailles (Article 231), and made it criminal for a government official to sign any treaty or agreement with a foreign power involving payments to it. This provision was levelled at the men who had just signed the Young Plan (Dec. 22, 1929). All these referenda were unsuccessful, the first and the third because they failed to bring out one-half the electorate as was required for constitutional referenda, the second because the Communists were unable to secure the support of 10 per cent of the electorate for their request. Four other referenda proposed by various groups were disallowed by the Ministry of the Interior, since they involved budgetary matters (which were excepted from the realm of direct popular action, under the constitution). As far as the first of these referenda was concerned, it answered to a sentiment so strongly felt by the German masses that its support far exceeded the radical elements who had initiated it. The original petition, which required about 4,000,000 signatures, was, in fact, signed by 12,523,939 voters. This figure is appreciably larger than the combined vote of the Social Democrats and the Communists had been in previous elections. Since the German Parliament rejected the proposed measure, and its provisions were held to alter the constitution (private property and equal protection of the law clauses), a majority of all registered voters had to be brought out. This the Socialists and Communists found impossible. For one thing, the constitutional requirement of a majority of the registered voters unintentionally made the referendum public, once the opposition decided to boycott the ballot (as they were apt to do). It is difficult, if not impossible, to determine the extent to which political pressure was used in keeping voters from the polls. It is a fair assumption that such pressure played a role in small towns and rural districts. The final result of the ballot showed 14,441,590 affirmative, 584,723 negative, and 559,406 void ballots. Of the 24,000,000 people who did not vote, about 8,000,000 were habitual non-voters. It appears, after deducting that many, that the margin between supporters and opponents of the measure was rather narrow. It also shows that after allowance for all qualifying considerations has been made, this referendum could not, very probably, have been carried. A more moderate proposal, giving the princes a limited life-estate, might have been accepted, and would have satisfied the popular sentiment. But the Communists, it is fair to say, did not care about that problem. To them the referendum simply appeared as a grand opportunity for stirring up passions and controversy; the Republic was doomed, anyway.

The nationalist implications of direct popular action: the referendum on the Young Plan.—The most striking illustration of the inherent dangers of direct popular action is provided by the third of the German referenda, held in December 1929 on the war guilt issue and the reparations problem. The content of this referendum was of doubtful constitutionality, and the particular issues involved were not definite enough to offer any clear alternatives. But the referendum proposal did quite distinctly voice the indignation of a considerable part of the German electorate at the international position of Germany. Who constituted this part of the German electorate? Apart from the groups which one would naturally expect to be on this side, there is a very clear indication, statistically, that the rural parts of Germany provided the mass support for this outburst of "emotional nationalism." The actual leadership came, of course, from other quarters. As already remarked, certain German Nationalist groups, fearing that the evacuation of the Rhineland might be construed as a victory for the moderates, were anxious to focus the attention of the public upon the sacrifices involved in bringing about this result. More specifically, the Steel Helmet, a veterans' organization, and the German Nationalist party requested the Minister of the Interior to open the lists of petitions for a referendum on a "law against the enslavement of the German people," briefly called the "Liberty Law." The proposed bill required the German government to notify the foreign powers involved that the war-guilt clauses of the Versailles Treaty were contrary to fact and not binding in law; to demand the unconditional withdrawal of all troops from occupied areas; and to declare any officer of the German government who would sign a treaty based upon the "war-guilt lie" guilty of treason. In his original speech delivered before the Arminius Monument and commemorating the victory over the Romans, Herr Hugenberg, the leader of the Nationalists, had declared: "The world will return our sword to us when our hearts have become pure and strong. Our revival will be easier than we imagine now in our despondency. We do not wish to be the slaves of foreign capital. Against this we must fight with the hardness of our hearts and the steadfastness of our will. These two will eventually produce an effect like that of the trumpets of Jericho. The plan of tributes agreed to in Paris must not become law." We have here a clear manifestation of heedless nationalism. Violent controversies were provoked within the Nationalist camp itself over the provision making criminals of any government officers who might sign the Young Plan. Hindenburg was reported to be strongly hostile to this aspect of the referendum. It would seem that the adoption of this extreme paragraph was due primarily to pressure from the radical elements, this time more particularly the National Socialists. As the *Frankfurter Zeitung* commented: "We must not deceive ourselves: there are today considerable groups in Germany which are so broken by the misery of the war and the inflation that they offer a fertile field for the activity of demagogues and agitators. . . . More particularly the drums and trumpets of Hitler and Goebbels excite those who are so down and out that they cannot consider such a question with sense." Goebbels himself confirmed this diagnosis in writing: "Now the moment has come when the so-called National Opposition must start to fight with all its might the person of Stresemann and his damnable foreign policy. . . . It is the task of our movement to give to this referendum a distinctly *revolutionary* bent. . . . Is it surprising that we mobilize our forces against this nonsense (the Young Plan), that we organize active resistance against this criminal system, and that we help the groaning of a martyrized people to be heard? Away with these traitors to German Liberty. Raise the banners of resistance and revolution." Moderates argued that the referendum itself was likely to retard the liberation of the German people. The government pointed out that no German government had ever recognized the war-guilt clauses of the treaty. On the contrary, this clause had time and again been solemnly denied. But evidently as far as this question was concerned, for the manipulators of the referendum, it was clearly a matter of emotionalizing the masses and of stimulating them to nationalist frenzy, rather than any specific material change of policy. Curiously enough, the difficulties of the German referendum procedure aided such purposes, though the intention had been to forestall them. The very fact that the referendum would hardly be carried made it safe for Hugenberg and his associates to initiate it. Yet, the results were actually rather discouraging to these demagogic leaders. Out of a total electorate of about 42,000,000 only about 6,300,000 or 15 per cent went to the polls. The opposition again boycotted the ballot altogether. It was therefore not a secret vote. Whether in this case the lack of secrecy increased or decreased the vote, it is hard to say; pressures were at work both ways. But the referendum undoubtedly stirred up popular passions, created consternation abroad by showing the fierceness of German nationalism, and contributed toward the disintegration of the constitutional order. It showed that matters of foreign affairs should certainly not be allowed to be part of any scheme for direct popular action, since they permit too large a scope to the irresponsible activity of demagogues.

The plebiscite under the Nazi dictatorship.—The vicissitudes of the referendum under the Weimar Republic do not attend direct popular action when it is called into play by Adolf Hitler. For only the government can invoke it (law of July 14, 1933). According to an official authority, "the meaning of such a 'consultation' of the people by the Leader is to be seen in the fact that the relation of confidence between the Leader and the people as followers receives tangible political expression on the occasion of important political decisions." The National Socialists have used the plebiscite primarily in the field of foreign affairs. Here direct consultation of the people has been made to serve the purpose of demonstrating a united front in support of the aggressive foreign policy of the government. When Hitler, in the fall of 1933, decided to quit the League of Nations and the Disarmament Conference, he appealed to the German people to sanction this act. The move essentially amounted to demonstrating to the whole world, presumably hostile to Hitler's action, that this demand for "equality of treatment" was a demand backed by the entire people. Such a plebiscite mobilizes the democratic myth of the "will of the people" for the attainment of international concessions. The issue of equality had, to be sure, been pushing forward with ever more threatening force after Stresemann first began to talk of the implied (moral) obligation of the allied powers to disarm, after Germany's entry into the League of Nations. Germany having disarmed, the road was now free, so it was argued, for the others to do likewise. Since nothing but talk resulted from such suggestions, the German public was getting more and more aroused over this issue, even under the Republic. Brüning's policy was already permeated by efforts to secure at least in principle the recognition of arms equality. It is, therefore, not surprising that the German masses should have supported the Nazi government in demanding it, and even in quitting the League in protest. The violent propaganda campaign put on by the Nazis in the fall of 1933 merely consolidated the attitudes which had already become dominating amongst Germans of all classes. The referendum, which was held on November 12, 1933, produced the desired results. Of 45,176,713 qualified voters 43,491,575 or 96.3 per cent participated in this ballot, and of these 40,622,628 or 95.1 per cent voted "yes," 2,101,191 or 4.9 per cent voted "no" and the remainder were invalid. As one recent commentator has remarked, "this overwhelming result was wholly without parallel in any other national election or referendum anywhere in the modern world, save in Fascist Italy. It was not achieved by dishonest counting, nor yet by open threats or bribery of voters." This "overwhelming result" had its internal as well as external advantages. It undoubtedly enhanced the majority the government was able to roll up in the "election" it proceeded to hold on the same day. The relation of the two votings is suggested by the fact that in the "election" the government only secured 92.2 per cent of the votes as against the 95.1 per cent in the referendum. To be sure, this election was nothing else than a repetition of the Napoleonic plebiscites; it was an opportunity for the voting masses to acclaim the regime of the Nazis; for only they and their friends were presented to the voters. The opposition had to make the fruitless gesture of turning in an invalid ballot. The technique worked out by the Nazis for this first "democratic" ballot has been applied several times since. After President Hindenburg's death on the last day of July, 1934, Hitler had all presidential powers transferred to himself as Chancellor and Führer, thus avoiding the choice between two undesirable alternatives; either to have a president over himself in form, or to have a chancellor beside himself in reality. This bold measure was secured against criticism by another appeal to the people. "Steeped in the conviction that all authority of the State must proceed from the people and by them be ratified in a free, secret election, I request you immediately to lay the decision of the cabinet before the German people for a free plebiscite." The results were somewhat less imposing than those of the previous plebiscite; of 45,474,157 eligible voters 43,530,232 or 95.7 per cent participated, and of these 38,368,195 or 89.9 per cent voted for, and 4,294,727 or 10.1 per cent voted against Hitler's proposal to take all power to himself. Since the invalid votes were mostly spoiled ballots, we get an opposition of almost 12 per cent. Nor is it possible to be so certain about the accuracy of the reports. Various statements have come out of Germany, and statistical evidence has been offered to indicate that the figures were distorted to a greater or less degree. There is little object in speculating upon the extent of such falsification; adequate evidence cannot be secured, anyway. What is noteworthy is that in certain urban centers, like Cologne, Hamburg, and Berlin, the opposition vote admittedly reached 20 per cent and more. Foreign affairs afford, under contemporary conditions, particularly in Germany, a more effective means of mass appeal to be utilized in plebiscitary acclaims. Consequently, when Hitler reoccupied the Rhineland in the spring of 1936, he immediately proceeded to appeal to the German masses, as he had done in the previous year, when announcing German re-armament in defiance of the Treaty of Versailles. In both cases, popular support did not fail to come forth in impressive and compact numbers, similar to those on the two previous occasions. In both cases, Hitler's international antagonists, particularly the French, were stunned and recoiled from forceful measures in the face of such solid national support. At critical moments in the life of the Nazi dictatorship one may, therefore, always look for some bold action in the international sphere, with a plebiscite following it to reintegrate the crumbling mass support. The limited supply of any safe outlets for that tendency augurs ill for the Nazis as well as for Europe.

The Fascist plebiscites.—The popular referendum or plebiscite does not form as essential a part of the Fascist pattern of government as it does of the National Socialist. Unlike the Nazis, who place the people above the state, the Fascists, proud of their Roman tradition, and with no appreciable numbers of their people outside the national boundaries (except in America) extoll the Machiavellian doctrine of the state as the ultimate value. But there is much practical politics hidden behind these ideological screens. The

Italian masses are not as extensively democratized as are the German masses. The high percentage of illiteracy in Italy has retarded that process. Nor does Italy face the same number of generally felt international grievances. Mussolini's Fascist organization was a relatively small body of determined men who supported him in imposing his conception of politics (Mussolini shall rule!) upon the rest of the Italians. There was no vast popular movement which had to be held together, a movement rent by violent conflicts of interest and principle. The pattern of Italian Fascism is, moreover, profoundly affected by the fact that the king, following Mussolini's conception of the monarchy, has conferred upon Fascism the legitimacy which the National Socialists must seek in popular plebiscites. "The monarchy," Mussolini has said, "is the sacred symbol, glorious, traditional, millenary, of the Nation; we have strengthened the Monarchy and made it more august." With his prestige thus heightened, the king helps to legalize the Fascist power. But the plebiscitary element is not wholly lacking. As Finer has aptly remarked: "Men have need for approval; the Fascists are grateful for it; in fact they even seek for it, and not merely with flickering candles. The Fascist regime is obsessed with the seeking for unanimity." In order to secure this measure of popular approval, the parliamentary "elections" provide a suitable occasion for the unloosing of official propaganda to drum up the desired "acclaim." All the machinations of modern propaganda are brought into play, but the voter remains indifferent, though he votes. To quote Finer once more, "It is the nemesis of dictatorships that they are more tormented morally by the defection of a single voter than democracies." And the Italian "Parliament," which seems such a grotesque and impotent parody of its English namesake, serves primarily, perhaps, the purpose of affording the Fascists the occasion for that periodic appeal for general popular acclaim, the need of which seems to be felt in this democratic age just as much by dictators as by the leaders of constitutional governments.

The contrast of the Soviet Union.—A different situation has seemed to prevail in the Soviet Union (until the recent proposals for constitutional reform along democratic lines). The elaborate tier of councils, governing soviets, trade unions, consumers' cooperatives, and so forth, escapes the classification in older terms. The Bolsheviks themselves designate this elaborate method of indirect election as democratic centralism. There is undoubtedly a very considerable measure of democracy in the local bodies, if by democracy is meant discussion and argument. But such discussion and argument can not, of course, extend beyond the scope of the actual autonomous sphere of the particular body. It may, at any time, be invaded by the higher-ups. The Soviet Union attempts, therefore, a somewhat different solution of the problem of how to combine the urge for popular participation with the need of autocratic direction. One authority recently remarked: "The soviet system left no room for a referendum, or even for a parliamentary general election. It was the reverse of government by the mob." This is, in a measure, true; though a little later the same authority cites the general discussion invoked about the change in family law as an instance of general popular consultation. Certainly in the more recent "consultation" held on a similar issue, there was much discussion, but the authorities calmly flouted the sentiments brought forth, and went ahead with their original proposals. These consultations, in other words, seem to resemble the cabinet consultations of the American Presidents: the ayes have it! There is a great deal of discussion, and as far as technical matters of strictly local concern are involved, these discussions are decisive. But as to any matter of policy, it is authoritatively decided by Stalin and his group. Let Stalin's own words not be cited against this, in comparison with those of Mussolini. Men vary in the candor with which they recognize their own situation. What is more, Stalin seems to be the type who reaches his decisions in consultation with others. But it is not without significance that one of his intimates has characterized him as a mountain with a head: he thinks but he does not move. The whole set-up in the Soviet Union is permeated by the fact that a carefully worked out intellectual pattern, the Marxist-Leninist conception of social life, provides the base-line upon which all action is molded. It is not the will of the people, but the ideas of Marx and Lenin, which ultimately legitimize action. Consequently those who most effectively interpret this creed are secure in the conviction of righteousness; they crave no popular acclaim. There is a profound strain of intellectualist aristocracy in the Marxist doctrine of the Communist believers as the *avant-garde* of the "proletariat." It is on behalf of the proletariat that these guardians in the true platonic sense wield their benevolent and yet autocratic power. It is, from the standpoint of political science, ostrich-like to go to a dictionary to discover that a dictator is "a ruler or governor whose word is law;

a person exercising absolute authority of any kind or in any sphere . . ."; for such a being has never existed in any literal sense. Yet if one recalls the rule of anticipated reactions, he will appreciate more clearly what "discussion" in the presence of a person like Stalin amounts to. It is exactly like the "discussion" in American faculty meetings over which the president of the institution presides. After a great deal of talk that which the president had decided is done, with minor modifications. The fiction of consent, when backed by the ever present threat of death (or starvation), is a sorry sham, and not worthy of thinking men in communities with a tradition of constitutional government.

Conclusion.—In theory and in practice modern democracy has been haunted by the spectre of direct popular action as an alternative to all kinds of representative schemes. The potential manipulation of mass psychology with a view to destroying any and all constitutional restraints in the name of His Majesty the People has taken concrete form in recurrent dictatorial regimes. These regimes have sought to legitimize themselves by securing popular majority support. Napoleon I, Napoleon III, Mussolini, and Hitler were all found to be alike in their search for popular acclaim. The suddenness with which these structures, apparently reared upon so broad a foundation of majority support in the past, have caved in under the impact of victorious foreign armies suggests the unrepresentative quality of this primitive substitute for more elaborate and more highly rationalized schemes of representation. Strange as it may seem at first glance, experience seems to suggest that the representative quality of an act is not at all enhanced by the numbers actually participating in it. This conclusion is equally deducible from the forms of direct popular action introduced into the pattern of constitutional government. The referendum and the initiative have worked with a reasonable degree of smoothness in both Switzerland and the United States; in both they serve a useful purpose in offering yet another technique for the division of power among several groups in the community. But the difficulty of placing effective restraints upon its exercise makes it a questionable device in communities not thoroughly seasoned in popular politics, and thoroughly attached to their constitutional morale.

All political power is subject to abuse, no matter what the legal form of its exercise. But concentrated power is very much more easily abused than divided power. Direct popular action, while not concentrated power under a constitutional set-up, is its nearest kin. If, on the other hand, fear of its possible abuse bars the employment of direct popular action for ordinary purposes, as was done under the German Republic, then its machinery will be used only for the purpose of providing an effective platform for radical propaganda campaigns. The damage done by these abortive efforts is not very easy to estimate. It seems clear enough, however, that they did not do any appreciable good, except in terms of the promoters of these campaigns, Communists and Nazis. At any rate, it may well be doubted whether Jean-Jacques Rousseau after watching the operation of modern plebiscites, nationally or internationally, would be inclined to consider them very useful tools for discovering the "general will." But then, it is only fair to add that he concluded his famous discussion of democracy by the apodictic remark: "If there were somewhere a people of gods, it would govern itself democratically. So perfect a government does not suit human beings." This observation is borne out by political experience. Contemporary American democracy is not an argument against Rousseau's conclusion. For as commonly used among us, the word democracy designates a constitutional government of divided powers. Rousseau would have called it a mixed government, following Polybius and the great writers of the seventeenth century in England. Such a government seems still the nearest possible approach to the government which would prevail among gods or angels. Direct popular action in its several forms serves to strengthen the democratic element of the mixture. If the dose is too strong, it will destroy the balance. That it provides "real democracy," as the German propaganda minister would try to make us believe, is a Utopian dream or a sorry sham.

BIBLIOGRAPHY

LIST OF ABBREVIATIONS

APSR—American Political Science Review
ASWandSP—Archiv für Sozialwissenschaft und Sozialpolitik
CD—Journal Officiel (Chambre des Députés)
ESS—Encyclopedia of the Social Sciences
HCD—Hansard, T. C. (ed.), *Parliamentary Debates*
HDSR—Handbuch des deutschen Staatsrechts
JoR—Jahrbuch des oeffentlichen Rechts
PSQ—Political Science Quarterly
RGZ—Reichsgerichts Entscheidungen, Zivilsachen
SWPSSQ—Southwestern Political and Social Science Quarterly

Chapter I

THE FORMS OF GOVERNMENT AND THE INSTRUMENTS OF POLITICAL ACTION

The problems of method in political science are, of course, part of the larger questions concerning method in the social sciences, in fact, they cannot be discussed without considering scientific method as such. It will unquestionably be noticed that the text adopts views with regard to the broader issues which are still highly controversial, and at variance with what was commonly accepted a few decades ago. Poincaré, Myerson, and Rickert among others, had raised questions concerning the nature of scientific knowledge which no searching student could neglect. The revolutionary developments in physics and other natural sciences after the war have increasingly focused the attention of everyone upon the crumbling edifice of scientific dogma. The great weakness of the imposing sociological structures which men like Pareto and Max Weber had erected before the war was, at least in part, due to the realization on their own part that the ground on which they were attempting to build showed signs of being merely drifting sands. The deeper justification for these efforts when viewed in the longer perspective of the movement of ideas will, it would now seem, be found in their endeavors to cope with the challenge of Marxism. They sought to oppose a more scientific science to the fiercely dogmatic social science of the prophet of social justice. It may be that such searching efforts were necessary in order to acquire the *scientia ignorantiæ*. For today it is fairly evident that the doctrinaire assumptions concerning human knowledge which underlie the various sociological efforts at a comprehensive science of human society are fallacious. Some of this insight is owed to Wilhelm Dilthey, who essayed to show why such a comprehensive science is logically impossible. But incomplete knowledge is more than complete ignorance; and if there are no laws, there may yet be reasonably accurate hypotheses concerning recurrrent regularities of social and political events. Such a hypothetical view of scientific effort has found its most penetrating expositor in Emile Meyerson. His *Identité et Realité* (1908) squarely faces the issue posited by the problem of cause. More recently, an American, Oliver L. Reiser, has put these matters rather well in a volume entitled *Philosophy and the Concepts of Modern Science* (1935). The whole range of difficulties is portrayed in *Reason and Nature—An Essay on the Meaning of Scientific Method* (1931), by Morris Cohen, whose general views are largely shared by the present author; they are simply and forcefully stated on pp. xii-xiii of the preface. It is obvious that in a matter of this kind all one's past reading is in a measure relevant to a bibliography. Kant's *Critique of Pure Reason* (all too frequently neglected in English-speaking countries in favor of his later works: even Kant had his weak moments), Schopenhauer's essay *On the Fourfold Basis of the Principle of Sufficient Causation,* John Stuart Mill's *A System of Logic,* and H. Bergson's writings all have reference. To these there must be added the views of Alfred N. Whitehead, as expressed in *Process and Reality* (1929) and in *Science and the Modern World* (1925); of C. S. Peirce, *Collected Papers* (1931-1935), particularly vol. ii, *Elements of Logic* (though I have not fully absorbed his complex thought); and finally John Dewey, to whom reference may be limited here to *The Public and Its Problems* (1927). The very mention of so heterogeneous a group of thinkers will indicate the author's disinclination to identify himself with any of them. But they all seem to have contributed toward a deeper understanding of "understanding" anything. Max Scheler's baroque intellectual edifice has always fascinated me, though I remain unaware of any permanent pattern except the philosophical traditions of the Roman Catholic faith (upon which Scheler hardly improved). Nevertheless, his *Die Wissensformen und die Gesellschaft* (1926) ought to be assimilated by those of our contemporaries who exude enthusiasm over Pareto and his ilk. If we must accept authority, let us return to the tradition-hallowed authority of the keepers of the Christian faith.

The problem of power as the focal point of political science has been adumbrated with reflective shrewdness by Charles Merriam. His book, *Political Power* (1934), voices with a certain Olympian detachment the aspirations of a large group of political scientists in this country, at least in purpose; for to set forth the rôle that political power plays in the process of social control, and not to consider whether power is moral or immoral, whether the state should do much, very little, or nothing at all, that is the objective of his volume. But the actual discussions reveal the dubious nature of these distinctions; all the way through it we hear of purposes, moral judgments are passed, and the difficulties of practical programs are related to their deeper strands of supporting social philosophy. In the view of the present writer, Merriam's efforts come to naught (and the unsophisticated reader is left with a sense of frustration), because the underlying concept of a science of social phenomena, regardless of objectives, purposes, ends, is misleading. The power situation itself is incomprehensible without a clear understanding of the community of purposes in terms of which the power is wielded. *Community* as the central phenomenon has recently been elaborated by R. MacIver in his volume by that name (1917). But the Achilles' heel of his neo-Aristotelian analysis is his theory of interests. Inherently the communal foundation of power need not at all imply a return to metaphysical speculations, as is usually contended. What ought to be, is a matter capable of a less subjective approach. The objectives of human beings are perhaps not as variable as the subtleties of philosophical speculation have implied. As a consequence, we need not be scared of values, purposes, objectives, ends; their subjectively variable margin is quite narrow when viewed in terms of effective social change. This fact has been more generally appreciated among legal philosophers. The problems of method are agitating the legal fraternity in the United States today to an extent never perhaps equalled before. It is significant that Merriam pays slight attention to the law. Pound, Llewellyn, and the Dewey-ites have been veering toward an interpretation of law or rather of legal science which would comprehend all the social sciences, if carried to its logical conclusion—except, perhaps, law. (See for an elaboration the author's article, "Remarks on Llewellyn's View of Law, Official Behaviour and Political Science," in *Political Science Quarterly,* vol. l, 1935. There is much of great value in these efforts to break through the crusts of legalistic formalism, particularly from a pedagogic point of view. Changing methods in the field of legal science are of vital importance to all the social sciences, and more particularly to political science. If constitutional law begins to ask what people actually do under a particular constitution, and not merely what battles of words they engage in for the settlement of conflicts among them, the constitutional lawyer becomes a political scientist (one hopes). The discussions of the present chapter have been greatly influenced by this whole methodological discussion in American jurisprudence (and the parallel though in many ways very different discussions on the Continent and in England: Duguit, Krabbe, del Vecchio, Kelsen, Smend, Kohler, Stammler, etc.). In spite of the fact that these discussions revolve around the problem of what is law, they must necessarily concern themselves with power as well, since law cannot readily be considered apart from the problem of enforcement (even if you treat it as irrelevant to the essence of law). Nowhere does the present writer feel the disjointedness of present intellectual work more keenly than in the lack of living contact between political science and legal science, as far as their concrete and positive work is concerned. And yet he feels also that legal terminology is the bane of much of political science writing, and thus sympathizes with Merriam's disregard of the law.

Special References

1. The "hypothetical" view of scientific knowledge is now accepted by a number of thinkers. A most explicit development of it is found in Emile Meyerson, *Identité et Réalité;* Cf. also M. Cohen, *Reason and Nature,* pp. 106 ff. The casual remarks of the text are not, of course, meant to take up the hoary question of induction vs. deduction. The faith in the order of nature implied in the former is well stated by Whitehead, *Science and the Modern World,* pp. 62 ff.

2. Cf. J. S. Mill, *A System of Logic,* particularly vol. ii, pp. 475 ff. and pp. 585 ff. For a thorough statement in support of quantitative methods in politics, see S. A. Rice, *Quantitative Methods in Politics* (1928), particularly pp. 20 ff.; and for the objections to it the author's review article, "Quantitative Methods in Politics," in *APSR,* vol. xxiii, pp. 1022 ff. Another forceful effort in a similar direction (this time an argument for the abstract deductive method) is found in V. Pareto, *The Mind and Society,* particularly vol. i. See also L. J. Henderson's expository essay, *Pareto's General Sociology* (1935), particularly pp. 7 ff. This essay is interesting because it shows precisely how and why the natural scientist fails to understand the epistemological problems involved: because he does not know the real problems of the social sciences. Nineteenth-century social philosophers, however, like Comte and Spencer, tended to take so extreme a view that Pareto must rather be considered a modification in the right direction. Still further in that direction goes Max Weber with

his insistence upon the fact of sympathetic understanding (*Verstehen*). See his *Gesammelte Aufsätze zur Wissenschaftslehre* (1922), pp. 403 ff. Cf. also H. Rickert, *Kulturwissenschaft und Naturwissenschaft* (1910; 5th ed., 1921), particularly pp. 20 ff. But as the next section shows, the essence of this point was already perceived by J. S. Mill and stated fairly acceptably. Through him it entered the work of W. Dilthey in a decisive way.

3. For an exposition of the inverse deductive method, see J. S. Mill, *op. cit.*, vol. ii, pp. 585 ff. Plato, to be sure, is replete with references to how politics proceeds from common-sense notions. See particularly *Protagoras* and *Meno*. J. R. Seeley, *Introduction to Political Science* (1896), pp. 13 ff., shares the belief in the simple nature of the base-line assumptions of political science. John R. Commons, *Institutional Economics* (1934), pp. 18 ff., has pointed out, however, how difficult it becomes to handle such common notions, once they are institutionalized.

4. This is the point Max Weber put well (*op. cit.*, pp. 503 ff.). See also Albert Salomon, "Max Weber's Sociology," in *Social Research*, vol. ii, pp. 60 ff., and the literature cited there. C. S. Peirce has perhaps done more than anyone else in exploding the notion of scientific work *free from preconceived ideas.*

5. The relation of psychology to political science has received a considerable amount of attention in recent years. Ideas concerning human nature have always profoundly affected man's political thought (note contrast between Machiavelli and Rousseau, for example). Ever since Hobbes, the interdependence of the two subjects has been clear. Yet not much progress has been made concerning the question stated in the text. Pragmatic, psychoanalytic, and behavioristic writers have appeared in recent political science, to be sure. Graham Wallas, *Human Nature in Politics* (1908) may be said to have opened up these discussions. Charles Merriam, *New Aspects of Politics* (1925) pushed them somewhat further. G. E. G. Catlin, *A Study of the Principles of Politics* (1930), particularly Part I, went into them on a more comprehensive scale.

6. See §3.

7. The importance of the materials modern historical scholarship has placed at the disposal of all the social sciences is reduced, but not destroyed, by the bias of the historical investigator himself. It is, in other words, necessary to guard against it, as against gravitation in physical experiments. But that is not impossible. What is more, many of the data with which the social scientist is concerned are beyond such controversy, which attaches itself to the interpretations. In this subject much interesting thought is found in the writings of English, French, and German scholars. Cf. the so-called *historical school* in economics, such as Cunningham, Schmoller, and Ashley. Cf. also the controversy between Max Weber and Eduard Meyer, the former expounding his views in *op. cit.*, pp. 215 ff., the latter in *Zur Theorie und Methodik der Geschichte* (1902).

8. That history is merely a fact-gatherer for the social sciences was once alleged by G. E. G. Catlin in *The Science and Method of Politics* (1927). For a profounder view, see W. Dilthey, *Einleitung in die Geistes-*

wissenschaften, Versuch einer Grundlegung für das Studium der Gesellschaft und der Geschichte (1883), pp. 93 ff.

9. For an elaboration of the argument of this paragraph, see the author's "Remarks on Llewellyn's View of Law, Official Behavior, and Political Science," in *APSR*, vol. l, pp. 419 ff. (1935). An important general discussion (in terms of the European usage of the word "sociological" which comprehends political science) is found in Hans Kelsen, *Der Soziologische und der Juristische Staatsbegriff* (2nd ed., 1928). It is based upon views roughly akin to those which underlie Dicey's distinction between legal and political sovereignty. John Dickinson's notions as expounded in his article, "A Working Theory of Sovereignty," *PSQ*, vol. xlii, pp. 524 ff. (1927), and vol. xliii, pp. 32 ff. (1928) are in turn related to both.

10. The discussion of the methodology of modern economics is so extensive that it does not seem practicable to give special references here. The controversy among various schools expounding classical, historical, marginal utility, institutional economics has been couched in terms of method, and this controversy is still vigorously being carried on. The definition by Hobbes is found in *Leviathan*, Book I, ch. x. The objections to defining scientific base-line concepts are stated well in A. N. Whitehead, *Process and Reality*, pp. 6 ff.

11. The axiom here stated is often seemingly denied by men striving after a "scientific" outlook, but what is denied under the heading of purpose, value, or objective reappears in another form. Recently Charles Merriam (*Political Power* [1934], p. 7) has said that "political power lies in a definite common pattern of impulse." A. F. Bentley took a somewhat similar view (*Process of Government* [1908], pp. 171-172). It has often been assumed that an introduction of objectives unavoidably plunges politics into the controversies of ethics and metaphysics. The fact that Plato (*Republic*, Book VI, for example) stressed the common purpose of all men seems to substantiate such a view, but it does not. For a correct modern statement, see M. R. Cohen, *Reason and Nature*, pp. 342 ff.

12. Locke's thoughts on power in the *Essay on Human Understanding*, Book II, are as follows: "Power, thus considered (namely, in reference to the change in perceivable ideas), is twofold, viz. able to make or able to receive any change: the one may be called active and the other passive power" (ch. xxi, §2). Locke then goes on to point out that we derive a clear idea of active power from our mind, not from external observation (perception). "This power which the mind has thus to order the consideration of any idea, or the forbearing to consider it; or to prefer the motion of any part of the body to its rest, and vice versa, in any particular instance; is that which we call the will." This statement is preceded by the important sentence: "This at least I think evident, that we find in ourselves a power to begin or to forbear, continue or end several actions of our minds, and motions of our bodies, barely by a thought or preference of the mind ordering, or, as it were, commanding the doing or not doing such a particular action" (*ibid.*, §5). And again: "All the actions that we have any idea of, reducing themselves, as has been said, to these two, viz. thinking and motion; so far as man has power to think or not to think, to

move or not to move, according to the preference or direction of his own mind, so far is a man free" (*ibid.*, §8). And further: "Liberty is not an idea belonging to volition, or preferring; but to the person having the power of doing, or forbearing to do, according as the mind shall choose or direct." And later, after his well-known argument on the so-called freedom of the will: "For *powers are relations*, not agents: and that (agent) which has the power, or not the power to operate, is that alone which is or is not free, and not the power itself. For freedom, or not freedom, can belong to nothing, but what has or has not the power to act" (*ibid.*, §17). Note that this view, rather dogmatically expressed, is found in Bentley, *op. cit.* The contrast between consent and constraint is implied in Tönnies' fundamental distinction between *Gemeinschaft* and *Gesellschaft*.

13. Consent is interpreted as a result of propaganda by Merriam, *Political Power,* pp. 307 ff., and H. D. Lasswell, *World Politics and Personal Insecurity* (1935), *passim.* On the other side, we may refer to A. F. Bentley, who, although in theory he admits government through force, in actual treatment fails to take it up; cf. his *Process of Government.* R. MacIver also tends in that direction in his *Community.* The notion of polarity as contrasted with logical consistency is developed by M. R. Cohen, *Reason and Nature,* particularly pp. 165 ff.

14. The problem of the intensity (tension level) of political situations is adumbrated in Lasswell, *Propaganda Technique in the World War* (1927), pp. 190 ff., but in a very general way. Merriam also mentions it as a question of significance. For some factual detail, see below, ch. xxv.

15. The dependence of government by consent upon agreement on fundamentals has received increasing attention in recent years. German and Austrian students of English government emphasized this throughout the nineteenth century. Joseph Redlich, in his admirable *The Procedure of the House of Commons* (German edition 1905, English 1908), adopted it as a central theme. The non-recognition of such consensus in England is indicative of the fact that communities seem to be as unaware of it when they have it as men are of health. The American Civil War should have produced some really searching thought on this subject.

16. The rule of anticipated reactions has not, to the author's knowledge, previously been stated in exact form, though occasional references to the facts are found throughout political literature. See, for example, A. N. Holcombe's discussion of the referendum in *State Government in the United States* (3rd ed., 1931), pp. 569 ff., or K. C. Cole, "The Rôle of the Senate in the Confirmation of Judicial Nominations," *APSR,* vol. xxviii (1934), pp. 875 ff.

17. The illustration of monarchy is elaborated in an article by the author and F. M. Watkins, "Monarchy," in the *ESS*. See also "Oligarchy" and "Tyranny." The "Spenglerian" touch of this paragraph must not be taken as an indication of the author's acceptance or approval of that writer's general philosophy of history, which he, in fact, rejects. The aspect brought into the analysis here was derived by Spengler from Burckhardt and Dilthey.

18. The dynamic nature of modern life generally is a recurring theme.

It runs like a red thread through all of A. N. Whitehead's books. Writers on evolutionary ethics, such as Julian Huxley, Leslie Stephen in his *Science of Ethics,* and Alexander in his *Moral Order and Progress,* are in point. But the idea is widespread at the present time, though it was fashionable a few years ago in certain French internationalist circles to attribute it to American and German writers and to insist that the French view is static. The opposite is more nearly correct, as far as emphasis is concerned.

Chapter II

THE CORE OF MODERN GOVERNMENT BUREAUCRACY

Special References

2. Thomas F. Tout, *Chapters in the Administrative History of Medieval England* (6 vols., 1920-1933); Jean Brissaud, *History of French Public Law* (tr. J. W. Garner, 1915); Gustav Schmoller, "Der Deutsche Beamtenstaat vom 16.-18, Jahrhundert," in *Jahrbuch für Gesetzgebung, Verwaltung und Volkswirtschaft,* vol. xviii (1894), and "Ueber Behördenorganisation, Amtswesen und Beamtentum," introduction to *Acta Borussica,* vol. i (1894), particularly chs. ii and vii; Otto Hintze, "Die Entstehung der modernen Staatsministerien," in *Historische Zeitschrift,* vol. c (1907), pp. 53-111; Hugo Preuss, *Verfassungspolitische Entwicklungen* (1927), particularly §§15 and 17.

3. See W. Cunningham, *The Progress of Capitalism in England* (1916); Adam Smith, *Wealth of Nations,* Book IV, ch. i, and Book V; Werner Sombart, *Der Moderne Kapitalismus* (1916), vol. i, 1, chs. xxi-xxviii; and R. H. Tawney and E. Power, *Tudor Economic Documents* (1924).

5. See Hans Delbrück, *Geschichte der Kriegskunst* (1900); M. Oppenheim, *A History of the Administration of the Royal Navy* (1896), vol. i; Sombart, *op. cit.,* vol. i, 2, ch. xlix, and H. T. Buckle, *History of Civilization in England* (1857).

6. R. Kjellen, *Grundriss zu einem System der Politik* (1920), and *Die Grossmächte der Gegenwart* (1916). See also Friedrich Ratzel, *Politische Geographie* (1897).

7. R. H. Tawney, *Religion and the Rise of Capitalism* (1926); C. J. Friedrich, *Introduction to Johannes Althusius' Politica* (1932), particularly chs. ii and iv; J. G. Droysen, *Geschichte der Preussischen Politik* (1868), vol. ii, pp. 2, 383 ff.; Otto Hintze, "Kalvinismus und Staatsräson in Brandenburg zur Anfang des 17. Jarhunderts," in *Historische Zeitschrift,* vol. cxliii (1931); E. Troeltsch, *The Social Teachings of the Christian Churches* (1923; tr. O. Wyon, 1931); Max Weber, *Protestant Ethic and the Spirit of Capitalism* (tr. T. Parsons, 1930).

8. H. Sidgwick, *The Development of European Polity* (1903); James Bryce, *The Holy Roman Empire* (1904), and *Modern Democracies* (1921).

9. C. J. H. Hayes, *Essays on Nationalism* (1926).

10. Georg von Below, *Die Ursachen der Rezeption des Römischen*

Rechts (1905); Otto von Gierke, *Das Deutsche Genossenschaftsrecht* (1868), particularly vol. ii; H. Sidgwick, *op. cit.*, Lectures XXII and XXIII.

11. Sidgwick, *op. cit.*

Chapter III

THE CORE OF MODERN GOVERNMENT: BUREAUCRACY

Special References

1. Besides the references cited in the previous chapter, §2, one may note: C. J. Friedrich and Taylor Cole, *Responsible Bureaucracy* (1932), particularly chs. i and ii (vol. i of *Studies in Systematic Political Science*, etc.); Max Weber, *Wirtschaft und Gesellschaft* (*Grundriss der Sozialökonomik*, vol. iii) (1925), ch. iii, §§3, 4, 5, of the first part, and ch. vi of the third part; Alfred Weber, *Der Beamte* (in *Ideen zur Staats- und Kultursoziologie*) (1927). These three attempts at systematic treatment are closely related to one another in their terminology and in the effort to avoid ideological distortions. Such distortions intrude themselves to some extent in: Herman Finer, "The Civil Service," in *The Theory and Practice of Modern Government* (1932), vol. ii, part vii; Leonard D. White, *Introduction to the Study of Public Administration* (1926). The latter work, while presenting a lucid summary of contemporary conditions, does not emphasize the historical perspective which is of paramount importance for the present treatment as showing that administration is not a special phrase of modern government, but its very core. Other general references are found in Sarah Greer, *A Bibliography of Civil Service and Personnel Administration* (1935).

2. W. Altmann, *Ausgewählte Urkunden zur Brandenburg-Preussischen Verfassungs- und Verwaltungsgeschichte*, vol. i. pp. 55 ff.; Gustav Schmoller, "Ueber Behördenorganisation, Amtswesen und Beamtentum . . . " which is the introduction to vol. i of *Acta Borussica* (1894).

3. W. Altmann, *op. cit.*, pp. 73 ff.

4. Leonard D. White, *op. cit.*, pp. 55-59.

5. C. J. Friedrich, *op. cit.*, pp. 29 ff.; Herman Finer, *op. cit.*, vol. ii, p. 1362; Leonard D. White, *op. cit.*, pp. 66 ff.

7. Otto Hintze, "Behördenorganisation und allgemeine Verwaltung in Preussen," the introduction to vol. vi of *Acta Borussica* (1901); Walter L. Dorn, "The Prussian Bureaucracy in the Eighteenth Century," *Political Science Quarterly*, vols. xlvi and xlvii (1931, 1932); C. J. Friedrich, *op. cit.*, pp. 36 ff.; René Hugot-Derville, *Le principe hiérarchique dans l'administration française* (1913).

8. C. J. Friedrich, and F. M. Watkins, "Monarchy," in *Encyclopedia of the Social Sciences*, vol. x; Max Weber, *op. cit.* (This problem of the conditions under which monocratic leadership occurs has not as yet received the attention it deserves. Certain phases are considered below in chs. xiv and xxiv.)

9. R. C. K. Ensor, *Courts and Judges in France, Germany, and England* (1933).

10. See the works cited in Greer, *op. cit.*, pp. 79 ff.

11. Walter R. Sharp, *The French Civil Service—Bureaucracy in Transition* (1931), chs. iv, v, vi and vii; Fritz M. Marx, "Civil Service in Germany," in *Civil Service Abroad* (1935), chs. vi, vii, viii; C. J. Friedrich, "Responsible Government Service under the American Constitution," in *Problems of the American Public Service* (1935), ch. vii; Harvey Walker, *Training Public Employees in Great Britain* (1935).

13. See again Max Weber and C. J. Friedrich. This matter has so far received very inadequate attention.

Chapter IV

THE OBJECTIVES OF MODERN GOVERNMENT

Special References

1. Henry Sidgwick, *Principles of Political Economy*, ch. xviii, §§4 and 5. Much of the most interesting material is found in the work of historians, parenthetically. A special treatment of great significance for this whole chapter is Hans Delbrück, *Geschichte der Kriegskunst im Rahmen der Politischen Geschichte* (1900-1926) Part IV. Besides this work, Alfred T. Mahan, *The Influence of Sea Power upon History* (1890) is of special interest. The influence of this epochal study is discussed by William L. Langer, *The Diplomacy of Imperialism* (1935), ch. xiii, which is itself an important historical contribution to the problem here considered, and is supplemented by a selected bibliography. These and many other works deal with the matter, but none of course from the systematic standpoint here envisaged.

2. See concerning this point the interesting observations in W. Thomas and F. Znaniecki, *The Polish Peasant* (1918), pp. 156 ff.; sociologists have also attempted more systematic studies, such as that given by G. Simmel in his *Soziologie*, ch. iv, and by P. Sorokin and C. C. Zimmerman in *Principles of Rural-Urban Sociology* (1929).

3. The duplicity of the language of diplomacy is a commonplace. Unfortunately, the moral objections to this practice have obscured the common *objective* of the words and actions. Cf. the sane outlook of Langer, *op. cit.*, ch. iii.

4. Arnold von Luschin und Ebengreuth, *Oesterreichische Reichs- und Rechtsgeschichte*, pp. 397, 411, 466-467 ff., 479.

5. M. Oppenheim, *A History of the Administration of the Royal Navy, 1509-1660* (1896). Cf. also Mahan, *op. cit.*

6. Delbrück, *op. cit.*, pp. 255 ff. Also Sombart, *Kapitalismus*, vol. i, 1, pp. 342 ff.

7. Delbrück, *op. cit.*, *passim.*

8. The generalization advanced in this paragraph is sometimes advanced by historians in their special treatments of a specific history. Thus

J. Beloch, in his *Griechische Geschichte* (1893-1904), explains the dispersion of political authority characteristic of the city-state in these terms.

9. Max Scheler, *Versuch zu einer Soziologie des Wissens* (1924), pp. 99 ff.

10. H. Nicolson, *Public Faces* (1932). See also *Geschichte der K. und K. Wehrmacht von 1618 bis Ende des XIX. Jahrhunderts* (her. v.d. Direktion des K. und K. Kriegsarchivs). Not exactly the point of the text, but related problems of the link between technology and science are touched upon in ch. xi of C. Bouglé's *Leçons de Sociologie sur l'Evolution des Valeurs* (tr. H. S. Sellars as *The Evolution of Values*, 1926); by E. Mach in *Erkenntnis und Irrtum* (1905; 1926); and the same author's *Die Mechanik in ihrer Entwicklung* (1883-1933) (trans. by T. J. McCormack, with later additions by P. E. B. Jourdain, 1915); and by Max Scheler, *Sociologie des Wissens,* pp. 129 ff., as well as the other authors cited there. Decisive is Werner Sombart, *Krieg und Kapitalismus* (1912).

12. Oppenheim, *op. cit.;* Sombart, *Krieg und Kapitalismus,* pp. 66 ff.; J. W. Fortescue, *A History of the British Army* (1899); and similar works for France, Germany, etc., cited by Sombart.

13. As in other parts of this chapter, considerable literature is provided by economic history, e.g., regarding the debasing of the coins. Regarding trading companies, G. Cawston and A. H. Keane, *Early Chartered Companies* (1896), and S. van Brakel, *De Hollandsche Handelscompagnieen der Sewentiende Eeuw* (1908) are worth consulting, along with the standard economic histories. Regarding the estimates on benefits derived from confiscation of ecclesiastical property, Thomas Tanner's *Notitia Monastica* (1744) has been consulted; see also F. A. Gasquet, *Henry VIII and the English Monasteries* (1888-1889). The figure regarding the price of the Ark Royal is found in E. Keble Chatterton, *Sailing Ships* (1909).

14. See particularly Georg von Below, "System und Bedeutung der landständischen Verfassung," in *Territorium und Stadt* (1900), pp. 163 ff., and the same author's *Landständische Verfassung von Jülich und Berg* (1885). For France, see Georges Picot, *Histoire des États Généraux* (2nd ed., 1888). A thorough comparative study based on the large new material throughout Europe does not exist; unfortunately, the article in the *ESS* is limited to France. But the essays on the several parliaments in the *ESS* afford some guidance. For the battle on the White Hill see Julius Krebs, *Die Schlacht am Weissen Berge* (1879), and the summary in Delbrück, *op. cit.,* vol. iv, pp. 223 ff.

15. The French *intendants* are treated with discrimination by G. Hanotaux, *Origines de l'Institution des Intendants des Provinces* (1884), of whose views an adequate summary is found in Herman Finer, *Modern Government,* vol. ii, pp. 1223 ff. See also Paul Rice Doolin, *The Fronde* (1935).

16. This problem is most acutely discussed by Gerhart Lütkens, "Das Kriegsproblem und die marxistische Theorie," in *ASW & SP*, vol. xlix (1922), pp. 467 ff. See also the author's forthcoming book on foreign relations. Acute specific comments are found in W. P. Maddox, *Foreign Relations in British Labour Politics* (1934), pp. 53 f., and elsewhere;

and in Merle Fainsod, *The Third International* (forthcoming). Much good material on this score is also found in Louis Fischer, *The Soviets in World Affairs* (1930), *passim.*

17. The enormous literature on disarmament cannot be cited here. For a convenient reference selection, see the article on disarmament in the *ESS*. Regarding Pan-European ideas, see R. N. Coudenhove-Kalergi, *Pan-Europa* (3rd ed., 1924), and Edouard Herriot, "Pan-Europa," in *Foreign Affairs*, vol. viii, pp. 237 ff.

18. This point is well stated by Erich Hunger, *Zur Idee und Tradition des Foederalismus* (1929). It is touched upon by many writers, lately in a somewhat similar mood by Harold D. Lasswell, *World Politics and Personal Insecurity* (1935), pp. 252-253. See also Felix Morley, *The Society of Nations* (1932), pp. 597 ff.; and Kant's essay, *Vom Ewigen Frieden* (1795), discussed there.

19. For literature on the Russian, German, Austrian and Italian events touched upon here, see the chapters below in Part IV. An essay deserving special consideration is C. Malaparte's *Coup d'État* (1932).

Chapter V

OBJECTIVES AND TECHNIQUES

General References

Among the many treatments of diplomacy in all modern languages, the political scientist will find three most suggestive. These are (1) Ernest Satow, *Guide to Diplomatic Practice* (1917); (2) Jules Cambon, *Le Diplomate* (1922); (3) Albrecht Mendelssohn-Bartholdi, *Diplomatie* (1927). Regarding the general problem of democracy and diplomacy, there are also a considerable number of works; among the more important ones in English may be noted: Arthur Ponsonby, *Democracy and Diplomacy* (1915); George Young, *Diplomacy Old and New* (1921); P. S. Reinsch, *Secret Diplomacy* (1922); Aubrey L. Kennedy, *Old Diplomacy and New* (1922); DeWitt C. Poole, *The Conduct of Foreign Relations under Modern Democratic Conditions* (1924). These and other points of view are considered in a forthcoming volume by the author, *The People and Its Representatives in Foreign Affairs.* For an able summary, see C. deLisle Burns' article in the *ESS.*

Special References

2. The importance of the distinction between policy determination and negotiation is emphasized by Harold Nicolson, *Curzon: The Last Phase, 1919-1925* (1934), in a terminal essay containing "some remarks on the practice of diplomacy." It is an old distinction, but in constant need of reemphasizing. D. J. Hill, *A History of Diplomacy in the International Development of Europe* (1905), vol. iii, gives significant critical comments on the failure of Louis XIV, pp. 282 ff., Frederick the Great, pp. 537 ff., but the judgments expressed in the text are *communis opinio*

doctorum. For Louis XIV, see G. Pagès, *La Monarchie d'Ancien Régime en France* (1928), pp. 134 ff. For Frederick the Great, see G. Küntzel, "Die Drei Grossen Hohenzollern," in *Meister der Politik,* ed. E. Marcks and K. von Müller (1923), vol. ii, pp. 391 ff. *Re* Napoleon, see J. H. Rose, *The Life of Napoleon I* (1901-1924), vol. ii, pp. 213 ff.

3. The general problem of this paragraph will be taken up at greater length in C. J. Friedrich, *The Balance of Power in Post-war Politics* (1937).

4. For the Franco-Russian alliance, see W. L. Langer's study, *The Franco-Russian Alliance, 1890-1894* (1929), p. 399. For the problem of Anglo-German relations see F. Meinecke, *Geschichte des deutsch-englischen Bundesproblems, 1890-1901* (1930).

5. For the problem of official language, see Satow, *op. cit.,* vol. i, pp. 58 ff. See *New York Times,* January 28, 1934, for the Soviet remark; for Curzon's breach, see Nicolson, *op. cit.,* p. 358.

6. See Otto Krauske, "Die Entwicklung der ständigen Diplomatie," *Staats- und sozialwissenschaftliche Forschungen,* vol. xxiii (1885). For a general summary, cf. F. L. Schuman, *International Politics* (1933). See also D. J. Hill, *History of Diplomacy in the International Development of Europe* (1905-1914), particularly vol. i, pp. 359-360.

7. See H. K. Norton, *Foreign Office Organization* (1929), and F. L. Schuman, *op. cit.* For detailed material on the organizational changes, cf. the author's forthcoming volume. The personal qualities are discussed in the general works mentioned above. The specific quotations are from Nicolson, *op. cit.,* pp. 402 ff.

8. See Charles Dupuis, *Le principe d'equilibre et le concert européen de la paix de Westphalie à l'acte d'Algesiras* (1909), a broad general treatment. The post-war situation is the subject of V. M. Dean, *Toward a New Balance of Power in Europe* (1934). See also F. L. Schuman's ingenious discussions, *op. cit.,* pp. 54 ff., and Ranke, "Die Grossen Mächte," vol. x of *Rankes Meisterwerke* (1914-1915.) The analysis of this chapter will be more fully developed in the author's *The Balance of Power in Post-war Politics* (1937).

9. Cecil Spring-Rice, *The Letters and Friendships of Sir Cecil Spring-Rice* (1929).

Chapter VI

OBJECTIVES AND TECHNIQUES

General References

Obviously, a general bibliography for this chapter would have to cover the entire field of modern economic history, manifestly an impossible task. Reference may be had to any one of the more recent and competent texts in the field. In addition to these, attention may specially be called to three somewhat controversial and yet very significant works: W. Cunningham, *The Progress of Capitalism in England* (1916), and his

The Growth of English Industry and Commerce (5th ed., 1910-1912); W. J. Ashley, *Introduction to English Economic History* (1888-1925); and Werner Sombart, *Der Moderne Kapitalismus* (5th ed., 1922), particularly vol. i, 1, pp. 334 ff. Besides these, Gustav Schmoller's Introduction to the first volume of *Acta Borussica* must be noted, as well as several of his essays reprinted in *Umrisse, Abhandlungen und Untersuchungen* (1898).

Special References

1. The entire controversy of the economic (materialistic) interpretation of history is evidently bound up with the few sentences of this paragraph. Suffice it, in lieu of references, to remind the reader that such an interpretation is not peculiar to Karl Marx, as is now often popularly assumed, but is found throughout the later eighteenth and the nineteenth century, and has become very common in the United States.

2. For an exposition of ideas of organic growth, see H. von Treitschke, *Politics* (1916), vol. i, pp. 15 ff., 45 ff., or Seeley, *Introduction to Political Science* (1896), pp. 43-44 and 53-76 as illustrations of what nineteenth-century historians are full of. Friedrich Ratzel, in his *Politische Geographie* (3rd ed., 1923), has given an elaborate exposition of this doctrine, pp. 59 ff. The controversy concerning the organic nature of groups is very extended. See Francis W. Coker, *Organismic Theories of the State* (1910), and W. Y. Elliott, *The Pragmatic Revolt in Politics* (1928), particularly Parts IV and V. The latter's ingenious attempt to surmount the difficulties by developing a coorganic conception of the state is deserving of more attention than it has received. For John of Salisbury, see John Dickinson, *The Stateman's Book of John of Salisbury* (1927), Introduction, particularly pp. xx-xxi.

3. The observations contained in this paragraph have been a recurrent theme in the writings of monarchists. The French Royalists under Charles Maurras have been particularly emphatic. See his *Enquête sur la Monarchie* (1909). For the point concerning England, see the eloquent passages placed by Oliver Goldsmith into the mouth of the Vicar of Wakefield in defense of monarchy. Cf. also Bolingbroke's *The Patriot King* (1749), and Frederick the Great (of Prussia), *Anti-Machiavel* (1741). It should not be forgotten, however, that monarchical society has no monopoly upon furthering the development of culture. Witness Athens, Florence, or Nuremberg.

4. For the general ideas of this paragraph, cf. G. Schmoller, "Der Deutsche Beamtenstaat vom 16. bis 18. Jahrhundert," *Jahrbuch für Gesetzgebung, Verwaltung und Volkswirtschaft,* vol. xviii; and Otto Hintze's article cited above, II, §2. See also the author's article, "Some Thoughts on the Politics of Government Control," in *Journal of Social Philosophy,* vol. i (1936), pp. 122 ff.

5. For Bodin's views and their relation to economics, see R. Chauviré, *Jean Bodin* (1914) particularly Book IV, ch. iii.

6. For the *Ordonnances du Roi,* see Esmein's *Cours Élémentaire d'Histoire du Droit Français* (1903) pp. 774 ff., and the official publication of the *ordonnances* by The Imprimerie Royale.

7. The extensive literature concerning mercantilism cannot be reviewed here; an admirable summary is given by Eli F. Heckscher in his article on the subject in the *ESS*, summarizing his able volumes entitled *Merkantilismen* (1931), now translated into English by M. Shapiro as *Mercantilism* (1935).

8. The commercial policy of the various countries has, of course, been treated in numerous monographs. Readily accessible sources of reference are Jacob Viner, "English Theories of Foreign Trade before Adam Smith," in *Journal of Political Economy*, vol. xxxviii (1930), pp. 249 ff. and 404 ff.; and Charles W. Cole, *French Mercantilist Doctrines before Colbert* (1931). For Colbert, see P. Clement, *Histoire de Colbert* (3rd ed., 1892).

9. Cf. E. Levasseur, *Histoire du Commerce de la France* (1911-1912), and the works cited in the general note. For special companies: William H. Price, *The English Patents of Monopoly* (1906), Paul Kaeppelin, *La Compagnie des Indes Orientales* (1908), etc.

10. See George L. Beer, *The Old Colonial System, 1660-1754* (1912), and Heckscher, *op. cit.*

11. A. von Luschin und Ebengreuth, *Allgemeine Munzkunde und Geldgeschichte des Mittelalters und der neueren Zeit* (1904), and Arthur R. Burns, *Money and Monetary Policy in Early Times* (1927).

12-13. For the quotation, see W. Cunningham, *Growth,* vol. ii, p. 434. See also general note, and previous paragraph, particularly Sombart, *op. cit.,* ch. xxvi, pp. 398 ff.

14. Cf. H. Brougham, *An Inquiry into the Colonial Policy of the European Powers* (1803), and Beer, *op. cit.*; S. L. Mims, *Colbert's West India Policy* (1912); C. G. Haring, *Trade and Navigation between Spain and the Indies in the Time of the Hapsburgs* (1918); Alfred Zimmermann, *Die Kolonialpolitik der Niederländer* (1903); A. Duchêne, *La Politique Coloniale de la France* (1928).

Chapter VII

OBJECTIVES AND TECHNIQUES

General References

The literature on the political phase of judicial methods is not very extensive. The standard legal histories give little or no aid in connection with this question. W. S. Holdsworth, *A History of English Law* (3rd ed., 1922), vol. i, and Frederick Pollock and F. W. Maitland, *History of English Law* (2nd ed., 1899) cannot be neglected, nor can the relevant section in Heinrich Brunner, *Deutsche Rechtsgeschichte* (2nd ed., 1906 and 1928) and Richard Schroeder, *Lehrbuch der deutschen Rechtsgeschichte* (6th ed., 1919-1922). Two articles in the *ESS,* one by Max Radin on the "Courts" and one by Harold Laski on the "Judiciary" summarize the problems very well indeed. Rudolf Smend's *Das Reichskammergericht* (1911), while unfinished and on a special subject, is very significant. To these may be added P. M. Viollet, *Droit Public: Histoire des Institutions Politiques et Administratives de la France* (1890-1903). Literature on recent judicial methods has tended to explore the psychological and sociological implications of judicial techniques in the complex modern society. Justice Cardozo's *The Nature of the Judicial Process* (1921) is perhaps the most widely known, but Edward S. Robinson's *Law and the Lawyers* (1935) should be added, particularly chs. viii-xii. There is also the analysis of German problems in Martin Beradt, *Der Deutsche Richter* (1930) and Friedrich Dessauer, *Recht, Richtertum und Ministerialbüreaukratie* (1928), and the broader comparative treatment by R. C. K. Ensor, *Courts and Judges in France, Germany and England* (1933). Cf. also the bibliography to Chapter XII.

Special References

1. On primitive government, anthropology is producing an increasing literature which is unfortunately lacking in orientation, because of the failure of political scientists and anthropologists to work together. However, efforts along such lines are being made, for example, by K. N. Llewellyn at Columbia. The standard sources of information remain: Sir J. G. Frazer, *The Golden Bough* (1890); Robert H. Lowie, *Primitive Society* (1920); and A. M. Hocart, *Kingship* (1927). On the judicial functions of parliament, following the older literature (Thomas Smith, etc.), see Julius Hatschek, *Englisches Staatsrecht* (1905), vol. i, pp. 241 ff.; Joseph Redlich, *Recht und Technik des Englischen Parlamentarismus* (1905); and Charles H. McIlwain, *The High Court of Parliament and Its Supremacy* (1910), where the problem is developed in its ramifications. For the relation of parliament to the courts, see H. B. Gerland, *Die Beziehungen zwischen dem Parlament und den Gerichten in England* (1928). For the judicial functions of the French parliament, see the recent study by Paul R. Doolin, *The Fronde* (1935), particularly chs. i and vi.

2. For literature on the Roman law phase, see above, II, § 10. On Bracton, see Holdsworth, *op. cit.*, vol. ii, pp. 230 ff., where the controversial questions of the extent of his "Romanism" are reviewed. For Coke's claim, see Roscoe Pound's *The Spirit of the Common Law* (1921), p. 61.

3. Dr. Bonham's case is found in *Famous State Trials*, or in *Reports*, vol. viii. Cf. also the comments in McIlwain, *op. cit.*, pp. 147-148. Regarding the statement of Bacon, see *The Works of Francis Bacon* (1842), vol. ii, p. 235. Cf. also Bacon's whole memorial on codification, *ibid.*, pp. 229 ff.

4. On Coke, see *Edward Coke, Oracle of the Law*, by Hastings Lyon and Herman Block (1929). For the King's statements, see *The Works of Francis Bacon*, vol. ii, pp. 493-494, as well as *Coke on Littleton*, §97b. "Artificial Reason" is also discussed in Pound, *loc. cit.*

5. On *stare decisis*, see the brilliant article by Herman Oliphant, "A Return to *Stare Decisis*," in 6 *American Law School Review*, 215 ff.; and K. N. Llewellyn, *Bramble Bush* (privately printed, 1930), pp. 63 ff. See also the author's "Remarks on Llewellyn's View of Law, Official Behavior, and Political Science," in *PSQ*, vol. 1 (1935). Further interesting reflections are found in Edward S. Robinson, *Law and the Law-*

yers (1935), p. 257, and in Max Radin, "Case Law and *Stare Decisis*—Concerning Präjudizienrecht in America," 33 *Columbia Law Review* 199 ff.

6. Cf. Ensor, *op. cit.*, and the able review of it by Wolfgang Kraus in 48 *Harvard Law Review* 873 ff. For a rationalistic theory, see A. L. Goodhart, *Precedent in English and Continental Law* (1934), and Roscoe Pound's review of it in the 48 *Harvard Law Review* 863 ff.

7. For this and the following paragraph, see the three striking articles, "Legal Profession and Legal Education," by H. D. Hazeltine, Max Radin, and A. A. Berle, Jr., and the literature cited there. Special mention may be made of Frederick Pollock, *The Origins of the Inns of Court* (1931), and T. F. T. Plucknett, "The Place of the Legal Profession in the History of English Law," in 48 *Law Quarterly Review* 328 ff.

8. Concerning the relation of bench and bar, see Charles A. Warren, *A History of the American Bar* (1911), and Thorstein Veblen, *The Theory of Business Enterprise* (1919), ch. viii. For the Act of Settlement, see Holdsworth, *op. cit.*, vol. vi, pp. 230 ff.

9. Concerning the case of the miller, see Rudolf Stammler, *Deutsches Rechtsleben in Alter und Neuer Zeit* (1932), § xxxi, "Der Prozess des Müllers Arnold 1779-1787," pp. 413 ff.

10. The reforms of Cocceji are treated in Max Springer, *Die Coccejische Justizreform* (1914).

11. The problem of the relationship between courts and classes has been much emphasized by Marxist writers. Cf. e.g., Ernst Fraenkel, *Zur Soziologie der Klassenjustiz* (1927), and the work of Beradt cited above. It is evident in Stammler's study of the miller's case. In the United States, this problem of special prejudice of the judges has often been brought forward in connection with the discussion of the Supreme Court's constitutional review (see below, ch. xii), and recent attacks have focused renewed attention upon it. A forceful statement of this point of view is Edouard Lambert, *Le Gouvernement des Juges et la Lutte contre la Législation Sociale aux États-Unis* (1921), but Beard, *The Supreme Court and the Constitution* (1912), F. J. Goodnow, *Social Reform and the Constitution* (1911), and John R. Commons, *The Legal Foundations of Capitalism* (1924), have leaned to similar interpretations, as has Veblen, *op. cit.*

12. The literature on administrative law is very extensive. Cf. the highly authoritative article by Ernst Freund on the subject in the *ESS*, and the literature cited there. See also F. F. Blachly's recent *Administrative Legislation and Adjudication* (1934), and the pamphlet of the American Bar Association on the subject.

13. For the Conseil d'État, cf. the authorities on French constitutional and administrative law, such as Esmein, Duguit, Hauriou. Rejecting the now admittedly untenable position of Dicey, two books are of primary interest, John Dickinson's *Administrative Justice and the Supremacy of Law in the United States* (1927), and William A. Robson, *Justice and Administrative Law* (1928).

14. See the two previous paragraphs. To these add Harold Laski's general treatment of "Administrative Tribunals" in the *ESS*.

15. The quotation from Robson is found in *op. cit.*, pp. 324 f.

Chapter VIII

THE MAKING OF A CONSTITUTION AS A POLITICAL PROCESS

General References

As stated in the text, much of the thought of this chapter is derived from the so-called classical constitutionalists of the seventeenth and eighteenth centuries, for they contain several of the most important hypotheses. Herman Finer has a chapter on constitutions, but it is built upon the broader concept of the constitution as "a system of fundamental political institutions." The same is true of most French and German writing, which is essentially legal in nature, and therefore preoccupied with the problems arising from the distinction between ordinary law and constitutional law. This is a distinction of no mean importance; but the political scientists' problem is that of distinguishing between constitutional and unconstitutional government. This problem was more clearly envisaged by the earlier writers than by nineteenth-century thinkers. But the dictatorial regimes of the present day have once more pushed the problem of restraints into the foreground. And while the literature is as yet rather scarce, there is probably more to it than is suggested by Walton H. Hamilton's engaging formula that "constitutionalism is the name given to the trust which men repose in the power of words engrossed on parchment to keep a government in order" (*ESS*, vol. iv, p. 255).

Special References

4. The textbooks are full of this wearisome discussion about written and unwritten constitutions, or rather of the distinction between constitutions embodied in one document and those in many documents. The most definitive discussion, perhaps, is found in James Bryce, *Constitutions* (1905).

5. See article, "Constitutions," by Howard Lee McBain in the *ESS*, vol. iv. Cf. also H. W. Horwill, *The Usages of the American Constitution* (1925), and H. L. McBain's *The Living Constitution* (1927).

6. See Charles H. McIlwain, *The High Court of Parliament and its Supremacy* (1910), particularly pp. 75 ff., 82 ff., 286 ff. The same point was stated earlier but much less well by Julius Hatschek, *Englisches Staatsrecht* (1905), where the author first encountered it.

9. In recent years, a vast amount of historical research has produced a juster estimate of medieval politics, and has brought to light the strictly constitutional nature of much of it. The list of works which may be cited is a long one; perhaps it will suffice to refer to Otto von Gierke, *Das deutsche Genossenschaftsrecht* (1868), particularly vols. i and ii; Charles H. McIlwain, *The Growth of Political Thought in the West* (1932), par-

ticularly chaps. v, vi, and vii; R. W. and A. J. Carlyle, *A History of Medieval Political Theory in the West* (1903), particularly vols. i and iii; and Henry O. Taylor, *The Medieval Mind* (1911), *passim*.

10. The literature on Cromwell is rapidly increasing. This we owe to the drift toward dictatorship. But Cromwell wanted a constitution, our present dictators do not. Cf. the bibliography given in the author's article on Cromwell in the *ESS*, vol. iv, pp. 605 f.

11. See Finer, *op. cit.*

12-17. See general remarks.

Chapter IX

THE CONSTITUENT POWER, THE AMENDING POWER, AND REVOLUTION

General References

The general problem of constitutional and political change, and of revolution, has received increasing attention in recent years. Aristotle's classic doctrine has not, however, usually served as the point of departure. Nor has a really comprehensive inventory of historical experience, such as probably underlies Aristotle's theory, been attempted. But even partial comparisons have yielded some striking results, like Crane Brinton's "Revolutions" in the *Encyclopedia of the Social Sciences*, Pitirim Sorokin's *Sociology of Revolutions* (1925), and Eugen Rosenstock's *Die Europäischen Revolutionen* (1931). Rosenstock's strongly Hegelian cast brings to light the fact that "philosophy of history" and of "sociology" in the Comtian sense implies a theory of revolution. The work of Hegel, Comte and Marx suggests at the same time that modern theories have been inclined to view change in a certain direction rather than change in any cyclical sense. Besides these, a large body of material regarding revolutions was gathered by writers in the sixteenth and seventeenth centuries who were interested in the "right of revolution." But this material is of little value from the standpoint of modern critical historical scholarship. Nevertheless, it suggests some data not ordinarily covered by modern works. Another body of uncritical dogmatic writings is offered by Socialists and Marxists. These authors attempt to "explain" revolutions in terms of economic changes, a point of view which is also found in certain rather more popular contemporary accounts, such as that of George Soule, *The Coming American Revolution* (1934), Part I, "The Nature of Revolution." A psychological view of revolution, on the other hand, is set forth by Everett Dean Martin, in his *Farewell to Revolution* (1935).

Special References

2. Internal plebiscites are vitally different from international plebiscites which are employed to determine changes of sovereignty, to use the language of international law. The international plebiscite always offers the

voter a real alternative, when it asks him whether he wishes the Saar, e.g., to be French or German. The literature on domestic plebiscites is quite scanty.

3. For the *Instrument,* see Samuel Rawson Gardiner, *Constitutional Documents* (2nd ed., 1889), pp. 405 ff. See also Gardiner's summary and comments in the Introduction, pp. liii ff. For Cromwell's speeches, see T. Carlyle, *Oliver Cromwell's Letters and Speeches* (1849). The first quotation is found on p. 423 f. of vol. ii, the second and third on pp. 424 and 425. The following sentences are from p. 433.

4. A. Esmein, *Éléments de Droit Constitutionnel Français et Comparé* (8th ed., revue par H. Nézard (1927-1928), vol. i, pp. 449 ff.

5. Concerning the Swiss constitution, see Ed. His, *Geschichte des neueren schweizerischen Staatsrechts* (1928), pp. 238 ff.

6. It is very important to keep in mind that the "constituent power" as here used is not identical with the *pouvoir constituant* of French constitutional law, which corresponds to the amending power of American constitutional law. See Esmein, *op. cit.,* vol. i, pp. 612 ff. However, the legal doctrine is confused, and often includes part of what is here called the constituent power, mingled with the amending power.

8. The problem of constitutional change through usage has occupied English and American students for a long time. A convenient summary of some of the prevailing views is found in W. B. Munro, *The Government of the United States* (1919), ch. v. See also Herbert W. Horwill, *The Usages of the American Constitution* (1925), and Karl Loewenstein, *Erscheinungsformen der Verfassungsänderung* (1931); also Oliver P. Field, *The Effect of an Unconstitutional Statute* (1935). Some of the most fundamental aspects of this problem have been stated in the course of the controversy concerning the significance of a written constitution, from Burke to Bryce. By far the most careful analysis of the Swiss referendum is offered by Axel Brusewitz' "Folkomröstningsinstitutet i den Schweiziska Demokratien," in *Statens Offentliga Utredningar* (1923). The figures are taken from A. L. Lowell, *Popular Government* (1930), ch. xii.

9. For a recent program of broad constitutional reform, see W. Y. Elliott, *The Need for Constitutional Reform* (1935).

10. The statement from Burgess occurs in *Political Science and Comparative Constitutional Law* (1890), vol. i, pp. 150 ff.

11. Information on the working of Dutch political institutions is extraordinarily poor. A fair summary is found in *Jahrbuch des Oeffentlichen Rechts,* vol. xviii (1930), and earlier accounts in vols. viii and xii. For England, see F. A. Ogg, *English Government and Politics* (1930); for France, see Esmein, *Droit Constitutionnel,* pp. 543 ff.

12. The question of possible limitations on the amending power is very controversial. For France the matter is stated with acuteness by most writers on constitutional law. See, e.g., Esmein, *Droit Constitutionnel,* vol. ii, pp. 543 ff. A more extended discussion is found in Charles Lefebure, *Études sur les Lois Constitutionnelles de 1875* (1882), pp. 217 ff. The general problem is considered by Egon Zweig, *Die Lehre vom Pou-*

voir Constituant (1909). The American situation is considered in an article by William Marbury, "The Limitations upon the Amending Power," 33 *Harvard Law Review* 323 ff. (1919), where it is argued that such limitations are valid. The opposite view is usually taken by political scientists; cf. Munro, *op. cit.*, p. 192. Whatever may be the logic of the matter, it is improbable that an amendment to Article V of the Constitution would not be accepted. For the use of the word "gang," cf. H. D. Lasswell's article in the *ESS*.

13. For Cromwell's remarks, see T. Carlyle, *op. cit.*, p. 435; Arthur N. Holcombe, *State Government in the United States* (3rd ed., 1931), pp. 129-130.

14. Cf. Leo Trotzki, *Mein Leben* (1930), p. 320. For Rosenstock, see General References, this chapter; the general theory is developed in the first part of the book.

16. Walter Lippmann, *The Method of Freedom* (1934).

17. The transition is described by Frederick L. Schuman, *The Nazi Dictatorship* (1935), pp. 214 ff. The German constitutional issue is stated by Otto Koellreuter and Carl Schmitt in *Deutsche Juristenzeitung*, April 1 and 15, 1933. See also Ulrich Scheuner, "Das Recht der Nationalen Revolution," in *Archiv des öffentlichen Rechts*, vol. xxiv, particularly pp. 292 ff. Scheuner, however, is silent regarding the exclusion of many deputies; on the contrary, he takes great pleasure in asserting the "legal" character of the revolution. *Dum tacent, clamant!* For the pre-revolutionary difficulties, see Herbert Kraus, *The Crisis of German Democracy* (1932), which gives a good summary. For the statement of Hugh Peters, see Carlyle, *op. cit.*, vol. i, pp. 353-354.

18. Aristotle's discussion occurs in the fifth book of the *Politics*. But an understanding of it is marred by a traditional inclination to render αἴτιογ by the English, "cause." Medieval scholasticism from which this terminology is derived was less wrong as long as the nominalist conception of *causa* prevailed. The fourfold scheme of *causa materialis, causa efficiens, causa formalis,* and *causa finalis* was, however, given a totally misleading turn when ontological considerations intruded themselves. The German *Grund* as distinguished from *Ursache* suggests the colorless English word "ground" or "basis" for αἴτιογ. But whatever the word, it is of decisive importance to realize that Aristotle's view was methodologically far superior to the uncritical ontological materialism or energeticism of modern "science" which has proceeded by first eliminating the *causa finalis*, then the *causa formalis*, then the *causa materialis*, and is now in the process of getting rid of the *causa efficiens*. When that is done, social scientists will be able to forget the exaggerated claims and materialistic nonsense of those who would foist the methods of natural science upon us, in their obsession to "discover" material (Marx) or at least efficient (Vitalists, Fascists) causes. Certainly, it is only now becoming once more possible to see Aristotle's political science in its true perspective. The "incomprehensible" order of the *Politics* becomes quite obvious when seen in this light. Cf., for an important landmark, Werner Jäger, *Aristoteles* (1923).

Chapter X

THE CONSTITUTION AS A POLITICAL FORCE

General References

The central theme of this chapter has not been stated elsewhere, as far as the author's knowledge goes, but it is adumbrated and to some extent implied in constitutionalist writings since the English constitutionalists began merging the medieval idea of a fundamental law with the basic pattern of governmental organization. Among modern writings, the author has particularly profited by W. Y. Elliott's *The Pragmatic Revolt in Politics* (1928), particularly pp. 407 ff. and 470 ff., and Rudolf Smend's *Verfassung und Verfassungsrecht* (1928).

Special References

1. The citation from Rousseau is found in *Social Contract*, Book II, ch. xii. Holcombe's phrase is from *State Government in the United States* (3rd ed., 1931).

2. The general idea of the bill of rights is discussed in its historical setting by Benjamin F. Wright, Jr., in his *American Interpretations of Natural Law* (1931). See also ch. iv, "The Bill of Rights and the Government Services," in "Responsible Government Service under the American Constitution," in *Problems of the American Public Service* by C. J. Friedrich, *et al.*, and the literature cited there.

3. The point of this paragraph is clearly implied in most writings since the eclipse of the law of nature school, but is often obscured by the squabble about sovereignty. A good statement of the American case can be found in Charles A. Beard's *The American Leviathan* (1930), but it too does not make out an argument for the maintenance of "rights" against elements in the community which would destroy them.

4. The problem of conflicts in written constitutions has vexed lawyers, particularly when reflecting upon judicial review. Herman Oliphant touches upon this point in his "A Return to *Stare Decisis*" in 6 *American Law School Review* 215 ff. The problem as a whole is treated comparatively by Charles G. Haines, *The Revival of Natural Law Concepts* (1930). See also Smend, *op. cit.*

5. A suggestive discussion of the implications of a preamble, though from a predominantly legal point of view, occurs in Edward S. Corwin's "We, the People" in *The Doctrine of Judicial Review* (1914), pp. 81 ff. The German preamble is ably discussed in Hugo Preuss, *Reich und Länder* (ed. Gerhard Anschütz, 1928).

7. See A. Lawrence Lowell, *Public Opinion in War and Peace* (1923); Walter Lippmann, *Public Opinion* (1922) and *The Phantom Public* (1925); and the large bibliography given by Lasswell and Casey, *A Bibliography of Public Opinion and Propaganda* (1935). Of Burke's, the most important essay in this connection is *An Appeal from the New to*

the Old Whigs (*Works*, Boston, 1839, vol. iii, pp. 333 ff.). Of de Maistre, consult *Considérations sur la France* (3rd ed., 1881).

8. The Marxist-Communist doctrine of class war is not so much the cause (as the Nazis would have it) as it is the manifestation of this cleavage in the community. The problem of conflicting loyalties is well put and investigated in Paul Kosok, *Modern Germany—A Study of Conflicting Loyalties* (1933). For pre-war Austria, see Oscar Jaszi, *The Dissolution of the Habsburg Monarchy* (1929). For Poland, see Malbone W. Graham, Jr., *New Governments of Eastern Europe* (1927), and R. Machray, *Poland, 1914-1931* (1932). For Czechoslovakia, see Malbone W. Graham, Jr., *New Governments of Central Europe* (1924), chs. xii-xiv. Most important is T. G. Mazaryk, *The Making of a State* (1926).

9. Sage remarks on the general problem of this paragraph are found in Charles E. Merriam, *The Making of Citizens* (1931), chs. ii and iii, and the same author's *Political Power* (1934), *passim.*

10. See Robert C. Brooks, *Civic Training in Switzerland* (1930). See also Ed. His, *Geschichte des neueren schweizerischen Staatsrechts, Die Zeit der Restauration und der Regeneration, 1814-1848* (1929), and E. Fueter, *Die Schweiz seit 1848* (1928), *passim.*

11. See Burke, *op. cit.*, vol. iii, p. 421. For the debate, see *Verhandlungen der Verfassungsgebenden Deutschen Nationalversammlung,* 1105A, and *Bericht und Protokolle des Achten Ausschusses über den Entwurf einer Verfassung des Deutschen Reichs*, pp. 24-25. For the imperial constitution, see Burt Estes Howard, *The German Empire* (1906), pp. 403 ff. For the controversy about "Reich," see also Gerhard Anschütz, *Die Verfassung des Deutschen Reichs* (14th ed., 1933), Introduction, and pp. 36 ff. Regarding the British Commonwealth, see W. Y. Elliott, *The New British Empire* (1932), pp. 42 ff.

12. Carlton J. H. Hayes, *Essays on Nationalism* (1926); Lippmann, *Public Opinion* (1922). See also Koppel S. Pinson, *A Bibliographical Introduction to Nationalism* (1935); and H. D. Lasswell and R. D. Casey, *A Bibliography of Public Opinion and Propaganda* (1935).

13. The statements from Burke are found in *Works*, vol. iii, pp. 52 and 137. The statement from Walter Lippmann's *Method of Freedom* (1934) is found on pp. ix-x.

Chapter XI

THE SEPARATION OF POWERS

General References

The separation of powers (and the concomitant checks and balances) have been part of the dead stock-in-trade of so-called political theory ever since Locke and Montesquieu. Yet, after they had served their purpose as platform planks of anti-monarchical agitation, they settled back into the dogmatic slumber of an "accepted principle of constitutional law." Hardly any attempt was made to explore the principle as a working hypothesis related to ascertainable matters of fact;[1] instead, it was treated as a more or less practicable norm in the particular form which the respective national constitutional law had given it. Practically all the "general" literature is either legal or doctrinal. Today the emergence of governments built upon an almost complete concentration of powers has once more set the stage for scientific reconsideration of the question: under what conditions and in what forms can a separation of powers occur and be maintained? This chapter does not answer that question, but adumbrates it. It restates the author's view as expressed in an article for the *ESS* in 1934.

Special References

2. Polybius' famous discussion occurs in his *History,* Book VI, chs. xi ff. Curiously, Mommsen's classic *Abriss des Römischen Staatsrechts* (1893) does not explicitly take up this problem at all. The most elaborate application of the doctrine to English constitutional law occurs in Sir Thomas Smith, *De Republica Anglorum* (1583); see, regarding him, the discussion in J. W. Allen, *A History of Political Thought in the Sixteenth Century* (1928), pp. 262 ff. Its generalized expansion is most extensively set forth by James Harrington in his *Oceana* (1656); the profound influence of his thought upon America is argued by T. W. Dwight in his "James Harrington," *Political Science Quarterly,* vol. ii (1887), pp. 1 ff.

3. See Locke, *An Essay Concerning the True Origin, Extent and End of Civil Government,* chs. x-xii. Here ch. x, dealing with the forms of government, is merely a brief preface to a statement of the doctrine of the separation of powers. For the city of Strassburg, see Gustav Schmoller, *Deutsches Städtewesen in älterer Zeit* (1922), pp. 214 ff.

4. See Ernst Klimowsky, *Die englische Gewaltenteilungslehre bis zu Montesquieu* (1927), and Leopold von Ranke, "Zur Geschichte der Doktrin von den drei Staatsgewalten," in his *Werke,* vol. xxiv.

5. For the *Instrument,* see Gardiner, *Constitutional Documents,* pp. 405 ff. For Cromwell's speeches, see Carlyle, *Cromwell,* vol. ii, pp. 415 and 464-465.

6. The citation from Blackstone is found in his *Commentaries* (1765), (ed., T. Cooley, 1876), vol. i, p. 146.

7. The point made in this paragraph has received insufficient attention in the extensive literature on Montesquieu. See Joseph Dedieu, *Montesquieu et la Tradition Politique Anglaise en France* (1909); H. Jansen, *Montesquieu's Theorie von der Dreitheilung der Gewalten im Staate auf Ihre Quellen Zurückgeführt* (1878). One difficulty has been the purely linguistic one that *power, pouvoir* and *Gewalt* are only roughly comparable.

8. See E. B. Greene, *The Provincial Governor in the English Colonies of North America* (1898); Benjamin F. Wright, Jr., "The Origins of the Separation of Powers in America," in *Economica,* vol. xiii (1933); and

[1] A notable exception: Herman Finer, *Theory and Practice of Modern Government,* cited above.

William S. Carpenter, "The Separation of Powers in the Eighteenth Century," in *American Political Science Review,* vol. xxii (1928).

9. The importance of the two-party system as a constitutional restraint was first clearly stated by Walter Bagehot in his epochal *The English Constitution* (1867, . . . 1928). It was systematically restated by Julius Hatschek, *Englisches Staatsrecht* (1905), vol. ii, pp. 1 ff. The crucial importance of the conventions concerning the parties for restraining the power of the government was made the touchstone of true parliamentary government by Robert Redslob in a brilliant essay, *Die Parlamentarische Regierung in Ihrer Wahren und Ihrer Unechten Form* (1918). The failure to recognize this restraint is an important factor in the destruction of crypto-parliamentary schemes, such as those of Italy and Germany.

10-11. See Benjamin Constant, *Cours de Droit Constitutionnel* (1814), and Erich Kaufmann, *Studien zur Staatslehre des Monarchischen Prinzipes* (1906), Esmein-Nézard, *Droit Constitutionnel* (8th ed.), vol. i; Robert von Mohl, *Staatsrecht, Völkerrecht und Politik* (1860), vol. i, pp. 3 ff., vol. ii, pp. 4 ff. Cf. also the convenient summary in Conrad Bornhak, *Genealogie der Verfassungen* (1935).

12. See the article, "Legislative Assemblies—Germany," by Otto Koellreuter, in the *ESS*, vol. ix, and the literature cited there. See also "The Development of the Executive Power in Germany," in *APSR,* vol. xxvii (1933), by Carl J. Friedrich. The transition to parliamentary government in France is brilliantly portrayed by Joseph Barthélemy in his *L'Introduction du Régime Parlementaire en France sous Louis XVIII et Charles X* (1904).

13. Regarding Sweden, see "Legislative Assemblies—Scandinavian States and Finland," by Herbert Tingsten, in the *ESS*, vol. ix; P. E. Fahlbeck, *Die Regierungsform Schwedens* (1911); and Axel Brusewitz, "Maktfördelning och demokrati i den konstitutionella utvecklingen," in *Statsvenska Tidskrift* (1923), as well as Nils Herlitz, *Grunddragen av det Svenska Statsskickets Historia* (1928), particularly pp. 177 ff.

14. See *Problems of the American Public Service* (ed. Commission of Inquiry into Public Personnel Problems), "Responsible Government Service in the United States," by Carl J. Friedrich, pp. 48 ff.

15. See John Dickinson, "Checks and Balances," in the *ESS*, vol. iii. See also W. Hasbach, "Gewaltentrennung, Gewaltenteilung und Gemischte Staatsform," in *Vierteljahrschrift für Sozial- und Wirtschaftsgeschichte* (1916), and the sane restatement by Herman Finer, *Theory and Practice of Modern Government* (1932), vol. i, pp. 153 ff.

16. See, e.g., Woodrow Wilson, *Congressional Government* (1887), pp. 265 ff.; Frank J. Goodnow, *The Principles of the Administrative Law of the United States* (1905), p. 53 and *passim.*

17. See John Adams, *A Defence of the Constitutions of Government of the United States of America* (1787), pp. 308-309: "All nations, under all governments, must have parties; the great secret is to control them. There are but two ways, either by a monarchy and standing army, or by a balance in the constitution. Where the people have a voice, and there is no balance, there will be everlasting fluctuations, revolutions and hor-

rors. . . ." For Constant, see *Cours de Politique Constitutionnelle* (1872), and the able little sketch by Edwin Mims, Jr., in the *ESS*, vol. iv. For the prerogative, see the author's article, "Prerogative" in the *ESS*; Dicey's statement is found in his *Law of the Constitution* (8th ed., 1926), p. 420, Cf. also the bibliography cited in the author's article. Laski's view is stated in a pamphlet entitled *The Crisis and the Constitution* (1932), ch. vi. For the English King's imperial position, see W. Y. Elliott, *The New British Empire* (1932), *passim.*

18. See Carl Schmitt, *Der Hüter der Verfassung* (1931). For the general questions of the separation of powers under the Constitution of Weimar, see Rudolf Smend, *Verfassung und Verfassungsrecht* (1928); Hans Bettmann, *Die Gewaltenteilung im demokratischen Rechtsstaate—Eine Untersuchung zum geltenden deutschen Staatsrecht* (1931); and Ernst von Hippel, *Die Lehre Montesquieu's von der Dreiteilung der Gewalten und der Grad ihrer Verwirklichung in den Verfassungen des Deutschen Reichs von 1871 und 1919 und den Verfassungen des Preussischen Staates von 1850 und 1920* (1921). On the whole, German thought was profoundly influenced by French ideas, rather than American and English notions. For the peculiar features of the French practice, see Antoine Saint Girons, *Droit Public Français: Essai sur la Séparation des Pouvoirs dans l'Ordre Politique Administratif et Judiciaire* (1881), as well as the leading text, A. Esmein, *Droit Constitutionnel,* vol. i, ch. iii.

19. For a more detailed discussion of judicial review, see the next chapter and the literature cited there.

Chapter XII

JUDICIAL REVIEW OF LEGISLATIVE ACTS

General References

General literature on this subject is considerable. In the United States, judicial review of legislation has always been considered one of the unique achievements of the country's constitutional scheme. Abroad it has not found any willing imitators. The literature reflects this cleavage. In recent decades the court's position as guardian of the Constitution has been the subject of violent attacks in the United States, too. The literature is thus divided into writers favoring and writers questioning and opposing the power of the courts to declare acts of the legislature unconstitutional. The related and more detached question, under what conditions can a court function as guardian of a constitution, has received only incidental treatment. Like most legal writers, those who have discussed judicial review have been preoccupied with the needs and rationalizations of the particular legal system with which they happened to be familiar. Typical examples are Charles Warren's *Congress, the Constitution and the Supreme Court* (1925), and E. S. Corwin, *The Doctrine of Judicial Review* (1914), on one hand; the discussion in Gerhard Anschütz, *Die Verfassung des Deutschen Reichs* (14th ed., 1933), vol. i, pp. 369 ff. and elsewhere, or in Esmein-Nézard *Droit Constitutionnel* (8th ed., 1928), vol. i, pp. 538 ff., on the other hand. The tendency in Germany after the war to adopt judicial review brought on a veritable avalanche of controversial writings on the subject, the more important part of which is surveyed in the author's article, "The Issue of Judicial Review in Germany," *PSQ,* vol. xliii (1928), pp. 188 ff., to which should be added the broader treatment by Charles G. Haines, "Some Phases of the Theory and Practice of Judicial Review of Legislation in Foreign Countries," in *APSR,* vol. xxiv, pp. 583 ff. This latter author wrote also a study of the American problem, *The American Doctrine of Judicial Supremacy* (1914), and he more recently analyzed the underlying philosophical problems in a significant volume, *The Revival of Natural Law Concepts* (1930). The critical social reformist view was expounded before the war by C. A. Beard, *The Supreme Court and the Constitution* (1912), and in a milder form by F. J. Goodnow, *Social Reform and the Constitution* (1911). The English point of view, similarly considered, was set forth by Harold Laski, "Judicial Review of Social Policy in England," in 39 *Harvard Law Review* 832 ff. (1925). It may, however, also be stated in terms of conservative preferences, as is shown by the treatment A. V. Dicey gave the subject in *Introduction to the Study of the Law of the Constitution* (8th ed., 1915), ch. iii. That the American tradition is part of an older liberal philosophy of government can be gleaned from such treatments as that given by Robert von Mohl, *Staatsrecht, Völkerrecht und Politik* (1860), vol. i, pp. 66 ff., "Ueber die rechtliche Bedeutung verfassungswidriger Gesetze"; his views, too, were influenced by the particular provision of such judicial review in the constitution of Württemberg, concerning which one may compare Mohl's own treatise, *Das Staatsrecht des Königreichs Württemberg* (1829), particularly vol. i, pp. 634 ff. Mohl was well acquainted with American constitutional doctrine.

Special References

1. The statements of Hamilton on behalf of judicial review (though the doctrine is not found in the Constitution) are given in the *Federalist,* Nos. 78-82.

2. *Re* literature on Coke, see above, VII, §§4 ff.

3. Holdsworth's view is found in vol. iv, pp. 174, 184-185. For McIlwain, see his *The American Revolution* (1924). The study of Robert L. Schuyler, *Parliament and the British Empire: Some Constitutional Controversies Concerning Imperial Legislative Jurisdiction* (1929), while full of interesting material, cannot be admitted to have undermined McIlwain's central argument, as is sometimes supposed; in fact, Schuyler did not deal with the fundamental constitutional issue at all. Cf. the review by George M. Wrong, *APSR,* vol. xxiii, p. 1011.

4. Adams' views are expounded in *Defence of the Constitutions of Government of the United States of America* (1787). *Marbury v. Madison* is 1 *Cranch* 137 (1803). Concerning this decision and the extensive literature dealing with it, see E. S. Corwin, "Marbury *v.* Madison and the Doctrine of Judicial Review," in *The Doctrine of Judicial Review* (1914),

pp. 1 ff. Case books on constitutional law are apt to contain this case. Gneist's statement is found in *Der Rechtsstaat und die Verwaltungsgerichte* (1879), pp. 237 f. Regarding Württemberg, see Mohl, *op. cit.*

5. See literature above, chs. viii and x.

6. For this, see above ch. ix. For the pocket veto, see 279 U.S. 655, and the comments by R. E. Cushman, *APSR,* vol. xxiv, pp. 67 ff.

7-9. The discussion of rigid versus flexible constitutions has been carried on for a long time. The most concise essay is found in James Bryce, *Studies in History and Jurisprudence* (1901), vol. i, pp. 124 ff. The question as to whether an independent amending power existed in Germany was always considered in the extensive discussions on judicial review. See Fritz Morstein Marx, *Variationen über richterliche Zuständigkeit zur Prüfung der Rechtmässigkeit des Gesetzes* (1927), for a general survey.

10-11. The question of constitutional change by interpretation is carefully considered in H. W. Horwill, *Usages of the American Constitution* (1925), and historically traced with a masterful hand by A. C. McLaughlin, *A Constitutional History of the United States* (1935). In terms of the German context, a searching special analysis is given by Karl Loewenstein, *Erscheinungsformen der Verfassungsänderung* (1931).

12. See Marx, *op. cit.,* and Friedrich, *op cit.*

13. See the literature cited above, VII, §11.

14. See the literature cited above, VII, §5. Also Justice Cardozo, *The Nature of the Judicial Process* (1921), and William A. Robson, *Justice and Administrative Law* (1928), ch. v.

15-16. On the subject of scientist and lawyer and the possibilities of a "naturalist" jurisprudence, see Edward S. Robinson, *Law and the Lawyers* (1935), ch. i. On representation, see the literature below, ch. xvi.

17. Concerning Siéyès' constitutional jury, see Esmein-Nézard, *Droit Constitutionnel* (8th ed., 1928), vol. i, pp. 638 ff., where Siéyès' great speech before the Convention is summarized. For this speech, still eminently worth reading, see *Réimpression de l'Ancien Moniteur,* vol. xxv, pp. 293 ff. Cf. also the study by Trouillard, *Le Sénat Conservateur du Consulat et du Premier Empire* (1912), and the recent study on Siéyès by G. G. van Deusen, *Siéyès; His Life and his Nationalism* (1932), particularly p. 61.

18. For Czechoslovakia, see O. Flanderka, *Le Controle de la Constitutionnalité des Lois en Tchecoslovaquie* (1926); on Austria, Charles Eisenmann, *La Justice Constitutionnelle et la Haute Cour Constitutionnelle de l'Autriche* (1928), and the article by Haines cited above.

19. The entire literature bears upon this point. Special mention may be made of Edouard Lambert, *Le Gouvernement des Juges et la Lutte contre la Legislation Sociale aux États-Unis* (1921), and the same author's essay (jointly with Halfred C. Brown), *La Lutte Judiciaire du Capital et du Travail Organizes aux États-Unis* (1923).

20. One might note the conclusion of Esmein, as set forth in Esmein-Nézard, *Droit Constitutionnel,* vol. i, p. 636: "Pours attribuer aux tribunaux un rôle si délicat et si important, il faut avant tout que la magistrature possède une bien haute autorité: il faut que le peuple ait une con-

fiance profonde dans sa sagesse et dans sa valeur professionnelle et scientifique." Similar views are found in R. Thoma's searching article, "Das Richterliche Prüfungsrecht," *Archiv für Öffentliches Recht,* vol. xliii, pp. 267 ff., and in the other material cited above, ch. vii, §11. See also the papers read at the round table discussion led by W. Y. Elliott in January, 1936 (*Proceedings of the American Academy of Political Science*), particularly "The States under the Constitution," by John Dickinson, and "The National Powers under the Constitution," by W. Y. Elliott.

Chapter XIII

FEDERALISM AND THE TERRITORIAL DIVISION OF POWER

General References

The literature on federalism is vast. Sobei Mogi has included, in his meritorious survey of *Federalism* (1931), a selected bibliography of twenty-three pages. Much of this literature, unfortunately, revolves around the question of how to combine various doctrines of sovereignty with the constitutional norms of a federal government. Since the two are inconsistent logically, these discussions partake of the aridity of the many learned discourses on the squaring of the circle. A new chapter opened when Hugo Preuss, following Gierke, proposed to eliminate the concept of sovereignty in his *Gemeinde, Staat, Reich als Gebietskörperschaften* (1889), particularly pp. 89 ff. Though Gierke himself disowned Preuss' views (see John D. Lewis, *The Genossenschaft Theory of Otto von Gierke* [1935], p. 100; see also *ibid.*, fn. 36, quoting E. Kaufmann), Preuss felt himself to be Gierke's true follower in maintaining that "the entire concept belongs to a set of ideas which is gone together with political institutions (*staatliche Erscheinungsform*) corresponding to it," and he could point to certain earlier German writers who had attempted to eliminate sovereignty, such as R. von Mohl (cf. *Enzyklopädie der Staatswissenschaften,* 2nd ed., pp. 43, 86). It is not without interest from our point of view that Mohl shares with Preuss a vivid sense of historical reality as contrasted with logical and normative problems. This side of the literature of federalism leaves much to be desired. Siegfried Brie's celebrated *Der Bundesstaat* (1874) is doctrinal, though in the words of R. Emerson's able summary of the whole body of German writings on the subject (cf. ch. iii, "Federalism," in *State and Sovereignty in Modern Germany* [1928]), Brie's volume "did much to clarify the issues involved in the debate over federalism." Doctrinal, too, are most of the other German writers on the subject. At the same time, historical scholarship began to accumulate an increasing body of data on past federations and federal "states." Swiss, American and German historians offered materials aplenty on which to base a more realistic view. This was attempted in a very comprehensive manner by Edward A. Freeman, in his *History of Federal Government in Greece and Italy* (1863), which was to be the first of several volumes dealing with the entire development. Stimulated by him, H. Sidgwick included several chapters (lectures) on federalism, new and old, in his *The Development of European Polity* (1903, and later editions). A detailed comparative account of American and German federal structures has recently been given by Herman Finer in his *The Theory and Practice of Modern Government* (1932), vol. i, ch. viii. Robert C. Binkley has made the struggle between unitary and federative polity a main theme of his volume, *Realism and Nationalism, 1852-1871* (1936), expounding the view that the period saw the ultimate defeat of federative plans. A compact survey of the institutional problem is offered by Arthur W. MacMahon in his article, "Federation," in the *ESS*. The notion of an administrative federalism is developed by Arnold Brecht, "Federalism and Business Regulation," in *Social Research*, vol. ii (1935). All this literature contains elements of the views set forth in the text, and there is a great deal of common historical material which is drawn from one or the other. But the particular synthesis of facts and theory set forth here is not afforded the comfort of a long line of predecessors, since it is an attempt to relate federal structures to the general lines of institutional development of modern constitutional government as seen by the author.

Special References

2. The significance of objectives (or purposes) was stressed by Heinrich Rosin, following R. von Jhering, *Der Zweck im Recht 1877-1883;* but unhappily Rosin proceeded to make purpose the exclusive criterion. Cf. Emerson, *op. cit.*, pp. 118 ff. For the analogy between federations of governments and those of associations, see MacMahon, *op. cit.*, and H. Preuss, *op. cit.*, particularly Part III, and Gierke, *Das Deutsche Genossenschaftsrecht*, vol. i, pp. 457 ff. Very valuable also is R. M. MacIver, *Community* (3rd ed., 1928), pp. 98 ff., 153 ff., 249 ff., where the problem is discussed in its general setting.

3. For literature on the several federations and leagues, see below, §6.

4. For the items on Swiss constitutional development, cf. Ed. His, *Geschichte des neueren Schweizerischen Staatsrechts* (1929), of which Volume I deals with "Die Zeit der Helvetik und der Vermittlungsakte 1798 bis 1813," while the second takes up "Die Zeit der Restauration und der Regeneration 1814 bis 1848." Cf. also W. Sulzbach, *Nationales Gemeinschaftsgefühl und Wirtschaftliches Interesse* (1929).

5. No good comparative study of the impact of economic forces exists. But the literature on the United States is considerable. For a challenging, though perhaps extreme, position one can still refer to Charles A. Beard's pathfinding study, *An Economic Interpretation of the Constitution of the United States* (1914). For Germany, the recent study published by the Friedrich-List-Stiftung concerning the founding of the *Zollverein*, Friedrich Lenz, *Friedrich List, der Mann und das Werk* (1935), is very illuminating on this score. E. Fueter has given much emphasis to this factor in dealing with Swiss history in his *Die Schweiz seit 1848* (1928).

This point is carried even further by E. Gagliardi, *Geschichte der Schweiz von den Anfängen bis auf die Gegenwart* (1927), particularly vol. iii.

6. Cf. Gierke, *op. cit.*, pp. 463 ff. (for the Hanse) ; *ibid.*, pp. 476 ff. (for the Rhenish League). See also the article by Fritz Rörig in the *ESS* for the former, and the literature cited there and in C. Brinkmann, "The Hanseatic League, a Survey of Recent Literature" in *Journal of Economic and Business History*, vol. ii, (1930), pp. 585 ff. For Switzerland, see Gagliardi, *op. cit.*, vol. i. For the Achaean League, see W. S. Ferguson, *Greek Imperialism* (1913), pp. 238 ff. and *passim*, as well as the monographs cited there. For the League of Nations, see Felix Morley, *The Society of Nations* (1932), *passim*, but particularly ch. x.

7. Same references as previous paragraph. For the Dutch United Provinces, see D. C. Niyhoff, *Staatkundige Geschiedenis van Nederland* (1893) ; for Althusius' ideas on federalism, see Otto von Gierke, *Johannes Althusius*, ch, v, now available in translation as Appendix B in John D. Lewis' *The Genossenschaft Theory of Otto von Gierke* (1935). For the text, see *Politica Methodica Digesta of Johannes Althusius*, ed. C. J. Friedrich (1932).

8. Cf. again Morley, *The Society of Nations* (1932). The citation is from p. 419. For other federations, see earlier citations.

9. Secession, like so many other things, has usually been discussed in terms of rights rather than facts. No people with a government common to them all will permit secession.

10. A general discussion of these representative assemblies is found in Sir J. A. R. Marriott, *Second Chambers* (1910). The ablest, though perhaps a bit partial, discussion of the United States Senate is found in Lindsay Rogers, *The American Senate* (1926). The unrepresentative quality of the Senate as it affects foreign affairs has recently been the subject of much constitutional analysis. See Royden J. Dangerfield, *In Defense of the Senate* (1933) ; E. S. Corwin, *The President's Control of Foreign Relations* (1917) ; Denna F. Fleming, *The Treaty Veto of the American Senate* (1930) ; James W. Garner, *American Foreign Policies* (1928) ; Quincy Wright, *The Control of American Foreign Relations* (1922). The quotation from Elliott is found in his *The Need for Constitutional Reform*, p. 191. The Swiss situation is analyzed in detail in Max Veith, *Der rechtliche Einfluss der Kantone auf die Bundesgewalt* (1902), particularly pp. 78 ff. The statistical figures are taken from *Statistical Abstract of the United States* (1925) and *Statistisches Jahrbuch der Schweiz* (1933). For the "representative" aspect, see below, xvi, particularly §§6, 11 and 12. See also Fritz Fleiner, *Schweizerisches Bundesstaatsrecht* (1922), No. 1, pp. 154 ff.; and R. C. Brooks, *Government and Politics of Switzerland* (1918), pp. 81 ff. J. M. Vincent's *Government in Switzerland* (1900) also goes into this problem with considerable care.

11. The figures for Germany are from *Statistisches Jahrbuch für das deutsche Reich* (1927). The data regarding the members of the *Reichsrat* are found in successive editions of the *Handbuch für das deutsche Reich.* See also Josef Held, *Der Reichsrat*, etc. (1926) ; K. Bilfinger, *Der Einfluss*

der Einzelstaaten auf die Bildung des Reichswillens (1923); and the *HDSR*, vol. i, §§46, 47; Gerhard Anschütz, *Die Verfassung des Deutschen Reichs* (14th ed.), pp. 338 ff.; F. Poetzsch-Heffter, "Vom Staatsleben unter der Weimarer Verfassung," *JoR*, vol. xiii (1927); Julius Hatschek, *Deutsches und Preussisches Staatsrecht* (1922), pp. 698 ff.; Herbert Kraus, *The Crisis of German Democracy* (1932), pp. 107 ff.; Johannes Mattern, *Principles of the Constitutional Jurisprudence of the German National Republic* (1928), pp. 402 ff., and the literature cited in these volumes. See also the competent discussion in Finer, *op. cit.*, pp. 369 ff.

12. Cf. Fritz Hummel, *Preussen und seine Provinzen im Reichsrat* (1928), besides the general commentaries cited under §11. See also Hugo Preuss, *Reich und Länder* (ed. G. Anschütz [1928]), particularly pp. 24 ff. The memorandum of the Minister of the Interior can be found in the published materials of the *Länderkonferenz Beratungsunterlagen*, pp. 11-12. The statistical tables are found in *ibid.*, on pp. 469 ff. Concerning the ousting of the Prussian government, see below, §§15, 16.

13. The question of functions and their distribution is at the core of much of the German juristic writing, particularly in connection with the controversy over *Kompetenz-Kompetenz*, for which compare Emerson, *op. cit.* See also the general commentaries cited under §11, but particularly Preuss, *op. cit.*, pp. 105 ff.

14. For the most vivid picture of the transition from federation to federal government in the United States, see *The Federalist*, Nos. 1-10. The problem of the participation of the *Länder* as units in the amending power was not clearly faced by the Weimar constituent assembly, nor did it receive much attention afterward; it was occasionally adduced as proof that the German constitution did not recognize such a power; cf. Anschütz, *op. cit.*, p. 401, where he discusses article 76. Regarding article 18, see the same commentary, pp. 139 ff. See also Hugo Preuss, *op. cit.*, pp. 154 f., and Kraus, *op. cit.*, p. 121.

15. The quotation is from Lindsay Rogers, *The American Senate*, p. 24; but compare the whole chapter. For Switzerland, see Fleiner, *op. cit.*, p. 183. For Germany, regarding article 15, see Kraus, *op. cit.*, pp. 119 f., and Anschütz, *op. cit.*, pp. 111 ff. For the problems of "execution," see Johannes Mattern, *Bavaria and the Reich* (1923), *passim;* Richard Grau, *Die Diktaturgewalt des Reichspräsidenten und der Landesregierungen auf Grund des Artikels 48 der Reichsverfassung* (1923). Regarding the same article, see also the extensive literature listed by Frederick F. Blachly and Miriam E. Oatman, *The Government and Administration of Germany* (1928), pp. 721 f. Regarding the conflict between the Reich and Prussia, see the next paragraph.

16. Regarding the Court of State, see Hans-Heinrich Lammers, *Das Gesetz über den Staatsgerichtshof* (1921), *passim,* where the law of July 9, 1921, is discussed. See also H. Nawiasky, *Bayerisches Verfassungsrecht* (1923), pp. 467 ff.; Richard Thoma in the *Festschrift zum 50 jährigen Bestehen des Reichsgerichts* (1929), vol. i, pp. 179 ff. Franz Jerusalem, *Die Staatsgerischtsbarkeit* (1930), and Kurt Ritter, *Die verfassungsrechtlichen Streitigkeiten vor dem Staatsgerichtshof für das deutsche*

Reich (1930); an article by Hans J. Wolff in the *Archiv des oeffentlichen Rechts,* vol. xviii, pp. 411 ff., and finally the decisions of the court itself, published as an appendix to the *RGZ.* Concerning the Prussian case, see *RGZ.* The literature on the Supreme Court is, of course, very large. It may be best to note only the most widely recognized standard works: Charles Warren, *The Supreme Court in United States History* (2nd ed., 1928), 3 vols.; and Felix Frankfurter and James M. Landis, *The Business of the Supreme Court* (1927). To these must be added Edward S. Corwin's recent estimate, *The Twilight of the Supreme Court* (1934). Regarding Switzerland, see Fleiner, *op. cit.* Concerning Britain, see W. Y. Elliott, *The New British Empire* (1932), pp. 57 ff.

17. For this paragraph, see Elliott, *op. cit., passim,* but particularly chs. i, ii, and viii, and the literature cited there. Regarding the Imperial Defense Committee, see Maurice Hankey, "The Origin and Development of the Committee of Imperial Defense," in the *Army Quarterly,* July, 1927. See also the parliamentary debates (*HCD*) on the subject, March 27, 1928. See below, xvi, §12.

18. See Finer, *op. cit.,* vol. i, pp. 243 ff. The quotation is from W. A. Robson, *The Development of Local Government* (1931), p. 189.

19. An interesting discussion of federalism along broad comparative lines is to be found in Erich Hunger, *Zur Idee und Tradition des Föderalismus* (1929), taking up ideas expounded by Constantin Franz, *Der Foederalismus als das leitende Prinzip für die soziale, staatliche und internationale Organisation* (1879). In both, the problem of constitutionalism is in the background. See also, Herriot, *The United States of Europe* (tr. R. J. Dingle, 1930), *passim,* and *L'Europe Fédéraliste* (ed. J. Hennessy).

Chapter XIV

CONSTITUTIONAL DICTATORSHIP AND EMERGENCY POWERS

General References

The literature on the subject of this chapter is quite limited, except for the historical treatment of Roman and other antecedents. To be sure, a considerable amount of controversial writing on this subject appeared in the 'thirties and 'forties of the last century in France; and Karl Marx, who has done more than anyone else to spread the idea of dictatorship in recent times, undoubtedly was influenced by this literature. A number of treatments of contemporary unconstitutional dictatorships contain more or less extensive comments on constitutional dictatorship. Particularly, Carl Schmitt's *Die Diktatur von den Anfängen des modernen Souveränitätsgedankens bis zum proletarischen Klassenkampf* (2nd ed., 1928) attempts a comprehensive synthesis, but unfortunately his theoretical analysis is marred by his preoccupation with "political" considerations of the moment—at that time the justification of more extended presidential powers. The other works one may mention in this connection are O. Forst de Battaglia, *Prozess der Diktatur* (1930), translated by H. Paterson as *Dictatorship on Its Trial* (1931); F. Cambo, *Les Dictatures* (1930); and E. Ortega y Gasset, *La Verdad sobre la Dictadura* (1925), all of them digested in H. R. Spencer's article on the subject for the *ESS*. The author, however, has profited most from a work which will shortly appear in print and which has been prepared at his suggestion by Frederick M. Watkins. Originally conceived as a translation of Schmitt's work, the inadequacies of the latter's essay made an independent and scientific treatment seem highly desirable.

Special References

1. See the bibliography of Chapter II, particularly §2. The most significant general discussion of constitutional dictatorship is given by J.-J. Rousseau, *Contrat Social,* Book IV, ch. vi.

2. For the ecclesiastical development, see J. Haller, *Papsttum und Kirchenreform* (1903), esp. vol. i. Cf. also for the general context the able summary by Clemens Bauer in the *ESS* under the heading, "Papacy." Much valuable material is found also in Albert Hauck, *Kirchengeschichte Deutschlands* (3rd ed., 1913). The whole problem is opened up in Otto Hintze's striking essay, "Der Kommissarius und seine Bedeutung in der allgemeinen Verwaltungsgeschichte," in *Festgabe für Karl Zeumer* (1910), who first emphasized the importance of the discussion in Bodin. Various aspects of this essay are further developed in Carl Schmitt, *op. cit.,* chs. i and ii. Bodin's discussion is to be found in ch. ii of Book III of his *De Republica* (Frankfurt ed., 1609), pp. 424 ff. On the intendants, see G. Hanotaux, *Origines de l'institution des intendants* (1884).

3. For the Roman problem, see Theodor Mommsen, *Römisches Staatsrecht* (ed. 1874), vol. ii, 1 pp. 125 ff. On Wallenstein, see the detailed study in Schmitt, *op. cit.,* pp. 79 ff. Concerning Cromwell's dictatorship, see S. R. Gardiner, *History of the Great Civil War* (1893) particularly vols. ii and iii. See also the essay by W. C. Abbott, "The Historic Cromwell," in *Adventures in Reputation* (1935).

4. The text of this paragraph is particularly directed against the central thesis of Schmitt's treatise. Spencer, *op. cit.,* avoids Schmitt's error and approaches the view maintained here. New confusion has arisen in connection with an article by Max Lerner, "The Pattern of Dictatorship," in *Dictatorship in the Modern World* (1935). Here the "constitutional dictatorship" is placed parallel to Communist and Fascist dictatorship in an undiscriminating way. The significant doctrine of Rousseau (*op. cit.*) is neglected. Confusion is worse confounded when S. and B. Webb try to persuade us that, according to the dictionary, "dictatorship means the absolute rule by one man," and since such a rule does not exist in Soviet Russia, there does not exist any dictatorship in that country. See *Soviet Communism* (1935), vol. i, ch. vi.

5. The ruling of the Supreme Court is found in *Ex parte Milligan,* 4 *Wall* 2 (1866). Regarding the statement of Judge Mackintosh, see Charles

M. Clode, *The Administration of Justice under Military and Martial Law* (1872), p. 166. For the subject of martial law in the United States, see Charles Fairman, *The Law of Martial Rule* (1930), and the brief discussion in A. V. Dicey, *Introduction to the Study of the Law of the Constitution* (8th ed., 1915), ch. vii and note x. See also the able article by Thurman Arnold in the *ESS*.

6. For the state of siege in France, see Esmein-Nézard, *Droit Constitutionnel* (8th ed., 1928), vol. ii, pp. 176 ff. See also *Das Recht des Ausnahmezustandes im Auslande* (1928) by various authorities, published as vol. ix of *Beiträge zum ausländischen öffentlichen Recht und Völkerrecht* (Berlin).

7. Concerning the Defense of the Realm Act and the Emergency Powers Act (1920), cf. Fairman, *op. cit.*

8. The article of the German constitution is 48, now famous in the annals of German constitutional history. The original conception of it is expounded by Hugo Preuss, "Verfassungsmässige Diktatur," in *Zeitschrift für Politik*, vol. xiii, (1923), pp. 97 ff. The leading constitutional authority was Richard Grau, *Die Diktatur des Reichspräsidenten und der Landesregierungen auf Grund des Artikels 48 der Reichsverfassung* (1922). See also the same author's more recent treatment of the subject in *Handbuch des deutschen Staatsrechts* (1932), vol. ii, pp. 274 ff., and the literature cited there, as well as Anschütz, *op. cit.*, art. 48. These problems are also treated by Harlow J. Heineman, *The Growth of Executive Power in Germany—A Study of the German Presidency* (1934). As far as the Brüning regime is concerned, very interesting supporting detail was offered by Dr. Brüning himself in a series of lectures at Harvard University in the spring of 1936, the Godkin Lectures; they will presently appear in print. The problems of presidential dictatorship were politically considered in the author's article, "Dictatorship in Germany," in *Foreign Affairs*, vol. ix (1930), and the historical perspective of these problems in "The Development of the Executive Power in Germany," *APSR*, vol. xxvii (1933), pp. 185 ff.

9. Concerning Poincaré's "dictatorship," see Esmein-Nézard, *op. cit.*, vol. ii, pp. 112 ff., and the literature cited there. See also the study of Dendias cited below §11.

10. A considerable body of highly controversial literature has recently appeared in the United States, and the epithet "dictator" has rather indiscriminately been applied to the American President. In order to forestall the recurrence of such a situation as arose in 1932-1933, constitutional reform has been urged by various writers, among them W. Y. Elliott who, in *The Need for Constitutional Reform* (1935), cast the problem into this framework. See particularly pp. 27 ff. and 73 ff. Lindsay Rogers had interpreted the Wilsonian position during the war as dictatorship also; see his "Presidential Dictatorship in the United States," *Quarterly Review* (1919).

11. The study by Michael Dendias, *Le Renforcement des Pouvoirs du Chef de l'État dans la Démocratie Parlementaire* (1932), contains much

valuable comparative material, but it fails to draw the necessary clear distinction between constitutional and unconstitutional trends.

13. The literature for the comparisons of this paragraph comprehends at least some reference to the extensive treatment of existing unconstitutional dictatorships. Besides the work of the Webbs cited above, one may note the following: Herman Finer, *Mussolini's Italy* (1935), esp. Part II; Gaetano Salvemini, *Under the Axe of Fascism* (1936), particularly the conclusion; Herbert W. Schneider, *Making the Fascist State* (1928), esp. chs. ii and iii; H. R. Spencer, *Government and Politics of Italy* (1932), esp. chs. iii, ix-xi; Fritz Ermarth, *The New Germany* (1936), esp. chs. i and ii; Fritz Morstein Marx, *Government in the Third Reich* (1936), esp. pp. 31-60; Frederick L. Schuman, *The Nazi Dictatorship—A Study in Social Pathology and the Politics of Fascism* (1935), esp. chs. iv-vi. To these may be added two personal accounts, each highly flavored and partisan, but interesting: *The Berlin Diaries, May 30, 1932-January 30, 1933,* edited by Helmut Klotz (1934); and Joseph Goebbels, *Vom Kaiserhof zur Reichskanzlei* (3rd ed., 1934). They both shed light upon the transition from constitutional to unconstitutional government in Germany, whether their specific allegations are true or not. Concerning the Swiss militia tradition, see the volume by Julian Grande, *A Citizens' Army* (1916). Concerning Machiavelli, see, e.g., *Discourses,* Book III. Cf. also O. Ferrara, *Machiavel* (French ed., 1928), pp. 123 ff., and elsewhere. This point was given central importance in J. L. de Lolme's *The Constitution of England,* etc. (new ed., 1807), particularly chs. xvii and xviii.

15. Concerning Hellenistic Greece, see William S. Ferguson, *Greek Imperialism* (1913); concerning Augustan Rome, Mason Hammond, *The Augustan Principate in Theory and Practice during the Julio-Claudian Period* (1933), and Ernest Barker, "The Conception of Empire," in *The Legacy of Rome* (ed. Cyril Bailey, 1924). Concerning Renaissance Italy, see J. C. L. Sismondi, *A History of the Italian Republics* (revised edition by William Boulting, 1906). For monarchical absolutism see above, chs. ii-vii. The quotation is from the essay by Max Lerner cited above, §4.

Chapter XV

RESPONSIBILITY AND ITS ENFORCEMENT

Special References

1. It is interesting to note that Robert von Mohl already noted the English trend toward "bureaucracy" in *Staatsrecht, Völkerrecht und Politik* (1860), vol. ii, p. 60 f. It was, of course, widely discussed in England in connection with civil service reform.

2. The *Myers Case* is found 272 U. S. 52 (1926); the *Humphreys Case,* correctly cited as Rathbun *v.* United States, 295 U. S. 602 (1935). See the able comment by Cushman, *APSR,* vol. xxx, pp. 72 ff., concerning this case. The *Myers Case* has also been extensively commented upon; see, e.g.,

W. W. Willoughby, *The American Constitutional System* (2nd ed., 1929), ch. lxxxiv; James Hart, *Tenure of Office under the Constitution* (1930); and E. S. Corwin, *The President's Removal Power under the Constitution* (1927).

3. The entire medieval literature on the prince is permeated by the idea of ecclesiastical sanctions for "just" conduct. See the essay by John Dickinson, "The Medieval Idea of Kingship and Some of its Limitations, as Developed in the *Polykraticus* of John of Salisbury," in *Speculum*, vol. i (1926), pp. 308 ff.; R. W. and A. J. Carlyle, *History of Medieval Political Theory in the West* (1903-1916), *passim;* and (for an authoritative source) Thomas Aquinas, *De regimine principum.* For Henry II, see Rosenstock-Wittig, *Das Alter der Kirche* (1928), pp. 561 ff. Concerning Protestantism, see Hintze's articles cited above, ch. ii, §7, as well as Max Weber's pointed essay, *The Protestant Ethic and the Spirit of Capitalism* (trans. T. Parsons, 1930), pp. 79 ff.

4. Concerning the *Anti-Machiavel,* see Friedrich Meinecke, *Die Idee der Staatsräson in der neueren Geschichte* (2nd ed., 1925), pp. 340 ff.

5. Concerning Botero, see Friedrich Meinecke, *op. cit.,* pp. 81 ff., and his own work, *De Ratione Status* (ed. Conring, 1666). Meinecke's work is of general importance here; but compare the author's review in *APSR,* vol. xxiv, pp. 1064 ff. Concerning the divine right of kings, see John N. Figgis' classical treatment of the subject *The Divine Right of Kings* (2nd ed., 1914). See also his *Churches in the Modern State* (1913).

6. For the wide ramifications of the issue of toleration, see the comprehensive monograph by W. K. Jordan, *The Development of Religious Toleration in England from the Beginning of the English Reformation to the Death of Queen Elizabeth* (1932). Charles A. Beard's volume, *The Idea of National Interest* (1934), was followed by another, *The Open Door at Home; A Trial Philosophy of National Interest* (1934). C. J. H. Hayes' views are set forth in *Essays in Nationalism* (1926), esp. ch. iv, "Nationalism as a Religion."

7. For Burke's views, see *Works* (Boston, 1839), vol. ii, pp. 12 ff. Cf. also the significant comments by M. Einaudi, *Edmundo Burke e L'Indirizzo Storico Nelle Scienze Politiche* (1930), particularly pp. 78 ff.

8. Robert de Jouvenel, *La République des Camarades* (1914).

9. Frank R. Kent, *The Great Game of Politics* (1930), represents the typical cynical American newspaperman's view. The view of the text is set forth in somewhat greater detail, and in relation to American problems, in the author's "Responsible Government Service under the American Constitution," in *Problems of the American Public Service* (1935), published by the Commission of Inquiry on Public Personnel Problems. This essay may also be consulted for the next few paragraphs.

10. The Report of the Commission of Inquiry on Public Personnel Problems published its report, *Better Government Personnel,* in 1935.

11. The statement here quoted is found on p. 45 ff. For the English situation, see Leonard D. White, "The British Civil Service," in *Civil Service Abroad,* published by the Commission of Inquiry (1935), particularly pp. 17 ff.

12-13. The problem of titles relates, sociologically, to prestige and honor.

See the able article by Hans Speier, "Honor and Social Structure," in *Social Research*, vol. ii (1935), pp. 74 ff. See also the convincing institutional comments by Arnold Brecht, "Civil Service," in *Social Research*, vol. iii (1936), pp. 202 ff.

14. Cf. here Leonard D. White, *Introduction to the Study of Public Administration* (1926), ch. xv. For the practice of German disciplinary bodies, see the author's "The German and the Prussian Civil Service," in *The Civil Service in the Modern State* (1930), ed. by L. D. White, and the literature cited there.

15. For this, see George C. S. Benson, *Financial Control and Integration* (1934), vol. ii of *Studies in Systematic Political Science and Comparative Government*, ed. by C. J. Friedrich; W. F. Willoughby, *Principles of Public Administration* (1927); W. F. Willoughby, *The Problem of a National Budget* (1918); A. E. Buck, *Public Budgeting* (1929); F. A. Cleveland and A. E. Buck, *Budget and Responsible Government* (1920); R. G. Hawtrey, *The Exchequer and the Control of Expenditure* (1921), and A. C. Saemisch, *Die Kontrolle der staatlichen Finanzwirtschaft* (1931). The advocated reforms are discussed in Benson, *op. cit.*, pp. 30 ff.

17-18. For the points of this paragraph, see the literature cited above.

20. The problem of responsibility as here treated remains in a relatively unsatisfactory state. It is typical of the present lack of interest that the *ESS* did not include an article on this all-pervasive problem. In looking for it, one is obliged to gaze desolately at "resorts" and "restaurants." The author knows of few occasions more revealing of the complete confusion of the modern mind as to what is important.

Chapter XVI

GENERAL PROBLEMS OF REPRESENTATION

General References

The literature of political science on representation is rather unsatisfactory. On the one hand, there is the philosophical literature ranging from Hobbes' *Leviathan* through Rousseau's *Contrat Social* to Greene and Bosanquet, discoursing in normative and speculative terms. On the other hand, lawyers or rather jurists have been splitting hairs over the distinction between representation and delegation. This latter trend, while already seen in Burke's previously cited passages, became particularly popular in post-war Germany, where it produced two voluminous studies of considerable merit. These are Gerhard Leibholz, *Das Wesen der Repräsentation unter besonderer Berücksichtigung des Repräsentativsystems* (1929), and Hans J. Wolff, *Organschaft und Juristische Person* vol. ii; *Theorie der Vertretung* (*Stellvertretung, Organschaft und Repräsentation als soziale und juristische Vertretungsformen*) (1934). Besides these, Rudolf Smend must also be mentioned because he has made representation the center of his whole constitutional theory in his *Verfassung und Verfassungsrecht* (1928), emphasizing its value for purposes of integration; see particularly pp. 93 ff. This (learned) insistence upon the difference between representation and delegation, after a long period of interchangeable use, arose out of strictly partisan considerations. Theorists appeared who maintained that "representation" denoted a wholly ideal relationship (this view was also developed by M. Hauriou in his *Leçons sur le Movement Social* [1899]), while the humbler *Vertretung* (delegation) was claimed to be a word describing the dirty work of a commercial representative or lobbyist. It was then shown that German (and other) parliamentary representatives were mere delegates, and the conclusion readily offered itself that representation had "deteriorated." It was the old trick of so exalting the ideal aspect of an institution as to make its actual operation appear in an unfavorable light. In fact, a sound and important distinction lies back of this facetious argument which has been carefully studied by historians, namely, the distinction between representatives bound by an imperative mandate, legally, and representatives not so bound. The detailed workings of such a system were ably discussed by Miss Alice M. Holden in "The Imperative Mandate in the Spanish Cortes of the Middle Ages," *APSR*, vol. xxiv (1930), pp. 886 ff. For England, the same material is analyzed in May McKisack, *Parliamentary Representation of the English Boroughs during the Middle Ages* (1932), with which one might supplement the standard work of A. F. Pollard, *The Evolution of Parliament* (2nd ed., 1926). See also H. J. Ford, *Representative Government.* To this should be added the convenient and lucid essay by Charles A. Beard on "The Teutonic Origins of Representative Government," in *APSR*, vol. xxvi (1932), pp. 28 ff., which demolishes the already faded authority of Montesquieu's celebrated claim that representative government originated in "the forests of Germany." A broad comparative and historical view underlies the essay, "Representation," by Francis W. Coker and Carlton C. Rodee in the *ESS*. It is built around a sound generalization resembling the more restricted political definition of representation given by Robert von Mohl in his "Recht und Politik der repräsentativen Monarchie" in *Staatsrecht, Völkerrecht und Politik* (1860), vol. i, pp. 8 f. In its historical sections it summarizes the profound essay by Otto Hintze, "Weltgeschichtliche Bedingungen der Repräsentativverfassung," in *Historische Zeitschrift*, vol. cxliii, pp. 1-47, to which should be added the same author's "Typologie der ständischen Verfassung," *ibid.*, vol. cxli, pp. 229 ff. Interesting controversial positions have been advanced by Wundt and Oppenheimer, but the discussion of the material upon which they are based lies beyond the scope of this volume. Even the quantitative aspects of representative behavior have in recent years begun to be explored; Stuart Rice has devoted Part V of his interesting volume on *Quantitative Methods in Politics* (1928) to "The Voting Behavior of Representative Groups" (pp. 189-241).

Special References

2. The discussion in J.-J. Rousseau here referred to is found in *Contrat Social*, Bk. III, ch. xv.

3. Hobbes' view is expounded in *Leviathan*, Bk. I, ch. xvi. For Locke's idea of power, see above, ch. i, §12.

4. For the estates, see Georg von Below, "System und Bedeutung der

landständischen Verfassung," in *Territorium und Stadt* (1900), pp. 163 ff.; Otto von Gierke, *Das Deutsche Genossenschaftsrecht,* vol. i, §51 and elsewhere. See also, for a comparative political view, Hugo Preuss, *Verfassungspolitische Entwicklungen in Deutschland und Westeuropa* (1927), §14. Rudolf Gneist's *Englische Verfassungsgeschichte* (1882), while subject to criticism in many respects, also helps through its discussion of parliamentary institutions as estates, as given in §§19-26. For the orthodox view, see William Stubbs' *English Constitutional History* (3rd ed., 1887), particularly ch. xv.

5. For the inspirational aspect of dictatorial regimes, consult the literature cited above, ch. xiv, §13.

6. The definition by Robert von Mohl is found in his *Staatsrecht, Völkerrecht und Politik* (1860), vol. i, pp. 8-9.

7. For literature on the Economic Councils, see below, ch. xxiv, §§4, 6. The subject of restrictive qualifications for the electorate is an unpopular one, but it has to be faced. See the discussion in Edward M. Sait, *American Parties and Elections* (1927), particularly pp. 18 ff. and 38 ff. The abuse made of such methods is, however, a very serious obstacle to any progress along this line.

8. Professor McIlwain has rightly insisted upon this emphasis on legislation in Bodin. See the article by Max A. Shepard, "Sovereignty at the Crossroads—A Study of Bodin," in *PSQ,* vol. xlv (1930), pp. 580 ff. For the identification of parliamentary deliberation and conversation, see Carl Schmitt, *Politische Romantik* (2nd ed., 1925), *passim,* and *Die geistesgeschichtliche Lage des heutigen Parlamentarisums* (1923), pp. 20 ff. For the remainder, see the bibliography below, ch. xxii.

9. Rousseau's quotation is found in *Contrat Social* (Everyman edition), Bk. I, ch. v, pp. 33-34; that of Locke, in *Of Civil Government* (Everyman edition), p. 183; that of Richard Hooker, in his *Of the Laws of Ecclesiastical Polity,* (Everyman edition), p. 232.

10. The power of the purse is a standpat argument in connection with the development of parliamentary institutions. Hence the literature cited below in chs. xxi and xxii contains extensive material on the subject.

11. Consult, for this paragraph, the literature on the division of power and federalism, given above, chs. xi and xiii.

12. Compare the brief survey of "Medieval Representative Institutions," in H. Sidgwick, *The Development of European Polity* (1903), ch. xxi. On Simon de Montfort, cf. Stubbs, *op. cit.,* pp. 96-98.

Chapter XVII

ELECTORAL SYSTEMS IN THEORY AND PRACTICE

General References

The theory of electoral systems has received rather scanty attention in contrast to the practice of it. Only the gradual extension of proportional representation schemes has stimulated efforts at generalization. Even these disquisitions have been largely in terms of "justice" rather than in those of generalized description. There is, of course, the special literature on proportional representation cited below. Walter Bagehot's classical discussion of this question, in his *English Constitution* (2nd ed., 1873), ch. v, and J. S. Mill's in *Representative Government* (1860), ch. vii, are the main approaches, going beyond the general theory of representation. The literature on majority rule is, to be sure, relevant in a measure. Wladislaw Konopczynski's able summary in the *ESS*, as well as his *Liberum Veto* (1918), tr. into French by Mme. Korwin-Piotrowska (1930), contains much genuine scientific theory; the same may be said for Georg Simmel's brief discussion in his *Soziologie* (2nd ed., 1923), pp. 142 ff. Besides these, historical treatments help considerably, such as Otto von Gierke's "Ueber die Geschichte des Majoritätsprinzips," in *Essays in Legal History*, ed. by Paul Vinogradoff (1913), ch. xvi; and the recent study by J. G. Heinberg, "History of the Majority Principle," in *APSR*, vol. xx (1926), pp. 52 ff., and the literature cited there. There is, of course, a certain amount of generalization found in the general discussions contained in volumes such as C. E. Merriam and H. F. Gosnell, *The American Party System* (rev. ed., 1929), and E. M. Sait, *American Parties and Elections* (1927), particularly pp. 487 ff. in the latter, but attention is focused upon the workings of particular institutions in specific contexts. H. F. Gosnell's comparative survey, *Why Europe Votes* (1930), while full of significant material is prevented from making the best of it by the method (statistical) this author favors. Much interesting material is contained in the volume edited by Johannes Schauff entitled *Neues Wahlrecht* (1929), but much of it is focused on the German problems. One author who contributed a general article, "Ueberblick über die Wahlformen," Adolf Tecklenburg, had previously devoted a number of articles to the general electoral problems; see particularly his article, "Der Wille des Wählers und das Mass seiner Verwicklichung," in *Schmollers Jahrbuch*, vol. l (1926), pp. 981 ff. Very important further material is to be found in a number of parliamentary reports. For England we have the *Report of the Royal Commission Appointed to Enquire into Electoral Systems* (1910), Cd. 5163, and the *Minutes of Evidence*, Cd. 5162. For France, see *Rapport fait au nom de la Commission de Suffrage universel sur les propositions de loi tendant a établir la représentation proportionnelle*; this report was made by Charles Benoist on April 7, 1904, and is printed in *CD* IX, Annexe No. 160 (1906). For Sweden there is (perhaps the ablest of the three and the most recent) *Proportionsvalssakunnigas Betänkande* (1921). Finally we may mention the thoughtful, but of course biased, literature published by the Proportional Representation Society in England, whose secretary, John H. Humphreys, has made many contributions through the pages of the society's journal, *Representation*, and whose study, *Proportional Representation: A Study in Methods of Election* (1911), remains the most authoritative treatment of its subject. For the opposite view, however, see George Horwill, *Proportional Representation, Its Dangers and Its Defects* (1925). Two comprehensive descriptive accounts of recent electoral experience must be constantly consulted: Charles Seymour and D. P. Frary, *How the World Votes; the Story of Demo-*

cratic Development in Elections (2 vols., 1918), and Karl Braunias, *Das Parlamentarische Wahlrecht* (1932). To these one may add two somewhat exceptional books which partly invalidate the remarks at the outset: Leo Wittmayer, *Die Organisierende Kraft des Wahlsystems* (1903), and F. A. Hermens, *Demokratie und Wahlrecht* (1933). The latter volume, which is in the author's possession in proof-sheets, was to be published by the Görres-Gesellschaft, but the advent of the Hitler regime prevented its appearance. An English edition is being prepared.

SPECIAL REFERENCES

1. For the problem of qualifications, see the sage remarks of Bagehot, *op. cit.* (2nd ed., 1873), pp. 209 ff.

2. For the English system, see the treatment in F. A. Ogg, *English Government and Politics* (2nd ed., 1936), ch. xiii, and the literature cited there. For the quotation, see pp. 298-299. The remarks of J. S. Mill are found in *op. cit.*, ch. x. The quotation from Bagehot is in *op. cit.*, p. 214.

3. The pamphlet by Thomas Hare is entitled *The Machinery of Representation* (2nd ed., 1857). The theme is more fully developed in his *Treatise on the Election of Representatives, Parliamentary and Municipal* (1859). Victor de Considérant's scheme is contained in *De la Sincérité du Gouvernement, Lettre á Mss. les Membres du Grand Conseil . . . de Genève* (reprinted, 1892). The title of Thomas Gilpin's pamphlet is *On the Representation of Minorities of Electors to Act with the Majority in Elected Assemblies* (1844). The quotation from Blackstone is found in *Commentaries on the Laws of England* (5th ed., 1773), bk. i, p. 159.

4. The statistics are from Schauff, *op. cit.*, p. 249. The statements from Bagehot are found in *op. cit.*, ch. v.

5. Regarding the apportionment controversy, see E. V. Huntington, "Methods of Apportionment in Congress," in *APSR*, vol. xxv (1931), pp. 961 ff., and the article on the subject by W. S. Carpenter in the *ESS*. For gerrymandering, see the discussions in Merriam-Gosnell, *op. cit.*, and in Sait, *op. cit.*, as well as E. C. Griffith, *Rise and Development of the Gerrymander* (1907), and C. O. Sauer, "Geography and the Gerrymander" in *APSR*, vol. xii, pp. 403 ff.

6. See the general literature. For this and the following paragraphs, the general works on proportional representation by J. H. Humphreys, C. G. Hoag and G. H. Hallet, and Horwill may be consulted.

7. For Belgium, see T. H. Reed, *Government and Politics of Belgium* (1924), pp. 44 ff., and the analysis in Karl Braunias, *op. cit.*, vol. i, pp. 24 ff.; finally, see Joseph-Barthélemy, *L'Organisation du Suffrage et l'Expérience Belge* (1912). For Holland, see Braunias, *op. cit.*, vol. i, pp. 379 ff. See also the Dutch Royal Commission's report (1917).

8. For Sweden and Norway, see Braunias, *op. cit.*, vol. i, pp. 399 ff. and 489 ff. The matter is summarized in the same author's article in Schauff, *op. cit.* See also (for Sweden) the Royal Commission's report of April 4, 1921, summarized in *Statsvetenskaplig Tidskrift* (1921), pp. 113 ff. For Denmark, see Braunias, *op. cit.*, vol. i, pp. 56 ff., and Seymour-Frary, *op. cit.*, vol. ii, pp. 179-180.

9. For Switzerland, see R. C. Brooks, *Government and Politics of Switzerland* (1918), pp. 349 ff.; Braunias, *op. cit.*, vol. i, pp. 508 ff.; and Seymour-Frary, *op. cit.*, vol. ii, p. 216.

10. For the Irish Free State, see Warner Moss, *Political Parties in the Irish Free State* (1933), as well as Braunias, *op. cit.*, vol. i, pp. 274 ff.

11. For Germany, see Horwill, *op. cit.;* and Braunias, *op. cit.*, vol. i, pp. 100 ff. See also "Die Entwicklung zum Proportionalwahlrecht in Deutschland," by Karin Schauff, in Schauff, *op. cit.;* and "Die Parteipolitische Struktur Deutschlands," by Johannes Schauff in *ibid.*, pp. 139-154; "Die Verhältniswahl im Einzelwahlkreis . . . ," by Richard Schmidt, *ibid.*, pp. 171-183; and finally, "Gesichtpunkte zur Wahlrechtsreform," by J. Schauff, *ibid.*, pp. 200-239. All books on German politics deal with this question; a clear exposition is found, for example, in Herbert Kraus, *The Crisis of German Democracy* (1932), pp. 137 ff. A definitive evaluation will have to await a thoroughgoing study of the Weimar Republic, which the author, together with others, is planning.

12. The criticism of the German system is excellently presented in an article by F. A. Hermens, "Proportional Representation and the Breakdown of German Democracy," in *Social Research*, vol. iii (1936), pp. 411-433. Rudolf Smend's article is "Die Verschiebung der Konstitutionellen Ordnung durch die Verhälniswahl," in *Festgabe für Karl Bergbohm* (1910), pp. 278 ff. Smend's views are further developed in *Verfassung und Verfassungsrecht* (1928), *passim.* These problems are central for Hermens, *op. cit.*, pp. 115 ff.

13. The case for proportional representation in Germany was ably stated by Carl Decker in "Die Grunde fur das Proportionalwahlsystem," in Schauff, *op. cit.*, pp. 55-63. Similar views are expressed in Humphreys', and Hoag-Hallett's works, of course.

Chapter XVIII

POLITICAL PARTIES: GENERAL PROBLEMS

General References

The problem of parties has received a considerable amount of attention, particularly since the publication of M. Y. Ostrogorski's volumes, *La Démocratie et l'Organisation des Partis Politiques* (1902, tr. by Frederick Clarke as *Democracy and the Organization of Political Parties*). The history of parties in various countries, as well as the general problems which they raise, have been studied by a large number of writers. It stands in the center of such general treatments as James Bryce's *Modern Democracies* (new ed., 1924). The recognition of the party as a problem has undermined the democratic dogma of the unity of the people. Robert Michels, following Max Weber, has analyzed the hierachical and bureaucratic tendencies of political parties, irrespective of their political faith, in his *Zur Soziologie des Parteiwesens in der modernen Demokratie* (2nd ed., 1925). Max Weber's own view is set forth in *Wirtschaft und Gesellschaft* (1922). For a somewhat more popular account, see "Politik als

Beruf," in his *Gesammelte Politische Schriften* (1921), pp. 396 ff. For the extensive historical literature, cf. the items for each country offered in the *ESS*, as well as in the several paragraphs for the next chapter. This entire literature is somewhat askew because of the shift in meaning which the concept of a party has undergone since the war. The rise of Communism and the several forms of Caesarism have been accompanied by the establishment and maintenance of parties of a novel kind: oligarchic factions claiming representative positions on the ground of a fervent faith in their particular creeds. Max Weber went perhaps furthest in recognizing the tendency of parties to claim such universality of appeal and hence representative importance. The last word in this whole matter has not yet been spoken, however.

Special References

1. For the change in outlook concerning parties, cf. John Adams, *Defense of the Constitutions* (1787). For the remarks on Washington, see, e.g., S. E. Morison, *The Oxford History of the United States* (1927), vol. i, p. 234. Bolinkbroke's ideas are set forth in *The Patriot King* (1749). For the whole problem of corruption, see the penetrating study by L. B. Namier, *The Structure of Politics at the Accession of George III* (1929), and the equally revealing monograph by Holden Furber, *Henry Dundas, First Viscount Melville, 1742-1811, Political Manager of Scotland, Statesman Administrator of British India* (1929, unpub.).

2. For the beginning of this paragraph, see the articles by W. C. Abbott, particularly "The Origin of English Political Parties," in the *American Historical Review*, vol. xxiv (1918-1919), pp. 578 ff. Consult also M. T. Blauvelt, *The Development of Cabinet Government in England* (1902); G. M. Trevelyan, *The Two-party System in English Political History* (1926); and the work by Namier quoted in the previous paragraph. For the statement from N. Wraxall, see his *Memoirs* (1779), vol. ii, pp. 498 ff.

3. For Sir Erskine May, see *The Constitutional History of England since the Accession of George the Third* (3rd ed., 1871), ch. xviii. Lord Macaulay's views are stated in his *The History of England* (ed. Firth, 1913), ch. i. A very able analysis of the emergence of party organization in the course of the Long Parliament is given in an (unprinted) dissertation by J. H. Hexter, *The Rise of the Independent Party* (1936), an abstract of which can be found in the volume of abstracts of doctral dissertations printed by the Harvard University Press each year.

4. The discussion in this paragraph is developed from the views of Max Weber and Robert Michels, but with significant modifications. The former's ideas are set forth in *Wirtschaft und Gesellschaft*. See, for both, the works cited in the general bibliography above. For the Prussian system, see the articles by Dorn cited above, ch. iii, §7.

5. For Holcombe's views, see his work cited above.

6. For Julius Hatschek's theory, see his *Englisches Staatsrecht*, vol. ii (1905), pp. 8 ff. Hume's "Essay on Parties," contained in *Essays and Treatises* (1760), vol. i, pp. 93 ff., has the quotation on p. 97.

7. For Michels' views, cf. *op. cit.*, pp. 400 ff., and *passim*, and his *Prob-*

leme der Sozialphilosophie (1914). The quotation is found in *Robinson's Diary*, vol. ii, p. 316. There are many other such observations; for example, the terse remarks of Single-Speech Hamilton, cited in the preface to the recent edition of his *Parliamentary Logic* (ed. 1927, by C. S. Kenny). Compare for the general subject, Joseph Redlich, *Procedure of the House of Commons* (1908), vol. ii, pp. 89 ff.

8. See again the works by Weber and Michels cited above.

9. For this concluding paragraph see the famous historical discussion by M. Ostrogorski, *op. cit.*, vol. i, pp. 117 ff.

Chapter XIX

POLITICAL PARTIES

Special References

(N.B. For general bibliographical note, see the previous chapter.)

1. A. Lawrence Lowell, *Public Opinion in War and Peace* (1923), ch. vii. The study by H. Rehm is entitled *Deutschlands Politische Parteien* (1912).

2. André Siegfried's study is contained in the well-known monograph, *Tableau Politique de la France de l'Ouest* (1913). See, for the German side, the article by Sigmund Neumann, "Die Bedeutung des gesellschaftlichen Aufbaus . . . ," in *Jahrbuch für politische Wissenschaft*, vol. i (1933); Arthur Dix, *Die deutschen Reichstagswahlen und die Wandlung der Volksgliederung* (1930); and finally Neumann's more comprehensive *Die Deutschen Parteien; Wesen und Wandel nach dem Kriege* (1932). For France as a whole, compare likewise André Siegfried's *Tableau des Partis en France* (1930), translated as *France: A Study in Nationality* (1930), a volume rich in glittering generalities as well as sound insight.

3. For the English development, see Trevelyan, *op. cit.* For France, see Joseph-Barthélemy, *Introduction du Régime Parlementaire en France* (1904); it deals with the early phase. Georges Weill's *Histoire du Parti Republicain en France, 1814-1870* (1928) is important after that, and following him Gabriel Hanotaux, *Historie de la France contemporaine 1871-1900* (1903-1908), as well as Roger H. Soltau, *French Parties and Politics, 1871-1921* (new ed., 1930). For Germany, see Neumann, *op cit.*, and Ludwig Bergsträsser, *Geschichte der politischen Parteien in Deutschland* (6th ed., 1932). For the social-democratic party in particular, cf. Franz Mehring, *Geschichte der deutschen Sozialdemokratie* (12th ed., 1922).

4. For England, see again Trevelyan, *op. cit.*, and M. H. Woods, *A History of the Tory Party in the Seventeenth and Eighteenth Centuries* (1924) (more particularly the chapter on the party in the nineteenth and twentieth centuries), as well as F. J. C. Hearnshaw, *Conservatism in England* (1933). Cf. also G. Lowes Dickinson, *The Development of Parliament during the Nineteenth Century* (1895).

5. For this, see Lorenz von Stein, *Geschichte der sozialen Bewegung in*

Frankreich von 1879 bis auf unsere Tage, 3 vols. (new ed., 1921). The original of this remarkable book appeared in 1850. There has for a long time been a controversy as to whether Karl Marx took his class doctrine from Lorenz von Stein. Though, on the best evidence, this appears improbable, the resemblance is certainly a striking one. See also Charles Trevelyan, *From Liberalism to Labor* (1921), a revealing personal account.

6. For Mirabeau and Siéyès, see G. G. van Deusen, *Siéyès; His Life and His Nationalism* (1932), pp. 74 ff.; and G. de Ruggiero, cited below, §7. See particularly Siéyès, *Qu'est-ce-que le Tiers État?* (1788). Nowhere has the doctrine of integral nationalism of the bourgeois been stated with greater force. For Napoleon, see the recent study by Hans E. Friedrich, *Napoleon I, Idee und Staat* (1935). For the foreign policy of Louis XVIII, see Frederick B. Artz, *Reaction and Revolution, 1814-1832* (1934), pp. 126 ff., and the literature cited there. The present impact of the French past has been depicted with much skill by C. J. H. Hayes, *France—A Nation of Patriots* (1930), particularly chs. i-v. For England, see Trevelyan, *op. cit.* See also Joseph Redlich, *Parliamentary Procedure in the House of Commons* (1908), vol. i, pp. 127-129 (trans. from the German *Recht und Technik des Englischen Parlamentarismus,* 1905), and J. L. Garvin, *The Life of Joseph Chamberlain* (1932-34), vol. ii, chs. xxx-xxxiii, xxxix-xli, xliv-xlv. See further, R. B. Haldane, *Autobiography* (1929), ch. vi, and Sir Edward Grey, *Twenty-five Years* (1925), vol. i, pp. 60 ff. Another source of vital importance is G. E. Buckle and W. F. Monnypenny, *The Life of Benjamin Disraeli, Lord Beaconsfield* (1910-1920), throughout. No individual statesman, however, is as indicative of the kinship between liberalism and imperialism as Lord Palmerston, whose biography by Anthony Ashley (1879) should be added without fail to any reading on this subject. For Labor, see the excellent monograph by William P. Maddox, *The British Labour Party in Foreign Affairs* (1934), particularly pp. 24 ff. For the impact of the Midlothian campaign, see the article by Eugene P. Chase, "Parliamentary Control of Foreign Policy in Great Britian," in *APSR,* vol. xxv (1931), pp. 861 ff. For the situation immediately before the war, see the article by H. Temperley, "The Coming of the War," in *Foreign Affairs,* vol. ix (1931), pp. 335 ff.

7. For this and the following paragraph (as for the whole question of liberalism), see the volume by Guido de Ruggiero, *The History of European Liberalism* (1927), particularly Parts I, III-IV. A really good history of German liberalism has never been written, but Friedrich Meinecke and his school have made important contributions toward such a history. Indeed, Meinecke's *Weltbürgertum und Nationalstaat* (7th ed., 1928) almost constitutes such a history, as far as the problem of the text is concerned. Cf. also several of the biographies of Meinecke's students, such as Siegfried A. Kaehler, *Wilhelm von Humboldt und der Staat* (1927); D. Gerhardt and W. Norwin: *Die Briefe Georg Niebuhrs* (vol. i, 1926; vol. ii, 1929); Hans Rothfels, *Carl von Clausewitz, Politik und Krieg* (1920), and the same author's *Stein und der Deutsche Staatsgedanke* (1931). To these must be added Meinecke's own *Radowitz und die Deutsche Revo-*

lution (1913), Hermann Oncken's *Rudolf von Bennigsen, Ein Deutscher Liberaler Politiker nach seinen Briefen und Hinterlassenen Papieren* (1910), and finally Veit Valentin's *Geschichte der Deutschen Revolution 1848-49* (1934), particularly vol. i, pp. 1 ff. and 297 ff. For Stresemann, see *Stresemann, Ein Vermächtnis* (1932), edited by H. Bernhard in 3 volumes.

8. For Cavour, see W. R. Thayer, *The Life and Times of Cavour* (1911). See also G. M. Trevelyan. *Garibaldi and the Thousand* (1909) and *Garibaldi and the Making of Italy* (1911). For Mazzini, see Gaetano Salvemini, *Mazzini* (4th ed., 1925); a study of this man in the light of problems raised by national socialism would be highly desirable. Cf. also, O. Vossler, *Mazzini's politisches Denken und Wollen* (1927).

9. See the work of Mehring cited above, as well as Michels, *op. cit.* An interesting special study is Eckart Kehr, *Schlachtflottenbau und Parteipolitik, 1894-1901* (1930). Cf. also the materials brought together by Werner Sombart in *Grundlagen und Kritik des Sozialismus* (1919), 2 vols. Concerning Lasalle, see the work by H. Oncken, *Lasalle: Eine politische Biographie* (3rd ed., 1920). The Paris Commune has been described by Edward S. Mason, *The Paris Commune* (1930); there is considerable socialist literature on the subject which Mason reviews in the course of his study. Alexandre Zévaès' extensive writings on the history of French socialism and the socialist party are rather diffuse; the most distinctive insight was afforded the author by the collected articles and speeches of Jean Jaurès, published under the title, *Œuvres de Jean Jaurès* (1931). Roger H. Soltau's previously cited volume contains, of course, an account of these developments. Concerning Jules Guesde, see A. Zévaès, *Jules Guesde* (1929), and D. J. Saposs, *The Labor Movement in Post-War France* (1931). Concerning the struggle of Bismarck with the socialists, see Mehring, *op cit.* on the socialist side, and Johannes Ziekursch, *Politische Geschichte des neuen deutschen Kaiserreiches* (1927), vol. ii, pp. 323 ff.; and A. Wahl, *Deutsche Geschichte, 1871-1914* (1926), vol. i, pp. 479 ff., for a more favorable statement.

10. For the British Labor Party's background, see Sidney and Beatrice Webb, *The History of Trade Unionism* (1920), as well as Maddox, *op. cit.*, and the literature cited there. To mention one or two, one may refer to Egon Wertheimer, *Portrait of the Labor Party* (1930), and William Stewart, *J. Keir Hardie: A Biography* (1921). For a proper context, one may compare J. M. Gaus, *Great Britain—A Study in Civic Loyalty* (1929).

11. Concerning this whole subject, see the excellent monograph by Merle Fainsod, *The Origins of the Third International, 1914-1919* (1934). Much interesting material is contained in Lloyd George's *War Memoirs, 1917* (1934), chs. iv and v.

12. For the German "revolution," see Arthur Rosenberg, *The Birth of the German Republic, 1871-1918* (1931), trans. by Ian F. D. Morrow. The literature on this subject is considerable, but no really first-rate study has so far appeared. For a brief comparative survey, see Agnes Headlam-Morley, *The New Democratic Constitutions of Europe* (1921). The blind

alley in which German socialist leaders found themselves in 1919 is best seen from two short contemporary analyses: Count U. Brockdorff-Rantzau, *Deutschlands auswärtige Politik* (1919), and Friedrich Lenz, *Staat und Marxismus* (1921). Articles depicting the dissatisfaction of the younger elements among socialists found their expression in the formation of a group known as Young Socialists (*Jungsozialisten*); their magazine, *Der Jungsozialist,* reveals the various aspects of this trouble. On the problem of national policy (and the war issue), Gerhart Lütkens' *Deutschlands Aussenpolitik* (1923) is useful, as well as the same author's article, "Das Kriegsproblem und die Marxistische Theorie," in *Archiv für Sozialwissenschaft und Sozialpolitik* vol. xlix (1922), pp. 467 ff.

13. The remark by Asquith is found *HCD*, vol. clxix, p. 860; for the next quotation, see *ibid.*, vol. clxxvi, p. 3066. The reference to Baldwin's speech is *ibid.*, vol. ccxix, pp. 62-63. The debate on Unemployment Insurance Bill No. 3 is found *HCD*, vol. cclv, July 18-31, 1931. For France, see the previously cited literature.

14. On Austria see Erich Hula, "Die autoritären Elemente in der neuen Oesterreichischen Verfassung," in *Mitteilungen des Verbandes österreichischer Banken und Bankiers* (1934), and the literature cited there, as well as K. G. Hugelmann, "Die politischen Parteien und die Anschlussfrage," in *Die Anschlussfrage*, etc. (1930), ed. by F. F. G. Kleinwächter and H. von Paller.

15. For the problem of Catholic parties, there is a considerable amount of special literature, but no comprehensive treatment at all. For Germany, we have the work of Karl Bachem, *Vorgeschichte, Geschichte und Politik der deutschen Zentrumspartei* (1927-1932). For the papal encyclicals, see *Les Documents Pontificaux sur la Démocratie et la Société Moderne* (with Introduction and Notes by Georges Michon) (1928). For the Action Française group, see the monograph by Madame Charlotte Muret, entitled *French Royalist Doctrines since the Revolution* (1933), and the unprinted thesis by F. M. Watkins, *The Political Theory of the Action Francaise* (1930) (in the Harvard University Library).

16. For the German side, see Bachem, *op. cit.,* as well as Ludwig Bergsträsser, *Der Politische Katholizismus* (1921-1923). For the German constitutional convention, see Friedrich Meinecke's *Radowitz* cited above, pp. 152 ff. On the Vatican problem, see R. de Cesare, *Roma e lo Stato del Papa dal Ritorno di Pio Nono al 20 Settembre* (1907), translated as *The Last Days of Papal Rome, 1850-1870* (1909); on its concordat policies, see an article by A. Géraud Pertinax, "The Lateran Treaties: A Step in Vatican Policy," in *Foreign Affairs*, vol. vii (1929), pp. 571 ff. There is also a special monograph on the problems raised by the advent of Hitler, by John B. Mason, "The Catholic Church and Hitlerism," in *Ecclesiastical Review*, vol. viii (1933). On the *Kulturkampf*, see Bachem, *op. cit.*, vol. iii, pp. 193 ff., for the Catholic view; the Protestant view is set forth in most of the Bismarck literature published in Germany; for a sane survey see Robert C. Binkley, *Realism and Nationalism, 1852-1871* (1935), pp. 312 ff. For the latest phase, cf. the work

by Brüning referred to above, ch. xiv, §8. See also Sigmund Neumann, *Die Deutschen Parteien* (1932). For Swiss Catholicism, see Robert C. Brooks, *Civic Training in Switzerland* (1930), ch. iii, and E. Fueter, *Die Schweiz seit 1848* (1928), pp. 23 ff. For Belgium, see Thomas H. Reed, *Government and Politics of Belgium* (1928), p. 41. For Holland, see A. C. Hoff, and others, *Onze Politieke Partijen* (1918), and the standard history by P. J. Blok. As far as Austria is concerned, I. Seipel's own view may be gleaned from his article, "Christlich-Soziale Partei in Oesterreich," in *Staatslexikon*, ed. by Hermann Sacher (1926), vol. i, cols. 1270 ff.

17. For the literature on Bonapartism, Fascism and National Socialism, see above, ch. xiv, §14 and below, ch. xxv. C. J. H. Hayes' *Essays in Nationalism* (1926) portrays the conflict. For the development of National Socialism, the volumes by K. Heiden, *A History of National Socialism* (2nd ed., 1936) are the best. Two German studies may be added, however, both of them stressing the ideological side: Theodor Heuss, *Hitler's Weg; eine historisch-politische Studie über den Nationalsozialismus* (1932), anti; and E. Czech-Jochberg, *Hitler: Eine Deutsche Bewegung* (1933), pro. The title of the latter is quite striking: Hitler *im*-personalized as a movement. Some other literature has been surveyed by the author in "German National Socialism," in *The Political Quarterly*, vol. ii (1931), pp. 2 ff.; again by Hajo Holborn, "National Socialism in Germany: A Short Bibliography," in *International Affairs*, vol. xiii (1934), pp. 93 ff., and once more by the author in "Germany, Hitler, Versailles," in *Harvard Graduates' Magazine*, vol. xlii (1934). The special problems of anti-semitism have not yet received a really searching treatment.

Chapter XX

CABINET SYSTEMS

General References

The only comprehensive comparative monograph on this subject is W. Hasbach, *Die parlamentarische Kabinettsregierung* (1919), though Herman Finer's part on the executive, in his *The Theory and Practice of Modern Government* (1932) (Part VI, pp. 949 ff.) is practically as comprehensive. While somewhat differently focused, Robert Redslob's *Die parlamentarische Regierung* (1918), translated into French as *Le régime parlementaire, Études sur les institutions d'Angleterre, de Belgique, de Hongrie, de France* (1924), advanced the much attacked thesis that the relation between cabinet and parliament in France is such that the system must be called "false" in terms of the older English doctrine. A good deal of important general thought on the subject is digested also in James Bryce's *Modern Democracies*. Much genuine political thought is also found in Max Weber's "Parlament und Regierung in neugeordneten Deutschland," in *Gesammelte Schriften*, p. 126 ff.

Special References

1. For the earlier bureaucratic council phase, see above, chs. ii and iii, and the literature cited there. For England especially, see T. F. Tout, *Chapters in the Administrative History of Medieval England* (6 vols., 1920-1933). On the cabinet phase, see Walter Bagehot, *The English Constitution* (1873), for the classical statement of the view that the cabinet is the executive committee of parliament.

4. See M. T. Blauvelt, *The Development of Cabinet Government* in England (1902), and A. Lawrence Lowell, *The Government of England* (1912), particularly chs. ii, iii, xvi, xviii, and xxiii, as well as F. A. Ogg, *English Government and Politics* (1930), chs. vi and vii. The quotation of Lowell is found in *op. cit.*, vol. i, p. 56. For a recent critical account of the decline in parliamentary power over the ministry, see Ramsay Muir, *How Britain Is Governed* (1930). For Lloyd George's views, see his *War Memoirs*, particularly vol. iii, ch. i and *passim*. Regarding the Imperial Defense Committee, see notes above, ch. xiii, §17. For the personnel aspect, see Harold Laski, *The British Cabinet: A Study of its Personnel, 1801-1924* (1928), and his article on the subject in *APSR*, vol. xxii (1928), pp. 12 ff. For the cabinet secretariat, see G. R. Starr, in *APSR*, vol. xxix (1935), pp. 390 ff.

5. See A. Esmein, *Éléments de Droit Constitutionnel,* vol. ii, pp. 4, 230 ff.; and E. M. Sait, *Government and Politics of France* (1926), chs. ii and iv, as well as the forthcoming volume on the same subject by Henry A. Yeomans, delivered this winter as lectures at the Lowell Institute. Robert de Jouvenel's comments are found in *La Républlique des Camarades* (1914), on pp. 93 ff.; the quotation, on p. 115. For the figures, see *Annuaire du Parlement,* vol. vii, pp. 795-826, vol. x, pp. 912-923; *Europa Yearbook* (1927), pp. 207-210; and John G. Heinberg, "The Personnel of French Cabinets, 1871-1930," *APSR,* vol. xxv (1931), pp. 389 ff. The quotation from Barthélemy is found in his *The Government of France* (authorized translation by J. Bayard Morris), pp. 105-106.

6. The ablest analysis of the Weimar system is found in Heinrich Herrfahrdt, *Die Kabinettsbildung nach der Weimarer Verfassung unter dem Einfluss der politischen Praxis* (1927), and in Fritz Poetzsch-Heffter, "Vom Staatsleben unter der Weimarer Verfassung, "I" and "II," in *Jahrbuch des oeffentlichen Rechts*, vol. xiii, pp. 162 ff., and vol. xvii, pp. 103 ff. Cf. also B. W. Maxwell, "The German Cabinet in Theory and Practice," in *SWPSSQ,* vol. xi; for the historical aspects, the author's article, "The Development of the Executive Power in Germany," *APSR,* vol. xxvii (1933), pp. 185 ff.; and those by Richard Thoma, "Die rechtliche Gestaltung des parlamentarischen Regierungssystems," in *Handbuch des oeffentlichen Rechts*, vol. i, pp. 503 ff.; and by E. Wolgast, *Zum deutschen Parlamentarismus* (1929), particularly pp. 70 ff. and 77 ff. As to the points concerning Dr. Brüning, they were contained in lectures given by him before the Lowell Institute and in the Godkin Lectures at Harvard. They will be embodied in a forthcoming volume on German politics. Cf. also the account given by Herbert Kraus in his *The Crisis of German Democracy*

(1932), and H. J. Heineman's views as set forth in *The Growth of Executive Power in Germany* (1934). For the historical difficulties of Prussia, cf. Seeley's *Life and Times of Stein* (1879) *passim.*

7. Robert C. Brooks' *Government and Politics of Switzerland* (1918), particularly when supplemented by his *Civic Training in Switzerland* (1930). To this must at least be added the leading constitutional text, Fritz Fleiner's *Schweizerisches Bundesstaatsrecht* (1922-1923). The specific references are to pp. 187, 222 ff. See also C. J. Friedrich and Taylor Cole, *Responsible Bureaucracy, a Study of the Swiss Civil Service* (1932), particularly pp. 29 ff. The closing quotation is from Brooks, *Government and Politics,* pp. 132-133.

8. Two monographs trace specially the development of the American cabinet: H. B. Learned, *The President's Cabinet* (1912), and M. L. Hinsdale, *History of the President's Cabinet* (1911). Charles A. Beard, whose ch. ix on the President in his *The American Leviathan* is admirable, rightly remarks that insight into the substance of presidential power is to be gained from a careful study of the letters and papers of Roosevelt and Wilson and their official biographies: J. B. Bishop, *Theodore Roosevelt and His Times* (2 vols., 1920); R. S. Baker, *Life and Letters of Woodrow Wilson* (so far 5 vols., 1927-1935); selections from the correspondence of Theodore Roosevelt and Henry Cabot Lodge; C. Seymour, *The Intimate Papers of Colonel House* (4 vols., 1926-1928). Lord Bryce's chapters on the Presidency are still worth reading: *American Commonwealth* (1924), chs. v, vi, vii, viii, ix, xx, xxv. The citation is from vol. i, p. 85. The quotation from Beard is found on p. 263. The concluding quotation from Bryce is found on p. 281.

9. An able bibliographical survey of the whole problem is given by Michael Dendias in his *Le Renforcement des Pouvoirs du Chef de L'État dans la Démocratie Moderne* (1932), followed by an adequate essay.

Chapter XXI

PARLIAMENTS AS REPRESENTATIVE ASSEMBLIES

General References

The general literature on parliaments is very considerable, as may be gleaned from a perusal of the monographs cited in the section on "Legislative Assemblies" in the *ESS*, vol. ix, pp. 395-398. Of the general and theoretical studies, Robert Luce's *Legislative Assemblies* (1924) and his *Legislative Procedure* (1922) may be put down together with Herman Finer's *The Theory and Practice of Modern Governments,* Part V (Parliaments), as the broadest comparative treatments of the subject in recent years. For the rest, the bibliography just cited, when supplemented by the notes which follow, will give an indication of the most promising avenues of approach to more detailed problems. However, in spite of its seemingly special focus, Joseph Redlich's *The Procedure of the House of Commons* (a translation of *Recht und Technik des englischen Parlamen-*

tarismus [1905]) is so broadly significant that no student of parlimentary problems can afford to neglect it. For the historical phases of the comparative development, Robert von Mohl's "Recht und Politik der repräsentativen Monarchie," in his *Staatsrecht, Völkerrecht und Politik,* vol. i, pp. 1 ff., remains valuable, as do the articles which follow. That this series of studies appeared in 1860 enhances rather than diminishes their interest from the standpoint of those who distinguish between constitutional government and democracy.

Special References

2. Though Finer starts his discussion, *op. cit.,* with the customary proposition that legislatures occupy themselves mainly with lawmaking, control of the executive and investigations, the body of his discussion tends to support strongly the conclusion that "the procedure of Parliament is directed to influencing the general body of the public rather than its members" (p. 830). For the breakdown of contact between government and citizen in Germany, see Fritz Morstein Marx, *Government in the Third Reich,* pp. 156 f. and *passim.* Regarding the difficulties encountered by Stresemann, see *Stresemann's Vermächtnis* (ed. Henry Bernhard, 1932), for example, vol. i, pp. 133 ff. Regarding Brüning, see his forthcoming volume. The technique of the United States Chamber of Commerce's referendum is competently described by Pendleton Herring, *Group Representation before Congress* (1929), pp. 89 ff.

3. The schemas of parliamentary seating arrangements are found in Joseph R. Starr, *Topical Analysis of Comparative European Government* (1934), pp. 30 and 115. Regarding seating arrangements in Congress, see Robert Luce, *Legislative Procedure* (1922), p. 241.

4. For this paragraph, see Joseph Redlich's masterly analysis in *Recht und Technik des Englischen Parlamentarismus* (1905), pp. 373 ff. The author cites from the German edition; reference to the English volumes can readily be made, because of the paragraphing throughout. Figures are given by Redlich on p. 385. An interesting comparative table for the year 1924 is given by Herman Finer, *op. cit.,* p. 657. Other interesting contributions are found in Walther Lambach, *Die Herrschaft der Fünfhundert* (1926), and in Sigmund Neumann, *Die deutschen Parteien; Wesen und Wandel nach dem Kriege* (1932). The special problems of the German parliament are treated statistically by Viktor Egelhardt, "Die Zusammensetzung des Reichstags nach Alter, Beruf und Religionsbekenntnis," in *Die Arbeit,* vol. viii (1931), pp. 31 ff. For the problems of the trade association officials, see these titles, and the interesting, though rather controversial account by G. T. Garratt, *The Mugwumps and the Labor Party* (1932).

5. For the general development discussed in this chapter, see Redlich, *op. cit.,* chs. i, ii. Cf. also E. Porritt, *The Unreformed House of Commons; Parliamentary Representation before 1832* (3rd ed., 1909), for the earlier phase. The quotation from Redlich is found in the English edition of *op. cit.,* vol. i, p. 207.

6. For the whole paragraph, compare the well-balanced discussion in

F. A. Ogg, *English Government and Politics* (1929), chs. xiv and xv, and the literature cited there. The general problem of second chambers is discussed by H. W. V. Temperley, *Senates and Upper Chambers* (1910), J. A. R. Marriott, *Second Chambers* (1910 and 1927), and H. B. Lees-Smith, *Second Chambers in Theory and Practice* (1923); it is treated more briefly in Finer, *op. cit.*, ch. xvii. The figures are found in Ogg, *op. cit.*, p. 331; the wisecrack was made by Aug. Birrell, a liberal leader. Lord Wemyss' proposal is summarized in Ogg, *op. cit.*, p. 359. The text of the Bryce Committee is reprinted (with omissions) in Howard L. McBain and L. Rogers, *The New Constitutions of Europe* (1922), pp. 573; its intellectual value is generally overrated, its proposals were weak and complicated. The quotation is from the Webbs' *A Constitution for a Socialist Commonwealth of Great Britain* (1920), p. 63. The proposal for proportional representation is found in R. Muir, *Peers and Bureaucrats* (1910), pp. 133 ff. The quotation from the *Labour Speakers' Handbook* is given in Ogg, *op. cit.*, p. 356. Bentham's views are set forth lucidly and convincingly by Lewis Rockow, "Bentham on the Theory of Second Chambers," *APSR*, vol. xxii (1928), pp. 576 ff. They are also succinctly stated in Bentham's *Essay on Political Tactics* (1816-1817), ch. i, §5 (followed by a statement of the advantages intended by Bentham, but actually supplied by his editor, Dumont; whether we should question the conclusions of Rockow on this account is doubtful, though Hatschek, *Englisches Staatsrecht*, vol. i, p. 435, takes it for granted).

7. The evaluation of Bentham is shared by Redlich, *op. cit.*, pp. 777 and 784 ff., and by Hatschek, *op. cit.*, p. 434 ff., though these authors disagree about many other points. The full title of Bentham's work is *An Essay on Political Tactics, or Inquiries Concerning the Discipline and Mode of Proceeding Proper to Be Observed in Political Assemblies: Principally Applied to the Practice of the British Parliament, and to the Constitution and Situation of the National Assembly of France*. This work was first published in French in 1816 by M. Dumont, and translated into German, etc., from this edition. Robert Mohl praised it highly and was himself, as chairman of the Committee on (Procedural) Rules in the National Assembly at Frankfurt, as well as through his active participation in the diets of Württemberg and the new German Empire, instrumental in spreading the gospel. See his comments in *Geschichte und Literatur der Staatswissenschaften* (1855), vol. i, pp. 310 ff.; in *Württembergisches Staatsrecht* (1836), vol. iii, pp. 627 ff.; and in *Staatsrecht, Völkerrecht und Politik*, vol. i, pp. 281 and 282, where he commences his noteworthy essay, "Die Geschäftsordnung der Ständeversammlungen," with it (1860). Bentham's ideas are set forth in Bowring's edition (1843) (hereafter referred to), vol. ii, pp. 302 ff. and 310 ff. The quotation is found on p. 313. Hamilton's book is entitled *Parliamentary Logic* (republished in 1927); its editor, Courtney S. Kenny, has offered some shrewd comments in an introduction and notes. Bentham's comments on Hamilton, quite vitriolic to be sure, are found in his *The Book of Fallacies* (ed. cit.), vol. ii, pp. 383 ff. For Redlich's view as stated, see *op. cit.*, pp. 390 ff. Bentham's recognition of parties is suggested in *op. cit.*, p. 361, and the quotation is in *ibid.*, p. 385. Even

the fragmentary English edition of Hitler's *Mein Kampf* contains a few passages, pp. 30 ff. (in the original 9th ed., pp. 81 ff.) Hatschek's views are found in *op. cit.*, vol. i, pp. 426 ff.

8. The statement from Bentham is found in *op. cit.*, vol. ii, p. 330. Regarding Speaker Onslow, see Edward Porritt, *The Unreformed House of Commons: Parliamentary Representation before 1832* (1903), pp. 448 ff. Cf. also generally *ibid.*, chs. xxi-xxii. The reference to Stubbs is found in his *Lectures* (1906), p. 314. For Edward Coke, see Hastings Lyon and H. Block, *Edward Coke: Oracle of the Law* (1929), pp. 60 ff. For the following quotations from Redlich, cf. *op. cit*, pp. 422 and 410 ff. The figures in parentheses for the National coalition and the combined opposition are due to by-elections between 1931 and 1934. The quotation is again from Redlich, *op. cit.* (in the author's own translation), p. 405. Cf. his entire discussion in the English edition, vol. ii, pp. 131-168.

9. For the American Speakership, the important historical study is M. P. Follett, *The Speaker of the House of Representatives* (1896). For a more recent study of the institution as it exists today, see Robert Luce's *Legislative Procedure* (1922) chs. xix-xxii. The quotation from Bryce (whose discussion of the problem is worth considering) is found in *American Commonwealth*, vol. i, p. 208. The next quotation is from an article by Elwood Mead in the *Independent*, January 8, 1917, which is cited by R. Luce, *op. cit.*, p. 486. Speaker Carlisle's statement is in *ibid.*, p. 466. This view was reasserted by Speaker Longworth in 1926: "I believe it to be the duty of the Speaker, standing squarely on the platform of his party, to assist in so far as he properly can the enactment of legislation in accordance with the declared principles and policies of his party, and by the same token to resist the enactment of legislation in violation thereof" *Cong. Record*, 69th Congress, 1st Sess., p. 382. The quotation from Reed is given by C. A. Beard, *The American Leviathan*, p. 302, in the course of a very brief but, as usual, perspicacious discussion of the speakership. Luce's criticisms of customary views on the Speaker's powers are found in *op. cit.*, pp. 455 ff. For reform suggestions, see W. Y. Elliott's highly controversial *The Need for Constitutional Reform* (1935), pp. 232 ff. For the relative neutrality of the Speaker in Massachusetts, see Luce, *op. cit.*, p. 456, where this author also criticizes the discussion of the speakership in American state legislatures as found in Arthur Holcombe's *State Government in the United States* (1916), p. 252 (see also later p. 465). Holcombe's views seem to have remained unaltered, however, for he makes the same statements in the third edition (1931), pp. 294 ff.

10. For Bryce's discussion, see *American Commonwealth*, vol. i, pp. 203 ff. (rev. ed., 1924). For the whips, cf. Redlich, *op. cit.*, pp. 364 ff.; A. L. Lowell, *Government of England* (1908), vol. i, pp. 448 ff. Viscount Gladstone's account is found in *APSR*, vol. xxi (1927), pp. 519 ff. Cf. also M. Ostrogorski, *Democracy and the Organization of Political Parties* (1902), vol. i, pp. 137 ff.

11. Lindsay Rogers, *The Senate* (1926), esp. chs. iv and v. Rogers' conclusions were challenged by Robert Luce in *Congress: An Explanation* (1926), as far as the House and its comparison with the Senate were

concerned. Cf. also G. R. Brown, *The Leadership of Congress* (1922). The discussion in the House of Commons to which references are made occurred on June 25, ff., 1929. See *HCD*, vol. ccxxix, pp. 50 ff.

12. This paragraph's point constitutes the central theme of Redlich's volume. The quotations (in the author's own translation) are found in the original, p. 799.

13. Cf. Stuart A. Rice, *Quantitative Methods in Politics* (1928), ch. xiv.

Chapter XXII

PARLIAMENTS AS DELIBERATIVE ASSEMBLIES

General References

The general literature is, of course, the same as that described in the note to ch. xxi. It may, however, be worth while to remark upon the absence of any studies bearing upon the social and political conditions of "deliberation." All the works referred to comment upon the problems connected with this central function of parliament, but no studies of this phenomenon as such have come to the author's attention.

Special References

1. The secrecy of parliamentary proceedings is described by Porritt, *op. cit.*, vol. i, pp. 589-596, and by Th. E. May, *Constitutional History of England* (7th ed., 1882), vol. ii. See also *HCD*, vol. xi (1808), cited by Redlich, *op. cit.*, p. 291.

2. The central importance of speech is brought out forcefully by Redlich, *op. cit.*, pp. 586 ff. The remarks of the Marquess of Hartington are to be found in *HCD*, vol. cclxvii (1882), p. 1327. The problems of parliamentary government in Britain without a majority party are discussed by Ramsay Muir, *How Britain Is Governed* (1930), particularly pp. 145 ff. For the most recent efforts at "reform," see R. D. Denman, "Procedure in the House of Commons," in *The Nineteenth Century* (1933). On motions, see Bentham, *Political Tactics*, chs. viii, ix and xi; *Works*, vol. ii, pp. 352 ff.

3. Closure is one of the most hotly contested issues of modern politics. For the "classical" doctrine of adjournment, see again Bentham, *op. cit.*, ch. xiii. See also Luce, *op. cit.*, ch. xii. Speaker Brand's statement is to be found in *HCD*, vol. cclvii (1881), pp. 2032-2033. Closure is searchingly discussed by Redlich, *op. cit.*, pp. 198 ff., 201 ff., 211 ff., 219 ff., 598 ff. For Finer's view, see his *op. cit.*, vol. ii, pp. 852 ff. For Speaker Reed's remark, see *Congressional Record*, January 31, 1890 (vol. xxi, p. 999). It may be observed in passing that Carl Schmitt, if he had familiarized himself with the actual operation of parliamentary bodies instead of certain theories about them, would not have made all the errors which underlie his "smart" insistence upon the kinship between parliamentarism and the Romantic "eternal conversation." If he had dug a bit deeper still, he would have discovered that the Romantics in England (where they had some familiar-

ity with parliamentary methods) were the spearhead of anti-parliamentary emotionalism. The true kinship is not between parliaments and Romantics, but between Romantics and anti-parliamentarism and irrationalism, as opposed to the kinship between parliamentarism, rationalism, utilitarianism and reform. Lindsay Rogers, *The American Senate* (1926), contains a provocative discussion of the problems of closure; for the particular quotation, see pp. 248-250.

4. Cf. Redlich, *op. cit.*, pp. 114 ff., 463 ff., 473 ff.; H. Finer, *op. cit.*, vol. ii, pp. 804 ff. The two quotations are found on pp. 797 and 809, respectively. See *Standing Order 41*. The remarks of Sir Courtenay Ilbert are found in his English edition of Redlich, vol. iii, pp. 215-216. Muir's views are found in *How Britain Is Governed* (1930), pp. 231 ff. The quotations are from p. 231.

5. For this paragraph cf. the thorough discussion in Luce, *op. cit.*, chs. iv-viii. For the early beginnings, see R. V. Harlow, *The History of Legislative Methods in the Period before 1825* (1917). Special references is had to p. 16. The first quotation from Luce is found, *op. cit.*, on p. 100 the second one on p. 151. For a scientifically detailed study of the activities of interest groups before Congress, see E. P. Herring, *Group Representation before Congress* (1929), particularly pp. 249 ff., although he probably overestimates the importance of the caucus, p. 248. See below, §12. For the figures, see Rogers, *op. cit.*, pp. 186-187. Cf. for England, Muir, *op. cit.*, pp. 205-211. On hearings, see Luce, *op. cit.*, pp. 142 ff. Cf. the recent Supreme Court case, *Jurney* v. *McCracken*, S. Ct. 55 [1935], for the issue of congressional power of investigation. The list of House Standing Committees in the 73rd Congress was as follows:

1. Accounts—11
*2. Agriculture—27, *19*
*3. Appropriations—35, *23*
*4. Banking and Currency—25, *20*
5. Census—21
*6. Civil Service—21, *10*
*7. Claims—21, *13*
8. Coinage, Weights and Measures—21
9. Disposition of Useless Executive Papers—2
*10. District of Columbia—21, *15*
*11. Education—21, *13*
*12. Election of Vice-President and Representatives in Congress—13, *17*
*13. Enrolled Bills—7, *3*
*14. Expenditures in the Executive Department—21, *7*
15. Flood Control—22
*16. Foreign Affairs—21, *23*
*17. Immigration and Naturalization—22, *14*
*18. Indian Affairs—22, *13*
19. Insular Affairs—22 (included by Senate with Territories)
*20. Interstate and Foreign Commerce—25, *20*
21. Invalid Pensions—21
*22. Irrigation and Reclamation—21, *17*
*23. Judiciary—25, *18*
24. Labor—21 (included by Senate with Education)
*25. Library—5, *10*
26. Memorials—3
27. Merchant Marine, Radio, and Fisheries—23
*28. Military Affairs—26, *17*
*29. Mines and Mining—22, *13*
*30. Naval Affairs—26, *17*
*31. Patents—21, *7*

*32. Pensions—21, *10*
*33. Post Office and Post Roads—26, *19*
*34. Printing—3, *6*
*35. Public Buildings and Grounds—21, *14*
*36. Public Lands—23, *14*
37. Revision of the Laws—13
38. Rivers and Harbors—25
39. Roads—21
*40. Rules—12, *13*
*41. Territories—23, *17*
42. War Claims—21
*43. Ways and Means—25, *20* (called Finance in the Senate)
44. World War Veterans' Legislation—21

The starred committees in the foregoing list (which is taken from *Official Congressional Directory,* 73d Congress, 1st Session) are also found in the Senate, the membership there being indicated by italics. Three committees—on Commerce, on Interoceanic Canals, and on Manufactures—seem to correspond to House committees Nos. 27, 38, and 39, but include other matters also. There is also a committee on the Audit and Control of the Contingent Expenses of the Senate, with 5 members.

6. The history of committee procedure in the French Chamber is sketched by Joseph-Barthélemy, *Essai sur le Travail Parlementaire et le Système des Commissions* (1934), ch. i. The author does not believe that it is necessary, or indeed desirable, to translate the French term *commission* as commission, inasmuch as that word has acquired a very different connotation in English, particularly in the United States. The fact that the French, who originally also called their standing committees *comités,* changed to *commission* is due to the horror which the committees of the revolutionary tribunals, and more particularly the *Comité du Salut Public,* had left behind. See, for this, Barthélemy, *op. cit.,* pp. 7 and 27. For the party basis of committees, see *ibid.,* pp. 82 ff. (we have omitted reference to the older system of *bureaux* because it is complicated and no longer significant). About committee leadership, see Barthélemy, *op. cit.,* p. 9 and *passim.* The story regarding the subsidy to the French line is told in *ibid.,* pp. 203 f. About the reportorial stage, Barthélemy gives examples on pp. 180-181, and he discusses the advisory reports in *ibid.,* p. 197. For the vote without debate, see *ibid.,* pp. 207 ff. As these references show (and many more could be given), no student of the French parliamentary system could afford to neglect Barthélemy's highly informative volume. Two studies of the French parliamentary government are being prepared in English, one by Henry A. Yeomans whose exposition at the Lowell Institute during Feburary, 1936, anticipated his major conclusions, the other by Lindsay Rogers. W. L. Middleton's brief account, *The French Political System* (1932), and Robert M. Gooch's recent articles also contribute valuable insights.

7. The problem of financial control is arousing an increasing amount of interest, and rightly so. The mass of public expenditures is ever greater, and some method of supervision seems essential. The literature, however, is quite diffuse; the subject was supposed to be part of public finance and therefore held to be explorable in terms of economics. This is only partially true. In recent years, however, budgetary problems have received

careful treatment by a number of scholars, among whom W. F. Willoughby and Buck stand out. To these might be added Gaston Jèze, the introduction to whose *Allgemeine Theorie des Budgets* (1927) commences with the striking (and probably correct) assertion, "Das Budget ist seinem Wesen nach ein politischer Akt." Buck's recent *The Budget in Governments of Today* (1934) is the most comprehensive study of budgetary problems we have. The statement from Ramsay Muir is found in *How Britain Is Governed* (1930), p. 228. Willoughby makes the same point in his *Principles of Public Administration* (1927), p. 481. The reference to the English parliamentary committee is *Reports from the Select Committee on National Expenditures* (1918), p. 115. For the *Budget and Accounting Act* and the methods prevailing since that time, see W. F. Willoughby, *Principles of Public Administration,* Part IV, which gives a broad comparative treatment; for the particular problems of the text, cf. ch. xxiii. For the particular technical matters of the audit, cf. G. C. S. Benson, *Financial Control and Integration,* in *Studies in Systematic Political Science and Comparative Government* (1934), vol. ii. See also above, ch. xv, §15.

8. The discussion in this paragraph follows ch. ix of Barthélemy's *Essai* as far as the facts are concerned, though the interpretation varies at times. Specific reference may be made to p. 278, where he discusses the special facilities; to pp. 283 ff., where he discusses the presidents and reporters; to p. 286, where the statement about government and opposition is made. That the reporter is actually controlling the government is alleged by A. Thibaudet, *La République des Professeurs* (1927), p. 243, as well as others. Barthélemy's remark about the leftist group is found on p. 354.

9. For this paragraph, cf. Barthélemy, *op. cit.,* ch. vi, "Le controle parlementaire par les commissions." He also emphasizes the suspicion of the bureaucracy as a central attitude behind the French public's and the parliament's interest in committees as a method of organizing effective control, for example, on pp. 24-25. For the control techniques of Frederick the Great, see W. L. Dorn, "The Prussian Bureaucracy in the Eighteenth Century," *Political Science Quarterly,* vol. xlvi (1931), pp. 403 ff. The resignations of Briand and Loucheur are described by Barthélemy, *op. cit.* pp. 233-234. The significance of investigations, politically, is considered by L. Rogers, *The American Senate* (1926), ch. vi.

10. The problems of this paragraph are highly controversial and will form the subject of a separate volume to be published by the author. Some of the bibliography is found above, attached to ch. v. In the United States, an extensive controversy has raged over the Senate's power in foreign affairs; E. S. Corwin, *The President's Control of Foreign Relations* (1917), and Q. Wright, *The Control of American Foreign Relations* (1922), have treated these problems for the United States, as well as R. J. Dangerfield in his *In Defense of the Senate* (1933). F. R. Flournoy gives an account of British practice in *Parliament and War* (1927), which is critically discussed by A. Ponsonby, *Democracy and Diplomacy* (1915). To these may be added George Young, *Diplomacy Old and New* (1921); P. S. Reinsch, *Secret Diplomacy* (1922); Walter Lippmann, *The Stakes*

of Diplomacy (1915); and Aubrey L. Kennedy, *Old Diplomacy and New* (1922), as well as the recent discussion by Harold Nicolson, called a terminal essay, concluding his trilogy, *Portrait of a Diplomatist* (1930), *Peace-Making 1919* (1933), and *Curzon: the Last Phase* (1934), and attached to the last volume. All three contain repeated references to the problem. Finally a broad treatment is undertaken by DeWitt C. Poole, *The Conduct of Foreign Relations under Modern Democratic Conditions* (1924), which blends experience nicely with theory. The French problem has repeatedly been treated by Joseph-Barthélemy, first in his *Démocratie et Politique Étrangère* (1916), then in his *La Conduite de la Politique Extérieure dans les Démocraties* (1930), and finally in ch. viii of his *Essai* already cited so often. The last represents the maturer view. The interpretation of the Dutch situation is based on interviews of the author.

11. Bentham's views on secrecy are set forth in his essay, ch. ii (*Works*, vol. ii, pp. 310 ff.). For Luce's views, see his *Legislative Procedure*, pp. 150-151. For Wilson, see *The New Freedom* (1913), pp. 125-129. The further reference to Bentham is found on pp. 315-316. For the rest, the problem of secrecy is of wide ramifications and awaits scientific study by a sociologically minded political scientist. At present we are groping in the dark, as far as answers to the question, "Under what conditions do men act secretly?" are concerned. Yet the matter is central to political science.

12. The importance of the caucus is quite controversial among students and observers of American politics. It would seem to the author that Luce's discussion of the matter, *op. cit.*, pp. 506 ff., is rather well balanced, but it should be supplemented by the observations of E. M. Sait, *American Parties and Elections* (1927); Charles E. Merriam, *The American Party System* (ed. with H. F. Gosnell, 1929); Arthur N. Holcombe, *The New Party Politics* (1933), and others. Obviously, the matter is in a state of flux at present.

Chapter XXIII

THE PRESS AS THE FOURTH ESTATE

General References

There is a considerable body of literature on the press and its problems, but much of it treats it without regard to the political and governmental implications of "public opinion." Studies on the latter, in turn, often fail to consider the institutional channels, and more particularly the press. A notable exception are the writings of Walter Lippmann, whose volumes *Public Opinion* (1922) and *The Phantom Public* (1925), but more particularly the former, clearly face the political issues. A. Lawrence Lowell's *Public Opinion in War and Peace* (1923), on the other hand, gives slight attention to the press. Perhaps the most comprehensive sketch of the varied political, economic and social ramifications of the press in our modern industrial society is offered by Dexter Merriam Keezer in his article for the *ESS* (1934), "Press," to which should be added R. E. Park's masterly essay, "The Natural History of the Newspaper," in the *American Journal of Sociology,* vol. xxix (1923), pp. 273 ff. Malcolm M. Willey and Stuart Rice have given a descriptive account of contemporary trends in *Communication Agencies and Social Life* (1933). A suggestive critical analysis is found in Norman Angell's *The Press and the Organization of Society* (1922). There is a considerable body of literature in French and German on these questions, of which Keezer, *op. cit.,* gives a careful selection. One might mention here Stephane Lauzanne, *Sa majesté la presse* (1925); E. Dovifat, *Die Zeitungen* (1925); Oskar Wettstein, *Über das Verhältnis zwischen Staat und Presse* (1904); J. Buchhorn, *Politik und Presse* (1920); and Karl Bömer, *Bibliographisches Handbuch der Zeitungswissenschaft* (1929), particularly pp. 192 ff., "Die Zeitung im Staatsleben." Karl Bücher, though he has done more than any other scholar to stimulate research in this field, never went very far into the problems which are of particular interest to us here. Ch. ix of the second volume of his *Die Entstehung der Volkswirtschaft* (1922), entitled "Die Anonymität in den Zeitungen," is, however, full of significant suggestions. To this should be added ch. vi of the first volume, "Die Anfänge des Zeitungswesens," and the literature cited there.

More or less a topic apart is the question of the press in foreign affairs. It is not taken up specially in the preceding chapter; parts of it are dealt with above in ch. v. Careful consideration will be given to it in a forthcoming study on foreign affairs. P. F. Douglass and Karl Bömer have dealt with it extensively in "The Press as a Factor in International Relations," in the *Annals of the American Academy of Political and Social Science,* vol. clxii (1932), pp. 241 ff. Special material is offered by S. B. Fay in "The Influence of the Pre-War Press in Europe," in Massachusetts Historical Society, *Proceedings,* vol. lxiv (1932), pp. 113 ff. Most textbooks in international relations also devote a chapter or more to this problem; besides these, one may note DeWitt C. Poole, *The Conduct of Foreign Relations under Modern Democratic Conditions* (1924), particularly chs. vii and viii.

Special References

1. The citation from Charles A. Beard is found in his *The American Leviathan,* p. 257. The view from Lippmann is found in his *Public Opinion,* p. 320. Jefferson's statement is cited by Keezer, *op. cit.,* p. 326, but without reference.

2. For the beginnings, see Bücher, *op. cit.* (1922), vol. i, pp. 229 ff. and the literature cited there. The quotation from Matthias A. Shaaber is from his *Some Forerunners of the Newspaper in England, 1476-1622* (1929), p. 325. Cf. also F. K. Hunt, *The Fourth Estate* (1850), chs. iv and v. For the *Gazette* see E. Hatin, *Histoire Politique et Littéraire de la Presse en France* (1859-1861), vol. i, pp. 28 ff. The later English development is well discussed also by Alexander Andrews, *The History of British Journalism* (1859), and by Stanley Morison, *The English Newspaper* (1932). See also literature cited below, §§ 3 and 9.

3. See again Andrews and Hunt, *op. cit.* Interesting also is Wilhelm Dibelius, *England* (1930), pp. 314 ff. The quotation is from Frederick B. Artz, *Reaction and Revolution, 1814-1832* (1934), p. 286.

4. See again Artz, *op. cit.*, pp. 263 ff., and the literature cited there.

5. The most detailed discussion is Lucy M. Salmon, *The Newspaper and Authority* (1923). See also William G. Hale, *Law of the Press* (1923); and for the fundamental issues, Zechariah Chafee, *Freedom of Speech* (1920). The publication of the British Foreign Office appeared in 1926 under the title, *The Press Laws of Foreign Countries,* edited by M. Shearman and O. T. Raynor. The figures are taken from Keezer, *op. cit.,* p. 341. Concerning the Zenger case, see C. A. Duniway, *The Development of Freedom of the Press in Massachusetts* (1906), and Isaiah Thomas, *The History of Printing in America* (1810).

6. The literature on these undertakings is considerable, but not very weighty. For Hearst, mention ought to be made of John Winkler, *Hearst, an American Phenomenon* (1928). An interesting special study was made by R. D. Casey, "Scripps-Howard Papers in the 1928 Presidential Campaign," *Journalism Quarterly* (1930), pp. 210 ff. Walter Millis' *The Martial Spirit* (1931), particularly chs. i-iv, is valuable for the historical rôle of Hearst and Pulitzer in bringing about the Spanish-American War. For Northcliffe and Beaverbrook, see the uncritical volumes by Kennedy Jones, *Fleet Street and Downing Street* (1920) and by W. M. Aitken, Baron Beaverbrook, *Politicians and the Press* (1925). For the Hugenberg concern, Ludwig Bernhard's peculiar and in many respects candid study, *Der "Hugenberg Konzern"; Psychologie und Technik einer Grossorganisation der Presse* (1928), is quite informative.

7. Besides the literature cited in the preceding paragraph, consult Keezer, *op. cit.,* for the figures. The broader implications of this development are well stated in R. E. Park's study cited above.

8. A brief descriptive survey of the British press is given by Harold E. Scarborough, "British Press," *Foreign Affairs,* vol. xii (1934), pp. 508 ff. To this should be added the appropriate section of *Political Handbook of the World; Parliaments, Parties and Press* (at present edited by Walter H. Mallory), an annual publication of the Council on Foreign Relations. A richly illustrated picture may be derived from Stanley Morison's *The English Newspaper* (1932). Kurt von Stutterheim's account, *The Press in England* (tr. W. H. Johnson, 1934), particularly ch. v, and Wilhelm Dibelius' chapter on the press as previously cited, add insight, as does the more recent discussion offered by Kingsley Martin in an article in the *Political Quarterly,* vol. i (1930), pp. 428 ff., entitled, "Public Opinion: Rationalization of the Press and Democracy." Much real benefit can also be derived from the biographies of such leading British newsmen as Spender and Steed. Colonel Repington's memoirs also are worth careful attention.

10. For this paragraph, see Park, *op. cit.;* Allan Nevins, *The Evening Post; a Century of Journalism* (1922); John LaPorte Given, *Making a Newspaper* (1907); O. G. Villard, *Some Newspapers and Newspapermen* (1923), and *The Press To-day* (1930); E. H. Davis, *History of the New*

York Times (1921), while quite informative is not entirely free from a natural partisanship. See also Emil Dovifat, *Der amerikanische Journalismus* (1927). The reference is to p. 311. The quotation from the report of the Interchurch Movement is found in Keezer, *op. cit.,* p. 339; the title of the pamphlet is *Public Opinion and the Steel Strike* (1921), where it appears on p. 147.

11. Besides Lauzanne's volume in French, ch. vi of Carlton J. H. Hayes' *France: A Nation of Patriots* (1930) gives an interesting survey of the press which is supplemented by three Appendices (C, D, and E) containing carefully annotated lists of periodicals and dailies; for both we are, according to Professor Hayes' preface, indebted to Miss Vera Mikol. Besides this chapter, Robert de Jouvenel's spicy comments in *La République des Camarades* (first published in 1914) under the heading, "Le Quatrième Pouvoir," pp. 201 ff., are worth while.

12. See Ludwig Salomon, *Geschichte des deutschen Zeitungswesens,* 3 vols. (1906); F. Bertkau and Karl Bömer, *Der wirtschaftliche Aufbau des deutschen Zeitungsgewerbes* (1932); E. Dovifat, *Die Zeitungen* (1925); and Karl Bömer, *Bibliographisches Handbuch der Zeitungswissenschaft* (1929). The references to particular German papers are found here on pp. 45 ff. The peculiar problem of the Norddeutsche is discussed by Joachim Bohmer, "Die Norddeutsche Allgemeine Zeitung," in *Zeitungswissenschaft,* vol. i (1926). For Hugenberg, see the reference above §6. For the partisan quality of the German press, see the instructive volume of Paul Roth, *Die Programme der politischen Parteien und die Tagespresse in Deutschland* (1913), and the imaginative monograph by Ludwig Kantorowicz, *Die Sozioldemokratische Presse Deutschlands* (1922).

13. Concerning Russia, see J. Botscharow, *Die Entwicklung der russischen Presse (1621-1928)* (1928); Arthur W. Just, *Die Presse der Sowietunion; Methoden diktatorische Massenführung* (1931). Concerning Italy, see *Italian Journalism under Fascism,* prepared for the International Press Exhibition (Pressa) at Cologne by Ermanno Amicucci for the National Fascist Union of Journalists. Also Francesco Luigi Ferrari, *Le Régime Fasciste Italien* (1928), pp. 155 ff.; Henry R. Spencer, *Government and Politics of Italy* (1932), ch. xiii. See also Herman Finer, *Mussolini's Italy,* pp. 234 ff. Concerning Germany, see Fritz Morstein Marx, *Government in the Third Reich* (1935), pp. 90 ff. The official point of view is set forth in Karl F. Schrieber, *Das Recht der Reichskulturkammer,* 2 vols. (1935). The quotations are from Marx. The remark about the constructive power is found in Keezer, *op. cit.,* p. 332. So are the circulation figures for *Pravda* and *Izvestia,* p. 333.

14. Besides Z. Chafee's volume cited above, consult Lucy M. Salmon's volume on *The Newspaper and Authority* (1923), and Lasswell's article in the *ESS* on censorship. The rambling literature on this subject has been compiled by Kimball Young and R. D. Lawrence, *Bibliography on Censorship and Propaganda* (1928). The constructive problems are well treated by Oscar Wettstein, *Ueber das Verhältnis zwischen Staat und Presse, mit besonderer Berücksichtigung der Schweiz* (1904). These problems have, of course, always been in the foreground of attention in the field of foreign

policy, as noted at the end of our general note. Here we may add Paul Eltzbacher's *Die Presse als Werkzeug der auswärtigen Poltik* (1918), which goes beyond the material indicated by its title. Highly controversial is the rôle of the press in war time; we note Harold D. Lasswell's *Propaganda Technique in the World War* (1927), and Will Irwin, *Propaganda and the News* (1936), particularly chs. x and later.

15. Walter Lippmann's statements are found in *Liberty and the News* (1920), pp. 72 ff.

Chapter XXIV

INTEREST GROUPS AND THE RELATION OF GOVERNMENT TO MODERN INDUSTRIAL LIFE

General References

The general topic of this chapter is involved in the huge corpus of socialist and related literature, and there is no sense in suggesting any kind of selection here. But the particular subject of the relation of the various associations and groups to government is of rather recent interest. The connection of this subject to representation has been stressed by the writers noted above under ch. xvi. The detailed examination of the actual behavior of different groups has been more particularly an American preoccupation. E. P. Herring, in his two volumes on *Group Representation before Congress* (1929) and *Public Administration and the Public Interest* (1936), has offered the broadest analysis. More special studies have been made by Peter Odegard, *Pressure Politics, the Story of the Anti-saloon League* (1928); H. Childs, *Labor and Capital in National Politics* (1930); E. E. Schattschneider, *Politics, Pressures and the Tariff* (1935), and others. European, particularly German, writers, have dwelt more upon the general problems, though E. Tatarin-Tarnheyden's *Die Berufstände* (1922) gives a sketch of the mass of German interest groups. H. Herrfahrdt's *Das Problem der Berufständischen Vertretung von der Französischen Revolution bis zum Gegenwart* (1921) traces the evolution of economic groups from the "estates" in the beginning of the nineteenth century to the situation after the World War. Unfortunately, the estates type of political representation has never been treated with much interest in the United States (and England). It was dismissed as "feudal." Actually, the estates period represents a phase in the evolution of modern constitutionalism, and deserves greater attention in view of the modern interest in functional representation. Hans Spangenberg's *Vom Lehnstaat zum Ständestaat* (1912) gives a broad introduction. Georg von Below in his somewhat controversial essay, "System und Bedeutung der Landständischen Verfassung," in his *Territorium und Staat* (1900), pp. 163 ff., and Otto von Gierke in his *Deutsches Genossenschaftsrecht*, vol. i, pp. 534 ff. and 819 ff., offer a broad sketch of the legal and institutional characteristics. The latter also perceived the intimate political and legal relation between these older forms and the modern associational concept and traced it through the study of the *Genossenschaft* concept. Gierke thus realized the significance of a political thinker who had built an associational theory of the government, Johannes Althusius, whose most important work, the *Politica Methodice Digesta* (1603), was republished, with an introduction by the present writer, in 1932. In this introduction the author showed the underlying connection between modern collectivist trends and these older patterns. Gierke's *Johannes Althusius* also deserves attention in this connection.

Special References

1. The quotation is taken from Wilson's *The New Freedom* (1913), p. 125. Bryce's discussion is given in *American Commonwealth*, vol. i pp. 691 ff. Regarding Bismarck's council, see Julius Curtius, *Bismarcks Plan eines deutschen Volkswirtschaftsrates* (1919), and the same author's article, "Der preussische Volkswirtschaftsrat, seine Errichtung, seine Tätigkeit, die Ursachen seines Eingehens," in *Wirtschaftliche Nachrichten aus dem Ruhrbezirk* (1921), pp. 593 ff.

2. The story about "One-Speech" Hamilton is told in C. S. Kenny's new edition of his *Parliamentary Logic* (1927). The interrelation between the general interest and the particular interests is set forth in chs. i and xxiii of Herring's *Public Administration and the Public Interest* (1936). K. C. Cole has for some time been engaged in studying the problem of "interest," and the author has profited from seeing some of his MSS. Cf. his article, "The Role of the Senate in the Confirmation of Judicial Nominations," in *APSR*, vol. xxviii (1934), pp. 875 ff.

3. Apart from the studies already mentioned in the general bibliography, attention should be called to the welter of articles and essays cited by Herring in *Group Representation*, particularly pp. 300 ff., and the relevant sections in Lasswell and Casey, *Propaganda and Promotional Activities: an Annotated Bibliography* (1935). The "purposes" of the various organizations are quoted from Herring, *op. cit.*, pp. 22-23.

4. The legal information on the chambers of agriculture, commerce, handicraft, etc., is contained in standard treatises on administrative law, such as W. Jellinek, *Verwaltungsrecht* (3rd ed., 1931), pp. 180 ff., or M. Hauriou, *Précis de Droit Administratif* (11th ed., 1927), pp. 236 ff. But descriptive accounts of their actual operation are rather unsatisfactory. A. J. Wolfe's studies for the *Special Agents Series* of the Department of Commerce, Bureau of Foreign and Domestic Commerce, Nos. 78, 98, 101, and 102, are of some help. See also Tatarin-Tarnheyden, *op. cit.*, pp. 62 ff.; H. E. Krüger, "Historische und Kritische Untersuchungen über die freien Interessen Vertretungen von Industrie, Handel und Gewerbe in Deutschland," in Schmoller's *Jahrbuch*, vols. xxxii and xxxiiii (1908-1909); Christian Eckert, *Die Stellung der Handelskammern* (1922); and E. P. Herring's study of the French chambers for *APSR*, vol. xxv (1931), "Chambres de Commerce en France." For the French government's interest in patriotic societies, see C. J. H. Hayes, *France, a Nation of Patriots* (1930), ch. viii. For Germany, see Eckart Kehr, *Schlachtflottenbau und Parteipolitik 1894-1901* (1930), particularly pp. 168 ff.

Concerning Gompers, see Louis Reed, *The Labor Philosophy of Samuel Gompers* (1930).

5. Regarding the situation in pre-war Russia see Leon Trotzki, *The History of the Russian Revolution* (tr. Max Eastman, 1932). Concerning the German development, see the literature on the revolution, A. Rosenberg and others, Tatarin-Tarnheyden, *op. cit.*, pp. 144 ff., and Georg Bernhard, *Wirtschaftsparlamente von den Revolutionsräten zum Reichswirtschaftsrat* (1923), pp. 43 ff. See also for further literature C. Hauschild, *Der vorläufige Reichswirtschaftsrat, 1920-1926* (1926), pp. 641 ff. Hugo Preuss' article appeared in *Berliner Tageblatt*, November 14, 1918, and was republished in *Staat, Recht und Freiheit* (1926), pp. 365 ff. Besides the National Economic Council, the bottom layer, the factory councils, were organized by the *Betriebsrätegesetz* of February 4, 1920. Concerning these factory councils, see C. Guillebaud, *The German Works Council* (1928).

6. For the German National Economic Council, see Dr. Hauschild's collection of materials just cited, and Friedrich Glum's *Der deutsche und der französische Reichswirtschaftsrat* (1929). Neither H. Finer's study, *Representative Government and a Parliament of Industry* (1923), nor the recent article by Lindsay Rogers and W. R. Dittmar, "The Reichswirtschaftsrat: De Mortuis," *PSQ*, vol. l (1935), pp. 481 ff., can be accepted, the former because it is too optimistic, the latter because it is too skeptical regarding its work. A more balanced view is found in Glum's article on the Council in *Handbuch des deutschen Staatsrechts*, vol. i (1930), pp. 578 ff. Similar balanced discussions of the French and Czechoslovak Councils are given by Edith C. Bramhall, "The French National Economic Council in France," *APSR*, vol. xx (1926), pp. 623 ff., and E. P. Herring, "The Czechoslovak Advisory Board for Economic Questions," *APSR*, vol. xxiv (1930), pp. 439 ff. The latter has a list of countries with councils. The English development is briefly described by Ogg in *English Government and Politics* (1936).

7. For the Fascist Corporate State, see Gaetano Salvemini, *Under the Axe of Fascism* (1936), particularly Part I; and H. Finer, *Mussolini's Italy* (1935), ch. xvii, pp. 492 ff.

8. For the German *ständische Aufbau*, see Fritz Ermath, *The New Germany*, Part IV, pp. 76 ff.; and F. M. Marx, *Government in the Third Reich* (1936), ch. v, pp. 134 ff. See also the further literature cited by these authors.

9. Regarding the Russian situation, see the comprehensive work of Sidney and Beatrice Webb, *Soviet Communism: A New Civilization?* (1935). Although it will be seen that the writer does not draw the same conclusions as the Webbs, their presentation of the facts is the most careful and elaborate yet available.

10. Concerning guild socialism, see G. D. H. Cole, *Guild Socialism Restated* (1920), and his article on guild socialism in the *ESS*. See also W. Y. Elliott, *The Pragmatic Revolt in Politics* (1928), ch. vi, and Niles Carpenter, *Guild Socialism* (1922). The corresponding actual developments (including some idealizing) are set forth in *Wirtschaftsdemokratie*

(1928), published by the German General Trades Unions' Union on the basis of the work of a group of specialists, and edited by Fritz Naphtali.

11. See above, §3. To this add the special supplement on "Pressure Groups and Propaganda" of *The Annals of the American Academy of Political and Social Science*, published in May, 1935.

12. See W. Y. Elliott, "Sovereign State or Sovereign Group," in *APSR*, vol. xix (1925), pp. 475 ff. In terms of the approach here used, this alternative is misleading, however.

Chapter XXV

DIRECT POPULAR ACTION

General References

Direct popular action has been dealt with primarily in connection with the specific issues of the referendum and initiative internally, and the plebiscites externally. A. L. Lowell, to be sure, went into the general phases of the problem both in his *Public Opinion and Popular Government* (1913) and in *Public Opinion in War and Peace* (1923). English writers such as Bagehot usually gave it just passing notice, to discard it in favor of the English representative system. The debates preceding the adoption of the German and Swiss programs are rather interesting sources for an elaborate argument both pro and con direct popular action within the context of a constitutional order. The expression "direct democracy" has often been used in continental Europe; it is rather misleading in view of the implied contention that the introduction of the initiative and referendum changes the whole tenor of the constitutional order. Carl Schmitt's *Volksentscheid und Volksbegehren, ein Beitrag zur Auslegung der Weimarer Verfassung und zur Lehre von der unmittelbaren Demokratie* (1927), and Klinghoffer's study, "Die Verankerung des Referendums in den europäischen Nachkriegsverfassungen," in *Archiv des oeffentlichen Rechts*, vol. xiv, pp. 1 ff., are significant and of somewhat more general scope. Carl Schmitt has developed his views on direct democracy more fully in his *Verfassungslehre* (1928), particularly pp. 204 ff. Likewise, Hans Kelsen, from a very different standpoint, has enlarged his views on democracy, as expounded in *Vom Wesen und Wert der Demokratie* (2nd ed., 1929), pp. 14 ff., in his magistral *Allgemeine Staatslehre* (1925), particularly pp. 356 ff. For France, where direct popular action had been widely favored during the revolution (following Rousseau), it has always found a place in general treatises, although its application has been discredited. It is here that the relationship to dictatorial plebiscites has most readily suggested itself, and both topics are treated, for example, in A. Esmein's well-known and oft-cited volumes, *Éléments de Droit Constitutionnel Français et Comparé,* particularly vol. i, pp. 435 ff. From the present writer's standpoint this is the most comprehensive treatment in contemporary literature, although it will be seen that different general views from those expounded in the present chapter underlie Esmein's discussion. A final word must be added concerning a treatise which appeared in a remote place, and which has therefore not received the recognition it deserves; and that is Prossor Axel Brusewitz' *Folkomröstningsinstitutet i den Schweiziska Demokratien—Dess Förutsättningar, Former och Functioner,* which was published by the Department of Justice of Sweden in 1923, the official reference being *Statens Offentliga Utredningar,* 1923:10. In spite of its specialized title (*The Institution of Popular Votes in the Swiss Democracies—Their Conditions, Forms and Functioning*), the general discussion is carried to an advanced point, the ideological background carefully examined, and a general conclusion reached which is comprehensive and accurate, as far as direct popular action within a constitutional framework is concerned. Unfortunately, the comparative aspects relating referenda to international and dictatorial plebiscites do not find room here.

Special References

1. Rousseau's argument against representation is found in *Contrat Social,* Book II, ch. xv.

2. For Napoleon I, see F. M. Kircheisen, *Napoleon I, sein Leben und seine Zeit* (1911-1932), particularly vols. v and vii. The figures are found in vol. v, p. 270, and vol. vii, pp. 10-12, respectively. Cf. also H. A. L. Fisher, *Napoleon* (1913); J. H. Rose, *The Life of Napoleon I* (8th ed., 1922); and Albert Sorel, *L'Europe et la Révolution Française* (9th ed., 1911), vols. vi-viii. None of these works could draw upon a careful study of the Napoleonic plebiscites, for such a study, as Kircheisen remarks, has unfortunately never been made. For the data concerning Napoleon III, see P. de la Gorce, *Histoire du Second Empire,* vols. i and vi. The particular data are found in the former on pp. 12-13 and 105, and in the latter in *livre* xxxviii, particularly pp. 115 ff. What is true of the plebiscites of the first Napoleon is equally true of those of the third. However, there seems to exist an unprinted study of these which is cited by Charles Seignobos, "La Révolution de 1848, le second Empire," in *Histoire de France contemporaine* (ed. Ernest Lavisse), vol. vi. See also Réné Arnaud, *Le Coup d'Etat du 2 Decembre* (1926).

3. For this paragraph see Theodore Curti, *Die Resultate des Schweizerischen Referendums* (2nd ed., 1911); Simon Deploige, *The Referendum in Switzerland* (tr. C. P. Trevelyan, 1898); Robert C. Brooks, *Government and Politics of Switzerland* (1918), ch. vi, and the same author's *Civic Training in Switzerland* (1930), pp. 107 ff. The most comprehensive study of the Swiss initiative and referendum has, however, appeared in Sweden: Axel Brusewitz, *op. cit.* The table of percentages, except for the decade 1923-1933, is found there, p. 212. The quotation from Brooks is from p. 164 of his *Government and Politics of Switzerland.* The discussion of the treaty referenda follows F. Fleiner, *Schweizerisches Bundesstaatsrecht* (1923), p. 755. A special study of the social and political aspects of the two referenda held so far would be very desirable.

4. The discussion of this paragraph is based on A. L. Lowell, *Public Opinion and Popular Government* (new ed., 1926), chs. xi, xiii and xiv;

W. B. Munro, *The Initiative, Referendum and Recall* (1912), chs. i-xi; and A. N. Holcombe, *State Government in the United States* (3rd ed., 1931), ch. xvi. Another valuable contribution to these problems is W. F. Dodd, *The Revision and Amendment of State Constitutions* (1910). Special reference is made to the figures on p. 268. The quotations at the end of the paragraph are found in Holcombe, *op. cit.*, pp. 551 and 569.

5. See Lowell, *Public Opinion and Popular Government*, ch. xv. Carl Schmitt, *Verfassungslehre*, §20, pushes matters to their logical extreme, a method by which he confuses all political problems which involve balance between extremes rather than following out one of them. Cf. also Esmein, *Droit Constitutionnel*, vol. i, pp. 435 ff.

6. For this paragraph, see Sarah Wambaugh, *A Monograph on Plebiscites, with a Collection of Official Documents* (1920), and Johannes Mattern, *The Employment of the Plebiscite in the Determination of Sovereignty* (1921).

7. See Sarah Wambaugh, *Plebiscites since the World War* (1933), and the literature cited there. The two maps in more elaborate form are found there, vol. i, pp. 87 and 266. The map showing the results of the Schleswig plebiscite is based on "Kort over Afstemnings-Resultaterne i Sønderjylland." That for the plebiscite in Upper Silesia is based on a map published by the British Section, Interallied Administrative and Plebiscite Commission. The Saar plebiscite has been described with detachment in a pamphlet of the Royal Institute of International Affairs, entitled *The Saar Plebiscite* (1935). See also James K. Pollock, "The Saar Plebiscite," in *APSR*, vol. xxix (1935), pp. 275 ff., supporting the appraisal given in the text.

8. A long list of references could be given for this paragraph, for the German constitutional provisions called forth a great deal of legal controversy as to their meaning and import. This literature is, however, given in the definitive statement of the matter published shortly before the advent of Hitler by the official actually in charge of these matters in the National Ministry of the Interior, Georg Kaisenberg, in *Handbuch des Deutschen Staatsrechts* (ed. Gerhard Anschütz and Richard Thoma, and published in 1930-1931) under the title, "Die formelle Ordnung des Volksbegehrens und des Volksentscheids in Reich und Ländern," *op. cit.*, vol. ii, pp. 204 ff. See also the analysis by H. F. Gosnell, "The General Referendum on the Princes' Property," *APSR*, vol. xxi (1927), pp. 119 ff.

9. The problems of this referendum are more extensively analyzed in an (hitherto unpublished) article by the author, entitled *The Agricultural Element in Mass Nationalism—An analysis of the Young Plan Referendum*. For the legal phases of this referendum see the article by Wilhelm Merk, "Volksbegehren und Volksentscheid," in *Archiv des oeffentlichen Rechts*, vol. xix (1930), pp. 83 ff.

10. For the use of the plebiscite under Hitler, see Frederick L. Schuman, *The Nazi Dictatorship* (1935), pp. 256 ff. and 462 ff.; Fritz Morstein Marx, *Government in the Third Reich* (1936), *passim* (the plebiscite is not recognized as a specific institution); and Otto Koellreuter, *Deutsches*

Staatsrecht (1935), who expounds the official Nazi view. For the quotation from him, see p. 146. For the quotation from Schuman, see p. 262.

11. The plebiscite under Fascism has not been as carefully analyzed as might be desired. Herman Finer's *Mussolini's Italy* (1935) contains a general discussion of the problem; the quotations are found on pp. 265-266. Cf. also H. R. Spencer, *The Government and Politics of Italy* (1932).

12. Instead of many references, cf. Sidney and Beatrice Webb, *Soviet Communism—A New Civilization?* (1936), particularly ch. vi, against which some of the remarks in the text are directed.

GENERAL INDEX

INDEX TO BIBLIOGRAPHY

(Arabic numbers refer to chapters; those in italics, to paragraphs. *G* refers to the General Bibliography.)